MODERN DATABASE
MANAGEMENT

Modern Database Management

FOURTH EDITION

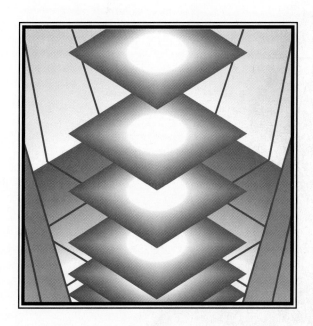

FRED R. McFADDEN · JEFFREY A. HOFFER

THE BENJAMIN/CUMMINGS PUBLISHING COMPANY, INC.

REDWOOD CITY, CALIFORNIA · MENLO PARK, CALIFORNIA
READING, MASSACHUSETTS · NEW YORK · DON MILLS, ONTARIO
WOKINGHAM, U.K. · AMSTERDAM · BONN · SYDNEY
SINGAPORE · TOKYO · MADRID · SAN JUAN

To our families and students, for their guidance and inspiration

Senior Sponsoring Editor: Michelle Baxter
Editorial Assistant: Mark Schmidt
Development Editor: Shelly Langman
Production Editor: Cathy Lewis
Text Design: Richard Kharibian
Cover Direction: Yvo Riezebos
Cover Design: Terry Hight
Illustrations: Rolin Graphics
Copy Editor: Nicholas Murray
Proofreader: Anna Huff
Composition: CRWaldman Graphic Communications

Apple Computer, Inc., IBM Canada, McDonnell Douglas Corporation, Sears, Roebuck and Co., and Taco Bell Corporation are not affiliated with Benjamin/Cummings Publishing Company, Inc.

Part I photos courtesy of Sears, Roebuck and Co.
Part II photos courtesy of IBM Canada.
Part III photos courtesy of Taco Bell Corporation.
Part IV photos courtesy of Apple Computer, Inc.
Part V photos courtesy of McDonnell Douglas Corporation.

Library of Congress Cataloging-in-Publication Data

McFadden, Fred R.
    Modern database management/Fred R. McFadden, Jeffrey A. Hoffer.
  --4th ed.
      p. cm.
    Rev. ed. of: Database management. 3rd ed. © 1991.
    Includes index.
    ISBN 0-8053-6047-6
    1. Data base management.   I. Hoffer, Jeffrey A.   II. McFadden,
Fred R.,   Database management.   III. Title.
QA76.9.D3M395   1993
005.74--dc20   93-31795
                                                                        CIP

ISBN 0-8053-6047-6
    4 5 6 7 8 9 10—CRW—98 97

The Benjamin/Cummings Publishing Company, Inc.
390 Bridge Parkway
Redwood City, CA 94065

Preface

This text is designed for an introductory course in database management. Such a course is usually required as part of an information systems curriculum in business schools, computer technology programs, and applied computer science departments. The Data Processing Management Association (DPMA), Association for Computing Machinery (ACM), and International Federation of Information Processing Societies (IFIPS) curriculum guidelines all outline this type of database management course. This book is an extensive revision of the third edition of *Database Management* by the same authors. *Database Management* has been used successfully for a decade at both the undergraduate and graduate levels, as well as in management and professional development programs.

NEW TO THIS EDITION

The fourth edition, *Modern Database Management*, updates and expands material in areas undergoing rapid change due to improved managerial practices, systems design methods and tools, and technology.

- **Client/server and other databases on computer networks:** A totally new chapter examining issues for peer-to-peer, client/server, and distributed databases. This discussion reflects the trends toward downsizing, redefining the role of mainframes, increased emphasis on local area networks, and end-user computing.

- **The object-oriented data model:** An entire chapter discusses how object-oriented constructs are used in the analysis and design of a database. This chapter parallels our coverage of the E-R model.

- **The entity-relationship data model:** A full chapter describes how the E-R data model is used to develop conceptual descriptions of enterprise and application area databases.

- **The Query-by-Example (QBE) language:** The text includes a chapter with a comprehensive overview of QBE, which has become a common interactive interface to databases. We use Paradox 4.0 to illustrate QBE.

- **Personal database systems:** A full chapter provides an overview of dBASE IV. In addition we include a second chapter on advanced PC database system topics of screen and report generation as well as developments in database systems for Microsoft® Windows.

- **The SQL relational database standard:** A complete chapter on the SQL language illustrates a wide variety of SQL concepts and commands and discusses the evolution of this international standard.

Modern Database Management puts considerable emphasis on the context in which databases are developed, showing the role of database analysis and design in the total systems development process. The book addresses information systems planning and the development of enterprise data models from planning matrices and other outputs of IS planning efforts. The framework for database development followed in this book parallels the typical development process used for information systems in general—from planning to analysis, design, implementation, and maintenance. To ensure that the database development process fits with the development of the total information system, we have coordinated our framework for database development in this text with that used to teach systems analysis and design text. Thus, students will be able to take both systems analysis and design and database courses using a common systems development framework.

Modern Database Management provides sound, clear, and current coverage of the concepts, skills, and issues needed to cope with an expanding organizational data resource. Since public and private organizations are populated with a wide variety of mainframe, personal computer, and networked database technologies, this text presents a balanced coverage of the computer technology (from the legacy systems of IBM's IMS and systems that follow the CODASYL standard to emerging graphical user interface systems like Paradox for Windows and client/server systems such as Sybase and Oracle). We place the greatest emphasis on the dominant technology of today—relational.

SCOPE OF THE BOOK

Modern Database Management is designed to fit within a variety of curricula on the development of information systems in public and private organizations. Many excellent texts and reference books emphasize issues relevant in a computer science curriculum (like the design of database management systems or the theory of particular database technologies) or concentrate on one particular technology (like SQL, dBASE, or Paradox). In contrast, the goal of this text is to provide adequate technical detail while emphasizing the management and implementation issues pertinent in a business information systems curriculum. Thus, the book stresses the design and use of databases, and the role of technology in meeting business information needs.

With this goal in mind, *Modern Database Management*

- Emphasizes the concepts of information as a corporate resource and of managers as stewards of this resource.

- Compares dominant technologies in parallel, so that business managers and information systems professionals can make intelligent choices about the application of different database technologies.

- Provides a chapter on database development, with an emphasis on database planning.

- Emphasizes data administration in a separate chapter (Chapter 12), and deals with issues related to managing organizations and technology throughout the text.

- Integrates the coverage of the concepts and notations for modeling organizational data, with reference to the now widely used entity-relationship notation.

- Provides coverage of database design, including normalization and view integration.

- Covers the major database processing standards (SQL, QBE, and XBase), as well as database development tools available on mainframe, LAN, and personal computer platforms.

- Provides coverage of data integrity, security, and other issues of special concern in multiple-user, shared database environments.

- Discusses options for the design of distributed databases and describes unique issues of this increasingly important database processing environment.

ORGANIZATION

We encourage instructors to customize their use of this book to meet the needs of both their curriculum and student career paths. The modular nature of the text (five logically sequenced sections), its broad coverage, extensive illustrations, and inclusion of advanced topics and emerging issues make customization easy. The many references to current publications make it possible to develop supplemental reading lists or to expand lecture discussion beyond the material in the text. In addition, since it is not the intent of the book to cover any particular database technology in depth, an instructor may wish to supplement this text with a tutorial on the specific database management system that students will use in the database course.

The modular nature of the book permits the instructor not only to reorganize the sequence of chapters, but also to skip or use chapters in different ways. For example, portions of Chapter 2, which presents an example of database application, can be read at various times during the database course. Students lacking exposure to database systems in prior courses can gain an early overview of the direction of the course by scanning Chapter 2. This approach can be especially helpful to students conducting a database development project. Those who have had some hands-on training on a PC relational DBMS can work through some of the examples in Chapter 2 on their own, using a data files disk available to adopters of this text. Since Chapter 2 uses dBASE IV to illustrate the development of a database, this chapter can also be read along with Chapter 9 on XBase language systems.

We strongly recommend that Chapter 1 on the database environment be read first. It provides a background and overview for the text. Chapter 2 can be read at various points in a database course. Chapter 3 on the database development process formalizes the presentation in Chapter 2 and links database development into the total systems development process from planning to maintenance. This chapter would typically be read early in a database course. For a course that emphasizes database programming skill development, however, Chapter 3 could be eliminated or read later as a capstone topic. Chapters 4 and 5 address alternative approaches to data modeling and conceptual design—E-R and object-oriented modeling, respectively. Due to the extensive use of E-R diagrams in practice and frequent reference to E-R diagrams in later chapters, we strongly recommend that students read Chapter 4. If the curriculum emphasizes object-oriented analysis and design principles, Chapter 5 provides a strong coverage of these principles in database development. Otherwise, this chapter may be scanned or skipped without loss of understanding in any subsequent part of the book.

Chapters 6 and 7 address logical and physical database design, respectively. Chapter 6 concentrates on the relational data model and data normalization. Thus, if students will design a relational database, they should read Chapter 6 before they try to create a database. Chapter 7 addresses database implementation issues that affect the performance and integrity of database processing. Issues raised in Chapter 7 are especially important in the development of shared databases, but are less critical for personal databases.

Another important modular feature of *Modern Database Management* is the concentrated coverage of each type of database technology in its own chapter. Thus, the instructor may choose to eliminate those technologies that do not match the educational objectives or time constraints of the course. The database technologies included follow:

Technology	Chapter
SQL	8
Xbase	9 (illustrated using dBASE IV)
QBE	10 (illustrated using Paradox 4.0)
Screen and report generators, as well as graphical user interfaces	11
Client/server and distributed databases	13
IMS	14
CODASYL systems	15

While Chapters 8–11 and 13–15 focus on specific database processing standards and environments, Chapter 12 covers administrative issues for data resources. This chapter addresses several advanced technical issues about organizational data. Parts of Chapter 12 can be read early in the course or immediately before any of the technology chapters (Chapters 8–11, and Chapters 13–15) to provide additional in-depth background on database technology.

LEARNING AIDS

To assist the student and instructor, *Modern Database Management* includes the following learning aids:

- Realistic **Case Examples** illustrate important concepts throughout the text. Pine Valley Furniture Company shows a typical manufacturing company, and Mountain View Community Hospital highlights a service-sector organization. Illustrations from these situations address production, marketing, accounting, customer service, and human resource management information needs. To provide variety and to illustrate points not inherent in the two primary case situations, three additional situations—Lakewood College, Vacation Property Rentals, and Hy-Tek Corporation—are included to a lesser degree. Case examples are identified by margin symbols.

 Pine Valley Furniture

 Mountain View Community Hospital

 Lakewood College

 Vacation Property Rentals

 Hy-Tek Corporation

- **Part Openers** appear at the beginning of each of the five sections of the text to preview the chapters in the parts. Each part opener describes an application in a real-world company. The following companies are described in the part openers: Sears, Roebuck and Co. (Leveraging the Value of Data), IBM Canada (Real-Time Process Monitoring and Control), Taco Bell (Managing Information Overload), Apple Computer (Distributed Databases), and McDonnell Douglas (Manufacturing Support with IMS).

- **Learning Objectives** appear at the beginning of each chapter to preview the major concepts and skills the student will gain after studying the chapter. The learning objectives are also a great study tool in preparing for assignments and examinations, as they reflect the major points of the text.

- A **Summary** at the end of each chapter encapsulates the main concepts of the chapter and links the chapter to related chapters.

- The **Chapter Review** tests student's knowledge. The list of **Key Terms** summarizes new concepts introduced in the chapter. The **Review Questions** check the student's grasp of important concepts, basic facts, and significant issues. **Problems and Exercises** require students to apply their knowledge to realistic situations and, in some cases, to extend this knowledge to new circumstances. These require discussion of issues, distinguishing key concepts, and practice of skills developed in the chapter.

- A **Glossary of Terms** is included in two convenient forms. First, the definition of each key term is placed in the page margin near where the term is defined or fully discussed in the text. Second, all the key terms are collected into a comprehensive glossary. In addition, the book index highlights glossary terms by showing in italics the page number where the matching margin glossary appears. Also included is a **Glossary of Acronyms** for abbreviations commonly used in database management.

SUPPLEMENTS

The text is a part of a complete educational package designed to provide a high level of support to the instructor.

- **Instructor's Guide:** A comprehensive supplement containing numerous instructional resources:

  Teaching Suggestions: These include lecture suggestions, teaching hints, and student project ideas that make use of the chapter content.

  Solutions: Sample answers are provided for all Review Questions, and Problems and Exercises.

  Multiple-Choice Questions: 300 multiple-choice questions (approximately 20 per chapter with answers).

  Examination Questions: 20 examination problems (similar to the Problems and Exercises from the text) with solutions. The Multiple-Choice and Examination questions form a test bank that can be used for in-class or take-home assignments, quizzes, or examinations.

  Transparency Masters: A set of masters for overhead transparencies of enlarged illustrations and tables from the text help the instructor tie lectures and class discussion to material in the text.

- **Data Disk:** Contains dBASE IV, Paradox, and ASCII files for databases illustrated in the text. All data files, screens, and reports shown in Chapter 2 are included on this diskette. The data files are provided in ASCII format for importing into any PC-DBMS that is used in the database course.

- **Case Book for Modern Database Management** (written by Donald A. Carpenter): A totally new Case Book containing a wide variety of realistic cases for course projects. Most of the cases are taken from actual company situations. The case solutions and implementations can be worked out using almost any DBMS. Solutions for these cases, including implementations in several popular packages, are available from the publisher.

- Because *Modern Database Management* does not teach any specific database system in depth, you may want to supplement this text with a tutorial book on the software students will use in the database course. Several excellent DBMS tutorial guides are listed below:

Projects for dBASE III + 30838	Marianne Fox/Larry Metzelaar
Projects for Paradox for Windows 34240	Ahmer Karim
Projects for Paradox 3.5 32967	Marianne Fox/Larry Metzelaar
Projects for dBASE IV 30834	Marianne Fox/Larry Metzelaar

ACKNOWLEDGMENTS

We are very grateful to numerous individuals who contributed to the preparation of *Modern Database Management*. First, we wish to thank our reviewers for their detailed reviews and many suggestions, characteristic of their thoughtful teaching style. Because of the extensive development of this text from prior editions of *Database Management*, analysis of topics and depth of coverage provided by the reviewers were crucial.

The reviewers were:

Mary Alexander,
University of South Florida

Dinesh Batra,
Florida International University

Michael Barrett,
Clarion University

James Buxton,
Tidewater Community College

Harvey Blessing,
Essex Community College

C. K. Carlson,
George Mason University

Kevin Gorman,
University of North Carolina, Charlotte

Herman Hoplin,
Syracuse University

Ramesh Kumar,
California State University, Fullerton

John Tower,
Oakland University, Michigan

Santosh Venkatraman,
Northeast Louisiana University

Next we wish to thank Joe Valacich from Indiana University and Joey George from Florida State University for their great insights on the relationship of database design and overall information systems development. Their careful attention and creative suggestions during our writing have contributed much to the ability to coordinate *Modern Database Management* with modern systems development methods.

We thank our typists and assistants, Libby Merry and Bethany Sprague at Indiana University and Karen Norris at University of Colorado–Colorado Springs, who were tireless and meticulous in capturing and editing our manuscript on word processing systems, so that the inevitable revisions could be accomplished with relative ease. Bethany Sprague also coordinated the development of the *Instructor's Manual*—a job that tests calmness, attention to detail, and working within a tight schedule. For those professional services and constant moral support we are eternally grateful.

W. Joseph Graves (Joseph Graves Associates, Indianapolis, Indiana) and Nancy Fox (Cummins Engine Company, Columbus, Indiana) were instrumental in the update of the chapters on the CODASYL data model and on IMS. Their careful review of our manuscript was invaluable in making sure that these chapters accurately depict the status of these technologies.

We are very grateful to the staff of Benjamin/Cummings for their support and guidance throughout the project. In particular, we wish to thank Michelle Baxter (Editor), Sally Elliott (General Manager), Mark Schmidt (Editorial Assistant), and Cathy Lewis (Production Editor) for their encouragement and attention to detail. We also wish to thank Shelly Langman (Development Editor) for helping us to set the overall tone and style, and for helping to make two authors appear to be one. We are also very thankful to our undergraduate and MBA students at Indiana

University and University of Colorado–Colorado Springs for tactful nudges that give us new insights on communicating ideas.

Finally, we give immeasurable thanks to our families—wives and children—who endure many evenings and weekends of solitude for the thrill of seeing a book cover hang on a den wall. Much of the value of this text is due to their support and love, but we alone bear the responsibility for any errors or omissions that remain between the covers.

Fred R. McFadden
Jeffrey A. Hoffer

Brief Table of Contents

Detailed Table of Contents

Part III   Relational Database Implementation   *280*

Taco Bell Corporation
MANAGING INFORMATION OVERLOAD

Part V   Legacy Database Systems   *490*

McDonnell Douglas Corporation
MANUFACTURING SUPPORT WITH IMS

MODERN DATABASE MANAGEMENT

PART **I**

The Context of Database Development

Sears, Roebuck and Co.

LEVERAGING THE VALUE OF DATA

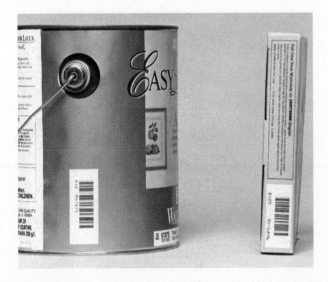

This first part of the text introduces you to the hypothetical Pine Valley Furniture Company and to the concept of data as a resource to be managed by the firm. As you read Part I, compare the data management methods available to Pine Valley Furniture with those of Sears, Roebuck and Co. Sears has developed numerous computer-based applications that support retail stores. These systems provide a very sophisticated degree of application integration that enables Sears to "leverage" the value of data to management.

The integrated systems include price look-up, credit, inventory replenishment and control, merchandise receiving, point-of-sale (POS) reservation, error correction, delivery, service, repairs, layaway, and COD as well as a mechanized hold for merchandise file, and both financial and management reporting by using a common set of databases. These systems provide managers with the information needed to support decision-making and to provide timely answers to a variety of possible customer inquiries. Managers are supported by an electronic mail facility. Data capture is through the latest technology available for barcode scanning at POS terminals.

As customers of Sears, many of you have seen these systems in action, although you might not be aware of the activities taking place behind the scenes. The price look-up system enables accurate price determination through the use of barcode scanning technology. The credit system can be used to answer queries on active customer accounts. Positive credit approval is available through POS terminals for instant approval on merchandise sales. The system accesses customer credit limit information stored in mainframe databases.

As sales are processed, the inventory replenishment system automatically updates product inventory databases. This system also supports queries about products. By entering a product item number, a salesperson can determine the quantity of items stocked in the retail store warehouse. For special orders or items not stocked at local retail stores, a POS reservation system automatically reserves merchandise for customers and processes customer orders for merchandise that is stored at central warehouse locations and sources throughout the country. This system ensures that accurate delivery-date information is provided to customers. If an item is out of stock at the central warehouse, the reservation system can even let managers know when the item is expected back in stock!

The error correction system is a back-office operation that enables personnel to correct data entry mistakes that are automatically flagged by the computer. This cleans up entry errors before they can affect "downstream" inventory management application systems. When goods are received, a receiving system automatically updates the databases that are accessed by the inventory system. Sears uses barcode reading devices to speed up processing at the loading dock by scanning the purchase order data for incoming shipments of products. Sears also uses EDI to transmit ordering information to its source.

These integrated systems support approximately 850 stores with 29 central inventory facilities primarily through use of the DB2 database management system. Literally thousands of transactions are processed in each store on a daily basis. By providing instant up-to-date information at the touch of a finger, the system provides customers with services not previously available, allows products to be delivered in less time than was previously required, and optimizes inventory management.

The Database Environment

LEARNING OBJECTIVES

After studying this chapter, you should be able to:

- Define the following key terms: *data, database, information, entity,* and *information resource management.*
- List six basic principles of information resource management.
- Contrast centralized and distributed databases, and describe two types of distributed databases.
- Describe the major characteristics of file processing systems, and list several typical shortcomings of these systems.
- Describe the major advantages of the database processing approach, compared to traditional file processing systems.
- Draw a high-level enterprise data model for a simple organization.
- Describe briefly the major components of a database environment.
- Contrast a process-driven approach to a data-driven approach to information systems development.

INTRODUCTION

This book is about the data resource of organizations and about the management of that resource. In today's highly competitive global economy, managers are increasingly aware that their data resources are essential to the survival of their organizations. Data (and information derived from data) are required for competitive initiatives such as improving customer satisfaction, facilitating teamwork, developing new products and markets, and providing faster response. Of course, data can be an asset only if they are accurate and available when needed. This is the reason an organization must purposely organize and manage its data. Databases have become the standard technique for structuring and managing much of the data and information in organizations today.

Data and information are used for a variety of purposes in organizations. Data are used to represent and track the status of customers, products, orders, and employees. For example, to determine whether a particular sofa is in stock, a salesperson in a furniture store would probably display an inventory record for the item rather than physically search for it in the warehouse. Also, information is used to measure performance and report on the financial health of the enterprise. For example, the furniture store manager would rely on monthly accounting reports to determine whether the store was profitable during each period and to determine patterns and trends.

A course in database management has emerged as one of the most important courses in the information systems curriculum today. As an information systems professional, you must be prepared to analyze database requirements and design and implement databases within the overall context of information systems development. Also, you must be prepared to consult with end users who are increasingly using database technology to prototype, design, and implement their own information systems. Managers and other end users in organizations must understand the potential competitive advantages available through the creative use of technology, including databases.

In this chapter we introduce the basic concepts of databases and database management systems. We describe the concept of information resource management, which views data as a shared corporate resource. We contrast the database approach with traditional file management systems, and point out the advantages and risks of this approach. We also provide a brief description of several typical database architectures, including centralized, distributed, and client/server. We introduce a realistic case example (Pine Valley Furniture Company) to illustrate the important concepts and issues of database management.

INFORMATION RESOURCE MANAGEMENT

Information resource management (IRM): The concept that information is a major corporate resource and must be managed using the same basic principles used to manage other assets.

Databases should be understood within the larger context of information resource management. **Information resource management (IRM)** is the concept that information is a major corporate resource and must be managed using the same basic principles that are used to manage other assets, such as employees, materials, equipment, and financial resources. McLeod and Brittain-White (1988) suggest the following basic principles of IRM:

1. A business organization is composed of resources that flow into the organization from its environment and then return to the environment.

2. There are two basic types of resources: (a) physical resources, such as personnel, materials, machines, facilities, and money; and (b) conceptual resources, consisting of data and information.

3. As the scale of operations grows, it becomes more difficult to manage the physical resources by observation. Thus the manager is forced to rely on the conceptual resources.

4. The same basic principles that have been developed for the management of physical resources can be applied to the management of conceptual resources.

5. Management of data and information includes acquisition prior to the time they are needed, security measures designed to protect the resources from destruction and misuse, quality assurance, and removal procedures that discharge the resources from the organization when they are no longer needed.

6. Management of data and information can be achieved only through organizational, not individual, commitment.

Data Versus Information

In this text we distinguish between data and information. The word **data** refers to facts concerning things such as people, objects, or events. For example, a listing of students showing student number, name, major, and GPA would qualify as data (see Figure 1-1a).

An organization collects and stores vast quantities of data from both internal and external sources, an amount that would generally be overwhelming if it were left in its original state. **Information** is data that have been processed and presented in a form suitable for human interpretation, often with the purpose of revealing trends or patterns. Student data, for example, could be analyzed and summarized through the use of statistical measures such as means and ranges and presented in graphic form (see Figure 1-1b). Managers and others in an organization use such information to support decision making. In the above example, the student information might be used to decide whether to introduce new courses or to hire new faculty members.

Data: Facts concerning things such as people, objects, or events.

Information: Data that have been processed and presented in a form suitable for human interpretation, often with the purpose of revealing trends or patterns.

Figure 1-1

Comparison of data and information

```
                    CLASS ROSTER

Course:  MGT 500                    Semester:  Spring 1994
         Business Policy
Section: 2


        Name              ID          Major      GPA

Baker, Kenneth D.       324917628      MGT        2.9
Doyle, Joan E.          476193248      MKT        3.4
Finkle, Clive R.        548429344      PRM        2.8
Lewis, John C.          551742186      MGT        3.7
McFerran, Debra R.      409723145      IS         2.9
Sisneros, Michael       392416582      ACCT       3.3
```

(a) Data

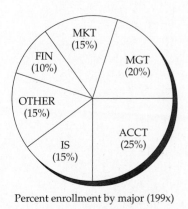

Percent enrollment by major (199x)

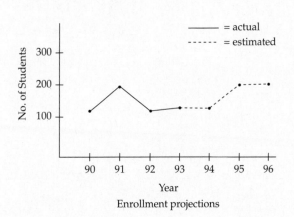

Enrollment projections

(b) Information

Databases

As we have seen, data provide the raw material that is used to produce information (the finished product). The following steps are required to convert data into information: acquisition, storage, manipulation, retrieval, and distribution. To perform these steps efficiently and effectively, organizations must often organize their data in the form of databases. A **database** is a shared collection of logically related data, designed to meet the information needs of multiple users in an organization. Later in this chapter we expand this definition, compare databases with conventional files, and discuss the objectives and advantages of databases.

The concept of a shared corporate database is illustrated in Figure 1-2. In this vision, all of the various functional areas operate from the same set of shared data contained in the corporate database. There is a standard set of data definitions, and a data administration group is custodian of this corporate resource.

The vision shown in Figure 1-2 has proved difficult to achieve in practice, for a variety of reasons. Databases in most organizations have evolved over a period of time, often without a comprehensive plan to guide their development. The ease of use of contemporary database software has encouraged end users to develop their own database applications, which often duplicate data already contained in other applications. According to Davydov (1993), "the current state of database applications is characterized by the fact that companies continue to deploy databases to meet isolated application needs. The end result is more redundant, incompatible data." Nevertheless, the goal of shared databases is not only valid but essential for the successful organizations of the future.

Database: A shared collection of logically related data, designed to meet the information needs of multiple users in an organization.

Figure 1-2

The concept of a shared corporate database

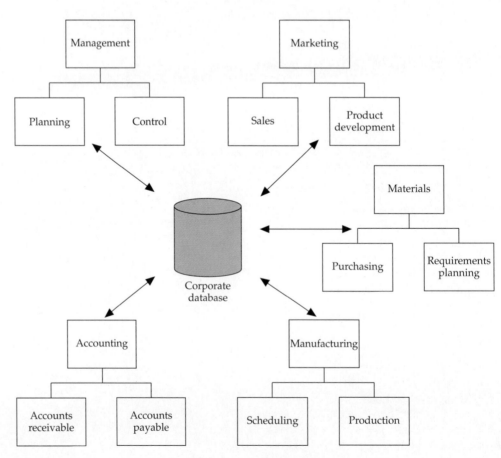

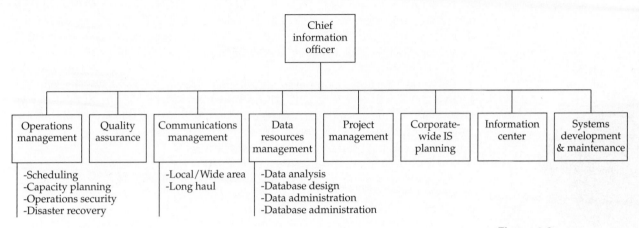

Figure 1-3

Functions of information resource management. Source: Reprinted with permission of Idea Group Publishing. From *Information Resources Management Journal* 1, no. 1. Copyright 1988.

Implementing Information Resource Management

Information resource management is a concept designed to elevate the importance of managing data and information in organizations. Successful implementation of IRM is the responsibility of an organization's senior management, but how does an organization go about implementing IRM? Proponents of information resource management suggest that there are eight functions of IRM that are absolutely necessary (see Figure 1-3): operations management, quality assurance, communications management, data resources management, project management, corporate-wide IS planning, information center (or user-computing support), and systems development and maintenance. We discuss many of these functions in this text, with emphasis on data resources management and its subfunctions: data analysis, database design, data administration, and database administration.

TYPES OF DATABASES

Several strategies are available for deploying and using databases in organizations. At one extreme, a single user may develop a simple accounting database on a personal computer to manage a small business. At the other extreme, a very large company may have databases at numerous locations around the country (or world) that are linked together.

There are two generic database architectures: centralized and distributed. In this section, we describe some of the most common examples of each and their advantages and potential disadvantages.

Centralized Databases

With a centralized database, all data are located at a single site. Users at remote sites may generally access the database using data communications facilities. Centralized databases provide greater control over accessing and updating data than distributed databases, but they are more vulnerable to failure since they depend on the availability of the resources at the central site. Figure 1-4 shows three common examples of centralized databases: a personal computer database, a central computer database, and a client/server database.

Personal Computer Databases   A personal computer database is the type that is most familiar to most students (Figure 1-4a). Personal computer databases normally have a single user who creates the database, updates and maintains the data, and produces reports and displays. Often the database supports one application, or at least a limited number of applications.

The most common applications of personal computer databases are in small businesses. Typical applications include simple accounting, inventory manage-

Figure 1-4

Centralized databases

(a) Personal computer database

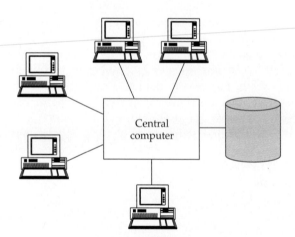

(b) Central computer database

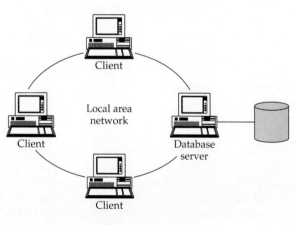

(c) Client/server database

ment, and customer billing. Personal computer databases are relatively simple to develop and use, especially with the graphical user interfaces that are common with current software products. We describe personal computer database systems in Chapters 9 and 10.

Personal computer databases are used in medium- and large-scale organizations, as well as in small businesses. In developing such applications, however, users risk creating "islands of automation," so that the data cannot readily be shared. If there is a need to share data, the database should be stored on a database server in a local area network (this client/server approach is described below).

Central Computer Databases   The data that most applications in large organizations access is stored on a central computer (Figure 1-4b). In many systems, users at remote locations can access the database using terminals and data communications links. Depending on the size of the organization, the central computer is usually a mainframe or a minicomputer. Central computer databases often involve very large, integrated databases that must be accessed by a large number of users. Usage is often intense, with several hundred transactions per second being processed (some systems support over one thousand transactions per second). Typical applications include airline reservation systems, financial institutions, and express delivery companies.

Client/Server Databases   Large central computers are very expensive compared to smaller microcomputers and workstations. As a result, many organizations are downsizing present applications to (or developing new applications on) these smaller, more cost-effective computers. As shown in Figure 1-4c, the computers are often linked together in a local area network so that they may share resources such as printers, storage devices, and so on.

The architecture shown in Figure 1-4c is called a *client/server architecture* and is discussed in detail in Chapter 13. A client/server architecture is designed for the distribution of work on a computer network in which many clients may share the services of a single server. A **server** is a software application that provides services (called *back-end functions*—printing, file or database management, communications management, etc.) to requesting clients. A **client** (which provides *front-end functions*) is a software application that requests services from one or more servers. Normally the server application (e.g., the database server in Figure 1-4c) is located on a separate computer on the network.

The main objective of a client/server architecture is to allow client applications to access server-managed data (McGoveran and White, 1990). The user interface and logic of the business application are processed on the server, while the database processing is performed on the database server.

Client/server systems (and the associated local area networks) are often used to support **work-group computing**, that is, the use of computing resources for decision support and other applications by a team. Several such networks can be linked together so that various work groups can share data (this would be an example of distributed databases, described below). Client/server systems are rapidly becoming the building blocks for enterprise-wide computing systems in many organizations.

Server: A software application that provides services (such as database management) to requesting clients.

Client: A software application that requests services (such as communications management) from one or more servers.

Work-group computing: The use of computing resources for decision support and other applications by a team.

Distributed Databases

Many organizations are spread out over various locations, such as different cities, states, and even countries. In such cases, centralized databases are often impractical and uneconomical. A *distributed database* is a single logical database that is spread physically across computers in multiple locations. We describe distributed databases in detail in Chapter 13.

There are two generic categories of distributed databases: homogeneous and heterogeneous. They are illustrated in Figure 1-5 and described briefly below.

Homogeneous Databases   When applied to databases, the term *homogeneous* means that the database technology is the same (or at least compatible) at each of the locations and that the data at the various locations are also compatible. In Figure 1-5a the databases are distributed over three nodes (or locations). For these databases to be homogeneous, the following conditions would probably exist:

1. The computer operating systems used at each of the locations are the same, or at least they are highly compatible.
2. The data models used at each of the locations are the same. (The relational model is most commonly used for distributed databases today.)
3. The database management systems used at each of the locations are the same, or at least they are highly compatible.
4. The data at the various locations have common definitions and formats.

Figure 1-5

Distributed databases

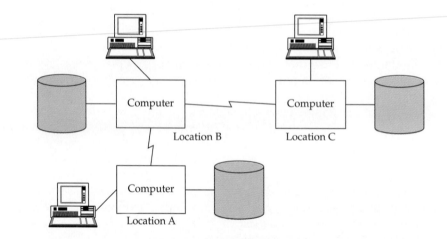

(a) Homogeneous databases

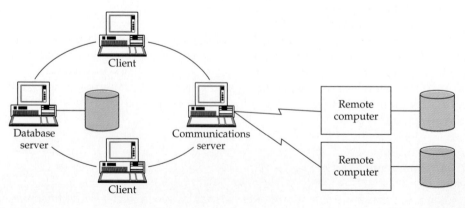

(b) Heterogeneous (federated) databases

Homogeneous databases simplify the sharing of data among the various users. In Figure 1-5a, a user at Location A could easily retrieve or update data stored at Locations B and C, for example. Thus homogeneous databases represent the design goal for distributed databases. Achieving this goal requires a high level of planning throughout the organization. We describe database planning in Chapter 3.

Heterogeneous Databases   In most organizations, databases evolve over a period of time without careful guidance or planning. Different computers and operating systems may be used at each of the locations. Different data models and database management systems are also very common. For example, one location may have the latest relational database management technology, while another location may store data using conventional files or older hierarchical or network databases.

To complicate matters further, the data across the locations are often incompatible. Typical conflicts would include syntactic differences (such as different representations of data fields at two locations) and semantic differences (such as different meanings for the term *account* at different locations). For a discussion of the problems of integrating heterogeneous databases, see Howe (1993).

Sooner or later, the users at the various locations discover that they need to share the data, despite the incompatibilities. One solution is to develop a completely new database that integrates all of the existing systems; however, this is often not technically or economically feasible. Instead, the databases are sometimes linked together, as shown in Figure 1-5b. The result is a set of heterogeneous databases (the term *federated* databases is also sometimes used). Such a system generally limits the types of processing that users may perform; for example, a user at one location may be able to read but not update the data at another location.

Case Example: Pine Valley Furniture Company

In this section, we describe the database approach and its advantages and disadvantages by means of a realistic case example. In this example, a small company progresses from manual information systems to a minicomputer using traditional files and finally to a contemporary relational database system.

Business Background

Pine Valley Furniture Company manufactures high-quality, all-wood furniture and distributes it to stores nationwide. There are several product lines, including dinette sets, stereo cabinets, wall units, living room furniture, and bedroom furniture. Pine Valley Furniture employs about 50 persons at the present time and is experiencing rapid growth.

Pine Valley Furniture was founded about 15 years ago by Donald Knotts, its general manager and majority owner. Mr. Knotts had made custom furniture as a hobby and started the business in his own garage. Pine Valley Furniture operated out of a rented warehouse until five years ago, when it moved to its present location.

Managing the data resources at Pine Valley Furniture was relatively simple during the first years of its operation. At first, Mr. Knotts kept most of the information needed to run the business in his head, although a few records were kept, mostly for tax purposes. When the business expanded into a rented warehouse, there were about 10 employees. Mr. Knotts hired a part-time bookkeeper to keep a small set of books, including a general ledger and accounts receivable and payable ledgers. The books amounted to a small, centralized database that provided most of the information needed to run the company at that time.

When Pine Valley Furniture moved into its present location, the company's product line had expanded, and its sales volume had doubled in two years. Its work force had grown to over 30 employees. This organizational growth and complexity meant that Mr. Knotts could no longer manage the operation by himself. He therefore organized the company into functional areas of responsibility. He organized manufacturing operations into three main sections: Fabrication, Assembling, and Finishing, each of which had a manager.

Separate departments were also established for several business functions: a

Figure 1-6

Manual information systems at Pine Valley Furniture

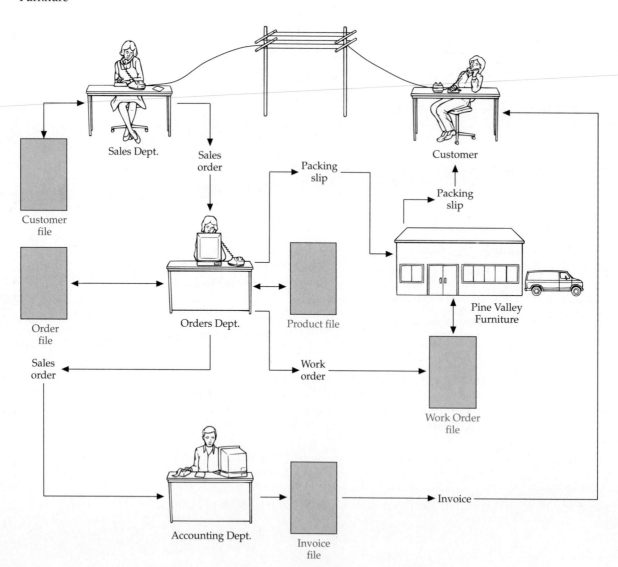

Sales Department, an Orders Department, an Accounting Department, and a Purchasing Department. Pine Valley Furniture thus emerged from the entrepreneurial mode of operation to become a formal organization with functional departments and managers.

Manual Information Systems

When Pine Valley Furniture organized into functional departments, it also changed its approach to managing its data resources. The single set of books that it had used previously was no longer adequate to run the business. Instead, each department now had its own books—files, ledgers, and so on—and informal lines of communication were established to transfer data between departments.

Figure 1-6 shows the manual information system at Pine Valley Furniture. The diagram depicts the flow of data for the mainstream functions: order processing, billing, shipping, and processing work orders. Most customer orders are received in the Sales Department by telephone. The Sales Department refers to a customer file to check the customer's credit and then prepares a sales order. The sales order is then sent to the Orders Department, which checks a product file to determine whether the requested item is in stock. If the item is in stock, the clerk prepares a packing slip. If the item is not in stock (or if the stock level has dropped below a predetermined level), the clerk prepares a work order to send to the Manufacturing Department to prepare a batch of the item. One copy of the sales order is sent to the Accounting Department, and another is filed in the Orders Department. The Accounting Department prices the sales order and prepares an invoice for items shipped to the customer. A packing slip is included with each customer shipment.

Notice in Figure 1-6 that each department has a separate file (or files) to support its operations and answer its questions. The files shown in Figure 1-6, and typical questions that might be answered by referring to these files, are shown in Table 1-1. Other departments also have files to support their operations. For example, the Purchasing Department has a file of purchase orders to indicate what materials are currently on order from vendors.

TABLE 1-1   Typical User Questions of Database

Department	File	Typical Questions
Sales	Customer	What is customer ABC's address and credit limit?
Orders	Product	How many chairs (product no. 123) do we have in stock?
Accounting	Invoice	How much does customer ABC owe us on invoice no. 567?
Manufacturing	Work Order	How many units of product no. 123 are we scheduled to build today?

The information system portrayed in Figure 1-6 is a manual system, in which the data files are decentralized, and each department works with a subset of the organization's data. Although the system works, it has a number of deficiencies or disadvantages:

1. A constant stream of intracompany paperwork (in the form of memos, reports, transactions, and so on) and telephone calls is required to communicate changes and keep the files synchronized.

2. The system cannot easily provide answers to complex operational questions. For example, answering the question, "What invoices are outstanding for order no. 123 from customer ABC?" would probably require some research on the part of the Orders Department.

3. Managers cannot easily obtain summary information required for decision making.

4. Duplicate data exist throughout the organization, resulting in a lack of consistency and poor communication. For example, information concerning customer orders is maintained in the Sales, Orders, Accounting, *and* Shipping departments at Pine Valley Furniture.

It is tempting to assume that a computer would automatically eliminate many of these typical shortcomings of a manual information system, and our assumption is generally true—a computer will often permit data to be processed faster and more accurately. When we consider the traditional file processing environment that has prevailed for decades, however, many of the preceding problems would remain and might even be amplified. This occurs because in the traditional approach the designer often essentially automates existing manual systems, as we explain in the following section.

FILE PROCESSING SYSTEMS

The traditional approach to information systems design focuses on the data processing needs of individual departments in the organization, instead of regarding the organization as a whole. The information systems (IS) group responds to user requests by developing (or acquiring) new computer programs, often one at a time, for individual applications such as accounts receivable, payroll, and inventory control. Each application program or system that is developed is designed to meet the needs of the particular department or user group. Thus, there is no overall map, plan, or model to guide the growth of applications.

Each new computer application is typically designed with its own set of data files. Much of the data in these new files may already be present in existing files for other applications. Unfortunately, to meet the needs of the new application, the existing files would have to be restructured, which, in turn, would require that existing programs that use these same files be revised or completely rewritten. For this reason, it is often far simpler (and also less risky) to design new files for each application.

 ### File Processing Systems at Pine Valley Furniture

Pine Valley Furniture Company has experienced numerous operating problems over the years, including declining customer service compounded by increasing inventory levels. Although the company has grown rapidly, profits have failed to keep pace. Mr. Knotts decided that the existing manual information system was no longer sufficient to manage a fast-growing business, and after some evaluation a minicomputer was selected and installed at Pine Valley Furniture in the early 1980s.

Most of the applications that have subsequently been installed on the computer are in the accounting and financial areas, such as order filling, invoicing, accounts receivable, inventory control, accounts payable, payroll, and general ledger. Most of these application programs were purchased from a software vendor who modified the programs to meet the requirements of the Pine Valley Furniture Company.

Three of the computer applications at Pine Valley Furniture are depicted in Figure 1-7. The systems illustrated are Order Filling, Invoicing, and Payroll, and the figure shows the major data files associated with each application system. Notice that each application system in Figure 1-7 has its own data files, which is typical of traditional applications. For example, the Inventory Master file used in the Order Filling System and the Inventory Pricing file used in the Invoicing System both contain identical data describing products made by Pine Valley Furniture. Also, these application systems both use a Customer Master file. Is this master file actually one file or two distinct files with duplicate information? In this case, the two applications happen to share a single Customer Master file, yet there is a large quantity of duplicated data in the files used by the various applications at Pine Valley Furniture.

By comparing Figures 1-6 and 1-7, we can see the similarity in design between the computer systems at Pine Valley Furniture and the manual systems they replaced. In each case, the approach was to develop procedures and associated data files to solve data processing problems for individual functional departments. Basically, the company just automated the existing manual procedures. With the computer systems, the data files are no longer physically located within the individual departments, as in the manual system. Yet, since they are tailored to the needs of each application or department, the files are generally regarded as "belonging" to that department or application, rather than as a resource to be shared by all departments or users.

Figure 1-7

Three application systems at Pine Valley Furniture

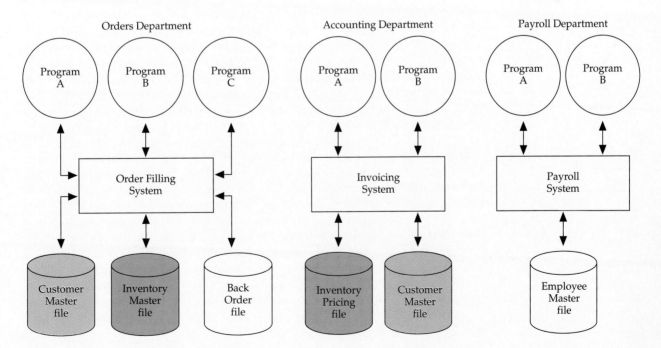

The computer applications at Pine Valley Furniture have generally been successful. The software has enabled the company to reduce its paperwork burden and improve its response to customer orders. In addition management is able to obtain better information concerning costs, sales, and profits. Nevertheless, managers at Pine Valley are dissatisfied with several aspects of the new computer system. While the applications have helped improve the operations management function, there has been little impact on middle management and still less on top management. Mr. Knotts and the other managers at Pine Valley Furniture have come to realize that there are basic limitations to traditional file processing systems. Some of these limitations are described next.

Disadvantages of File Processing Systems

The basic disadvantages of file processing systems are uncontrolled redundancy, inconsistent data, inflexibility, limited data sharing, poor enforcement of standards, and excessive program maintenance.

Uncontrolled Redundancy   In file processing systems, each application has its own files, an approach that inevitably leads to a high level of data redundancy (that is, duplication of data). There are several disadvantages to recording the same data item in multiple files: first, valuable storage space is wasted; second, the same data may have to be input several times to update all occurrences of a data item; and third, inconsistencies (or various versions) often result, as described below. As we shall see, some replication of data can be useful, but careful control is required.

Inconsistent Data   When the same data are stored in multiple locations, inconsistencies are inevitable. For example, several of the files at Pine Valley Furniture contain customer data. Suppose that there is an address change for one of the customers. If the files are to be consistent, this change must be made simultaneously (and correctly) to each of the files containing the customer address data item. Since the files are controlled by different users, however, it is likely that some files will contain the old address, while others contain the new address.

Inconsistencies in stored data are one of the most common sources of errors in computer applications. They lead to inconsistent documents and reports and undermine the confidence of users in the integrity of the information system. The outdated customer address just described, for example, may cause an invoice to be mailed to the wrong location. As a result, the invoice may be returned, and the customer payment delayed or lost.

Inflexibility   A file processing system resembles a mass-production facility. It produces numerous documents and reports routinely and efficiently, provided that these outputs were anticipated in the original design of the system. Such systems, however, are often quite inflexible and cannot easily respond to requests for a new or redesigned product. In other words, an application system cannot readily satisfy demands for information in a format that was not anticipated in the original design. This often leads to considerable frustration on the part of the users, who cannot understand why the computer system cannot give them information in a new format when they know it exists in the application files.

For example, the Order Filling System at Pine Valley Furniture contains three files: Customer Master, Inventory Master, and Backorder (see Figure 1-7). Suppose that the Orders Department manager wants to obtain a list of back-ordered items for a given customer. Unless the system design anticipated this request, it will be difficult to satisfy. If the request represents a new requirement, the firm may need a new application program to extract the required records from each file and produce the desired report. Depending on the backlog in the Information Systems Department, it may take months to complete the request.

Limited Data Sharing   With the traditional applications approach, each application has its own private files, and users have little opportunity to share data outside of their own applications. Notice in Figure 1-7 that users in the Accounting Department have access to the Invoicing System and its files but they may not have access to the Order Filling System files, which are used primarily by the Orders Department.

One consequence of limited data sharing is that the same data may have to be entered several times to update files with duplicate data. For example, at Pine Valley Furniture, a change in the description for an inventory item would have to be entered separately into both the Order Filling and Invoicing systems, since each contains its own version of an inventory file.

Another consequence of limited data sharing is that in developing new applications, the designer often cannot (or does not) exploit data contained in existing files. Instead, new files are designed that duplicate much of the existing data. Suppose that the manufacturing manager at Pine Valley Furniture requests a new system for scheduling production orders. Such a system would undoubtedly require an inventory file to provide economical order quantities, status of existing orders, and related inventory information. Of course, an Inventory Master file already is being used in the Order Filling System, but this file would have to be redesigned to meet the requirements of the scheduling application. Any change to the file would also probably require a complete rewrite of Programs A, B, and C in the Order Filling System (see Figure 1-7). Instead, the designer usually specifies a new Inventory File for the Production Scheduling System. In file processing systems, the cycle of limited data sharing and redundancy is perpetuated in this manner.

Poor Enforcement of Standards   Every organization requires standard procedures so that it may operate effectively. Within information systems, standards are required for data names, formats, and access restrictions. Unfortunately, data standards are difficult to make known and enforce in a traditional file processing environment, mainly because the responsibility for system design and operation has been decentralized. Two types of inconsistencies may result from poor enforcement of standards: synonyms and homonyms. A **synonym** results when two different names are used for the same data item—for example, student number and matriculation number. A **homonym** is a single name that is used for two different data items—for example, in a bank the term *balance* might be used to designate a checking account balance in one department and a savings account balance in a different department.

Enforcement of standards is particularly difficult in larger organizations with decentralized responsibility and decision making. Without centralized control or coordination, users in various departments may purchase their own computers and develop their own private applications without regard for compatibility or the sharing of data. Even in a small company, however, the achievement of standards is often difficult in an applications environment. At Pine Valley Furniture, the individual applications purchased from the software vendor were of a standalone variety and were not really compatible with one another (although all the applications were linked to the Accounting General Ledger System). The various

Synonym: Two different names that are used to describe the same data item (for example, *car* and *automobile*).

Homonym: A single name that is used for two different data items (for example, the term *invoice* used to refer to both a customer invoice and a supplier invoice).

application programs often used different names and formats for the same data items, which made modifications more difficult and precluded data sharing.

Excessive Program Maintenance   In file processing systems, descriptions of files, records, and data items are embedded within individual application programs. Therefore, any modification to a data file (such as a change of data name, format, or method of access) requires that the program (or programs) also be modified. Suppose that the data item CUSTOMER NAME had to be expanded from a 20-character field to a 25-character field in the Customer Master file at Pine Valley Furniture. As a result of this simple change, several programs in the Order Filling System and Invoicing System would have to be modified. The process of modifying existing programs is referred to as *program maintenance*. Many organizations today devote 80% or more of their programming effort to this activity. Much of the shortage of computer programmers and the large backlog of new applications can be attributed to the burden of maintaining programs in file processing systems.

The disadvantages of file processing systems discussed here were especially pronounced in earlier application systems. In newer systems, a number of powerful support packages and tools have been introduced to help overcome (or at least minimize) some of the disadvantages. These software support packages include graphical user interfaces, generalized file management and report writers, on-line query processing, transaction processing systems, data dictionaries, and high-level programming languages. Even with these facilities, however, many of the fundamental deficiencies of file processing systems persist: redundant data, low sharing of data, lack of standards and control, and low productivity.

THE DATABASE APPROACH

The database approach emphasizes the integration and sharing of data across the organization. This approach requires a major reorientation in thought process (sometimes referred to as a *paradigm shift*), starting with top management. Such a reorientation is difficult for most organizations; still, many are making this shift today and are learning in the process that information can be used as a competitive weapon.

Data-Driven Versus Process-Driven Design

With file processing systems, a process-driven approach has traditionally been used to design information systems. However, with the database approach, information systems professionals have discovered that a data-driven approach is often preferable. Figure 1-8 presents a simplified comparison of these two approaches.

With the process-driven approach (Figure 1-8a), organizational processes (such as Order Processing, Accounts Receivable, and Inventory) are first identified and analyzed. Processes and the data flows between processes are described using tools such as data flow diagrams (see Chapter 3). Designers work backward from the required outputs of the system to determine the required inputs. They use flowcharts to specify the program logic required to convert inputs into outputs. Finally, they design data files as a by-product of process design. This approach results in traditional file processing systems such as those described for Pine Valley Furniture Company.

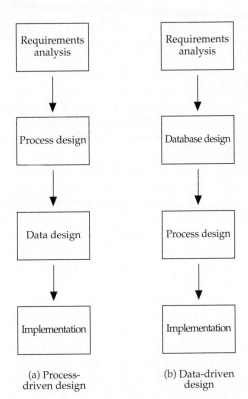

Figure 1-8

Process-driven versus
data-driven design

(a) Process-
driven design

(b) Data-driven
design

In contrast, the data-driven approach (Figure 1-8b) first focuses on the entities (or things) that the organization must manage: for example, employees, products, and customers. This approach identifies the attributes (or properties) of those entities and the relationships among them. The data-driven approach also identifies the business rules that govern how the entities are managed or used. After creating suitable models of the data structures and related business rules, designers develop the applications required to manage the data. We illustrate this approach in the next section.

Designers have discovered that a balanced approach that combines the data-driven and process-driven approaches is usually the most appropriate. Chapter 3 describes a framework for such an approach. Throughout this text we emphasize the data-driven approach to information systems development. Most of the concepts and techniques we describe can be applied equally well to either approach.

Database Approach for Pine Valley Furniture

By the early 1990s competition in furniture manufacturing had intensified, and competitors seemed to respond more rapidly than Pine Valley Furniture to new business opportunities. While there were numerous reasons for this trend, the managers felt constrained by their data processing systems, for reasons described earlier. At the suggestion of their data processing manager, Sharon Larson, the company formed a task group to investigate the potential of the database approach at Pine Valley Furniture Company. The task group (chaired by Ms. Larson) consisted of a mix of end-user managers and information specialists, plus a consultant who was hired to assist with the preliminary study.

Enterprise Data Model After evaluating the existing system, the task group decided to develop a preliminary enterprise data model for Pine Valley Furniture. First, the group identified the major functions and processes in the company. Next, the group identified the major entities that are associated with these functions and processes. An **entity** is a thing (e.g., person, place, event, or concept) about which an organization chooses to record data. The entities identified by the group were customers, customer orders, invoices, products, work orders, raw materials, and vendors. At the same time, the group identified the business rules that describe the relationships among the entities.

Next, the group developed an enterprise data model. An **enterprise data model** is a high-level conceptual data model for an organization that shows the entities and the relationships among those entities. Figure 1-9 shows the preliminary enterprise data model for Pine Valley Furniture in the form of a simplified entity-relationship diagram. (We describe entity-relationship diagrams in detail in Chapter 4.) In this diagram, we use special lines to specify the relationships between entities. A descriptive label is placed on each line to describe the relationship (for example, a customer Places an order).

The lines in Figure 1-9 also indicate the number of one entity that is (or may be) associated with a related entity. For example, look at the line leading from CUSTOMER to ORDER. The notation on the line near ORDER indicates that for each customer, there may be a minimum of zero orders (as indicated by the open circle symbol) and a maximum of many (as specified by the crow's foot symbol). (*Many* means an unspecified number such as one, two, three, or more.) The notation on this same line near CUSTOMER indicates that each order must be for

Entity: A thing (e.g., person, place, event, or concept) about which an organization chooses to record data.

Enterprise data model: A high-level conceptual data model for an organization. An enterprise data model shows the entities and the relationships among the entities.

Figure 1-9

Enterprise data model (preliminary) for Pine Valley Furniture

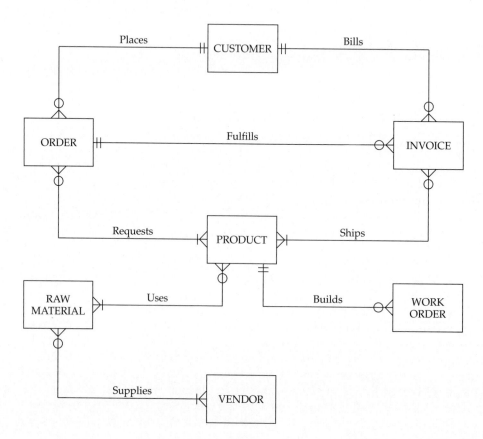

exactly one customer (since the minimum and maximum are both one). This stipulates the business rule that an order can never apply to more than one customer.

Now look at the line from ORDER to PRODUCT, which represents the Requests relationship. The symbols indicate that an order must request at least one product, and may request more than one. In the other direction, the notation indicates that a product may not be sold on (or appear on) any order, or it may appear on several orders. You should examine the remaining relationships and state the business rule for each symbol that is used.

Notice the following characteristics of the enterprise data model:

1. The enterprise data model is a model of the organization that provides valuable information about how the organization functions as well as important constraints.

2. The enterprise data model stresses the *integration* of data and processes by focusing on both relationships and entities.

Relational Database   The results of Pine Valley Furniture's preliminary study convinced management of the advantages of the database approach. The company decided to implement a modern relational database management system that views all data in the form of tables. Figure 1-10 shows tables describing three entities from the enterprise data model (PRODUCT, CUSTOMER, and ORDER) at Pine Valley Furniture. Each column of a table represents an attribute (or characteristic) of the entity, and each row is an instance (or occurrence) of that entity. This chapter introduces the relational model only briefly; we define it in detail in subsequent chapters.

PRODUCT

PRODUCT NO.	DESCRIPTION	FINISH	ROOM	UNIT PRICE
0100	Table	Oak	DR	500
0350	Table	Maple	DR	625
0625	Chair	Oak	DR	100
0975	Wall Unit	Pine	FR	750
1000	Dresser	Cherry	BR	800
1250	Chair	Maple	LR	400
1425	Bookcase	Birch	LR	250

CUSTOMER

CUSTOMER NO.	NAME	ADDRESS
C100	Contemporary Casuals	100 Oak Palo Alto CA
C150	Value Furniture	200 Walnut Cupertino CA
C325	Home Furnishings	300 Maple San Jose CA
C468	Western Furniture	400 Locust San Francisco CA
C500	Impressions	500 Pine Redwood City CA

ORDER

ORDER NO.	DATE	CUSTOMER NO.
A1000	9/16/9X	C325
B2500	10/15/9X	C468
C3000	8/20/9X	C325
D1500	11/1/9X	C500

Figure 1-10

Three relations at Pine Valley Furniture

An important property of the relational model is that it represents relationships between entities by values stored in the columns of the corresponding tables. Figure 1-9 shows that each customer may have several orders. Notice that customer number is one of the attributes in the ORDER table in Figure 1-10. As a result, we can easily link orders to customers. The ORDER table shows two orders (order A1000 and C3000) for customer C325. There is one order each for customers C468 and C500, and no orders for customers C100 or C150. These linkages allow users to retrieve data from the various tables by means of a powerful query language, as we will see in Chapter 2.

Implementing the Relational Database

The database approach offers a number of potential advantages compared to the older file processing approach. Few of these advantages will be realized, however, if the organization simply implements a series of stand-alone databases, which does not permit data sharing by members of the organization. In fact, stand-alone databases have many of the disadvantages common to file processing systems. To allow for data sharing, Pine Valley Furniture installed a local area network that links the personal computers in the various departments to a database server, as shown in Figure 1-11. A **local area network (LAN)** is a system that permits computing devices to communicate with one another over distances that range from a few feet to several miles (Palmer and Raines, 1991). The arrangement of the computers in this network forms a client/server architecture, as described earlier in this chapter.

Local area network (LAN): A system that permits computing devices to communicate with one another over distances that range from a few feet to several miles.

Figure 1-11

Client/server system for Pine Valley Furniture

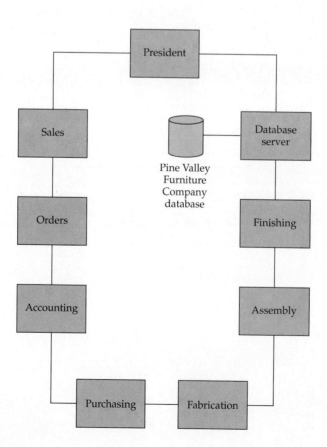

For example, when the Sales Department receives a new customer order for furniture, the order is captured and entered into this database. An accountant can view the monthly financial statements by querying the portion of the database that contains financial information, and the president can obtain market share projections using data from the database. These are examples of the use of the shared data that are stored in the Pine Valley Furniture Company database. We describe the development of these applications in detail in Chapter 2.

Benefits of the Database Approach

The database approach offers a number of potential advantages compared to traditional file approaches. These benefits include minimal data redundancy; consistency of data; integration of data; sharing of data; ease of application development; uniform security, privacy, and integrity controls; data accessibility and responsiveness; data independence; and reduced program maintenance.

Minimal Data Redundancy With the database approach, previously separate (and redundant) data files are integrated into a single, logical structure. In addition, each occurrence of a data item is recorded (ideally) in only one place in the database. For example, the fact that the address for a specific customer of Pine Valley Furniture is 300 Maple Street might be recorded in two separate files in a file processing system (see Figure 1-7). In a database system, however, this fact will normally be recorded only once (as shown in Figures 1-9 and 1-10) by the system that captures the data.

We are not suggesting that *all* redundancy can or should be eliminated. Sometimes there are valid reasons for storing multiple copies of the same data (for example, data access efficiency and data validation checks). In a database system, however, redundancy is *controlled*. It is designed into the system to improve performance (or provide some other benefit), and the system is (or should be) aware of the redundancy.

Consistency of Data By eliminating (or controlling) data redundancy, we greatly reduce the opportunities for inconsistency. For example, if each address is stored only once, we cannot have disagreement on the stored values. When controlled redundancy is permitted in the database, the database system itself should enforce consistency by updating each occurrence of a data item when a change occurs. If an address is stored in two separate records, the database system should update this data value in both records whenever a change occurs. Unfortunately, many systems today do not enforce data consistency in this manner.

Integration of Data In a database, data are organized into a single, logical structure, with logical relationships defined between associated data entities. This makes it easy for users to relate one item of data to another. For example, look again at Figure 1-9. Suppose a user is interested in information for a particular product. Since this entity is logically related to the raw material entity, the user can easily determine what raw materials are required to build the product. Also, the user can check to see what raw materials are on order from a vendor, since the RAW MATERIAL entity is logically related to the VENDOR entity. Data management software (described later) performs the function of associating logically related data items, regardless of the physical organization or location of the items in the database.

Sharing of Data A database is intended to be shared by all authorized users in the organization. For example, the database at Pine Valley Furniture is designed to satisfy the information needs of Accounting, Sales, Manufacturing, Purchasing, and other departments. The company thus has essentially re-created the single set of books that it had when it was first founded. Most database systems today (such as the client/server system shown in Figure 1-11) permit multiple users to share a database concurrently, although certain restrictions are necessary, as described in later chapters.

In a database system, each functional department is provided with its own view (or views) of the database. Each such departmental view (or *user view*) is a subset of the conceptual database model. Figure 1-12 shows three possible user views for Pine Valley Furniture. The first is for the Sales Department and shows the relationship between the CUSTOMER and ORDER entities. The second is for the Accounting Department and shows the relationships among the CUSTOMER, ORDER, and INVOICE entities. The third is for the Purchasing Department and shows the relationships among the PRODUCT, VENDOR, and RAW MATERIAL entities. These user views simplify the sharing of data by providing each user with the precise view of data required to make a decision or perform some function, without making the user aware of the overall complexity of the database.

Ease of Application Development A major advantage of the database approach is that it greatly reduces the cost and time for developing new business applications. This advantage applies to end users who develop applications using fourth-generation tools, as well as to information systems professionals. There are two important reasons that database applications can often be developed much more rapidly than conventional file applications:

1. Assuming that the database and the related data capture and maintenance applications have already been designed and implemented, the programmer need only develop the applications to query the database.

2. A number of aids, such as graphical user interface tools, report generators, and high-level languages, are available for developing database applications. (We describe many of these tools in subsequent chapters.)

Uniform Security, Privacy, and Integrity Controls The data administration function has complete jurisdiction over the database and is responsible for establishing controls for accessing, updating, and protecting data. In a database environment, these controls are often part of the database definition. Centralized con-

Figure 1-12

Three possible user views for Pine Valley Furniture

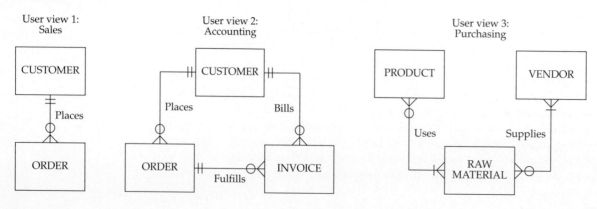

User view 1:
Sales

User view 2:
Accounting

User view 3:
Purchasing

trol and standard procedures can improve data protection, compared to that provided by a dispersed data file system. If proper controls are not applied, however, a database probably will be *more* vulnerable than conventional files, since a larger user community is sharing a common resource. We describe measures for database security, privacy, and integrity in Chapter 12.

Data Accessibility and Responsiveness   A database system provides multiple retrieval paths to each item of data, giving a user much greater flexibility in locating and retrieving data than with data files. Retrieval of data can cross traditional departmental boundaries. Refer to the enterprise data model for Pine Valley Furniture (Figure 1-9). Suppose that a customer calls requesting information about several items that have been back-ordered. While on the phone, the salesperson can look up the customer record, display the particular order in question, and then display the product record for each item on that order. Finally, the salesperson can display the work order status for each back-ordered item to determine its completion date. In fact, some organizations establish data communications links with their customers, so customers can obtain this information through a direct query into their supplier's database.

This example represents a routine, planned sequence of retrievals. But a database system (especially a relational database) allows end users to satisfy many ad hoc (one-time) requests for data through the use of a query language or report writer. For example, the manager of the Product Department at Pine Valley Furniture wanted a listing of all wall units that sold for more than $500. He was able to obtain such a listing quickly by entering the following command at a terminal:

```
SELECT PRODUCT_NO, DESCRIPTION, UNIT_PRICE
FROM PRODUCT
WHERE DESCRIPTION = 'Wall Unit'
            AND UNIT_PRICE > 500;
```

The language for this command is called **structured query language** (or **SQL**), which is a standard fourth-generation query language for relational database systems. It specifies the columns or attributes to be listed (PRODUCT_NO, DESCRIPTION, and UNIT_PRICE), the table from which the data are to be extracted (PRODUCT), and the conditions for selecting rows from the table. You will study how SQL can be used to build and manipulate databases in Chapter 2 and in subsequent chapters.

Structured query language (SQL): A standard fourth-generation query language for relational database systems.

Data Independence   The separation of data descriptions from the application programs that use the data is called **data independence**. As a result of this, an organization's data can change and evolve (within limits) without necessitating a change in the application programs that process the data. Data independence is one of the major objectives of the database approach.

In traditional systems, the descriptions of the data and the logic for accessing those data are built into each individual application program; thus, the program is *dependent* on the data files. Any change to the data file requires modifying or rewriting the application program. In contrast, in the database approach all data descriptions are stored separately from application programs, in a central location called the *repository*. (At Pine Valley Furniture Company, the repository is stored on the database server; see Figure 1-11.) The contents of the repository are under the control of the database administration group. We describe the properties of the repository in Chapter 12.

Data independence: The separation of data descriptions from the applications that use the data.

Reduced Program Maintenance Stored data must be changed frequently for a variety of reasons: new data item types are added, data formats are changed, new storage devices or access methods are introduced, and so on. In a data file environment, these changes require modifying the application programs that access the data. The term *maintenance* refers to modifying or rewriting old programs to make them conform to new data formats, access methods, and so forth.

In a database system, data are independent of the application programs that use them. Within limits, we can change either the data or the application programs that use the data without necessitating a change in the other factor. As a result, program maintenance can be significantly reduced in a modern database environment.

This section identifies nine major potential benefits of the database approach; however, we must caution you that many organizations have been frustrated in attempting to realize some of these benefits. For example, the goal of data independence (and therefore reduced program maintenance) has proven elusive due to the limitations of older data models and database management software. Fortunately, the relational model provides a significantly better environment for achieving these benefits. Another reason for failure to achieve the intended benefits is poor organizational planning and database implementation—even the best data management software cannot overcome such deficiencies. For this reason, we stress database planning and implementation.

Costs of the Database Approach

As with any business decision, the database approach entails some additional costs and risks that must be recognized and compared with the potential benefits.

New, Specialized Personnel Frequently, organizations that adopt the database approach or purchase a database management system (DBMS) need to hire or train individuals to maintain the new database software, develop and enforce new programming standards, design databases to achieve the highest possible performance, and manage the staff of new people. This personnel increase may be more than offset by other productivity gains, and an organization should not minimize the need for these specialized skills, which are required to obtain the most from the potential benefits. We discuss these staff requirements for database management in Chapter 12.

Need for Explicit Backup Minimal data redundancy, with all its associated benefits, must also allow for backup copies of data. Such backup or independently produced copies are helpful in restoring damaged data files and in providing validity checks on crucial data. To ensure that data are accurate and available whenever needed, either database management software or additional procedures have to provide these essential capabilities. A database management system usually automates many more of the backup and recovery tasks than a file system. This book covers database security, integrity, and recovery throughout.

Interference with Shared Data The concurrent access to shared data via several application programs can lead to some problems. First, when two concurrent users both want to change the same or related data, inaccurate results can occur if access to the data is not properly synchronized. Second, when data are used exclusively for updating, different users can obtain control of different segments of the database and lock up any use of the data (so-called deadlock). Database management software must be designed to prevent or detect such interferences in a way that is transparent to the user.

Organizational Conflict   A shared database requires a consensus on data definitions and ownership as well as responsibilities for accurate data maintenance. Experience has shown that conflicts on how to define data, data length and coding, rights to update shared data, and associated issues are frequent and difficult to resolve. Handling these organizational issues requires organizational commitment to the benefits of the database approach, organizationally astute database administrators, and a sound evolutionary schedule for database development.

If strong top management support of and commitment to the database approach is lacking, end-user development of stand-alone databases is likely to proliferate. These databases do not follow the general database approach that we have described: There is no enterprise model, no repository, no data capture-transfer-distribution system, and so on. Thus, they are unlikely to provide the benefits described earlier.

COMPONENTS OF THE DATABASE ENVIRONMENT

The major components of a typical database environment and their relationships are shown in Figure 1-13. You have already been introduced to some (but not all) of these components in previous sections. Following is a brief description of the nine components shown in Figure 1-13.

1. **Computer-aided software engineering (CASE) tools:** Automated tools used to design databases and application programs. We describe the use of CASE tools for database design and development throughout the text.

2. **Repository:** Centralized knowledge base containing all data definitions, screen and report formats, and definitions of other organizations and system components. We describe the repository in Chapter 12.

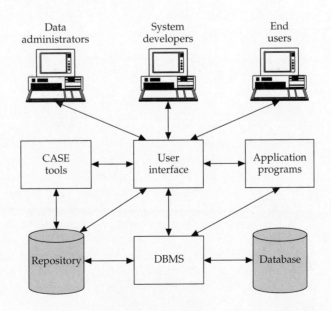

Figure 1-13

Components of the database environment

3. **Database management system (DBMS):** Commercial software (and occasionally, hardware and firmware) system used to create, maintain, and provide controlled access to the database and also to the repository. We describe the functions of a DBMS in Chapter 12.

4. **Database:** A shared collection of logically related data, designed to meet the information needs of multiple users in an organization. It is important to distinguish between the database and the repository: The repository contains *definitions* of data, while the database contains *occurrences* of data.

5. **Application programs:** Computer programs that are used to create and maintain the database and provide information to users.

6. **User interface:** Languages, menus, and other facilities by which users interact with various system components, such as CASE tools, application programs, the DBMS, and the repository.

7. **Data administrators:** Persons who are responsible for the overall information resources of an organization. Data administrators use CASE tools to improve the productivity of database planning and design. We describe the functions of data administration in detail in Chapter 12.

8. **System developers:** Persons such as systems analysts and programmers who design new application programs. System developers often use CASE tools for system requirements analysis and program design.

9. **End users:** Persons throughout the organization who add, delete, and modify data in the database and who request or receive information from it. All user interactions with the database must be routed through the DBMS.

With advances in software, the user interface is becoming increasingly user-friendly. Examples of such advances are menu-driven systems, use of a mouse, and voice-recognition systems. These systems promote *end-user computing*, which means that users who are not computer experts can define their own reports, displays, and simple applications. In fact, some organizations are creating *information centers*—organizational units that can be consulted to assist users in this endeavor. Of course, in such an environment, database administration must ensure the enforcement of adequate security measures to protect the database.

In summary, the DBMS operational environment shown in Figure 1-13 is an integrated system of hardware, software, and people that is designed to facilitate the storage, retrieval, and control of the information resource and to improve the productivity of the organization.

SUMMARY

Information is a major corporate resource and must be managed using the same basic principles used to manage other assets, such as employees, materials, equipment, and financial resources. Information is an asset only if it is accurate and available when needed; this can occur only if an organization purposely organizes and manages its data. Databases have become the standard technique for structuring and managing data in most organizations today.

A database is a shared collection of logically related data, designed to meet the information needs of multiple users in an organization. Data consist of raw facts concerning people, objects, events, or other entities; information is data that have been organized and presented in a form suitable for human interpretation.

Although some organizations have manual databases, in this text we restrict our attention to computer databases.

The traditional approach to information systems focuses on the data processing needs of individual departments or work groups. Each computer application is designed with its own set of files, which often duplicate data already stored in other files. This duplication (or redundancy) often results in inconsistent data in the various files; in addition, the files cannot be easily shared among the various users. Another disadvantage of file processing systems is that they are inflexible—users cannot request data in a new format without waiting for new application programs.

The database approach is designed to overcome many of the disadvantages of file processing systems. With this approach, databases are designed from an organization-wide viewpoint to minimize data redundancy. All data definitions are stored in a central location called a *repository*. Databases are managed by a commercial software system called the *database management system* (DBMS), and all user requests for data must be routed through the DBMS. Objectives of the database approach include improved data consistency, better sharing of data, easier access to data, and improved productivity for both end users and information system specialists.

To implement the database approach, organizations must establish a data administration function. The data administration group is responsible for developing an overall database plan, designing and implementing databases, and establishing policies concerning database security and quality assurance.

CHAPTER REVIEW

Key Terms

Client	Enterprise data model	Local area network (LAN)
Data	Entity	Server
Data independence	Homonym	Structured query language (SQL)
Database	Information	Synonym
Distributed database	Information resource management (IRM)	Work-group computing

REVIEW QUESTIONS

1. Define each of the following terms:
   a. data
   b. information
   c. database
   d. information resource management (IRM)
   e. application program
   f. repository
   g. synonym
   h. enterprise data model
   i. data independence
   j. database management system (DBMS)
   k. client/server architecture
   l. homonym
2. Contrast the following terms:
   a. data dependence; data independence
   b. database management system; user interface
   c. database; repository
   d. data; information
   e. synonym; homonym
   f. centralized database; distributed database
   g. homogeneous database; heterogeneous database

3. List and briefly describe six disadvantages of many traditional application systems.
4. Explain why data redundancy is so common in traditional application systems.
5. List and briefly describe nine benefits that can often be achieved with the database approach, compared to traditional application systems.
6. Briefly describe nine components in a database environment.
7. What is a client/server architecture?
8. Where are data definitions maintained in each of the following environments?
   a. traditional file processing system   b. database system
9. List eight functions of information resource management. In what courses are these functions covered in your information systems programs?
10. Briefly describe three types of centralized databases and two types of distributed databases.

PROBLEMS AND EXERCISES

1. Match the following terms and definitions:

____ IRM	a. data processed for human interpretation
____ entity	b. graphic model of entities and relationships
____ CASE	c. raw facts
____ relationship	d. integrated collection of data
____ DBMS	e. information considered as a resource
____ repository	f. person, place, or concept
____ data	g. commercial software system
____ information	h. automated design tools
____ database	i. central collection of data definitions
____ enterprise data model	j. logical association between entities

2. Diagram each of the following situations:
   a. A student takes several COURSEs; each COURSE has many STUDENTs.
   b. An INSTRUCTOR teaches several COURSEs, but each COURSE is taught by one INSTRUCTOR.
   c. A COURSE has several SECTIONs; each SECTION pertains to one COURSE.
   d. A COURSE may have several TEXTBOOKs; a given TEXTBOOK is used in only one COURSE.
3. Draw an enterprise data model for each of the following situations (state any assumptions you make):
   a. Football team: entities are TEAM, COACH, PLAYER, AGENT, GAME
   b. Family: entities are MOTHER, FATHER, HOME, CHILDREN, CAR, CLOTHES
   c. Bank: entities are BRANCH, CUSTOMER, TELLER, ACCOUNT, DEPOSIT, WITHDRAWAL
4. Add the entity EMPLOYEE to the enterprise data model for Pine Valley Furniture Company (Figure 1-9). Assume that a given work order may require one or more employees. Also, assume an employee may work on zero, one, or more than one work order.
5. Draw a user view (similar to those in Figure 1-12) for a production scheduling system at Pine Valley Furniture Company. This new application requires information about the following entities: PRODUCT, WORK ORDER, RAW MATERIAL, ORDER. (*Hint:* see Figure 1-9 for the relationships among these entities.)
6. Write a SQL command to produce a listing of the following data from Figure 1-10:
   a. List the product number and description for all dining room furniture (ROOM = 'DR').
   b. List the order number and customer number for all orders whose date is 10/15/9X.
   c. List the name and address for customer number C325.

7. Draw an enterprise data model for an organization you are familiar with (Girl Scouts, fast-food restaurant, and so on). First, list about six major entities for the organization, and then draw the relationships between the entities.
8. Visit an organization that has installed a database system. Talk to a person in data administration and determine each of the following:
   a. Which of the benefits of the database approach have been realized by the organization? Which have not been realized?
   b. Is this a centralized or distributed database system?
   c. What major components of a database system (Figure 1-13) are present in the organization?
   d. Does the organization have an enterprise data model? If so, in what form is it represented?

REFERENCES

Amoroso, D. L., F. R. McFadden, and Kathy Brittain-White. 1990. "Disturbing Realities Concerning Data Policies in Organizations." *Information Resources Management Journal* 3 (Spring):18–28.

Davydov, M. M. 1993. "Capitalizing on Information Assets." *Database Programming & Design* 6 (February):34–41.

Guimaraes, T. 1988. "Information Resources Management: Improving the Focus." *Information Resources Management Journal* 1 (Fall):10–21.

McGoveran, D., and C. J. White. 1990. "Clarifying Client/Server." *DBMS* 3 (November):78–90.

McLeod, Raymond, Jr., and Kathy Brittain-White. 1988. "Incorporation of IRM Concepts in Undergraduate Business Curricula." *Information Resources Management Journal* 1 (Fall):28–38.

Palmer, Michael J., and Alvin R. Raines. 1991. *Local Area Networking with NOVELL Software.* Boston: Boyd & Fraser.

Vetter, M. 1987. *Strategy for Data Modeling.* New York: Wiley.

CHAPTER

2

A Database Application for Pine Valley Furniture

LEARNING OBJECTIVES

After reading this chapter, you should be able to:

- Identify the steps in the development of a database.
- Understand the variety of skills needed to design and develop a database application.
- Use the rudimentary features of a database management system.
- Explain the various components of a database management system (DBMS), including tools to assist in nonprocedural programming.
- Begin to design and build a database for a class project.
- Understand several basic styles of relational database management systems and relational database query languages.
- Read entity-relationship diagrams, and draw simple entity-relationship diagrams to describe a database.
- Write simple queries using the dBASE IV Control Center.

INTRODUCTION

Chapter 1 introduced the operations of Pine Valley Furniture Company, a manufacturer of all-wood furniture. Chapter 2 illustrates a database application that satisfies some of the transaction processing and management information system needs of this company.

There are several reasons for presenting this chapter at this point. First, you have probably not used or developed an information processing application based upon database technology, nor are you familiar with how such applications are developed. The goal of this text is to introduce you to the concepts and many of the skills you will use to design and build database applications. This chapter briefly illustrates what you will be able to do after you complete a database course using this text.

Second, most students learn best from a text full of concrete examples. Although all of the chapters in this book contain numerous examples, illustrations, and actual database diagrams and code, each chapter concentrates on a specific aspect of database management. We have designed this chapter to provide you with an overview of database management and how the various aspects of database management are related. This chapter is the closest we can come to a demonstration of a working system in the format of the printed page.

Finally, many instructors want you to begin the initial steps of a database development group or individual course project early in your database course. Due to the logical progression of topics in this book (database planning, data analysis, logical database design, physical design, and implementation), you will study many pages before you will see your target for the project. This chapter gives you an idea of where you are headed. From this illustration, you can begin using some basic skills now before a more rigorous treatment of topics is presented later in the book. Thus, this chapter provides the information you need to begin developing a database application in your course. Obviously, since this is only Chapter 2, many of the examples we will use will be much simpler than the database requirements in your project, other course assignments, or a real organization.

This chapter illustrates the development and operation of a working information system; that is, all the sample screens and reports shown here are generated from a system that has actually been implemented. The chapter also illustrates the use of automated tools to assist in the development of a database. The example database application includes both transaction processing and management information and decision support requirements. These system requirements tell us what type of data must be stored in a database and the necessary space and response time to meet business expectations. Thus, we begin this chapter with an illustration of the data analysis of these processing requirements for Pine Valley Furniture, followed by an illustration of the necessary database and associated computer programs for transaction and information processing. First, however, we provide an overview of the database development process and of the Pine Valley Furniture enterprise.

THE DEVELOPMENT OF A DATABASE APPLICATION

Database application system: The data definitions, stored data, transactions, inquiries, screens, reports, and other programs needed to capture, maintain, and present data from a database.

A **database application system** includes the data definitions, stored data, transactions, inquiries, screens, reports, and other programs needed to capture, maintain, and present data from a database. Like any other application system you might have encountered in practice or analyzed and designed in a systems analysis and design course, a database application is developed in steps. These steps involve analysis of business needs, functional design of a system that meets these requirements, physical design of a working system that efficiently meets time and space expectations, and programming (using a combination of programming and database processing languages). In addition, testing, documentation, installation, and training must occur. We will not attempt in this chapter to illustrate all of these activities. Instead we give the essence of this process, so you can put the more detailed coverage of these topics later in the book into perspective.

Table 2-1 provides a simple outline of a typical database development project. We will elaborate this process and link database development into the overall information systems development process in Chapter 3. We will illustrate most, but not all, of these steps in this chapter. Also, we will study only a very small portion of the database requirements at Pine Valley Furniture.

TABLE 2-1 Database Development Project Outline

Enterprise modeling
- Analyze current data processing.
- Analyze the general business functions and their database needs.
- Plan database development project.

Conceptual data modeling
- Analyze overall data requirements for business function(s) supported by database.
- Develop preliminary conceptual data model.

Logical database design
- Analyze in detail the business function(s) supported by database.
- Normalize transactions and reports.
- Integrate views into conceptual data model.
- Design screens, reports, and applications.
- Identify data integrity and security requirements.

Physical database design and creation
- Define database to DBMS.
- Decide on physical organization of data.
- Design programs.

Database implementation
- Code and test programs.
- Complete database documentation.
- Install database and convert from prior systems.

Database maintenance
- Analyze database and database applications to ensure that information requirements are met.
- Tune database for improved performance.
- Fix errors in database and database applications.

A database development project begins with **enterprise modeling**, which is where you set the range and general contents of organizational databases. This step occurs within *information systems planning* for an organization. In this step you review current systems, analyze the nature of the business area to be supported, describe the data needed at a very high level of abstraction, and plan one or more database development projects. Database planning, described in Chapter 3, is conducted in this phase. Figure 2-1, a duplicate of Figure 1-9, shows a preliminary enterprise data model for part of Pine Valley Furniture.

In *conceptual database design* you analyze the overall data requirements for a specific information system. This system might be the topic of a particular user request to modify an existing system or to build a new system, or it might be the result of the identification of a new database from enterprise modeling. The result of conceptual database design also is a figure like Figure 2-1, but the scope of such a figure is restricted to data needed for one information system. It helps for subsequent analysis, however, to define the scope involved. As in enterprise modeling, such a chart is preliminary, since the transactions, reports, screens, and inquiries have not been detailed.

In *logical database design* you perform the detailed review of the business processes supported by the database. You analyze the individual reports, transactions, screens, and so on required by these processes, and determine exactly what data are to be maintained in the database and the nature of that data. The analysis of each individual report, transaction, and so on represents a particular, limited view of the database. These individual views must be combined, or integrated, into a comprehensive database structure. The result is a complete picture of the database without any reference to a particular database management system for

Enterprise modeling: The first step in database development, in which the scope and general contents of a database are specified.

Figure 2-1

Preliminary Pine Valley Furniture enterprise data model

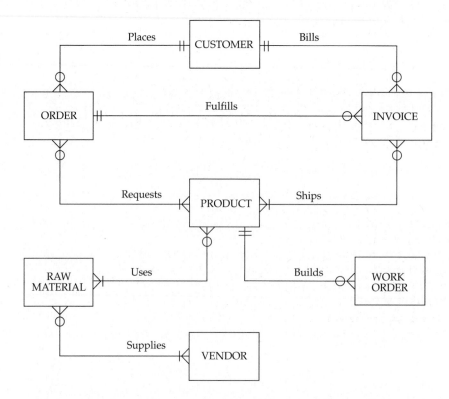

managing this data. This logical database design is then compared with the conceptual design, and discrepancies are reconciled. With a final logical database design in place, we can also begin to identify the needs for particular computer programs and queries to maintain and report the database contents.

In *physical database design and creation*, you decide on the organization of the database in computer storage (usually disk) and define the physical structures to the database management system. You outline the programs to process transactions and to generate anticipated management information and decision support reports.

In *database implementation*, you write, test, and install the programs that process the database for data capture and reporting. You might program in standard programming languages (like COBOL or C), in special database processing languages (like SQL or the dBASE IV query language), or using special-purpose nonprocedural languages to produce stylized reports and screens, possibly including graphs. We illustrate several of these options in this chapter.

In *database maintenance*, you evolve the database. In this step, you add, delete, or change characteristics of the structure of a database in order to meet changing business conditions, to correct errors in database design made in earlier steps, or to improve the processing speed of database applications. You might also need to rebuild a database if it becomes contaminated or destroyed due to a program or computer system malfunction. This is typically the longest step of database development, since it lasts throughout the life of the database and its associated applications.

Figure 1-13 introduced the components of the database environment, and we illustrate several components in this chapter. Obviously, the database itself as well as a database management system (DBMS) and application programs are essential, and we illustrate them here. We also show a simple repository, associated with the DBMS we will use, and we use several forms of user interfaces. Specifically, we illustrate the following:

- *Menu system* module of the DBMS, which helps us to define the database, to write queries and programs, and to maintain and report data
- *Report writer* module of the DBMS, which provides special commands for summarizing and aggregating data, as well as for producing custom-designed column headings and other report layout features
- *Screen painter* module of the DBMS, which assists us in creating readable and easy-to-use CRT screens (or forms) for data entry, maintenance, and simple queries

The DBMS used in this chapter to illustrate a database application for Pine Valley Furniture is dBASE IV, Version 1.5, from Ashton-Tate (a Borland Company) (1992). This has been one of the most popular personal computer database systems, starting with the original dBASE II package. A student version of dBASE IV (see Senn, 1990, and Krumm, 1990) is available. The student version provides all the functionality of the full package but places a few restrictions on the size of the database that can be created. Chapter 9 covers dBASE IV in detail. We could have implemented our database using any personal computer DBMS. We illustrate another major system, Paradox, in Chapter 10. For our dBASE implementation, we use the SQL subsystem, the dBASE menu system, and the proprietary dBASE language to introduce the variety of languages available. SQL is a standard for database programming languages that has been adopted by many of the mainframe and personal computer DBMS vendors. We cover SQL in Chapter 8.

THE CONCEPTUAL DATA MODEL FOR PINE VALLEY FURNITURE

Some of the data and information processing requirements at Pine Valley Furniture were described in Chapter 1. Figure 2-1 depicts a preliminary enterprise data model for some of these requirements. We limit our discussion in this chapter to the requirements shown in Figure 2-2.

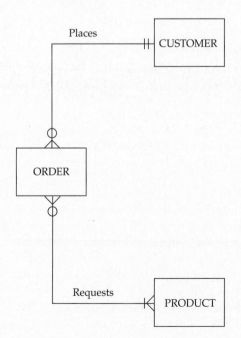

Figure 2-2

Pine Valley Furniture sample conceptual data model

To create a more manageable model for use at this point in the text, we have dropped from Figure 2-1 the RAW MATERIAL, WORK ORDER, INVOICE, and VENDOR data entities, along with any processing requirements associated with them. Figure 2-2 uses a version of a standard notation called *entity-relationship* (*E-R*) diagramming (we expand on this notation in Chapter 4). Such charts can be generated from a variety of computer-assisted software engineering (CASE) tools, such as E-R Designer (Chen and Associates, 1988), which is a personal computer tool for developing such database descriptions.

TRANSACTION PROCESSING REQUIREMENTS FOR PINE VALLEY FURNITURE

In this and the next section on management information requirements, we show the development of a logical database design for Pine Valley Furniture. We first develop the logical database using E-R diagramming, and at the end of the next section we show the equivalent relational database design. For simplicity, we will not discuss the important but detailed topics of data normalization and view integration, which are done during logical database design. These topics are reviewed in detail in Chapter 6.

Business transaction: All the data about one business event, which might cause several database transactions to add, delete, or change database records.

A **business transaction** is the data about a business event, such as receipt of a customer order, notice of an employee address change, or the issuance of a customer sales invoice. Such transactions change the contents of a database (add, delete, or modify data), so we usually associate transaction processing with populating and maintaining a database. Some simple inquiries (such as displaying the status of a customer order, determining the on-hand inventory of a product, or checking the credit status of a customer) may also be considered transactions. A crucial feature of a transaction is its integrity; that is, only correct and consistent data should be permitted in the database. For example, if we discover some error during the input of a new customer order or are unable to complete the input, the whole order should probably be rejected. The careful control of business transactions is central to transaction processing applications. We will illustrate some simple controls in this chapter.

We will concentrate our attention on the order entry, customer service, and product management areas at Pine Valley Furniture (PVF). The basic business transactions include entry and maintenance of customer and product data (such as changing a customer's address or entering data about a new product), as well as entry of new customer orders. The identification of all the business transactions would happen during the logical design phase of the database development project, as a detailed systems analysis of the business is conducted. Detailed procedures for the analysis of database requirements are outlined in Chapters 4 through 6.

Pine Valley Furniture has decided that all transaction processing will be done on-line, so data entry and maintenance will use CRT screen displays. The database will reside on the server on Pine Valley Furniture's local area network. We will ignore in this introductory chapter many issues of data security, access control, and recovery that must be considered in a real application. Later in this chapter we give some examples of how to include such data integrity controls when the database is defined. A data analyst would identify the need for such controls during the logical design step of developing the database.

Product and Customer Data Entry

Figure 2-3a shows the design for a product display screen that PVF employees use for data entry, maintenance, and simple status checks on products. Each product is uniquely identified by a number (PRODUCT NO.), called a *primary key*, and is defined in the DESCRIPTION data element. The product's standard price (UNIT PRICE), type of wood finish (FINISH), and intended application (ROOM) are also shown. In addition, the quantity of the product in stock (QUANTITY ON HAND) is shown.

The product display is summarized in E-R notation in Figure 2-3b. The bubbles attached to the PRODUCT entity rectangle indicate facts, or data elements, about each Pine Valley product. The primary key data elements are underlined. One requirement for the product display screen (as well as for the customer, to be shown next) is that during data entry, duplicate products (or customers) may not be entered. Similarly, the typical process for deleting or modifying product (or customer) data is to display a formatted screen that shows all the data names for product (or customer) data and then enter the primary key (for example, PRODUCT NO. for product data). The data entry program would then display the remainder of the data for that record for visual verification that the correct

```
              PRODUCT DISPLAY


    PRODUCT NO.:          M128
    DESCRIPTION:          Bookcase
    ROOM:                 Study
    FINISH:               Birch
    UNIT PRICE:           $200.00
    QUANTITY ON HAND:     10
```

Figure 2-3

Sample product display

(a) Product display screen

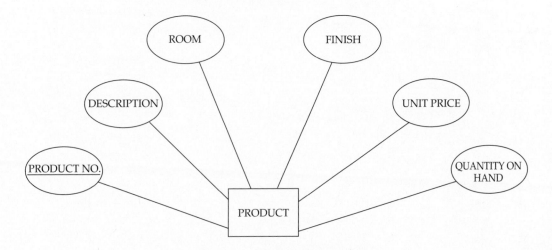

(b) E-R diagram for product display screen

Figure 2-4

Design for product data management menu

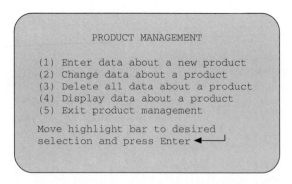

key was entered. Only when the user verifies that the correct record has been retrieved would it be deleted or changed, thus avoiding errors in maintaining the database.

Use of the product display screen is to be controlled by a menu system that asks the employee to select from five options: (1) enter a new product, (2) change product data, (3) delete a product, (4) display data about a product, or (5) exit the product data management function. For simplicity, we will not deal with authority to perform these actions (database security) in our illustration.

Figure 2-4 shows a design for a main product data management menu screen. We can quite easily develop such a menu with the dBASE IV Application Generator. We use a mouse to move the cursor to the desired option and then select

Figure 2-5

Sample customer display

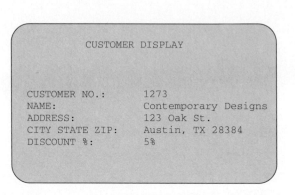

(a) Customer display screen

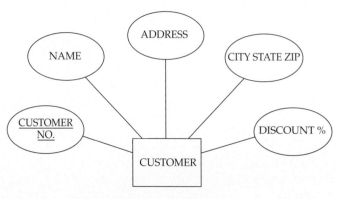

(b) E-R diagram for customer display screen

that option by clicking a mouse button. Later in the chapter we will show you how to use the product display for each of the five product data management options on this menu.

Figure 2-5a shows a sample customer display screen that Pine Valley wants to use for entry and maintenance of customer data. Each customer is assigned a unique number (CUSTOMER NO.). Other customer data included are the customer's full name (NAME), street address (ADDRESS), city information (CITY STATE ZIP), and agreed-upon price discount (DISCOUNT%). The price discount is applied across the board on all purchases by the customer.

This customer display is summarized using E-R notation in Figure 2-5b. CUSTOMER NO. is underlined because it is the primary key. Note that we have combined the city information into one data element. We chose this format only after verifying that these are not three separate pieces of data. For simplicity, we assume that there will be no use for city, state, or zip code separately (although in most circumstances this would not be true).

Customer Order Entry

A design for the Pine Valley Furniture customer order entry screen appears in Figure 2-6a. Orders are entered on-line from paper documents (either official Pine Valley order forms or, more typically, orders printed by customers in their own formats). Each order is assigned a unique number (ORDER NO.), to track each customer request. ORDER NO. is an internal Pine Valley number; any order number that a customer might provide is not to be included in the database. The date that the order is received (ORDER DATE) and the date Pine Valley expects to ship all the products ordered (PROMISED DATE) also appear on this screen. Obviously, each order is from some customer, indicated by CUSTOMER NO. on the screen. The other customer data (NAME, ADDRESS, and CITY STATE ZIP) are not actually entered for each order. Rather, they are automatically displayed on this screen when the CUSTOMER NO. is entered by referencing the previously entered customer data. Thus, an order can only be entered if the data for the associated customer has already been entered. Also, there is no distinction between the sold-to, bill-to, and ship-to customers. Given the nature of the Pine Valley Furniture business, these three addresses are always the same. Similarly, product data (DESCRIPTION and UNIT PRICE) are displayed from the associated product record as each line on the order is entered by PRODUCT NO. The QUANTITY ORDERED must, of course, be entered for each line item. QUANTITY ORDERED is neither a characteristic of the order (how much of which product?) nor of the product (on which order?). This property of QUANTITY ORDERED will affect how we display the data for this screen in an E-R diagram.

Note that the customer order contains more complex data than do the customer or product display transaction screens, because we may need to show more than one product on an order. Further, a customer order actually refers to existing customer and product data, as well as new order and order line item data. Figure 2-6b depicts this set of data associated with the different data entities. For example, an order is placed by one customer, so the customer data is shown as being attached to the related customer, not to the order directly. In Chapter 6 we describe a process called *data normalization*, by which we organize data to simplify data maintenance. Associating customer data with only the customer entity and associating product data with only the product entity is the result of normalization.

Also note in Figure 2-6 that we use a diamond for the Requests relationship, since a data element is associated with Requests. An order may include many line

Figure 2-6

Sample customer order

```
           PVF CUSTOMER ORDER

ORDER NO.:  61384    CUSTOMER NO.:  1273

NAME:                Contemporary Designs
ADDRESS:             123 Oak St.
CITY STATE ZIP:      Austin, TX 28384

ORDER DATE:          PROMISED DATE:
11/04/93             11/21/93
```

PRODUCT NO.	DESCRIPTION	QUANTITY ORDERED	UNIT PRICE
M128	Bookcase	4	200.00
B381	Cabinet	2	150.00
R210	Table	1	500.00

(a) Order entry screen

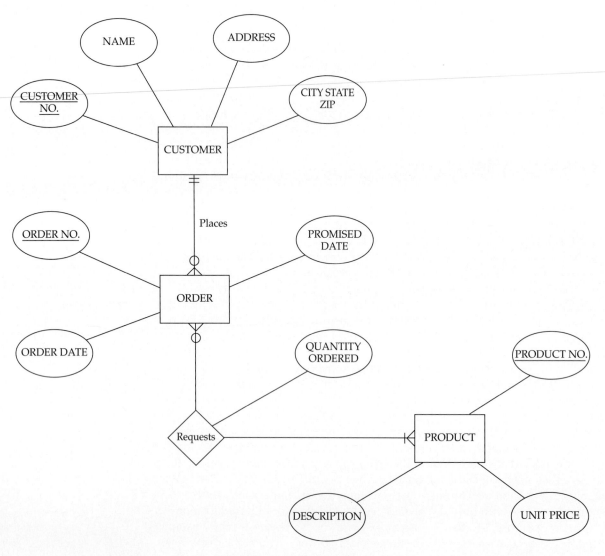

(b) E-R diagram for order entry screen

items (and a given product may appear on many orders). The quantity ordered is a characteristic of neither the order nor the product but rather relates jointly to a product on an order, which is the meaning of the Requests relationship. The type of relationship, like Requests, that occurs many times for each of the entities to which it relates is called a *many-to-many relationship*. Another way to state this is that one or many products are associated with each order, and zero, one, or many orders are associated with each product. Figure 2-6b clearly shows that QUANTITY ORDERED is neither order nor product data per se. QUANTITY OR-DERED occurs for each instance of the Requests relationship. A Requests instance exists for each line item on each order. That is, an instance of Requests is associated with exactly one ORDER instance and exactly one PRODUCT instance.

The same order entry screen design could also be used to show the content of existing orders. By entering the ORDER NO., we can retrieve all the associated data into the form on a CRT.

Now that all the transaction processing requirements have been analyzed, we form the consolidated database by combining the requirements of each of the transactions. Figure 2-7 contains the E-R diagram for the database, which includes

Figure 2-7

E-R diagram for all transaction processing

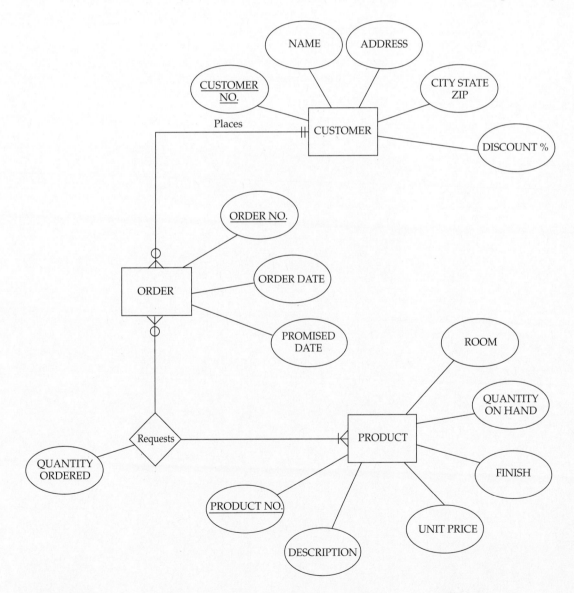

all of the data referenced so far. Each of the previous E-R diagrams is a subset of this figure. At least until we analyze additional reporting requirements that support management information and decision support, Figure 2-7 represents a logical model of the database needed by Pine Valley Furniture. At this point a data analyst would also collect all of the integrity control statements mentioned above (for example, no two customers can have the same CUSTOMER NO., and PROMISED DATE cannot be earlier than ORDER DATE), so later stages of database development can ensure that these rules are met. The next step is to analyze the management reporting requirements to determine if we need additional data.

MANAGEMENT INFORMATION REQUIREMENTS FOR PINE VALLEY FURNITURE

Management information requirements include information to check the status of business activities as well as that needed to make informed business decisions. Some information is simply data retained in the database. Other information is produced by summarizing, aggregating, comparing, or combining various pieces of data stored in the database.

An example of a simple management need for information at Pine Valley Furniture is the review of an individual customer's discount rate. The business question would be, "What discount are we giving customer X?" Figure 2-8a shows a

Figure 2-8

Discount rate query

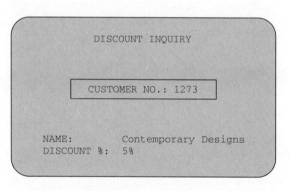

(a) Discount rate inquiry screen

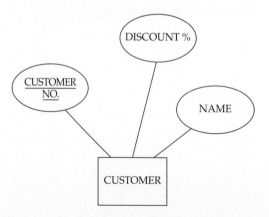

(b) E-R diagram for discount rate inquiry

design for a sample CRT screen for this inquiry. For this query, the manager enters the appropriate CUSTOMER NO., and then the application system retrieves the corresponding customer record and displays the NAME and DISCOUNT% data. In this situation, only one database record, from the CUSTOMER data entity of Figure 2-7, is required. Figure 2-8b shows the data required for this query using E-R notation.

Another rather simple management information requirement at PVF is the daily customer order log. This report, depicted in Figure 2-9a, lists all the orders submitted to PVF on a specified date, in sequence by customer name. Only customers who placed an order on the specified date would appear on this log. The head of the Customer Service Department scans this report, and it is used as a printed copy of daily order activity. Each row of the report is an extract of data from one customer order. As Figure 2-7 shows, however, the customer NAME is not stored with the ORDER but in the CUSTOMER record related to it. Thus, this report requires access to data in both the ORDER and CUSTOMER entities, which is depicted in E-R notation in Figure 2-9b.

Each sales manager at PVF is responsible for a set of major customers. As part of this job, each manager occasionally checks on the order activity of a given customer assigned to him or her and uses this information to identify low- and high-activity customers and to obtain a general understanding of a customer's buying pattern. This information is also available as a sales manager is getting

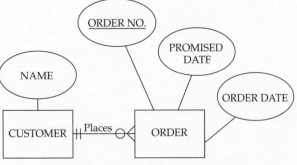

Figure 2-9

Daily order log report

(a) Sample daily order log

```
                                                          PAGE 1
                        DAILY ORDER LOG
                           11/10/93


        CUSTOMER NAME        ORDER NO.      PROMISED DATE
     ABC Office Supply         61397          11/20/93
     Commonwealth Builder      61398          11/12/93
```

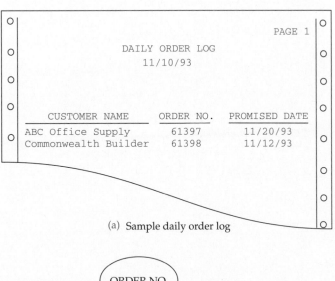

(b) E-R diagram for daily order log

ready to call or visit a customer. Figure 2-10a shows a layout for a customer order history report, which is displayed on the sales manager's CRT and can be printed at the manager's option. For this report, a sales manager specifies the desired customer and the period of time (start and end order dates) over which orders are to be reviewed. Data from CUSTOMER, Places, ORDER, Requests, and PRODUCT entities and relationships are needed to produce this report, as shown in the E-R diagram of Figure 2-10b.

Although PVF requires numerous other management reports, we will wait to introduce these later in the book. Since the E-R diagrams for the management information requirements we have outlined so far do not introduce any new data, the E-R diagram of Figure 2-7 also represents a comprehensive logical description of the database required at PVF. To keep our example simple, we also do not introduce any decision support applications at this point. Given the approach we have taken for logical database design, the next step would be to translate the E-R logical database into relational notation. The details of this process are beyond the scope of this chapter. Thus, we simply present below a list of the four database

Figure 2-10

Customer order history query

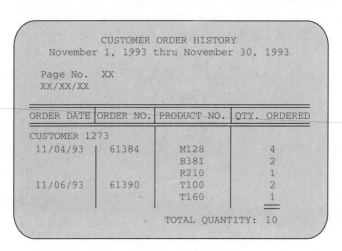

(a) Sample customer order history screen

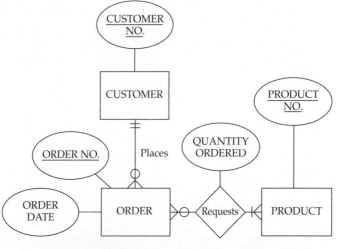

(b) E-R diagram for customer order history

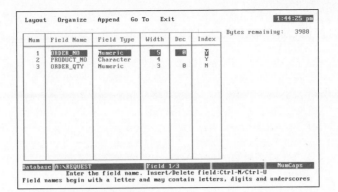

Figure 2-16

REQUEST table definition

has a predefined format). We have chosen to index this table on both the primary key, ORDER_NO (which was defined as unique, as above), and ORDER_DATE (for which we left the default as nonunique, which is appropriate). The second index was chosen after analyzing transaction and management information processing. We determined that the ORDER DATE field is frequently used to qualify which orders are to be retrieved, and an index will speed up the searching of records.

It might be desirable to impose other integrity rules on the data; for example, the PROM_DATE should not be earlier than the ORDER_DATE. dBASE does not have a facility to define this integrity rule with the table definition, but we can include such rules later when we define data entry screens for this file. Cross-reference key control is another restriction that we would like to specify here. That is, the CUST_NO field in each row of the CUORDER table should match some existing value in the CUSTOMER table. Again, we cannot place this *referential integrity* rule with the table definition in dBASE, but we can handle referential integrity in data entry application programming. Some other relational systems support including such restrictions with the table definition, so that the restrictions apply to any user of the database, not just those using a particular screen definition or program. Storing all integrity controls with the table defintions would be a more desirable integrity feature.

Figure 2-16 shows the definition of the tables for the Requests (REQUEST in dBASE) relationship. We include the primary keys of the two related tables (ORDER_NO and PRODUCT_NO are included and indexed), along with the data element associated with the relationship (ORDER_QTY instead of QUANTITY ORDERED).

We will not take the space here to include security controls on this database definition, but when many people will use the database, such controls are desirable. We might want to limit update of the database to authorized users only (for example, only order entry clerks can update an order). Chapters 12 and 13 illustrate such security features, which we would normally implement at this point in the database development.

PROCESSING TRANSACTIONS IN dBASE IV

We have now completed two of the three steps in the physical database design and creation phase outlined in Table 2-1. The next step is to design programs. First we will design the programs that enter data into the tables we just defined.

Recall that we identified three transactions for our example database: entry and maintenance of (1) product data, (2) customer data, and (3) customer orders. All transactions will be processed on-line, so we must design screen displays that match the desired input format presented in earlier sections. Fortunately, dBASE provides a screen design and processing module in the Control Center as well as other commands to handle the entry, editing, and display of data from stylized screen formats. In fact, dBASE automatically generates a default screen display for each file that is defined in a database.

Product and Customer Transactions

Figure 2-17 shows the layout of the default screen (or, in dBASE terms, a *form*) for the PRODUCT file. This form shows one *record*, or row, from the PRODUCT table on the screen at a time. Each field appears on a separate line, and a default status line appears at the top. The number of the next available blank record is also automatically placed on this form. This format is obviously rather plain, and the computer field names, not user-meaningful prompts, are used for each field. Using the custom forms design editor, we can move the fields around and add headings and more meaningful field labels to produce a screen that resembles the design for a product display from Figure 2-3.

We will not outline the step-by-step process involved in using the forms designer to produce a more readable screen layout. Instead we will show a few of the key form definition screens. The starting point is the default form. The "quick layout" of the default form appears in Figure 2-18. This form is shown on what dBASE calls the *form design work surface*, on which we can arrange the form con-

Figure 2-17

Blank PRODUCT default form

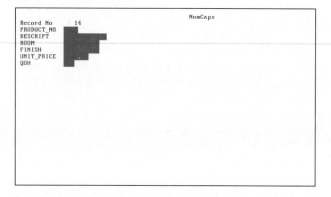

Figure 2-18

PRODUCT default form definition

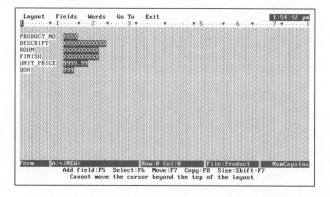

tents. The form designer menu line is at the top, a ruler is on line 2, and the field names and default templates are placed as in Figure 2-17. The cursor of this form design surface is currently in the upper left-hand corner character cell (row 0, column 0). The bottom line lists the hot keys for certain functions that can be performed on the form design work surface.

The final form design (meant to resemble Figure 2-3) appears in Figure 2-19. We have added a screen title, labeled each field with a clear phrase, and included a description, or *template*, indicating the valid format of each field. Although the PRODUCT_NO field is a character field, we redefined its input template for this screen as A999, meaning that the first position is alphabetic and the next three must be digits. We added a dollar sign in front of the UNIT_PRICE field to clarify the unit of measure.

Figures 2-20 through 2-22 show how some of these and other data-editing and validation rules are defined for a form. In Figure 2-20 the PRODUCT_NO field space on the form is changed to a new template. We produced this screen by placing the cursor on the form design work surface anywhere on the PRODUCT_NO field (which starts in row 4, column 41). Then we selected the Fields menu and the Modify Field submenu. We next moved the menu cursor to highlight the Template option (the large help box lists the possible characters for each position of the template). We entered the A999 format, which represents the coding scheme for product numbers.

Figure 2-21 illustrates other options, this time for the UNIT_PRICE field (which is located at row 8, column 42 of the product display form). First, we have specified that this field may be edited (changed), so for this form UNIT_PRICE is a read/write field. On another form we could make this a read-only field; users who were not allowed to change values for this field would have to use this form.

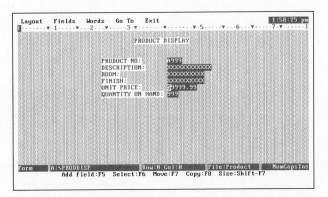

Figure 2-19

Final PRODUCT form layout

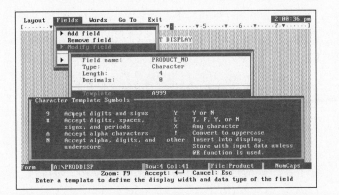

Figure 2-20

Template for PRODUCT_NO field

Figure 2-21

Editing rules for
UNIT_PRICE field

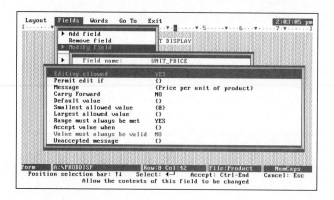

Figure 2-22

Editing rules for QOH
field

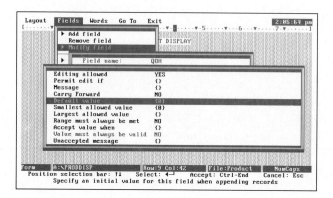

Second, for this field we have added a message to be displayed on a screen status line that gives a more descriptive explanation of the field. This message will be shown when the cursor is on the UNIT_PRICE field. Further, we defined the field to have 0 as its smallest allowed value, to restrict erroneous entry of a negative number. If a user tried (by mistake) to enter a negative quantity, dBASE would forbid this entry, generate a standard error message, and request a new value. Also, the YES value in "Range must always be met" means that this smallest value cannot be overridden. Many more complex editing rules could be defined by utilizing the other editing options.

Figure 2-22 illustrates editing for a minimum value for the QOH field (which is located at row 9, column 42 of the product display form) and also the use of a default value that will be automatically stored if the user fails to enter any value. We specified NO for "Range must always be met" to allow (under special conditions) negative on-hand values. Some database operations may be sensitive to missing data, so entry of a default may be both natural (a new product is likely to have zero on hand to begin with) and helpful for subsequent processing. Since zero is not the only possible default in all circumstances, we must take care in selecting a default value. We discuss the handling of missing data in Chapter 7.

The complete description of the product form is stored in the PVF catalog under the PRODDISP name. A sample product display screen using this form for the PRODUCT file appears in Figure 2-23. This screen shows the data for product number M128, which was entered previously. The top line shows that both NumLock and CapsLock are active on the keyboard. The cursor has been placed on the UNIT_PRICE field, which is why the prompt line appears at the bottom of the screen. We could create much more complex screen formats with multiple pages, automatic display of date and time, and other editing rules. This same

Figure 2-23

Sample PRODUCT display transaction

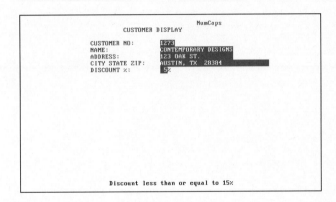

Figure 2-24

Sample CUSTOMER display transaction

screen format can be used to enter new records, to update existing records, to delete records, and to display records one record at a time.

We decided to build the customer display screen similarly, following the design in Figure 2-5. The result appears with sample data in Figure 2-24. In this screen, the cursor is currently sitting on the DISCOUNT field, for which a special display message was defined to appear on the bottom status line, as is shown. For the integrity of customer data, it is important to ensure valid entry of the price discount percentage field. We accomplished this integrity control by using the field editing screen in the form design module to limit this field to values between and including 0 and 15%. The editing window for this rule, which also shows the status message for this field, is shown in Figure 2-25. Finally, Figure 2-26 shows that if a user tries to enter an inadmissible discount value of 22%, dBASE generates a standard error message on the status line, indicating the proper range. Clearly, this value-range editing capability is helpful. It only works, however, for continuous ranges of values and not, for example, for a discrete list of possible character field codes.

Standard functions like adding, editing, and deleting records are often provided by a database management system without special programming. In dBASE, the product data management functions are supported directly in the dBASE Control Center (without the customized style of a tailored menu). When a form is displayed, such as the product form in Figure 2-23, the record on this form may be edited; changing product data is as simple as typing over the existing data on the form.

Other data management functions can be invoked by pressing the F10 key to access the menu bar while a form is displayed. Figure 2-27 shows the product

Figure 2-25

Editing rules for
DISCOUNT field

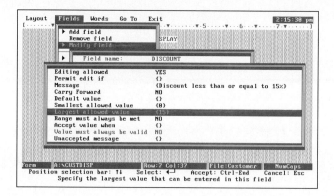

Figure 2-26

Sample entry of invalid
discount

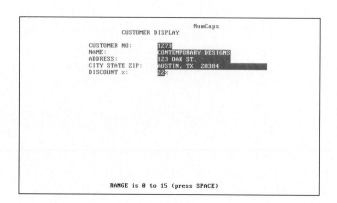

Figure 2-27

Product data
management through
dBASE Control Center

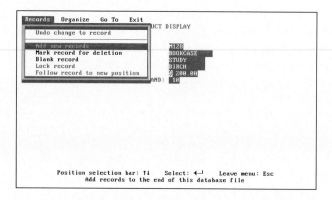

form of Figure 2-23 after pressing ⟨F10⟩; the first submenu, the Records submenu for data maintenance, appears. From this submenu, you may add new records to the product file, mark the current record for deletion, make all fields of the current record blank, or lock the current record. Locking is used when several people are accessing the same file on a LAN, so that no one else can change the current record until you are done with it.

Deleting a record requires two steps in dBASE. First, we tell dBASE to place a special symbol, or mark, on the record indicating that it is to be deleted. Then, usually after many records are marked, we tell dBASE to eliminate the marked records and reclaim the space they used. These steps are called MARK and PACK. Until the file is PACKed, any marked record can be RECALLed to unmark it.

Once a record is changed and before another record is retrieved, you may select "Undo change to record" to restore the changed record to its original contents.

The final submenu option here is "Follow record to new position." In the case of the PRODUCT file, if you were to change the product number field, since the file is indexed on PRODUCT_NO, the record is logically moved to a new position in the file. The issue here is, where do you want dBASE to continue processing the file: at the old location of the record or at its new location? The choice will determine which record is retrieved if you press ⟨PageUp⟩ (for next record) or ⟨PageDown⟩ (for prior record).

You use the Organize submenu to arrange the records in the order you want to see them. Here, you can invoke certain indexes, create new indexes, and sort the records, among other options. The Go To submenu allows you to move to any record in the file. Options here include moving to the first or last record in the file, moving to a specific record number in the file, or skipping a specified number of records, among other choices. The Exit menu takes you back to the Control Center main screen. Again, all of these data management functions are provided, in a fixed style, within dBASE. To build a custom style, we use the dBASE Application Generator and, in most cases, the proprietary dBASE programming language.

Order Transaction

The product and customer transactions were relatively straightforward to implement; each involved the maintenance of one record at a time in only one file. The order transaction is, however, more complicated. As shown in Figure 2-6, all four of the dBASE files must be accessed: ORDER, CUSTOMER, PRODUCT, and REQUEST. Further, two of these, ORDER and REQUEST, must be changed when a new order is added or an order is changed. The dBASE forms subsystem permits only one file to be used per form. Thus, we will not be able to use just one form for this transaction in a dBASE implementation. dBASE does permit us to work with data from multiple related files in a *view*, but we still cannot produce a layout similar to Figure 2-6 from a view.

We must also ensure the data integrity of each transaction. Suppose that during order entry or update the user decides to abort the transaction (or the computer system malfunctions). The application program must ensure that none of that transaction's data are stored in the database, even what may have already been accepted and confirmed as accurate. All of these circumstances suggest that we need a much more complex transaction processing approach than we have seen above.

Figure 2-28 outlines a minimal sequence of steps needed to properly process an order transaction. An experienced database programmer would suggest many other features, but we will stick with the basics here. The BEGIN TRANSACTION and END TRANSACTION commands are used to control transaction and database integrity. Suppose a fatal error occurs or the user aborts the transaction after a BEGIN TRANSACTION but before an END TRANSACTION command is executed. In this case, a ROLLBACK command can be given to restore the database to its contents just before the BEGIN TRANSACTION was executed. These commands ensure that either the whole transaction or none of the transaction impacts the database.

The main logic of the process is as follows:

- First, a value for ORDER_NO is entered, and the program verifies that an order with this ORDER_NO does not exist. The While loop keeps requesting an ORDER_NO until a new one is entered.

- Second, the CUST_NO for the order is entered, and a While loop is used again to request entry of a CUST_NO until one is entered for an existing CUSTOMER record. Optionally, the procedure might allow the user to add a new CUSTOMER record at this point, using the format presented earlier for this purpose.

- Third, the CUSTOMER record for the entered CUST_NO is displayed, and the user confirms that this is the customer who actually placed the order; if not, the CUST_NO entry sequence is restarted.

- Fourth, the remainder of the data for the ORDER record is entered, and the ORDER record is stored (it is stored in a kind of suspense file until the END TRANSACTION makes the addition permanent).

- Fifth, each line item on the order is entered in turn. Within this part of the program, the PRODUCT_NO is entered, and the While loop continues to prompt the user for an existing PRODUCT_NO. As with the customer cross-reference, a visual verification for the correct product is made by displaying the DESCRIPTION and UNIT_PRICE fields and looping back to the entry of a PRODUCT_NO if an incorrect PRODUCT_NO has been entered. Then the order quantity is entered, and the REQUEST record is stored. This process repeats until all lines (REQUEST records) for this order have been entered. Then the END TRANSACTION makes the changes to the database permanent, and the full integrity of the transaction is guaranteed.

The full programming of this transaction is beyond our scope at this point in the text. Implementation would require that we use the proprietary dBASE pro-

Figure 2-28

Order transaction processing

```
      CLEAR SCREEN
      BEGIN TRANSACTION
      Accept ORDER_NO entry from keyboard
      Do While ORDER_NO already exists
         Display Duplicate order error message
         Accept ORDER_NO entry from keyboard
      End While
CUST: Accept CUST_NO from keyboard
      Do While CUSTOMER does not exist
         Display Customer does not exist message
         Accept CUST_NO from keyboard
      End While
      Display CUSTOMER record for verification of correct customer record
      If incorrect customer, GOTO CUST:
      Accept ORDER_DATE and PROM_DATE
      Store CUORDER record
      Do While more lines to add to order
PROD:    Accept PRODUCT_NO from keyboard
         Do While PRODUCT does not exist
            Display Product does not exist message
            Accept PRODUCT_NO from keyboard
         End While
         Display DESCRIPT and UNIT_PRICE for verification of correct PRODUCT record
         If incorrect product, GOTO PROD:
         Accept ORDER_QTY
         Store REQUEST record
      End While
      END TRANSACTION
```

gramming language, a structured language (examples appear in Chapter 9). Besides the record processing logic above, the program would have to write the data to the screen in the format outlined in Figure 2-6. You can think of this figure as having two windows. The top window contains data from one record in the CUORDER file. The bottom window contains as many of the REQUEST file records associated with the order as will fit. The bottom window should scroll, to allow showing more line items than can fit at once on the screen. This screen handling adds greater complexity to the program for this transaction. Thus, we will assume for now that the order transaction has been implemented and the associated data entered in the CUORDER and REQUEST files.

We have now examined the transactions for our sample application. We now turn to the management reporting requirements.

PROCESSING INFORMATION REQUESTS IN dBASE IV

In this section we use various modules of dBASE IV to illustrate how Pine Valley Furniture could use a database and database management system to meet its management information retrieval and analysis needs. We use three dBASE modules: the query and report writer parts of the dBASE Control Center, and the SQL interactive programming language. The dBASE query module allows us to quickly and intuitively retrieve data. This style, called *Query-by-Example*, is used in many PC and mainframe database systems, primarily for end-user ad hoc queries and the development of simple applications. We discuss this query language style in Chapter 10. The dBASE report writer feature is similar to comparable modules in other personal computer database management systems. This module allows the definition of highly customized printed reports. SQL is an international, standard language used primarily by professional programmers. We will use an interactive version of SQL to introduce the use of this language for ad hoc inquiry.

This section illustrates how both SQL and the dBASE query module serve as concise languages for data access. The output from an SQL or dBASE query command is in the form of a single table, where the columns are the requested data elements and the rows are composed from records that we select via qualification statements. When we want to customize the layout of reports (add subtotals and page numbers, change column headings, add titles, and so on), the dBASE report writer is useful.

We will use SQL, since it is a standard programming language, as the primary language in illustrations. We will show some dBASE queries as comparisons. Also, the dBASE query language will be necessary to prepare data for the report writer.

Introduction to SQL

SQL, or Structured Query Language, is a language in which the programmer (or manager writing ad hoc queries) specifies which data she wants, not how to retrieve data record by record. SQL is a fourth-generation, nonprocedural language that was designed for database processing. It is a command-driven language; that is, programming involves entering keywords and parameters. SQL includes many different commands to perform input, data retrieval, and modification, as well as other commands to control data accuracy and security, but the most common command for information processing is SELECT.

The general structure of the SELECT command follows:

```
SELECT <list of desired data elements>
   FROM <list of tables or views in which data is stored>
   WHERE <qualification on what records to include>;
```

We will examine how other parts of the SELECT command can sort the result, group and subtotal data, and store the results in a temporary table to avoid the cost of repeatedly recalculating the same intermediate results.

Simple Queries at Pine Valley Furniture

Figure 2-8 shows the discount rate inquiry, which is an example of a very simple management information requirement. For this request, the desired data elements are NAME and DISCOUNT%, the single table involved is the CUSTOMER table, and only one record is needed, the record identified by a specific CUST_NO value. We will not concern ourselves with the precise display format shown in Figure 2-8. Thus, the SQL command to produce the data for this inquiry for Customer 1273 would be

```
SELECT NAME, DISCOUNT
   FROM CUSTOMER
      WHERE CUST_NO=1273;
```

and SQL would respond with

```
NAME                    DISCOUNT
CONTEMPORARY DESIGNS           5
```

To emphasize the power of such database access, imagine the programming necessary to produce this result in COBOL, BASIC, FORTRAN, C, or some other third-generation programming language with which you are familiar. Your program would have specified *how* to retrieve this data (which record to retrieve first, in what sequence to search for the desired record, and so on). Although SQL is certainly not natural English and is still a command-driven language, the SQL style of querying requires less special training and less technical understanding of computer data processing than do third-generation languages.

In contrast, consider the same inquiry produced from the query module of the dBASE Control Center. Figure 2-29a shows the dBASE query, and Figure 2-29b

Figure 2-29

dBASE query for discount rate inquiry

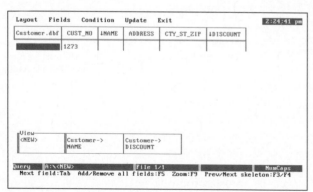

(a)   Query and view templates

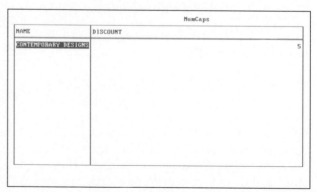

(b)   Resultant answer table

shows the answer screen. (Because dBASE uses the full screen width, the DISCOUNT field is unnecessarily wide on the answer screen.) We develop a dBASE query as follows. First, a template of the table from which data are to be retrieved (the CUSTOMER table) is placed (from the Layout menu) on the top of the screen. Second, the fields to be displayed are picked (using the F5 key or the Fields menu), and dBASE automatically places these in the answer template, or view, at the bottom of the screen. The picked fields in the top template are marked by a down arrow next to the field names. Finally, qualifications are entered in the top template to limit which rows of the CUSTOMER table to display. In our case, we want to see only those (actually only one row) with a CUST_NO value of 1273. If this query is run repeatedly, it would be wise to save the query rather than construct it each time. For many nonprogrammers, this dBASE query interface can be easier to use than a command language like SQL. The programming is quite visual, because it is accomplished by picking items from menus or placing data names and constants in understandable forms.

We handle the discount rate query via a dBASE customer screen form. A copy of this form, with data for customer number 1273, appears in Figure 2-30. We can use this form in a dBASE program that would read the customer number a user enters, retrieve the associated record, and display the name and discount as shown.

The daily order log of Figure 2-9 is a slightly more complex inquiry example for Pine Valley Furniture, because it requires qualified data from two database tables, CUSTOMER and ORDER. We will use SQL not only to specify what data we want but also to indicate on what basis to associate an order with its customer. For simplicity, we will not concern ourselves with the precise display format outlined in Figure 2-9a for this information request.

This request specifies three data elements for display: the NAME from the CUSTOMER table and the ORDER_NO and PROM_DATE from the CUORDER table. Thus, two tables, CUSTOMER and CUORDER, must be referenced in the command. Qualification involves two parts: first, selecting orders placed on a certain ORDER_DATE, and second, specifying on what basis to match an order with a customer. The results are to be sorted by NAME. Thus, the SQL command becomes

```
SELECT CUSTOMER.NAME, ORDER_NO, PROM_DATE
  FROM CUORDER, CUSTOMER
    WHERE ORDER_DATE=CTOD('''11/10/93''') AND
      CUORDER.CUST_NO=CUSTOMER.CUST_NO
        ORDER BY CUSTOMER.NAME;
```

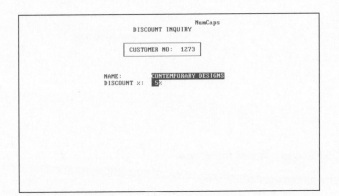

Figure 2-30

dBASE form for discount rate query

Since the FROM clause involves two tables, we need to specify in which table to find each data element. The dBASE version of SQL assumes the first table listed, and data from other tables need to be clarified by prefixing the field name with the table name (for example, CUSTOMER.NAME). CTOD (character-to-date) is a built-in function in dBASE that translates a character date into the internal date format used to store date type fields so the date qualification can be processed. Thus, the first part of this WHERE clause specifies the day (ORDER_DATE) for which the daily order log is to be generated. The second part of the WHERE clause specifies the means for associating the two tables in the query. This association is via the cross-reference provided by the CUST_NO fields stored in both tables. For each order, there is one customer number, so the cross-reference from the CUORDER table to the CUSTOMER table is unambiguous. The ORDER BY clause indicates the desired sequence for data. The result, for the sample data we have entered, is

CUSTOMER→NAME	CUORDER→ORDER_NO	CUORDER→PROM_DATE
ABC OFFICE SUPPLY	61397	11/20/93
COMMONWEALTH BUILDER	61398	11/12/93

Obviously, this format is somewhat awkward (cryptic column labels, lack of blank lines and spaces to make the result more readable, and so on). The results were obtained more directly by stating what data were desired and under what conditions.

The dBASE query module can also be used to prepare this data. Figure 2-31a shows the query that produces this same result. Two templates are required at the top of the screen, one for each of the two source tables. The fields to appear in the result (the template at the bottom) are marked, and the qualification on orders placed on November 10, 1993, is entered under the ORDER_DATE field. The example value of CC is used to link the two tables on the common field, CUST_NO. A sorting code is included under the NAME column in the Customer template to cause rows in the answer table to appear in the desired sequence. Figure 2-31b shows the resultant answer table. This table could then be input to a custom report that would handle numbering pages, more readable column headings, and other desired printing options to make the data appear as in Figure 2-9a.

The last query we will cover is the customer order history query of Figure 2-10. The E-R diagram of Figure 2-10b implies that this query will involve four tables: CUSTOMER, ORDER, REQUEST, and PRODUCT. But as we discussed earlier, the database definition for each ORDER record contains the CUST_NO as a cross-reference from ORDER to CUSTOMER. Since we need only the

Figure 2-31

dBASE query for daily order log

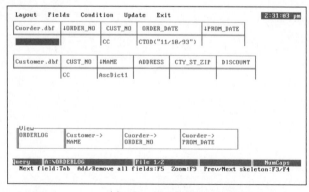

(a) Query and view

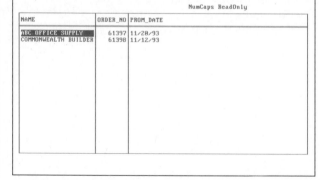

(b) Resultant answer table

CUST_NO for this query (because we only want to select orders for a given customer), the CUSTOMER file will not be needed. Similarly, since the REQUEST file has the relevant PRODUCT_NO in it, the PRODUCT file will not be needed. Thus, this query also involves only two tables, ORDER and REQUEST. The ORDER_NO field will be used to join the two tables together to form the answer table.

We will illustrate two ways to write this query. The first approach, as in the previous information processing examples, is to write a specific and complete SQL query for the desired CUST_NO. Thus, for the example of Figure 2-10a, the query would be

```
SELECT ORDER_DATE, CUORDER.ORDER_NO,
   REQUEST.PRODUCT_NO, REQUEST.ORDER_QTY
     FROM CUORDER, REQUEST
    WHERE CUST_NO=1273 AND
      ORDER_DATE BETWEEN CTOD(''11/01/93'') AND CTOD(''11/30/93'') AND
      CUORDER.ORDER_NO=REQUEST.ORDER_NO;
```

As before, we must prefix each field name with the table name, unless the field comes from the first table listed. Since ORDER_NO is in both tables, it must always have a table name prefix to clarify which ORDER_NO is to be used. The first part of the WHERE clause says that orders for only one particular customer are sought. The second part states the relevant date range, using the BETWEEN key word to define the smallest and largest values. The third part specifies on what basis to relate rows from the two tables. The answer to this query, given the sample data in our database, follows:

CUORDER→ORDER_DATE	CUORDER→ORDER_NO	REQUEST→PRODUCT_NO	REQUEST→ORDER_QTY
11/04/93	61384	M128	4
11/04/93	61384	B381	2
11/04/93	61384	R210	1
11/06/93	61390	T100	2
11/06/93	61390	T160	1

We can reduce the amount of query writing required to produce this query result for any customer and for any date range by using an SQL view. A **view** is a virtual, or imaginary, table. The other tables that we have defined so far are real and are called **base tables**. A view is constructed by forming a table from fields in one or more related base tables. Thus, you can query or report data from a single virtual table, or view, without having to select and append the desired data each time you submit the query or report. A view gives a current, but restricted, "window" into the database; that is, a view is not a temporary table that has to be rebuilt when changes are made to the original data. Because its contents are derived (by the DBMS) as needed from base tables, a view always reflects the latest changes made in any of its base tables. The advantage of an SQL view is that we can use it just like a table for subsequent data retrieval.

For the customer order history query, as in Figure 2-10, an SQL view table would contain not only the four fields displayed above but also the fields used to select rows from the view to display. Thus, the CUST_NO field would also be needed. All five fields are in either the ORDER or REQUEST table. We would define the appropriate view table as follows:

View: A virtual table in the relational data model in which data from real (base) tables are combined so programmers can work with just one (virtual) table instead of the several or more complete base tables.

Base table: A table in the relational data model that most likely corresponds to one physical file in secondary storage.

```
CREATE VIEW HISTORY
   (CUSTOMER, DATE, ORDER, PRODUCT, QUANTITY)
      AS SELECT CUST_NO, ORDER_DATE, CUORDER.ORDER_NO,
        REQUEST.PRODUCT_NO, REQUEST.ORDER_QTY
     FROM CUORDER, REQUEST
        WHERE CUORDER.ORDER_NO=REQUEST.ORDER_NO;
```

The customer order history query based upon this view then becomes

```
SELECT DATE, ORDER, PRODUCT, QUANTITY
   FROM HISTORY
     WHERE CUSTOMER=1273 AND
        DATE BETWEEN CTOD(''11/01/93'') AND CTOD(''11/20/93'');
```

and the result would be similar to the above:

```
DATE          ORDER     PRODUCT    QUANTITY
11/04/93      61384     M128              4
11/04/93      61384     B381              2
11/04/93      61384     R210              1
11/06/93      61390     T100              2
11/06/93      61390     T160              1
```

This query based upon the history view is simpler than the original customer order history query for three reasons:

1. Since all the data appear to come from one table, field names do not need prefixes.
2. The more technical cross-reference fields are not needed in the WHERE clause.
3. Field names local to this view are easier to remember.

Furthermore, the view provides additional convenience and security, especially for those involved in end-user computing who are not programmers. For example, we could restrict end users from accessing base tables and give them access only to the views pertinent to their information rights and needs.

Report Writer Features for Database Processing

The above customer order history query result does not resemble the format of Figure 2-10a. To produce a report that is more readable and closer to the desired format, we can use the dBASE report writer module. This module helps the report designer to develop a stylized report, like the screen painter (or forms) module we used earlier for transactions. A form lays out *one* row of a table on a screen. In contrast, a report includes *all* the rows of the table or view, with the appropriate summary figures, using as many pages as necessary to print all the data.

One report writer restriction is that all the data must be in one table or view. Also, the view must be created from a dBASE query, not an SQL view. Moreover, since a dBASE report prints *all* the data in a view in the desired format with control breaks, headings, and so on, we must develop a separate view for each time period; we cannot produce a dBASE report for qualified rows in a view. To illustrate the general features of the report writer, we have chosen to include all customers in the report (with a separation of the report detail grouped for each cus-

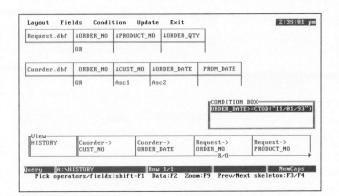

Figure 2-32

dBASE view for customer order history query

tomer), so the view will only limit ORDER and REQUEST data to the desired ORDER_DATE range.

As before, we will not outline every step in the construction of a dBASE view. Figure 2-32 shows the view definition screen after we composed the view. The two templates at the top of the screen show the layout of each of the base tables from which the view is derived. The bottom template lists the fields that we have placed into the view. As before, one additional field, ORDER_QTY, does not fit on the screen.

The ORDER_NO fields in the two base tables are used to match rows from the tables—the example value 'OR' shows this linkage. Also, we decided to sort the view data (in ascending sequence) first on CUST_NO and then on ORDER_DATE, as specified by the 'Asc' codes under these fields in the templates. Finally, we use a condition box to specify which rows of the CUORDER table to include in the view (that is, those for orders that fall within the desired date range). Figure 2-33 zooms in on this box to show its complete contents. Thus, the view table, HISTORY, contains all the fields we need for the report, and just those rows for orders during the desired period.

dBASE can generate a standard default report format for a table or view, as shown in Figure 2-34 for the HISTORY view. Each report format is arranged into *bands*. The *page header band* specifies what will appear on the top of each page. The *report intro band* lays out text that usually describes and provides an explanation of the contents of the report. The *detail band* represents the fields that will be printed for each row in the view. The *summary band* specifies the fields for which subtotals, averages, counts, or other summary data are to appear at the end of the report. The *page footer band* specifies text or data that are to appear at the bottom of each printed page. Each field is identified by a template format, just as we saw with forms.

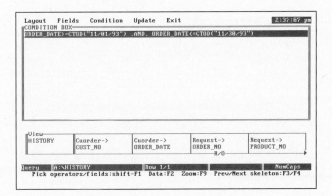

Figure 2-33

Condition box for customer order history view

Figure 2-34

Default customer order
history report format

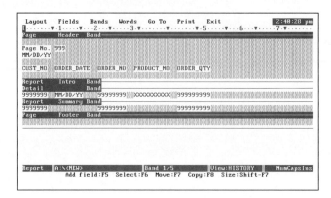

Figure 2-35 shows our final report layout for this application. The layout includes more descriptive column headings, and only the necessary fields appear in the detail band. Furthermore, since rows in the detail band are grouped by customer, we created a *group intro band* and an associated *group summary band*. These bands will help us highlight each time the customer changes on the report. We have also placed the CUST_NO on a separate line in the group intro band. A group summary, the total quantity of all products ordered by a customer, appears in the group summary band. We defined this summary field by adding a calculated field into the group summary band via the Fields menu at the top of the report design work surface.

One final feature that we decided to include was to suppress the printing of the ORDER_DATE and ORDER_NO fields, since they repeat for the different products on an order. We specified field-value suppression by using the Modify

Figure 2-35

Final customer order
history report format

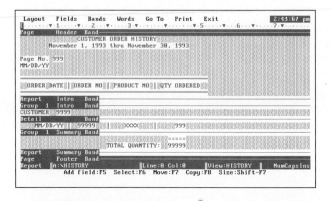

Figure 2-36

"Suppress repeated
values" menu window

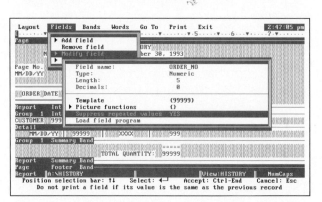

```
 O                    CUSTOMER ORDER HISTORY                  O
             November 1, 1993 thru November 30, 1993
 O   Page No.   1                                            O
     12/25/93
 O   ┌──────────┬───────────┬────────────┬──────────────┐   O
     │ORDER DATE│ ORDER NO. │PRODUCT NO. │QTY. ORDERED  │
 O   └──────────┴───────────┴────────────┴──────────────┘   O
     CUSTOMER 1069
 O    11/10/93 │   61397   │    O800    │      2        │   O
                               O625           3
 O    11/22/93 │   61396   │    O100    │      2        │   O
                                               ══
 O                              TOTAL QUANTITY:   7          O
     CUSTOMER 1256
 O    11/10/93 │   61398   │    O100    │     10        │   O
                               M128          10
 O    11/11/93 │   61399   │    M128    │     20        │   O
                                               ══
 O                              TOTAL QUANTITY:  40          O
     CUSTOMER 1273
 O    11/04/93 │   61384   │    M128    │      4        │   O
                               R210           1
 O                             B381           2              O
      11/06/93 │   61390   │    T160    │      1
 O                             T100           2              O
                                               ══
 O                              TOTAL QUANTITY:  10          O
     CUSTOMER 2345
 O    11/20/93 │   61395   │    B975    │      3        │   O
                               B985           4
 O                             B381           6              O
                                               ══
 O                              TOTAL QUANTITY:  13          O
     CUSTOMER 3434
      11/02/93 │   61401   │    E350    │      4
 O    11/24/93 │   61402   │    E125    │     12        │   O
                                               ══
 O                              TOTAL QUANTITY:  16          O
```

Figure 2-37

Customer order history report

Field menu and the "Suppress repeated values" option. Figure 2-36 shows the window menu on which we specify that option for ORDER_NO field values. The final report for all customers with orders during November 1993 appears in Figure 2-37.

SUMMARY

This chapter has illustrated the development of a database application. After completing a course using this text, you will be able to develop even more complex applications using a variety of database systems. Our example shows that the development of a database application is a multiple-step process with considerable discretion in the design of the database, data entry screens, and reports. The choices available at each step allow extensive customization but also require careful consideration to avoid poor choices (for both computer system performance as well as human ease of use).

Chapter 3 begins the discussion of the concepts and tools needed to organize data for computer efficiency and understandable use of the organizational data resource. This chapter introduced many of these concepts and tools through the example application. By now you should have a general understanding of data entities, elements, relationships, a database, an application, a transaction, integrity constraints, queries, reports, and database programming. We also briefly introduced (through the order transaction processing illustration) the control of concurrent access to data and the recovery of a contaminated or destroyed database. We consider all of these topics more fully later in the text.

This chapter also introduced the relational type of database management system, which is today the most popular style for developing new database applications. Although dBASE IV, the specific program we used, is very popular, it does not provide all the features we might like. In fact, no one package is superior to all others in every respect. This early application and illustration of some of the features of dBASE, however, can make you more alert to comparative advantages and disadvantages as you see other systems demonstrated in class or illustrated in this text.

CHAPTER REVIEW

Key Terms

Base table

Business transaction

Database application system

Enterprise modeling

View

REVIEW QUESTIONS

1. Define each of the following terms:
   a. database
   b. database application
   c. database management system
   d. business transaction
   e. database transaction
   f. enterprise data model
   g. report writer
   h. entity
   i. relationship
   j. one-to-many relationship
   k. data integrity
   l. many-to-many relationship
   m. SQL
2. Contrast each of the following terms:
   a. table; file
   b. database; file
   c. file; index
   d. primary key; index
   e. form; report
   f. base table; view
   g. view; temporary table
3. What purpose do the commands START TRANSACTION and END TRANSACTION achieve in a database program?
4. What are the four major steps in the development of a database application?
5. What is the purpose of drawing an E-R diagram?
6. What characteristics of data and a database are defined when a database is created in dBASE IV?

PROBLEMS AND EXERCISES

1. In this chapter we illustrated one method for handling missing data during data entry: using a default value. What other methods can you think of, and why would you want to use each method?
2. What purpose does a field template serve in defining a data entry form/screen?
3. This chapter claims that although controlling data integrity during data entry via edit and range rules stored with a form is helpful, this is not the most desirable place to store these rules. Where would be a better place to store the data-editing rules, and why?

4. Why were so many of the queries for the sample application of this chapter written in the SQL language? Why was this the best instructional choice, as opposed to using the proprietary dBASE language, in which we could have done everything?
5. Write an SQL query to display the complete contents of the PRODUCT table. Write the same query through the dBASE Control Center or similar interface with another DBMS.
6. Write an SQL query to display the promised date for each request involving Product B975. Write the same query through the dBASE Control Center or similar interface with another DBMS.
7. Construct a view in SQL that would allow the question of Problem 6 to be answered for any product number.
8. Design a menu for managing customer data (similar to the Product menu in Figure 2-4).

REFERENCES

Ashton-Tate. 1992. *Using dBASE IV*. Scotts Valley, Calif.: Borland International, Inc.

Chen and Associates. 1988. *E-R Designer Reference Manual*. Baton Rouge, La.

Krumm, R. 1990. *The Student Edition of dBASE IV, Programmer's Version*. Reading, Mass.: Addison-Wesley.

Senn, J. A. 1990. *The Student Edition of dBASE IV*. Reading, Mass.: Addison-Wesley.

CHAPTER

3

The Database Development Process

LEARNING OBJECTIVES

After studying this chapter, you should be able to:

- Define the following key terms: *information systems architecture, methodology, business function, business process, functional decomposition*, and *repository*.
- List six benefits of an information systems architecture.
- Describe the three components of the Zachman framework for an information systems architecture.
- Describe the four stages of information engineering, and the purpose of each stage.
- Describe the three major components of an enterprise model.
- Describe the major entity types that appear in the metamodel for strategic information systems planning.
- Briefly describe five planning matrices that are used in strategic information systems planning.

INTRODUCTION

The scope of information systems today is the whole enterprise. Managers, knowledge workers, and others in an organization expect easy access and retrieval of information regardless of its location. According to Morton (1992), "earlier systems with their islands of information are being retired in favor of cooperative, integrated, interoperable enterprise systems." While this goal will take some time to achieve completely, it represents a clear direction for information systems development.

The goal of enterprise-wide computing presents significant challenges for information systems (IS) management. Given the proliferation of personal and departmental databases (islands of information), how can IS possibly control and maintain all of the data that are created and stored throughout the organization? In many cases they simply cannot, because it is nearly impossible to track who has what data, where there are overlaps, or how accurate the information is. Personal and departmental databases abound because users are either unaware of

73

what information exists in the corporate databases or they can't get at it, so they create and maintain their own information (Reingruber and Spahr, 1992).

In this chapter we describe several key components that are required to develop information systems that support the goal of enterprise computing. First, we introduce the concept of an information systems architecture and describe an emerging framework for such an architecture. Next we describe information engineering, which is a formal methodology for developing information systems (including databases) within the information systems architecture. Then we describe strategic information systems planning, which is supported by the information engineering methodology and links strategic information systems planning with strategic business planning. We describe the role of CASE tools and a repository throughout the chapter, and introduce a case example for a hospital to illustrate many of the key concepts.

A FRAMEWORK FOR INFORMATION SYSTEMS ARCHITECTURE

If you were planning to build a new home, you would certainly want a blueprint or set of architectural plans before starting construction. Also, if you were writing a textbook, you would want an architectural plan (in the form of a detailed table of contents) before proceeding very far with the actual writing. The successful completion of almost any large-scale creative endeavor requires the early development of a vision or architectural plan.

Designing and building effective information systems is one of the greatest challenges facing most organizations today. You may be surprised to learn that (unfortunately) many organizations do not have a comprehensive architectural plan for their information systems development. There are a variety of reasons for this: there is no standard format for an information systems architecture, developing an architecture is costly in terms of time and other resources, and it may seem difficult (perhaps even counterproductive) to develop an architecture when conditions change so rapidly. Yet with the increased scope and complexity of information systems, an architecture is essential in order to avoid chaos.

Information systems architecture (ISA): A conceptual blueprint or plan that expresses the desired future structure for the information systems in an organization.

An **information systems architecture (ISA)** is a conceptual blueprint or plan that expresses the desired future structure for the information systems in an organization. This architecture creates the context within which managers can make consistent decisions concerning their information systems. According to Martin, DeHayes, Hoffer, and Perkins (1994), an information systems architecture offers the following benefits:

1. Provides a basis for strategic planning of information systems (we introduce strategic IS planning later in this chapter)
2. Provides a basis for communicating with top management and a context for budget decisions concerning IS
3. Provides a unifying concept for the various stakeholders in information systems
4. Communicates the overall direction for information technology and a context for major decisions in this area
5. Helps achieve information integration when systems are distributed (increasingly important in a global economy)
6. Provides a basis for evaluating technology options (for example, downsizing and distributed processing)

Overview of the Framework

As we noted earlier, at present there is no standard means for portraying an information systems architecture; however, in 1987 John Zachman (then of IBM) developed a comprehensive framework for developing such an architecture (see Zachman, 1987). An overview of this framework (called information systems architecture, or ISA) is shown in Figure 3-1. It is important to understand that this diagram does not represent an information systems architecture, but rather a framework or context within which you can develop an architecture.

Architecture Components   The Zachman ISA framework includes three major components (represented by the columns in the diagram) in an information systems architecture: data, process, and network. That is, every information system is visualized as a combination of these three components. The data column represents the ''what'' in an information system. In manufacturing systems (for example), the ''what'' corresponds to a bill of materials listing the components required to assemble a finished product. In information systems, the ''what'' consists of data entities and the relationships among those entities.

The process column represents the ''how'' in an information system. In a manufacturing system, the ''how'' corresponds to a list of instructions that specify how a finished product is assembled from its components. In information systems, a process is a sequence of steps that converts inputs into outputs (or data into information).

The network column represents the ''where'' in an information system. In manufacturing systems, the ''where'' describes the locations where various components and items are manufactured. In information systems, the ''where'' describes the locations where data are stored and processing is performed, as well as the links connecting the locations.

Business rules (in the form of logic, constraints, and knowledge) are embedded throughout all three columns of the framework. These rules may be stated in the form of expert systems, constraints, assertions, and in other forms. We describe means for capturing and stating business rules in subsequent chapters.

In this text we are most directly concerned with the data column in the framework. However, in both developing and using information systems we realize that there is a close interrelationship among data, process, and network components. Thus, it is essential for you to understand the overall context of the information systems architecture.

Architecture Roles and Perspectives   There are six rows in the information systems architecture framework (Figure 3-1). Each row represents the role or perspective of an individual concerning the three components (data, process, and network). Figure 3-2 summarizes each row by listing the model name for that row, the person who is most concerned with that model, and a brief description of the role each person plays in developing the model. For example, row 2, the business model, represents the role (or perspective) of the architect, who is concerned with developing models that describe the business scope, mission, and direction. Zachman uses a construction-industry analogy to describe the individual roles, reflected in the role names (architect, builder, etc.).

Each cell of the framework contains a representation of a model for a component (data, process, or network) and for an individual. For example, in Figure 3-1, the perspective of the information systems model is represented by a detailed entity-relationship diagram for the data component, by a data flow diagram for

Figure 3-1

Information systems
architecture framework
Source: Adapted from
Moriarty (1991)

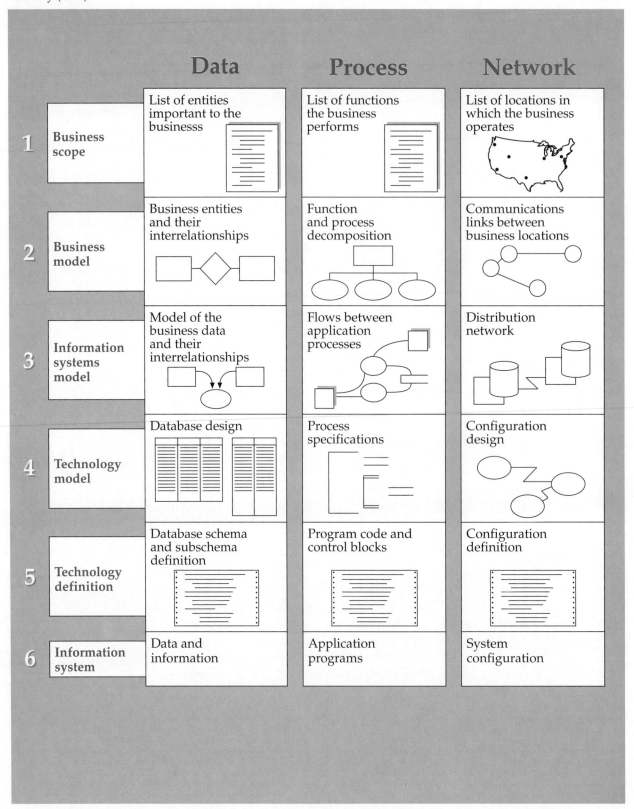

Model Name	Role or Perspective	Role Description
Business scope	Owner	Provides a strategic overview including business scope, mission, and direction
Business model	Architect	Develops business models that describe the business scope, mission, and direction
Information systems model	Designer	Develops information systems models that support the business
Technology model	Builder	Converts information systems models into a design that conforms to the features and constraints of the technology
Technology definition	Contractor	Converts technology models into statements to generate the actual information system
Information system	User	Manages, uses, and operates the completed information system

Figure 3-2

Models and roles in the ISA framework
Source: Adapted from Moriarty (1991)

the process component, and by a distribution network diagram for the network component. The framework is flexible, however, and an organization can use any model representation it chooses in each of the cells. In fact, more than one model may be constructed within each cell or perspective. For example, the information systems model for data may contain two levels of detail: a high-level summary entity-relationship diagram, and a very detailed entity-relationship diagram. Von Halle (1992) describes several options for developing models within the information systems architecture framework.

Evolution Through the Framework

During development, an information system should evolve through the cells of the framework from the top of the table to the bottom. This rule is true for simple systems such as spreadsheets as well as for complex transaction processing systems, although, of course, the amount and level of detail will differ. For a simple system such as a spreadsheet, one person may assume several (or all) of the roles in the table; for a complex system, several people may collaborate in performing one of the roles.

As shown in Figure 3-1, the model or representation in each cell differs considerably from the model in the cell directly above it. That is, each model in general is not developed by simply adding detail to the model in the previous cell. Instead, each model is developed by *transforming* the model in the previous cell to a new one that best represents the view of the person concerned with that row. Of course, the new model must be consistent with previous models (in higher rows), and may contain additional detail as well as a new representation.

The framework should be used to enforce a discipline in developing new systems. This approach can be accomplished by following two simple rules:

1. Objects within rows are mapped horizontally. Each process is mapped to the data it uses, and both data and processes are mapped to the network

locations or objects where they are distributed. This approach helps ensure that the various components are integrated with each other.

2. Ideally, the transformation of data, process, and network proceeds simultaneously from one row to the next. For example, all three components of the business model should be completed before starting work on any components of the information systems model. This approach helps avoid inconsistencies and the resulting rework.

Role of Methodologies and Tools

The information systems architecture framework that we have described presents a context for developing integrated information systems. The framework suggests the type of model (or models) that are appropriate for each cell in the table (representing an IS component and stakeholder perspective). It does not provide a means, however, to develop these models (that is, to fill the cells).

An organization needs a methodology (one or more) and related set of tools to develop the architectural representations required for each perspective. A **methodology** is a process (or related series of steps) to accomplish a stated goal, together with a set of design objects (described below) that are manipulated to support the process. The methodology should provide a discipline to help ensure that a consistent set of standards and procedures is used throughout the overall development process and that the resulting systems support the stated business goals and objectives.

Conceptually a methodology is similar to a recipe, which includes a set of instructions (a process) and a set of ingredients (the objects that are manipulated by the process). We describe one data-oriented methodology (information engineering) in detail in the next section.

A variety of tools (both manual and automated) are required to support the development of information systems. **Computer-aided software engineering (CASE) tools** are software products that provide automated support for some portion of the system development process. Figure 3-3 shows typical functions performed by CASE tools. Some of these functions (such as diagramming, screen and report painters, and checking and analysis) are designed primarily to support the earlier stages of system development (rows 1 through 4 in Figure 3-1). Other functions (such as code generation and maintenance) are designed primarily to support the later stages (rows 5 and 6 in Figure 3-1). Repository functions are designed to support all stages of the development process. We describe the role of the repository later in this chapter.

An **integrated CASE (I-CASE) toolset** is a CASE tool that provides all (or at least most) of the functions shown in Figure 3-3, and therefore can support all phases of the system development process. These I-CASE toolsets are emerging as the state-of-the-art in the industry.

CASE tools and methodologies are often used in concert in the system development process. A CASE tool is generally designed to support one or more methodologies. For example, both the KnowledgeWare Application Development Workbench and the Texas Instruments Information Engineering Facility are designed to support the information engineering methodology. Excelerator II (Intersolv Corporation) is designed to support several methodologies, including structured analysis and design, information engineering, and rapid application development. In turn, most methodologies are supported by one or more CASE tools to speed system development and improve the quality of the delivered products.

Methodology: A process (or related series of steps) to accomplish a design goal, together with a set of design objects that are manipulated to support the process.

Computer-aided software engineering (CASE) tools: Software tools that provide automated support for some portion of the system development process.

Integrated CASE (I-CASE) toolset: A set of CASE tools that can support all phases of the system development process.

Figure 3-3
Tasks performed by
CASE tools
Source: McClure (1989)

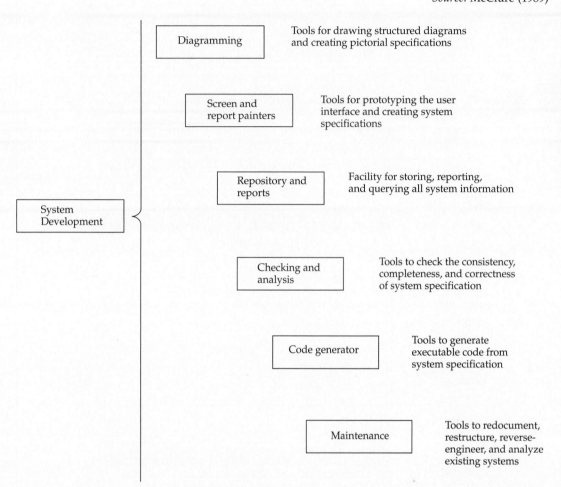

INFORMATION ENGINEERING METHODOLOGY

To pursue the goal of enterprise computing, organizations need both an information systems architecture and a methodology that supports developing that architecture. **Information engineering** is a formal methodology that is used to create and maintain information systems. It is a top-down methodology that starts with business models and then supports the building of data models and process models that link to and support the business models.

We emphasize the information engineering methodology in this chapter for three important reasons. First, the methodology is enterprise-wide in scope (at least during the planning stages), in contrast with most IS development methodologies, which tend to deal with only one application or organizational subunit at a time. Second, information engineering is data-driven (data models are generally developed before process models). We believe this approach is appropriate

Information engineering: A formal, top-down methodology that uses a data orientation to create and maintain information systems.

since it is logical to determine the "what" before the "how" in systems design. Information engineering, however, does include process models, and results in a balanced approach. Third, information engineering is compatible with the information systems architecture framework described in the previous section. Information engineering addresses all of the cells in the data and process columns of the framework (Figure 3-1) (we are not aware of any general IS methodology that addresses the network column at the present time).

Phases in Information Engineering

Figure 3-4 presents an outline of the major phases in information engineering: planning, analysis, design, and implementation. Each phase is divided into steps. The figure also shows some of the important design objects, such as goals, critical

Figure 3-4

Major phases in information engineering

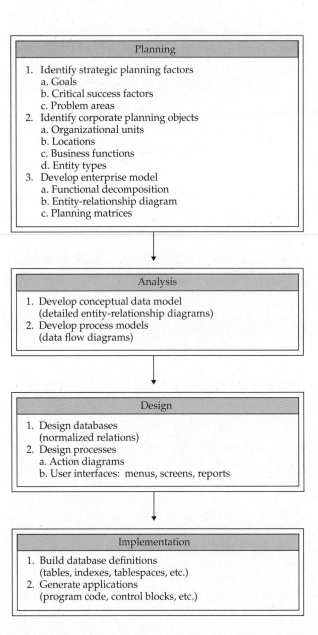

Planning
1. Identify strategic planning factors
   a. Goals
   b. Critical success factors
   c. Problem areas
2. Identify corporate planning objects
   a. Organizational units
   b. Locations
   c. Business functions
   d. Entity types
3. Develop enterprise model
   a. Functional decomposition
   b. Entity-relationship diagram
   c. Planning matrices

Analysis
1. Develop conceptual data model
   (detailed entity-relationship diagrams)
2. Develop process models
   (data flow diagrams)

Design
1. Design databases
   (normalized relations)
2. Design processes
   a. Action diagrams
   b. User interfaces: menus, screens, reports

Implementation
1. Build database definitions
   (tables, indexes, tablespaces, etc.)
2. Generate applications
   (program code, control blocks, etc.)

Product	Vendor
Excelerator II	Intersolv, Inc.
Foundation	Anderson Consulting
IE: Expert	Information Engineering Systems Corp.
Information Engineering Facility	Texas Instruments
Information Engineering Workbench	KnowledgeWare

Figure 3-5

Some information engineering implementations

success factors, functions, locations, entities, and organizational units. There is a relationship between information engineering as shown in Figure 3-4 and the database development process presented in Table 2-1. Although there is not a one-to-one match, the similar phases are:

Information Engineering	Database Development
Planning	Enterprise modeling
Analysis	Conceptual data modeling and part of logical database design
Design	Parts of both logical and physical database design
Implementation	Database implementation
No similar phase	Database maintenance

Our intention in this chapter is to present an overview, rather than a detailed description, of information engineering. There are several CASE tools that support the information engineering methodology (see Figure 3-5). The CASE tools differ in their definitions of information engineering, and the steps shown in Figure 3-4 are typical but do not necessarily correspond to any given implementation. For a detailed description of the information engineering methodology see Finkelstein (1989) and Martin (1990).

We will briefly describe each of the four phases of the methodology shown in Figure 3-4, using examples from the Pine Valley Furniture Company. Some of these examples were presented in Chapters 1 and 2; others are presented here for the first time. As we describe each of the phases, we relate the models and information developed to the information systems architecture framework described in the previous section.

PLANNING

A major strength of information engineering is its emphasis on strategic planning for information systems. As Figure 3-4 shows, the first phase of information engineering is planning. The goal of the planning phase is to align information technology with the business strategies of an organization. This requires close cooperation between business managers and information systems managers. Organizations can achieve a competitive advantage when they are able to develop sound strategic information systems plans and convert those plans into a series of practical information systems projects.

As shown in Figure 3-4, information systems planning is accomplished in three steps. The first step is to identify strategic planning factors such as organizational goals, critical success factors, and problem areas. The purpose of this step is to develop the planning context and to link information systems plans to the strategic business plans. The second step is to identify the important objects in the planning environment, such as organizational units, locations, and high-level business functions and entity types. This step corresponds to the first row (business scope) in the ISA framework (Figure 3-1). The third step is to develop an enterprise model. This model, which corresponds to the second row (business model) of the framework, includes the following submodels:

1. A functional decomposition diagram, showing the breakdown of high-level business functions into lower-level supporting functions
2. A high-level entity-relationship diagram (like Figure 2-2)
3. A set of planning matrices that link the various components in the submodels

Strategic Planning Factors

Figure 3-6 shows some of the strategic planning factors for Pine Valley Furniture. Corporate goals are stated for growth (10% per year), return on investment (15% per year before taxes), personnel management (no layoffs), and corporate citizenship. Critical success factors in achieving these goals include maintaining high product quality, providing fast response and on-time deliveries to customers, and maintaining high productivity as a means to control costs. Current problem areas that need to be addressed include inaccurate sales forecasts, increasing competition from both domestic and foreign producers, and stockouts that sometimes lead to backorders or (worse) lost sales.

Corporate Planning Objects

The second step in planning is to identify the major corporate planning objects, which in turn define the business scope. Corporate planning objects generally

Figure 3-6

Strategic planning factors (Pine Valley Furniture)

```
1. Goals
     a. Maintain 10% per year growth rate
     b. Maintain 15% before-tax ROI
     c. No layoffs
     d. Responsible corporate citizenship
2. Critical success factors
     a. High-quality products
     b. On-time deliveries
     c. High productivity
3. Problem areas
     a. Inaccurate sales forecasts
     b. Increasing competition
     c. Stockouts
```

include organizational units, functions, entity types, and organizational locations. Figure 3-7 shows some of the relevant planning objects for Pine Valley Furniture.

Organizational Units   Organizational units consist of the various departments (or other components) from the organizational chart. Several of the major departments at Pine Valley Furniture appear in Figure 3-7.

Organizational Locations   For an organization that has operations or organizational components at more than one location, Figure 3-7 would also show a list of these locations. At the present, however, Pine Valley Furniture exists at only one location, so such a list is not relevant.

Business Functions   A **business function** is a related group of business processes that support some aspect of the mission of the enterprise. The business functions listed in Figure 3-7 are high-level functions such as business planning, product development, and so forth, that are associated with nearly any manufacturing company. Notice that these functions are not the same as organizational units (although in some cases they may have the same names). In fact, a function may be assigned to more than one organizational unit (or conversely, an organizational unit may perform more than one function). For example, product development (a function) is the joint responsibility of the Sales and Manufacturing departments together with top management.

Business function: A related group of business processes that support some aspect of the mission of an enterprise.

Entity Types   We first discussed many of the entity types listed in Figure 3-7 in Chapter 1 (see Figure 1-9). Three additional entities have been added to the list in Figure 3-7: WORK CENTER, EMPLOYEE, and EQUIPMENT. These entity types were identified through interviews with key managers in each of the business areas. We should expect that this list will expand as more detailed analysis occurs in later stages of information engineering.

Figure 3-7

Corporate planning objects (Pine Valley Furniture)

```
Sales Department
Orders Department
Accounting Department
Manufacturing:
    Fabrication Department
    Assembly Department
    Finishing Department
Purchasing Department
Receiving/Shipping Department
    . . .
```
Organizational units

```
Business planning
Product development
Materials management
Marketing and sales
Production operations
Finance and accounting
Human resources
    . . .
```
Business functions

```
CUSTOMER
PRODUCT
VENDOR
RAW MATERIAL
ORDER
WORK CENTER
WORK ORDER
INVOICE
EQUIPMENT
EMPLOYEE
```
Entity types

As we indicated earlier, the planning data that have been developed during this first phase of planning address the first row (business scope) of the ISA model. If you compare Figure 3-7 with the first row of Figure 3-1, you will find that (except for locations) this component of the architecture is now completed (although we may refine it in subsequent steps).

Enterprise Model

The last planning step in information engineering is to develop an enterprise model. As Figure 3-4 shows, this step consists of three substeps: functional decomposition, entity-relationship diagram, and planning matrices.

Functional decomposition: The process of breaking the functions of an organization down into progressively lower levels of detail.

Functional Decomposition   In information engineering, **functional decomposition** is the process of breaking the functions of an organization down into progressively greater levels of detail. During the planning stage of information engineering, each high-level function is typically broken down into a second level of supporting functions. We show a functional decomposition for Pine Valley

Figure 3-8

Functional decomposition (Pine Valley Furniture)

Functions   Supporting functions

- Business planning
  - Market analysis
  - Sales forecasting
- Product development
  - Concept analysis
  - Product design
- Marketing and sales
  - Marketing research
  - Order fulfillment
  - Distribution
- Materials management
  - Material requirements planning
  - Purchasing
  - Receiving
- Finance and accounting
  - Capital budgeting
  - Accounts receivable
  - Accounts payable
- Human resources
  - Recruiting
  - Training
- Production operations
  - Production scheduling
  - Fabrication
  - Assembly
  - Finishing

Furniture in Figure 3-8. For example, business planning consists primarily of two component functions: Market analysis and Sales forecasting. Materials management consists primarily of three components: Material requirements planning, Purchasing, and Receiving.

Entity-Relationship Diagram   A high-level entity-relationship diagram includes the entity types that were identified during the second planning step and the relationships among those entities. Figure 3-9 is an expanded version of the diagram shown in Figure 1-9; it includes the following additional entity types: WORK CENTER, EMPLOYEE, and EQUIPMENT. This diagram will continue to expand as new entity types are identified.

Planning Matrices   The last step in enterprise modeling is to develop a series of planning matrices that link the various components that have been developed to this point. The matrix shown in Figure 3-10 maps five of the functions in the

Figure 3-9

Entity-relationship diagram (Pine Valley Furniture)

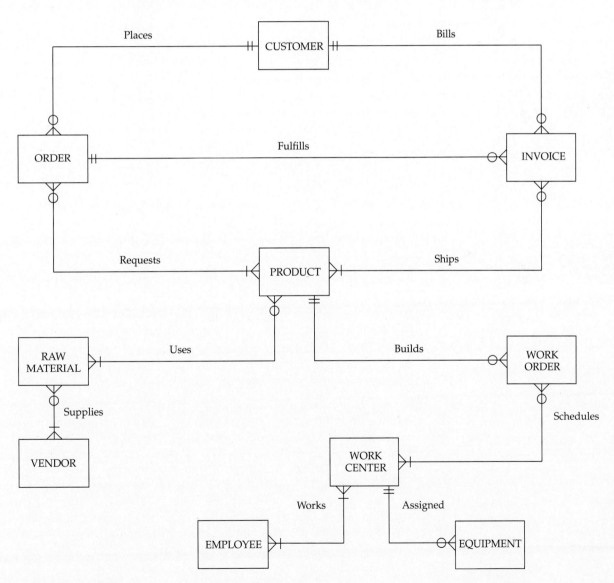

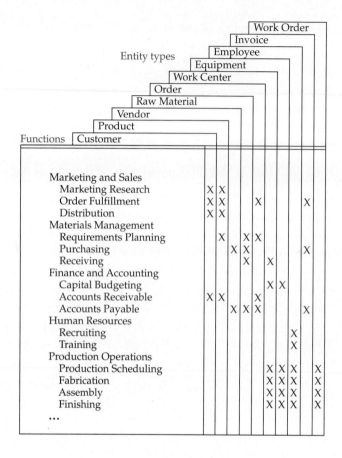

Figure 3-10

Mapping functions to entity types (Pine Valley Furniture)

functional decomposition (Figure 3-8) to the entity types (Figure 3-9). Since this matrix shows which functions use which entities, it can serve several purposes:

1. Identify orphans: that is, indicate which entities are not used by any functions, or which functions do not use any entities.

2. Spot missing entities: employees from each function who examine the matrix can identify any entities that may have been missed.

3. Prioritize development: if a given functional area has a high priority for systems development, then the entities used by that area also have a high priority in database development.

The enterprise model that we have described briefly in this section corresponds to the business model (row 2) of the information systems architecture framework (Figure 3-1). The functional decomposition in Figure 3-8 is a process model, the entity-relationship diagram in Figure 3-9 is a data model, and the matrix in Figure 3-10 links the process and data models. Notice that our terminology refers to row 2 as a business model (rather than an information systems model). The enterprise model is a model of the business, and the objects we use in building the model (functions, entity types, etc.) are familiar to managers throughout the organization. The business model becomes the foundation for building the information systems model in the next phase of information engineering.

ANALYSIS

As Figure 3-4 shows, the second phase of information engineering is *analysis* (sometimes called *requirements analysis*). The purpose of this phase is to develop detailed specifications for the information systems required to support the organization. Specifications include decision support and executive information systems, as well as transaction processing systems. Analysis covers both a study of the current business situation and information systems as well as the determination of requirements for the new system.

Whereas the scope of information systems planning is the whole enterprise, analysis often deals with one business area at a time. A **business area** is a cohesive grouping of functions and entities that forms the basis for information systems development. Business areas are normally broader in scope than the individual departments or business units that request the development of new or improved applications. Martin (1990:184) suggests the following criteria for defining a business area:

1. Clear-cut with definable boundaries
2. Small enough to be well understood and easily manageable
3. Large enough to require shared databases
4. Does not overlap other business areas

Business areas can be selected and prioritized using the planning matrices, critical success factors, problem areas, and other data developed during the planning phase. Some of the criteria used to prioritize business areas are potential benefits, strategic and organizational impact, demand from business users, adequacy of existing systems, degree of risk, and probable cost.

Steps in Analysis

Analysis corresponds to row 3 (information systems model) of the information systems architecture framework (see Figure 3-1). Figure 3-4 shows that there are two major steps in analysis: develop a conceptual data model and develop process models. These steps correspond respectively to the data and process columns of the framework (Figure 3-1).

Develop Conceptual Data Model   A **conceptual data model** is a detailed model that captures the overall structure of organizational data, while being independent of any database management system or other implementation consideration. A conceptual data model includes the relevant entities, relationships, and attributes, as well as the business rules and constraints that define how the data are used. The conceptual data model may be expressed in one of several forms; the most common are detailed entity-relationship diagrams and object-oriented models. We describe conceptual data modeling in detail in the next two chapters.

Develop Process Model   Process models provide logical descriptions of the processes performed by organizational functions and the flow of data between processes. A **process** is a well-defined set of logical tasks performed repeatedly in support of one or more business functions. A process converts inputs into outputs, and has definite boundaries (beginning and ending points). Examples of processes are Admit Patient (hospital), Ticket Passenger (airline), Assemble Bicycle (manufacturing), and Process Customer Order (mail order firm). Notice that in naming

Business area: A cohesive grouping of functions and entities that forms the basis for information systems development.

Conceptual data model: A detailed model that captures the overall structure of organizational data, while being independent of any database management system or other implementation consideration. A conceptual data model includes the relevant entities, relationships, and attributes, as well as the business rules and constraints that define how the data are used.

Process: A well-defined set of logical tasks performed repeatedly in support of one or more business functions. A process converts inputs into outputs, and has definite boundaries (beginning and ending points).

processes, we use an action verb followed (usually) by a noun. The action verb distinguishes a process from functions (whose names are usually nouns), and also highlights the action-oriented nature of processes. The noun that is the object of the verb (such as patient, passenger, bicycle) is an important entity that is used in the process. This naming convention helps identify the entities associated with processes.

Physical process: A process that converts tangible inputs into tangible outputs.

Information process: A process that converts data into information.

There are two basic types of processes: physical processes and information processes. A **physical process** (such as Assemble Bicycle) converts tangible inputs into tangible outputs, while an **information process** (such as Process Customer Order) converts data into information. Many processes are a combination of physical and information processes. In information engineering, we are interested primarily in information processes.

In information engineering, we identify processes by decomposing business functions (identified during the planning phase) into their component (or supporting) processes. For example, one of the functions identified for Pine Valley Furniture is Material requirements planning (see Figure 3-8). Two processes within this function are Determine gross requirements and Determine net requirements (see Figure 3-11). A given process may then be decomposed into lower-level processes. In Figure 3-11, Determine gross requirements is decomposed into three processes: Determine firm demand, Determine forecasted demand, and Calculate gross requirements.

Data flow diagram (DFD): A graphic model of the flow, use, and transformation of data through a set of processes.

Data Flow Diagrams After the processes have been identified and decomposed into lower-level processes, the next step is to develop models that show the flow of data between related processes (for example, all of the processes that support a given function). The most common means for modeling these flows is to use data flow diagrams. A **data flow diagram (DFD)** is a graphic model of the flow, use, and transformation of data through a set of processes. The diagram shows the external agents that are the sources or destinations of data, the processes that transform (or act on) the data, and the data stores where data are collected and held. A DFD differs from a data model, in which we use entity-relationship notation; an E-R diagram shows the natural structure of data. There is, however, a connection between the most detailed DFDs and E-R diagrams: the names of data stores in the DFDs correspond to the names of the data entities in the E-R diagrams.

Figure 3-11

Decomposing a function into processes

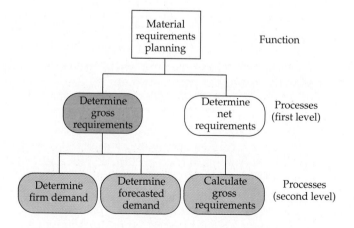

You usually develop many different data flow diagrams during the analysis for a new information system. First, you might draw a *physical* DFD of the current system, showing the people, technology, and media used to move, process, and store data. Second, you draw a *logical* DFD of the current system, which removes all references to system implementation. Third, you build a *logical* DFD of the new system, showing new inputs, outputs, data, and processing capabilities. Finally, you develop a *physical* DFD for the new information system, which clearly shows automated and manual steps, as well as media for data flows and storage. The names used for major data categories, called *data stores*, on the physical DFDs for the new system correspond to the data entity names in an entity-relationship model for the same system.

Analysis Example: Pine Valley Furniture

In Chapter 2 we developed a detailed database application for Pine Valley Furniture that illustrates many of the concepts described in this section. The business area selected was order fulfillment (one of the functions shown in Figure 3-8).

Process Decomposition   A decomposition of the information processes within order fulfillment appears in Figure 3-12. The top-level (or level-0) information process is named Fill Customer Orders. Another level-0 process (Ship Customer Orders, a physical process) is also shown for reference. Fill Customer Orders is decomposed into six level-1 processes: Process Sales Order, Check Customer Credit, Create New Customer, Check Product Availability, Create Invoice, and Create Backorder. Working together, these processes handle most of the transaction processing required to fill customer orders at Pine Valley Furniture. Processes to satisfy management queries or other requests for information are not included in the figure (such applications, often termed *decision support* or *executive information systems*, generally require a somewhat different analysis approach).

Data Flow Diagram   Figure 3-13 shows a logical data flow diagram using the six processes. We show processes as rounded rectangles and data flows by labeled arrows. We represent an external agent, such as Customer, by a rectangle. Finally, we show data stores, such as Product and Customer Order, as open rectangles.

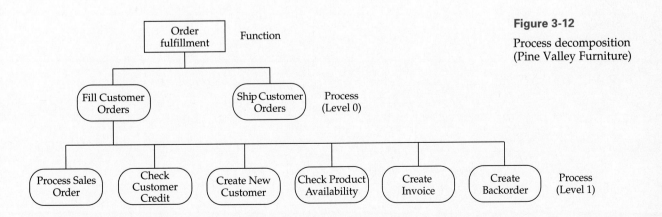

Figure 3-12

Process decomposition (Pine Valley Furniture)

Figure 3-13

Data flow diagram (Pine Valley Furniture)

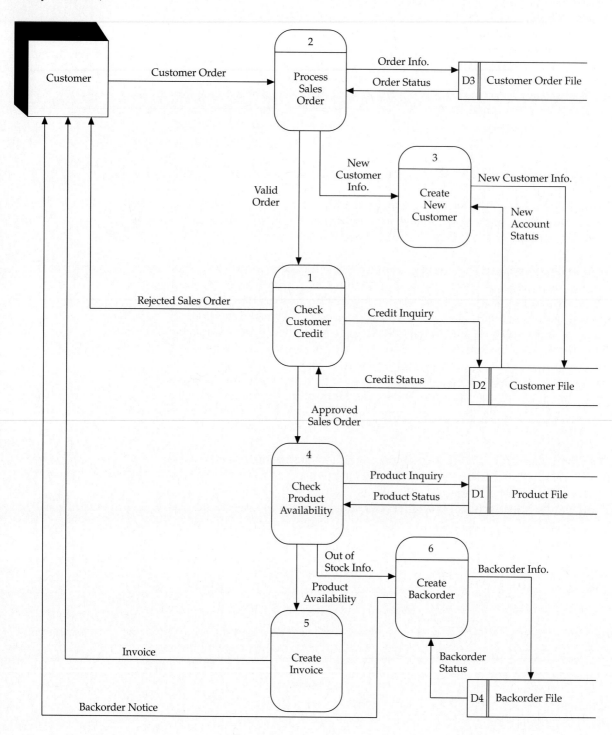

Remember that we will use these same data store names later in the E-R model for this application.

Each data flow in this diagram represents a view of data based on an entity type (or possibly more than one entity type) and its associated attributes. Through detailed analysis of the data flows, we can specify the data required by the processes in each diagram. There are formal techniques for performing this analysis; for example, see Shoval (1990). Since these techniques are beyond the scope of this text, we will use a simple (but effective) approach: we will construct a matrix that maps the processes in the data flow diagram to the entity types they use (see Figure 3-14).

The notation in Figure 3-14 indicates whether a process creates (C), reads (R), updates (U), or deletes (D) entities. Some processes perform more than one action on an entity. For example, Check Product Availability reads a Product instance (or record) and then updates that instance by deducting the quantity ordered from quantity on hand (assuming the latter is adequate). Notice that the Product entity is not created by any of the processes shown in Figure 3-14. This entity must be created by some process in a different data flow diagram (probably within the materials management function).

Entity-Relationship Diagram   The second major component of analysis is a detailed entity-relationship diagram. From the high-level entity relationship diagram developed during the planning phase (Figure 3-9) we are able to determine that the entity types required for Order Fulfillment are CUSTOMER, ORDER, PRODUCT, and INVOICE. We need much more detail, however, to develop an information model, including all relevant attributes, primary keys, new entity types and subtypes, and new relationships (or gerunds). As we indicated in Chapter 1, there are two basic approaches to this task:

1. *Process-oriented:* Start with the relevant data flow diagrams (Figure 3-13) and Process-Entity matrices (Figure 3-14). Analyze the data flows, and then synthesize the data model from the flows.

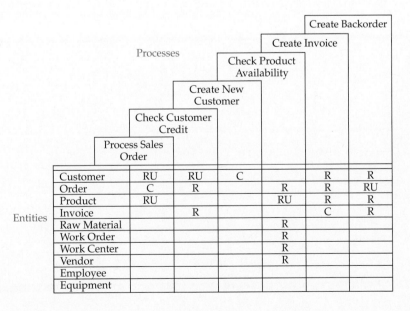

Figure 3-14

Mapping processes to entity types (Pine Valley Furniture)

2. *Data-oriented:* Start with the relevant user views (screens, reports, etc.), then develop a mini–data model for each view, and then synthesize the mini–data models to form an overall model.

We used a data-oriented approach in Chapter 2 to develop a detailed entity-relationship diagram for order fulfillment (see Figure 2-7). Figure 3-15 repeats this diagram for ease of reference.

The information engineering methodology supports both data and process models. We recommend that these models be developed concurrently, and that they be linked using the appropriate matrices. This approach will provide a quality check on the result and help ensure that the data and process models are

Figure 3-15

Detailed entity-relationship diagram (Pine Valley Furniture)

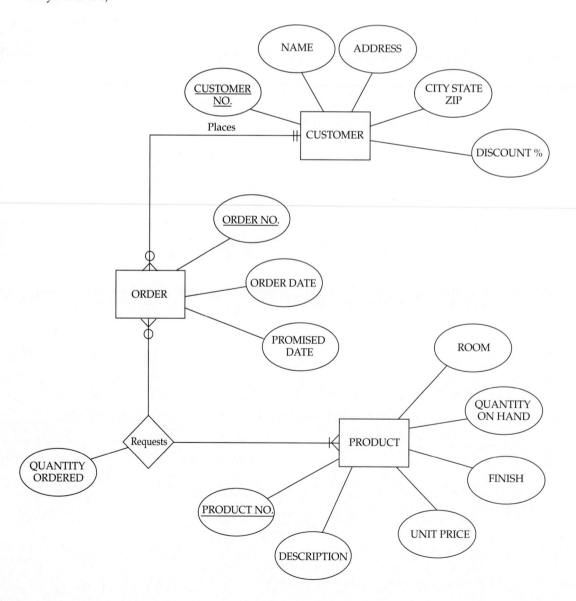

integrated. For example, in developing the process-entity matrix (Figure 3-14), we discovered a candidate entity type (BACKORDER) that was omitted in the data-oriented entity-relationship diagram (Figure 3-15). Pine Valley Furniture will have to decide whether to introduce BACKORDER as a separate entity type to make the models consistent.

These models may also be linked in a CASE tool that supports information engineering. This linkage occurs because the same entries will appear as data entities on E-R diagrams and as data stores on DFDs. Later we discuss the concept of the repository for a CASE tool, where the definitions of these entities and data stores are kept.

DESIGN

The third major stage in information engineering is design (see Figure 3-4). The purpose of this stage is to transform the information models that were developed during analysis to models that conform to the target technology we will use for information systems implementation. For example, if we use relational database technology, then the detailed data models developed during analysis must be transformed to normalized relations (and related business rules) during design. Design corresponds to the technology model (row 4) of the information systems architecture.

There are two steps within design: design databases and design processes (corresponding to the data and process columns of the framework). Each of these steps is described below, and illustrated for Pine Valley Furniture.

Database Design

The major objective of database design is to map the conceptual data model to an implementation model that a particular DBMS can process with performance that is acceptable to all users throughout the organization. In today's competitive economy, database users require information that is complete and up-to-date, and they expect to be able to access this information quickly and easily. Database design can be divided into the following two phases:

1. **Logical database design:** The process of mapping the conceptual data models (from analysis) to structures that are specific to the target DBMS. If the target environment is a relational DBMS, then the conceptual data models are mapped to normalized relations. We describe logical design in detail in Chapter 6.

2. **Physical database design:** The process of mapping the database structures from logical design into physical storage structures such as files and tables. Indexes are also specified, as well as access methods and other physical factors. A major objective of physical design is to provide adequate performance for user applications in terms of response times, throughput rates, and so on. Also, physical design is concerned with security, backup, and recovery. We describe physical design in detail in Chapter 7.

We illustrate logical and physical database design briefly here with examples from Pine Valley Furniture. The detailed entity-relationship diagram for Order Fulfillment was shown in Figure 3-15. During logical database design, this model is transformed into six normalized relations. Four of these relations (for

Logical database design:
The process of mapping logical data models to structures that are specific to a target DBMS.

Physical database design:
The process of mapping the database structures from logical design to physical storage structures such as files and tables. Indexes are also specified, as well as access methods and other physical factors.

CUSTOMER, ORDER, PRODUCT, and REQUESTS) are shown with sample data in Figure 3-16.

During physical database design, we specify the characteristics for each of the attributes in the logical database (including field name, type, and width), as well as editing rules and other constraints that apply to the attributes. We specify indexes for selected attributes. Menu screens for most of these design characteristics were shown in Chapter 2 for Pine Valley Furniture, as follows:

Figure 3-16

Normalized relations (Pine Valley Furniture)

CUSTOMER

CUSTOMER NO.	NAME	ADDRESS	CITY STATE ZIP	DISCOUNT
1273	Contemporary Designs	123 Oak St.	Austin, TX 28384	5
1269	ABC Office Supply	426 Main St.	Buffalo, NY 16829	5
1256	Commonwealth Builders	200 Locust	San Francisco, CA 91284	10
2345	Fred's Furniture	50 High St.	Denver, CO 80617	5

ORDER

ORDER NO.	ORDER DATE	PROMISED DATE	CUSTOMER NO.
61396	6/14/9X	6/20/9X	1256
61200	7/3/9X	7/10/9X	2345
64219	6/19/9X	6/28/9X	1273

PRODUCT

PRODUCT NO.	DESCRIPTION	ROOM	FINISH	UNIT PRICE	QUANTITY ON HAND
M128	Wall Unit	LR	Birch	200	9
B382	Bookcase	FR	Pine	125	4
D200	Dresser	BR	Maple	350	2

REQUESTS

ORDER NO.	PRODUCT NO.	QUANTITY ORDERED
61396	B382	3
61200	M128	1
61200	D200	2

- Table definitions: Figures 2-12 and 2-14 through 2-16
- Index organizations: Figure 2-13
- Editing rules: Figures 2-20 through 2-22, and 2-25

To conserve space we do not repeat these figures in this chapter, but you might want to review them in the context of our overall discussion of information engineering.

Process Design

The information processes required and the flows between those processes were specified during analysis (see Figures 3-12 and 3-13). The purpose of process design is to specify the detailed logic for each of these processes. This logic will include, among other details, all references to the relevant entity types, so that again the data and process models are linked during design. As with database design, process design can be divided into two closely related phases:

1. Specify the detailed logic for each process. (This logic must process all transactions for users sharing the database.)
2. Design user interfaces (menus, forms, and reports).

One of the key processes within Order Fulfillment is Process Sales Order (see Figure 3-13). This process captures the data that are associated with a given customer order (see Figure 2-6 for a sample customer order). The logic for this process is shown in Figure 2-28, so we do not repeat it here.

The other component of process design is the design of user interfaces, including menus, forms, and reports. User interfaces are especially important, since they are the primary point of contact between users and database applications. Whether an application is considered user-friendly often depends on the care given to the design of the user interface. Facilities for user interface design are improving through the use of windows, icons, and other graphical user interface products. Besides the examples in Chapter 2, additional illustrations of user interface design for personal computers appear in Chapters 9–11.

We introduced the design of forms in Chapter 2 for Pine Valley Furniture. Figure 2-19 shows the layout of a form for the PRODUCT display, while Figure 2-23 shows the use of that form for a sample product display transaction. These two figures are repeated for ease of reference in Figure 3-17.

Figure 3-17

Product display form (Pine Valley Furniture)

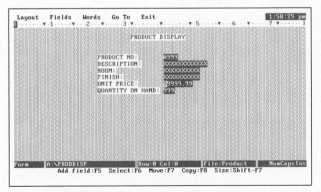

(a) Form layout

(b) Display transaction

IMPLEMENTATION

The last stage in information engineering is implementation (see Figure 3-4). The purpose of this stage is to construct and install the information systems according to the plans and designs from the preceding steps. Implementation corresponds to rows 5 and 6, technology definition and information system, of the information systems architecture.

Implementation involves a series of steps leading to operational information systems that includes creating database definitions, creating program code, testing the systems, developing operational procedures and documentation, training, and populating the databases. In the context of information engineering, we are concerned with only two of these steps: creating database definitions and creating applications (corresponding to the data and process columns of the framework).

Figure 3-18

Summary of the database development process

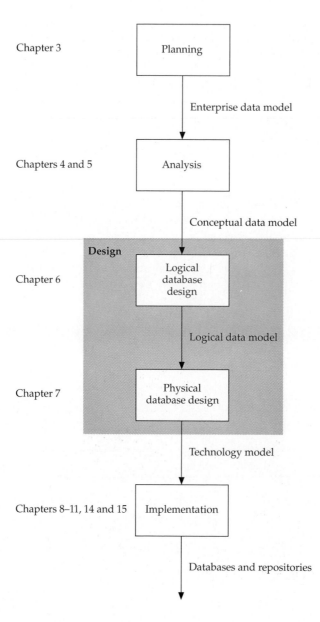

Database definitions are ordinarily expressed in the form of schemas and subschemas. A **schema** is a description of the overall logical structure of a database. Schemas are expressed in a language called the *data definition language* (DDL), which may range from a few simple menu choices for a personal computer DBMS to a complete language implementation for a mainframe computer. A **subschema** is a logical description of a user's view (or program's view) of the data that are used. A subschema is derived from an associated schema, and we normally define numerous subschemas for each database schema.

The database schema and subschemas are read and processed by the DBMS. Each is checked for accuracy, and the compiled (or processed) versions are stored in the repository or data dictionary. These definitions constitute an important part of the metadata for an organization and the DBMS refers to them whenever it accesses data in the database.

Application program code (and related control blocks, indexes, etc.) represents the last step in the process column. Program code for complex transactions such as processing a customer order are often implemented using procedural languages such as COBOL or C. The standard language for queries in relational databases is SQL, and SQL statements are often embedded in this code for accessing the entities (or records).

With the information engineering methodology, some CASE tools can generate (in part or completely) both the database definitions (schema and subschema) and the program code. Thus, while CASE tools are used to support the previous steps (planning, analysis, and design), they can be used to automate this final step. Using CASE tools improves the quality of the delivered information systems as well as the productivity of the development process.

A summary of the database development process (ignoring ongoing maintenance and enhancement activities) appears in Figure 3-18, which shows the four phases of development (planning, analysis, design, and implementation). It also shows the two stages of design related to databases: logical database design and physical database design. The output of each phase corresponding to the database is shown, as well as the chapter (or chapters) that describes each of the topics in detail. Although this figure shows that the database development process is linear, often there is feedback in practice. For example, work in logical database design might identify inadequacies that necessitate further analysis and refinement of the conceptual data model.

> **Schema:** A description of the overall logical structure of a database, expressed in a special data definition language.

> **Subschema:** A logical description of a user's view (or program's view) of data, expressed in a special data definition language.

STRATEGIC INFORMATION SYSTEMS PLANNING

Earlier in this chapter we described information systems planning in the context of information engineering. In this section we provide greater detail, and the last section illustrates strategic planning with a realistic case example.

Strategic information systems planning is an orderly means of assessing the information needs of an organization and defining the systems and databases that will best satisfy those needs. Strategic information systems planning (hereafter called *strategic IS planning*) is a top-down process that takes into account the outside forces that drive the business and the factors critical to its success. Strategic IS planning looks at data and systems in terms of how they help a business to achieve its objectives.

> **Strategic information systems planning:** An orderly means of assessing the information needs of an organization and defining the systems and databases that will best satisfy those needs.

The Importance of Strategic IS Planning

Traditionally, organizations have not actually planned information systems at all; they have evolved in a bottom-up fashion from stand-alone systems to solve isolated organizational problems. In effect, traditional information systems development asks, "What procedure (application program) is required to solve this particular problem as it exists today?" The problem with this approach is that the required organizational procedures are likely to change over time as the environment changes. For example, a company may decide to change its method of billing customers, or a university may change its procedures for registering students. When such changes occur, it is usually necessary to modify existing application programs.

In contrast, data resource management asks, "What database requirements will satisfy the information needs of the enterprise today and well into the future?" A major advantage of this approach is that an organization's data are less likely to change (or will change more slowly) than its procedures. Unless an organization changes its business fundamentally, its underlying data structures will remain reasonably stable over a 10-year period, although the procedures used to access and process the data may change many times during that period. Thus, the challenge of data resource management is to design stable databases that are relatively independent of the languages and programs used to update them.

To benefit from this database approach, the organization must analyze its information needs and plan its databases carefully. To attempt a database approach without such planning may produce disastrous results: the databases may support individual applications but fail to provide a resource that users throughout the organization can share.

The need for improved information systems planning in organizations today is readily apparent when we consider factors such as the following:

1. The cost of information systems has risen steadily and approaches 40% of total expenses in some organizations.

2. Systems cannot handle applications that cross organizational boundaries.

3. Systems often do not address the critical problems of the business as a whole nor support strategic applications.

4. Data redundancy is often out of control, and users may have little confidence in the quality of data.

5. Systems maintenance costs are out of control, because old, poorly planned systems must constantly be revised.

6. Application backlogs often extend three years or more, and frustrated end users rush to create (or purchase) their own systems, often creating redundant databases in the process.

Strategic information systems planning will certainly not solve all of these problems in itself. Such planning, however, driven by top management commitment, is a prerequisite in order to realize the benefits of information resource management.

Planning Prerequisites

Before the planning process can begin, three important preliminary steps must be accomplished.

1. *Top management should be committed.* Top management must be fully committed and prepared to become actively involved in the planning process.

2. *A project team should be selected.* A project team comprised of user-managers and information systems specialists should be appointed to perform strategic information systems planning. The team should have a strong leader (preferably a user-manager) and should act under the guidance of top management.

3. *A planning methodology should be selected.* The team should select a planning methodology (such as information engineering) that is consistent with corporate needs and is supported by comprehensive CASE tools.

The Planning Metamodel

The first step in the planning process is to decide what data to collect and how to organize them. Figure 3-19 is a *metamodel* that shows the major entity types and relationships that are normally involved in the planning process. We refer to this as a metamodel because it shows only generic entity types that apply to any organization. The metadata form a template for collecting data during the planning process. The data are collected and stored in the repository using a CASE tool that supports the planning methodology.

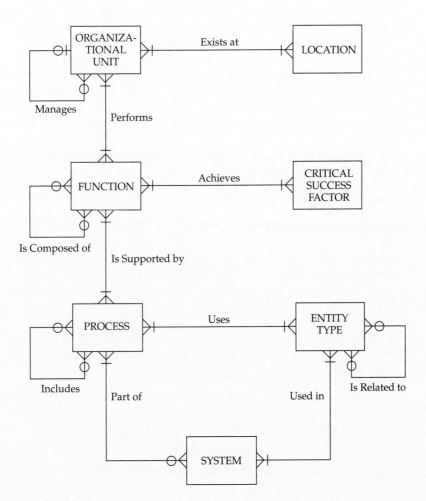

Figure 3-19

Metamodel for strategic information systems planning

Following is a brief definition of each entity type shown in Figure 3-19 (we have defined some of these terms earlier in this chapter).

1. *Organizational unit*: An administrative subdivision of an organization. Examples: information systems department, pediatrics unit.

2. *Location*: A geographical position where one or more administrative units are located. Examples: Bloomington, New York City.

3. *Function*: Related groups of business activities that support some aspect of the mission of the enterprise. Examples: software design, patient care.

4. **Critical success factor (CSF):** An internal or external business-related result that is measurable and has a major influence on whether an organization meets its goals (Martin, 1990). Examples: delivered defect rate (errors per thousand lines of code), patient complaint rate (number of complaints per month).

5. *Process*: A well-defined set of logical tasks that are performed repeatedly in support of one or more business functions. Examples: define user requirements, treat patients.

6. *Entity type*: A collection of entities that share similar properties or characteristics. Examples: vendors, patients.

7. *System*: An application program or other component of an information system. Examples: accounts payable, patient information.

Figure 3-19 also shows the significant relationships among the various entity types. Most of the relationships are many-to-many: for example, a function is supported by one or more processes, and a given process (such as Recruit New Personnel) may support more than one function. Notice that some of the entity types are related to themselves (a *recursive* relationship; see Chapter 4). For example, high-level functions (or functional areas) are often composed of lower-level functions (for an example, see Figure 3-8).

We can easily include additional entity types in our metamodel. Some entity types that are often included are PROJECT, BUSINESS MANAGER, GOAL, and PROBLEM AREA. Most CASE tools allow the user to easily add or delete entity types in the planning metamodel.

Planning Matrices

We have already noted that the planning metamodel (Figure 3-19) shows the relationships among the planning entities. We can represent each of these relationships as a matrix. For example, one matrix shows which functions are performed by which organizational units. Figure 3-20 shows six typical matrices; we can add others as needed.

The planning team can use a CASE tool to construct the planning matrices and analyze the relationships. A typical sequence for this analysis follows:

1. Prioritize the organizational critical success factors (CSFs), and use the function-versus-CSF matrix (Figure 3-20d) to prioritize business functions.

2. Use the organizational-unit-versus-function matrix (Figure 3-20b) to identify management responsibility for high-priority functions.

3. Use the function-versus-process matrix (Figure 3-20c) to identify processes that support critical functions.

Critical success factor (CSF): An internal or external business-related result that is measurable and has a major influence on whether an organization meets its goals.

Figure 3-20

Typical planning
matrices

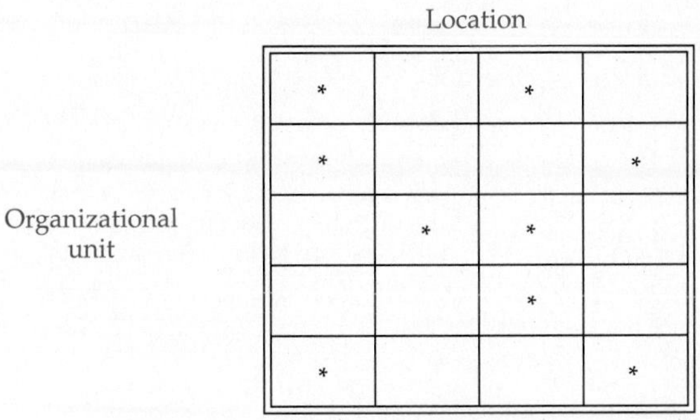

Location

*		*	
*			*
	*	*	
		*	
*			*

Organizational
unit

This matrix shows the geographical
location of organizational units
(* = organizational unit at location).

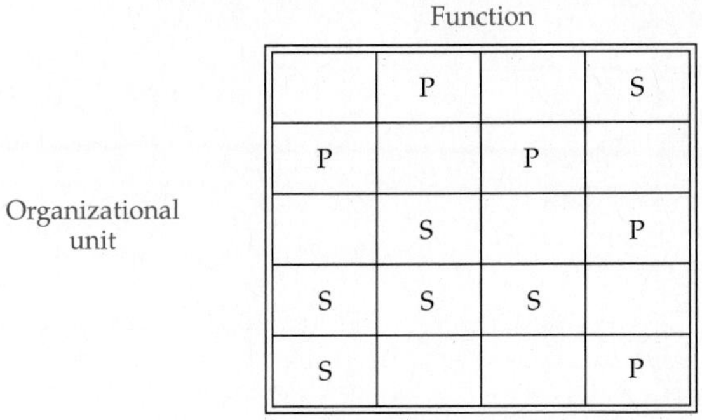

(a) Organizational-unit-versus-location

Function

	P		S
P		P	
	S		P
S	S	S	
S			P

Organizational
unit

This matrix shows which functions
are performed by organizational
units (P = primary responsibility;
S = secondary responsibility).

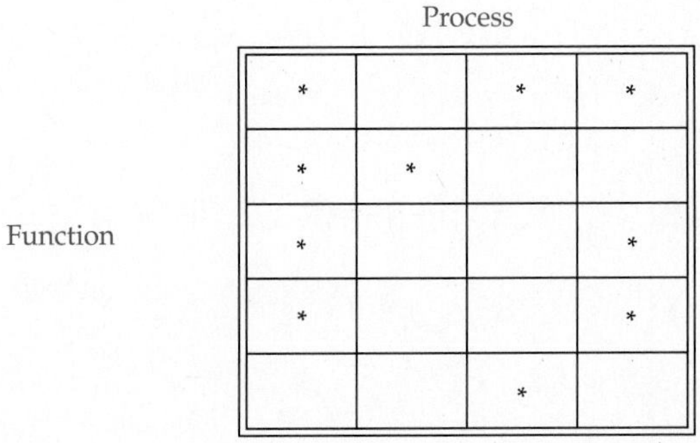

(b) Organizational-unit-versus-function

Process

*		*	*
*	*		
*			*
*			*
		*	

Function

This matrix shows which processes
support business functions
(* = process supports this function).

(c) Function-versus-process

(continues)

4. Use the process-versus-entity-type matrix (Figure 3-20e) to identify data
   entities created and used by high-priority processes. (This step in essence
   allows the organization to prioritize database development projects.)

5. Use the system-versus-entity-type matrix (Figure 3-20f) to identify system
   applications that input, process, and output high-priority data entities.

Although the above steps represent a typical sequence, in reality the planning
team will use the CASE tool repetitively to perform a series of "what-if" analyses.
The CASE tool does not automate the planning process, but provides the team
with a powerful tool for structuring and analyzing the planning data. The objective is to translate organizational goals, objectives, and critical success factors into
a series of prioritized projects for databases and information systems.

Figure 3-20 Continued

Critical success factor

Function

E		D	D
	E	E	
D		D	E
		E	
	D		

This matrix shows which business functions help to achieve which critical success factors (E = essential; D = desirable).

(d) Function-versus-CSF

Entity type

Process

C	U	R	U
U	R	U	
R	C	R	U
R	D		U
R	U	C	C

This matrix shows the use of entity types by business processes (C = creates; R = reads; U = updates; D = deletes).

(e) Process-versus-entity-type

Entity type

System

	P		I
O		P	I
	I		P
P	O	O	I
O	P	I	

This matrix shows the use of entity types by application systems (I = input; P = process; O = output).

(f) System-versus-entity-type

Benefits of CASE Tools in Planning

The planning process that we have described requires collecting, organizing, and analyzing vast amounts of data. Realistically, this process can only be accomplished with the support of CASE tools. Some of the important benefits of using CASE tools in strategic IS planning follow:

1. CASE tools provide a structured environment with a common database, a common approach, a standard vocabulary, and a standard user interface.

2. Various users can work on different parts of the study at the same time, with the CASE tools providing the necessary communication and integration.

3. Case tools provide a repository (described below) for storing vast quantities of information about information systems.

4. CASE tools provide a decision support environment for analyzing complex relationships and asking "what-if" system design questions.

5. CASE tools simplify the process of updating the strategic plan as business conditions change.

6. The database developed during strategic planning can become the basis for the subsequent stages (analysis, design, implementation, and maintenance) of systems development.

THE ROLE OF A REPOSITORY

Throughout this chapter we have emphasized the role of CASE tools in information systems development. Typically, different tools and methods are used for different stages of the development process. For example, one tool is used for planning, another for analysis, still another for design, and so on. If these tools and methods are to be effective, they must be integrated. In particular, the tools must be able to share the metadata that are developed during each stage of the process. Unfortunately, the ability to share such information among CASE tools has not been common, especially among tools from different vendors.

Such tool integration depends on a formal, detailed architecture for building and maintaining information systems. This architecture includes formal definitions of interfaces between tools, data model standards among tools, and common controls across the life cycle. The principal tool for providing this integration is an information repository (or *repository* for short). A **repository** is a knowledge base of information about the facts that an enterprise must be able to access and the processes it must perform to be successful (Moriarty, 1991). Thus, for example, all of the information that is collected during the four stages of information engineering is maintained in a repository.

Repository: A knowledge base of information about the facts that an enterprise must be able to access and the processes it must perform to be successful.

Figure 3-21 shows the role of a repository in information systems development. Notice that the repository supports and links all stages of the development process. As information is collected during the planning stage (or enterprise modeling), for example, it is stored in the repository by the CASE tool that supports planning. Then the CASE tool that supports the analysis stage retrieves and builds on the planning information. In this way the repository becomes a central source of information for all of the data and information resources in an organization.

As you would expect, over a period of time a vast amount of information is stored in a typical repository. The specialized software component required to manage and protect this important resource is called the *repository manager* (an IBM term) or, more generally, an *information resource dictionary system (IRDS)*. Repositories are becoming the key strategic component for building systems for enterprise-wide computing.

Case Example: Mountain View Community Hospital

This section illustrates the strategic IS planning process we have described with the case example of a hospital, an organization familiar to most people. Although the example is hypothetical, it does contain many of the elements of a real hospital environment. We use the same case in later chapters to illustrate detailed database design and implementation.

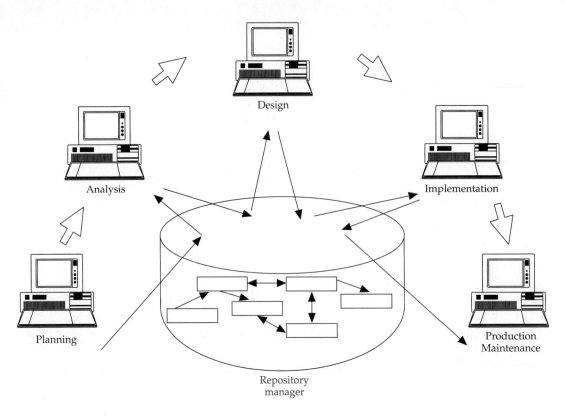

Figure 3-21

Repository-based
development

Identifying the Business Environment

Mountain View Community Hospital is a not-for-profit, short-term, acute-care general hospital. It is a small hospital, with 100 beds at the present time. Mountain View Community is the only hospital in the city of Mountain View, a rapidly growing city in the heart of the Rocky Mountains with a population of about 25,000 people.

Figure 3-22 shows an organizational chart for Mountain View Community Hospital. Like most hospitals, Mountain View Community is divided into two organizational groups. The physicians, headed by Dr. Browne (chief of staff), are responsible for the quality of medical care provided to their patients. The group headed by Ms. Baker (administrator) provides the nursing, clinical, and administrative support the physicians need to serve their patients.

Understanding the Business Direction

Mountain View Community Hospital has a long-range plan that was prepared two years ago with the assistance of a management consulting firm. The plan, which covers a 10-year period, defines the hospital's service area and its forecasted growth, identifies basic goals and objectives, and identifies the capacity and resources that will be required to meet future needs.

Although most admissions to Mountain View Community Hospital are from the city of Mountain View, some patients are also admitted from the surrounding rural areas. As a result, the entire county in which Mountain View is located (Mesa

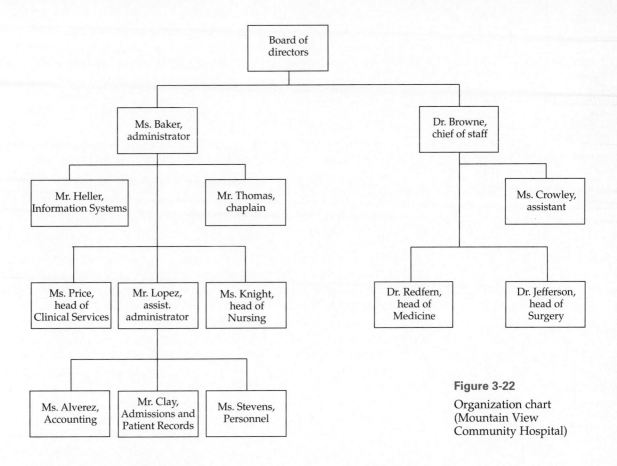

Figure 3-22

Organization chart
(Mountain View
Community Hospital)

County) was defined as the hospital's service area. The population of Mesa County is about 40,000 at present and has been growing at an annual rate of 8%, a trend that is expected to continue for several years.

The basic goal of Mountain View Community Hospital is to continue to meet the needs of Mountain View and Mesa County for high-quality health care, while containing costs that have been rising in accordance with national trends in recent years. To support the expected demand for services, the long-range plan calls for the expansion and modernization of facilities, including the addition of a new wing in five years, allowing expansion from the present 100 to 150 beds. Adequate land already exists for this expansion, as well as for additional parking facilities. Also, several existing facilities are to be renovated, including the Admitting and Outpatient registration areas. Two new service facilities are planned over a five-year period: Ultrasound and Occupational Therapy.

Existing Information Systems

Mountain View Community leased a minicomputer several years ago. The system has 12MB central memory and 300MB on-line disk storage capacity. Plans call for adding a faster processor and additional memory and disk storage capacity during the coming year; the extent of these additions, however, has yet to be determined.

Present information systems are batch-oriented and include application programs for patient accounting, billing and accounts receivable, and financial accounting. These application packages were obtained from a software vendor specializing in hospital applications.

Mr. Heller, who was recently appointed manager of Information Systems, identified the following deficiencies in the present systems:

1. The systems do not support the medical staff by recording or reporting the results of laboratory tests and procedures.

2. Since the systems are batch-oriented, they do not support on-line procedures such as patient registration or inquiries regarding billing.

3. The systems do not accumulate costs by department or cost centers.

4. The systems are inflexible and do not respond well to changing management needs or to the frequent changes in reporting requirements of external health agencies.

Management at Mountain View Community had for some time recognized that the present information systems were not responsive to their needs. Mr. Lopez (assistant administrator), who had previous experience with the database in a large city hospital, had advocated that Mountain View Community investigate this approach. Mr. Heller was hired as manager of Information Systems partly because of his experience with database systems. A new systems analyst (Mr. Helms) also was recently hired. Mr. Helms had experience in database design, and is regarded as a candidate for the data administrator position if and when it is approved by the board of directors.

At a meeting of the board of directors, Mr. Heller explained the concept of data resource management. Ms. Baker (hospital administrator) proposed that Mountain View Community adopt this approach and that Mr. Helms be appointed data administrator. The board of directors agreed with the concept but insisted on a study to estimate costs and benefits as well as develop an overall strategic information systems plan. Ms. Baker formed a study team with the following members: Mr. Lopez, assistant administrator (leader); Ms. Knight, head of nursing; Mr. Crowley, assistant chief of staff; Mr. Heller, manager of Information Systems; and Mr. Helms, systems analyst. An outside consultant was hired to assist them, and spent several days helping the team outline the study approach and establish schedules.

Critical Success Factors

The study team interviewed Ms. Baker (hospital administrator) and other top managers to determine critical success factors (CSFs) for the hospital. CSFs usually include between three and six key factors that are crucial to an organization's success. For example, in a microelectronics company, critical success factors might include product innovation, high quality, and strict cost controls.

The study team identified three CSFs for Mountain View Community Hospital: excellence in patient care, cost control, and recruitment and retention of skilled personnel (especially nurses). Each CSF can be broken down into several lower-level objectives. For example, three objectives were identified for cost control:

1. Improved inventory control

2. Improved staff scheduling

3. Improved vendor selection

Using a CASE tool, the team entered information describing the organization, existing information systems, and CSFs into the repository.

Enterprise Modeling

The study team reviewed Mountain View Community Hospital's long-range plan and proceeded to model the business functions and processes. First, the team identified the following major functions of a small general hospital (see Figure 3-23):

- *Patient care administration*, to manage the logistical and record-keeping aspects of patient care
- *Clinical services*, to provide laboratory testing and procedures, and patient monitoring and screening
- *Patient care services*, to provide patients with medical care and support services
- *Financial management*, to manage the financial resources and operations of the hospital
- *Administrative services*, to provide general management and support services

Having identified the major functions, the team's next step was to decompose each function into its supporting functions. The project team spent considerable time interviewing managers and other key staff members throughout the hospital to define the supporting functions performed within each business function. In total, 22 supporting functions were identified for Mountain View Community Hospital. The resulting decomposition of functions is shown in Figure 3-24, in a diagram called an *enterprise chart*. For example, the following functions were identified within patient care services: Dietary, Nursing, Surgery, Rehabilitation, and Blood banking. As the functions were defined, their descriptions were entered into the repository. Also, the team members entered data defining relationships among the organizational areas, functions, entities, and critical success factors.

As each function was defined, the team members also defined several of the key processes within each function. For example, one of the processes within Rehabilitation is Perform physical therapy. Some of these processes are shown in the enterprise chart (Figure 3-24). Processes are normally defined in detail during the analysis (rather than planning) stage. However, there is considerable flexibility in information engineering, and the planning team may choose to define key processes within the planning stage. As the processes were defined, their descriptions were also added to the repository.

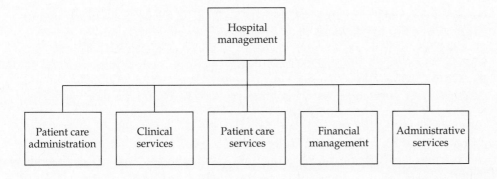

Figure 3-23

Business functions (Mountain View Community Hospital)

Figure 3-24

Enterprise chart
(Mountain View
Community Hospital)

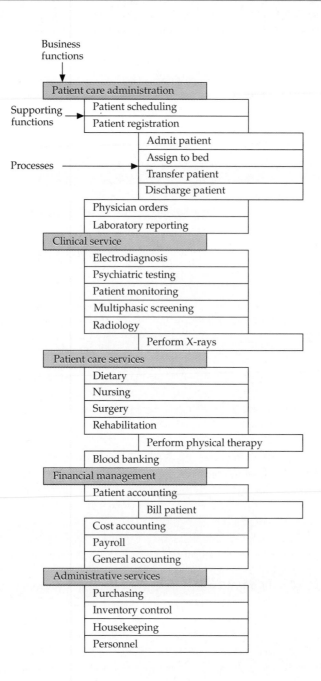

As the functions and processes were defined, the study team also identified 10 entity types for the hospital that are directly related to them: HOSPITAL, PHYSICIAN, PATIENT, WARD, STAFF, LABORATORY, TEST, MEDICAL/ SURGICAL ITEM, SUPPLY ITEM, and VENDOR. These are broad classes of data that will be further refined during logical database design. The study team entered descriptions of these entity types into the repository together with process-versus-entity and system-versus-entity data.

After entering all of the planning data into the repository, the planning team proceeded to analyze the data and integrate the various models. This step included constructing an entity-relationship diagram for the hospital and analyzing the planning matrices.

The Entity-Relationship Diagram

The team analyzed the relationship among the 10 entity types and constructed an entity-relationship diagram (see Figure 3-25). Following is a brief description of the relationships shown in the figure.

1. A HOSPITAL Maintains a number of LABORATORY(ies): radiology, electrodiagnosis, hematology, and so on. (*Note:* the E-R diagram handles the future possibility that Mountain View Community Hospital might operate multiple units called *hospitals*. As long as there is only one hospital facility, the HOSPITAL entity will have only one instance; hence, it is not necessary in the data model.)

2. A HOSPITAL Contains a number of WARDs (obstetrics, emergency, rehabilitation, etc.).

3. Each WARD Is Assigned a certain number of STAFF members (nurses, secretaries, etc.).

4. A HOSPITAL Staffs a number of PHYSICIANS on its medical staff. A PHYSICIAN may be on the staff of more than one HOSPITAL, and a PHYSICIAN may be independent.

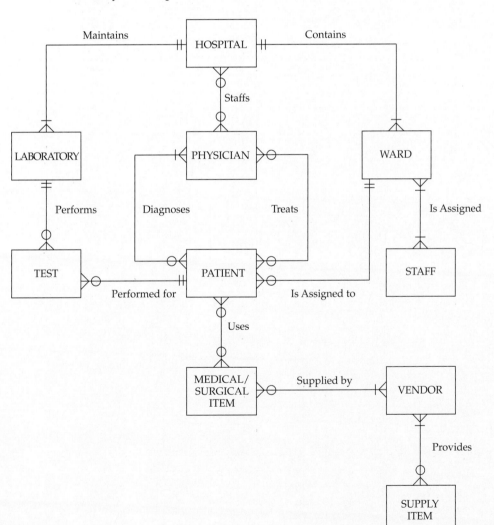

Figure 3-25

Entity-relationship diagram (Mountain View Community Hospital)

5. There are two associations between PHYSICIAN and PATIENT: Diagnoses and Treats (that is, prescribes treatments). Each PATIENT may be diagnosed and/or treated by more than one PHYSICIAN.

6. A PATIENT Is Assigned To a WARD. (*Note*: each PATIENT is in exactly one WARD, so there are no outpatients, and there is no need to track the movement of PATIENTs if they are transferred between WARDs.)

7. A PATIENT Uses MEDICAL/SURGICAL ITEMs, which are Supplied by the VENDORs. A VENDOR also Provides items called SUPPLY ITEMs that are used for housekeeping and maintenance.

8. A LABORATORY Performs TESTs for PATIENTs.

The study team recognized that the E-R diagram of Figure 3-25 was preliminary. Some additional entity types that will have to be added to the model in the future include the following: EQUIPMENT, BLOOD DONOR, VOLUNTEER, and BENEFACTOR. The present model, however, represents an important subset of the information resources for a small hospital.

The Function-Versus-Entity-Type Matrix

The study team used the CASE tool to produce a first version of a function-versus-entity-type matrix (see Figure 3-26). This matrix maps the 22 functions in Figure 3-24 versus the 10 entity types shown in Figure 3-25. A C indicates that a function

Figure 3-26

Function-versus-entity-type matrix (first version) (Mountain View Community Hospital)

Function \ Entity Type	Hospital	Physician	Patient	Ward	Staff	Laboratory	Test	Medical/ surgical item	Supply item	Vendor
Patient registration			C	R						
Patient scheduling		R	R			R				
Physician orders		R	R				R			
Laboratory reporting			R			R	R			
Electrodiagnosis							C			
Psychiatric testing							C			
Patient monitoring			R							
Multiphasic screening			R			R	C			
Radiology						R	C			
Dietary			R							
Nursing			R							
Surgery		R	R							
Rehabilitation			R							
Blood banking			R			R				
General accounting	C			C		C				
Cost accounting	R		R	R		R				
Patient accounting			R	R		R	R			
Payroll		R		R	R					
Purchasing								C	C	C
Inventory control								R	R	
Personnel		C			C				R	
Housekeeping									R	

creates an entity, while an *R* indicates that a function reads an entity. For simplicity, we do not show update or delete activities. For example, in Figure 3-26 we see that the Patient registration function creates a PATIENT entity and reads the WARD entity. By *create* we mean that the function creates an instance of the entity. A creating function may also update and delete an instance. A function that reads an entity may not create, update, or delete that instance.

Each row in Figure 3-26 indicates how the various entity types are used by a particular function, and each column of the figure shows all of the functions that use a particular entity type. The matrix can be made more useful, however, by rearranging the columns as shown in Figure 3-27. We accomplish this rearrangement as follows: select the first function in Figure 3-26 that creates an entity (Patient registration, which creates the PATIENT entity). Move that entity to the first column, as shown in Figure 3-27. Now select the next function that creates an entity (Electrodiagnosis, which creates a TEST entity) and move that entity to the second column. Proceed in this manner, moving entity types to the left as you proceed downward through the functions.

The purpose of rearranging the matrix is to group the functions and data into major subsystems, which are shown as boxes along or near the main diagonal in Figure 3-27. For example, the first box indicates a patient administration subsystem that includes four functions: Patient registration, Patient scheduling, Physician orders, and Laboratory reporting. This subsystem uses the PATIENT entity (the four functions also use entities in other subsystems). The second subsystem consists of a package of clinical service functions (Electrodiagnosis, Psychiatric

Function \ Entity Type	Patient	Test	Hospital	Ward	Laboratory	Vendor	Medical/surgical item	Supply item	Physician	Staff
Patient registration	C			R						
Patient scheduling	R			R					R	
Physician orders	R	R							R	
Laboratory reporting	R	R		R						
Electrodiagnosis		C								
Psychiatric testing		C								
Patient monitoring	R									
Multiphasic screening	R	C			R					
Radiology		C			R					
Dietary	R									
Nursing	R									
Surgery	R								R	
Rehabilitation	R									
Blood banking	R			R						
General accounting			C	C	C					
Cost accounting	R		R	R	R					
Patient accounting	R	R		R	R					
Payroll				R						
Purchasing						C	C	C		
Inventory control							R	R		
Personnel								R	C	C
Housekeeping								R		

Figure 3-27

Function-versus-entity-type matrix (revised version) (Mountain View Community Hospital)

Figure 3-28

Function-versus-critical success factor matrix (Mountain View Community Hospital)

Function / CSF	Excellent care	Cost control	Staff retention
Patient scheduling	D		
Patient registration			
Physician orders	D		
Laboratory reporting	D		
Electrodiagnosis			
Psychiatric testing	D		
Patient monitoring	E		
Multiphasic screening	E		
Radiology	D		
Dietary	E		
Nursing	E	E	E
Surgery	D	D	
Rehabilitation	E		
Blood banking	D		
Patient accounting	D	E	
Cost accounting		E	
General accounting			
Purchasing			
Inventory control		E	
Housekeeping		D	
Personnel			E

E=essential D=desirable

testing, Patient monitoring, Multiphasic screening, and Radiology) that create instances of the TEST entity. Examine Figure 3-27 and identify three additional subsystems. These subsystems provide the basis for subdividing the overall development into manageable projects.

Strategy Formulation

The project team decided to use critical success factors (CSFs) for Mountain View Community Hospital as a basis for planning IS projects (Shank, Boynton, and Zmud, 1985). They produced a function-versus-CSF matrix with the CASE tool, showing the functions that are essential (E) and desirable (D) to achieve each CSF (see Figure 3-28). For example, five functions were considered essential to achieve Excellent care: Patient monitoring, Multiphasic screening, Dietary, Nursing, and Rehabilitation. Eight other functions (shown in the figure) were considered desirable but not essential for this CSF.

The project team listed the five essential functions for the Excellent care CSF. They then used the function-versus-entity matrix (Figure 3-27) to identify the entities that are created and read by these functions: PATIENT, TEST, and LABORATORY (see Figure 3-29). However, the PATIENT and LABORATORY entities are read (but not created) by any of the five essential functions; thus, it was necessary to add the two functions (Patient registration and General accounting) that create (C) PATIENT and LABORATORY, respectively.

Function	Entity Type		
	PATIENT	TEST	LABORATORY
Patient monitoring	R		
Multiphasic screening	R	C	R
Dietary screening	R		
Nursing	R		
Rehabilitation	R		
Patient registration	C		
General accounting			C

Figure 3-29

Functions and entity types essential for Excellent patient care (Mountain View Community Hospital)

If Excellent care is the most important CSF, then Figure 3-29 shows the highest-priority functions and entity types for development, needs that can also be stated in terms of the subsystems (boxes) shown in Figure 3-27. The functions in Figure 3-29 require the first subsystem (patient care administration), the second subsystem (clinical service), and General accounting from the third subsystem. Since our greatest interest is in database planning, we conclude from Figure 3-22 that for Excellent care, the following three entity types are essential: PATIENT, TEST, and LABORATORY.

Final Report

The study team completed their IS strategic plan in approximately three months and prepared a report summarizing the plan for Mountain View Community Hospital. Much of the documentation for the plan was prepared using the CASE tool. The report included a statement of business direction, critical success factors, an enterprise model (functional decomposition, high-level entity-relationship diagram, and several planning matrices), and a prioritized list of IS projects. The entity-relationship diagram provided an overall map for database design and implementation, and the prioritized list of projects included a set of priorities for database design. The report concluded with a timetable for data and information systems design and implementation over the next three years.

The study team presented the strategic IS plan to the board of directors at their regular meeting the following month. The board endorsed the plan and shortly thereafter approved the creation of the data administration position. Ms. Baker appointed Mr. Helms to this position, to report initially to Mr. Heller.

PITFALLS IN STRATEGIC IS PLANNING

There are numerous risks and pitfalls in strategic IS planning, and successful planning requires that we manage these risks and overcome the pitfalls. We describe some of these hazards briefly. For an extended discussion, see Hoffer, Michaele, and Carroll (1989) and Lederer and Sethi (1989).

1. Top management is not committed to strategic IS planning or to implementing the plan. In the former case, the plan will be inadequate or incomplete; in the latter, it will collect dust and never be implemented.

2. There is lack of clarity in organizational direction, or the direction shifts abruptly. Thus, strategic IS plans cannot be integrated with business plans.

3. Planning is decentralized among business units, and lack of coordination may result in inconsistent or incomplete plans.

4. Tools to assist in the transition from planning to development may not exist. Tools are needed to provide a continued linkage between IS planning and ongoing development.

5. System- and user-managers who feel ownership of current applications frequently resist a new system architecture. Involvement of key personnel throughout the planning process is essential to overcome this resistance.

6. The strategic IS plan is not kept up-to-date as business conditions change, so that the plans become obsolete.

SUMMARY

In this chapter we have presented an overall framework and methodology for information systems development. The goal of IS development with this approach is to allow managers, knowledge workers, and other employees to access and retrieve information easily, regardless of its geographical location or storage method. The development methodology must allow end users (as well as information system specialists) to develop components of the target information systems within the organization's overall information systems architecture.

An information systems architecture is a conceptual blueprint or plan that expresses the desired future structure for the information systems in an organization. It creates the context within which managers can make consistent decisions concerning their information systems. Although there is no standard structure or format for expressing an information systems architecture, Zachman has defined a framework, ISA, that is very useful in developing an architecture. The three components of the Zachman framework (data, process, and network) are represented by columns. The six rows of the framework represent the roles or views of the different developers and users of the systems. The ISA framework provides a template for developing information systems to satisfy the goal of enterprise-wide computing.

A methodology is a process for developing information systems, together with a set of design objects that are manipulated to describe the systems. In this chapter we describe the information engineering methodology, which is a top-down approach for systems development. There are four stages in information engineering: planning, analysis, design, and implementation. The purpose of planning is to develop strategic information systems plans that are linked to strategic business plans. This stage results in developing an enterprise model that includes a decomposition of business functions and a high-level entity-relationship diagram.

The purpose of analysis is to develop detailed descriptions of required information systems that are independent of the technology that will be used to implement them. The major products of this stage are detailed logical descriptions of both data and processes (as well as network components, if applicable). The purpose of design is to map the logical descriptions to models that conform to the target technology that will be used to implement the systems (for example, relational database management systems). During implementation, detailed definitions of the processes and data are prepared in the languages of the target systems. CASE tools are typically used throughout the information engineering life cycle.

Strategic information systems planning is an orderly means for assessing the information needs of an organization and defining the systems and databases that will best satisfy those needs. Strategic IS planning is a top-down process that takes into account the outside forces that drive the business and the factors critical to the success of the firm.

Strategic IS planning is essential if organizations are to realize the benefits of information resource management. The need for improved IS planning is apparent for the following reasons: the cost of information systems is rising rapidly, systems cannot handle applications that cross organizational boundaries, systems often do not address critical success factors, data redundancy is often out of control, and system maintenance costs continue to rise. Strategic IS planning is itself a critical success factor in addressing these problems.

There is no single standard methodology for strategic IS planning. This chapter takes the information engineering approach, which begins by identifying the business direction and organizational CSFs and then identifies and summarizes the business functions and processes in the form of an enterprise chart. Entity types are also identified, and an entity-relationship diagram is prepared. A series of planning matrices is also developed to integrate the models and analyze the data. All of these organizational metadata are captured and stored in a repository using a suitable CASE tool. The end result of the methodology is a series of prioritized projects for data and information systems design and implementation.

There are numerous risks and potential pitfalls in strategic IS planning. These hazards include lack of top-management commitment, fragmentation of responsibility for planning, inadequate methodologies and CASE tools, resistance to change, and failure to update the IS plan as business conditions change. Those responsible for strategic IS planning must anticipate these problems and ensure that they do not undermine the planning process.

CHAPTER REVIEW

Key Terms

Business area
Business function
Computer-aided software
  engineering (CASE) tools
Conceptual data model
Critical success factor (CSF)
Data flow diagram (DFD)
Functional decomposition

Information engineering
Information process
Information systems
  architecture
Integrated CASE (I-CASE)
  toolset
Logical database design
Methodology

Physical database design
Physical process
Process
Repository
Schema
Strategic information
  systems planning
Subschema

REVIEW QUESTIONS

1. Define each of the following terms:
   a. business function
   b. business area
   c. business process
   d. methodology
   e. critical success factor
   f. schema
   g. subschema
   h. functional decomposition
   i. entity type
2. Contrast the following terms:
   a. business function; business process
   b. schema; subschema
   c. methodology; CASE tool
   d. CSF; CASE
   e. information systems architecture; information systems architecture framework
   f. organizational unit; function

3. List six factors that show the need for improved information systems planning today.
4. Describe three important prerequisites for strategic IS planning.
5. List six benefits of an information systems architecture.
6. Briefly describe three submodels in an enterprise model.
7. What are critical success factors, and how do they relate to the strategic IS planning process?
8. In the information systems architecture framework,
   a. which column represents the "how" in information systems development?
   b. which column represents the "what" in information systems development?
   c. which column represents the "where" in information systems development?
9. Describe six benefits of using CASE tools in strategic IS planning.
10. The planning metamodel described in this chapter contains information about what organizational entities?
11. Briefly describe six planning matrices that are used in strategic IS planning.
12. Briefly describe two phases of the design stage of information engineering.
13. Why is the function-versus-entity matrix (Figure 3-26) rearranged as shown in Figure 3-27?
14. Briefly describe six risks or pitfalls in strategic IS planning.
15. Briefly describe the four main stages of information engineering.

PROBLEMS AND EXERCISES

1. Match the following terms and their definitions:

   ____ business function   a. logical description of a user's view of data

   ____ business process   b. a process and a set of design objects

   ____ business area   c. influences whether goals are achieved

   ____ entity type   d. breaking down functional areas into functions

   ____ schema   e. related groups of business activities

   ____ methodology   f. cohesive grouping of functions and entities

   ____ information engineering   g. set of logical tasks performed repeatedly

   ____ critical success factor   h. formal methodology for IS development

   ____ subschema   i. knowledge base of corporate data

   ____ repository   j. logical description of overall database

   ____ functional decomposition   k. objects that share common properties

2. A family can be regarded as a small business organization.
   a. Define several major functions and processes of a family, and draw an enterprise chart.
   b. Define the family entity types, and draw an E-R diagram.
   c. Define three critical success factors (CSFs) for a family.
3. Examine the enterprise chart for Mountain View Community Hospital (Figure 3-24). List three processes for each of the following functions:
   a. nursing   b. payroll   c. housekeeping
4. List three additional entities that might appear in the entity-relationship diagram for Mountain View Community Hospital (Figure 3-25).

5. A professional football team is a business organization.
   a. Define several functions and processes of a football team, and draw a preliminary enterprise chart.
   b. Define several entity types, and draw a preliminary E-R diagram.
   c. Draw a matrix mapping the processes versus the entity types.
   d. Define three critical success factors (CSFs) for a professional football team.
6. Consider your business school or other academic unit as a business enterprise.
   a. Define several functions and processes, and draw a preliminary enterprise chart.
   b. Define several major entity types, and draw a preliminary E-R diagram.
   c. Map the processes versus the entity types.
   d. Define four critical success factors (CSFs) for the academic unit.
7. Examine the enterprise chart for Mountain View Community Hospital (Figure 3-24). List three processes for each of the following functions:
   a. patient accounting   b. blood banking   c. rehabilitation
8. Expand the E-R diagram for Mountain View Community Hospital (Figure 3-25) by adding the following entity types (and associated relationships): EQUIPMENT, VOLUNTEER, BLOOD DONOR.
9. Figure 3-29 shows the functions and entity types that are essential for the Excellent care CSF. Expand this table by including the functions and entity types that are both essential (E) and desirable (D) for this CSF (refer to Figure 3-28).
10. Develop a table (similar to Figure 3-29) of functions and entity types that are essential (E) for the Cost control CSF (refer to Figure 3-28).
11. Develop a table (similar to Figure 3-29) of functions and entity types that are essential (E) for the Staff retention CSF (refer to Figure 3-28).
12. Develop a composite table (similar to Figure 3-29) of functions and entity types that are essential (E) to all three CSFs: Excellent care, Cost control, and Staff retention. (*Note:* this problem combines Figure 3-29 with the results of Problems 10 and 11.)

REFERENCES

Business Systems Planning: Information Systems Planning Guide. 1975. White Plains, N.Y.: IBM Corporation.

Finkelstein, Clive. 1989. *An Introduction to Information Engineering.* Reading, Mass.: Addison-Wesley.

Goodhue, D. L., J. A. Quillard, and J. F. Rockart. 1986. "The Management of Data: Preliminary Research Results." Center for Information Systems Research, Sloan School of Management, MIT. Working Paper No. 140 (May).

Hoffer, J. A., S. J. Michaele, and J. C. Carroll. 1989. "The Pitfalls of Strategic Data and Systems Planning: A Research Agenda." *Proceedings of the Twenty-Second Annual Hawaii International Conference on System Sciences.* Vol. 4. *Emerging Technologies and Applications,* 348–56. Kona, Hawaii: IEEE Computer Society Press.

Lederer, A. L., and V. Sethi. 1989. "Pitfalls in Planning." *Datamation* 35 (June 1):59–63.

Martin, E. W., D. W. DeHayes, J. A. Hoffer, and W. C. Perkins. 1994. *Managing Information Technology: What Managers Need to Know.* 2d ed. New York: Macmillan.

Martin, J. 1990. *Information Engineering: Planning and Analysis.* Englewood Cliffs, N.J.: Prentice Hall.

McClure, C. 1989. *CASE Is Software Automation.* Englewood Cliffs, N.J.: Prentice Hall.

Moad, J. 1989. "Navigating Cross-Functional Waters." *Datamation* 35 (March 1):38–43.

Moriarty, Terry. 1991. "Framing Your System." *Database Programming & Design* 4 (June): 57–59.

Morton, Carol. 1992. "Information Competition: Can OLTP and DSS Peacefully Coexist?" *Data Base Management* 2 (June):24–28.

Reingruber, Michael J., and Daniel L. Spahr. 1992. "Putting Data Back in Database Design." *Data Base Management* 2 (March):19–21.

Shank, M. E., A. C. Boynton, and R. W. Zmud. 1985. "Critical Success Factor Analysis as a Methodology for IS Planning." *MIS Quarterly* 9 (June):121–29.

Shoval, Peretz. 1990. "An Integrated Methodology for Functional Analysis, Process Design, and Database Design." *Information Systems* 16 (January):49–64.

Von Halle, Barbara. 1992. "A Catalyst for Better Business." *Database Programming & Design* 5 (June):13–15.

Zachman, J. A. 1987. "A Framework for Information Systems Architecture." *IBM Systems Journal* 26 (March):276–92.

PART **II**

Data Modeling and
Database Design

IBM Canada

REAL-TIME PROCESS MONITORING AND CONTROL

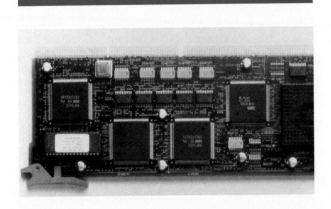

In Part II we examine the concepts of data modeling and database design. Entity-relationship data modeling, described in Chapter 4, is the approach most commonly used today. Object-oriented modeling is also becoming very common, however, and we describe this approach in Chapter 5. Once data modeling is completed, the resulting conceptual model must be translated into a database design we can implement using a contemporary database management system. We can divide database design into two phases: logical design (described in Chapter 6) and physical design (described in Chapter 7).

Selecting an appropriate data model is an important decision for any organization. The relational data model, which is most commonly used today, is most appropriate for tabular data with relatively simple relationships (such as accounting data). However, the object-oriented model is often more appropriate for complex data (such as images and maps). IBM Canada's Technical Products Division considered these factors and selected an object-oriented data model when it developed a real-time process monitoring and control system called DACS (Data Acquisition and Control System).

The DACS system is used to collect and analyze data about printed circuit boards and the processes that are used to manufacture and test those boards. Most of the data is captured from automated testers and other manufacturing devices. The data is very complex due to the nature of the printed circuit boards. Each board is composed of hundreds of parts and requires a series of intricate manufacturing steps. IBM estimated that the data coming from the testers would require between 30 and 40 tables to represent in a relational data model.

Instead, IBM selected an object-oriented database management system (OODBMS) to manage the data.

At the present time the database contains over 3 million objects, which are grouped into about 300 classes of similar objects. IBM estimates that in the future, the database may grow to nearly 10 million objects. As many as 200 users will use the DACS system when it is fully operational. Future plans call for modeling picture and video data, as well as character data.

IBM is realizing several advantages by using an object-oriented data model (and DBMS) for the DACS system. Complex objects are modeled more naturally and easily using this approach. The library of objects that is being built for this application can be reused in future projects, thereby speeding up application development. Surprisingly, it is estimated that complex queries can be performed faster with this system than with an equivalent relational system because multiple-table joins are not required. The object-oriented model includes the ability to maintain version control over the various circuit boards and the supporting processes and test equipment. In Part II, you will study the relational and object-oriented models in greater detail and gain greater understanding of the factors that led IBM Canada to select an object-oriented approach for this mission-critical application.

CHAPTER

4

The Entity-Relationship Model

LEARNING OBJECTIVES

After studying this chapter, you should be able to:

- Concisely define each of the following key terms: *entity type, attribute, relationship, cardinality, weak entity, gerund, generalization, supertype, subtype, inheritance.*
- Draw an entity-relationship (E-R) diagram to represent common business situations.
- Distinguish between unary, binary, and ternary relationships, and give an example of each.
- Model multivalued attributes and repeating groups in an E-R diagram.
- Model simple time-dependent data using time stamps in an E-R diagram.
- Model ISA relationships in an E-R diagram.
- Define four basic types of business rules in an E-R diagram.
- List several advantages of locating business rules in the repository, rather than in application programs.

INTRODUCTION

You have already been introduced to the entity-relationship model through simplified examples of its use in the first three chapters of this text. In this chapter we describe the entity-relationship (E-R) model in detail. After some years of use, the E-R model remains the mainstream approach for conceptual data modeling. Its popularity stems from factors such as relative ease of use, widespread CASE tool support, and the belief that entities and relationships are natural modeling concepts in the real world.

The E-R model is most often used as a tool for communications between database designers and end users during the analysis phase of database development (which we described in Chapter 3). The E-R model is used to construct a conceptual data model, which is a representation of the structure of a database that is independent of the software (such as a database management system) that will be

123

Figure 4-1

Summary of the database development process

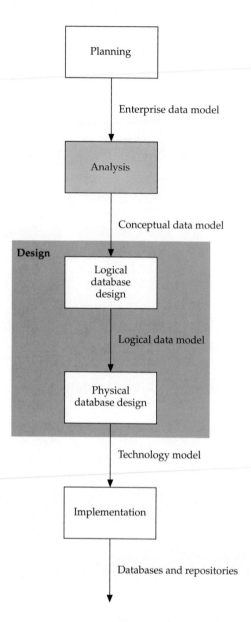

used to implement the database. Data modeling and the use of the E-R model correspond to the information systems model (row three) of the ISA framework described in Chapter 3 (see Figure 3-1).

The entity-relationship model was introduced in a key article by Chen (1976), in which he described the main constructs of the E-R model—entities and relationships—and their associated attributes. The model has subsequently been extended to include additional constructs by Chen and others; for example, see Teorey et al. (1986) and Storey (1991). The E-R model continues to evolve, but currently there is no standard notation for E-R modeling. In this chapter we present the main features of E-R modeling, using common notation and conventions.

INTRODUCTION TO THE E-R MODEL

Entity-relationship data model (E-R model): A detailed, logical representation of the entities, associations, and data elements for an organization or business area.

An **entity-relationship data model** (or **E-R model**) is a detailed, logical representation of the data for an organization or for a business area. The E-R model is expressed in terms of entities in the business environment, the relationships (or

Basic symbols

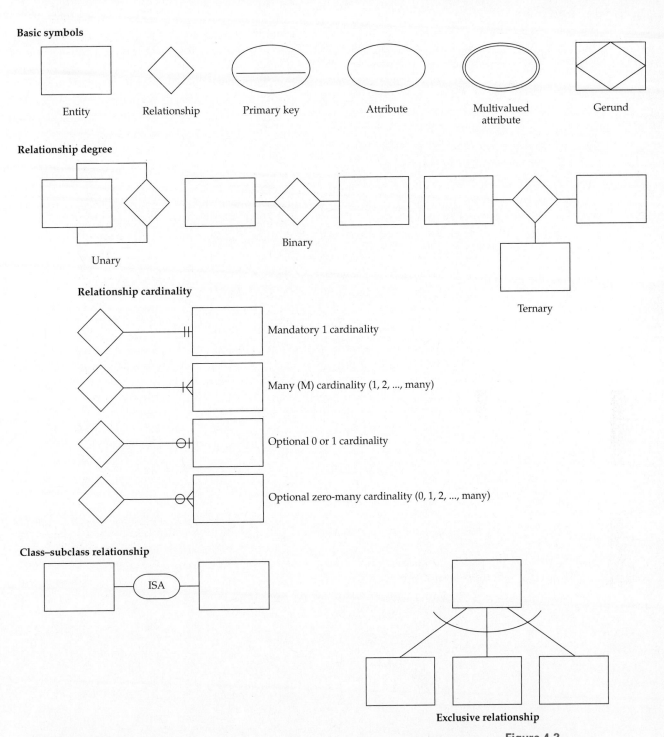

| Entity | Relationship | Primary key | Attribute | Multivalued attribute | Gerund |

Relationship degree

Unary

Binary

Ternary

Relationship cardinality

Mandatory 1 cardinality

Many (M) cardinality (1, 2, ..., many)

Optional 0 or 1 cardinality

Optional zero-many cardinality (0, 1, 2, ..., many)

Class–subclass relationship

ISA

Exclusive relationship

Figure 4-2

Entity-relationship notation

Entity-relationship diagram (E-R diagram): A graphical representation of an E-R model.

associations) among those entities, and the attributes (or properties) of both the entities and their relationships. An E-R model is normally expressed as an **entity-relationship diagram** (or **E-R diagram**), which is a graphical representation of an E-R model.

Entity-relationship models are usually constructed during the analysis phase of the database development process (see Figure 4-1, where we have shaded the analysis box to highlight this fact). An E-R model may also be used to represent an enterprise data model. The output of the analysis phase is a conceptual data model expressed in the form of a detailed entity-relationship diagram.

The major constructs of E-R models are entities, relationships, and associated attributes. We describe each of these components below, and then introduce other constructs in later sections. Figure 4-2 introduces the notation that we will use throughout the chapter, using symbols that are very similar to those found in the E-R Designer CASE tool (Chen and Associates, 1988). Even within this CASE tool, there are alternatives for representing some of the constructs. Rather than explain these symbols here, we explain and illustrate them throughout the chapter.

ENTITIES

We have defined an entity as a person, place, object, event, or concept in the user environment about which the organization wishes to maintain data. Some examples of each of these types of entities follow:

- Person: EMPLOYEE, STUDENT, PATIENT
- Place: STATE, REGION, COUNTRY
- Object: MACHINE, BUILDING, AUTOMOBILE
- Event: SALE, REGISTRATION, RENEWAL
- Concept: ACCOUNT, COURSE, WORK CENTER

Entity type: A collection of entities that share common properties or characteristics.

There is an important distinction between entity types and entity instances. An **entity type** (sometimes called an *entity class*) is a collection of entities that share common properties or characteristics. Each entity type in an E-R model is given a name. Since the name represents a class (or set), it is singular. We use capital letters in naming an entity type. In an E-R diagram, the name is placed inside the box representing the entity:

Entity instance (instance): A single occurrence of an entity type.

An **entity instance** (or **instance**) is a single occurrence of an entity type. Figure 4-3 illustrates the distinction between an entity type and two of its instances. An entity type is described just once (in the form of metadata) in a database, while many instances of that entity type may be represented by data stored in the database. For example, there is one EMPLOYEE entity type in most organizations, but there may be hundreds (or even thousands) of instances of this entity type that are stored in the database.

Figure 4-3

Comparison of entity type and instances

Entity type: EMPLOYEE
Attributes:
        EMPLOYEE NUMBER
        NAME
        ADDRESS
        CITY
        STATE
        ZIP
        YEAR HIRED
        BIRTHDATE

Instances of EMPLOYEE:
642-17-8360	534-10-1971
Michelle Brady	David Johnson
100 Pacific Ave.	450 Redwood Dr.
San Francisco	Redwood City
CA	CA
98173	97142
1989	1986
6-19-64	9-4-60

ATTRIBUTES

Each entity type has a set of attributes associated with it. An **attribute** is a property or characteristic of an entity that is of interest to the organization (relationships may also have attributes, as we will see in the section on "Relationships"). Following are some typical entity types and associated attributes:

STUDENT: STUDENT NO., NAME, ADDRESS, PHONE NO.
AUTOMOBILE: VEHICLE ID, COLOR, WEIGHT, HORSEPOWER
EMPLOYEE: EMPLOYEE NO., NAME, ADDRESS, SKILL

We use capital letters in naming an attribute. In E-R diagrams, we represent an attribute by placing its name in an ellipse with a line connecting it to its associated entity.

Attribute: A named property or characteristic of an entity that is of interest to the organization.

Candidate Keys and Primary Keys

Every entity type must have an attribute or set of attributes that uniquely identifies each instance and clearly distinguishes that instance from other instances of the same type. A **candidate key** is an attribute (or combination of attributes) that uniquely identifies each instance of an entity type. A candidate key for the STUDENT entity type shown above is STUDENT NO. (What is a candidate key for AUTOMOBILE?)

Candidate key: An attribute (or combination of attributes) that uniquely identifies each instance of an entity type.

Sometimes more than one attribute is required to identify a unique entity. For example, consider the entity type GAME for a basketball league. The attribute TEAM NAME is clearly not a candidate key, since each team plays several games. If each team plays exactly one home game against each other team, then the combination of the attributes HOME TEAM and VISITING TEAM is a candidate key. In the chapter exercises, we ask you to suggest a candidate key if more than one home game is played against each other team.

Some entities may have more than one candidate key. One candidate key for EMPLOYEE is EMPLOYEE NO.; a second is the combination of NAME and ADDRESS (assuming that no two employees with the same name live at the same address). If there is more than one candidate key, the designer must choose one of the candidate keys as a primary key. A **primary key** is a candidate key that has been selected as the identifier for an entity type. Bruce (1992) suggests the following criteria for selecting primary keys:

Primary key: A candidate key that has been selected as the identifier for an entity type. Also called an *identifier*. Primary key values may not be null.

1. Choose a candidate key that will not change its value over the life of each instance of the entity type. For example, the combination of NAME and ADDRESS would probably be a poor choice as a primary key for EMPLOYEE because the values of ADDRESS and NAME could easily change during an employee's term of employment.

2. Choose a candidate key such that for each instance of the entity, the attribute is guaranteed to have valid values and not be null. If the candidate key is a combination of two or more attributes, make sure that all parts of the key will have valid values.

3. Avoid the use of so-called intelligent keys, whose structure indicates classifications, locations, and so on. For example, the first two digits of a key may indicate the warehouse location. Such codes are often changed as conditions change, which renders the primary key values invalid.

4. Consider substituting single-attribute surrogate keys for large composite keys. For example, an attribute called GAME NO. could be used for the

entity GAME instead of the combination of HOME TEAM and VISITING TEAM.

For each entity, the name of the primary key is underlined on an E-R diagram. The following diagram shows the representation for the STUDENT entity type using E-R notation:

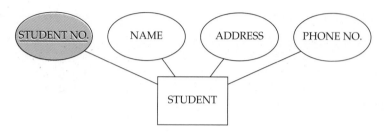

Multivalued Attributes

Multivalued attribute: An attribute that can have more than one value for each entity instance.

A **multivalued attribute** can have more than one value *for each entity instance*. For example, SKILL is one of the attributes of EMPLOYEE in the preceding entity examples. Each employee may have more than one skill, so that SKILL is a multivalued attribute. During the first pass of conceptual design, it is common to use a special symbol or notation to highlight multivalued attributes. We use a double-lined ellipse for this purpose, so that the EMPLOYEE entity with its attributes is diagrammed as follows:

In a subsequent step of conceptual design, we usually normalize the entity data by removing multivalued attributes and placing them in a separate entity type or in a relationship. We describe this process later in this chapter.

RELATIONSHIPS

Relationship: An association between the instances of one or more entity types that is of interest to the organization.

Relationships are the glue that holds together the various components of an E-R model. A **relationship** is an association between the instances of one or more entity types that is of interest to the organization. For example, a training department in a company is interested in tracking which training courses each of its employees has completed. This leads to a relationship (called Completes) between the EMPLOYEE and COURSE entity types that we diagram as follows:

As indicated by the arrows, this is a many-to-many relationship: each employee may complete more than one course, and each course may be completed by more than one employee. More significantly, we can use the Completes relationship to determine the specific courses that a given employee has completed. Conversely, we can determine the identity of each employee who has completed a particular course.

A relationship is indicated by a diamond shape, as shown in the preceding diagram. Earlier in the text we have shown a relationship by leaving out the diamond and placing the relationship name on the line connecting the entities. Both formats are used in practice. What is important is that you use a consistent format in all E-R diagrams. In either case, we suggest using a short, descriptive verb phrase that is meaningful to the user to name the relationship.

Attributes (or properties) may be associated with a many-to-many relationship, as well as with an entity. For example, suppose the organization wishes to record the date (month and year) when an employee completes each course. Some sample data follow:

EMPLOYEE NO.	COURSE NAME	DATE COMPLETED
549–23–1948	Basic Algebra	March 1994
629–16–8407	Software Quality	June 1994
816–30–0458	Software Quality	February 1994
549–23–1948	C Programming	May 1994

From this limited data you can conclude that the attribute DATE COMPLETED is not a property of the entity EMPLOYEE (since a given employee such as 549–23–1948 has completed courses on different dates). Nor is DATE COMPLETED a property of COURSE, since a particular course (such as software quality) may be completed on different dates. Instead, DATE COMPLETED is a property of the relationship between EMPLOYEE and COURSE. That is, there is a DATE COMPLETED for each instance of an employee and a course. The attribute is associated with the relationship and diagrammed as follows:

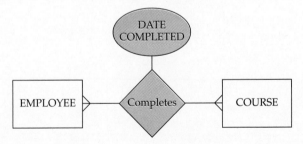

Degree of a Relationship

The **degree** of a relationship is the number of entity types that participate in that relationship. Thus, the relationship Completes is of degree two, since there are two entity types: EMPLOYEE and COURSE. The three most common relationships in E-R models are *unary* (degree one), *binary* (degree two), and *ternary* (degree three). Higher-degree relationships are possible, but they are rarely encountered in practice, so we restrict our discussion to these three cases. Examples of unary, binary, and ternary relationships appear in Figure 4-4.

Degree: The number of entity types that participate in a relationship.

Figure 4-4

Examples of relationships of different degrees

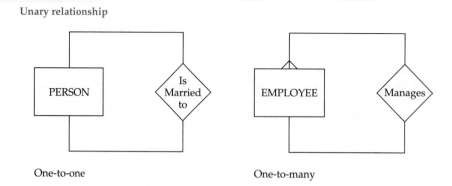

Unary relationship

PERSON — Is Married to

One-to-one

EMPLOYEE — Manages

One-to-many

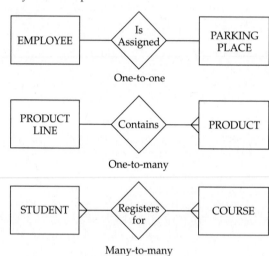

Binary relationship

EMPLOYEE — Is Assigned — PARKING PLACE

One-to-one

PRODUCT LINE — Contains — PRODUCT

One-to-many

STUDENT — Registers for — COURSE

Many-to-many

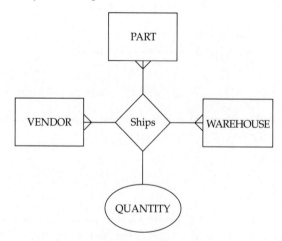

Ternary relationship

PART

VENDOR — Ships — WAREHOUSE

QUANTITY

Unary Relationship   Also called a *recursive relationship*, a **unary relationship** is a relationship between the instances of one entity type. Two examples are shown in Figure 4-4. In the first example, Is married to is shown as a one-to-one relationship between instances of the PERSON entity type. In the second example, Manages is shown as a one-to-many relationship between instances of the EMPLOYEE entity type. Using this relationship, we could identify (for example) the employees who report to a particular manager. (*Note*: in these examples, we ignore whether these are mandatory- or optional-cardinality relationships, as shown in the notation of Figure 4-2; we will introduce these concepts in a later section of this chapter.)

Figure 4-5 shows an example of another unary relationship, called a *bill-of-materials structure*. Many manufactured products are made of subassemblies, which in turn are composed of other subassemblies and parts, and so on. As shown in Figure 4-5a, we can represent this structure as a many-to-many unary relationship. In this figure, we use Has components for the relationship name. The attribute QUANTITY, which is a property of the relationship, indicates the number of each component that is contained in a given assembly.

Two occurrences of this structure are shown in Figure 4-5b. Each of these diagrams shows the immediate components of each item as well as the quantities of that component. For example, item X consists of item U (quantity 3) and item V (quantity 2). You can easily verify that the associations are in fact many-to-many. Several of the items have more than one component type (for example, item

Unary relationship (recursive relationship): A relationship between the instances of one entity type.

Figure 4-5

Bill-of-materials unary relationship

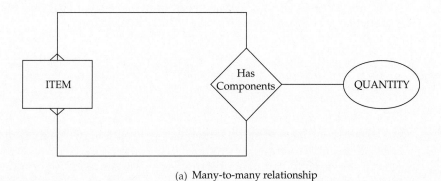

(a) Many-to-many relationship

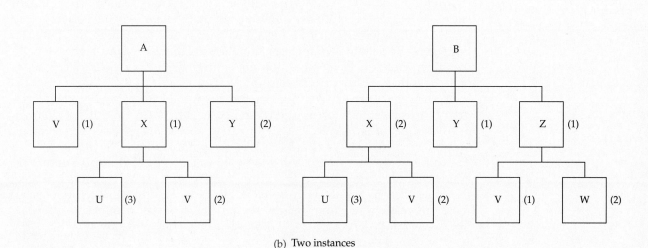

(b) Two instances

A has three immediate component types: V, X, and Y). Also, some of the components are used in several higher-level assemblies. For example, item X is used in both item A and item B. The many-to-many relationship guarantees that, for example, the same subassembly structure of X is used each time item X goes into making some other item.

Binary Relationship   A **binary relationship** is a relationship between instances of two entity types and is the most common type of relationship encountered in data modeling. Figure 4-4 shows three examples. The first (one-to-one) indicates that an employee is assigned one parking place, and each parking place is assigned to one employee. The second (one-to-many) indicates that a product line may contain several products, and each product belongs to only one product line. The third (many-to-many) shows that a student may register for more than one course, and that each course may have many student registrants.

Ternary Relationship   A **ternary relationship** is a *simultaneous* relationship among instances of three entity types. In the example shown in Figure 4-4, the relationship Ships tracks the quantity of a given part that is shipped by a particular vendor to a selected warehouse. Each entity may be a "one" or a "many" participant in a ternary relationship (in Figure 4-4, all three entities are "many" participants).

Note that a ternary relationship is not the same as three binary relationships. For example, QUANTITY is an attribute of the Ships relationship in Figure 4-4. QUANTITY cannot be properly associated with any of the three possible binary relationships among the three entity types (such as that between PART and VENDOR) because QUANTITY is the amount of a particular PART shipped from a particular VENDOR to a particular WAREHOUSE.

Gerunds

Since many-to-many relationships may have associated attributes, the E-R data model poses an interesting dilemma: is a many-to-many relationship (diamond symbol) actually an entity in disguise? Often the distinction between entity and relationship is simply a matter of how you view the data. A **gerund** (sometimes called a *composite entity*) is a many-to-many relationship that the data modeler chooses to model as an entity type with several associated one-to-many relationships. For example, Figure 4-6 shows an alternative (and equally correct) representation of the ternary relationship shown in Figure 4-4. In Figure 4-6, the entity type (gerund) SHIPMENT replaces the Ships relationship from Figure 4-4. The diamond symbol is included within the entity rectangle as a reminder that the entity was derived from a relationship.

Each instance of SHIPMENT represents a real-world shipment by a given vendor of a particular part to a selected warehouse. The QUANTITY of that shipment is an attribute of SHIPMENT. A shipment number is assigned to each shipment and is the primary key of SHIPMENT, as shown in Figure 4-6.

Note that we do not use a diamond along the lines from the gerund to the entities. This is because these lines *do not* represent binary relationships. To keep the same meaning as the ternary relationship of Figure 4-4, we cannot break the Ships relationship from Figure 4-4 into three binary relationships between SHIPMENT and VENDOR, PART, and WAREHOUSE, respectively.

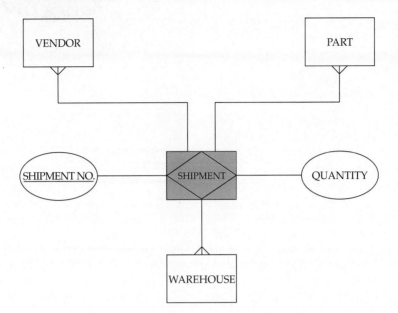

Figure 4-6
SHIPMENT entity type
(a gerund)

In a binary many-to-many relationship, it does not matter whether we represent the relationship as a gerund or as an entity. With a relational DBMS, we implement a many-to-many relationship as a gerund or as an entity in the same way—as a database table. For ternary and higher-order relationships, if any part of the relationship is not a "many," then we cannot show the relationship as an entity. Consider the following diagram of a ternary relationship between PATIENTs, LOCATIONs, and TREATMENTs in a hospital.

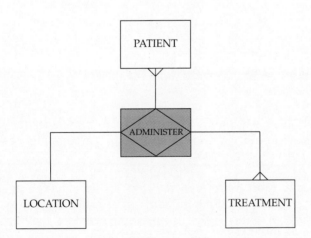

This is a one-many-many relationship, which shows a business rule that a given PATIENT must always be administered a given TREATMENT in the same LOCATION. Now, consider this same situation shown as an entity and three binary relationships:

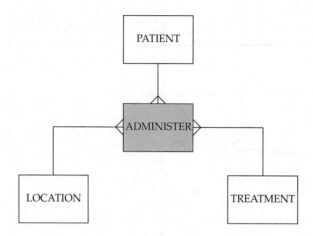

Each of the three binary relationships is, in fact, correctly shown as one-to-many. In this format, however, we have lost the business rule (or *semantic*) about where patients are administered treatments. This example emphasizes that three binary relationships are not the same as one ternary relationship. Thus, representing a relationship as an entity is not suitable when one or more of the branches of a relationship has only one associated entity occurrence.

Cardinalities in Relationships

Cardinality: The number of instances of entity B that can (or must) be associated with each instance of entity A.

Suppose there are two entity types, A and B, that are connected by a relationship. The **cardinality** of a relationship is the number of instances of entity B that can (or must) be associated with each instance of entity A. For example, consider the following relationship for video movies:

$$\boxed{\text{MOVIE}} \quad \diamond\!\!\begin{array}{c}\text{Is}\\ \text{Stocked}\\ \text{as}\end{array}\!\!\diamond\!\!\!< \quad \boxed{\text{MOVIE COPY}}$$

Clearly, a video store may stock more than one copy of a given movie. In the terminology we have used so far, this example is intuitively a "many" relationship. Yet it is also true that the store may not have a single copy of a particular movie in stock. We need a more precise notation to indicate the *range* of cardinalities for a relationship. This notation was introduced in Figure 4-2, which you may want to review at this point.

Minimum and Maximum Cardinalities   The *minimum* cardinality of a relationship is the minimum number of instances of entity B that may be associated with each instance of entity A. In the preceding example, the minimum number of movie copies available for a movie is zero. The *maximum* cardinality is the maximum number of instances. For our example, this maximum is "many" (an unspecified number greater than one). Using the notation from Figure 4-2, we diagram this relationship as follows:

$$\boxed{\text{MOVIE}} \quad +\!\!+\!\!\diamond\!\!\begin{array}{c}\text{Is}\\ \text{Stocked}\\ \text{as}\end{array}\!\!\diamond\!\!-\!\!\circ\!\!< \quad \boxed{\text{MOVIE COPY}}$$

The zero through the line near the MOVIE COPY entity means a minimum cardinality of zero, while the crow's foot notation means a "many" maximum cardinality.

A relationship is, of course, bidirectional, so there is also cardinality notation next to the MOVIE entity. Notice that the minimum and maximum are both one. This is called a *mandatory* one cardinality. In other words, each copy of a movie that is stocked must be a copy of exactly one movie. In general, participation in a relationship may be optional or mandatory for the entities involved. If the minimum cardinality is zero, participation is optional; if the minimum cardinality is one, participation is mandatory.

Examples of three relationships that show all possible combinations of minimum and maximum cardinalities appear in Figure 4-7. All of them have been discussed earlier in this chapter. A brief description of each relationship follows.

1. PATIENT Has PATIENT HISTORY (Figure 4-7a). Each patient has one or more patient histories (we assume that the initial patient visit is always recorded as an instance of PATIENT HISTORY). Each instance of PATIENT HISTORY "belongs to" exactly one PATIENT (another mandatory one cardinality).

2. EMPLOYEE Is assigned to PROJECT (Figure 4-7b). Each PROJECT has at least one assigned EMPLOYEE (some projects have more than one). Each EMPLOYEE may or (optionally) may not be assigned to any existing PROJECT, or may be assigned to several PROJECTs.

3. PERSON Is married to PERSON. This is an optional zero or one cardinality in both directions, since a person may or may not be married.

It is possible for the maximum cardinality to be a fixed number, not an arbitrary "many" value. For example, suppose corporate policy states that an employee

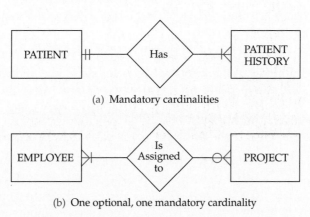

(a) Mandatory cardinalities

(b) One optional, one mandatory cardinality

(c) Optional cardinalites

Figure 4-7

Examples of cardinalities in relationships

may work on at most five projects at the same time. We could show this business rule by placing a five above or below the crow's foot next to the PROJECT entity in Figure 4-7b.

Existence Dependency   A consequence of the mandatory one cardinality is that an instance of the entity type cannot exist (at least as far as the organization is concerned) unless there is an instance of the related entity type. For example, an instance of MOVIE COPY cannot exist unless the related MOVIE entity already exists. We use the term **existence dependency** to mean that an instance of one entity cannot exist without the existence of an instance of some other (related) entity.

> **Existence dependency:** An instance of one entity cannot exist without the existence of an instance of some other (related) entity.

Another term that is often used for entity types that have a mandatory one cardinality is *weak entity*. A **weak entity** is an entity type that has an existence dependency. Thus, an instance of a weak entity cannot exist independently, but depends on the existence of another entity instance. In our example, MOVIE COPY is a weak entity. (Which entity in Figure 4-7 is a weak entity?)

> **Weak entity:** An entity type that has an existence dependency.

Identifying Relationship   Weak entities often do not have a natural identifier (or candidate key). Instead, the primary key of the *parent* entity (on which the dependent entity depends) is often used as part of the primary key of the dependent *child* entity. For the video example, this would result in the following choice of primary keys:

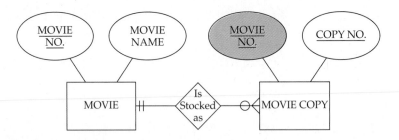

In this example, the primary key of the parent entity MOVIE (MOVIE NO.) is also part of the primary key of the dependent entity MOVIE COPY (COPY NO. is the other part). An **identifying relationship** is one in which the primary key of the parent entity is used as part of the primary key of the dependent entity. Such a relationship is the result of a conscious choice of primary keys by the data modeler. There are two benefits of an identifying relationship:

> **Identifying relationship:** A relationship in which the primary key of the parent entity is used as part of the primary key of the dependent entity.

1. *Data integrity.* Existence dependencies are enforced since the primary key is shared (therefore a weak entity cannot exist unless the parent entity exists).
2. *Ease of access of the dependent entity.* In the above example, we can locate a movie copy if we know the movie number and copy number.

MODELING MULTIVALUED ATTRIBUTES

In our discussion of attributes, we used SKILL as an example of a multivalued attribute of the EMPLOYEE entity type. We used a double-lined ellipse to highlight this attribute (see Figure 4-8a). During a subsequent step of conceptual design, multivalued attributes are often removed from the entities for which they appear. Each multivalued attribute (or more generally, each repeating group) is

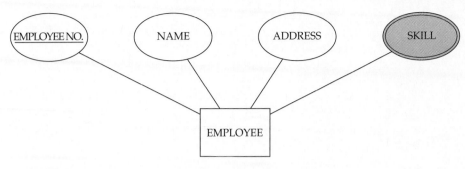

(a) Entity with multivalued attribute

Figure 4-8
Removing a multivalued attribute from an entity

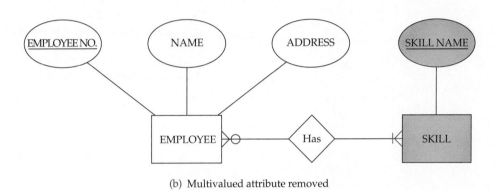

(b) Multivalued attribute removed

converted to a separate entity type that has a relationship to the entity type from which it was removed. In Figure 4-8b the new entity type SKILL replaces the attribute SKILL. There is now a many-to-many relationship between EMPLOYEE and SKILL, and SKILL NAME has been chosen as the primary key of SKILL. The logic behind this process is that SKILL is an entity type that is of independent interest to the organization, rather than just an attribute of other entity types. Typically, to become an entity, SKILL would have some nonkey attributes besides the primary key SKILL NAME.

Repeating Groups

A **repeating group** is a set of two or more multivalued attributes that are logically related. For example, Figure 4-9a is a patient chart that shows typical data for a patient and a log of that person's visits to a medical clinic. Figure 4-9b is an initial E-R representation of the PATIENT entity type with three multivalued attributes for each patient: DATE OF VISIT, PHYSICIAN, and SYMPTOM. These three attributes are logically related and form a repeating group (we assume that there is only one visit on a given date and that a patient sees one physician and is treated for one symptom during each visit).

Figure 4-9c shows the result of removing the repeating group from PATIENT. A new entity type called PATIENT HISTORY is created, and the three multivalued attributes that compose the repeating group are moved to this entity. DATE OF VISIT is chosen as the primary key of this new entity type (another option is

Repeating group: A set of two or more multivalued attributes that are logically related.

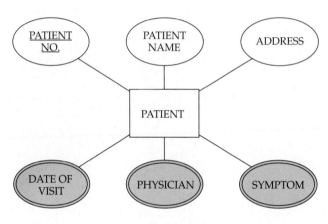

(a) Sample data

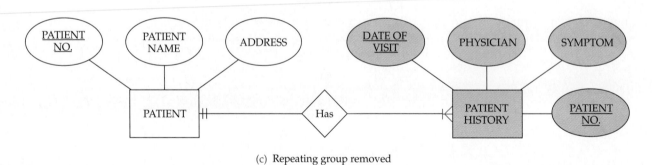

(b) Entity with repeating group

(c) Repeating group removed

Figure 4-9

Removing repeating groups

discussed below). There is a one-to-many relationship from PATIENT to PATIENT HISTORY, and PATIENT HISTORY is a weak entity.

We have just described an intuitive approach to normalization. In Chapter 6 we will describe the formal rules of normalization. During conceptual data modeling, the designer could leave multivalued attributes within the E-R model, as in Figure 4-9b. In this case, normalization would occur during logical design (described in Chapter 6). Removing the repeating groups during conceptual design, however, results in an E-R representation that is clearer to the user and that better models the real-world situation.

MODELING TIME-DEPENDENT DATA

Database contents vary over time. For example, in a database that contains product information, the unit price for each product may change as material and labor costs and market conditions change. If only the current price is required, then only that value needs to be represented. For accounting, billing, and other purposes, however, we are likely to need a history of the prices and the time period over which each was in effect. As Figure 4-10a shows, we can conceptualize this requirement as a series of prices and the effective date for each price. This results in a repeating group that includes the attributes PRICE and EFFECTIVE DATE. In Figure 4-10b, this repeating group has been replaced by a new (weak) entity named PRICE HISTORY. The relationship between PRODUCT and PRICE HISTORY is named Has.

In Figure 4-10, each value of the attribute PRICE is time stamped with its effective date. A **time stamp** is simply a time value (such as date and time) that is associated with a data value. A time stamp may be associated with any data value that changes over time when we need to maintain a history of those data values. Time stamps may be recorded to indicate the time the value was entered (transaction time), the time the value becomes valid or stops being valid, or the time when critical actions were performed (such as updates, corrections, or audits).

The use of simple time stamping (as in the above example) is often adequate for modeling time-dependent data. However, time often introduces more subtle complexities in data modeling. For example, Figure 4-11a represents a portion of an E-R diagram for Pine Valley Furniture Company. Each product is assigned to a product line (or related group of products). Customer orders are processed throughout the year, and monthly summaries are reported by product line and by product within product line.

Suppose that in the middle of the year, due to a reorganization of the sales function, some products are reassigned to different product lines. The model

Time stamp: A time value (such as date and time) that is associated with any data value.

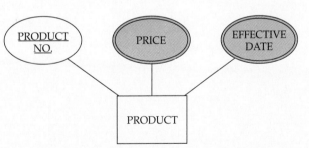

(a) PRODUCT entity with repeating group

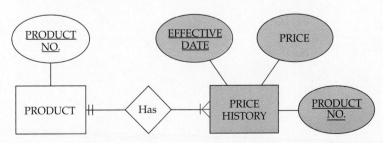

(b) PRODUCT entity with PRICE HISTORY

Figure 4-10

Example of time stamping

shown in Figure 4-11a is not designed to accommodate the reassignment of a product to a new product line. Thus, all sales reports will show cumulative sales for a product based on its *current* product line, rather than the one at the time of the sale. For example, a product may have total year-to-date sales of $50,000 and be associated with product line B, yet $40,000 of those sales may have occurred while the product was assigned to product line A. This fact will be lost using the model of Figure 4-11a.

The simple design change shown in Figure 4-11b will correctly recognize product reassignments. A new relationship (called Sales for product line) has been added between ORDER and PRODUCT LINE. As customer orders are processed, they are credited to both the correct product and product line as of the time of the sale.

We have discussed the problem of time-dependent data with managers in several organizations who are considered leaders in the use of data modeling and database management. These discussions revealed that current data models (and database management systems based on those models) are generally inadequate

Figure 4-11

Pine Valley Furniture product database

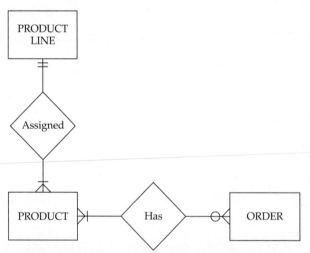

(a) E-R diagram not recognizing product reassignment

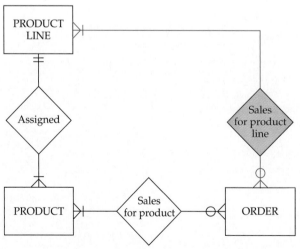

(b) E-R diagram recognizing product reassignment

in handling time-dependent data, and that organizations often ignore this problem and hope that the resulting inaccuracies balance out. The object-oriented model (described in Chapter 5) promises greater facility for managing time-dependent data. You need to be alert to the complexities posed by time-dependent data as you develop data models in your organization.

GENERALIZATION

One of the unique aspects of human intelligence is its ability to classify objects and experiences and to generalize their properties. If we see a robin or an eagle, for example, we immediately classify each as a bird. Even if the bird is searching for worms in the grass, we know it can fly, since most birds can fly (we memorize the exceptions at an early age). Similarly, if we see a Porsche we assume that it is both fast and expensive, since these are properties of luxury sports cars. Business entities are often best modeled using the concepts of generalization and categorization. **Generalization** is the concept that some things (entities) are subtypes of other, more general things. For example, to an airline a business passenger is one subtype of the more general type called *passenger*. **Categorization** is the opposite concept that an entity comes in various subtypes (much as ice cream comes in different flavors). For example, there are different subtypes of automobiles: sedans, convertibles, sports cars, compacts, and so on.

Generalization as a formal construct has been studied primarily within the field of artificial intelligence. Until recently its application was limited to the semantic and object-oriented data models (described in the next chapter). Fortunately, the entity-relationship model has been extended to include generalization constructs as well. We introduce the major concepts in this section.

Generalization: The concept that some things (entities) are subtypes of other, more general things.

Categorization: The concept that an entity comes in various subtypes.

Subtypes and Supertypes

One of the major challenges in data modeling is to recognize and clearly represent entities that are almost the same; that is, entity types that share common properties but also have one or more distinct properties. For example, suppose an organization has three basic types of employees: hourly employees, salaried employees, and contract consultants. Some of the important attributes for these types of employees are the following:

1. Hourly employees: EMPLOYEE NO., NAME, ADDRESS, DATE HIRED, HOURLY RATE
2. Salaried employees: EMPLOYEE NO., NAME, ADDRESS, DATE HIRED, ANNUAL SALARY, STOCK OPTION
3. Contract consultants: EMPLOYEE NO., NAME, ADDRESS, DATE HIRED, CONTRACT NO., DAILY RATE

Notice that all of the employee types have several attributes in common (EMPLOYEE NO., NAME, ADDRESS, DATE HIRED). In addition, each type has one or more unique attributes that distinguishes it from the other types (for example, HOURLY RATE is unique to hourly employees). If you were developing a conceptual data model in this situation, you might consider three choices:

1. Define a single entity type called EMPLOYEE. Although conceptually simple, this approach has the disadvantage that EMPLOYEE would have

to contain *all* of the attributes for the three entities. For an instance of an hourly employee (for example), attributes such as ANNUAL SALARY and CONTRACT NUMBER would not apply and would be null or not used. To deal with the many variations, programs that use this entity type would necessarily be complex.

2. Define a separate entity type for each of the three entities. This approach would fail to exploit the common properties of employees, and users would have to be careful to select the correct entity type when using the system.

3. Define a supertype called EMPLOYEE, with subtypes for HOURLY EMPLOYEE, SALARIED EMPLOYEE, and CONSULTANT. This approach exploits the common properties of all employees, yet recognizes the distinct properties of each type.

Figure 4-12 shows a representation of the EMPLOYEE supertype with its subtypes, using E-R notation. A **supertype** is a generic entity type (such as EMPLOYEE) that is subdivided into subtypes. A **subtype** is a subset of a supertype that shares common attributes or relationships distinct from the other subsets. Entity subtypes behave in exactly the same way as any entity type. For example, entity subtypes have attributes and may have relationships with other entity types.

In Figure 4-12, common attributes for all employees are included with the EMPLOYEE entity type. The primary key for EMPLOYEE, as well as for each of the subtypes, is EMPLOYEE NO. Attributes that are peculiar to each subtype are included with that subtype only.

Supertype: A generic entity type that is subdivided into subtypes.

Subtype: A subset of a supertype that shares common attributes or relationships distinct from other subsets.

Figure 4-12

EMPLOYEE supertype with subtypes

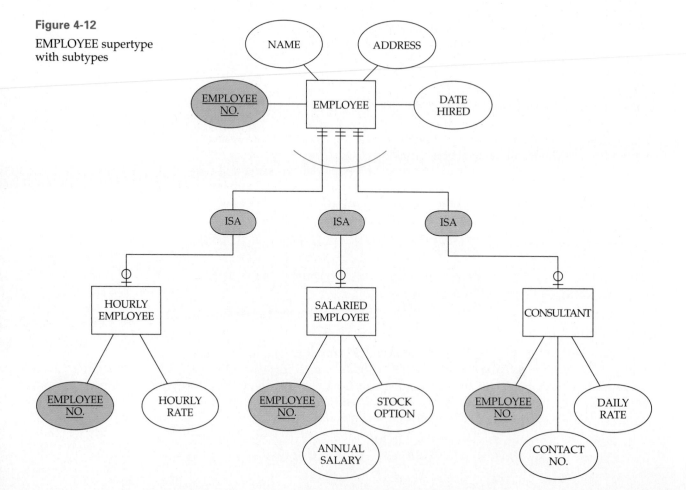

The relationship between each subtype and supertype is called an **ISA relationship**. A rectangle with rounded ends is used to designate ISA relationships. This relationship is read from the subtype to the supertype; for example, "HOURLY EMPLOYEE ISA EMPLOYEE" (correct grammar is not enforced). As shown in Figure 4-12, the cardinality of the relationship from a subtype to the supertype is mandatory one. The cardinality is mandatory one because an instance of a subtype is *always* an instance of the supertype (a salaried employee is always an employee). On the other hand, the relationship from the supertype to a subtype is optionally zero or one (an employee may or may not be a salaried employee). Since these cardinality relationships are always the same in ISA relationships, we will omit the cardinality notation in subsequent diagrams.

There is one additional symbol in Figure 4-12 we would like to discuss. The curved line just below the EMPLOYEE box that extends across the three lines for the ISA relationships denotes an exclusive relationship. An **exclusive relationship** means that the subtypes are mutually exclusive, and that exactly one is required for each instance of EMPLOYEE. That is, each employee must be an hourly employee, a salaried employee, or a consultant. We describe other relationship options below.

Whether to use subtype relationships or not is a decision that the data modeler must make in each situation. Subtypes are indicated for each (or both) of the following circumstances:

1. Different attributes are used to describe each entity subtype, as in the EMPLOYEE example.

2. Each entity subtype participates in different relationships.

Figure 4-13 is an example of the use of subtype relationships that illustrates both of these situations. The hospital entity type PATIENT has two subtypes:

ISA relationship: The relationship between each subtype and its supertype.

Exclusive relationship: The subtypes of a supertype are mutually exclusive, and each instance of the supertype is categorized as exactly one subtype.

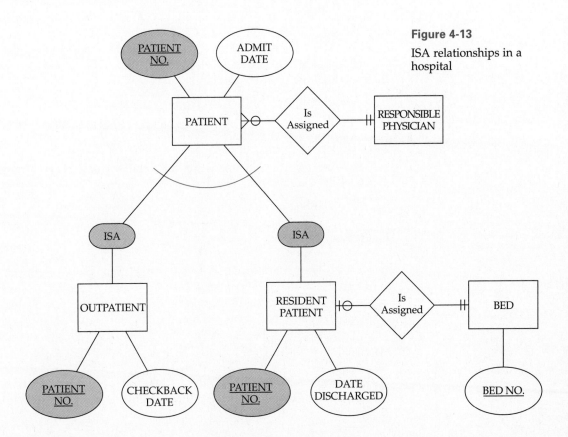

Figure 4-13

ISA relationships in a hospital

OUTPATIENT and RESIDENT PATIENT (the primary key is PATIENT NO.). All patients (of both subtypes) have an ADMIT DATE attribute, and each is assigned a RESPONSIBLE PHYSICIAN. Outpatients have a CHECKBACK DATE, while resident patients have a DATE DISCHARGED. Only resident patients are assigned a BED (and each bed may or may not be assigned to a patient). The exclusive relationship symbol indicates that each patient must be either an outpatient or a resident patient (there are no other types of patients).

Inheritance

All patients of a hospital (outpatients as well as resident patients) know that sooner or later they will be billed. This is a privilege they inherit by virtue of being a patient. **Inheritance** is the property by which all attributes of a supertype become attributes of its subtypes. Thus in Figure 4-12, the attributes NAME, ADDRESS, and DATE HIRED are inherited by all three employee subtypes (which is why these attributes are not explicitly attached to the subtypes). Except for the primary key, only attributes that are unique to a subtype are associated with that subtype.

A consequence of inheritance is that each attribute should be located at the highest logical level in a hierarchy. For example, suppose that an organization has identified three entity types with the following initial list of attributes (Storey, 1991):

1. PERSON: SSN, NAME, ADDRESS, BIRTHDAY, PHONE
2. EMPLOYEE: EMPLOYEE NO., NAME, BIRTHDAY, DEPARTMENT, PHONE
3. MANAGER: TITLE, DEPARTMENT, NAME, ADDRESS, PHONE, BIRTHDAY

The above list shows that EMPLOYEE can inherit the attributes NAME, BIRTHDAY, and PHONE from PERSON. Also, MANAGER can inherit the attributes NAME, ADDRESS, PHONE, and BIRTHDAY from PERSON and DEPARTMENT from EMPLOYEE. If we assume that SSN is the primary key for all entities, then the final list of attributes is:

1. PERSON: SSN, NAME, ADDRESS, BIRTHDAY, PHONE
2. EMPLOYEE: SSN, EMPLOYEE NO., DEPARTMENT
3. MANAGER: SSN, TITLE

This example also illustrates that ISA relationships can be arranged in a hierarchy of any depth. You will be asked to develop a hierarchy in the chapter exercises.

Exclusive Subtypes

In each of the examples of ISA relationships that we have considered (Figures 4-12 and 4-13), the subtypes have been mutually exclusive and exhaustive (explained below). As a result, each instance of the supertype was required to be a member of exactly one subtype. A special symbol (curved line) was used to express this constraint. In this section and the next we consider variations on this constraint.

Exhaustive Subtypes   In Figure 4-12 the subtypes are **exhaustive**; that is, there are no subtypes in addition to the three that are shown in the figure. As a result,

Inheritance: The property that, when entity types or object classes are arranged in a hierarchy, each entity type or object class assumes the attributes and methods of its ancestors (that is, those higher up in the hierarchy).

Exhaustive subtype: All subtypes are defined for a supertype.

each instance of EMPLOYEE must be a member of exactly one subtype. Similarly, in Figure 4-13 each PATIENT must be either an OUTPATIENT or a RESIDENT PATIENT, since there are no other types. The situation of exhaustive subtypes is likely to result when the business situation being modeled is reasonably well structured and familiar to the data modeler.

Nonexhaustive Subtypes   When subtypes are **nonexhaustive**, some (but not all) of the subtypes have been defined for a supertype. For example, in Figure 4-14a three subtypes (AUTOMOBILE, TRUCK, and MOTORCYCLE) have been defined for the entity type VEHICLE. To indicate that there are subtypes not defined, a rectangle has been left blank in the diagram. Together with the curved line, this notation indicates that each instance of VEHICLE is either in no subclass that has been defined or else is in exactly one subclass. In other words, a vehicle is either an automobile, a truck, a motorcycle, or else it is none of those things. The use of nonexhaustive subtypes allows data modeling to proceed even when the business situation is not fully developed or understood.

> **Nonexhaustive subtype:** Some (but not all) of the subtypes have been defined for a supertype.

Nonexclusive Subtypes

Another situation occurs when the subtypes are **nonexclusive**. In other words, the subtypes may overlap, and an instance of the supertype may simultaneously

> **Nonexclusive subtype:** Subtypes may overlap, and an instance of the supertype may simultaneously belong to more than one subtype.

Figure 4-14

Variations on subtype relationships

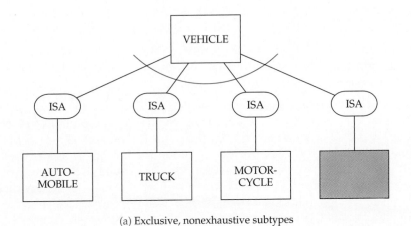

(a) Exclusive, nonexhaustive subtypes

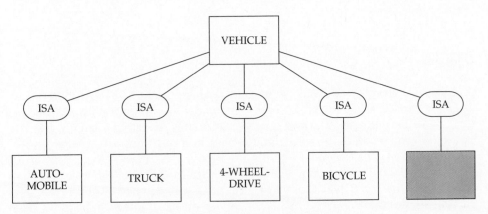

(b) Nonexclusive, nonexhaustive subtypes

belong to more than one subtype. An example of this situation is shown in Figure 4-14b. The defined subtypes of VEHICLE are AUTOMOBILE, TRUCK, 4-WHEEL-DRIVE, and BICYCLE (an empty box is included to indicate possible undefined subtypes).

In this example, an instance of VEHICLE may of course be an instance of more than one subtype (for example, both TRUCK and 4-WHEEL-DRIVE). In creating the E-R model, we simply omit the curved line to indicate the possibility of an instance belonging to more than one subtype. The subtypes may be exhaustive or nonexhaustive (in the former case we omit the empty box).

Nonexclusive subtypes may result when the business situation is not well understood or is quite complex. An alternative method of structuring the subtypes and relationships might be available to eliminate the overlaps among the subtypes.

BUSINESS RULES

Business rules: Specifications that preserve the integrity of the logical data model.

Conceptual data modeling is a step-by-step process for documenting information requirements that is concerned both with the structure of data and with rules about the integrity of that data. **Business rules** are specifications that preserve the integrity of the logical data model. There are four basic types of business rules.

1. *Entity integrity:* Each instance of an entity type must have a unique identifier (or primary key value) that is not null.
2. *Referential integrity constraints:* Rules concerning the relationships between entity types. We describe referential integrity in detail in Chapter 6.
3. *Domains:* Constraints on valid values for attributes.
4. *Triggering operations:* Other business rules that protect the validity of attribute values.

The entity-relationship model we have described in this chapter is concerned primarily with the structure of data, rather than with expressing business rules (although some elementary rules are implied in the E-R model). These rules should be identified and documented during the conceptual design process, concurrent with E-R modeling. Generally the business rules are stored in the repository (described in Chapter 3) as they are documented. In this section we briefly describe two types of rules: domains and triggering operations. These rules are illustrated with a simple example from a banking environment, shown in Figure 4-15a. In this example, an ACCOUNT entity has a relationship (named Is for) with a WITHDRAWAL entity. Notice the cardinalities on the relationship. What type of entity is WITHDRAWAL?

Domains

Domain: The set of all data types and ranges of values that an attribute may assume.

A **domain** is the set of all data types and ranges of values that attributes may assume (Fleming and von Halle, 1990). Domain definitions typically specify some (or all) of the following characteristics of attributes: data type, length, format, range, allowable values, meaning, uniqueness, and null support (whether an attribute value may or may not be null).

Figure 4-15b shows two domain definitions for the banking example. The first definition is for ACCT NO. Since ACCT NO. is a primary key attribute, the definition specifies that ACCT NO. must be unique and also must not be null (these specifications are true of all primary keys). The definition specifies that the attribute data type is character and that the format is nnn-nnnn. Thus any attempt

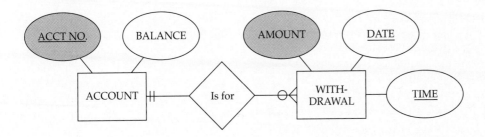

(a) Simple banking relationship

Name: ACCT NO.
Meaning: Customer account number in bank
Data type: Character
Format: nnn-nnnn
Uniqueness: Must be unique
Null support: Non-null

Name: AMOUNT
Meaning: Dollar amount of transaction
Data type: Numeric
Format: 2 decimal places
Range: 0–10,000
Uniqueness: Nonunique
Null support: Non-null

(b) Typical domain definitions

User rule: WITHDRAWAL AMOUNT may not exceed ACCOUNT BALANCE
Event: Insert
Entity Name: WITHDRAWAL
Condition: WITHDRAWAL AMOUNT > ACCOUNT BALANCE
Action: Reject the insert transaction

(c) Typical triggering operation

Figure 4-15

Examples of business rules

to enter a value for this attribute that does not conform to its character type or format will be rejected, and an error message will be displayed.

The domain definition for the AMOUNT attribute (dollar amount of the requested withdrawal) also may not be null, but is not unique. The format allows for two decimal places to accommodate a currency field. The range of values has a lower limit of zero (to prevent negative values) and an upper limit of 10,000. The latter is an arbitrary upper limit for a single withdrawal transaction.

The use of domains offers several advantages:

1. Domains verify that the values for an attribute (stored by insert or update operations) are valid.

2. Domains ensure that various data manipulation operations (such as joins or unions in a relational database system) are logical.

3. Domains help conserve effort in describing attribute characteristics.

Domains can conserve effort because we can define domains and then associate each attribute in the data model with an appropriate domain. To illustrate, suppose a bank has three types of accounts, with the following primary keys:

Account Type	Primary Key
CHECKING	CHECKING ACCT NO.
SAVINGS	SAVINGS ACCT NO.
LOAN	LOAN ACCT NO.

If domains are not used, the characteristics for each of the three primary key attributes must be described separately. Suppose, however, that the characteristics for all three of the attributes are identical. Having defined the domain ACCT NO. once (as shown in Figure 4-15b), we simply associate CHECKING ACCT NO., SAVINGS ACCT NO., and LOAN ACCT NO. with ACCT NO. Other common domains such as DATE, SOCIAL SECURITY NUMBER, and TELEPHONE NUMBER also need to be defined just once in the model.

Triggering Operations

Triggering operation (trigger): An assertion or rule that governs the validity of data manipulation operations such as insert, update, and delete.

A **triggering operation** (or **trigger**) is an assertion or rule that governs the validity of data manipulation operations such as insert, update, and delete. The scope of triggering operations may be limited to attributes within one entity, or it may extend to attributes in two or more entities. Complex business rules may often be stated as triggering operations.

A triggering operation normally includes the following components:

1. *User rule:* A concise statement of the business rule to be enforced by the triggering operation
2. *Event:* The data manipulation operation (insert, delete, or update) that initiates the operation
3. *Entity name:* The name of the entity being accessed and/or modified
4. *Condition:* Condition that causes the operation to be triggered
5. *Action:* Action taken when the operation is triggered

Figure 4-15c shows an example of a triggering operation for the banking situation. The business rule is a simple (and familiar) one: the amount of an attempted withdrawal may not exceed the current account balance. The event of interest is an attempted insert of an instance of the WITHDRAWAL entity type (perhaps from an automated teller machine). The condition is:

AMOUNT (of the withdrawal) > ACCOUNT BALANCE.

When this condition is triggered, the action taken is to reject the transaction. You should note two things about this triggering operation: first, it spans two entity types; second, the business rule could not be enforced through the use of domains.

Locating Business Rules

The use of triggering operations is an increasingly important component of database strategy. With triggering operations, the responsibility for data integrity lies within the scope of the database management system, rather than with application programs or human operators. In the banking example, tellers could conceivably check the account balance before processing each withdrawal. Human operators would be subject to human error, and in any event manual processing would not work with automated teller machines. Alternatively, the logic of integrity checks could be built into the appropriate application programs, but integrity checks in application programs would require duplicating the logic in each program. There is no assurance that the logic would be consistent (since the application programs may have been developed at different times by different people), or that the application programs will be kept up to date as conditions change.

According to Wood (1990), removing business rules from application programs and incorporating them in the repository (in the form of domains, refer-

glance, it might appear that Beach Property and Mountain Property represent separate entities, but on closer inspection we see that these entities share several common attributes. In fact, only the last attributes (BLOCKS TO BEACH, SKIING) are different. We conclude that BEACH PROPERTY and MOUNTAIN PROPERTY are subtypes of PROPERTY (a supertype). We represent this as two ISA relationships, as shown in Figure 4-17b.

In the E-R diagram, the primary key of all three entities is the composite key consisting of STREET ADDRESS and CITY STATE ZIP. Only PROPERTY contains the common attributes, whereas BEACH PROPERTY and MOUNTAIN PROPERTY each contain the nonkey attribute that is unique to that subtype.

Rental Agreement   Figure 4-18a shows the Rental Agreement view. This view associates a renter with a rental property during a specific interval of time (called the BEGIN DATE and END DATE).

The E-R diagram for RENTAL AGREEMENT appears in Figure 4-18b. Notice that the primary key for this entity type is the combination of STREET ADDRESS, CITY STATE ZIP, and BEGIN DATE. This combination of attributes uniquely identifies a rental agreement, since a given property cannot have two agreements for the same date (unless a mistake has been made). Another approach would be to assign a new attribute (called AGREEMENT NUMBER) as the primary key for this entity type.

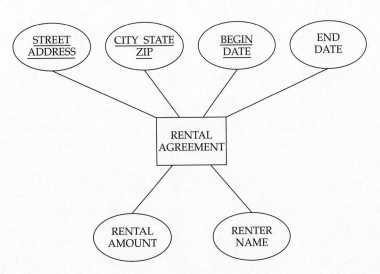

RENTAL AGREEMENT

Name: Arnold Thomas	Date: 12/3/9X
Street-Address: 360 Sail St.	
City-State-Zip: Orlando, FL 10389	
Begin-Date: 1/15/9X	
End-Date: 1/29/9X	
Rental-Amount: 350	

Rental agreement

E-R diagram

Figure 4-18

Rental agreement view and E-R diagram

Conceptual Data Model At this point we have developed a separate E-R diagram for each of the user views. We create a conceptual data model by merging the separate views into a single E-R diagram (see Figure 4-19). Following is a brief description of the relationships in the diagram.

1. There is an ISA relationship between PROPERTY and BEACH PROPERTY, and another between PROPERTY and MOUNTAIN PROPERTY.

2. There is a relationship called Signs between RENTER and RENTAL AGREEMENT. The cardinality is optional zero-many from RENTER to RENTAL AGREEMENT, and mandatory one from RENTAL AGREEMENT to RENTER. Thus, there cannot be a rental agreement signed without a valid renter.

3. There is a relationship called Is rented by between PROPERTY and RENTAL AGREEMENT. The cardinalities are the same as for the Signs relationship, for the same reasons.

Triggering Operations Figure 4-20 shows three typical triggering operations related to the conceptual data model. These operations are intended to implement the following business rules:

Figure 4-19

Conceptual data model (Vacation Property Rentals)

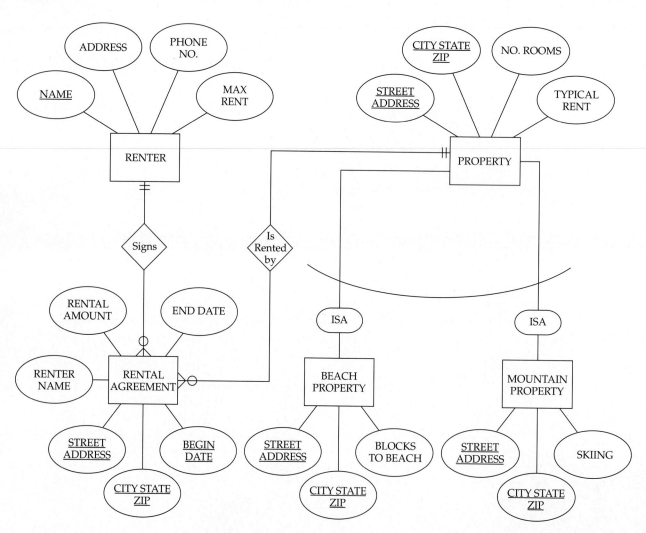

User rule:	An END DATE for a RENTAL AGREEMENT must be later than the BEGIN DATE.
Event:	Insert.
Entity name:	RENTAL AGREEMENT.
Condition:	END DATE < = BEGIN DATE for a RENTAL AGREEMENT
Action:	Reject the insert transaction.

Figure 4-20

Triggering operations (Vacation Property Rentals)

(a) Basic integrity constraint

User rule:	Do not insert a new RENTAL AGREEMENT unless there exists a valid occurrence of RENTER to sign that agreement.
Event:	Insert.
Entity name:	RENTAL AGREEMENT.
Condition:	RENTER NAME on RENTAL AGREEMENT does not exist on an instance of RENTER.
Action:	Reject the insert transaction.

(b) Referential integrity constraint

User rule:	Do not create a new RENTAL AGREEMENT for a property whose rental dates overlap an existing RENTAL AGREEMENT for the same property.
Event:	Insert.
Entity name:	RENTAL AGREEMENT.
Condition:	BEGIN DATE for a new RENTAL AGREEMENT is between the BEGIN DATE and END DATE for an existing RENTAL AGREEMENT for the same property.
Action:	Reject the insert transaction.

(c) Overlap constraint

1. An END DATE for a RENTAL AGREEMENT must be later than the BEGIN DATE (basic integrity constraint).

2. Do not insert a new RENTAL AGREEMENT unless there exists a valid RENTER to sign that agreement (referential integrity constraint).

3. Do not create a new RENTAL AGREEMENT for a property whose dates overlap an existing rental agreement for the same property (integrity constraint).

The second rule illustrates the use of a triggering operation to enforce a referential integrity constraint. We discuss some of the options for enforcing referential integrity in Chapter 6.

Case Example: Mountain View Community Hospital

The entity-relationship modeling process described in this chapter is illustrated here for Mountain View Community Hospital (this case was introduced in Chapter 3). We will discuss E-R modeling within the context of logical database design. This process was performed under the direction of Mr. Dave Helms, the data administrator, who was assisted in this effort by Ms. Ann Green, whose title was data analyst. Ms. Green was previously a systems analyst with Mountain View Community Hospital and had recently attended a college class on database analysis and design. A database consultant assisted in organizing the overall data modeling approach, but logical design was performed almost entirely by the design team of Mr. Helms and Ms. Green over a period of approximately four months.

The design team initiated this effort by reviewing the enterprise data model (or high-level E-R diagram) for the hospital that was developed during the planning phase (see Figure 3-25). This diagram is shown again in Figure 4-21, using the notation of this chapter.

Figure 4-21

Enterprise data model (Mountain View Community Hospital)

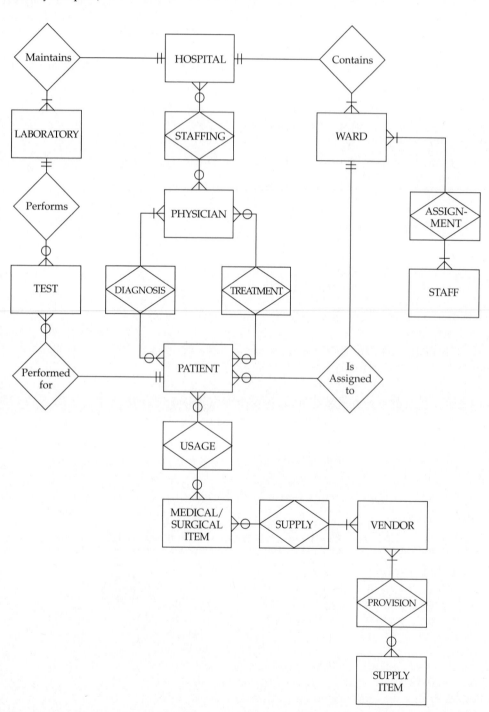

Define Database Scope

The E-R diagram (Figure 4-21) and other documents developed during the planning process proved helpful in defining the scope of the design effort. In particular, Figure 3-29 shows the hospital processes and entity types that are important to achieve excellent care, an important critical success factor (CSF) for the hospital. Since excellent care was a priority CSF, the project team decided to focus its initial effort on the PATIENT entity and other entity types related to PATIENT, such as PHYSICIAN, TEST, and MEDICAL/SURGICAL ITEM. However, the project team also planned to broaden logical design to other areas as time permitted.

Select Logical Design Methodology

The design team decided to use E-R diagrams as the basic tool for modeling data structure during logical design. A PC-based CASE tool was used to draw E-R diagrams and record descriptive data in a repository. The team also decided to document key business rules (or integrity constraints) as they were identified. Many of these constraints could not be recorded directly as part of the E-R diagrams but were instead entered in the repository.

Identify User Views

The design team interviewed users throughout Mountain View Community Hospital, including nurses, doctors, administrators, technicians, and clerks. They obtained samples of existing reports and other operating documents, as well as the formats of forms and displays, and drew an overview diagram identifying the various user views to be analyzed during logical design. The portion of this overview diagram that appears in Figure 4-22 identifies four significant user views of data for the hospital: Patient Bill, Room Utilization Report, Patient Display, and Physician Report. When the overview diagram was completed, with a total of 20 views, the design team reviewed it with users to ensure that they had identified all significant views within the present scope of the design effort.

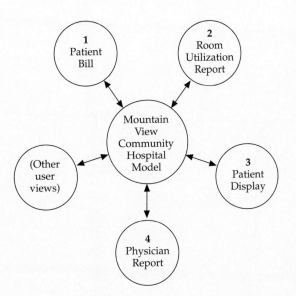

Figure 4-22

User views for Mountain View Community Hospital

Model Data Structure and Constraints

We select the four user views shown in Figure 4-22 to further illustrate the logical design process.

Figure 4-23

Patient Bill and E-R diagram

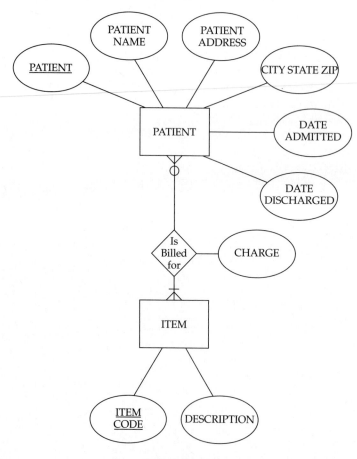

Mountain View Community Hospital
200 Forest Dr. Mountain View, CO

Statement of account for:

Patient name: Baker, Mary
Patient address: 300 Oak St.
City-State-Zip:
  Mountain View, CO 80638

Patient No.: 3249
Date admitted: 09-10-9X
Date discharged: 09-14-9X

Item Code	Description	Charge
200	Room semi-pr	150.00
205	Television	10.00
307	X-ray	25.00
413	Lab tests	35.00
	Balance due	220.00

(a) Patient bill

(b) E-R diagram

USER VIEW 1: PATIENT BILL

The first user view is that of the Patient Bill (see Figure 4-23a). Charges incurred by each patient are accumulated during the patient's stay at the hospital (we consider only resident patients). After the patient is discharged, a statement is mailed. The Patient Bill shown in Figure 4-23a is a simplified version of this statement.

Figure 4-23b shows an E-R diagram representing the structure of the Patient Bill. The Patient Bill represents the combination of attributes from two entities: PATIENT and ITEM (those items for which a patient is billed). The instances of ITEM form a repeating group within each Patient Bill. The primary key of PATIENT is PATIENT NO., while the primary key of ITEM is ITEM CODE. The relationship between PATIENT and ITEM is named Is billed for. The cardinality from PATIENT to ITEM is many (a Patient Bill must contain at least one item and may contain more than one). The cardinality from ITEM to PATIENT is optional zero-many (since a given item may or may not appear on a Patient Bill at a given time).

The relationship Is Billed For has an attribute called CHARGE that represents the amount a given patient is billed for this particular item. If every patient were billed the same amount for a given item, then CHARGE would be an attribute of ITEM; however, since we assume that two different patients may be billed different amounts for the same item, the attribute CHARGE is an attribute of the relationship instead. Notice how business policy often affects the structure of the model.

Domains   Several domain definitions for Mountain View Community Hospital are shown in Figure 4-24. Some of these domains are for attributes from the Patient Bill, and others are for other user views described later in this chapter.

DOMAIN NAME: Patient Name
　　　Definition: Names of Mountain View Community Hospital patients
　　　Type/Length: Character 32
　　　Format:
　　　　　Last Name Character 18
　　　　　First Name Character 12
　　　　　Middle Initial Character 2
　　　Allowable Values: May not be null

DOMAIN NAME: Item Code
　　　Definition: Unique identifier for a hospital supply item
　　　Type/Length: Character 6
　　　Allowable Values: May not be null

DOMAIN NAME: Charge
　　　Definition: Amount billed to a patient for a supply item
　　　Type/Length: Decimal 8
　　　Format: $DDDDD.DD

DOMAIN NAME: Location
　　　Definition: Unique identifier for a hospital bed location
　　　Type/Length: Character 5
　　　Format: RRR-B
　　　　　RRR = room number
　　　　　B = bed location in room
　　　Allowable Values: May not be null

DOMAIN NAME: Accommodation
　　　Definition: Designator for type of room accommodation
　　　Type/Length: Character 2
　　　Allowable Values: PR (= private), SP (= semiprivate)

Figure 4-24

Selected domain definitions

Business Rule   The project team identified the following business rule for the Patient Bill, which is to be specified as a triggering operation: DATE ADMITTED may not be later than DATE DISCHARGED.

USER VIEW 2: ROOM UTILIZATION REPORT

The Room Utilization Report (Figure 4-25a) is a daily report that shows the status of each room and bed location at Mountain View Community Hospital. This report is used primarily for bed scheduling and to track room and bed utilization.

The LOCATION column in this report indicates the room number and bed number. For example, location 102-2 means room number 102, bed number 2. The ACCOM column indicates type of accommodations (PR = private, SP = semi-

Figure 4-25

Room Utilization Report and E-R diagram

```
                    Room Utilization Report
                        Date: 10-15-9X

Location Accom Patient No. Patient Name Exp Discharge Date

  100-1    PR      6213     Rose, David      10-17-9X
  101-1    PR      1379     Cribbs, John     10-15-9X
  102-1    SP
  102-2    SP      1239     Miller, Ruth     10-16-9X
  103-1    PR      7040     Ortega, Juan     10-19-9X
```

(a) Room utilization report

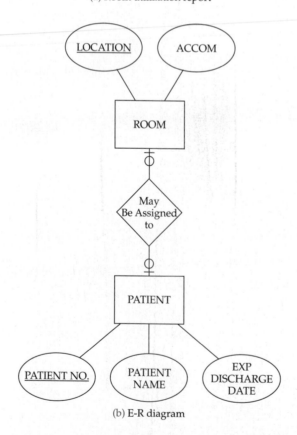

(b) E-R diagram

private). The remaining columns contain information about the patient (if any) assigned to the bed location at the time the report was prepared.

Figure 4-25b shows an E-R diagram for the Room Utilization Report. There are two entity types: ROOM and PATIENT. The relationship between these entities is named May be assigned to. The cardinalities on this relationship are optional 0 or 1 in both directions. That is, a room/bed location may be assigned to a patient at a given point in time, or it may not be assigned. Similarly, a patient may or may not be assigned to a bed (for example, an outpatient). The primary key of ROOM is LOCATION, while PATIENT NO. is the primary key of PATIENT.

USER VIEW 3: PATIENT DISPLAY

The Patient Display (Figure 4-26a) is presented on demand to any doctor, nurse, or other qualified person who uses a video display. We will assume that the user must enter the patient number to display data for a particular patient (in practice, the system would probably support look-up based on the patient's name as well).

Figure 4-26b shows an E-R diagram for Patient Display. PATIENT is the only entity type contained on this diagram. A business rule enforcing the integrity of DATE ADMITTED and DATE DISCHARGED was stated previously (see description under Patient Bill).

Figure 4-26

Patient Display and E-R diagram

```
Patient No.: 3249
Patient Name: Baker, Mary
Patient Address: 300 Oak St.
City-State-Zip: Mountain View, CO 80638
Date Admitted: 09-12-9X
Date Discharged: XX-XX-XX
Location: 437-2
Extension: 529
Third Party: Blue Cross
```

(a) Patient display

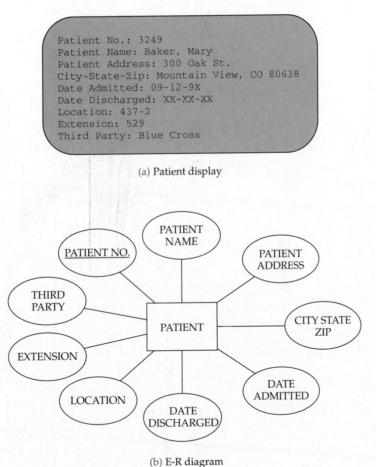

(b) E-R diagram

USER VIEW 4: PHYSICIAN REPORT

The Physician Report is prepared daily for each physician on the staff of Mountain View Community Hospital (see Figure 4-27a), showing the patients who have been treated and the name of the treatment (or procedure). To simplify the analysis, we assume that each patient may receive only one treatment from a given physician on a particular day.

Figure 4-27b shows an E-R diagram representing the Physician Report. There are two entities: PHYSICIAN and PATIENT. The relationship between these entity types is named Attends. The cardinalities of Attends are optional zero-many in both directions. A given physician may not have treated a patient during a given period, or may have treated one or more patients. Also, a patient may not have

Figure 4-27

Physician Report and E-R diagram

```
          Mountain View Community Hospital
                  Physician Report

Date: 10-17-9X           Physician ID: Wilcox
                         Physician Phone: 329-1848

Patient   Patient Name   Location     Procedure

 6083     Brown, May     184-2      Tonsillectomy
 3157     Miller, Ruth   216-1      Observation
 4139     Majors, Carl   107-3      Chemotherapy
```

(a) Physician report

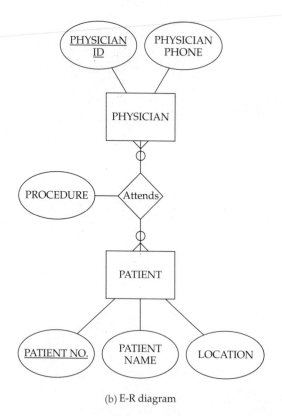

(b) E-R diagram

seen a physician (for example, was just admitted), or may have been seen by one or more physicians. Notice that PROCEDURE is an attribute of Attends, since it is not an attribute of either the PHYSICIAN entity or the PATIENT entity.

Build Conceptual Data Model

We have developed E-R diagrams for each of four key user views at Mountain View Community Hospital. We merge the four diagrams into a single E-R diagram to develop a conceptual data model (in actuality, the scope of a conceptual data model would be the whole enterprise rather than a limited set of views). The resulting E-R diagram appears in Figure 4-28. Notice that all redundancy has been

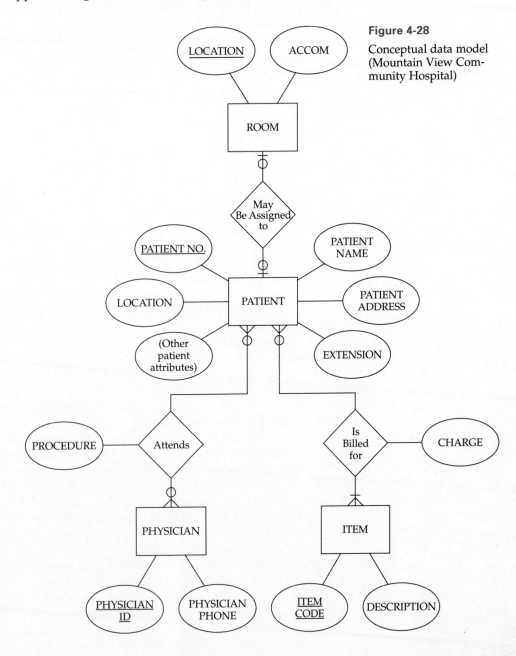

Figure 4-28

Conceptual data model (Mountain View Community Hospital)

eliminated in this diagram, and each of the individual E-R diagrams is a subset of this entity-relationship model.

SUMMARY

This chapter has described the entity-relationship (E-R) model and the use of this tool within the context of logical data modeling. The entity-relationship model was introduced by Chen in 1976 and has become the most commonly used technique for describing the logical structure of data. The model has been extended to include constructs such as subtypes and supertypes. However, at the present time there is no standard notation for E-R modeling.

The basic constructs of entity-relationship modeling are entity types, relationships, and associated attributes. An entity is a person, place, object, event, or concept in the user environment about which the organization wishes to maintain data. An entity type is a collection of entities that share common properties, while an entity instance is a single occurrence of an entity type. An attribute is a property or characteristic of an entity (or of a relationship) that is of interest to the organization. A multivalued attribute is an attribute that can have more than one value for each entity instance.

A candidate key is an attribute (or combination of attributes) that uniquely identifies each instance of an entity type. A primary key is a candidate key that has been selected to be used as an identifier for an entity type. It is best to choose primary keys whose values do not change and that do not carry intelligence such as part shape or warehouse location.

A relationship is an association between the instances of one or more entity types that is of interest to the organization. The degree of a relationship is the number of entity types that participate in the relationship. The most common relationship types are unary (degree one), binary (degree two), and ternary (degree three). A gerund is a relationship that has been modeled as an entity type.

The cardinality of a relationship is the number of instances of entity B that can (or must) be associated with each instance of entity A. Cardinality is often expressed in terms of the minimum and maximum number of instances. Relationship cardinalities include mandatory 1, many (1, 2, . . .), optional 0 or 1, and optional zero-many.

Generalization is the concept that some entities are types of other things. Categorization is the concept that an entity comes in various types. A supertype is a generic entity type that is subdivided into subtypes. A subtype is a subset of the instances of a supertype that share common attributes or relationships. Subtypes and supertypes are implemented in E-R diagrams using ISA relationships.

Business rules are specifications that preserve the integrity of the logical data model. There are four basic types of business rules: entity integrity, referential integrity, domains, and triggering operations. A domain is a specification of the types and ranges of values that attributes may assume. A triggering operation is an assertion or rule that governs the validity of data manipulation operations such as insert, delete, and update.

There are several important advantages to incorporating integrity constraints into the database description, rather than in application programs. Some of these advantages are faster application development, reduced maintenance effort, faster response to business changes, and greater end-user involvement in application development. Unfortunately, many commercial database management systems today provide only limited facilities for database integrity constraints.

CHAPTER REVIEW

Key Terms

Attribute
Binary relationship
Business rules
Candidate key
Cardinality
Categorization
Degree
Domain
Entity instance (instance)
Entity-relationship data
   model (E-R model)
Entity-relationship diagram
   (E-R diagram)

Entity type
Exclusive relationship
Exhaustive subtypes
Existence dependency
Generalization
Gerund
Identifying relationship
Inheritance
ISA relationship
Multivalued attribute
Nonexclusive subtype
Nonexhaustive subtype

Primary key
Relationship
Repeating group
Subtype
Supertype
Ternary relationship
Time stamp
Triggering operation
   (trigger)
Unary relationship
   (recursive relationship)
Weak entity

REVIEW QUESTIONS

1. Define each of the following terms:
   - a. entity
   - b. entity-relationship model
   - c. entity type
   - d. attribute
   - e. relationship
   - f. primary key
   - g. multivalued attribute
   - h. gerund
   - i. cardinality
   - j. weak entity
   - k. generalization
   - l. categorization
   - m. subtype
   - n. supertype
   - o. triggering operation

2. Contrast the following terms:
   - a. generalization; categorization
   - b. entity type; entity instance
   - c. candidate key; primary key
   - d. entity; relationship
   - e. subtype; supertype
   - f. degree; cardinality

3. Describe six advantages of incorporating integrity rules into the database definition (instead of within applications).

4. What is inheritance? Give two examples of inheritance (in addition to those in the text).

5. What are triggering operations? Give an example of a triggering operation for Mountain View Community Hospital.

6. List the four types of relationship cardinality, and draw an example of each.

7. What is meant by an existence dependency? What is the name for an entity type that has an existence dependency?

8. What is the degree of a relationship? List the three types of relationship degrees described in the chapter, and give an example of each.

9. What is generalization? Give an example.

10. List four criteria for selecting primary keys.

11. What is a business rule? List the four major types of business rules.

12. What is a subtype? A supertype? An ISA relationship? Give an example of each.

PROBLEMS AND EXERCISES

1. Match the following terms to the appropriate definitions.

   _____ supertype
   _____ gerund
   _____ generalization

   a. uniquely identifies entity instances
   b. generic entity type that is subdivided
   c. usually stated as a range of values

_____ weak entity

d. relationship modeled as an entity type

_____ attribute

e. association between entity types

_____ entity

f. collection of similar entities

_____ relationship

g. number of entity types in relationship

_____ cardinality

h. property of an entity

_____ degree

i. concept that some entities are subtypes

_____ candidate key

j. has an existence dependency

_____ entity type

k. relationship of degree three

_____ ternary

l. many-to-many unary relationship

_____ bill-of-materials

m. person, place, object, concept, event

2. Draw an E-R diagram for each of the following situations:
   a. A company has a number of employees. The attributes of EMPLOYEE include NAME, ADDRESS, and BIRTHDATE. The company also has several projects. Attributes of PROJECT include CODE, DESCRIPTION, and START DATE. Each employee may be assigned to one or more projects, or may not be assigned to a project. A project must have at least one employee assigned, and may have several employees assigned.
   b. A university has a large number of courses in its catalog. Attributes of COURSE include NO., NAME, and UNITS. Each course may have one or more other courses as prerequisites, or may have no prerequisites.
   c. A laboratory has several chemists who work on various projects and who may use certain kinds of equipment on each project. Attributes of CHEMIST include NAME and PHONE NO. Attributes of PROJECT include PROJECT ID and START DATE. Attributes of EQUIPMENT include NUMBER and COST.
   d. A college course may have one or more scheduled sections, or may not have a scheduled section. Attributes of COURSE include COURSE ID, NAME, and UNITS. Attributes of SECTION include COURSE ID, SECTION NO., and INSTRUCTOR.

3. Draw an E-R diagram to represent the following entity types and the natural relationships among them: VEHICLE, LAND VEHICLE, AIR VEHICLE, WATER VEHICLE, OCEAN VESSEL, RIVER RAFT, HELICOPTER, RAIL VEHICLE, BICYCLE, AIRPLANE, ROAD VEHICLE, CAR.

4. Figure 4-29 shows a Grade Report that is mailed to students at the end of each semester.
   a. Prepare an E-R diagram for Grade Report. Assume that each course is taught by one instructor.
   b. Prepare sample domain descriptions for the following attributes: NAME, ID, GRADE.

Figure 4-29

Grade report

```
LAKEWOOD COLLEGE
GRADE REPORT
FALL SEMESTER 199X

NAME:            Emily Williams          ID: 268300458
CAMPUS ADDRESS:  208 Brooks Hall
MAJOR:           Information Systems

COURSE ID     TITLE         INSTRUCTOR     INSTRUCTOR    GRADE
                            NAME           LOCATION

IS 350    Database Mgt.     Codd           B104          A
IS 465    System Analysis   Parsons        B317          B
```

5. The entity type STUDENT has the following attributes: NAME, ADDRESS, PHONE, AGE, ACTIVITY, and NO. OF YEARS. A given student may have more than one value for ACTIVITY and NO. OF YEARS.
   a. Draw an E-R diagram using a single entity type.
   b. Remove the repeating group from the E-R diagram.
6. There are three types of accounts in a bank, with the following attributes:
   CHECKING: ACCT NO., DATE OPENED, BALANCE, SERVICE CHARGE
   SAVINGS: ACCT NO., DATE OPENED, BALANCE, INTEREST RATE
   LOAN: ACCT NO., DATE OPENED, BALANCE, ACCT LIMIT
   Draw an E-R diagram that best represents this situation.
7. Draw an E-R diagram for each of the following situations in a zoo:
   a. Entity types are CREATURE, ANIMAL, FISH, and BIRD
   b. Entity types are CREATURE, DOG, HIPPO, ELEPHANT, HORSE, ???
8. The entity type GAME has the following attributes: HOME TEAM, VISITING TEAM, DATE, SCORE, ATTENDANCE. Suggest a primary key, assuming that each team may play more than one home game with each other team, but never more than one on a given date.
9. For the Patient Bill and E-R diagram shown in Figure 4-23 we have the following business rule: DATE ADMITTED may not be later than DATE DISCHARGED. Write the specifications for a triggering operation to implement this rule.
10. Add minimum and maximum cardinality notation to each of the following, as appropriate:
    a. Figure 4-4 (all examples)   b. Figure 4-5a   c. Figure 4-6
11. Obtain a common user view such as a credit card statement, phone bill, or some other common document. Prepare an E-R diagram for this document.
12. Draw an E-R diagram for the following situation (Batra, Hoffer, and Bostrom, 1988). Projects, Inc., is an engineering firm with approximately 500 employees. A database is required to keep track of all employees, their skills, projects assigned, and departments worked in. Every employee has a unique number assigned by the firm, required to store his or her name and date-of-birth. If an employee is currently married to another employee of Projects, Inc., the date of marriage and who is married to whom must be stored; however, no record of marriage is required if an employee's spouse is not also an employee. Each employee is given a job title (for example, engineer, secretary, foreman, and so on). We are interested in collecting more data specific to the following types: engineer and secretary. The relevant data to be recorded for engineers is the type of degree (e.g., electrical, mechanical, civil, etc.); for secretaries, it is their typing speed. An employee does only one type of job at any given time, and we only need to retain information for an employee's current job.

    There are 11 different departments, each with a unique name. An employee can report to only one department. Each department has a phone number.

    To procure various kinds of equipment, each department deals with many vendors. A vendor typically supplies equipment to many departments. We are required to store the name and address of each vendor and the date of the last meeting between a department and a vendor.

    Many employees can work on a project. An employee can work in many projects (for example, Southwest Refinery, California Petrochemicals, and so on) but can only be assigned to at most one project in a given city. For each city, we are interested in its state and population. An employee can have many skills (preparing material requisitions, checking drawings, and so on), but she or he may use only a given set of skills on a particular project. (For example, an employee MURPHY may prepare requisitions for Southwest Refinery project and prepare requisitions as well as check drawings for California Petrochemicals.) Employees use each skill that they possess in at least one project. Each skill is assigned a number, and we must store a short description of each skill. Projects are distinguished by project numbers, and we must store the estimated cost of each project.

REFERENCES

Batra, D., J. A. Hoffer, and R. B. Bostrom. 1988. "A Comparison of User Performance Between the Relational and Extended Entity Relationship Model in the Discovery Phase of Database Design." *Proceedings of the Ninth International Conference on Information Systems.* Minneapolis, Minn., Nov. 30–Dec. 3, 295–306.

Bruce, Thomas A. 1992. *Designing Quality Databases with IDEF1X Information Models.* New York: Dorset House.

Chen, P. P-S. 1976. "The Entity-Relationship Model—Toward a Unified View of Data." *ACM Transactions on Database Systems* 1 (March):9–36.

Chen and Associates. 1988. *E-R Designer Reference Manual.* Baton Rouge, La.: Chen and Associates.

Fleming, C. C., and B. von Halle. 1990. "An Overview of Logical Data Modeling." *Data Resource Management* 1 (Winter):5–15.

Storey, Veda C. 1991. "Relational Database Design Based on the Entity-Relationship Model." *Data and Knowledge Engineering* 7 (1991):47–83.

Teorey, Toby J., Dongqing Yang, and James P. Fry. 1986. "A Logical Design Methodology for Relational Databases Using the Extended Entity-Relationship Model." *Computing Surveys* 18 (June):197–221.

Wood, D. 1990. "A Primer of Features and Performance Issues of Relational DBMSs." *Data Resource Management* 1 (Winter):66–71.

The Object-Oriented Data Model

LEARNING OBJECTIVES

After studying this chapter, you should be able to:

- Define the following key terms: *object, object class, inheritance, encapsulation, domain,* and *message.*
- Draw an object-oriented data model (OODM) to represent common business situations.
- Describe some of the important data types that can be managed using object-oriented technology.
- Describe five limitations or concerns regarding object-oriented database management systems.
- Give examples of several object classes and instances.
- Give examples of generalization, specialization, and inheritance.
- Draw a message map on an object-oriented data model.

INTRODUCTION

Database and application development are undergoing a revolution that is based on objects. Most future database management systems will be based on objects, or at least will incorporate object-oriented functionality. This means that users will be able to create generic, all-purpose components that can be reused in multiple applications. In many situations, this will greatly speed up application development and also reduce maintenance effort.

Object-oriented technology is not simply a vision of the future. It has been estimated that there are more than 20 vendors of object-oriented database products throughout the world at the time of this writing (English, 1992). In addition, several vendors of mainstream relational database systems are incorporating object-oriented features into their products. Many organizations have already benefited from object-oriented applications. Only the lack of standards for object-oriented technology appears to prevent more rapid growth of this promising technology.

In this chapter we describe the use of the object-oriented data model (OODM) for representing both the data and processing requirements of an organization.

167

The OODM is being used for such diverse applications as geographic information systems, computer-aided design, real-time process monitoring and control, network management, and computer-aided manufacturing. Some of the advantages of using this model (compared to other database models) include closer representation of real-world problem domains, greater productivity in developing applications (in some cases by a factor of 5), and the ability to model complex data types such as images and documents.

INTRODUCTION TO THE OBJECT-ORIENTED DATA MODEL

In this chapter we focus on the object-oriented data model and its use during the analysis phase of the database development process (see Figure 5-1). The object-oriented data model has been formed from the merging of two different fields of study: data modeling and object-oriented programming languages (Coad and Yourdon, 1990). As a result, there is no standard definition for all of the terms that are used; however, there is a set of generally accepted core concepts for the object-oriented data model (OODM) (English, 1992). In the remainder of this section, we describe these core concepts as well as some of the key application areas for the OODM.

Core Concepts

The major concepts of the OODM include objects, encapsulation, classes, inheritance, identity, and domains. Each of these terms is described briefly and illustrated below.

Object: A structure that encapsulates (or packages) attributes and methods that operate on those attributes.

Objects   An **object** is a structure that encapsulates (or packages) attributes and methods that operate on those objects. Objects are abstractions of real-world entities that exhibit states and behaviors. The state of an object is expressed in the values of the *attributes* of the object. The behavior of an object is expressed by a set of *methods* (or operations) that operate on its attributes.

For example, College Office Supply (COS) sells writing pens. The object BIC Stic is an abstraction of one such pen. Typical attributes of this object are Item Name (BIC Stic pen), Color (Blue), Style (medium point), and Item Price ($.99 each, $9.99/dozen, and $9.49/dozen for three dozen or more). One method for this object is DisplayOrderPrice, which computes and displays the total price for a given order based on the quantity ordered and the attribute Item Price.

Encapsulation The property that the attributes and methods of an object are hidden from the outside world and do not have to be known to access its data values or invoke its methods.

Encapsulation   **Encapsulation** is the property that the attributes and the methods of an object are hidden from the outside world and do not have to be known to access its data values or invoke (or use) its methods. Instead, each object has a published *interface* that is made known to the outside world. An outside agent (such as another object) may request that a method be performed by sending a message to the object.

If a customer places an order with College Office Supply for two dozen BIC Stic pens, for example, an ORDER object is created for that customer. The ORDER object contains one or more ORDER ITEM objects (depending on how many different items the customer has ordered). The ORDER ITEM object for two dozen

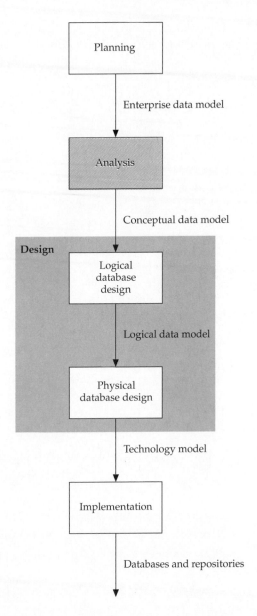

Figure 5-1
Role of database analysis in the database development process

BIC Stic pens sends the message DisplayOrderPrice to the BIC Stic object. That method is performed by the object, which returns the correct Order Price ($9.99/ dozen) and Total Price ($19.98) to the requesting object. Because of encapsulation, the method used to calculate this result is hidden from the requestor.

Classes   Objects that have the same (or similar) attributes and behavior (or methods) may be grouped into the same **object class**. For example, the object Pentel Color Pen has attributes and behavior that are common to the BIC Stic and to other writing pens. That is, each such object has attributes such as Item Name, Color, Style, and Item Price, and each has methods such as DisplayOrderPrice. Therefore, all such objects may be grouped into a class named WRITING PEN or a more general class, OFFICE SUPPLIES.

Object class: A logical grouping of objects that have the same (or similar) attributes and behavior (or methods).

Inheritance *Inheritance* (defined in Chapter 4) is the property that, when classes are arranged in a hierarchy, each class assumes the attributes and methods of its ancestors (that is, those higher up in the hierarchy). For example, at College Office Supply the class WRITING PEN is a member of the more general class named OFFICE SUPPLIES, which in turn is a member of a higher class named ITEM. The class WRITING PEN may inherit attributes such as Item Name and Item Price from the ITEM class, and an attribute such as Unit of Measure from the OFFICE SUPPLIES class. On the other hand, an attribute such as Color may be an attribute of WRITING PEN but not of the ancestor classes. Similarly, the WRITING PEN class may inherit a method such as DisplayOrderPrice from a higher-level class.

Identity: An external identi-fier for each object that is not accessible to and cannot be modified by any other object or application.

Identity Each object in an object-oriented database has an **identity** that is external to the data values stored within the object. Thus, there is no concept of a primary key used as a unique identifier, as in other database models. Instead, the object-oriented database management system (ODBMS) maintains an external identifier for each object that is not accessible to and cannot be modified by any other object or application. As a result, the identity of an object does not change, even though the values of any of its attributes may change.

Domains A unique feature of the OODM is that the *domain* (defined in Chapter 4) for any attribute may be of any data type. Thus, a domain may be any of the simple data types associated with other data models such as integer, character, decimal, or date. In addition, it can be some abstract data type defined by the user. Further, the values of an attribute may be an atomic (or single) data value, multiple data values (such as an array), or another object or set of objects from any class.

Following are some of the data types that can be managed by contemporary ODBMS technology, and typical applications (English, 1992):

1. Graphic (2D and 3D): Computer-aided design (CAD) and computer-aided manufacturing (CAM)

2. Spatial: Geographic information systems (GIS)

3. Documents: Office automation (OA), computer-aided publishing (CAP), workgroup computing

4. Images, video, audio: Multimedia, hypermedia

5. Heuristics, rules: Expert systems

6. Events: Process control, network management

7. Multidimensional: simulation, computer modeling

Typical Products and Applications

The first commercial ODBMS became available in 1987 with the introduction of Gemstone from Servio Corporation, and Vbase (the predecessor of Ontos) from Ontos, Inc. To date there are over twenty ODBMS products on the market, as well as numerous ODBMS research projects at several universities around the world (English, 1992). Figure 5-2 lists some commercial ODBMS products, together with some typical applications that have been developed or are under development with each of these products.

Notice that the vendors of ODBMS products include both mainstream computer vendors (such as Hewlett-Packard, Digital Equipment Corporation, and

Product	Vendor	Typical Applications
Gemstone	Servio Corporation	Office automation, CAD/CAM, CASE, manufacturing, heterogeneous databases
ITASCA	Itasca Systems	Geographic information systems, CAD/CAM
Level 5 Object	Information Builders, Inc.	Expert systems
Open ODB	Hewlett-Packard	Manufacturing, CAD/CAM
Object/DB	Digital Equipment Corp.	CASE, manufacturing, CAD/CAM
Object Store	Object Design, Inc.	Imaging, CASE, expert systems
Objectivity/DB	Objectivity, Inc.	CAD/CAM, multimedia
Statice	Symbolics	Office automation, hypertext, business and finance applications
Versant Object-Base	Versant Object Technology	Heterogeneous databases, CAD/CAM, office automation, expert systems
Zeitgeist	Texas Instruments	CAD/CAM, manufacturing, CASE

Figure 5-2

Typical ODBMS products and applications

Texas Instruments) as well as a number of start-up software companies. Undoubtedly there will be a shakeout of ODBMS vendors over time, just as there has been with vendors of relational DBMS products.

ODBMS technology is still very young, just as relational DBMS products were in the mid-1980s. Some of the current limitations or concerns regarding these products are the following:

1. *Lack of accepted standards.* Standard initiatives are underway at the national and international levels, as well as through industry groups, but it will probably be some time before such standards are adopted.

2. *Lack of development tools.* Tools such as computer-aided software engineering (CASE) and fourth-generation languages are under development, but not yet widely available.

3. *Performance.* The performance of ODBMS technology with large numbers of concurrent users and frequent transactions has not been tested or demonstrated.

4. *Data management facilities.* Some of the products do not have adequate facilities for concurrency control, backup and recovery, and so on. We discuss such data management issues in Chapter 12.

5. *Query languages.* One of the strengths of the OODM is encapsulation—the ability to hide data structures within objects. This strength becomes a weakness for a user who wants to retrieve data about one or more objects based on user-defined criteria.

All of the above problem areas are being addressed in various ways by vendors of the ODBMS products and in various research projects.

OBJECTS

Objects are fundamental components of our real-world experiences. The Encyclopaedia Britannica points out that in apprehending the real world, people constantly employ three methods of organization (Coad and Yourdon, 1990):

1. The differentiation of experience into particular objects and their attributes—for example, distinguishing between a car as an object and its size or color as attributes.

2. The distinction between whole objects and their component parts—for example, contrasting a car with its parts.

3. The formation of and distinction between different classes of objects—for example, being able to distinguish between the class of all trees and the class of all human beings.

The notation and approach of the object-oriented data model builds on these paradigms that people constantly use to cope with complexity.

Objects are the fundamental building blocks of the OODM and have a precise definition: an *object* (defined above) is a structure that encapsulates (or packages) attributes and methods that operate on those attributes. An object may contain any type of data, such as text, numbers, pictures, voice, or video. An object may contain other objects, which may contain other objects, and so forth. Also, an object may be a superclass or a subclass of other objects.

Attributes are properties or characteristics of objects that are of interest to the organization (we use the same definition for attributes in the OODM as in the entity-relationship model). For example, attributes of an object named EMPLOYEE would include Employee Number, Name, Address, and Date of Birth.

Method (or service): A processing routine that is encapsulated in an object and operates on the data described within that object.

Methods (sometimes called *services*) are the processing routines that are encapsulated in an object and operate on the data described within that object. We describe methods in detail in a later section.

Object Classes and Instances

Object instance: One occurrence (or materialization) of an object class.

In the object-oriented data model, we distinguish between object classes and instances, much as we did between entity types and instances in the entity-relationship model. We have defined an object class as a logical grouping of object instances that share the same attributes and methods. An **object instance** is one occurrence (or materialization) of an object class. CAR is an example of an object class, while your commuter car is an instance of that class. When we use the term *object* by itself, we are referring to an object class.

Figure 5-3 shows the notation that we use to represent objects. A rectangle with rounded corners (Figure 5-3a) is used to represent each object class. As shown in Figure 5-3b, each object class is divided into three sections: an object name, a list of attributes, and a list of methods for those attributes. Figure 5-3c shows examples of three sample object classes. We use capital letters for object names, and capitalize the first letter of each word in the names for attributes and methods.

The attribute definitions and methods for each object are stored in an object repository. Object instances contain data values and are stored in an object database. Object instances may contain attributes or methods that are just for that instance and hence are not shared with other instances of the same class. We illustrate this feature in a subsequent section.

Identifying and Describing Objects

We can use two basic approaches to identify and describe candidate objects: top-down and bottom-up (McFadden, 1991). A *top-down approach* begins with a high-level description of the problem domain (or environment) and proceeds from the

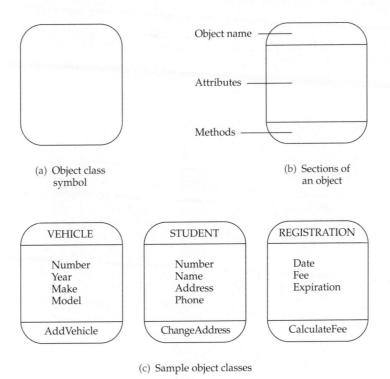

Figure 5-3

The representation of objects

(a) Object class symbol

(b) Sections of an object

(c) Sample object classes

general to the specific. Studying written material and talking with users are activities associated with a top-down approach. Locating nouns in written material (employee, account, etc.) often provides clues about potential objects. Pictures and diagrams are also sources of information concerning candidate objects.

The *bottom-up approach* begins with system detail, especially reports, video forms, and other detail documents and displays. By sifting through this detail (and again talking with users), the analyst identifies the candidate objects and their properties.

In reality, the top-down and bottom-up approaches should be used in concert to identify and describe candidate objects (as well as in the remaining steps of object-oriented data modeling). We illustrate both of these approaches below.

As candidate objects are identified, the analyst must decide whether to include them in the OODM. Coad and Yourdon (1990) suggest that the following criteria be considered:

1. *Needed remembrance.* Is there something about each instance (or occurrence) of this object that the system needs to remember? For a COURSE object, for example, the system is expected to remember attributes such as Course Name, Number of Units, and Prerequisite Courses.

2. *Needed methods.* Does the system need to provide processing on behalf of this object? For a COURSE object, for example, the system will be expected to maintain occurrences of this object, drop occurrences, and so on.

3. *More than one attribute.* If a candidate object has only one attribute (such as Length), that attribute should probably be included in one (or more) other objects, instead of being defined as an independent object.

4. *Common attributes.* Is there a set of attributes that applies to every instance of the object? For a COURSE object (for example), attributes such as Course

Number, Course Name, and Number of Units apply to every instance. On the other hand, if some attributes apply only to certain instances, this indicates that a classification structure (or generalization hierarchy) exists. We describe this structure below.

Example: Customer Order

We illustrate the bottom-up approach to describing objects with a simple example. Figure 5-4a shows a typical customer order entry form for Pine Valley Furniture Company. (The customer order was first introduced in Chapter 2; see Figure 2-6.) Each order is assigned a unique order number when it is entered into the system. As shown in Figure 5-4a, each order may request several products for shipment. The quantity ordered for each product is displayed on the screen. (The extended amount, which is computed by multiplying quantity ordered by unit price, is not shown.)

By analyzing the order entry screen, we can identify three candidate objects: ORDER, CUSTOMER, and PRODUCT (Figure 5-4b). Notice that ORDER contains three simple attributes that directly describe the order: Order No., Order Date, and Promised Date. CUSTOMER (an object) is also contained within ORDER, since when we view an order, we normally associate a customer with that order. However, the details (or attributes) about that customer are contained within CUSTOMER rather than within ORDER.

Figure 5-4

Sample customer order and object classes

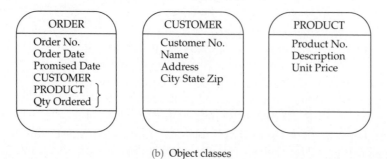

(a) Customer order

(b) Object classes

If you examine the order entry form, you will note that information about each product and the quantity ordered for that product is repeated at the bottom of the form. This information is captured in the ORDER object: PRODUCT (an object) and the attribute Qty Ordered are shown as a repeating group within ORDER. We use the } symbol to indicate repeating attributes and/or objects. As with CUSTOMER, the attributes for PRODUCT are contained within that object, rather than within ORDER. In general, we assign attributes to the objects with which they are most directly associated.

The three candidate objects in Figure 5-4b each meet all four of the criteria for objects described above. (Methods are omitted from the objects to simplify the discussion at this point, but will be included later.) Of course in a real problem environment, we would analyze many views such as the customer order form in order to identify and describe objects.

Connecting Objects

A **connection** is a mapping from one object class to another. It indicates some relationship between the instances of the first object class and those of the second. For example, there would be a connection between STUDENT and COURSE object classes, as well as between AIRLINE and PASSENGER object classes. In general, when a connection exists between object classes, we expect that these object classes exchange messages (described below).

Figure 5-5a shows the notation that we use to record connections. This is the same notation that we used for the entity-relationship model in Chapter 4. With an optional (zero-one) connection, each instance of object A is either connected to exactly one instance of object B, or else it is not connected to an instance. For example, an airline seat is either assigned to a passenger or is unassigned. With a mandatory one connection, each instance of object A must be connected to exactly one instance of object B. For example, an exam is taken by exactly one student. The optional and mandatory "many" connections are similarly defined.

Connection: A mapping from one object class to another.

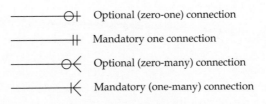

Optional (zero-one) connection

Mandatory one connection

Optional (zero-many) connection

Mandatory (one-many) connection

(a) Notation for object connections

Figure 5-5

Object connections

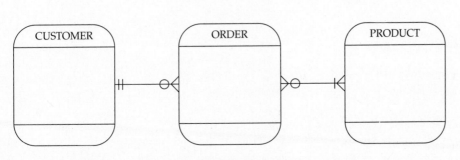

(b) Example of object connections

Figure 5-5b shows the use of the object connections for the customer order example. Each customer may (optionally) be connected to no orders, or to one or more orders. Each order must be connected to exactly one customer. An order must be connected to at least one product, while a product may be connected to zero, one, or more orders.

Notice that the notation and meaning are similar to those of the entity-relationship model. For the object model, however, unlike the E-R model, there is no special relationship symbol or relationship name in the notation we use here.[1]

GENERALIZATION

One of the most powerful features of the object-oriented data model is that it explicitly models class-subclass relationships, which show generalization and specialization of real-world entities.

Generalization (defined in Chapter 4) is the concept that some things (objects) are types of other things. For example, to an airline the object class BUSINESS PASSENGER is one type of the more general object class called PASSENGER. By this we mean that business passengers share attributes and require services (or methods) that are common to all passengers. (Of course, they may also have attributes and require services that are unique to business passengers.) *Specialization* (or *categorization*, also defined in Chapter 4) is the opposite concept: that an object comes in various types (as ice cream comes in different flavors). For example, there are different types of automobiles, such as sedans, convertibles, sports cars, compacts, and so on.

Generalization Hierarchy

Generalization hierarchy: A hierarchical grouping of objects that share common attributes and methods.

To express generalization relationships, objects are arranged into a hierarchy. A **generalization hierarchy** is a hierarchical grouping of objects that share common attributes and methods. For example, suppose that an organization has three basic types of employees: hourly employees, salaried employees, and contract consultants. Figure 5-6a shows a simple hierarchy in which the object class EMPLOYEE is at the top, and the three subclasses are arranged below it.

Exhaustive subclasses: There are no other subclasses.

Exclusive subclasses: Each instance of an object must be an instance of exactly one of the subclasses.

Figure 5-6 introduces the basic notation we will use to represent generalization hierarchies. The circle with the double line immediately below it indicates that the three subclasses are **exhaustive** (there are no other subclasses of EMPLOYEE). The fact that the lines from the three subclasses connect to the one circle indicates that the subclasses are **exclusive** (each instance of EMPLOYEE must be an instance of exactly one of the subclasses). We describe variations of this notation below.[2]

Inheritance

Inheritance is an important principle (and benefit) of the object-oriented data model. Inheritance (defined earlier in this chapter) means that all properties (both

---

[1]There is at the present time no standard notation for the OODM. The notation that we use here follows closely (with some modifications) that which appears in Coad and Yourdon (1990).

[2]This notation is based on the IDEF1X modeling language. See Bruce (1992) for a complete description of this language.

attributes and methods) of an object class become the properties of its subclasses. This property is illustrated in Figure 5-6b for the employee example, in which typical attributes and methods have been added to the structure. The attributes of EMPLOYEE (Employee No., Name, Address, Date Hired, and Date of Birth) apply to all three subclasses (with one exception described below). Also, the method named CalculateAge applies to all employees (age is computed by using Date of Birth). Therefore, these properties are assigned to the EMPLOYEE object and do not appear in the subclasses.

Figure 5-6

Simple generalization hierarchy

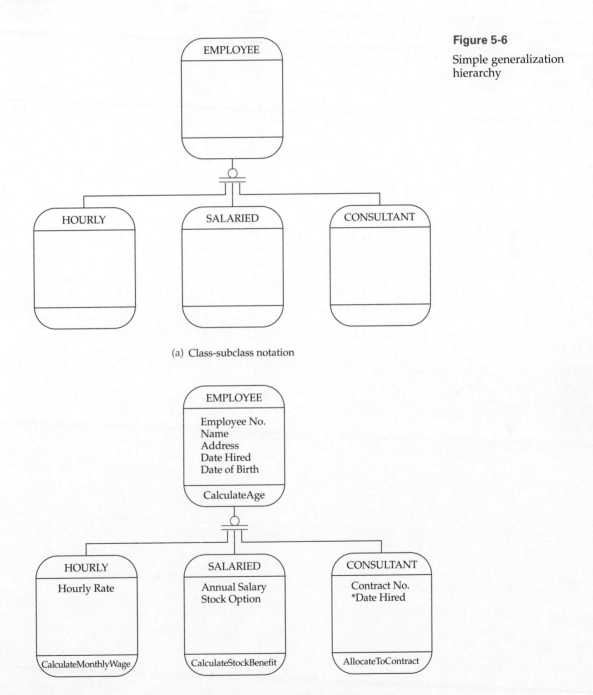

(a) Class-subclass notation

(b) Objects with attributes and methods

Properties that are unique to each subclass are assigned to that subclass. For example, the attributes Annual Salary and Stock Option apply only to instances of SALARIED EMPLOYEE, as does the method CalculateStockBenefit. All properties of EMPLOYEE are inherited by SALARIED EMPLOYEE, as well as by the other two subclasses.

Sometimes an attribute applies to most (but not all) subclasses of an object class. In this case, the attribute can be assigned to the class object, with an override for the subclass (or subclasses) to which it does not apply. For example, the

Figure 5-7

Exclusive versus nonexclusive subclasses

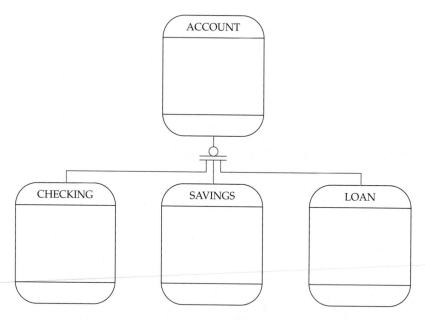

(a) Exclusive subclasses (OR structure)

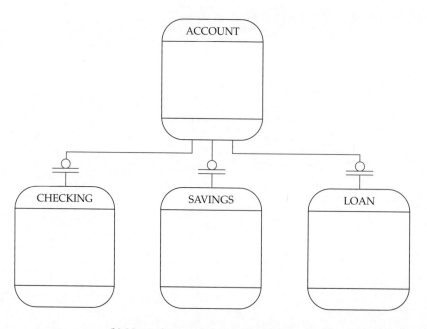

(b) Nonexclusive subclasses (AND structure)

attribute Date Hired applies to hourly and salaried employees, but not to consultants. In Figure 5-6b we have assigned this attribute to EMPLOYEE, but the * symbol before Date Hired in the CONSULTANT object indicates that this attribute does not apply to instances of that subclass and is therefore not inherited by them.

Variations on Generalization Hierarchies

The subclasses in Figure 5-6 are exclusive; that is, each instance of EMPLOYEE may be an instance of only one subclass. Note that while these subclasses are exclusive at a given time, over a period of time, a salaried employee (for example) might become a consultant. In other situations, an instance of a class might simultaneously be an instance of more than one subclass. The banking example in Figure 5-7 shows how to represent each of these cases.[1]

In Figure 5-7a, the object class ACCOUNT has three subclasses: CHECKING, SAVINGS, and LOAN. These subclasses are exclusive; an account must be one of the three types. This exclusive structure is sometimes referred to as an *OR* structure, since an account is either checking *or* savings *or* loan (but never more than one). The OR structure is represented by connecting all subclasses to one circle below the class, as in Figure 5-7a.

In modern banking, multipurpose accounts are common. Thus an account may simultaneously be a savings account and a checking account (perhaps a loan account as well). This situation is shown in Figure 5-7b. In this example, the subclasses are nonexclusive. This is referred to as an *AND* structure, since an account may be a checking account *and* a savings account (*and* perhaps a loan account) at the same time.

Another situation that may occur in a generalization hierarchy is that the object subclasses for a class may not be exhaustive (that is, there may be other subclasses not yet identified). This situation can be represented with a small variation in the notation we have used so far. For example, Figure 5-8 shows an object class named

---

[1]This example was suggested by Bruce (1992).

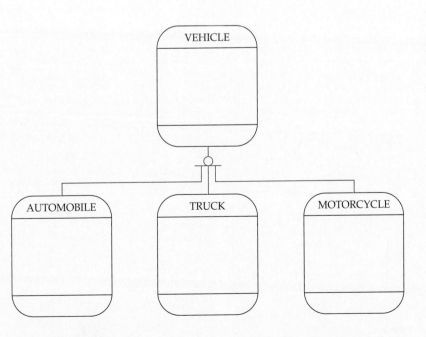

Figure 5-8

Nonexhaustive subclasses

VEHICLE with three subclasses: AUTOMOBILE, TRUCK, and MOTORCYCLE. There are other subclasses (such as BICYCLE) not included in the model. This exclusion is indicated by the single line (rather than double line) below the circle representing the class-subclass relationship. The hierarchy in Figure 5-8 is an OR structure. An AND structure can be used with nonexhaustive subclasses as well. In fact, combinations of these structures can be used in the same diagram.

Example: Vacation Property Rentals

Vacation Property Rentals (VPR) is a company that rents desirable vacation units throughout the country. There are two basic types of properties: mountain properties and beach properties. Most rentals are made on a weekly basis.

There are four user views that illustrate object-oriented data modeling: Renter, Rental Agreement, Beach Property, and Mountain Property.

Renter   The Renter view is shown in Figure 5-9a. This view is simply a list of persons who have rented properties from VPR in the past, are renting properties at the present time, or are prospective customers. The view shows the renter name, address, phone number, and maximum weekly rental the person is willing to pay.

We have chosen to represent RENTER as a single object class, as shown in Figure 5-9b. Since renters may be past, present, or prospective customers, should we create a generalization hierarchy in which each of these is represented as a subclass of RENTER? This decision depends on whether each subclass has unique properties (attributes or methods). There is not enough information given to determine this, so for the present time we are satisfied with RENTER as shown in the figure.

Beach Property and Mountain Property   Figure 5-10a shows the Beach Property and Mountain Property views. The Beach Property listing includes an attribute that records the number of blocks to the closest beach, while the Mountain

---

Figure 5-9

Renter view and object class

RENTER

NAME	ADDRESS	PHONE NO.	MAX RENT
Margaret Simpson	15 Ridge St., Dallas, TX 75083	219-473-4928	200
Arnold Thomas	50 Main St., Cupertino, CA 95014	408-123-0195	350
Phyllis Martinez	114 Maple Ave., Denver, CO 80328	303-111-4891	400

(a) Renter view

(b) Object class

Property listing shows what type of skiing is available at nearby resorts (Nordic, Alpine, or both). At first glance, it might appear that Beach Property and Mountain Property represent separate objects, but on closer inspection we see that these objects share several common attributes. In fact, only the last attributes (Blocks to Beach, Skiing) are different. We conclude that BEACH and MOUNTAIN are subclasses of the object class PROPERTY. Figure 5-10b shows the generalization hierarchy for this relationship. Examine this diagram and see if you can answer the following questions: are BEACH and MOUNTAIN exclusive or nonexclusive subclasses? Are they exhaustive or nonexhaustive?

One method is shown for PROPERTY. RentProperty is a processing routine that (when invoked by a user) creates a rental agreement for a specific property for a stated begin date, end date, and rental rate. We will describe the technique

Figure 5-10

Property views and object classes

BEACH PROPERTY

STREET ADDRESS	CITY STATE ZIP	NO. ROOMS	TYPICAL RENT	BLOCKS TO BEACH
120 Surf Drive	Honolulu, HI 99987	3	500	2
360 Sail Street	Orlando, FL 10389	4	400	1/2

MOUNTAIN PROPERTY

STREET ADDRESS	CITY STATE ZIP	NO. ROOMS	TYPICAL RENT	SKIING
400 Hill Road	Aspen, CO 87394	3	300	A, N
100 Mogul Drive	Jackson, WY 89204	3	250	N

(a) Property views

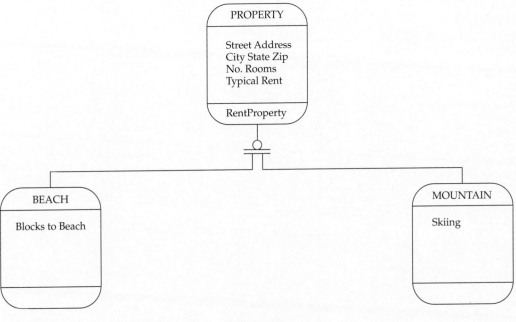

(b) Object classes

to implement this method in more detail in a later section. The method should provide an integrity check to ensure that a new rental agreement does not conflict with a prior rental agreement for the same property and rental dates.

Rental Agreement   Figure 5-11a shows the Rental Agreement view. This view associates a renter with a rental property during a specific interval of time (designated by the Begin Date and End Date). The RENTAL AGREEMENT object class is shown in Figure 5-11b. A rental agreement instance associates a renter instance with a property instance. Since RENTER and PROPERTY have been defined as object classes, they are included in the RENTAL AGREEMENT object. Attributes included in the object are Begin Date, End Date, and Rental Rate.

One method, ComputeTotalRent, is shown in RENTAL AGREEMENT. When ComputeTotalRent is invoked by a user (or another object), it computes the total rent for a particular rental agreement by multiplying the rental period (End Date minus Begin Date) by the Rental Rate. The total rent can then be displayed and/ or stored in the RENTAL AGREEMENT instance. If total rent is to be stored, then another attribute, called Total Rent, must be added to the RENTAL AGREEMENT object class.

Object-Oriented Data Model   Vacation Property Rentals is another example of the bottom-up approach, since we started with detailed user views and developed object-oriented structures for each view. We produce an object-oriented conceptual data model by merging the individual diagrams into an overall object-oriented model. Figure 5-12 shows the object-oriented model for VPR.

The object connections in the resulting model are obtained by analyzing the relevant relationships between objects. For VPR, there are two connections (in addition to the previously described class-subclass relationships):

1. There is an optional zero-many connection from RENTER to RENTAL AGREEMENT, since any renter may have no current rental agreement or may have one or more rental agreements. The connection from RENTAL

Figure 5-11

Rental agreement view and object class

RENTAL AGREEMENT

```
Name:  Arnold Thomas                    Date: 12/3/9X
Street Address:  360 Sail St.
City State Zip:  Orlando, FL 10389
Begin Date:  1/15/9X
End Date:  1/29/9X
Rental Rate:  350
```

(a) Rental agreement

RENTAL
AGREEMENT

RENTER
PROPERTY
Begin Date
End Date
Rental Rate

ComputeTotalRent

(b) Object class

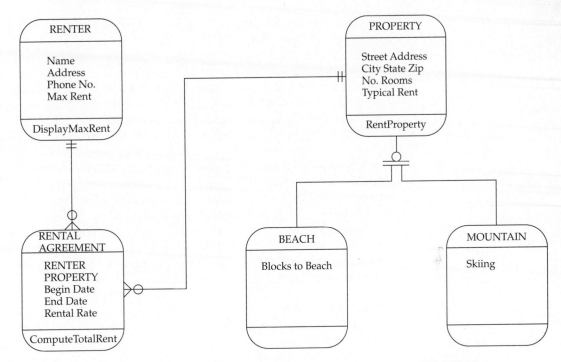

Figure 5-12

Object-oriented data model (Vacation Property Rentals)

AGREEMENT to RENTER is mandatory one, since we assume a rental agreement is for one renter. (If there could be more than one renter for a rental agreement, then this connection would be mandatory one-many.)

2. The same connection exists between RENTAL AGREEMENT and PROPERTY, for the same reasons.

Closely examine the object-oriented data model in Figure 5-12 to check whether objects and connections have been accurately defined, and whether attributes and methods have been assigned to the correct objects and levels (in the case of class-subclass structures).

ASSEMBLY STRUCTURES

Combining objects to form an assembly (or whole) is one of the most common of experiences. For example, a physical object such as a bicycle consists of a frame, wheels, sprockets, seat, and a number of other parts. Less obvious is that an organization is an assembly of people, procedures, and other objects. Also, an airline flight is an assembly of passengers, baggage, crew, and other items.

We have already encountered assembly structures in some of the examples in this chapter, but have not used that terminology to describe them. For example, we can regard a customer order (Figure 5-4a) as an assembly that includes a customer and some number of products. We represented this fact in Figure 5-4b by showing the CUSTOMER and PRODUCT objects encapsulated within the ORDER object. Also, we can view the Rental Agreement (Figure 5-11a) as an assembly that includes a renter and a property. Again, we represented this fact by encapsulating RENTER and PROPERTY within the RENTAL AGREEMENT object (Figure 5-11b).

Explicit Assembly Structure

In this section we introduce an alternate notation that explicitly represents assembly structures. Figure 5-13 shows this notation for the customer order. Figure 5-13a (which is the same as Figure 5-4b) shows CUSTOMER and PRODUCT contained in ORDER. We refer to this as an *implicit* assembly structure. Figure 5-13b shows ORDER represented as an *explicit* assembly structure. Notice that a line with an upward pointing arrow connects each component object class to its assembly. The type of connection (optional, mandatory) is indicated with the connection.

Each order may be associated with one or more products. Also, there is a quantity ordered associated with each product on the order. Therefore, the attributes Product No. and Qty Ordered are associated with the ORDER object class. They appear as a repeating group within that object.

The implicit and explicit representations of assembly structures are logically equivalent. The implicit structure has the advantage of being somewhat more concise; however, the explicit structure captures more meaning, since it shows the nature of each connection between assembly and part.

Bill of Materials   One of the most common assembly structures is the bill-of-materials structure (introduced in Chapter 4). With a bill-of-materials structure, there is only one object class. Each instance of the object is assembled from other instances of the same object, and the assemblies may be nested to any depth. Most manufactured products have this type of structure, and it frequently applies in other situations as well.

Figure 5-14 shows a representation of a typical bill-of-materials structure using both the implicit and explicit assembly notations. The object class is called ITEM. With the implicit structure (Figure 5-14a), ITEM and the attribute Quantity are

Figure 5-13

Representing assembly structures

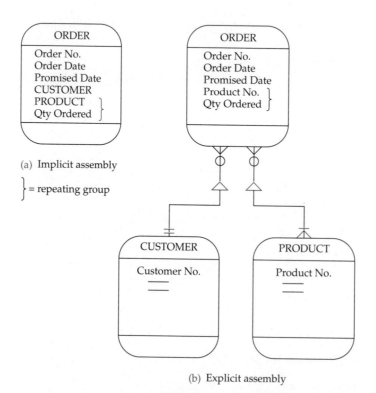

(a) Implicit assembly

$\left.\rule{0pt}{12pt}\right\}$ = repeating group

(b) Explicit assembly

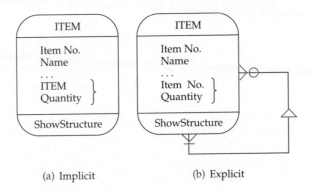

Figure 5-14

Bill-of-materials
structure

(a) Implicit   (b) Explicit

paired as a repeating group within ITEM. A repeating group is referred to as a **recursive structure**. With the explicit structure (Figure 5-14b), the attributes Item No. and Quantity are paired as a repeating group within ITEM. The line with the upward pointing arrow indicates the assembly structure. The connection at the top is optional zero-many, since a particular item may or may not be part of a higher-level assembly. The connection at the bottom is mandatory one-many, since an assembly by definition must have at least one component part.

Recursive structure: A repeating group.

One method (named ShowStructure) is shown in the ITEM object. When invoked by a user, this method will prepare a listing of all of the component items for a given item. This listing is usually prepared in indented form for ease of reading, and shows the quantity of each component item. For example, for a bicycle the first few lines might look like this:

```
.Bicycle (1)
  ..Seat (1)
  ..Wheel (2)
    ...Tire (1)
    ...Spoke (32)
```

Other methods for ITEM might compute total cost for the item, keep track of different versions over time, and so on. In fact, if an object-oriented database management system is used to implement the object-oriented data model, the system could store any of the following for each item: a drawing, a picture, and an audio or video description of how to use the item.

METHODS

A unique feature of the object-oriented data model is the encapsulation of methods (or processing routines) within objects. We have introduced methods briefly by pointing out typical methods in some of the object classes we have used as examples. In this section we examine methods in greater detail, describe the various types of methods, and point out the role of messages.

Methods encapsulated within an object class define the processing that the object provides. Ultimately, methods define the behavior of an object. Methods can only process data within the object class in which they are defined. They can receive requests from methods in another object class, but cannot process data in another object class.

Types of Methods

We can divide the basic methods that are defined for object classes into the following categories: Occur, Calculate, and Monitor. (Other types of methods can be added as needed.) These categories are described briefly below.

Occur Methods   The Occur methods provide basic maintenance for the instances of each object class and each classification structure (generalization or assembly). There are four basic Occur methods: instance add, instance change, instance delete, and instance select (Coad and Yourdon, 1990). For convenience these methods are named *Occur.Add, Occur.Change, Occur.Delete,* and *Occur.Select,* respectively. Occur.Add creates an instance of an object class. Occur.Change modifies an instance, while Occur.Delete deletes an instance. Occur.Select locates an instance (or instances) and returns requested attribute values to the sender.

Occur methods are included with every object class. They provide standard functions such as the following:

1. *Integrity control.* Each method checks incoming messages to determine whether they are valid. All message arguments (or attribute values) are checked against the corresponding domain definitions for those attributes. When an error occurs, an error message is returned to the sender.

2. *Instance connections.* Each method maintains instance connections as appropriate. For example, Occur.Add will establish a connection between a new instance and instances of another object class, if appropriate. Occur.Delete will prevent a delete from occurring if it will violate an instance constraint.

3. *Respond to sender.* Each method "gets back" to a sender by returning requested data values, acknowledgements of actions taken, error messages, and so on.

Calculate Methods   The Calculate methods perform calculations on the data values encapsulated in the same object class. These calculations may range from simple (debit an account) to very complex (a large spreadsheet).

Monitor Methods   The Monitor methods provide for the ongoing surveillance (or monitoring) of some system or system characteristic. For example, one characteristic of an inventory system is the stock level for each inventory item. A method called InventoryCheck could be used to monitor the stock level of each item and warn the user when the stock level falls below a predetermined limit. Thus, Monitor methods can be used to implement the principle of management by exception by producing signals when predetermined limits are exceeded in a system.

Message Connections

Message connection: A communications path between sending and receiving object classes.

In the object-oriented data model, a method is activated by sending a message from one object class (the sender) to another object class (the receiver). A **message connection** is a communications path between sending and receiving object classes. We use a dashed arrow (with arrow heads on both ends) to represent a message connection in an object-oriented diagram.

Following are simple rules for establishing message paths between object classes:

1. Establish message connections between each pair of object classes that are already connected by instance connections.
2. Establish message connections between other object class pairs not already connected that will need to exchange messages.

Figure 5-15 is an example of adding message connections to an object-oriented data model. This example is for the customer order (see Figures 5-4 and 5-5). Since connections were already established between CUSTOMER and ORDER, and between ORDER and PRODUCT (Figure 5-5), we insert message connections also between these object pairs in Figure 5-15. In addition, a USER (a new type of object) is included in Figure 5-15, with message connections between USER and CUSTOMER, and between USER and ORDER.

Messages

Messages are sent over message connections to request that a method be performed. A typical message pattern is the following:

1. A sender (object class) sends a message.
2. A receiver (object class) receives the message, and a method (one or more) is performed.
3. The receiver returns some response to the sender.

Messages must be formatted so that they reach the intended receiver. A common format is to use the name of the receiver as a prefix, followed by the name

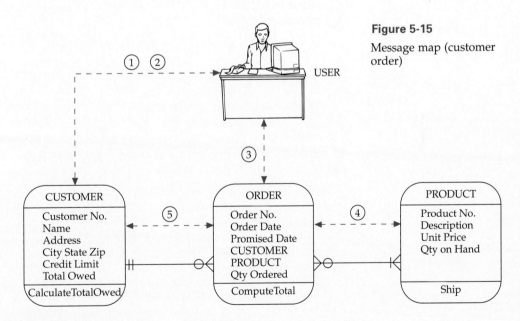

Figure 5-15

Message map (customer order)

Messages:

1. CUSTOMER. DisplayInformation
2. CUSTOMER. Occur. Add
3. ORDER. Occur. Add
4. PRODUCT. Ship
5. CUSTOMER. CalculateTotalOwed

of the requested service. For example, consider the message connection between EMPLOYEE and PROJECT object classes. If the EMPLOYEE object class wants to send a message to the PROJECT object class to display project information, the message would be formatted as follows:

```
PROJECT.DisplayInformation
```

This format resembles a telephone number, in which the name of the receiving object class (PROJECT) is an area code, and the name of the requested method (DisplayInformation) is the local telephone number. The requesting object class (EMPLOYEE) has no information about *how* the DisplayInformation method is accomplished within PROJECT. The requesting object class only has information about the interface with that object—how a message must be formatted, and what type of message to expect in return.

In this example, the PROJECT object may have a number of instances. How will DisplayInformation know which instance to select for display? This information must be included in the message that is sent. Suppose that information is to be displayed for project number 25. In this case, the project number would be included as an argument in the message, as follows:

```
PROJECT.DisplayInformation(25)
```

In general, each message may (optionally) include a list of one or more arguments that are required to complete the message. As we mentioned above, the method that receives and processes the message performs an integrity check to ensure that the included arguments conform to the relevant domain definitions (for example, is 25 a legal project number?). An error message is returned if any argument is not legal.

Example: Customer Order

Message map: A diagram that shows the flow of messages superimposed on the message connections.

Figure 5-15 is an example of the use of messages for the customer order. We refer to this diagram as a **message map**, since the diagram shows the flow of messages superimposed on the message connections. The five messages that are shown in the figure support the Enter Customer Order transaction. A general description of this transaction is the following:

> Customer orders arrive by mail, fax, or telephone. A customer sales representative (the user) checks the order manually. The salesperson then displays information for the customer by selecting a customer display form from a list of menu choices, and entering a customer number. If the customer order is from a new customer, the salesperson enters information to add that customer to the database. If the order is from an existing customer, the user checks the accuracy of the existing information and makes any necessary changes.
>
> The user next selects an order display form from the list of menu choices. The system assigns an order number to the new order and then prompts the user to enter the following information for the order: order date, promised date, and customer number. For each line item (product) on the order, the system then prompts the user to enter the product number and quantity ordered. As each product is added to the order, the system consults the quantity on hand for that item and computes the quantity that can be shipped. The product number, description, and quantity shipped are then added to a shipping notice for the order.

The system also computes the extended amount (quantity shipped times unit price) for each item on the order and adds it to the total owed (total credit extended) for that customer. If the total owed exceeds the customer's credit limit, a message is sent to the user, who then decides on what action to take.

The five messages that support this transaction processing are numbered in Figure 5-15, and the message names are given at the bottom of the figure. Following is a brief description of each message.

1. CUSTOMER.DisplayInformation. A request from USER to CUSTOMER. The argument in the message is Customer No. The response is a full screen of information for the selected customer.

2. CUSTOMER.Occur.Add. A request from USER to CUSTOMER. Assuming this is a new customer, a full screen of information for a new customer is sent to the CUSTOMER object. The response is an acknowledgement that a new customer has been created.

3. ORDER.Occur.Add. A message from USER to ORDER. The arguments are Order Date, Promised Date, and Customer No. The response is a request for the first Product No. and Qty Ordered. This request is repeated until there are no more products. An acknowledgement is then sent that the order is complete.

4. PRODUCT.Ship. A request from ORDER to PRODUCT. The arguments are Product No. and Qty Ordered. The response is Product No., Qty Shipped, and Unit Price.

5. CUSTOMER.CalculateTotalOwed. A request from ORDER to CUSTOMER. The argument is Extended Amount. The response is a message to USER if the credit limit has been exceeded.

In developing an object-oriented data model, we suggest that the level of detail shown in the message map (Figure 5-15) is sufficient to specify processing requirements at a high level. A more detailed specification of the processing for each method will be developed during the physical design. Figure 5-16 shows some of the detailed logic for the PRODUCT.Ship method. This method compares the quantity ordered for a product with the quantity on hand. If quantity on hand is adequate, the entire amount ordered is shipped. If quantity ordered exceeds quantity on hand, the quantity on hand is shipped, and the shortage is backordered (for simplicity, we do not show backorders in Figure 5-16). Other logic for Ship (not shown in Figure 5-16) would be required to perform integrity checking.

Example: Vacation Property Rentals

Figure 5-17 shows a message map for Vacation Property Rentals. This map is based on the object-oriented data model shown in Figure 5-12. An additional

Figure 5-16

Sample logic for a method

```
Method: Ship (Product No., Qty Ordered)
    IF Qty Ordered < = Qty on Hand
       THEN
          Qty Shipped = Qty Ordered
          Qty on Hand = Qty on Hand – Qty Ordered
       ELSE
          Qty Shipped = Qty on Hand
          Qty Backordered = Qty Ordered – Qty on Hand
          Qty on Hand = 0
    ENDIF
```

Figure 5-17

Message map (Vacation Property Rentals)

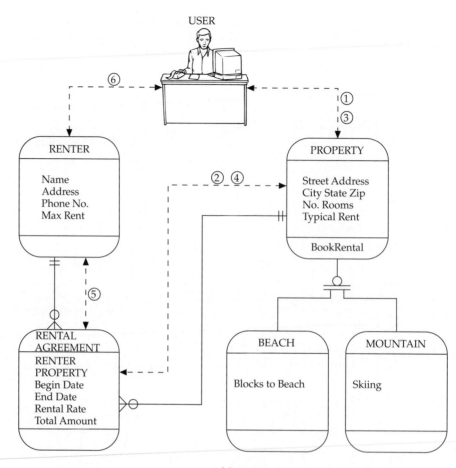

Messages:

1. PROPERTY. DisplayInformation
2. RENTAL AGREEMENT. ProvideAvailability
3. PROPERTY. BookRental
4. RENTAL AGREEMENT. Occur. Add
5. RENTER. Occur. Select
6. RENTER. Occur. Add

attribute called Total Amount (for the rental period) has been added to the RENTAL AGREEMENT object for illustration. Message connections are shown between object classes already connected, as well as between USER and RENTER, and USER and PROPERTY.

The messages that are shown in the figure are to support the transaction Create Rental Agreement. We assume that this is an on-line transaction, with the user (a salesperson) taking the necessary information from a customer (or prospective customer) during a telephone conversation. The messages shown in the figure are summarized below.

1. PROPERTY.DisplayInformation. Using a form (screen display), the user requests information for a particular property. Arguments are Address and City State Zip. The response is a complete screen of information (including available dates) for the property.

2. RENTAL AGREEMENT.ProvideAvailability. The PROPERTY object does not have information about availability for each property. Therefore, the

PROPERTY object sends this request to the RENTAL AGREEMENT object, which stores all information concerning rental dates. Arguments are Address and City State Zip. The response is a list of available dates for the property (alternatively, dates not available could be returned). This information becomes part of the response in message 1 (above).

3. PROPERTY.BookRental. A request by the user to PROPERTY to book a rental for a customer. The user calls up a screen display that prompts the user to provide values for the following: Address, City State Zip, Name, Begin Date, End Date, and Rental Rate. The response is either an acknowledgement that a rental agreement has been created, or a message that this is a new customer and that information describing the customer must be entered before a rental agreement can be completed.

4. RENTAL AGREEMENT.Occur.Add. A request sent from PROPERTY to RENTAL AGREEMENT to create a new instance of RENTAL AGREEMENT. Arguments are Name, Begin Date, End Date, and Rental Rate. The response is either an acknowledgement that a rental agreement has been created for the property on the requested dates, or a message that this is a new customer who does not yet exist in the database.

5. RENTER.Occur.Select. A request sent by AGREEMENT to RENTER, to determine if this customer exists in the database. The argument is Name. The response is a yes (renter exists) or no (renter does not exist).

6. RENTER.Occur.Add. A request from the user to RENTER, to create a new instance of RENTER (if a new customer). The user calls up a form on the screen that prompts for the following: Name, Address, Phone No., and Max Rent. The response is an acknowledgement that a new renter has been created.

Case Example: Mountain View Community Hospital

We introduced the Mountain View Community Hospital case in Chapter 3 in the context of strategic database planning. An organization chart for the hospital appears in Figure 3-22. The major business functions appear in Figure 3-23, and Figure 3-24 shows a decomposition of these functions into an enterprise chart. We will not repeat these figures or the related introduction to the case in this chapter.

An enterprise data model (in the form of an entity-relationship diagram) for the hospital appears in Figure 3-25, and is repeated in Figure 5-18 for ease of reference.

In this section we illustrate a top-down approach to developing an object-oriented data model; using a bottom-up approach is left as an exercise. In Figure 5-19, the enterprise data model has been transformed into a high-level object-oriented data model by simply mapping entities (from the E-R model) to objects. The object connections in Figure 5-19 show both lower and upper bounds. Also, Figure 5-19 shows the objects MED/SURG and SUPPLY as subtypes of the ITEM object class.

To complete the model shown in Figure 5-19, additional detail must be added to the objects in the form of both attributes and methods. This detail will be discovered through the examination of detailed reports and other data sources, and through discussions with users. This model illustrates that the object-oriented data model provides a convenient means for rapidly prototyping the major components of databases.

Figure 5-18

Enterprise data model
(Mountain View
Community Hospital)

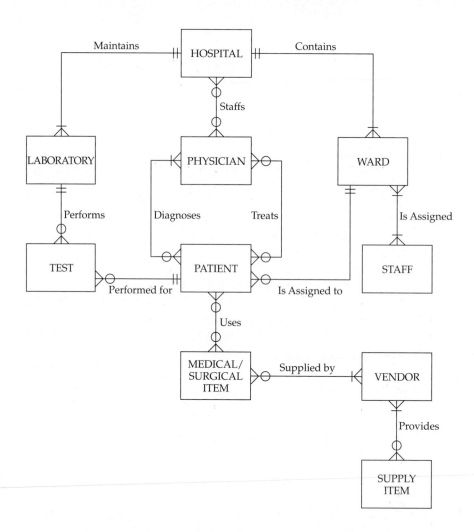

SUMMARY

This chapter describes the use of the object-oriented data model to represent both the data and processing requirements for an organization. Objects are structures that encapsulate data and exclusive methods for that data. An object may contain any type of data such as text, images, and video scenes. The object-oriented data model provides the following advantages:

1. *Methods:* The processing requirements for each object are packaged with the attributes and treated as an intrinsic whole.

2. *Inheritance:* Objects inherit (or receive) both attributes and methods from higher-level objects.

3. *Messages:* Objects exchange messages through an interface between objects.

4. *Structure:* Formal constructs are provided for representing both classification and assembly structures.

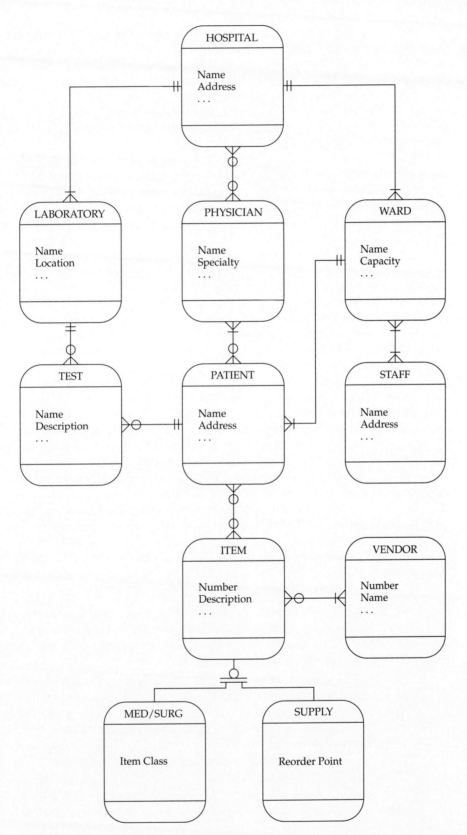

Figure 5-19
High-level, object-oriented model (Mountain View Community Hospital)

Attributes are properties of objects that are of interest to the organization. Methods are processing routines that are encapsulated in objects and operate on the data described in those objects. An object class is a logical grouping of object instances that share the same attributes and methods. Both top-down and bottom-up approaches may be used to define objects.

Connections between objects indicate some relationship between those objects. The notation used to represent connections is similar to that for relationships in the entity-relationship model.

Class-subclass relationships are explicitly represented in the object-oriented data model. A generalization hierarchy is a hierarchical grouping of objects that share common attributes and methods. Through the property of inheritance, all attributes and methods of an object class become the properties of its subclasses. Subclasses may have unique attributes and methods that are not properties of the parent class.

Objects may contain other objects; for example, an object called CLASS may contain another object called STUDENT. In an object-oriented data model this structure may be portrayed implicitly by simply including the object name STUDENT within the CLASS object. This type of relationship may also be viewed as an assembly structure, and object-oriented data models often include explicit notation for representing these structures. An important type of assembly structure is the bill of material, which is a recursive structure that contains only one object class.

Three basic types of methods are encapsulated in objects: Occur, Calculate, and Monitor. Occur methods (included in every object) are used to add, delete, modify, and select object instances. They also provide integrity control and maintain necessary connections between objects. Calculate methods provide some kind of calculation on the data encapsulated in objects, while Monitor methods provide surveillance of one or more characteristics of an object.

In the object-oriented data model, methods are activated by sending messages from a sending object to a receiving object. A message connection is a communications path between sending and receiving objects. A message map consists of notation that shows the flow of messages superimposed on the message connections.

The object-oriented approach is not just for data modeling, but is also the basis for several database management systems. Compared to the relational model, the object-oriented data model offers several important advantages:

1. *Reusability.* Generic objects can be defined for a variety of functions and then reused in numerous applications. For example, most screen objects in a Windows environment (icons, buttons, etc.) are defined once and managed as objects for all applications.

2. *Complex data types.* An object-oriented database can store and manage complex data such as documents, graphics, images, voice messages, and video sequences. For example, suppose that we desire to store an image of the conceptual data model for Mountain View Community Hospital (Figure 4-28). This image would be difficult to store in relational tables, but could be stored as a natural object in most object-oriented databases.

3. *Distributed databases.* Because of the mode of communication between objects, object-oriented databases can support distribution of data across a network more readily than most other database systems. Further, the object-oriented data model can be used to facilitate communications between different computers, operating systems, and database management systems.

CHAPTER REVIEW

Key Terms

Connection
Encapsulation
Exclusive subclasses
Exhaustive subclasses
Generalization hierarchy

Identity
Message connection
Message map
Method (or service)

Object
Object class
Object instance
Recursive structure

REVIEW QUESTIONS

1. Define each of the following terms:
   a. object
   b. object class
   c. object instance
   d. connection
   e. method
   f. generalization
   g. inheritance
   h. message connection
   i. message map
2. Contrast the following terms:
   a. object class; object instance
   b. generalization; specialization
   c. method; connection
   d. message connection; message map
   e. inheritance; generalization hierarchy
3. List six core concepts of the OODM.
4. Describe three methods of organization that people use to deal with complexity.
5. List four criteria that can be applied in deciding whether to include a candidate object in an object-oriented data model.
6. What is the distinction between an implicit and explicit assembly structure?
7. List three categories of methods in object classes.
8. List three standard functions that are provided by Occur methods.
9. List two rules for establishing message paths between object classes.
10. List six data types that can be managed with ODBMS technology, and give at least one application for each type.

PROBLEMS AND EXERCISES

1. Match each term with the appropriate definition:

   ____ object
   ____ object class
   ____ methods
   ____ connection
   ____ inheritance
   ____ attributes
   ____ message connection
   ____ specialization
   ____ object instance
   ____ generalization

   a. objects come in various types
   b. communications path between objects
   c. properties of objects
   d. grouping of object instances
   e. encapsulates attributes and methods
   f. processing routines in objects
   g. occurs with classes and subclasses
   h. one occurrence of an object class
   i. mapping between object classes
   j. STUDENT is a type of PERSON

2. Draw a diagram (using object-oriented notation) for each of the following situations. Use explicit notation for assembly structures where required.
   a. A company has a number of employees. The attributes of EMPLOYEE include Name, Address, Birthdate, and Date Hired. One method that is required of all employees is CalculateYearsOfService. The company also has several projects.

Attributes of PROJECT include Code, Description, and Start Date. Each employee may be assigned to one or more projects, or may not be assigned to a project. A project must have at least one employee assigned, and may have several employees assigned. One method required of all projects is CalculateTotalCostToDate.

b. In a vehicle-licensing application, there are three types of vehicles: passenger, truck, and trailer. Vehicle ID is an attribute of all vehicle types. Truck and trailer (but not passenger) vehicles have an attribute named Gross Capacity. The passenger and truck vehicle types require a method named PerformSmogCheck.

c. In a military operation, a mission consists of (or is assembled from) a number of flights. Each flight in turn consists of (or is assembled from) a number of shipments. There are two types of shipments: passenger and cargo item. Following are some attributes of each of these entities:

MISSION: Codename, Description, Date
FLIGHT: No., Origin, Destination
SHIPMENT: No., Location
PASSENGER: Name, Rank
CARGO ITEM: Weight, Dimensions, Description

d. A college course may have one or more scheduled sections, or may not have a scheduled section. Attributes of COURSE include Course ID, Name, and Units. Attributes of SECTION include Section No. and Instructor. A method that is required of all courses is ChangeCourseDescription. A method that is required of all sections is one that will delete a section.

3. Draw an object-oriented diagram to represent the following object classes: vehicle, land vehicle, air vehicle, water vehicle, ocean vessel, river raft, helicopter, rail vehicle, bicycle, airplane, train, road vehicle, car.

4. Figure 5-20 shows a Grade Report that is mailed to students at the end of each semester. Prepare an object-oriented diagram to represent this user view. Include at least one method in each object.

5. There are three types of accounts in a bank, with the following attributes:

CHECKING: Acct No., Date Opened, Balance, Service Charge
SAVINGS: Acct No., Date Opened, Balance, Interest Rate
LOAN: Acct No., Date Opened, Balance, Acct Limit

Draw an object-oriented diagram that best represents this situation.

6. Develop an object-oriented diagram for Mountain View Community Hospital using a bottom-up approach. Use the following steps:

a. Prepare object-oriented diagrams for each of the four user views: Patient Bill (Figure 4–23), Room Utilization Report (Figure 4–25), Patient Display (Figure 4–26), and Physician Report (Figure 4–27).

b. Merge the diagrams to form a single object-oriented data model. Be sure to include all object connections and message connections.

Figure 5-20

Grade report

```
                    LAKEWOOD COLLEGE
                      GRADE REPORT
                    FALL SEMESTER 199X

NAME:             Emily Williams        ID: 268300458
CAMPUS ADDRESS:   208 Brooks Hall
MAJOR:            Information Systems

COURSE    TITLE           INSTRUCTOR    INSTRUCTOR    GRADE
  ID                        NAME         LOCATION

IS 350    Database Mgt.   Codd          B 104           A
IS 465    System Analysis Parsons       B 317           B
```

7. In a library application, there are three types of books: text, reference, and trade. Draw an object-oriented diagram to represent each of the following situations:
   a. Any book must be exactly one of the three types of books.
   b. Any book may be one or more of the three types of books.
8. In an athletic club there are several classes of memberships. Some of these classes are: single, couples, and family.
   a. Draw an object-oriented diagram to represent this situation if there are no classes of memberships other than those listed above.
   b. Draw an object-oriented diagram to represent this situation if there are classes of memberships other than those listed above.
9. A segment of the object-oriented data model for Mountain View Community Hospital is shown in the accompanying figure. You are to draw a message map to represent the transaction associated with admitting a new patient to the hospital. A simplified description of this process follows. A user selects a patient screen form from a set of menu choices. The user fills in information for the new patient, which is used to create a patient record. The user then checks the availability of rooms in the desired section of the hospital. Assuming a room is available, the user assigns the patient to a specific room (A METHOD within ROOM named RegisterPatient is used for this purpose.) Finally, the user requests that the admitting physician schedule an appointment with the newly registered patient. (A method within PHYSICIAN named SchedulePatient is used for this purpose.)

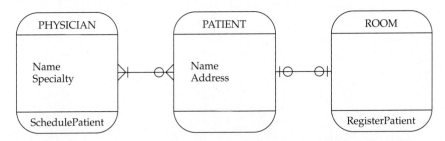

10. Obtain a common user view such as a credit card statement, phone bill, or some other common document. Prepare an object-oriented model to represent this view.
11. Draw an object-oriented diagram for the following situation (Batra, Hoffer, and Bostrom, 1988).

    Projects, Inc., is an engineering firm with approximately 500 employees. A database is required to keep track of all employees, their skills, projects assigned, and departments worked in. Every employee has a unique number assigned by the firm, required to store his or her name and date-of-birth. If an employee is currently married to another employee of Projects, Inc., then it is required to store the date of marriage and who is married to whom. However, no record of marriage need be maintained if the spouse of an employee is not an employee of the firm. Each employee is given a job title (for example, engineer, secretary, foreman, and so on). We are interested in collecting more data specific to the following types: engineer and secretary. The relevant data item to be recorded for engineers is the type of degree (e.g., electrical, mechanical, civil, etc.); for secretaries, it is their typing speeds. An employee does only one type of job at any given time, and we need to retain information for only the current job for an employee.

    There are 11 different departments, each with a unique name. An employee can report to only one department. Each department has a phone number.

    To procure various kinds of equipment, each department deals with many vendors. A vendor typically supplies equipment to many departments. It is required to store the name and address of each vendor and the date of the last meeting between a department and a vendor.

    Many employees can work on a project. An employee can work in many projects (for example, Southwest Refinery, California Petrochemicals, and so on) but can only be assigned to at most one project in a given city. For each city, we are interested in its state and population. An employee can have many skills (preparing material requisitions, checking drawings, and so on), but she or he may use only a given set of skills on a particular project. (For example, an employee MURPHY may prepare requisitions for Southwest Refinery project and prepare requisitions as well as check drawings for California Petrochemicals.) An employee uses each skill that she or he possesses in at least one project. Each skill is assigned a number. A short description must be stored for each skill. Projects are distinguished by project numbers.

It is required to store the estimated cost of each project.

REFERENCES

Batra, D., J. A. Hoffer, and R. B. Bostrom. 1988. "A Comparison of User Performance Between the Relational and Extended Entity-Relationship Model in the Discovery Phase of Database Desgn." *Proceedings of the Ninth International Conference on Information Systems.* Minneapolis, Minn., Nov. 30–Dec. 3, 295–306.

Bruce, Thomas A. 1992. *Designing Quality Databases with IDEF1X Information Models.* New York: Dorset House.

Coad, Peter, and Edward Yourdon. 1990. *Object-Oriented Analysis.* Englewood Cliffs, N.J.: Yourdon Press; Prentice Hall.

English, Larry P. 1992. "Object Databases at Work." *DBMS* 5 (October):44–58.

McFadden, Fred R. 1991. "Conceptual Design of Object-Oriented Databases." *Journal of Object-Oriented Programming* (September):8–11.

CHAPTER

6

Logical Design and the Relational Model

LEARNING OBJECTIVES

After studying this chapter, you should be able to:

- Define the following key terms: *logical database model, relation, relational data model, well-structured relation, anomaly, normalization, functional dependency, determinant, composite key, partial functional dependency, transitive dependency, foreign key, multivalued dependency,* and *recursive foreign key.*
- Describe four steps in logical database design.
- List five properties of relations.
- Define two properties that are essential for a candidate key.
- Give a concise definition for each of the following: first normal form, second normal form, third normal form, Boyce-Codd normal form, and fourth normal form.
- Briefly describe four problems that may arise when merging relations.
- Transform an entity-relationship diagram to a logically equivalent set of relations.
- Transform a relation in first normal form to a set of relations in any of the following: third normal form, Boyce-Codd normal form, or fourth normal form.

INTRODUCTION

In this chapter we describe logical database design, with special emphasis on the relational data model. *Logical database design* is the process of transforming the conceptual data model (described in Chapters 4 and 5) into a logical database model. There are four major logical database models in use today: hierarchical, network, relational, and object-oriented. Our emphasis in this chapter is on the relational data model for two reasons. First, the relational data model is most commonly used in contemporary database applications. Second, some of the principles of logical database design for the relational model apply to the other logical models as well.

199

We have introduced the relational data model informally through simple examples in earlier chapters. In this chapter, we define the important terms for this model. (We will often use the abbreviated term *relational model* when referring to the relational data model.) We also describe the concepts of normalization in detail. Normalization (the process of designing well-structured relations) is an important component of logical design for the relational model, and we can apply normalization concepts to designing hierarchical and network models as well.

In Chapter 4, we described conceptual design using the entity-relationship (E-R) data model. In this chapter, we describe and illustrate the process of transforming an E-R model to the relational model. Some CASE tools support this transformation today; however, it is important that you understand the underlying principles and procedures.

The objective of logical design is to translate the conceptual design (which represents an organization's requirements for data) into a logical database design that can be implemented on a chosen database management system. The resulting databases must meet user needs for data sharing, flexibility, and ease of access. The concepts presented in this chapter are essential to your understanding of the database development process.

LOGICAL DATABASE DESIGN

Figure 6-1 shows the position of logical database design in the overall database development process. Logical database design is the process of transforming the conceptual data model into a logical database model. The conceptual data model is a statement of the data requirements for an organization that is independent of the target database management system. A **logical database model** is a design that conforms to the data model for a class of database management systems.

Logical database model: A design that conforms to the data model for a class of database management systems.

Types of Logical Database Models

As Figure 6-2 shows, four logical database models are commonly used today. These are the hierarchical, network, relational, and object-oriented models. The hierarchical and network models are older models that are still in widespread use today as legacy systems. The relational model is a contemporary model that is the most widely used of the four. The newer object-oriented model is an increasingly important model for future database applications. Each of these models is described briefly below for comparison. The use of the hierarchical and network data models is discussed in Chapters 14 and 15, respectively. We discussed the object-oriented model in Chapter 5. We develop the principles and notations of the relational data model in this chapter, and then use this model extensively in the remainder of the book.

Hierarchical database model: A data model in which records are arranged in a top-down structure that resembles a tree.

Hierarchical Model   In the **hierarchical database model** (Figure 6-2a), records are arranged in a top-down structure that resembles an upside-down tree. The terms *parent* and *child* are often used in describing a hierarchical model. For example, in Figure 6-2a, DEPARTMENT is the parent of EMPLOYEE and PROJECT, while EMPLOYEE is the parent of SKILL and DEPENDENT. An important property of the hierarchical model is that a child may be related to only one parent. In Figure 6-2a, since EQUIPMENT is a child of PROJECT, it cannot also be a child of EMPLOYEE.

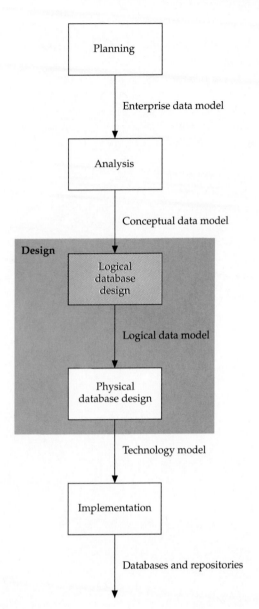

Figure 6-1

Role of logical database
design in the database
development process

The hierarchical database model was the first important logical database model
and is still in use today in some legacy systems, primarily on mainframe computers. We describe the hierarchical data model in detail in Chapter 14.

Network Model   In the **network database model** (Figure 6-2b), there is no
distinction between parent and child record types as in the hierarchical model.
Any record type may be associated with an arbitrary number of different record
types. For example, in Figure 6-2b, EQUIPMENT is associated with both the
EMPLOYEE and PROJECT record types. The arrows in this diagram indicate that
each project may be assigned more than one item of equipment. Similarly, each
employee may be responsible for several items of equipment.
The network model was developed to overcome the limited scope of the

Network database model:
A data model in which each
record type may be associated with an arbitrary number of different record
types.

Figure 6-2

Logical database models

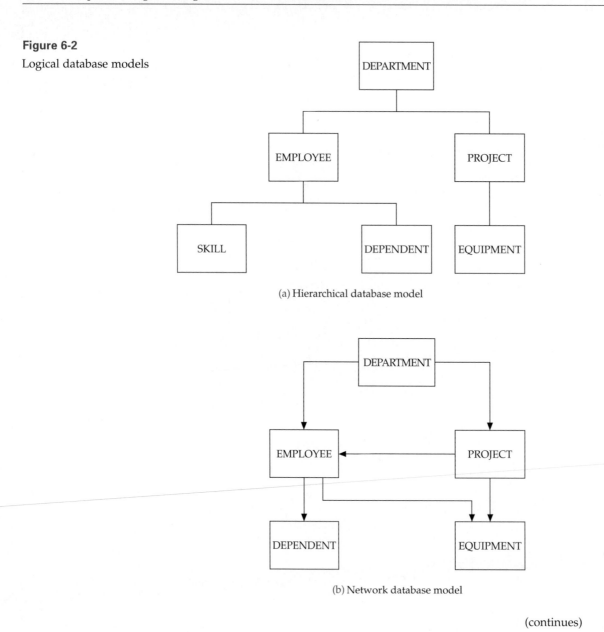

(a) Hierarchical database model

(b) Network database model

(continues)

hierarchical model. In reality, the distinctions between these two models are minimal today due to enhancements of each of the models. We describe the network model in detail in Chapter 15.

Relational Model   In the relational model, data are represented in the form of tables with rows and columns. Figure 6-2c shows two tables (or relations): DEPARTMENT and EMPLOYEE. Notice that there are no physical data structures (indicated by the lines in Figures 6-1a and 6-1b) representing associations between tables. Instead, associations are represented logically by the values that are stored within table columns. For example, in Figure 6-2c, the department number (DEPT NO.) for each employee is stored in the EMPLOYEE table. These values allow a user to link data from the two tables. We describe the relational database model in detail in this chapter.

Figure 6-2 continued

DEPARTMENT

DEPT NO.	NAME	LOCATION
D100	Engineering	West
D200	Accounting	South
D300	Marketing	East

EMPLOYEE

EMP NO.	NAME	PHONE	DEPT NO.
E10	Charles	418	D200
E20	Mary	236	D100
E30	Eldon	179	D300
E40	Paul	522	D100

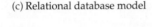

(c) Relational database model

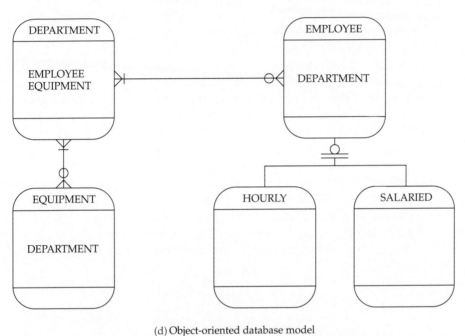

(d) Object-oriented database model

Object-Oriented Model   In the **object-oriented database model**, data attributes and methods that operate on those attributes are encapsulated in structures called *objects* (see Figure 6-2d). Objects may contain complex data types such as text, pictures, voice, or video. An object may request data or processing from another object by sending a message to that object. The object-oriented database model represents a new paradigm for storing and manipulating data, since objects may be generalized to form other, more complex objects, and may be reused in many applications. We described the object-oriented database model in detail in Chapter 5.

Object-oriented database model: A database model in which data attributes and methods that operate on those attributes are encapsulated in structures called *objects*.

Overview of Logical Database Design

Entity-relationship diagrams are the most common means of expressing conceptual data models in organizations today. Moreover, the relational model is the most commonly used data model for database implementation in organizations. The logical design process is concerned with transforming the conceptual data model (such as E-R diagrams) to a logical data model (such as relational). We describe the transformation in this chapter, with special emphasis on these two models.

Figure 6-3 presents an overview of the logical design process. Input to the process is a conceptual data model (assumed to be in the form of one or more E-R diagrams). The output of the process is a set of normalized relations (defined and illustrated later in this chapter).

Figure 6-3 shows four steps in logical design. We summarize these steps briefly here and then describe them in detail in the remainder of this chapter.

1. *Represent entities.* Each entity type in the E-R diagram is represented as a relation in the relational data model. The identifier of the entity type becomes the primary key of the relation, and other attributes of the entity type become nonkey attributes of the relation.

2. *Represent relationships.* Each relationship in an E-R diagram must be represented in the relational model. How we represent a relationship depends on its nature. For example, in some cases we represent a relationship by making the primary key of one relation a foreign key (described below) of another relation. In other cases, we create a separate relation to represent a relationship. This chapter describes each of the important variations.

3. *Normalize the relations.* The relations that are created in steps 1 and 2 may have unnecessary redundancy and may be subject to anomalies (or errors) when they are updated. Normalization is a process that refines the relations to avoid these problems. We describe normalization in detail in this chapter.

4. *Merge the relations.* In some cases, relations may have been created using separate E-R diagrams or even other types of views, such as reports or input forms. In these cases, there may be redundant relations (that is, two or more

Figure 6-3

Overview of the logical database design process

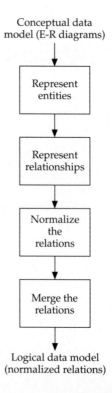

Conceptual data model (E-R diagrams)

Represent entities

Represent relationships

Normalize the relations

Merge the relations

Logical data model (normalized relations)

relations that describe the same entity type) that must be merged to remove the redundancy. We describe rules for merging relations later in the chapter.

THE RELATIONAL DATA MODEL

The relational data model was first introduced in 1970 by E. F. Codd, then of IBM (Codd, 1970), and it has continued to evolve through the efforts of Codd and numerous other researchers. Today, most organizations are implementing relational databases or at least investigating their possible use.

The **relational database model** represents data in the form of tables or relations. The relational model is based on mathematical theory, and therefore has a solid theoretical foundation. We need only a few simple concepts, however, to describe the relational model, and it is therefore easily understood and used by those unfamiliar with the underlying theory.

The relational data model consists of the following three components (Fleming and von Halle, 1989):

1. *Data structure.* Data are organized in the form of tables or relations.
2. *Data manipulation.* Powerful operations (such as those incorporated in the SQL language) are used to manipulate data stored in the relations.
3. *Data integrity.* Facilities are included to specify business rules that maintain the integrity of data when they are manipulated.

Relational database model: A data model that represents data in the form of tables or relations.

Relation: A named, two-dimensional table of data. Each relation consists of a set of named columns and an arbitrary number of unnamed rows.

Relations

A **relation** is a named, two-dimensional *table* of data. Each relation (or table) consists of a set of named *columns* and an arbitrary number of unnamed *rows*. Each column in a relation corresponds to an attribute of that relation. Each row of a relation corresponds to a record that contains data values for an entity.

Figure 6-4 shows an example of a relation named EMPLOYEE1. This relation contains the following attributes describing employees: EMPID, NAME, DEPT, and SALARY. There are five rows in the table, corresponding to five employees. It is important to understand that the sample data in Figure 6-4 are intended to illustrate the EMPLOYEE1 relation; they are not the relation itself. For example, if we add another row of data to the figure, it is still the same EMPLOYEE1 relation. Also, deleting a row does not change the relation. In fact, we could delete *all* of the rows shown in Figure 6-4, and the EMPLOYEE1 relation would still exist. Stated differently, Figure 6-4 is an *instance* of the EMPLOYEE1 relation.

We can express the *structure* of a relation by a shorthand notation in which the

Relation: A named, two-dimensional table of data. Each relation consists of a set of named columns and an arbitrary number of unnamed rows.

EMPLOYEE1

EMPID	NAME	DEPT	SALARY
100	Margaret Simpson	Marketing	42,000
140	Allen Beeton	Accounting	39,000
110	Chris Lucero	Info Systems	41,500
190	Lorenzo Davis	Finance	38,000
150	Susan Martin	Marketing	38,500

Figure 6-4

EMPLOYEE1 relation with sample data

name of the relation is followed (in parentheses) by the names of the attributes in the relation. For EMPLOYEE1 we would have

```
EMPLOYEE1(EMPID,NAME,DEPT,SALARY)
```

Properties of Relations

We have defined relations as two-dimensional tables of data; however, not all tables are relations. Relations have several properties that distinguish them from nonrelational tables. We summarize these properties in Figure 6-5, and briefly describe each property below.

Entries in Columns Are Atomic   An entry at the intersection of each row and column is *atomic* (or single-valued). There can be no multivalued attributes or repeating groups in a relation. (These terms were defined in Chapter 4.)

Notice that EMPLOYEE1 (Figure 6-4) has only single-valued entries. In Figure 6-6a, however, the employee data have been extended to include courses taken by each employee. The attributes COURSE and DATE COMPLETED form a repeating group for each employee in this table. Thus, for example, there are two courses for employee number 100. Since this table violates the property of atomic entries, it is not a relation.

In Figure 6-6b, we have eliminated the repeating groups by extending the attribute values into the previously vacant cells of Figure 6-6a. As a result, Figure 6-6b has only single-valued entries and now satisfies the atomic property of relations. The name EMPLOYEE2 is given to this relation to distinguish it from EMPLOYEE1. We will return to this relation later in the chapter.

Entries in Columns Are from the Same Domain   As we saw in Chapter 4, a *domain* is a definition of the types and ranges of values that attributes may assume. In a relation, all entries in a given column are drawn from the same domain. In the EMPLOYEE2 relation, for example, all of the values in the EMPID column must be drawn from the domain that defines employee IDs (such as three-digit integers). Also, all of the values in the DATE COMPLETED column must be drawn from the domain that defines dates.

Each Row Is Unique   No two rows in a relation are identical. Thus, in the EMPLOYEE1 relation (Figure 6-4), there cannot be two rows for the same employee. In EMPLOYEE2, there cannot be two rows for the same employee and course. This property assures that each row in the table is meaningful and that a user can easily locate the desired data.

Uniqueness in a relation is guaranteed by the designation of a primary key for each relation. A *candidate key* (defined in Chapter 4) in a relation is an attribute (or combination of attributes) that uniquely identifies a row in that relation. A

Figure 6-5

Properties of relations

> 1. Entries in columns are atomic (or single-valued).
>
> 2. Entries in columns are from the same domain.
>
> 3. Each row is unique (no duplicate rows).
>
> 4. The sequence of columns (left to right) is insignificant.
>
> 5. The sequence of rows (top to bottom) is insignificant.

EMPID	NAME	DEPT	SALARY	COURSE	DATE COMPLETED
100	Margaret Simpson	Marketing	42,000	SPSS	6/19/9X
				Surveys	10/7/9X
140	Alan Beeton	Accounting	39,000	Tax Acc	12/8/9X
110	Chris Lucero	Info Systems	41,500	SPSS	1/12/9X
				C++	4/22/9X
190	Lorenzo Davis	Finance	38,000	Investments	5/7/9X
150	Susan Martin	Marketing	38,500	SPSS	6/19/9X
				TQM	8/12/9X

(a) Table with repeating groups

EMPLOYEE2

EMPID	NAME	DEPT	SALARY	COURSE	DATE COMPLETED
100	Margaret Simpson	Marketing	42,000	SPSS	6/19/9X
100	Margaret Simpson	Marketing	42,000	Surveys	10/7/9X
140	Alan Beeton	Accounting	39,000	Tax Acc	12/8/9X
110	Chris Lucero	Info Systems	41,500	SPSS	1/12/9X
110	Chris Lucero	Info Systems	41,500	C++	4/22/9X
190	Lorenzo Davis	Finance	38,000	Investments	5/7/9X
150	Susan Martin	Marketing	38,500	SPSS	6/19/9X
150	Susan Martin	Marketing	38,500	TQM	8/12/9X

(b) EMPLOYEE2 relation

Figure 6-6

Eliminating repeating groups

primary key is a candidate key that has been selected to be the unique identifier for each row. Primary key values cannot be null (or empty), since they would then not identify a row.

There are two candidate keys for EMPLOYEE1, EMPID and NAME, although a name may not always uniquely identify an employee. If EMPID is selected, it becomes the primary key for EMPLOYEE1. There are also two candidate keys for EMPLOYEE2: the combination of EMPID and COURSE and the combination NAME and COURSE. We need a combination of attributes, since two (or more) rows may have the same values for EMPID. Assume in this relation that we select the combination of EMPID and COURSE as the primary key. We describe the rules for identifying keys below.

The Sequence of Columns (Left to Right) Is Insignificant   The columns of a relation can be interchanged without changing the meaning or use of the relation. Thus, for example, in Figure 6-4 we could make EMPID the last column in the table rather than the first. As a consequence of this property, there is no hidden meaning implied by the order in which columns occur. For example, the first column of a table may or may not be the primary key attribute. Another consequence is that columns of a table can be stored in an arbitrary sequence, and users can also retrieve columns in any sequence. A final consequence is that columns must be referenced by name and not by position within the table, since position is not significant.

The Sequence of Rows (Top to Bottom) Is Insignificant   As with columns, the rows of a relation may be interchanged or stored in any sequence. Users may view the rows of a relation in different logical sequences. For example, if we want to insert a new row in the EMPLOYEE2 table (Figure 6-6b), it is immaterial whether we insert it at the beginning, at the end, or in the middle of the table.

Well-Structured Relations

Well-structured relation: A relation that contains a minimum amount of redundancy and allows users to insert, modify, and delete the rows in a table without errors or inconsistencies.

To prepare for our discussion of normalization, we need to address the following question: What constitutes a well-structured relation? Intuitively, a **well-structured relation** contains a minimum amount of redundancy and allows users to insert, modify, and delete the rows in a table without errors or inconsistencies. EMPLOYEE1 (Figure 6-4) is such a relation. Each row of the table contains data describing one employee, and any modification to an employee's data (such as a change in salary) is confined to one row of the table.

In contrast, EMPLOYEE2 (Figure 6-6b) is not a well-structured relation. If you examine the sample data in the table, you will notice a considerable amount of redundancy. For example, the EMPID, NAME, DEPT, and SALARY appear in two separate rows for employees 100, 110, and 150. Consequently, if the salary for employee 100 changes, we must record this fact in two rows (or more, for some employees).

Anomalies: Errors or inconsistencies that may result when a user attempts to update a table that contains redundant data. There are three types of anomalies: insertion, deletion, and modification anomalies.

Redundancies in a table may result in errors or inconsistencies (called **anomalies**) when a user attempts to update the data in the table. Three types of anomalies are possible: insertion, deletion, and modification.

1. *Insertion anomaly.* Suppose that we need to add a new employee to EMPLOYEE2. The primary key for this relation is the combination of EMPID and COURSE (as noted earlier). Therefore, to insert a new row, the user must supply values for both EMPID and COURSE (since primary key values cannot be null or nonexistent). This is an anomaly, since the user should be able to enter employee data without supplying course data.

2. *Deletion anomaly.* Suppose that the data for employee number 140 is deleted from the table. This will result in losing the information that this employee completed a course (Tax Acc) on 12/8/9x. In fact, it results in losing the information that this course had an offering that completed on that date.

3. *Modification anomaly.* Suppose that employee number 100 gets a salary increase. We must record the increase in each of the rows for that employee (two occurrences in Figure 6-6b); otherwise the data will be inconsistent.

These anomalies indicate that EMPLOYEE2 is not a well-structured relation. The problem with this relation is that it contains data about two entities: EMPLOYEE and COURSE. We will use normalization theory (described below) to divide EMPLOYEE2 into two relations. One of the resulting relations is EMPLOYEE1 (Figure 6-4). The other we will call EMP COURSE, which appears with sample data in Figure 6-7. The primary key of this relation is the combination of EMPID and COURSE, and we underline these attribute names in Figure 6-7 to highlight this fact. Examine Figure 6-7 to verify that EMP COURSE is free of the types of anomalies described above and is therefore well-structured.

Figure 6-7

EMP COURSE relation

EMP COURSE

EMPID	COURSE	DATE COMPLETED
100	SPSS	6/19/9X
100	Surveys	10/7/9X
140	Tax Acc	12/8/9X
110	SPSS	1/12/9X
110	C++	4/22/9X
190	Investments	5/7/9X
150	SPSS	6/19/9X
150	TQM	8/12/9X

CONCEPTS OF NORMALIZATION

We have presented an intuitive discussion of well-structured relations; however, we need formal definitions of such relations, together with a process for designing them. **Normalization** is a process for converting complex data structures into simple, stable data structures. For example, we used the principles of normalization to convert the EMPLOYEE2 table (with its redundancy) to EMPLOYEE1 (Figure 6-4) and EMP COURSE (Figure 6-7).

Normalization: The process of converting complex data structures into simple, stable data structures.

Steps in Normalization

Normalization is often accomplished in stages, each of which corresponds to a normal form (see Figure 6-8). A **normal form** is a state of a relation that can be determined by applying simple rules regarding dependencies (or relationships between attributes) to that relation. We describe these rules briefly in this section and illustrate them in detail in the following sections.

Normal form: A state of a relation that can be determined by applying simple rules regarding dependencies to that relation.

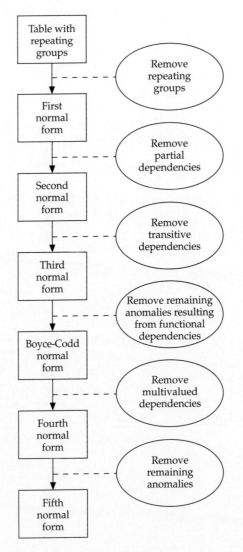

Figure 6-8

Steps in normalization

1. *First normal form (1NF)*. Any repeating groups have been removed, so there is a single value at the intersection of each row and column of the table (as in Figure 6-6b).

2. *Second normal form (2NF)*. Any partial functional dependencies have been removed.

3. *Third normal form (3NF)*. Any transitive dependencies have been removed.

4. *Boyce-Codd normal form (4NF)*. Any remaining anomalies that result from functional dependencies have been removed.

5. *Fourth normal form (4NF)*. Any multivalued dependencies have been removed.

6. *Fifth normal form (5NF)*. Any remaining anomalies have been removed.

Functional Dependence and Keys

Functional dependency: A particular relationship between two attributes. For any relation R, attribute B is functionally dependent on attribute A if, for every valid instance of A, that value of A uniquely determines the value of B. The functional dependence of B on A is represented as A→B.

Normalization is based on the analysis of functional dependence. A **functional dependency** is a particular relationship between two attributes. For any relation R, attribute B is *functionally dependent* on attribute A if, for every valid instance of A, that value of A uniquely determines the value of B (Dutka and Hanson, 1989). The functional dependence of B on A is represented by an arrow, as follows: A→B.

An attribute may be functionally dependent on two (or more) attributes, rather than on a single attribute. For example, consider the relation EMP COURSE (<u>EMPID,COURSE</u>,DATE COMPLETED) shown in Figure 6-7. We represent the functional dependency in this relation as follows: EMPID,COURSE→DATE COMPLETED.

Common examples of functional dependencies are the following:

1. SSN→NAME,ADDRESS,BIRTHDATE: A person's name, address, and birthdate are functionally dependent on that person's Social Security number.

2. VIN→MAKE,MODEL,COLOR: The make, model, and color of a vehicle are functionally dependent on the vehicle identification number.

3. ISBN→TITLE: The title of a book is functionally dependent on the book's international standard book number (ISBN).

Determinant: The attribute on the left-hand side of the arrow in a functional dependency; a is a determinant in the following functional dependency: A→B.

The attribute on the left-hand side of the arrow in a functional dependency is called a **determinant**. SSN, VIN, and ISBN are determinants (respectively) in the above three examples. In the EMP COURSE relation, the combination of EMPID and COURSE is a determinant.

You should be aware that the instances (or sample data) in a relation do not prove that a functional dependency exists. Only knowledge of the problem domain is a reliable method for identifying a functional dependency. However, we can use sample data to demonstrate that a functional dependency does *not* exist between two (or more) attributes. For example, consider the sample data in the relation EXAMPLE(A,B,C,D), shown in Figure 6-9. The sample data in this relation

Figure 6-9

EXAMPLE relation

EXAMPLE

A	B	C	D
X	U	X	Y
Y	X	Z	X
Z	Y	Y	Y
Y	Z	W	Z

STUDENT

STUDENT ID	STUDENT NAME	CAMPUS ADDRESS	MAJOR
268300458	Williams	208 Brooks	IS
543291073	Baker	104 Phillips	Acctg
. . .			

(3NF)

COURSE INSTRUCTOR

COURSE ID	COURSE TITLE	INSTRUCTOR NAME	INSTRUCTOR LOCATION
IS 350	Database Mgt	Codd	B 104
IS 465	Systems Analysis	Parsons	B 317
IS 350	Database Mgt	Codd	B 104
Acctg 201	Fund Acctg	Miller	H 310
Mktg 300	Intro Mktg	Bennett	B 212
. . .			

(2NF)

REGISTRATION

STUDENT ID	COURSE ID	GRADE
268300458	IS 350	A
268300458	IS 465	B
543291073	IS 350	C
543291073	Acctg 201	B
543291073	Mktg 300	A
. . .		

(3NF)

2. *Deletion anomaly.* Suppose we decide to delete the course Acctg 201 from the table. If there is only one row for Acctg 201, we may lose the information that the instructor Miller is located in H310.

Identify at least one example of an insertion anomaly in COURSE INSTRUCTOR.

The anomalies in the COURSE INSTRUCTOR relation exist because data concerning the entity INSTRUCTOR are "hidden" within COURSE INSTRUCTOR. The functional dependencies in this relation are the following:

1. COURSE ID→COURSE TITLE,INSTRUCTOR NAME, INSTRUCTOR LOCATION

2. INSTRUCTOR NAME→INSTRUCTOR LOCATION

Since INSTRUCTOR LOCATION is functionally dependent on INSTRUCTOR NAME (a nonkey attribute), this relation is an example of a transitive dependency. Therefore, we conclude that COURSE INSTRUCTOR is not yet in third normal form. To remove the transitive dependency from COURSE INSTRUCTOR, we divide it into the two relations shown in Figure 6-18: COURSE and INSTRUCTOR. COURSE contains the following attributes: COURSE ID (key), COURSE TITLE,

Figure 6-18

Relations obtained from
COURSE INSTRUCTOR

COURSE

COURSE ID	COURSE TITLE	INSTRUCTOR NAME
IS 350	Database Mgt	Codd
IS 465	Systems Analysis	Parsons
Acctg 201	Fund Acctg	Miller
Mktg 300	Intro Mktg	Bennett
. . .		

(3NF)

INSTRUCTOR

INSTRUCTOR NAME	INSTRUCTOR LOCATION
Codd	B 104
Parsons	B 317
Miller	H 310
Bennett	B 212
. . .	

(3NF)

and INSTRUCTOR NAME. INSTRUCTOR contains two attributes: INSTRUCTOR NAME (key) and INSTRUCTOR LOCATION. Thus the attribute INSTRUCTOR NAME becomes the primary key in the new INSTRUCTOR relation, and a foreign key in the new COURSE relation.

The normalization process is now completed. We transformed the Grade Report user view (Figure 6-13) through a series of simple steps to a set of four relations in third normal form. The 3NF relations are summarized in Figure 6-19, both in tabular form and in shorthand notation. These 3NF relations are free of the anomalies described earlier. Since each entity is described in a separate relation, we can easily insert or delete data concerning that entity without reference to other entities. Also, updates to the data for a particular entity are easy to accomplish, since changes are confined to a single row within a relation.

In the process of normalizing Grade Report, no information is lost from the original user view. In fact, the Grade Report in Figure 6-13 can be re-created by combining the data from the 3NF relations in Figure 6-19.

Normalizing Summary Data

Databases to support management control and strategic levels of an organization often contain subsets and summaries of data from operational databases. These "information bases" used to support higher levels of management also need to be normalized to avoid all the same anomalies found in operational databases.

Consider the Grade Report database of Figure 6-19. Deans, degree program heads, and department chairs may be concerned only with grade summaries by department or major. For example, one report view for summarized data of grades by major would be represented by:

```
MAJOR GRADES(MAJOR,NO. STUDENTS,AVG GPA)
```

Figure 6-19

Summary of 3NF
relations from GRADE
REPORT

STUDENT ID	STUDENT NAME	CAMPUS ADDRESS	MAJOR
268300458	Williams	208 Brooks	IS
543291073	Baker	104 Phillips	Acctg
. . .			

STUDENT (<u>STUDENT ID</u>, STUDENT NAME, CAMPUS ADDRESS, MAJOR)

COURSE ID	COURSE TITLE	INSTRUCTOR NAME
IS 350	Database Mgt	Codd
IS 465	Systems Analysis	Parsons
Acctg 201	Fund Acctg	Miller
Mktg 300	Intro Mktg	Bennett
. . .		

COURSE (<u>COURSE ID</u>, COURSE TITLE, <u>INSTRUCTOR NAME</u>)

INSTRUCTOR NAME	INSTRUCTOR LOCATION
Codd	B 104
Parsons	B 317
Miller	H 310
Bennett	B 212
. . .	

INSTRUCTOR (<u>INSTRUCTOR NAME</u>, INSTRUCTOR LOCATION)

STUDENT ID	COURSE ID	GRADE
268300458	IS 350	A
268300458	IS 465	B
543291073	IS 350	C
543291073	Acctg 201	B
543291073	Mktg 300	A
. . .		

REGISTRATION (<u>STUDENT ID</u>, <u>COURSE ID</u>, GRADE)

Here, NO. STUDENTS is the number of students in a given major, and AVG GPA is the average grade point for students in a given major. This relation is in 3NF. Note that AVG GPA, although *mathematically* related to NO. STUDENTS, is *functionally dependent* only on MAJOR.

We can derive the MAJOR GRADES table from the STUDENT and REGISTRATION tables of Figure 6-19. Whether MAJOR GRADES is a view on an operational database or an independent table for an information base is a decision to be made later during physical design. This decision will be based on such factors as time to derive MAJOR GRADES and response time required when MAJOR GRADES is requested, cost of data storage for this table, and costs to keep MAJOR GRADES contents consistent with operational data from which it is derived (for integrity).

At the requirements definition and logical design stages, a database designer should determine normalized relations for user views where possible, even of summarized data. Thus, MAJOR GRADES would be added as another table to the Grade Report database, and the designer should note how NO. STUDENTS and AVG GPA are derived from data in other tables.

New data elements may also appear in summary tables. For example, MAJOR GRADES might also include data on the home department and its head or chairperson for each major, which would be represented by:

MAJOR GRADES(<u>MAJOR</u>,DEPT,HEAD,NO. STUDENTS,AVG GPA)

Since it is very likely that each department has only one head (therefore, HEAD is functionally dependent on DEPT), MAJOR GRADES is not in 3NF (but is in 2NF). MAJOR GRADES can be put into 3NF as follows:

```
MAJOR GRADES(MAJOR,DEPT,NO. STUDENTS,AVG GPA)
DEPARTMENT (DEPT,HEAD)
```

Since information bases are frequently designed after operational databases are implemented (especially if databases are *not* planned as described in Chapter 3), a database analyst must be careful to clearly identify derived data and recognize the associated operational data source. If this is not done, the result can be unplanned redundancy and inconsistency within the database.

ADDITIONAL NORMAL FORMS

Relations in third normal form are sufficient for most practical database applications. However, 3NF does not guarantee that all anomalies have been removed. As Figure 6-8 shows, there are several additional normal forms that are designed to remove these anomalies: Boyce-Codd normal form, fourth normal form, and fifth normal form. We describe each of these normal forms (as well as domain-key normal form) in this section.

Boyce-Codd Normal Form

When a relation has more than one candidate key, anomalies may result even though the relation is in 3NF. For example, consider the ST MAJ ADV relation shown in Figure 6-20. The semantic rules for this relation follow:

1. Each student may major in several subjects.
2. For each major, a given student has only one advisor.
3. Each major has several advisors.
4. Each advisor advises only one major.
5. Each advisor advises several students in one major.

From this information, we note that there are two functional dependencies in this relation:

```
STUDENT ID,MAJOR→ADVISOR
ADVISOR→MAJOR
```

Figure 6-20

ST MAJ ADV relation

ST MAJ ADV

STUDENT ID	MAJOR	ADVISOR
123	Physics	Einstein
123	Music	Mozart
456	Biol	Darwin
789	Physics	Bohr
999	Physics	Einstein

In this relation, no single attribute is a candidate key; that is, no single attribute is a determinant for the remaining two attributes. The combination (STUDENT ID,MAJOR) is one candidate key, since ADVISOR is functionally dependent on this key. Applying the augmentation rule of functional dependencies (Figure 6-10) to the second functional dependency above gives STUDENT ID,ADVISOR→ MAJOR. Therefore, the combination STUDENT ID,ADVISOR is also a candidate key for relation ST MAJ ADV.

In Figure 6-20, we have arbitrarily selected (STUDENT ID,MAJOR) as the primary key for the relation ST MAJ ADV. (STUDENT ID,ADVISOR) would serve equally well. Therefore, we represent the relation as follows:

`ST MAJ ADV(STUDENT ID,MAJOR,ADVISOR)`

The relation ST MAJ ADV is clearly in 3NF, since there are no partial functional dependencies and no transitive dependencies; nevertheless, there are still anomalies in the relation. For example, suppose that student number 456 changes her major from Biology to Math. When the row for this student is updated, we lose the fact that Darwin advises in Biology (modification anomaly). Also, suppose we want to insert a row with the information that Babbage advises in Computer Science. This, of course, cannot be done until at least one student majoring in Computer Science is assigned Babbage as an advisor (insertion anomaly). Finally, if student number 456 withdraws from school, we lose the information that Darwin advises in Biology (deletion anomaly).

The type of anomalies that exist in this relation can only occur when there are two (or more) overlapping candidate keys. For example, as we have noted, there are two candidate keys in ST MAJ ADV: (STUDENT ID,ADVISOR) and (STUDENT ID,MAJOR). These candidate keys overlap (since they share STUDENT ID). This situation is relatively rare, but it can occur, as shown in this relation.

R. F. Boyce and E. F. Codd identified this deficiency and proposed a stronger definition of 3NF that remedies the problem. Their definition relies on the use of determinants (defined earlier). We say a relation is in **Boyce-Codd normal form (BCNF)** if and only if every determinant is a candidate key. Applying this rule to ST MAJ ADV, we see that this relation is *not* in BCNF (even though it is in 3NF). The relation is not in BCNF because although ADVISOR is a determinant, it is not a candidate key (since each advisor advises several students).

We can convert the ST MAJ ADV relation into BCNF by dividing it into two relations. The attribute that is a determinant but not a candidate key (in this case, ADVISOR) must be placed in a separate relation and must be the key of that relation. The following two relations result (see Figure 6-21):

1. ST ADV(STUDENT ID,ADVISOR)

2. ADV MAJ(ADVISOR,MAJOR)

> **Boyce-Codd normal form (BCNF):** A relation in which every determinant is a candidate key.

ST ADV

STUDENT ID	ADVISOR
123	Einstein
123	Mozart
456	Darwin
789	Bohr
999	Einstein

ADV MAJ

ADVISOR	MAJOR
Einstein	Physics
Mozart	Music
Darwin	Biol
Bohr	Physics

Figure 6-21

Relations in BCNF

These two relations are in Boyce-Codd normal form and are free of the types of anomalies associated with ST MAJ ADV. Verify that these statements are true. The ST MAJ ADV relation can be re-created by joining the two relations shown in Figure 6-21.

Fourth Normal Form

When a relation is in BCNF, there are no longer any anomalies that result from functional dependencies. However, there may still be anomalies that result from multivalued dependencies (defined below). For example, consider the table shown in Figure 6-22a. This user view shows for each course the instructors who teach that course and the textbooks that are used (these appear as repeating groups in the table). In this relation the following assumptions hold:

1. Each course may have several instructors.
2. Each course uses several textbooks.
3. The text that is used for a given course is independent of the instructor.

In Figure 6-22b, this table has been converted to a relation (named OFFERING), which is in first normal form. Thus, for each course, all possible combinations of instructor and text appear in the resulting table. Notice that the primary key of this relation consists of all three attributes (COURSE, INSTRUCTOR, and TEXT-BOOK). Since there are no determinants (other than the primary key itself), the relation is actually in BCNF. Yet, it does contain much redundant data, which, in turn, can easily lead to update anomalies. For example, suppose that we want to add a third textbook (author: Middleton) to the Management course. This change would require the addition of *three* new rows to the table in Figure 6-22b, one for each Instructor (otherwise that text would apply only to certain instructors).

The type of dependency shown in this example is called a **multivalued dependency**, which exists when there are at least three attributes (for example, A, B, and C) in a relation, and for each value of A there is a well-defined set of values of B and a well-defined set of values of C. However, the set of values of B is independent of set C, and vice versa.

To remove the multivalued dependency from a relation, we divide the relation into two independent attributes. Figure 6-23 shows the result of this division for the OFFERING relation of Figure 6-22b. Notice that the relation called TEACHER

> **Multivalued dependency:**
> A type of dependency that exists when there are at least three attributes (for example, A, B, and C) in a relation, and for each value of A there is a well-defined set of values for B and a well-defined set of values for C, but the set of values of B is independent of set C.

Figure 6-22

Table with multivalued dependencies

OFFERING

COURSE	INSTRUCTOR	TEXTBOOK
Management	White	Drucker
	Green	Peters
	Black	
Finance	Gray	Weston
		Gilford

(a) Table

OFFERING

COURSE	INSTRUCTOR	TEXTBOOK
Management	White	Drucker
Management	Green	Drucker
Management	Black	Drucker
Management	White	Peters
Management	Green	Peters
Management	Black	Peters
Finance	Gray	Weston
Finance	Gray	Gilford

(b) Relation

TEACHER	
COURSE	INSTRUCTOR
Management	White
Management	Green
Management	Black
Finance	Gray

TEXT	
COURSE	TEXTBOOK
Management	Drucker
Management	Peters
Finance	Weston
Finance	Gilford

Figure 6-23

Relations in fourth normal form (4NF)

contains the INSTRUCTOR attribute, while TEXT contains the TEXTBOOK attribute (these two attributes are independent of each other in Figure 6-22b). A relation is in **fourth normal form (4NF)** if it is in BCNF and contains no multivalued dependencies. You can easily verify that the two relations in Figure 6-23 are 4NF, and you could easily reconstruct the original relation (OFFERING) by joining these two relations.

> **Fourth normal form (4nf):** A relation is in fourth normal form if it is in BCNF and contains no multivalued dependencies.

Fifth Normal Form (5NF)

Fifth normal form is designed to cope with a type of dependency known as a **join dependency.** When a relation has a join dependency, it cannot be divided into two (or more) relations such that the resulting tables can be recombined to form the original table. For example, throughout the discussion of normalization in this chapter, we have repeatedly used the technique of dividing a relation that has two (or more) smaller relations, in order to eliminate anomalies. In each of the examples, since there were no join dependencies present, it was possible to re-create the original tables. However, it is possible to create examples of relations with join dependencies where the original table cannot be re-created without spurious results.

> **Join dependency:** A relation that has a join dependency cannot be divided into two (or more) relations such that the resulting tables can be recombined to form the original table.

Fifth normal form (5NF) provides a definition for removing join dependencies if they exist and can be described. Yet, according to Date (1981), ''It is tempting to suggest that such relations are pathological cases and are likely to be rare in practice.'' For this reason we do not provide an example of 5NF.

> **Fifth normal form (5NF):** A relation is in fifth normal form if it is in fourth normal form and does not have a join dependency.

Domain-Key Normal Form (DK/NF)

Fagin (1981) has proposed a conceptually simple normal form called **domain-key normal form (DK/NF).** According to this definition, a relation is in DK/NF if and only if every constraint on the relation is a logical consequence of key constraints and domain constraints. Fagin shows that any relation that is in DK/NF is automatically in 5NF, 4NF, and so on. Fagin's definition is an important contribution, since it provides an all-encompassing definition of the various normal forms. Unfortunately, the definition does not provide a methodology for converting a given relation to DK/NF. Thus, we do not pursue the definition of DK/NF in this text.

> **Domain-key normal form (DK/NF):** A relation is in domain-key normal form if and only if every constraint on the relation is a logical consequence of key constraints and domain constraints.

TRANSFORMING E-R DIAGRAMS TO RELATIONS

Our discussion of normalization set the stage for a discussion of the logical design process. An overview of this process was shown in Figure 6-3. In this section we describe how to transform E-R diagrams to relations. As Figure 6-3 shows, this transformation consists of two steps: represent entities, and then represent relationships. The relations that result from this transformation can then be normalized (as necessary) using the techniques described in the previous sections.

Represent Entities

Each entity type in an E-R diagram is transformed into a relation. The primary key (or identifier) of the entity type becomes the primary key of the corresponding relation. You should check to make sure that this key satisfies the following two properties of a candidate key for a relation described earlier:

1. The value of the key must uniquely identify every row in the relation.
2. The key should be nonredundant; that is, no attribute in the key can be deleted without destroying its unique identification.

Each nonkey attribute (or descriptor) of the entity type becomes a nonkey attribute of the relation. The relations that are formed from entity types may be modified as relationships are represented, as described in the next section.

Figure 6-24a shows a representation of the CUSTOMER entity type for Pine Valley Furniture Company. The corresponding CUSTOMER relation is represented as follows:

CUSTOMER(<u>CUSTOMER NO.</u>,NAME,ADDRESS,CITY STATE ZIP,DISCOUNT)

This relation is represented as a table with sample data in Figure 6-24b.

Represent Relationships

The procedure for representing relationships depends on both the degree of the relationship (unary, binary, ternary) and the cardinalities of the relationship. We describe and illustrate the important cases in the following discussion.

Figure 6-24

Transforming an entity type to a relation

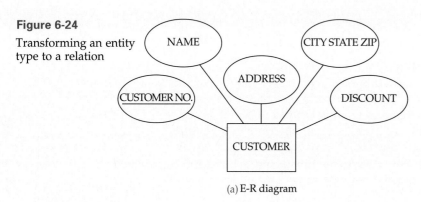

(a) E-R diagram

CUSTOMER

<u>CUSTOMER NO.</u>	NAME	ADDRESS	CITY STATE ZIP	DISCOUNT
1273	Contemporary Designs	123 Oak St.	Austin, TX 38405	5%
6390	Casual Corner	18 Hoosier Dr.	Bloomington, IN 45821	3%
. . .				

(b) Relation

Binary 1:N Relationship   A binary one-to-many (1:*N*) relationship in an E-R diagram is represented by adding the primary key attribute (or attributes) of the entity on the one-side of the relationship, as a foreign key in the relation that is on the many-side of the relationship.

Figure 6-25 shows an example of this rule. Figure 6-25a shows the Places relationship (1:*N*) linking CUSTOMER and ORDER at Pine Valley Furniture Company. Two relations, CUSTOMER and ORDER, were formed from the respective entity types. CUSTOMER NO., which is the primary key of CUSTOMER (on the one-side of the relationship) is added as a foreign key to ORDER (on the many-side of the relationship).

Figure 6-25

Representing a (1:*N*) relationship

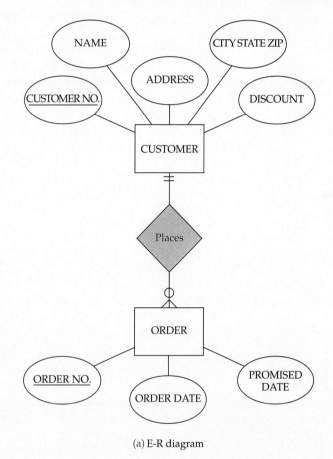

(a) E-R diagram

CUSTOMER

CUSTOMER NO.	NAME	ADDRESS	CITY STATE ZIP	DISCOUNT
1273	Contemporary Designs	123 Oak St.	Austin, TX 38405	5%
6390	Casual Corner	18 Hoosier Dr.	Bloomington, IN 45821	3%
. . .				

ORDER

ORDER NO.	ORDER DATE	PROMISED DATE	CUSTOMER NO.
57194	3/15/9X	3/28/9X	6390
63725	3/17/9X	4/01/9X	1273
80149	3/14/9X	3/24/9X	6390

(b) Relations

A special case of the above rule applies for a binary one-to-one (1:1) relationship between two entities A and B. In this case, the relationship can be represented by:

1. Adding the primary key of A as a foreign key of B.
2. Adding the primary key of B as a foreign key of A.
3. Both of the above (Storey, 1991).

Binary *M:N* Relationship   Suppose that there is a binary many-to-many (*M:N*) relationship between two entity types A and B. For such a relationship, we create a separate relation C. The primary key of this relation is a composite key consisting of the primary key for each of the two entities in the relationship. Any nonkey attributes that are associated with the M:N relationship are included with the relation C.

Figure 6-26 shows an example of this rule. Figure 6-26a shows the Requests relationship (*M:N*) between the entity types ORDER and PRODUCT for Pine Valley Furniture Company. Figure 6-26b shows the three relations (ORDER, PRODUCT, and ORDER LINE) that are formed from the entity types and the Requests relationship. First, a relation is created for each of the two entity types in the relationship (ORDER and PRODUCT). Then a relation (called ORDER LINE in Figure 6-26b) is created for the Requests relationship. The primary key of ORDER LINE is the combination (ORDER NO.,PRODUCT NO.), which are the respective primary keys of ORDER and PRODUCT. The nonkey attribute QUANTITY ORDERED also appears in ORDER LINE.

Figure 6-26

Representing an (*M:N*) relationship

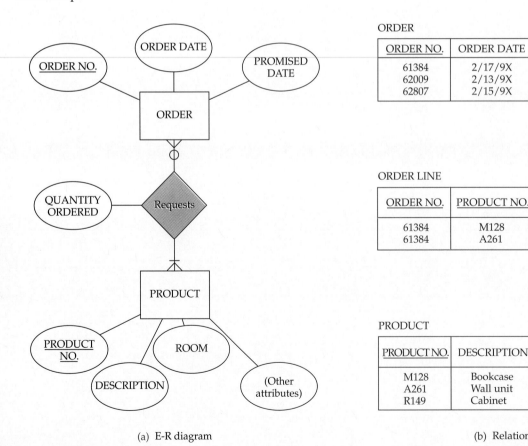

(a) E-R diagram

ORDER

ORDER NO.	ORDER DATE	PROMISED DATE
61384	2/17/9X	3/01/9X
62009	2/13/9X	2/27/9X
62807	2/15/9X	3/01/9X

ORDER LINE

ORDER NO.	PRODUCT NO.	QUANTITY ORDERED
61384	M128	2
61384	A261	1

PRODUCT

PRODUCT NO.	DESCRIPTION	(OTHER ATTRIBUTES)
M128	Bookcase	- - -
A261	Wall unit	- - -
R149	Cabinet	- - -

(b) Relations

Occasionally, the relation created from an *M:N* relationship requires a primary key that includes more than just the primary keys from the two related relations. Consider, for example, the following situation:

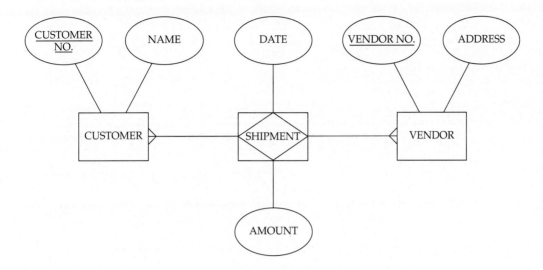

In this case, DATE must be part of the key for the SHIPMENT relation to uniquely distinguish each row of the SHIPMENT table, as follows:

```
SHIPMENT(CUSTOMER NO.,VENDOR NO.,DATE,AMOUNT)
```

In some cases, there may be an *n*-ary relationship among three or more entities. In such cases, we create a separate relation that has as a primary key the composite of the primary keys of each of the participating entities (plus any necessary additional key elements). This rule is a simple generalization of the rule for a binary *M:N* relationship.

Unary Relationships In Chapter 4, we defined a *unary* relationship as a relationship between the instances of a single entity type, which are also called *recursive relationships*. Figure 6-27 shows two common examples. Figure 6-27a shows a one-to-many relationship named Manages that associates employees of an organization with another employee who is their manager. Figure 6-27b shows a many-to-many relationship that associates certain items with their component items. This relationship (which was introduced in Chapter 4) is called a *bill-of-materials structure*.

For a unary 1:*N* relationship, the entity type (such as EMPLOYEE) is modeled as a relation. The primary key of that relation is the same as for the entity type. Then a foreign key is added to the relation that references the primary key values. A **recursive foreign key** is a foreign key in a relation that references the primary key values of that same relation. We can represent the relationship in Figure 6-27a as follows:

Recursive foreign key: A foreign key in a relation that references the primary key values of that same relation.

```
EMPLOYEE(EMP ID,NAME,BIRTHDATE,MANAGER ID)
```

In this relation, MANAGER ID is a recursive foreign key that takes its values from the same domain of worker identification numbers as EMP ID. We could easily query the above relation to identify employees who work for a particular

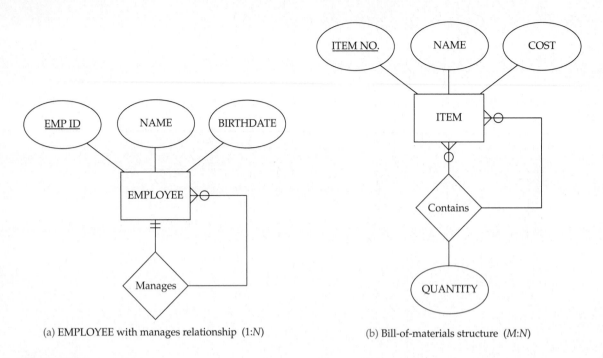

(a) EMPLOYEE with manages relationship (1:N)   (b) Bill-of-materials structure (M:N)

Figure 6-27

Two unary relationships

manager. For example, the following SQL command will display a list of employees who work for the manager with EMP ID = 500:

```
SELECT EMP_ID,NAME
FROM EMPLOYEE
WHERE MANAGER_ID=500;
```

For a unary *M:N* relationship, we model the entity type as one relation. Then we create a separate relation to represent the *M:N* relationship. The primary key of this new relation is a composite key that consists of two attributes. These attributes (which need not have the same name) both take their values from the same primary key domain. Any attribute associated with the relationship (such as QUANTITY in Figure 6-27b) is included as a nonkey attribute in this new relation. We can express the result for Figure 6-27b as follows:

```
ITEM(ITEM-NO.,NAME,COST)
ITEM BILL(ITEM NO.,COMPONENT NO.,QUANTITY)
```

We can easily manipulate the above relations (for example) to determine the components of an item. The following SQL query will list the immediate components (and their quantity) of the item with ITEM NO. = 100:

```
SELECT COMPONENT_NO,QUANTITY
FROM ITEM_BILL
WHERE ITEM_NO=100;
```

ISA Relationships (Class/Subclass)   The relational data model does not directly support class/subclass (or ISA) relationships. Fortunately, there are various strategies that database designers can use to represent ISA relationships using relations (Chouinard, 1989). For our purposes we use the following strategy:

1. Create a separate relation for the class and for each of the subclasses.

2. The table (relation) for the class consists only of the attributes that are common to all of the subclasses.

3. The table for each subclass contains only its primary key and the columns unique to that subclass.

4. The primary keys of the class and each of the subclasses are from the same domain.

An ISA relationship (with two subclasses) appears in the E-R diagram for Vacation Property Rentals (see Figure 4-17b). This relationship is repeated in Figure 6-28a, and the relations that are derived by applying the above rules are shown in Figure 6-28b. Notice that there are three relations: PROPERTY, BEACH, and MOUNTAIN. The primary key of each of these relations is the composite key (STREET ADDRESS,CITY STATE ZIP). Although the primary key of a subclass does not have to have the same name as the primary key of the class (as in this example), they must be from the same domain.

The PROPERTY relation contains those descriptors (or nonkey attributes) that are common to both subclasses: NO. ROOMS and TYPICAL RENT. The relations

Figure 6-28

Representing ISA relationships

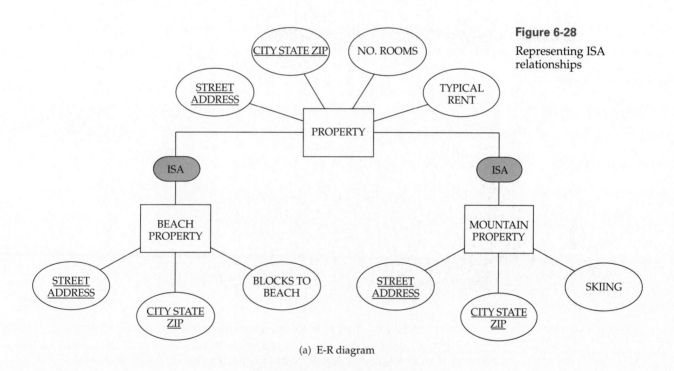

(a) E-R diagram

PROPERTY

STREET ADDRESS	CITY STATE ZIP	NO. ROOMS	TYPICAL RENT
120 Surf Dr.	Honolulu, HI 99987	3	500
100 Mogul Dr.	Jackson, WY 89204	3	250

BEACH

STREET ADDRESS	CITY STATE ZIP	BLOCKS TO BEACH
120 Surf Dr.	Honolulu, HI 99987	2

MOUNTAIN

STREET ADDRESS	CITY STATE ZIP	SKIING
100 Mogul Dr.	Jackson, WY 89204	N

(b) Relations

BEACH and MOUNTAIN (representing the subclasses) have the same primary key as PROPERTY. Each relation contains an attribute, however, that is unique to the subclass (BLOCKS TO BEACH for BEACH, SKIING for MOUNTAIN). We can form a subclass with its inherited attributes by joining the subclass relation with the class relation.

Several other strategies are available for representing ISA relationships with the relational model. Each strategy offers advantages and disadvantages in terms of performance, referential integrity, ease of retrieval, and other factors. For an extended discussion, see Chouinard, 1989, and Storey, 1991.

MERGING RELATIONS

In the previous section, we described how to transform E-R diagrams to relations. We should then check the resulting relations to determine whether they are in third (or higher) normal form, and perform normalization steps if necessary.

As part of the logical design process, normalized relations may have been created from a number of separate E-R diagrams and (possibly) other user views. Some of the relations may be redundant; that is, they may refer to the same entities. If so, we should merge those relations to remove the redundancy. This section describes merging relations (also called *view integration*), which is the last step of the logical design process in Figure 6-3.

An Example

Suppose that modeling a user view results in the following 3NF relation:

    EMPLOYEE1(EMPLOYEE NO.,NAME,ADDRESS,PHONE)

Modeling a second user view might result in the following relation:

    EMPLOYEE2(EMPLOYEE NO.,NAME,ADDRESS,JOBCODE,NO. YEARS)

Since these two relations have the same primary key (EMPLOYEE NO.), they describe the same entity and may be merged into one relation. The result of merging the relations is the following relation:

    EMPLOYEE(EMPLOYEE NO.,NAME,ADDRESS,PHONE,JOBCODE,NO. YEARS)

Notice that an attribute that appears in both relations (such as NAME in this example) appears only once in the merged relation.

View Integration Problems

When integrating relations as in the above example, the database analyst must understand the meaning of the data and must be prepared to resolve any problems that may arise in that process. In this section we describe and briefly illustrate four problems that arise in view integration: *synonyms, homonyms, transitive dependencies,* and *class/subclass relations.*

Synonyms   In some situations, two (or more) attributes may have different names but the same meaning, as when they describe the same characteristic of an entity. Such attributes are called *synonyms* (defined in Chapter 1). For example, EMPLOYEE ID and EMPLOYEE NO. may be synonyms.

When merging the relations that contain synonyms, you should obtain agreement (if possible) from users on a single, standardized name for the attribute and eliminate the other synonym. (Another alternative is to choose a third name to replace the synonyms.) For example, consider the following relations:

```
STUDENT1(STUDENT ID,NAME)
STUDENT2(MATRICULATION NO.,NAME,ADDRESS)
```

In this case, the analyst recognizes that both the STUDENT ID and MATRICULATION NO. are synonyms for a person's Social Security number and are identical attributes. One possible resolution would be to standardize on one of the two attribute names, such as STUDENT ID. Another option is to use a new attribute name, such as SSN, to replace both synonyms. Assuming the latter approach, merging the two relations would produce the following result:

```
STUDENT(SSN,NAME,ADDRESS)
```

Often when there are synonyms, there is a need to allow some database users to refer to the same data by different names. Users may need to use familiar names that are consistent with terminology in their part of the organization. An **alias** is an alternative name used for an attribute. Many database management systems allow the definition of an alias that may be used interchangeably with the primary attribute label.

Alias: An alternative name given an attribute.

Homonyms   In other situations, a single attribute, called a *homonym* (defined in Chapter 1), may have more than one meaning or describe more than one characteristic. For example, the term *account* might refer to a bank's checking account, savings account, loan account, or other type of account (therefore, *account* refers to different data, depending on how it is used).

You should be on the lookout for homonyms when merging relations. Consider the following example:

```
STUDENT1(STUDENT ID,NAME,ADDRESS)
STUDENT2(STUDENT ID,NAME,PHONE NO.,ADDRESS)
```

In discussions with users, the analyst may discover that the attribute ADDRESS in STUDENT1 refers to a student's campus address, while in STUDENT2 the same attribute refers to a student's permanent (or home) address. To resolve this conflict, we would probably need to create new attribute names, so that the merged relation would become:

```
STUDENT(STUDENT ID,NAME,PHONE NO.,CAMPUS ADDRESS,
PERMANENT ADDRESS)
```

Transitive Dependencies   When two 3NF relations are merged to form a single relation, *transitive dependencies* (described earlier in this chapter) may result. For example, consider the following two relations:

```
STUDENT1(STUDENT ID,MAJOR)
STUDENT2(STUDENT ID,ADVISOR)
```

Since STUDENT1 and STUDENT2 have the same primary key, the two relations may be merged:

```
STUDENT(STUDENT ID,MAJOR,ADVISOR)
```

However, suppose that each major has exactly one advisor. In this case, ADVISOR is functionally dependent on MAJOR:

```
MAJOR→ADVISOR
```

If the above dependency exists, then STUDENT is 2NF but not 3NF, since it contains a transitive dependency. The analyst can create 3NF relations by removing the transitive dependency (MAJOR becomes a foreign key in STUDENT):

```
STUDENT(STUDENT ID,MAJOR)
MAJOR ADVISOR(MAJOR,ADVISOR)
```

Class/Subclass (ISA)   These relationships may be hidden in user views or relations. Suppose that we have the following two hospital relations:

```
PATIENT1(PATIENT NO.,NAME,ADDRESS)
PATIENT2(PATIENT NO.,ROOM NO.)
```

Initially, it appears that these two relations can be merged into a single PATIENT relation. However, the analyst correctly suspects that there are two different types of patients: inpatients and outpatients. PATIENT1 actually contains attributes common to *all* patients. PATIENT2 contains an attribute (ROOM NO.) that is a characteristic only of inpatients. In this situation, the analyst should create *class/subclass (ISA)* relationships for these entities:

```
PATIENT(PATIENT NO.,NAME,ADDRESS)
INPATIENT(PATIENT NO.,ROOM NO.)
OUTPATIENT(PATIENT NO.,DATE TREATED)
```

For an extended discussion of view integration in database design, see Navathe et al. (1986).

Case Example: Mountain View Community Hospital

 The project team at Mountain View Community Hospital reviewed the conceptual data model (E-R diagram) that was developed during requirements analysis. This diagram was shown in Figure 4-28, and is repeated in Figure 6-29.

There are four entities in this data model: ROOM, PATIENT, PHYSICIAN, and ITEM. Of course, more entities will be added to the model when other user views are included. There are two *M:N* relationships: Attends (linking PATIENT and PHYSICIAN) and Is billed for (linking PATIENT and ITEM). There is also a 1:1 optional relationship (linking ROOM and PATIENT).

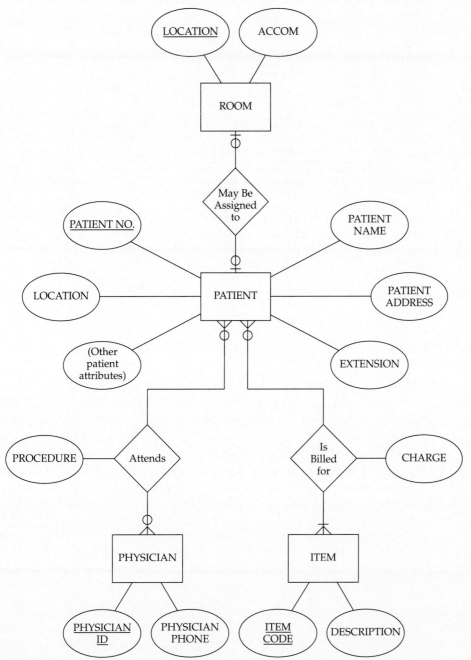

Figure 6-29
Conceptual data model
(Mountain View
Community Hospital)

Transforming the E-R Diagram to Relations

The project team used the rules described earlier in this chapter to transform the
E-R diagram to a set of relations (see Figure 6-30). Following is a brief description
of this process:

1. The four entities in the E-R diagram are transformed to relations: ROOM,
    PHYSICIAN, ITEM, and PATIENT. (The primary keys for these relations
    are the same as for the corresponding entities.)

ROOM   (3NF)

LOCATION	ACCOM
100-1	PR
101-1	PR
102-1	SP
...	...

PHYSICIAN   (3NF)

PHYSICIAN ID	PHYSICIAN PHONE
Wilcox	329-1848
Nusca	516-3947
...	...

ITEM   (3NF)

ITEM CODE	DESCRIPTION
200	Room semi-pr
205	Television
307	X-ray
413	Lab tests
...	...

PATIENT   (2NF)

PATIENT NO.	PATIENT NAME	LOCATION	EXTENSION	...
3249	Baker, Mary	137-2	248	
6213	Rose, David	100-1	137	
1379	Cribbs, John	101-1	142	
...	...	...	...	

CHARGES   (3NF)

PATIENT NO.	ITEM CODE	CHARGE
3249	200	150.00
3249	205	10.00
3249	307	25.00
6213	205	15.00
...	...	...

TREATMENT   (3NF)

PATIENT NO.	PHYSICIAN ID	PROCEDURE
3249	Wilcox	X-ray
1379	Gomez	Tonsillectomy
...	...	...

Figure 6-30

Relations derived from conceptual data model (Mountain View Community Hospital)

2. The *M:N* relationship Attends (between PATIENT and PHYSICIAN) is converted to a relation (TREATMENT) with the composite key (PATIENT NO.,PHYSICIAN ID). The attribute PROCEDURE is functionally dependent on this key.

3. Similarly, the *M:N* relationship Is billed for is converted to the relation CHARGES. The primary key of this relation is (PATIENT NO.,ITEM CODE), and the attribute CHARGE is a nonkey attribute.

4. The relationship May Be Assigned to (1:1) was represented by adding the attribute LOCATION as a foreign key in the PATIENT relation (LOCATION is the primary key of ROOM).

Normalizing the Relations

The project team examined each of the relations created from the conceptual data model to check for third normal form. As Figure 6-30 shows, all of the relations except PATIENT are in 3NF. Verify this statement by examining the functional dependencies in each relation. By using a systematic procedure in documenting the entities, attributes, and relationships during requirements analysis, the project team had intuitively normalized much of the data.

The PATIENT relation (Figure 6-30) is in second (not third) normal form. There is a transitive dependency, which may be illustrated as follows:

```
PATIENT NO.→PATIENT NAME,LOCATION,EXTENSION
LOCATION→EXTENSION
```

In other words, each bed location in the hospital has its own telephone extension. To convert the PATIENT relation to 3NF, we move the EXTENSION attribute to the ROOM relation. We can summarize the 3NF relations for Mountain View Community Hospital as follows:

```
ROOM(LOCATION,ACCOM,EXTENSION)
PHYSICIAN(PHYSICIAN ID,PHYSICIAN PHONE)
ITEM(ITEM CODE,DESCRIPTION)
PATIENT(PATIENT NO.,PATIENT NAME,PATIENT ADDRESS,CITY STATE ZIP,
  DATE ADMITTED,DATE DISCHARGED,THIRD PARTY,LOCATION)
CHARGES(PATIENT NO.,ITEM CODE,CHARGE)
TREATMENT(PATIENT NO.,PHYSICIAN ID,PROCEDURE)
```

SUMMARY

Logical database design is the process of transforming the conceptual data model into a logical database model. There are four major logical database models in use today: hierarchical, network, relational, and object-oriented. Our emphasis in this chapter has been on the relational data model, because of its importance in contemporary database systems.

In this chapter, we described a four-step process for logical database design. This process is based on transforming E-R diagrams to normalized relations. The four steps in this process are the following: represent entities, represent relationships, normalize the relations, and merge the relations.

Each entity type in the E-R diagram is transformed to a relation that has the same primary key as the entity type. A one-to-many relationship is represented by adding a foreign key to the relation that represents the entity on the many-side of the relationship. (This foreign key is the primary key of the entity on the one-side of the relationship.) A many-to-many relationship is represented by creating a separate relation. The primary key of this relation is a composite key, consisting of the primary key of each of the entities that participate in the relationship.

The relational model does not directly support class/subclass (ISA) relationships, but we can model these relationships by creating a separate table (or relation) for the class and for each subclass. The primary key of each subclass is the same (or at least from the same domain) as for the class.

The purpose of normalization is to derive well-structured relations that are free of anomalies (inconsistencies or errors) that would otherwise result when the relations are updated or modified. Normalization is generally accomplished in several stages. Relations in first normal form (1NF) contain no multivalued attributes or repeating groups. Relations in 2NF contain no partial dependencies, and relations in 3NF contain no transitive dependencies. Boyce-Codd normal form, which guarantees that a relation is free of anomalies that result from functional dependencies, is a stronger definition than 3NF. Fourth normal form (4NF) defines relations that have no multivalued dependencies. Domain-key normal form (DK/NF) is a generalized definition that subsumes all of the other normal forms but does not provide a practical mechanism for implementation.

We must be careful when combining relations to deal with problems such as synonyms, homonyms, transitive dependencies, and class/subclass relationships.

CHAPTER REVIEW

Key Terms

Alias	Composite key	Fifth normal form (5NF)
Anomalies	Determinant	First normal form (1NF)
Boyce-Codd normal form	Domain-key normal form	Foreign key
(BCNF)	(DK/NF)	Fourth normal form (4NF)

Functional dependency
Hierarchical database
  model
Join dependency
Logical data model
Multivalued dependency
Network database model
Normal form

Normalization
Object-oriented database
  model
Partial functional dependency
Recursive foreign key
Relation
Relational database model

Second normal form
  (2NF)
Third normal form (3NF)
Transitive dependency
Well-structured relation

REVIEW QUESTIONS

1. Define each of the following terms concisely:
   a. determinant
   b. functional dependency
   c. transitive dependency
   d. recursive foreign key
   e. normalization
   f. composite key
   g. multivalued dependency
   h. relation
   i. normal form
   j. logical database design
2. Contrast the following terms:
   a. normal form; normalization
   b. candidate key; primary key
   c. functional dependency; transitive dependency
   d. composite key; recursive foreign key
   e. determinant; candidate key
3. Summarize the four steps of logical database design.
4. Summarize four important properties of relations.
5. Describe two properties that must be satisfied by candidate keys.
6. Fill in the blanks in each of the following statements:
   a. A relation that has no partial functional dependencies is in _____ normal form.
   b. A relation that has no multivalued dependencies is in _____ normal form.
   c. A relation that has no repeating group is in _____ normal form.
   d. A relation that has no transitive dependencies is in _____ normal form.
   e. A relation that has no anomalies due to functional dependencies is in _____ normal form.
7. What is a well-structured relation? Why are well-structured relations important in logical database design?
8. If every determinant in a relation is a candidate key, the relation is said to be in _____ normal form.
9. Describe how the following components of an E-R diagram are transformed to relations:
   a. entity type
   b. relationship (1:N)
   c. relationship (M:N)
   d. relationship (class/subclass)
10. Briefly describe four typical problems that often arise in merging relations, and common techniques for addressing those problems.
11. Briefly describe four logical database models that are commonly used today.
12. List three conditions that you can apply to determine whether a relation that is in first normal form is also in second normal form.

PROBLEMS AND EXERCISES

1. Match the following terms to the appropriate definitions:

   ____ well-structured relation   a. relationship between two attributes

   ____ anomaly   b. multivalued dependencies eliminated

   ____ functional dependency   c. uniquely identifies rows

___ determinant

___ candidate key

___ 1NF

___ 2NF

___ 3NF

___ 4NF

___ recursive foreign key

___ relations

___ transitive dependency

d. repeating groups removed

e. inconsistency or error

f. contains little redundancy

g. contains two (or more) attributes

h. attribute on left-hand side of a functional dependency

i. contains no partial functional dependencies

j. transitive dependencies eliminated

k. functional dependency between nonkey attributes

l. named, two-dimensional table of data

2. Transform each of the following E-R diagrams from Chapter 4 into relations in 3NF:
   a. Figure 4-8b.   c. Figure 4-12.
   b. Figure 4-9c.   d. Figure 4-15a.

3. The conceptual data model for Vacation Property Rentals is shown in Figure 4-19.
   a. Transform this E-R diagram to a set of relations.
   b. Normalize the relations (BCNF).

4. Suppose that we have a relation R(A,B,C,D) with the following functional dependencies: A→B, A→C. Which of the following dependencies are implied by the rules of functional dependency (Figure 6-10)? If a dependency is implied, state the appropriate rule.
   a. A→D   d. BC→A
   b. AD→B   e. A→BC
   c. AB→B

5. Suppose that we have a relation R(A,B,C,D) with the following functional dependencies: A→B, BC→D. Which of the following dependencies are implied by the rules of functional dependencies (Figure 6-10)? If a dependency is implied, state the appropriate rule.
   a. C→D   d. AC→D
   b. A→D   e. B→CD
   c. AD→C

6. Consider the relation EXAMPLE(A,B,C,D) (see Figure 6-9). Sample data are shown below:

EXAMPLE

A	B	C	D
X	U	X	Y
Y	X	Z	X
Z	Y	Y	Y
Y	Z	W	Z

Determine which of the following functional dependencies do *not* hold:
A→B, A→C, B→A, D→C, C→D, D→A

7. For each of the following relations, indicate the normal form for that relation. If the relation is not in third normal form, decompose it into 3NF relations. Functional dependencies (other than those implied by the primary key) are shown where appropriate.
   a. CLASS(COURSE NO.,SECTION NO.)
   b. CLASS(COURSE NO.,SECTION NO.,ROOM)
   c. CLASS(COURSE NO.,SECTION NO.,ROOM,CAPACITY)
      ROOM→CAPACITY
   d. CLASS(COURSE NO.,SECTION NO.,COURSE NAME,ROOM,CAPACITY)
      ROOM→CAPACITY, COURSE NO.→COURSE NAME

Figure 6-31

Class list (Lakewood College)

```
┌─────────────────────────────────────────────────┐
│              LAKEWOOD COLLEGE                     │
│                CLASS LIST                         │
│              FALL SEMESTER 199X                   │
├─────────────────────────────────────────────────┤
│ COURSE NO.:  IS 350                               │
│ COURSE TITLE:  DATABASE                           │
│ INSTRUCTOR NAME: CODD                             │
│ INSTRUCTOR LOCATION:  B104                        │
├───────────┬──────────────┬──────────┬───────────┤
│STUDENT NO.│ STUDENT NAME │  MAJOR   │   GRADE   │
│   38214   │    Bright    │   IS     │     A     │
│   40875   │    Cortez    │   CS     │     B     │
│   51893   │    Edwards   │   IS     │     A     │
│   . . .   │              │          │           │
└───────────┴──────────────┴──────────┴───────────┘
```

8. Figure 6-31 shows a class list for Lakewood College. Convert this user view to a set of 3NF relations. Assume the following:
   a. An instructor has a unique location.
   b. A student has a unique major.
   c. A course has a unique title.
9. Figure 6-32 shows an E-R diagram for a simplified credit card environment. There are two types of card accounts: debit cards and credit cards. Credit card accounts accu-

Figure 6-32

E-R diagram for credit card

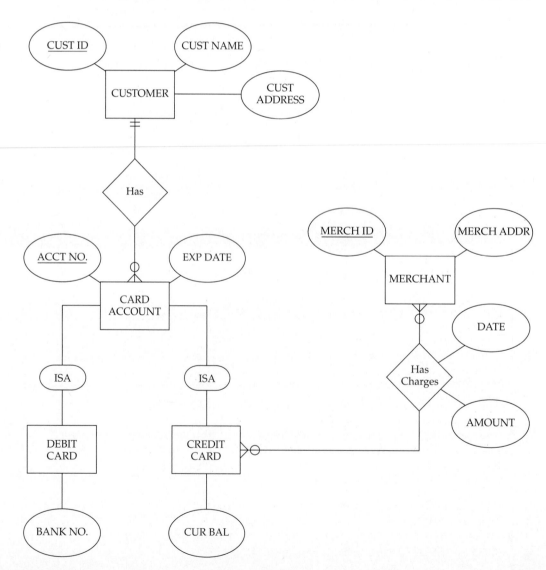

mulate charges with merchants. Each charge is identified by the date and amount of the charge. Your assignment is to transform the E-R diagram into a set of relations in third normal form. Be sure to identify both the primary and foreign keys in the resulting relations.

10. The table below contains sample data for parts and for vendors who supply those parts. In discussing this data with users, we find that part numbers (but not descriptions) uniquely identify parts, and that vendor names uniquely identify vendors.

PART NO.	DESCRIPTION	VENDOR NAME	ADDRESS	UNIT COST
1234	Logic chip	Fast Chips	Cupertino	10.00
		Smart Chips	Phoenix	8.00
5678	Memory chip	Fast Chips	Cupertino	3.00
		Quality Chips	Austin	2.00
		Smart Chips	Phoenix	5.00

a. Convert this table to a relation (named PART SUPPLIER) in first normal form. Illustrate the relation with the sample data in the table.
b. List the functional dependencies in PART SUPPLIER, and identify a candidate key.
c. For the relation PART SUPPLIER, identify each of the following: an insert anomaly, a delete anomaly, and a modification anomaly.
d. Convert PART SUPPLIER to a set of relations in third normal form.
e. Are the relations you developed in part (d) in Boyce-Codd normal form? Fourth normal form? Explain your reasons.

11. Consider the following relation:

EMPLOYEE

EMP NO.	COURSE	INTEREST
123	COMM. I	Bowling
123	COMM. II	Bowling
456	Q.C.	Skiing
456	Q.C.	Bowling

Assume that there is no relationship between the courses an employee takes and his or her interests.
a. In what normal form is this relation?
b. Give an example of an insertion and a deletion anomaly, if any exist.
c. Further normalize the relation, if necessary, to eliminate anomalies.

12. Consider the following relation:

PLAYER	POSITION	COACH
Earl	FB	Joe
John	G	Ed
Tony	FB	Pete
Carl	T	Jim
Mack	FB	Joe

Assuming that each coach coaches only one position, answer the following questions:
a. In what normal form is this relation?
b. Give an example of an insertion and a deletion anomaly, if any exist.
c. Further normalize the relation, if necessary, to eliminate anomalies.

REFERENCES

Chouinard, P. 1989. "Supertypes, Subtypes, and DB2." *Database Programming & Design* 2 (Oct.):50–57.

Codd, E. F. 1970. "A Relational Model of Data for Large Relational Databases." *Communications of the ACM* 13, no. 6.

Date, C. J. 1981. *Introduction to Database Systems.* 3d ed. Reading, Mass.: Addison-Wesley.

Dutka, A. F., and H. H. Hanson. 1989. *Fundamentals of Data Normalization.* Reading, Mass.: Addison-Wesley.

Fagin, R. 1981. "A Normal Form for Database That Is Based on Domains and Keys." *ACM Transactions on Database Systems* 6 (Sept.):387–415.

Fleming, C. C., and B. von Halle. 1989. *Handbook of Relational Database Design.* Reading, Mass.: Addison-Wesley.

Navathe, S., R. Elmasri, and J. Larson, 1986. "Integrating User Views in Database Design." *Computer* (Jan.):50–62.

Storey, V. C. 1991. "Relational Database Design Based on the Entity-Relationship Model." *Data and Knowledge Engineering* 7:47–83.

CHAPTER 7

Physical Database Design

LEARNING OBJECTIVES

After studying this chapter, you should be able to:

- Define physical database design and the major objectives of this last stage of database design.
- Describe five major components of physical database design.
- Describe the purpose of data volume and usage analysis.
- Briefly describe four basic data distribution strategies.
- Describe several important factors in selecting a file organization.
- Briefly describe four important file organizations.
- Describe the basic purpose of indexes and the important considerations in selecting attributes to be indexed.
- Define referential integrity, and state the basic rules for insertion and deletion that assure referential integrity.

INTRODUCTION

Physical design is the last stage of the database design process. The major objective of physical database design is to implement the database as a set of stored records, files, indexes, and other data structures that will provide adequate performance and ensure database integrity, security, and recoverability.

In this chapter you will study the basic steps that are required to develop an effective physical database design. You will learn how to estimate the amount of data that users will require in the database, and how data are likely to be used. Since databases are often distributed among multiple physical locations, you will study data distribution techniques. You will also learn about different file organizations and about the use of indexes, which are important in speeding up the retrieval of data. Finally, you will study the design of referential integrity constraints that are necessary to assure the quality of data in the database.

Physical database design must be performed carefully, since the decisions made during this stage have a major impact on data accessibility, response times,

243

security, user friendliness, and similar factors. Database administration (described in Chapter 12) plays a lead role in physical database design.

THE PHYSICAL DATABASE DESIGN PROCESS

Physical database design, as defined in Chapter 3, is the process of mapping the logical database structures developed in previous stages into an internal model (or set of physical database structures). As Figure 7-1 shows, physical database design is the last step in the database design process.

There are three major inputs to physical database design:

1. Logical database structures that were developed during logical design (described in Chapter 6). These database structures may be expressed as hier-

Figure 7-1

Role of physical database design in the database development process

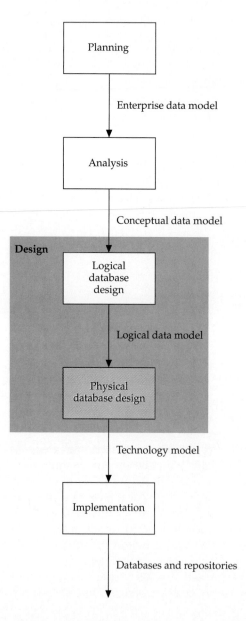

archical, network, and/or relational data models. In this chapter (as in Chapter 6) we emphasize the relational data model; however, we do provide a brief description of mapping the logical model to hierarchical and network structures.

2. User processing requirements that were identified during requirements definition, including size and frequency of use of the database, and requirements for each of the following: response times, security, backup, recovery, and retention of data.

3. Characteristics of the database management system (DBMS) and other components of the computer operating environment.

The steps that are required for physical database design depend on a number of factors: the nature of the target DBMS, characteristics of the organization's computing environment, extent of usage of distributed processing and data communications, types of organizational applications, and so on. In this chapter we emphasize the generic aspects of physical database design that are common to most database development projects. The following sections describe the following five components of physical database design:

1. Data volume and usage analysis
2. Data distribution strategy
3. File organizations
4. Indexes
5. Integrity constraints

DATA VOLUME AND USAGE ANALYSIS

The first step in physical database design is to estimate the size (or volume) and the usage patterns of the database. Estimates of database size are used to select physical storage devices and estimate the costs of storage. Estimates of usage paths or patterns are used to select file organizations and access methods, to plan for the use of indexes, and to plan a strategy for data distribution. We illustrate a simple process for this analysis below.

Data Volume Analysis

Figure 7-2 shows a simplified picture of the logical data model for Mountain View Community Hospital. Each entity is represented by a rectangle, but the attributes have been omitted. Inside each rectangle is a number representing the estimated average volume for that entity. For example, an estimated average of 1,000 PATIENT entities must be accommodated in the database at any one time. The numbers adjacent to the arrowheads are estimates of the average number of a given entity type associated with a related entity type. For example, Figure 7-2 indicates an average of ten charges associated with each patient at any given time.

The database design team at Mountain View Community Hospital made the estimates in consultation with users. Since there are 100 beds at the hospital, the maximum number of admitted patients at any one time is limited to 100. However, the accounting staff indicated that the records for an average patient would probably be kept active for about 30 days. Since the average length of stay for a patient

Figure 7-2

Logical data model with
volumes and ratios
(Mountain View
Community Hospital)

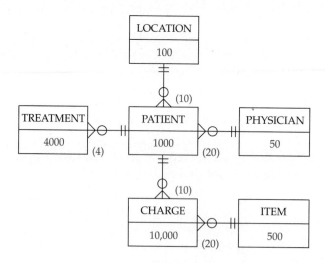

is 3 days, the total number of active patient records is expected to be $100 \times 30/3$, or 1,000. After an average period of 30 days, a patient record would be archived.

Further discussions with the hospital accounting staff revealed that each PATIENT incurs an average of ten charges during a hospitalization. Thus, the number of CHARGE entities is expected to be $10 \times 1,000$, or 10,000. Also, there are 500 separate items that may appear on a patient's bill. Thus, the average number of charges outstanding for a given item is 10,000/500, or 20, as shown in Figure 7-2.

The design team also conferred with the medical staff and discovered that each PATIENT receives an average of four treatments. Thus, the average number of TREATMENT entities in the database is $4 \times 1,000$, or 4,000.

Data Usage Analysis

In data usage analysis, the analyst identifies the major transactions and processes required against the database. Each transaction and process is then analyzed to determine the access paths used and the estimated frequency of use. When all transactions have been analyzed, the composite load map is prepared, showing the total usage of access paths on the conceptual model.

The database design team used a transaction analysis form to analyze each transaction at the hospital. Figure 7-3 shows how this form is used to analyze the transaction CREATE PATIENT BILL, which causes a PATIENT record to be read, along with the detail of patient charges, and also causes a patient bill to be printed. After talking with people in accounting, the analysts estimated an average transaction volume of 2 per hour and a peak volume of 10 per hour.

The number of logical references per transaction and per period are recorded on the form. CREATE PATIENT BILL requires only one PATIENT reference per transaction, which, at peak volume, translates to 10 references per hour. Each PATIENT has an average of 10 CHARGES. Therefore, the average number of times the PATIENT-CHARGE path is used per transaction is 10. This data usage translates to a peak volume of 10×10, or 100 per hour. Since the CHARGE-ITEM path is traversed once for each CHARGE, this data usage also results in a peak usage of 100 per hour. The analysts chose to use peak volumes to estimate references per period, since this would measure the maximum load on the database.

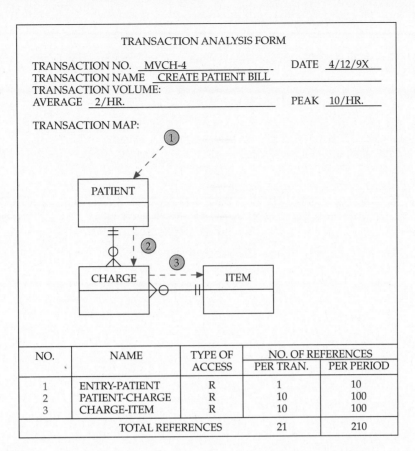

Figure 7-3

Analysis of the transaction CREATE PATIENT BILL (Mountain View Community Hospital)

Transaction Map   The **transaction map** in the middle of Figure 7-3 shows the sequence of logical database accesses required for CREATE PATIENT BILL. The dashed line on this map shows the access path for this transaction. The entry point is at the PATIENT entity; then the path goes to the entity CHARGE; then it proceeds from each CHARGE to ITEM to pick up the description for that CHARGE.

A detailed analysis of each step in the access path is entered at the bottom of the form. The type of access to each entity is recorded using the following codes:

C: create (or insert) a new entity

R: read an entity

U: update an entity

D: delete an entity

For the CREATE PATIENT BILL transaction, each access is coded with an R, since this transaction requires read only.

Composite Usage Map   There are many other transactions for the database in addition to CREATE PATIENT BILL: for example, CREATE TREATMENT, RECORD NEW PATIENT CHARGE, and DISPLAY PATIENT DATA. When all these transactions have been analyzed, the analysts can combine the data and display them in the form of a composite usage map. Figure 7-4 shows a sample composite usage map for Mountain View Community Hospital. The number in each rectangle shows the estimated number of entities of that type (for example, 1,000 PATIENTS). The number at the head of each dashed arrow is an estimate of

Transaction map: A diagram that shows the sequence of logical database accesses.

Figure 7-4

Composite usage map
(Mountain View
Community Hospital)

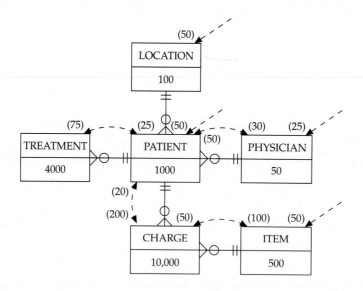

the total number of references on a given access path at a peak volume. For example, the number of references to the entity TREATMENT from the entity PATIENT is estimated at 75 per hour. Also, the number of references to PATIENT from outside the model is estimated at 50 per hour.

Composite usage map: A concise reference to the estimated volume and usage of data in the database.

The **composite usage map** is a concise reference to the estimated volume and usage of data in the database. It provides a basis for the remaining steps of physical database design, during which the analysts must design storage structures and access strategies to optimize performance.

We have described data volume and usage analysis as a component of physical database design, since it is most closely related to that design phase. However, when a hierarchical or network data model is to be used, at least a preliminary data volume and usage analysis should be performed *before* implementation design, since the products of data volume and usage analysis (especially the composite usage map of Figure 7-4) can help the analysts make better implementation decisions. For an extended discussion of data volume and usage analysis, see (Hogan, 1988).

DATA DISTRIBUTION STRATEGY

Many organizations today have distributed computing networks. For these organizations, a significant problem in physical database design is deciding at which nodes (or sites) in the network to physically locate the data.

Basic Data Distribution Strategies

There are four basic data distribution strategies:

Centralized data distribution: All data are located at a single site.

1. **Centralized.** All data are located at a single site. Although this simplifies the implementation, there are at least three disadvantages: (a) Data are not readily accessible to users at remote sites, (b) data communication costs may

be high, and (c) the database system fails totally when the central system fails.

2. **Partitioned.** With this approach, the database is divided into disjoint (non-overlapping) partitions. Each partition (also called a *fragment*) is assigned to a particular site. The major advantage of this approach is that data is moved closer to local users and so is more accessible.

3. **Replicated.** With this approach, a full copy of the database is assigned to more than one site in the network. This assignment maximizes local access to data but creates update problems, since each database change must be reliably processed and synchronized at all of the sites.

4. **Hybrid.** With this strategy, the database is partitioned into critical and non-critical fragments. Noncritical fragments are stored at only one site, while critical fragments are stored at multiple sites.

When all of the possible variations are considered, the problem of distributing data in a network is quite complex. In this chapter we discuss a relatively simple case of data distribution. An extended description of distributed database management is presented in Chapter 13.

An Example of Data Distribution

Hy-Tek Corporation manufactures a line of electronic products that are distributed through nationwide marketing channels. The company has five principal manufacturing locations, which are linked by a distributed processing network, a schematic of which is shown in Figure 7-5. Each of the five sites (labeled S1, S2, and so on) has a computer that is linked to the remaining nodes in the network (this example is adapted from Teorey, Chaar, Olukotun, and Umor (1989).

A description of the major components of this example follows.

Relations As shown in Table 7-1, Hy-Tek has three major relations that are to be located in the distributed processing network. The first relation (R1) is a CUSTOMER relation that contains information about Hy-Tek's customers. The

Partitioned data distribution: The database is divided into disjoint (nonoverlapping) partitions. Each partition (also called a *fragment*) is assigned to a particular site.

Replicated data distribution: A full copy of the database is assigned to more than one site in the network.

Hybrid data distribution: The database is partitioned into critical and noncritical fragments. Noncritical fragments are stored at only one site, while critical fragments are stored at multiple sites.

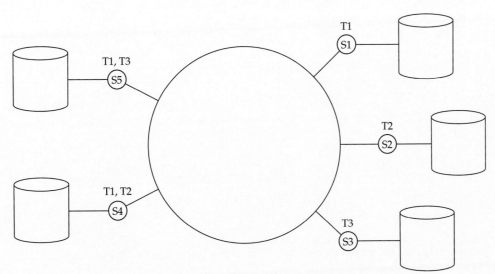

Figure 7-5

Distributed computing network (Hy-Tek Corporation) (Source: Copyright © *Database Programming & Design*, April 1989, Vol. 2, No. 4. Reprinted by Permission of Miller Freeman Publications.)

TABLE 7-1   Three Relations to Be Located in Distributed System

Relation	Size	Ave. Local Time (ms)		Ave. Remote Time (ms)	
		Query	Update	Query	Update
R1	300KB	100	150	500	600
R2	500KB	150	200	650	700
R3	1.0MB	200	250	1000	1100

Source: Copyright © *Database Programming & Design*, April 1989, Vol. 2, No. 4. Reprinted by permission of Miller Freeman Publications.

second relation (R2) is a PRODUCT relation, while the third relation (R3) is a SHIPMENT relation. The table shows the size of each relation and the average time (milliseconds) to query and update each relation from both a local site and a remote site. For example, the average time to query R1 is 100 milliseconds from a local site and 500 milliseconds from a remote site (the additional time represents the communications overhead). The average time to update R1 is 150 milliseconds from a local site and 600 milliseconds from a remote site.

Transactions   Table 7-2 shows the major transactions that access and update the three relations in the database. (Figure 7-5 shows the location for each of these transactions.) Transaction T1 originates at sites S1, S4, and S5. Transaction T1 is executed with an average frequency of one time per second at *each* of these sites. Transaction T1 accesses relation R1 an average of four times each time T1 is executed; three of these accesses are reads (R) and one is a write (W), which updates the relation. Also, transaction T1 accesses relation R2 two times (both reads) each time it is executed. Transaction T2 originates at sites S2 and S4 an average of two times per second at each site. Transaction T2 accesses relation R1 (two reads) and R3 (three reads, one write). Finally, transaction T3 originates at sites S3 and S5, and has a frequency of three per second at each site. Transaction T3 accesses relation R2 (three reads, one write) and R3 (two reads).

Assumptions   We can now state the data distribution problem for Hy-Tek as follows: Given the network with five sites shown in Figure 7-5, the relations shown in Table 7-1, and the transactions shown in Table 7-2, at which of the sites should

TABLE 7-2   Transactions That Access the Relations

Transaction	Originating Site	Frequency (Each Site)	Relation Access (R = Read, W = Write)
T1	S1, S4, S5	1 per sec.	R1: 3R, 1W R2: 2R
T2	S2, S4	2 per sec.	R1: 2R R3: 3R, 1W
T3	S3, S5	3 per sec.	R2: 3R, 1W R3: 2R

Source: Copyright © *Database Programming & Design*, April 1989, Vol. 2, No. 4. Reprinted by permission of Miller Freeman Publications.

1) Only updates to R₁ is via T₁

2) Updates to R₂ is via T₃

3) updates to R₃ is via T₂

the relations be located? We will make two assumptions to simplify the solution to this problem:

1. The major objective in placing the data is to maximize the number of *local* references to the data (this approach will also minimize the number of remote references).

2. None of the relations will be partitioned, so that each relation will be located in its entirety at one (or more) sites.

Methodology   The method we will use for allocating relations to sites is called the *all beneficial sites* method, which selects all sites for a relation where the benefit is greater than the cost for locating a relation at that site. Table 7-3 shows the calculations for the relations at Hy-Tek. The top of Table 7-3 shows the costs, and the bottom of the table shows the benefits.

The *cost* at each site is the *additional remote updates* from other sites for the given relation at that site. The *benefit* at each site is measured by the difference in cost to do a *remote read* (when no copy is located at the site) *versus a local read* (when a copy is located at the site).

First, we consider whether relation R1 should be located at S1. From Table 7-3, we see that the additional cost will be that of updating R1 with transaction T1, from the remote locations S4 and S5. Thus, there are transactions from two sites that originate at a rate of one per second and require 600 ms (milliseconds) each. The total cost (from the first line of Table 7-3) is:

```
2 sites * 1 transaction/second * 600 ms = 1200 ms
```

[handwritten note: T1 is the only transaction that updates R1. Hence we evaluate the cost of T1 at all sites.]

Now we consider locating R1 at site S2. Transaction T1 must now update R1 at S2 from three remote locations: S1, S4, and S5. The total cost is:

```
3 sites * 1 transaction/second * 600 ms = 1800 ms
```

The calculations for R1 at the remaining sites (S3, S4, and S5) also appear in Table 7-3. We recommend that you perform each of these calculations to make sure you understand the process.

Now we consider relation R2 at site S1. The additional cost will be due to remote updates by transaction T3 originating at sites S3 and S5 (transaction T3 is the only one that *updates* R2). The additional cost will be:

[handwritten note: T3 is the only transaction that updates R2. Hence we evaluate the cost of T3 at all sites.]

```
2 transactions * 3 transactions/second * 700 ms = 4200 ms
```

The remaining calculations for the costs for relations R2 and R3 appear in Table 7-3. Again, you should verify each of the calculations.

Now we consider the *benefit* of assigning each relation to each site (shown in the bottom half of Table 7-3). First, suppose that relation R1 is assigned to site S1. Notice that transaction T1 originates at S1 (frequency of one per second) and reads R1 (three times per transaction). With a copy of R1 at S1, each of these reads is a local reference (rather than a remote reference). Thus, we compute the benefit as follows:

[handwritten note: T2 is the only transaction that updates R3. Hence we evaluate the cost of T2 at all sites]

```
3 reads * 1/second * (500 - 100) = 1200 ms
```

If instead R1 is assigned to S2, then the benefit arises from local references for transaction T2. As shown in Table 7-3, we calculate as follows:

TABLE 7-3 **Cost and Benefit for Each Relation Located at Five Possible Sites**

Relation	Site	Remote Update Trans.	Remote Update Trans. *Freq. *Time =	Cost
R1	S1	T1 from S4 and S5	2*1*600 ms	1200 ms
	S2	T1 from S1, S4, S5	3*1*600 ms	1800 ms
	S3	T1 from S1, S4, S5	3*1*600 ms	1800 ms
	S4	T1 from S1 and S5	2*1*600 ms	1200 ms
	S5	T1 from S1 and S4	2*1*600 ms	1200 ms
R2	S1	T3 from S3 and S5	2*3*700 ms	4200 ms
	S2	T3 from S3 and S5	2*3*700 ms	4200 ms
	S3	T3 from S5	1*3*700 ms	2100 ms
	S4	T3 from S3 and S5	2*3*700 ms	4200 ms
	S5	T3 from S3	1*3*700 ms	2100 ms
R3	S1	T2 from S2 and S4	2*2*1100 ms	4400 ms
	S2	T2 from S4	1*2*1100 ms	2200 ms
	S3	T2 from S2 and S4	2*2*1100 ms	4400 ms
	S4	T2 from S2	1*2*1100 ms	2200 ms
	S5	T2 from S2 and S4	2*2*1100 ms	4400 ms

Relation	Site	Query (Read) Sources	No. of Reads* freq* (Remote-Local-Time) =	Benefit
R1	S1	T1 at S1	3*1*(500 − 100)	1200 ms
	S2	T2 at S2	2*2*(500 − 100)	1600 ms
	S3	None	0	0
	S4	T1 and T2 at S4	(3*1 + 2*2)* (500 − 100)	2800 ms
	S5	T1 at S5	3*1*(500 − 100)	1200 ms
R2	S1	T1 at S1	2*1*(650 − 150)	1000 ms
	S2	None	0	0
	S3	T3 at S3	3*3*(650 − 150)	4500 ms
	S4	T1 at S4	2*1*(650 − 150)	1000 ms
	S5	T1 and T3 at S5	(2*1* + 3*3)* (650 − 150)	5500 ms
R3	S1	None	0	0
	S2	T2 at S2	3*2*(1000 − 200)	4800 ms
	S3	T3 at S3	2*3*(1000 − 200)	4800 ms
	S4	T2 at S4	3*2*(1000 − 200)	4800 ms
	S5	T3 at S5	2*3*(1000 − 200)	4800 ms

Source: Copyright © *Database Programming & Design*, April 1989, Vol. 2, No. 4. Reprinted by permission of Miller Freeman Publications.

```
2 reads * 2/second * (500 - 100) = 1600 ms
```

The remaining benefit calculations for R1, as well as those for R2 and R3, appear in Table 7-3. Again, you should verify that each of these calculations is correct and that you understand the benefit of these calculations.

Distributing the Relations   Once we have done the calculations in Table 7-3, we assign a relation to a site whenever the benefit of this assignment exceeds the cost. This rule leads to the following assignments (see Figure 7-6):

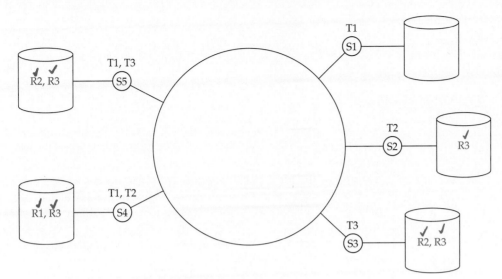

Figure 7-6

Final allocation of data for Hy-Tek (Source: Copyright © *Database Programming & Design*, April 1989, Vol. 2, No. 4. Reprinted by permission of Miller Freeman Publications.)

Assign relation R1 to site S4 only.

Assign relation R2 to sites S3 and S5.

Assign relation R3 to sites S2, S3, S4, and S5.

When the costs and benefits for an assignment are equal (as for R1 at S1), the organization is indifferent as to whether the relation is assigned to that site. In Figure 7-6 we did not assign a relation to a site when the costs and benefits were equal. The organization may choose to make such assignments for other reasons, however, such as when greater availability of data is important.

FILE ORGANIZATION

A **file organization** is a technique for physically arranging the records of a file on secondary storage devices. In selecting a file organization, the system designer must recognize several constraints, including the physical characteristics of the secondary storage devices, available operating system and file management software, and user needs for storing and accessing data.

The criteria that are normally important in selecting file organizations include:

1. Fast access for retrieval
2. High throughput for processing transactions
3. Efficient use of storage space
4. Protection from failures or data loss
5. Minimizing need for reorganization
6. Accommodating growth
7. Security from unauthorized use

Often these objectives are conflicting, and the designer must select a file organization that provides a reasonable balance among the criteria within the resources available.

File organization: A technique for physically arranging the records of a file on secondary storage devices.

In this chapter we consider the following basic file organizations: sequential, indexed, and hashed. Figure 7-7 illustrates each of these organizations with the names of popular video games.

Sequential File Organization

Sequential file organization: The records in the file are stored in sequence according to a primary key value.

In a **sequential file organization**, the records in the file are stored in sequence according to a primary key value (Figure 7-7a). The location of a particular record in the file is not known by the storage organization. To locate a particular record, the user must normally scan the file from the beginning until the desired record is located. An everyday example of a sequential file is the alphabetical list of persons in the white pages of a phone directory (ignoring any index that may be included with the directory pages).

Figure 7-7

Comparison of file organizations

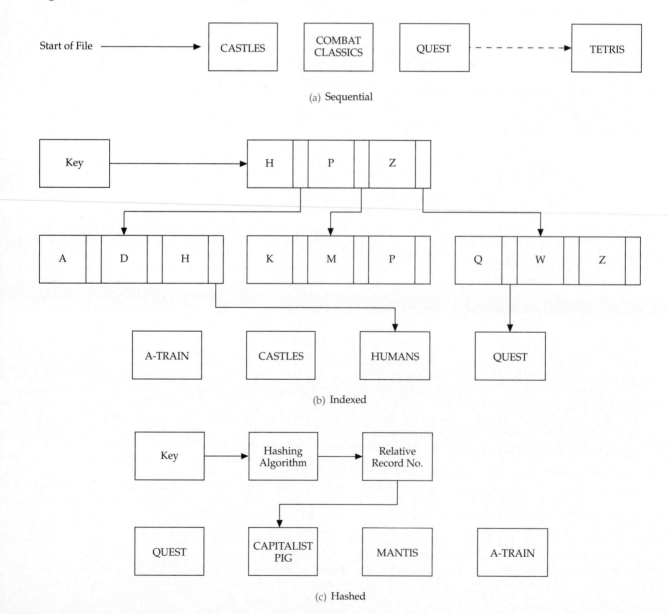

(a) Sequential

(b) Indexed

(c) Hashed

Indexed File Organizations

In an **indexed file organization**, the records are either stored sequentially or non-sequentially, and an index is created that allows the user to locate individual records. An **index** is a table or other data structure that is used to determine the location of rows in a table (or tables) that satisfy some condition.

There are two basic types of indexed file organizations: indexed sequential and indexed nonsequential.

Indexed Sequential   When the records are stored sequentially by primary key value, a simple index (called a *block index*) may be used (Figure 7-7b). This approach (called **indexed sequential**) has been the most common file organization for predatabase systems. An everyday example of a simple indexed sequential file is again the list of persons in the white pages of a phone directory. The top of each page usually shows the last name of the first person on that page, followed by the last name of the last person on that page. This is a simple block index that allows the user to quickly locate the page that contains a desired name. The user then scans that page to locate that name.

Indexed Nonsequential   When the records in an indexed organization are stored nonsequentially, a full index (frequently called an *inverted index*) is required. This file organization is especially significant for our purposes, since relations are often stored using this approach. (Recall from Chapter 6 that one of the properties of the relational model is that the order of rows is insignificant.) We describe and illustrate the index structure that is commonly used with relational systems in the section on "Indexes" later in this chapter.

The arrangement of books in a library, and the accompanying computerized indexes (or catalogs) provide an everyday example of an indexed nonsequential file organization. The books are shelved in sequence according to catalog number, but are not in sequence according to author name or title. The author and title catalogs are full indexes that allow a person to quickly locate the shelf position for a particular author or title.

Hashed   In a **hashed file organization** the address for each record is determined using a hashing algorithm (Figure 7-7c). A **hashing algorithm** is a routine that converts a primary key value into a relative record number (or relative file address). As a result of using a hashing algorithm, in general the records are located nonsequentially in the file (for example, see the records in Figure 7-7c).

A typical hashing algorithm uses the technique of dividing each primary key value by a suitable prime number and then using the remainder of the division as the relative storage location. For example, suppose that an organization has a set of approximately 1,000 employee records to be stored on magnetic disk. A suitable prime number for this problem is 997 (since it closely approximates 1,000). Now consider the record for employee number 12396. When we divide this number by 997, the remainder is 432 (check this result). Thus this record is stored at location 432 in the file. Another technique (not discussed here) must be used to resolve duplicates (or overflow) that can occur with the division/remainder method when two or more keys hash to the same address.

INDEXES

Most database manipulations require locating a row (or collection of rows) that satisfies some condition. For example, we may want to retrieve all customers in a given zipcode or all students with a particular major. Scanning every row in a

Indexed file organization: The records are either stored sequentially or non-sequentially, and an index is created that allows the user to locate individual records.

Index: A table or other data structure that is used to determine the location of rows in a table (or tables) that satisfy some condition.

Indexed sequential: The records are stored sequentially by primary key value, and a simple index (called a *block index*) is used.

Indexed nonsequential: The records in an indexed organization are stored non-sequentially, and a full index (frequently called an *inverted index*) is required.

Hashed file organization: The address for each record is determined using a hashing algorithm.

Hashing algorithm: A routine that converts a primary key value into a relative record number (or relative file address).

table looking for the desired rows may be unacceptably slow, particularly when the tables are large, as they often are in real-world applications. Using indexes can greatly speed up this process, and defining indexes is an important part of physical database design.

An *index* is a table or other data structure that is used to determine the location of rows in a table (or tables) that satisfy some condition. Indexes may be defined on both primary key values and nonkey attribute values. We illustrate each of these types of indexes below.

Indexes are more compact than the data records (or rows) they reference. Often, indexes can be kept in computer main memory for extended periods in order to reduce secondary memory access costs to retrieve them. However, indexes for files with many rows (or records) can also be very large. An index, then, can be viewed as a file itself on which an index can be created. Later in this section we will review several popular schemes used as file organizations for an index file.

Primary Key Indexes

Figure 7-8 shows a portion of the PRODUCT file for Pine Valley Furniture Company. The primary key of the table represented by this file is PRODUCT NO. In Figure 7-8, the rows are arranged in ascending sequence according to PRODUCT NO. You may recall from Chapter 6 that one of the properties of relations is that the order of the rows is unimportant. However, when a relation is physically implemented as a file, there is a physical ordering of the records. In Figure 7-8, a field called RECORD NO. contains the relative position of each record within the file. For example, record number 5 in the file contains data for product number 1000. These relative record numbers are used by the DBMS to directly access a record in the file, but are not visible to users of the system.

Figure 7-9 shows an index for the PRODUCT file based on PRODUCT NO. The index (named PRODINDX) is at the top of the figure. This index associates values for product number (PRODUCT NO.) with their relative record number (RECORD NO.) in the file. Notice that the values for PRODUCT NO. are stored in ascending sequence in the index (as well as in the PRODUCT table). This ordering allows for faster searching for the required values. (Remember that the index is stored in main memory, while the file is stored in much slower secondary storage.) The figure highlights product number 1425 in the index, and provides a link to relative record number 7 in the file, where the data for this product is located. File access methods use rapid search methods to perform this type of search.

Figure 7-8

PRODUCT file (Pine Valley Furniture)

PRODUCT

RECORD NO.	PRODUCT NO.	DESCRIPTION	FINISH	ROOM	PRICE
1	0100	Table	Oak	DR	500
2	0350	Table	Maple	DR	625
3	0625	Chair	Oak	DR	100
4	0975	Wall Unit	Pine	FR	750
5	1000	Dresser	Cherry	BR	800
6	1250	Chair	Maple	LR	400
7	1425	Bookcase	Pine	LR	250
8	1600	Stand	Birch	BR	200
9	1775	Dresser	Pine	BR	500
10	2000	Wall Unit	Oak	LR	1200

PRODINDX

PRODUCT NO.	RECORD NO.
0100	1
0350	2
0625	3
0975	4
1000	5
1250	6
1425	7
1600	8
1775	9
2000	10

PRODUCT

RECORD NO.	PRODUCT NO.	DESCRIPTION	FINISH	ROOM	PRICE
1	0100	Table	Oak	DR	500
2	0350	Table	Maple	DR	625
3	0625	Chair	Oak	DR	100
4	0975	Wall Unit	Pine	FR	750
5	1000	Dresser	Cherry	BR	800
6	1250	Chair	Maple	LR	400
7	1425	Bookcase	Pine	LR	250
8	1600	Stand	Birch	BR	200
9	1775	Dresser	Pine	BR	500
10	2000	Wall Unit	Oak	LR	1200

Figure 7-9

Index for PRODUCT file on PRODUCT NO.

Since PRODUCT NO. is the primary key of PRODUCT, values for this attribute must be unique; that is, no two rows may contain the same values for PRODUCT NO. In most relational DBMSs, you can create an index by specifying you want a column indexed at the time you define a table. You may also create the index in Figure 7-9 (called PRODINDX) directly by issuing the following SQL command:

```
CREATE UNIQUE INDEX PRODINDX ON PRODUCT (PRODUCT_NO);
```

The word UNIQUE in this command indicates that the system is to maintain uniqueness of product numbers. The DBMS will not permit two products with the same product number to exist in the PRODUCT table. Thus we see that a unique index performs two important functions: it provides fast access to specific records and enforces uniqueness of primary key values.

Indexes for Nonkey Attributes

Database users often wish to retrieve rows of a relation based on values for non-key attributes. For example, in the PRODUCT table, users may want to retrieve records that satisfy any combination of the following conditions:

1. All tables (DESCRIPTION = 'Table')

2. All oak furniture (FINISH = 'Oak')

3. All dining room furniture (ROOM = 'DR')

4. All furniture priced below $500 (PRICE<500)

To speed up such retrievals, we can define an index on each nonkey attribute that we use to qualify a retrieval. For example, Figure 7-10 shows an index (called DESCINDX) defined on the DESCRIPTION attribute of the PRODUCT table. In general, there is more than one record that satisfies each value (for example, in Figure 7-10, records numbered 5 and 9 contain data for dressers). More sophisticated index designs are generally used than the one shown in Figure 7-10, but this figure conveys the general structure of indexes for nonkey attributes.

The index illustrated in Figure 7-10 is created with the following SQL command:

```
CREATE INDEX DESCINDX ON PRODUCT (DESCRIPTION);
```

Notice that the term UNIQUE should not be used with nonkey attributes, since each value of the attribute may be repeated, as in the above example.

Clustering Indexes

When the records in a file are often retrieved based on the values of a nonkey attribute, retrievals can be sped up by physically ordering the file on that nonkey attribute. For example, suppose that Pine Valley Furniture frequently needs product reports that list the products in alphabetical order by DESCRIPTION. Figure 7-11 shows the PRODUCT file rearranged so that the records are in ascending order according to DESCRIPTION.

Clustering attribute: Any nonkey attribute in a record (or row) that is used to cluster (or group together) the rows that have a common value for this attribute.

When the records of a file are physically ordered on a nonkey attribute that does not have a distinct value for each record (as for DESCRIPTION in this example), that attribute is called the *clustering attribute* of the file (Elmasri and Navathe, 1989). Thus a **clustering attribute** is any nonkey attribute in a record (or row) that is used to cluster (or group together) the rows that have a common

Figure 7-10

Index for PRODUCT file on DESCRIPTION

DESCINDX

DESCRIPTION	RECORD NO.
Bookcase	7
Chair	3, 6
Dresser	5, 9
Stand	8
Table	1, 2
Wall Unit	4, 10

PRODUCT

RECORD NO.	PRODUCT NO.	DESCRIPTION	FINISH	ROOM	PRICE
1	0100	Table	Oak	DR	500
2	0350	Table	Maple	DR	625
3	0625	Chair	Oak	DR	100
4	0975	Wall Unit	Pine	FR	750
5	1000	Dresser	Cherry	BR	800
6	1250	Chair	Maple	LR	400
7	1425	Bookcase	Pine	LR	250
8	1600	Stand	Birch	BR	200
9	1775	Dresser	Pine	BR	500
10	2000	Wall Unit	Oak	LR	1200

Figure 7-11

Clustering index for
PRODUCT file on
DESCRIPTION

CLUST_INDX

DESCRIPTION	RECORD NO.
Bookcase	1
Chair	2
Dresser	4
Stand	6
Table	7
Wall Unit	9

PRODUCT

RECORD NO.	PRODUCT NO.	DESCRIPTION	FINISH	ROOM	PRICE
1	1425	Bookcase	Pine	LR	250
2	0625	Chair	Oak	DR	100
3	1250	Chair	Maple	LR	400
4	1000	Dresser	Cherry	BR	800
5	1775	Dresser	Pine	BR	500
6	1600	Stand	Birch	BR	200
7	0100	Table	Oak	DR	500
8	0350	Table	Maple	DR	625
9	0975	Wall Unit	Pine	FR	750
10	2000	Wall Unit	Oak	LR	1200

value for this attribute. These rows are physically clustered together in storage for rapid retrieval. Thus, for example, all rows for Wall Units would be clustered in a physical block or subdivision of storage.

We can create a different type of index to speed up retrieval of records that have a common value for the clustering field. A **clustering index** is an index defined on the clustering attribute of a file. This index (named CLUST_INDX) is illustrated in Figure 7-11, and is defined with the following SQL command:

Clustering index: An index defined on the clustering attribute of a file.

```
CREATE INDEX CLUST_INDX
  ON PRODUCT (DESCRIPTION)
  CLUSTER;
```

The CLUST_INDX index names the clustering attribute (DESCRIPTION), and will cause the DBMS to cluster (or physically order) the rows of the PRODUCT file according to that attribute.

Notice in Figure 7-11 that each index value points to the *first* record in the cluster for that value (for example, the first record for a table). The cluster of records containing that row is then scanned to locate the remaining records for other tables. Each DBMS will have its own technique for implementing the clustering index.

Only one clustering index may be defined on each file, since in general it is impossible to physically arrange the records according to two (or more) clustering attributes. We can expect that the clustering shown in Figure 7-11 will permit rapid retrievals based on DESCRIPTION, while retrievals based on another attribute (such as FINISH) will be much slower. The designer must understand how the data will be used and be prepared to make trade-offs when designing such indexes.

Trees

The preceding discussion describes simple ordered index files (see Figures 7-9 through 7-11). In practice, such indexes are usually implemented in multiple levels, which provides faster search techniques for the required data. Trees are the most common data structures for index files, and we briefly introduce the terminology for trees in this section.

Tree: A data structure that consists of a set of nodes that branch out from a node at the top of the tree (thus the tree is upside down).

Root node: The node at the top of a tree.

Leaf node: A node in a tree that has no child nodes.

Subtree: A node and all the descendants of that node.

Pointer: A field containing data that can be used to locate a related record.

Structure of Trees   Figure 7-12 shows a typical tree data structure. A **tree** is a data structure that consists of a set of nodes that branch out from a node at the top of the tree (thus the tree is upside down!). The **root node** is the node at the top of a tree. Each node in the tree, except for the root node, has exactly one parent, and may have zero, one, or more than one child nodes. In Figure 7-12, for example, node H has a parent node (D) and two child nodes (K and L). Nodes are defined in terms of levels: the root node is level zero, and the children of this node are at level one, and so on.

A **leaf node** is a node in a tree that has no child nodes. In Figure 7-12, you should verify that nodes J, F, C, G, K, L, and I are leaf nodes.

A **subtree** of a node consists of that node and all the descendants of that node. A subtree of node D appears in Figure 7-12.

One way to implement trees is to include within each node a special field called a **pointer** to each of its child nodes. For example, node D (Figure 7-12) would have pointers to nodes G, H, and I. Often, each node (except the root node) also has a pointer to its parent node.

Figure 7-12

Example of a tree data structure

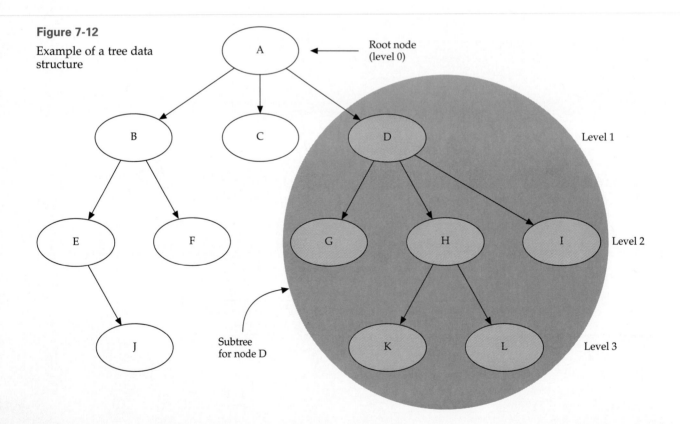

Properties of Trees   In this section we introduce several important properties of trees that suggest the possible applications of different tree structures as well as desirable properties for all trees. The properties we discuss are uniform accessibility, branching factor, and depth.

In certain types of trees, some records are closer to the root node than others. This means that a different number of comparisons and branches will be required to access different records. Placing frequently accessed records close to the root node would improve overall database performance. Most types of trees build uniform accessibility by requiring that all leaf nodes be an equal distance from the root node.

The **branching factor** (or **degree of a tree**) is the maximum number of children allowed per parent. Large branching factors, in general, create broader, more shallow trees. Since access time in a tree depends more often on depth than on breadth, and since movement between levels usually means a disk access, it is usually advantageous to have bushy, shallow trees.

Depth is the number of levels between the root node and a leaf node in the tree. Depth may be the same from the root node to each leaf node, producing a tree called a *balanced tree* (discussed below), or depth may vary across different paths. Notice that the tree shown in Figure 7-12 is *not* a balanced tree, since the depth from the root node to the leaf nodes varies. Balanced trees are democratic in that all leaf nodes have about the same access costs; however, balancing can be costly to maintain as the tree contents are updated.

Branching factor (degree of a tree): The maximum number of children allowed per parent in a tree.

Depth: The number of levels between the root node and a leaf node in a tree.

Balanced Trees

Index files are most commonly organized using a balanced tree data structure. In a **balanced tree**, or **B-tree**, all leaves are the same distance from the root. For this reason, B-trees have a predictable efficiency that many other types of trees do not. Hashing (discussed in the previous section) may yield fewer accesses for random record retrieval than B-trees. However, unlike hashing, B-trees also support sequential retrieval of records (for example, retrieval of employee records in alphabetical order). Many database management systems now use B-trees as the principal method for primary and nonkey access.

Balanced tree (B-tree): A tree in which all leaves are the same distance from the root.

There are several varieties of B-trees, with the standard B-tree and the B+-tree being the most common (Comer, 1979). Since most B-tree implementations are of the B+-tree, we illustrate this type briefly in this section. An example of a B+-tree of degree 3 for the PRODUCT file of Pine Valley Furniture (Figure 7-8) appears in Figure 7-13. In this diagram, each vertical arrow represents the path followed for values that are equal to the number to the left of the arrow, but less than the number to the right of the arrow. For example, in the nonleaf node that contains the values 625 and 1000, the middle arrow leaving the bottom of this node is the path followed for values equal to 625, but less than 1000. The existence of the horizontal arrows in the leaf nodes is what distinguishes a B+-tree from a B-tree.

Suppose you wanted to retrieve the data record for product number 1425. Notice that the value in the root node is 1250. Since 1425 is greater than 1250, you follow the arrow to the right of this node down to the next level. In this node you find the target value (1425), so you follow the middle arrow down to the leaf node that contains the value 1425. This node contains a pointer to the data record for product number 1425, so this record can now be retrieved. You should trace a similar path to locate the record for product number 1000.

As with any index structure, the data records may be stored in any physical

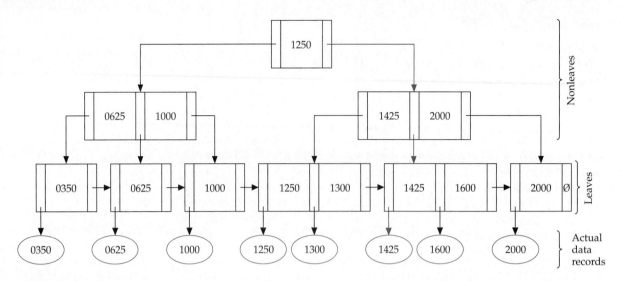

Figure 7-13

Example of a B+-tree

sequence, and the index permits retrieval in a sequence desired by the user. Since the data records are stored outside the index, multiple B+-tree indexes can be maintained on the same data. For example, we could define one B+-tree index on the primary key, and a second on a nonkey field. The B+-tree index is maintained automatically by the DBMS as values in the index change.

When to Use Indexes

During physical database design, you must choose which attributes to use to create indexes. There is a trade-off between improved performance for retrievals through the use of indexes, and degraded performance for inserting, deleting, and updating the records in a file. Thus indexes should be used generously for databases that are used primarily to support data retrievals, such as for decision support applications. Indexes should be used judiciously for databases that support transaction processing and other applications with heavy updating requirements, since the indexes impose additional overhead.

Following are some rules of thumb for choosing indexes for relational databases.

1. Specify a unique index for the primary key attribute of each table. This selection ensures the uniqueness of primary key values and speeds retrievals based on those values. Random retrieval based on primary key value is common for answering multiple-table queries and for simple data maintenance tasks.

2. Specify an index for foreign keys that are used in joining tables. As in point 1, this speeds processing multiple-table queries.

3. Specify an index for nonkey attributes that are referred to in qualification, sorting, and grouping commands (in SQL, these are WHERE, ORDER BY, and GROUP BY clauses, respectively).

To illustrate the use of these rules, consider the following relations for Pine Valley Furniture Company:

```
PRODUCT(PRODUCT_NO,DESCRIPTION,FINISH,ROOM,PRICE)
ORDER(ORDER_NO,PRODUCT_NO,QUANTITY)
```

You would normally specify a unique index for each primary key: PRODUCT_NO in PRODUCT and ORDER_NO in ORDER. Other indexes would be assigned based on how the data are used. For example, consider the following SQL retrieval command:

```
SELECT PRODUCT.PRODUCT_NO,DESCRIPTION,ORDER_NO,QUANTITY
  FROM PRODUCT,ORDER
  WHERE PRICE < 500
  AND PRODUCT.PRODUCT_NO=ORDER.PRODUCT_NO
  GROUP BY PRODUCT.PRODUCT_NO;
```

To speed up this retrieval, you could consider specifying indexes on the following nonkey attributes:

1. PRICE in PRODUCT (used in the WHERE clause to qualify the retrieval)
2. PRODUCT_NO in ORDER (foreign key referred to in the WHERE clause, used to join the two tables)

The challenge for the database designer is that users may direct a potentially large number of different queries against the database. You will probably have to be selective in specifying indexes to support the most common or frequently used queries. The data volume and usage analysis described earlier in this chapter can assist you in this process. The interested reader is referred to Gibson et al. (1989) for a discussion of the trade-offs made when selecting indexes.

INTEGRITY CONSTRAINTS

In Chapter 4, we described *business rules*, which are specifications that preserve the integrity of the database. There are four such types of business rules: entity integrity, referential integrity, domains, and triggering operations. Each category is implemented using various features of the DBMS. In this section we describe referential integrity in more detail, since there are often various options that may be specified by the database designer.

A **referential integrity constraint** is a business rule that addresses the validity of references by one object in a database to some other object (or objects) in the database. We can illustrate the requirement for referential integrity by a simple example (see Figure 7-14). The PART table contains a list of parts, and the VENDOR table contains a list of vendors. In this example, each part has exactly one vendor (but a vendor can supply many parts). VENDOR NO. is a foreign key in the PART relation. For each row in the PART relation VENDOR NO. references the vendor who supplies that part in the VENDOR relation.

Referential integrity constraint: A business rule that addresses the validity of references by one object in a database to some other object (or objects) in the database.

PART

PART_NO.	PART_NAME	VENDOR_NO.
100	Gizmo	10
200	Widget	40
300	Thumzer	30
400	Whatsit	10

VENDOR

VENDOR_NO.	VENDOR_NAME
10	Artcraft
20	Bakeright
30	Choicetops
40	Deskmate

Figure 7-14

Two associated relations

A referential integrity constraint requires the following: Each value in the foreign key column in the referencing table must be the same as a value in the corresponding primary key column in the referenced table, or else it must be null. In Figure 7-14, the PART table is the referencing table, and the VENDOR table is the referenced table. Notice that at the present time, all referential integrity constraints are satisfied. Thus for part number 100, the vendor number (10) matches the primary key for the first vendor in the VENDOR table. Similarly, there is a match on vendor number for each of the other parts.

Referential Integrity Rules

Referential integrity considerations arise primarily in the context of insertions and deletions, and we limit our discussion to these operations.

Insertion rule: A row should not be inserted in the referencing table unless there already exists a matching entry in the referenced table.

Insertion Rule   The insertion rule states that row should not be inserted in the referencing table unless there already exists a matching entry in the referenced table. In Figure 7-14, suppose an attempt is made to enter the following row for a new part:

    500 Kluge 50

This insertion request should be disallowed, since there is no entry for vendor number 50 in the VENDOR table. The user will have to create a new row for vendor number 50 in that table, before inserting any part referencing vendor number 50 in the PART table.

In some circumstances, an organization may wish to allow the insertion of part information, even though a vendor has not yet been determined for that part. This insertion can be accomplished without violating referential integrity constraints by leaving the vendor number null in the referencing table. Thus, the following insertion request would be allowed (the symbol "—" designates a null or missing value):

    500 Kluge —

The result of inserting this row in the PART table is shown in Figure 7-15. Referential integrity is not violated, since the vendor number is not yet determined.

Deletion rule: A row should not be deleted from the referenced table if there is a matching row (or rows) in the referencing table.

Deletion Rule   The deletion rule is that a row should not be deleted from the referenced table if there is a matching row (or rows) in the referencing table. In Figure 7-14, none of the rows in VENDOR can be deleted since there are matching rows in PART.

Consider the following SQL request:

Figure 7-15

Foreign key with nulls allowed

PART

PART_NO.	PART_NAME	VENDOR_NO.
100	Gizmo	10
200	Widget	40
300	Thumzer	30
400	Whatsit	10
500	Kluge	—

```
DELETE
  FROM VENDOR
  WHERE VENDOR__NO = 10;
```

This request should be disallowed, since there are matching rows in PART for vendor number 10. However, considering the possible use of nulls, there are three delete rules that might apply:

1. *Restrict.* Disallow the delete request.
2. *Nullify.* Reset to null any vendor number 10 in the PART relation, then delete vendor number 10 from VENDOR (see Figure 7-16a).
3. *Cascade.* Delete any part in the PART table for vendor number 10, then delete vendor number 10 from VENDOR (see Figure 7-16b).

The choice of delete rule in a given case depends on the nature of the business situation. For example, the restrict rule is appropriate if the intent is to remove only vendors with whom no business is being done. The nullify rule (Figure 7-16a) is appropriate if the intent is to remove any vendor and all traces (that is, part references) to that vendor. The cascade rule (Figure 7-16b) is appropriate if the intent is to stop using any part supplied by a deleted vendor.

Enforcing Referential Integrity

Referential integrity constraints can be enforced through two possible mechanisms:

1. Each application program must contain logic to independently enforce integrity constraints.
2. Referential integrity options are declared when relational tables are defined, and then enforced by the DBMS.

The first of these approaches is not reliable, since individual application programs may or may not have included the necessary logic to enforce referential integrity. Also, application programs that do contain referential integrity rules may conflict with each other. Thus we prefer the second approach (declarative referential integrity), since it provides consistent enforcement of rules. The current version of SQL (SQL-92) provides syntax and semantics for declaring referential integrity rules that implement each of the above options (Melton and Kulkarni, 1992).

PART

PART_NO.	PART_NAME	VENDOR_NO.
100	Gizmo	—
200	Widget	40
300	Thumzer	30
400	Whatsit	—

VENDOR

VENDOR_NO.	VENDOR_NAME
20	Bakeright
30	Choicetops
40	Deskmate

(a) Nullify

PART

PART_NO.	PART_NAME	VENDOR_NO.
200	Widget	40
300	Thumzer	30

VENDOR

VENDOR_NO.	VENDOR_NAME
20	Bakeright
30	Choicetops
40	Deskmate

(b) Cascade

Figure 7-16

Two delete rules

DENORMALIZATION

The logical database design process outlined in Chapter 6 results in the specification of normalized tables for a relational database. You do not, however, have to implement the database in its normalized form. Some database developers occasionally choose to implement a relational database that purposely violates the principles of normalization. Their goal is to reduce the number of physical database tables that must be accessed to retrieve the desired data by reducing the number of joins needed to derive a query answer. As we know from the discussion in Chapter 6, denormalization induces anomalies into the database that could require the extra work of updating redundant data. As Finkelstein (1988) points out, denormalization can also increase the chances of errors and inconsistencies, and can force reprogramming systems if business rules change.

Denormalization can actually cause extra query processing, not reduce query time. For example, consider the following denormalized table adapted from Figure 7-15:

PART NO.	PART NAME	VENDOR NO.	VENDOR NAME
100	Gizmo	10	Blendmore
200	Widget	40	Deskmate
300	Thumzer	30	Choicetops
400	Whatsit	10	Blendmore
500	Kluge	—	—

In this example, an update query to change the name of vendor 10 would cause two rows in this table to be accessed, whereas only one row in a normalized VENDOR table would be accessed. Further, denormalized rows are larger, which means that fewer rows can fit into a given secondary memory block, and fewer can reside in the same RAM storage space. These characteristics cause slower processing time for a variety of processing operations. Also, when normalized tables are intelligently indexed, as discussed in the prior section, rows can be quickly accessed and combined from multiple tables. Thus, denormalization from the logical to the physical database must be done with great care and for very specific reasons.

One common issue in normalization is whether a set of columns using the same domain of values constitute a repeating group, and hence violate first normal form. For example, consider the following SQL table definition:

```
CREATE TABLE CUSTOMER
    (CUST_NO          CHAR(7),
    CUST_NAME         CHAR(20),
    BILL_ADDRESS      CHAR(50),
    SHIP_ADDRESS      CHAR(50),
    CONTACT_ADDRESS   CHAR(50));
```

In this situation, there are three address columns from the same domain of values. The issue is whether the address columns in the CUSTOMER table should be split out into a separate table, as:

```
CREATE TABLE CUST_ADDRESS
   (CUST_NO         CHAR(7),
   ADDRESS_TYPE     SMALLINT,
   ADDRESS          CHAR(50));
```

Although any of the addresses in the CUSTOMER table might be null, there appears to be a fixed number of address fields. If there is a fixed number of columns from the same domain, then there is no need to split out these columns into a separate table. You must consider, however, whether there might be additional columns from this same domain at some time in the future. A common example of the need for additional columns in the future would be a student database in which you wish to store parents' names. A student may have an arbitrary number of parents, due to changing marital status. In this situation, splitting parents' names into a separate table would allow for changing conditions.

There are no hard-and-fast rules for deciding when to denormalize data from the logical data model. Rodgers (1989) discusses the general trade-offs. Some of the more common situations for which you should consider denormalization follow:

- *Two entities with a one-to-one relationship*. Even if one of the entities is an optional participant, if the matching entity exists most of the time, then it may be wise to combine these two entities into one table.

- *A many-to-many relationship with nonkey attributes*. Rather than causing three tables to be joined to extract data from the two entities in the relationship, it may be advisable to combine columns from one of the entities into the table representing the many-to-many relationship, thus avoiding one join in many queries.

- *Reference data*. Reference data exists in an entity on the one-side of a one-to-many relationship, and this entity participates in no other database relationships. You should especially consider merging the two entities in this situation when there are very few instances of the entity on the many-side for each entity instance on the one-side.

HIERARCHICAL AND NETWORK MODELS

In this chapter we have emphasized physical design for the relational data model. Since the hierarchical and network models are still used (especially as legacy systems), we conclude by briefly describing how to map the logical data model to either of these two data models.

Hierarchical Data Model

The hierarchical data model is an example of the tree structure introduced earlier in this chapter. Hierarchies are familiar structures. We usually view an organization as a hierarchy of positions and authority; we can view a computer program as a hierarchy of control and operating modules; and various taxonomies of animal and plant life place elements in a hierarchical set of relationships.

The *hierarchical database model*, as defined in Chapter 6, represents data as a set of nested one-to-many relationships. (One-to-one relationships are also permitted.) For example, Figure 7-17 shows a hierarchical database structure for Pine Valley Furniture Company. The record type CUSTOMER "owns" the record type

Figure 7-17

Example of a hierarchical data model (Pine Valley Furniture)

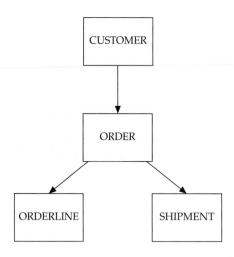

ORDER. CUSTOMER is referred to as the *parent* in this relationship, while ORDER is the *child*. In turn, ORDER is the parent of two record types: ORDERLINE and SHIPMENT. The single-headed arrow in this diagram denotes a one-to-many relationship (there is no need to use a more complicated notation, since each relationship in a hierarchy is presumed to be 1:*M*).

In summary, the following rules govern a hierarchical data structure:

1. A parent record type may "own" an arbitrary number of child record types. For example, in Figure 7-17 ORDER owns both ORDERLINE and SHIPMENT.

2. No single occurrence of a record type may have more than one parent record type (or occurrence) in the hierarchy.

The second rule is an obvious limitation of hierarchical data structures. For example, as shown in Figure 7-18a, ORDERLINE has two "natural" parents: PRODUCT and ORDER. This structure violates the single-parent rule of hierarchical structures.

As Figure 7-18b shows, we can resolve the problem of multiple parentage by splitting the relation in Figure 7-18a into two hierarchical data structures. Unfortunately, this solution produces redundancy, since ORDERLINE is now repeated under PRODUCT and ORDER. Some hierarchical implementations (such as the one described in Chapter 14) allow the designer to implement the structure shown in Figure 7-18a without redundancy, although this requires some processing overhead.

Network Data Model

In the preceding section we saw how the single-parent rule of the hierarchical data model forces redundant and excessive data and structure. When we allow this rule to be violated, we can create a *network data model* and further eliminate redundancy. The network model permits as much or as little structure as we desire. We can even create a hierarchy (a special case of a network). As with the hierarchical data model, if a certain relationship is not *explicitly* included in the database definition, then it cannot be used by a DBMS in processing a database.

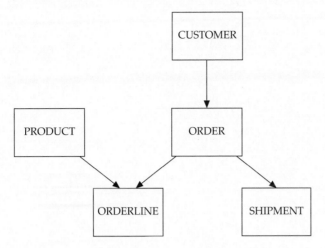

Figure 7-18

Resolving multiple
parentage

(a) ORDERLINE has multiple parents

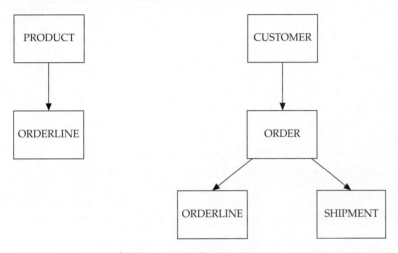

(b) Two separate database structures

An example of a network data model appears in Figure 7-18a, where the ORDERLINE record type has two parent record types: PRODUCT and ORDER. In general, a record type may have an arbitrary number of parents in the network data model.

The **simple network data model** supports 1:*N* but not *M:N* relationships. (All the relationships in Figure 7-18a are 1:*N*.) The simple network data model is the most common implementation of the network data model. We discuss this model in Chapter 15. The **complex network data model** supports *M:N* (as well as 1:*N*) relationships. Only few DBMS products support the complex network data model.

In the following sections, we illustrate mapping the conceptual data model first to a network, and then to a hierarchical data model. We use a conceptual data model for Mountain View Community Hospital (Figure 7-19) to illustrate this process. The mapping is relatively straightforward, since the E-R diagram shown in the figure already resembles a network data model. However, this model contains two *M:N* relationships (Attends to and Is Billed for) that must be trans-

Simple network data model: A type of network data model that supports 1:N (but not *M:N*) relationships.

Complex network data model: A type of network data model that supports M:N (as well as 1:*N*) relationships.

Figure 7-19

Conceptual data model
(Mountain View
Community Hospital)

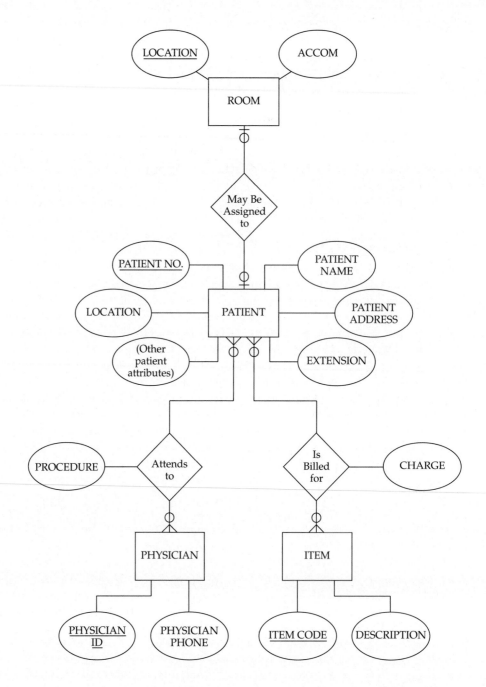

formed to 1:*N* relationships. If this transformation results in multiple parents for
a given record type, we must resolve the multiple parentage in the hierarchical
data model.

Mapping to a Network Data Model

The most common implementation of the network model is the CODASYL model
(described in Chapter 15). The CODASYL model usually requires the following
steps:

1. Define record types and associations.
2. Define sets (owner-member relationships).
3. Eliminate redundant keys (if unneeded).
4. Define record access strategies.

Figure 7-20 shows the result of transforming the conceptual data model of Figure 7-19 to a network data model. Following is a brief description of each of the four steps.

Define Record Types   Each entity in the conceptual data model becomes a CODASYL record type. The primary keys for each record type are underlined in Figure 7-20 (nonkey data are omitted for simplicity). Also, each many-to-many relationship is transformed to a record type. Figure 7-20 includes two such record types: TREATMENT, which is derived from the Attends to relationship, and CHARGES, which is derived from the Is Billed for relationship. This transformation is similar to the transformation for the relational model described in Chapter 6.

In the CODASYL model, a one-to-many association between record types is usually represented by an arrow with a single head. We use this convention in Figure 7-20. For example, there is a 1:M association from PATIENT to TREATMENT.

There is no provision in the CODASYL model to enforce the optional and mandatory characteristics of associations that appear in the conceptual (or logical) data model. Instead, these constraints must be enforced through the application programs that access the database. There are, however, clauses in the CODASYL data definition language for rules to control the insertion and retention of records in relationships. We cover these rules in Chapter 15.

Define Sets   The set is the basic building block in the CODASYL model. A **set** is a one-to-many association between two record types, where the first record

Set: In a network data base model a one-to-many association between two record types, where the first record type is called the *owner* and the second is called the *member*.

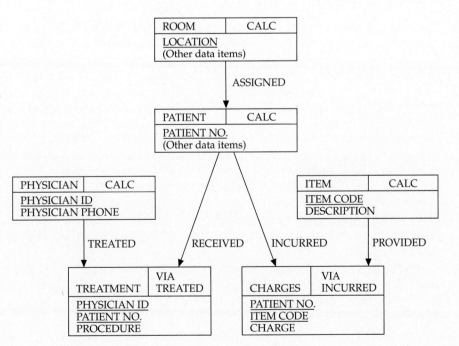

Figure 7-20

Network data model (Mountain View Community Hospital)

type is called the *owner*, and the second is called the *member*. Each set type is given a unique name.

In mapping to a network data model, we define a set for each 1:*M* association in the logical data model. For example, in Figure 7-20 the 1:*M* association between PHYSICIAN and TREATMENT is defined as a CODASYL set with the name TREATED. PHYSICIAN is the owner record type for this association, while TREATMENT is the member record type. For each occurrence of a PHYSICIAN record type, there may be zero, one, or more than one occurrence of a TREATMENT record type.

In the conceptual data model (Figure 7-19), the association from ROOM to PATIENT is optional 1:1. This means that each bed location is either assigned to a patient or is unassigned. The CODASYL model makes no provision for directly enforcing only one patient per location; this provision must be handled by the application program for room assignment.

Eliminate Redundant Keys   In the conceptual data model, composite primary keys and foreign keys are normally redundant. For example, in Figure 7-20 the composite key for CHARGES is (PATIENT NO., ITEM CODE). The PATIENT NO. data item is contained in the parent PATIENT record type, while ITEM CODE is contained in the parent ITEM record type. When mapping to a CODASYL data model, these duplicate keys are candidates for elimination because the associations they imply are represented by the CODASYL sets. For example, the composite key (PATIENT NO.,ITEM CODE) can be eliminated from the CHARGES record type.

Whether keys should in fact be eliminated (to avoid redundancy) is a design decision. In general, these keys should *not* be eliminated if any of the following three conditions hold:

1. The key in question is required for direct access to a record.
2. The key in question is normally required for reference purposes, and removing it will often necessitate referencing the owner record occurrence.
3. The key is used to sort the member records of a set.

As an example of the first case, the composite key (PATIENT NO.,ITEM CODE) could be used for direct access to CHARGES records if this is a requirement. To illustrate the second situation, suppose that in examining an occurrence of the CHARGES record, we normally need to identify the PATIENT NO. If PATIENT NO. were removed from the CHARGES record type, we would have to reference a PATIENT record occurrence (owner record) to determine this information. For the third case, consider the need to display CHARGES records in PATIENT NO. sequence for each ITEM. If CHARGES records are sorted in PATIENT NO. order within the PROVIDED set, we can avoid using a sort utility to arrange the records into the desired sequence.

In summary, deciding whether or not to eliminate keys requires a trade-off between redundancy and performance. The designers must consider the anticipated usage patterns to evaluate each individual case. In Figure 7-20, we have retained the redundant data items so that they can be used for reference purposes.

Define Record-Access Strategies   The last major step in mapping to a network model is to define the basic techniques for accessing occurrences of each record type in the model. Although there are many variations, there are two basic record-access (or location mode) strategies in the CODASYL model:

1. **CALC.** We access records directly by supplying a primary key value.
2. **VIA.** We access records through a set relationship. Thus, we first access an owner record occurrence (often using CALC), and then we access each set-member occurrence for that owner. VIA results in a *physical* clustering of member records near to the associated owner record.

The access strategies used depend on the way data will be accessed by various users and their applications. In Figure 7-20, notice that four of the record types are accessed directly in CALC mode: ROOM, PATIENT, PHYSICIAN, and ITEM. Thus, we can access an instance of each of these records by supplying a primary key value. The other two record types (CHARGES and TREATMENT) are accessed using VIA set relationships. TREATMENT is normally accessed by means of the TREATED relationship, while CHARGES is accessed primarily by means of the INCURRED relationship.

The VIA clause defines the primary access path to records, but we can also access records through secondary access paths. For example, we can access CHARGES records by using the PROVIDED as well as the INCURRED set relationship. However, secondary access paths are nearly always slower and less efficient. We describe the details of various CODASYL access strategies in more detail in Chapter 15.

In essence, the CODASYL approach to database implementation provides efficient, rapid access, provided that predefined access paths are used. Since the CODASYL approach is somewhat less flexible, it is more resistant to change than some other models (especially the relational model).

CALC: A record-access strategy in the CODASYL data model in which records are stored and accessed by supplying a primary key value.

VIA: A record-access strategy in the CODASYL data model in which records are stored and accessed through a set relationship.

Mapping to a Hierarchical Model

When we examined the hierarchical and network models earlier in this section, we noted that they are similar, except that the hierarchical model does not permit multiple parentage. Therefore, mapping to a hierarchical model may be performed in two stages:

1. Map the conceptual model to a network model (as described above).
2. Map the network model to a hierarchical model by introducing redundancy as needed to resolve multiple parentage and to provide ease of access to the data.

An initial transformation of the network data model, resulting in three hierarchical structures (with some redundancy), is shown in Figure 7-21a. These structures are true hierarchical models, since there is no multiple parentage. However, with the hierarchical data model we must access all data by starting at the root node (specific implementations often permit more flexible access). Thus, in the model in Figure 7-21a, to access PATIENT, TREATMENT, or CHARGES data, we must start with a ROOM reference, which would undoubtedly be quite awkward. To eliminate this restriction, it may be necessary to decompose the hierarchy into the four structures shown in Figure 7-21b. Notice that this solution introduces further redundancy (the PATIENT record type appears twice). In using the hierarchical data model, designers must make numerous trade-offs such as this to arrive at an acceptable solution. We describe an implementation of the hierarchical data model in detail in Chapter 14.

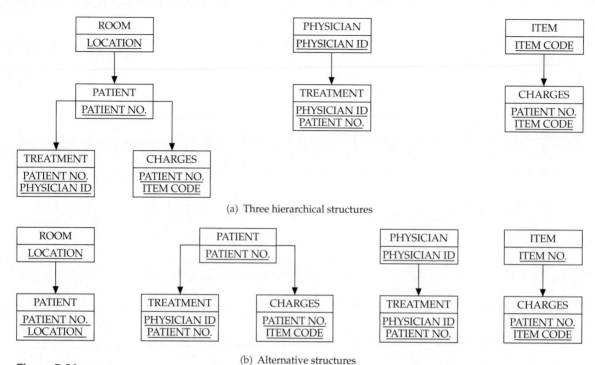

(a) Three hierarchical structures

(b) Alternative structures

Figure 7-21

Hierarchical data structure (Mountain View Community Hospital)

SUMMARY

Physical database design is concerned with transforming the logical database structures into an internal model consisting of stored records, files, indexes, and other physical structures. The objective of physical design is to implement the database to meet user needs in terms of performance, security, integrity, and related factors.

Some implementation design is required when the target DBMS supports a hierarchical or network data model. In this case, we must map the logical data model to either hierarchical or network structures. Mapping to a hierarchical data model involves identifying the root node types, identifying dependent node types, and resolving multiple parentage. Mapping to a network data model includes defining record types, defining sets, eliminating redundant keys (if desired), and defining record-access strategies.

Many of the decisions in physical database design depend on estimates of the size and probable usage patterns of the data. Data volume analysis is the process of estimating database size by estimating the number and size of each database entity or record type. Data usage analysis identifies the major database transactions and the access paths required for each transaction. A composite usage map provides a concise reference to the estimated volume and usage of data in the database.

One of the more interesting problems in physical database design is deciding on the distribution of data among the nodes of a network. There are three basic data distribution strategies: centralized, partitioned, and replicated. With the partitioned approach, the central database is partitioned into disjoint (nonoverlapping) partitions, called *fragments*. Each partition is assigned to a particular site. With a replicated approach, a full copy of the database (or at least some subset of the database) is assigned to *each* site in the network. A hybrid approach combines the elements of both the partitioned and replicated approaches. We base the data distribution decision on an analysis of information describing data usage and the characteristics of the network.

In most relational databases, we can specify an index for any attribute in a given table. Indexes are usually implemented in the form of tree structures, with the B+-tree (where the B stands for balanced) being the most common. Although indexes improve performance for data retrievals, they do tend to degrade performance for inserting, deleting, and updating the rows of a table. Also, indexes increase the cost of table reorganization, backup, and recovery. As a result, we must choose indexes carefully to balance performance trade-offs.

Although it is most common to implement a relational database in normalized form, there are situations for which you should consider whether denormalizing would improve database processing performance. Denormalization reintroduces the types of anomalies eliminated by the normalization process, so it must be done with care.

CHAPTER REVIEW

Key Words

Balanced tree (B-tree)	File organization	Pointer
Branching factor (degree of a tree)	Hashed file organization	Referential integrity constraint
CALC	Hashing algorithm	Replicated data distribution
Centralized data distribution	Hybrid data distribution	Root node
Clustering attribute	Index	Sequential file organization
Clustering index	Indexed file organization	Set
Complex network data model	Indexed nonsequential	Simple network data model
	Indexed sequential	Subtree
Composite usage map	Insertion rule	Transaction map
Deletion rule	Leaf node	Tree
Depth	Partitioned data distribution	VIA

REVIEW QUESTIONS

1. Give concise definitions for each of the following terms:
   a. tree
   b. branching factor
   c. leaf node
   d. depth
   e. balanced tree
   f. hashing algorithm
   g. index
   h. clustering attribute
   i. file organization
   j. fragment
   k. physical design
   l. clustering index
2. Contrast the following terms:
   a. leaf node; root node
   b. clustering attribute; clustering index
   c. tree; subtree
   d. branching factor; depth
   e. CALC; VIA
3. List and briefly describe four basic data distribution strategies.
4. What are the major inputs to physical database design?

5. What is the purpose of data volume and usage analysis?
6. What is meant by the "all beneficial sites" method of data distribution?
7. List seven important criteria in selecting file organizations.
8. Describe two important functions that are performed by unique (primary key) indexes.
9. What is the main advantage of balanced trees over other types of indexes?
10. State three rules of thumb for choosing indexes.
11. Define denormalization, and explain the hazards of denormalizing data.

PROBLEMS AND EXERCISES

1. Match the following terms to the appropriate definitions.

___ physical design   a. maximum number of child nodes

___ root node   b. used to group rows with common values

___ branching factor   c. partition of a database

___ depth   d. maps logical model to internal model

___ fragment   e. has no child nodes

___ index   f. all leaves are at the same depth

___ clustering index   g. data structure that branches out

___ hashing algorithm   h. node at the top of a tree

___ tree   i. number of levels between root and leaves

___ subtree   j. a node and its descendants

___ leaf node   k. converts primary key values to addresses

___ balanced tree   l. data structure that helps locate records

2. Consider the following two relations for Lakewood College:

```
STUDENT(STUDENT ID,STUDENT_NAME,CAMPUS_ADDRESS,GPA)
REGISTRATION(STUDENT ID,COURSE ID,GRADE)
```

Following is a typical query against these relations:

```
SELECT STUDENT.STUDENT_ID,STUDENT_NAME,COURSE_ID,GRADE
   FROM STUDENT,REGISTRATION
     WHERE  STUDENT.STUDENT_ID=REGISTRATION.STUDENT_ID
     AND    GPA>3.0
   ORDER BY STUDENT_NAME;
```

   a. On what attributes should indexes be defined to speed up the above query? Give the reason for each attribute selected.
   b. Write SQL commands to create indexes for each attribute you identified in (a).
3. Consider the logical data model with volumes and ratios for Mountain View Community Hospital (Figure 7-2). After a period of time, the assumptions for this model have changed as follows:
   a. There is an average of 12 (rather than 10) charges for each patient.
   b. The records for each patient are kept active for an average of 15 (rather than 30) days.
   c. The average length of stay in the hospital is 5 (rather than 3) days.
   Draw a new diagram reflecting this new information to replace Figure 7-2.
4. Create a transaction analysis form (similar to the one shown in Figure 7-3) for the CREATE TREATMENT transaction. Following is a summary of this transaction:

a. The transaction volume averages 5 per hour, with a peak of 12 per hour. (Base your calculations on the average volume.)

b. The user first accesses the relevant PATIENT record (once per transaction), then the relevant PHYSICIAN record (once per transaction), and finally creates a new TREATMENT record (once per transaction).

5. Figure 7-22 shows a conceptual data model for a simple purchasing database. Map this conceptual model to a CODASYL logical model. Assume the following access patterns:

a. SUPPLIER, BUYER, and PURCH ORDER require direct access.

b. INVOICE occurrences are retrieved by first retrieving a PURCH ORDER occurrence and then retrieving all related INVOICE occurrences.

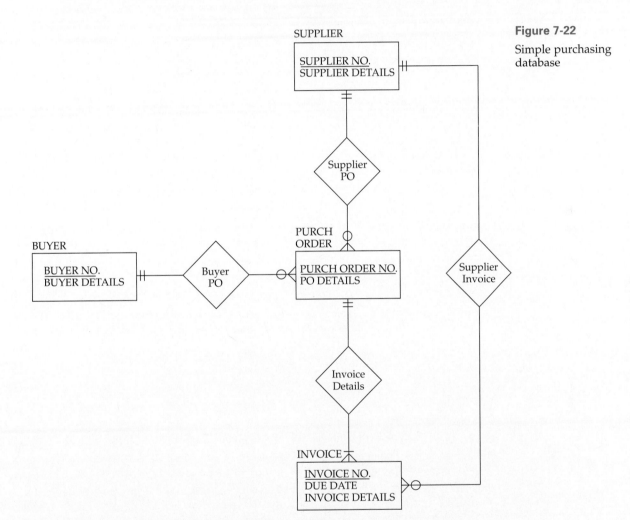

Figure 7-22

Simple purchasing database

6. Map the conceptual data model shown in Figure 7-22 to a hierarchical model (see assumption in Problem 5).

7. A fourth relation (R4) is to be added to the database for Hy-Tek Corporation (see Tables 7–1 and 7–2). Relation R4 (which will be 1.0MB in size) has the following average query and update times (in milliseconds):

	Query	Update
Local	50	100
Remote	300	500

All three of the transactions in Table 7-2 will access relation R4 as follows:

Transaction	Access to R4
T1	2R, 1W
T2	4R, 1W
T3	1R, 1W

Your assignment is to decide where to locate R4 for Hy-Tek Corporation using the "all beneficial sites" method.

8. A new transaction (T4) is to be added to the distributed data processing system for Hy-Tek Corporation. Transaction T4 has the following characteristics (see Table 7-2):

Originating sites: S1, S3, S4

Frequency (each site): 1 per second

Relation accesses: R1: 2R, 1W
R2: 4R, 1W
R3: 1R, 1W

Your assignment is to recalculate and (if necessary) redistribute the three relations R1, R2, and R3 for Hy-Tek Corporation. (*Note:* This problem is *independent* of Problem 7.)

9. Hy-Tek Corporation is considering changes to its distributed processing system that would reduce the times required for remote query and updates as follows (see Table 7-1):

Relation	Size	Ave. Local Time (ms)		Ave. Remote Time (ms)	
		Query	Update	Query	Update
R1	1MB	100	150	300	400
R2	3MB	150	200	200	400
R3	5MB	200	250	500	700

Your assignment is to recalculate and (if necessary) redistribute the data for Hy-Tek Corporation based on these revised access times. (*Note:* This problem is *independent* of Problems 7 and 8.)

REFERENCES

Comer, D. 1979. "The Ubiquitous B-tree." *ACM Computing Surveys* 11 (June):121–37.

Elmasri, R., and S. Navathe. 1989. *Fundamentals of Database Systems.* Redwood City, Calif.: Benjamin/Cummings.

Finkelstein, R. 1988. "Breaking the Rules Has a Price." *Database Programming & Design* 1 (June):11–14.

Gibson, M., C. Hughes, and W. Remington. 1989. "Tracking the Trade-Offs with Inverted Lists." *Database Programming & Design* 2 (Jan.):28–34.

Hogan, R. 1988. "Usage Path Analysis." *Database Programming & Design* 1 (Sept.):37–43.

Melton, J., and K. Kulkarni. 1992. "Out With the Old." *Database Programming & Design* 5 (Aug.):26–27.

Rodgers, U. 1989. "Denormalization: Why, What, and How?" *Database Programming & Design* 2(12) (Dec.):46–53.

Teorey, T. J., J. Chaar, K. Olukotun, and A. Umar. 1989. "Allocation Methods for Distributed Database." *Database Programming & Design* 2 (Apr.):34–42.

PART **III**

Relational Database
Implementation

Taco Bell Corporation

MANAGING INFORMATION OVERLOAD

In Part III we describe implementations of relational database systems. Chapter 8 describes SQL (Structured Query Language), which has become a standard language for creating and processing relational databases. Chapter 9 provides an introduction to implementing a dBASE IV database, while Chapter 10 introduces a different approach (called Query-by-Example) using a Paradox database. Finally, Chapter 11 describes some advanced features of database systems, including graphical user interfaces (GUIs), forms designers, and report generators.

Taken together, the four chapters in Part III provide a foundation for understanding how organizations can exploit relational database systems to develop new, mission-critical applications. Taco Bell Corporation is using this approach to help manage the information overload that results from its rapid growth. Taco Bell (a division of PepsiCo) has some 3,500 fast-food outlets in the United States that generate annual sales of nearly $3 billion. New units are opened almost daily, as the company continues its rapid growth pattern.

Taco Bell's central information system is based on DB2 relational databases running on IBM series 9000 mainframes. This system is linked to individual food outlets by telecommunications and is used to track sales and manage the logistics of supplying stores. However, the company's growth rate had threatened to overcome the capacity of the centralized system to support the opening of new outlets. Each new outlet represents a substantial investment; therefore, the site must be chosen carefully and the project must be managed to maximize the productivity of employees in the field.

To meet these objectives, Taco Bell developed two new applications called Construction Manager Workbench and Real Estate Manager Workbench. They were developed using a relational DBMS and implemented on laptop computers. Taco Bell real estate and construction managers use these applications in the field to assist them in opening new locations. Both workbench applications replace manual procedures. For example, Real Estate Manager Workbench assists managers in selecting building sites and performing purchase-versus-lease studies based on various criteria. It lets the real estate manager collect data on demographics, population count, competitors' sales volumes, traffic counts, and other factors. The Construction Manager Workbench assists managers in super-vising the construction process, including project planning, budgets, and schedules.

The workbench applications all have user-friendly graphical user interfaces that operate under Microsoft Windows. In particular, a forms designer allows users to place buttons, check boxes, and paint fields on the form that are tied to the relational databases. The applications are also integrated with Microsoft Windows productivity tools such as Excel, Word, and MS Project. Future plans call for joining the workbench data with the mainframe DB2 databases through telecommunications. This will allow the graphical data to be shared by users throughout the whole organization, which will further enhance Taco Bell's ability to manage its rapid growth.

SQL: A Standard
for Database Processing

LEARNING OBJECTIVES

After studying this chapter, you should be able to:

- Define a database using the SQL data definition language.
- Write single and multiple table queries using SQL commands.
- Create a view in SQL, and know when and why views are created.
- Define three types of join commands, and be able to use SQL to directly or indirectly write queries for each of these types of joins.
- Write noncorrelated and correlated subqueries, and know when to write each.
- Write SQL commands to add, delete, and change database contents.
- Explain the benefits and hazards of having a standard database language like SQL.
- Explain the general capabilities of relational database management systems.

INTRODUCTION

This chapter is the first of four chapters on relational database management systems (RDBMSs). Many different database management systems built for the relational data model (see Chapter 6 and Codd, 1970, 1982) exist. More than one type of relational DBMS is available; however, most products now include a particular relational language called the Structured Query Language (SQL) (introduced in Chapter 2). Thus, we concentrate in this chapter on the SQL standard of data creation and manipulation. Although the basics of SQL and the relational data model are present in a wide selection of products, the style of relational data manipulation languages and the extent of vendor-introduced enhancements vary across products.

The primary purpose of this chapter is to review in depth the most common language for relational systems, SQL, which has been accepted as a standard by the American National Standards Institute (ANSI) and the International Organization for Standardization. The ANSI SQL standards were published first in 1986 and updated in 1989 and 1992. A new SQL3 standard is under development at the time of this writing. Melton (1993) and Melton and Kulkarni (1992a, 1992b) present a thorough analysis of the evolution of the SQL standard.

SQL has been implemented in both mainframe and personal computer systems, so this chapter is relevant to both computing environments. SQL is available under the IBM OS/2 operating system as the Extended Edition Database Manager, on the IBM AS/400 as the Database Manager, and as DB2 under the MVS and as SQL/DS under the VM operating systems. Other products that provide an SQL language include Oracle from Oracle Corporation, SQL Server from Microsoft, SQLBase from Sybase, Ingres from Relational Technologies, R:Base from Microrim, IDMS/R from Computer Associates, and the DBC/1012 database machine from Teradata.

An originally non-SQL database system that now includes an SQL capability is dBASE IV. In this chapter, we use the dBASE IV version of SQL where possible; we use SQL/DS, the SQL sublanguage in Ingres, or Oracle when dBASE IV is missing some SQL feature.

In Chapter 9 we review the non-SQL parts of dBASE in depth. The original, proprietary dBASE language was developed from a style of relational languages called *relational algebra systems* (SQL follows the relational calculus style). Relational algebra was the dominant style for PC systems until SQL was introduced into these products. In Chapter 10 we explain a third type of relational system, Query-by-Example (similar to the dBASE query module introduced in Chapter 2), using Paradox 4.0 for illustrations. Finally, in Chapter 11 we discuss and illustrate the form- and report-generation features of relational systems, and we introduce the type of relational database interface possible in a Microsoft® Windows operating environment.

SQL: A STANDARD FOR RELATIONAL SYSTEMS

Many DBMSs are said to be relational. In fact, without even trying to generate an exhaustive list, we can safely say that more data management products claim to be relational than claim to be all other data models combined. For practical purposes it does not matter what a DBMS is called; what matters is that the DBMS has the features required for our data processing. Nevertheless, a careful attempt to distinguish relational from nonrelational systems will highlight the important features of relational implementations (Codd, 1985a, 1985b). Of course, a system that obeys the rules of a *truly* relational DBMS has certain desirable properties and capabilities that give it tremendous power and provide integrity of database processing. (See Appendix A, "Codd's 12 Rules for a Truly Relational System," for a discussion of what constitutes a *truly* relational DBMS.)

Relational DBMS (RDBMS): A database management system that manages data as a collection of tables in which all data relationships are represented by common values in related tables.

Most people agree that a relational database is one perceived by its users as a collection of tables in which all data relationships are represented by common values, not links. A **relational DBMS (or RDBMS)**, then, is a data management system that uses this view of data, which was illustrated in Chapter 2 for the Pine Valley Furniture database system.

To provide some direction for the development of RDBMSs, the American National Standards Institute (ANSI) and the International Organization for Standardization have approved a standard for the SQL relational query language (functions and syntax) proposed originally by the X3H2 Technical Committee on Database (Technical Committee X3H2—Database, 1986; ISO, 1987). The 1986 standards have been updated to form SQL2 (Technical Committee X3H2—Database, 1989; ISO, 1989, 1991), and new standards are being written in 1992 at the time of this writing.

The purposes of the SQL standard follow:

1. To specify the syntax and semantics of SQL data definition and manipulation languages

2. To define the data structures and basic operations for designing, accessing, maintaining, controlling, and protecting an SQL database

3. To provide a vehicle for portability of database definition and application modules between conforming DBMSs

4. To specify both minimal (Level 1) and complete (Level 2) standards, which permit different degrees of adoption in products

5. To provide an initial standard, although incomplete, that will be enhanced later to include specifications for handling such topics as referential integrity, transaction management, user-defined functions, join operators beyond the equi-join, and national character sets (among others)

An indirect effect, which may not have been intended, is that acceptance of *an* SQL standard has been interpreted by many as acceptance of SQL as *the* approved RDBMS query language. Even before the Technical Committee began its work, several SQL-based products were on the market (for example, SQL/DS and DB2 from IBM, and Oracle from Oracle Corp.). Since the adoption of the SQL standard, various mainframe and PC RDBMS vendors have announced that their packages will be enhanced to include an SQL language interface to their existing product. Thus, the market is accepting SQL as a necessary structured query language, although certainly not the only programming language, for relational database access. In addition, the SQL standard is being reviewed by the International Standards Organization (ISO) and may become the international standard for relational query languages.

The benefits of such a standardized relational language include the following:

- *Reduced training costs.* Training in an organization can concentrate on one language, and a large labor pool of IS professionals trained in a common language reduces retraining when hiring new employees.

- *Productivity.* IS professionals can learn SQL thoroughly and become proficient with it from continued use; the organization can afford to invest in tools to help IS professionals become more productive; programmers can more quickly maintain existing programs since they are familiar with the language in which programs are written.

- *Application portability.* Applications can be moved from machine to machine when each machine uses SQL; further, it is economical for the computer software industry to develop off-the-shelf application software when there is a standard language.

- *Application longevity.* A standard language tends to remain so for a long time, so there will be little pressure to rewrite old applications; rather, applications will simply be updated as the standard language is enhanced or new versions of DBMSs are introduced.

- *Reduced dependence on single vendor.* When a nonproprietary language is used, it is easier to use different vendors for the DBMS, training and educational services, application software, and consulting assistance; further, the market for such vendors will be more competitive, which may lower prices and improve service.

• *Cross-system communication.* Different DBMSs and application programs can more easily communicate and cooperate in managing data and processing user programs.

On the other hand, a standard can stifle creativity and innovation; one standard is never enough to meet all needs, and an industry standard can be far from ideal since it may be the offspring of compromises between many parties. A standard may be difficult to change (because so many vendors have a vested interest in it), so fixing such deficiencies may take considerable effort. Another hazard is that when you use special features added to SQL by a particular vendor, you may lose some of the advantages listed above.

SQL is not without its critics, who claim that the *initial* SQL standard, although a good start, has definite flaws. Date (1987b) claims that important features (such as referential integrity rules and certain relational operators) are omitted and that the language is extremely redundant (that is, there is more than one way to write the same query). These limitations will become clear in this chapter. It can be expected that the SQL standard will be further modified, probably led by the capabilities of SQL-based DBMSs.

RELATIONAL DATA DEFINITION IN SQL

In this section we discuss various SQL commands for defining the structure of a database. We show the commands available in dBASE IV, along with some examples of extensions to the basic SQL data definition language (DDL) available in several other products or newer versions of the SQL standard. In Chapter 6 we learned how to design a relational database using normalization to derive the relations to be defined. In this section we assume that this design has occurred, and we concentrate on the translation of these relations into DDL.

To illustrate the use of typical relational DDLs, we again refer to the Mountain View Community Hospital (MVCH) database of Figure 4-28. Figure 8-1 contains a list of the commands necessary to define this database using the SQL DDL of dBASE IV.

dBASE limits table (and view) names to up to 8 characters and column names to up to 10 characters; therefore, the table and column names from Figure 4-28 have been abbreviated as necessary in Figure 8-1.

Not shown in Figure 8-1 or subsequent SQL commands is a special symbol used in some SQL implementations—a line-continuation character. For example, in interactive mode, SQL/DS (IBM Corp., 1991) interprets each 80-character line as one free-format text command. Thus, if a command cannot all fit on one line, it must be continued, and SQL/DS must be told to wait to process the command until all lines for that command have been entered. In SQL/DS this continuation symbol is the hyphen (-), which is placed at the end of a continued line. In most SQL versions, a semicolon designates the end of the command, as in the dBASE version of SQL.

Data Types

Each DBMS will support various types of data for columns in a relational table. The choice of data type should be made to allow any legal value for the column to be entered. In addition, a wise choice for data type helps to control the integrity

```
CREATE TABLE ROOM
   (LOCATION                        CHAR(4),
    ACCOM                           CHAR(2),
    EXTENSION                       SMALLINT,
    PATIENT_NO                      INTEGER);

CREATE TABLE PATIENT
   (PATIENT_NO                      INTEGER,
    DATE_DISCH                      DATE,
    ...Other data elements...);

CREATE TABLE PHY
   (PHY_ID                          CHAR(10),
    PHY_PHONE                       CHAR(8));

CREATE TABLE ITEM
   (ITEM_CODE                       SMALLINT,
    DESCRIPT                        CHAR(15));

CREATE TABLE ATTENDS
   (PHY_ID                          CHAR(10),
    PATIENT_NO                      INTEGER,
    PROCEDURE                       CHAR(15));

CREATE TABLE BILLED
   (PATIENT_NO                      INTEGER,
    ITEM_CODE                       SMALLINT,
    CHARGE                          DECIMAL(7,2));
```

Figure 8-1

SQL database definition for Mountain View Community Hospital

of data by causing invalid values to be rejected by the DBMS. The types for the dBASE SQL system follow:

DECIMAL(m,n) Signed numbers, where m is the total number of digits (including sign), and n is the number of digits to the right of the decimal point (examples: a part's unit weight or dimensions).

INTEGER Large (up to 11 digits) positive or negative whole numbers (examples: a country's population or the quantity on hand of a part).

SMALLINT Small (5 or 6 digits, depending on the DBMS) positive or negative whole numbers. By specifying this data type, less storage space is required (examples: age, temperature, or an airline flight number).

FLOAT(m,n) Whole and fractional numbers represented in scientific notation, where m is the total number of digits (including sign), and n is the number of digits to the right of the decimal point (example: engineering specifications).

CHAR(n) Alphanumeric (character) data, where n is the maximum length for this character string; n character positions are allocated to each instance of a CHAR column (examples: customer name or product description).

DATE Calendar dates. A system variable can be used to set the format for the date data type—for example, month/day/year or year/month/day (examples: order date or subscription anniversary date).

LOGICAL True or false values.

Other SQL systems often include additional data types of

VARCHAR(n)	Character data that vary significantly in length. Such data are stored in a variable-length format, to reduce wasted space (examples: detailed product description or an address).
LONG VARCHAR	Variable-length character data that can be longer than the VARCHAR data type allows (examples: comments on a customer order or instructions for building a custom product).

The SQL92 standard has added data types of time, bit, timestamp, and interval. It also allows specification of the valid character set for each column. For example, if Mountain View Community Hospital opened a branch in Japan, the NAME of a patient might be defined as

```
NAME CHAR(40) CHARACTER SET IS KANJI
```

Data Definition Commands

Including CREATE TABLE, seven SQL DDL commands are typically available in SQL DBMSs:

CREATE TABLE	Defines a new table and its columns.
DROP TABLE	Destroys a table (definition and contents as well as any views and indexes associated with it). Usually only the table creator may delete the table.
ALTER TABLE	Adds one or more new columns to a table. (In some RDBMSs this would also permit deleting columns or redefining the column's data type.) Usually only the table creator may add columns to the table.
CREATE INDEX	Defines an index on one column (or a concatenation of columns) that enables rapid access to the rows of a table in a sequence or randomly by key value. A table may have many indexes, and each index may be specified to be UNIQUE (primary key) or not and may be sequenced in ascending or descending order.
DROP INDEX	Destroys an index. Usually only the table creator may delete an index of that table.
CREATE VIEW	Defines a logical table from one or more tables or views. (Views may not be indexed.) There are limitations on updating data through a view, but some updating of data through a view is permitted.
DROP VIEW	Destroys a view definition (and any other views defined from the deleted view). Usually only the creator of the view's base tables may delete a view.

We illustrate these commands and other data definition features in the following sections.

Null value: A special column value, distinct from 0, blank, or any other value, that indicates that the value for the column is missing or otherwise unknown.

Column Controls   A column may assume a special value, called a **null value**, when the value for that column in a given row is missing or unknown. Null is distinct from 0 or blank, which may be legitimate, known values for a column.

NOT NULL is an integrity control in some SQL systems (but not in dBASE) that tells the DBMS not to permit a null value for a specific column of any row in the table. For example, in the definition of the ITEM table in Figure 8-1, the ITEM_CODE column should be NOT NULL. The NOT NULL control is enforced on all data update statements. You usually apply NOT NULL to key fields (the relational data model requires that primary key columns be not null), but you may apply NOT NULL to any column as appropriate (for example, a cross-reference key may be NOT NULL).

UNIQUE is another column integrity control that specifies that the values of a column must be unique across all rows of the table. You use UNIQUE only with single columns, so unique concatenated keys (like PATIENT_NO + ITEM_CODE for the BILLED table in Figure 8-1) can only be handled by creating a unique index, which we illustrate later in this chapter.

Changing Table Definitions You may change table definitions in many SQL RDBMSs by ALTERing column specifications. In dBASE IV, the ALTER TABLE command adds new columns to an existing table. For example, we could add a patient name column to the PATIENT table by

```
ALTER TABLE PATIENT
  ADD (NAME CHAR(20));
```

The NAME column is added to the end of existing rows, and values are initialized with blanks. We may not drop previously defined columns or change the data type of an existing column. To drop a column, you must define a view (see the following section on view definition) on the base table that omits the column no longer desired, or you may create a new table, leaving out the column to be dropped, and then insert the data from the previous table into the new one. The ALTER command is invaluable for adapting the database to inevitable modifications due to changing requirements, prototyping, evolutionary development, and mistakes. Some relational systems do support column dropping and data type changes.

Additional Table Definition Features Like many SQL-based systems, dBASE provides several commands to assist in documenting table definitions and with the flexibility of using defined data:

CREATE SYNONYM	Specifies an alternative name for a table or view; often used to define an abbreviation to reduce the number of keystrokes needed when referring to a table or view.
DROP SYNONYM	Destroys a synonym declaration.
DBDEFINE	Creates SQL database definitions for tables that have already been defined under the dBASE proprietary system; this is needed to allow access to the same data files by both dBASE and its SQL sublanguage.

SQL/DS has two additional features to make data definitions more flexible:

LABEL	Defines a column heading to be used in place of the column name in query results; an advantage is the uniform heading of columns across all applications.
COMMENT	Provides an explanatory remark for table columns that is stored as part of the internal system tables and can be queried via SQL, thus extending the built-in data dictionary features of SQL/DS.

The following are examples of the use of some of these commands for the ITEM table and its DESCRIPT column, defined in Figure 8-1:

```
COMMENT ON ITEM COLUMN DESCRIPTION
   IS 'Selected from medical dictionary of terms';
CREATE SYNONYM IT FOR ITEM;
DROP SYNONYM IT;
LABEL ON TABLE ITEM COLUMN DESCRIPT
   IS 'Standard Description';
```

View Definition

The often-stated purpose of a view (defined in Chapter 2) is to simplify query commands, but a view may also provide valuable data security and significantly enhance programming productivity for a database. To highlight the convenience of a view, consider the Patient Bill of Figure 4-23. Construction of the lines of this bill requires access to three tables from the MVCH database of Figure 8-1: PATIENT, BILLED, and ITEM. A novice database user may make mistakes or be unproductive in properly formulating queries involving so many tables. A view allows us to predefine this association into a single virtual table as part of the database. With this view, a user who wants only Patient Bill data does not have to reconstruct the joining of data to produce the report or any subset of it.

We define a view, DET_BILL, by specifying an SQL query that has the view as its result. For the Patient Bill, this would be

```
CREATE VIEW DET_BILL AS
     SELECT BILLED.PATIENT_NO, BILLED.ITEM_CODE,
       DESCRIPT, CHARGE, NAME and other columns as required
     FROM PATIENT, BILLED, ITEM
     WHERE PATIENT.PATIENT_NO = BILLED.PATIENT_NO
       AND ITEM.ITEM_CODE = BILLED.ITEM_CODE;
```

The SELECT clause specifies what data elements (columns) are to be included in the view table. The FROM clause lists the tables involved in the view development. The WHERE clause specifies the names of the common columns used to join BILLED to ITEM and to PATIENT. Because a view is a table, and one of the relational properties of tables is that the order of rows is immaterial, the rows in a view may not be sorted (the ORDER BY clause in SQL). However, queries that refer to this view may display their results in any desired sequence.

A view is not maintained as real data; rather it is constructed automatically as needed by the DBMS. Therefore, a view is a virtual table. A view always contains the most current derived values and is thus superior in terms of data currency to constructing a temporary real table from several base tables. Also in comparison to a temporary real table, a view obviously consumes very little storage space. A view is costly, however, since its contents must be calculated each time they are requested.

A view may join multiple tables or other views together and may contain derived (or virtual) columns. For example, a user in Mountain View Community Hospital may simply want to know the total charges by patient for room and special items in the room (item codes between 200 and 300). A view for just this aggregate data can be created from the DET_BILL view as follows:

```
CREATE VIEW ROOM__CHG (OCCUPANT, RM__CHGS) AS
   SELECT NAME, SUM (CHARGE)
      FROM DET__BILL
      WHERE ITEM__CODE BETWEEN 200 AND 300
      GROUP BY NAME;
```

As this view shows, we can assign a different name to a view column than the associated base table or expression column name. Here, OCCUPANT is a renaming of NAME, local to only this view, and RM__CHGS is the column name in this view given the expression for total charges by patient. Now this expression can be referenced via this view in subsequent queries as if it were a simple column.

We can see the power of such a view in the following example of a query that asks for the names of all patients with total charges greater than $500. The RM__CHG-based query is:

```
SELECT OCCUPANT FROM ROOM__CHG
   WHERE RM__CHGS > 500;
```

which would be translated by the DBMS into a more complex, equivalent query on the DET__BILL view:

```
SELECT NAME FROM DET__BILL
   WHERE ITEM__CODE BETWEEN 200 AND 300
   GROUP BY NAME
   HAVING SUM (CHARGE) > 500;
```

Of course, a query involving the base tables of PATIENT, BILLED, and ITEM would be even more complex.

You may restrict access to a view with GRANT and REVOKE statements (security statements). For example, you could grant some users access rights to aggregated data (for instance, averages) in a view and deny access to base, detailed data. We further explain security commands in Chapter 12.

Some people advocate the creation of a view for every single base table, even if that view is identical to the base table. They suggest this approach because views can contribute to greater programming productivity as databases evolve. Consider a situation where 50 programs all use the BILLED table. Suppose that the MVCH database evolves to support new functions that require the BILLED table to be renormalized into two tables. If these 50 programs refer directly to the BILLED base table, they will all have to be modified to refer to one of the two new tables, or to join the tables together. On the other hand, if these programs all use the view on this base table, then only the view has to be re-created, saving considerable reprogramming effort. You should remember, however, that views require considerable run-time computer processing, since the virtual table of a view is re-created each time the view is referenced. Therefore, referencing a base table through a view rather than directly can add considerable time to query processing. This additional operational cost must be balanced against the potential reprogramming savings of a view.

Updating data directly from a view rather than from base tables is possible under certain limitations outlined in a later section, "Modifying Data Through a View." Some update operations to data in a view are permitted, as long as the update is unambiguous in terms of data modification in the base table.

Internal Schema Definition in RDBMSs

The internal schema of a relational database can be controlled for processing and storage efficiency. Typically a database designer can tune the operational performance of the internal data model of a relational database by one or more of the following techniques:

1. Choosing to index primary and/or secondary keys to increase the speed of row selection, table joining, and row ordering (and to drop indexes to increase speed of table updating). You may want to review the section in Chapter 7 on selecting indexes.

2. Selecting file organizations for base tables that match the type of processing activity on those tables (for example, keep table physically sorted by a frequently used reporting sort key).

3. Selecting file organizations for indexes (which are also tables) suitable for how the indexes are used, and allocating extra space for an index file, so that an index can grow without having to be reorganized.

4. Clustering data, so that related rows of frequently joined tables are stored close together in secondary storage to minimize retrieval time.

5. Maintaining statistics about tables and their indexes, so that the DBMS can find the most efficient ways to perform various database operations.

Not all of these techniques are available in all SQL systems. Techniques 1 and 4 are typically available, so we discuss these in the following sections.

Indexes   You can create indexes in most RDBMSs to provide rapid random and sequential access to base-table data. (Although users do not directly refer to indexes when writing any SQL command, the DBMS recognizes when and which existing indexes would improve query performance.) You can usually create indexes for both primary and secondary keys and often on both single and concatenated (multiple-column) keys. In some systems, you can choose between ascending or descending sequence for the keys in an index.

For example, to create an index on the ATTENDS relation for the PHY_ID column (a secondary key) in dBASE's SQL, we would write

```
CREATE INDEX PHYS
   ON ATTENDS (PHY_ID);
```

To create a concatenated key index on the BILLED relation for PATIENT_NO and ITEM_CODE (a primary key), we would write

```
CREATE UNIQUE INDEX PAT_ITEM
   ON BILLED (PATIENT_NO, ITEM_CODE);
```

Indexes may be created at any time. If data already exist in the key column(s), index population will automatically occur for the existing data. If an index is defined as UNIQUE and the existing data violates this condition, the index creation will be rejected. Indexes will remain up to date with subsequent data maintenance.

When we no longer need tables, views, or indexes, we can use the associated DROP statements. For example, to delete the PHYS index above, we would use

```
DROP INDEX PHYS;
```

Several cautions should be applied when deciding on index creation. First, an index consumes extra storage space and requires maintenance time when indexed data change value. Together, these costs may noticeably retard retrieval response times and cause annoying delays for on-line users. Second, some RDBMSs do not use all indexes available for a query. A system may use only one index even if several are available for keys in a complex qualification. The database designer must know exactly how indexes are used by the particular RDBMS to make wise choices on indexing. With SQL/DS, the Relational Design Tool understands the SQL/DS query-processing algorithms and can be very helpful in picking the right combination of indexes.

Row Clustering A feature now becoming common in RDBMSs is the ability to cluster rows of different tables into adjacent physical storage to minimize access between related tables. Remember, the relational data model assumes that a table is a logical construct, so a table need not correspond to a physical file of contiguous records. For example, in Oracle (Oracle Corp., 1988) we can specify that we want ATTENDS rows for a given PATIENT to be clustered with the associated PATIENT table row for that patient, as follows:

```
CREATE CLUSTER PATIENT_DATA
  (PATIENT_NO INTEGER NOT NULL)
ALTER CLUSTER PATIENT_DATA
  ADD TABLE PATIENT
  WHERE PATIENT.PATIENT_NO = PATIENT_DATA.PATIENT_NO
ALTER CLUSTER PATIENT_DATA
  ADD TABLE ATTENDS
  WHERE ATTENDS.PATIENT_NO = PATIENT_DATA.PATIENT_NO
```

In this case, each distinct value of PATIENT_NO will be associated with a separate page of secondary storage, and all PATIENT and ATTENDS data for a given PATIENT_NO will be stored together. Note that physical contiguity is used, not pointers, to tie together related rows. This is similar to the VIA SET file organization in the CODASYL guidelines for network DBMSs (see Chapter 15). Sometimes row clustering is accomplished through indexing, as was discussed in Chapter 7.

Data Integrity Controls

With data integrity controls, we try to ensure that only valid data are entered and that data are consistent across all tables of a database. One type of data integrity is transaction integrity, or making sure that complete units of work are properly terminated and do not interfere with each other. We discuss transaction integrity in a later section, "Transaction Integrity Facilities."

The type of integrity discussed here is data validity. Relational systems control such validity by data type specification, valid ranges or lists of values, limitations on allowing null values (especially for primary key columns), and forcing values of foreign and cross-reference keys to exist in other tables.

Other than the data type specification and UNIQUE and NOT NULL qualifications on table columns that we have already illustrated, integrity assertions were not defined in the ANSI SQL 1986 standard. Consequently, many products today (for example, SQL/DS and dBASE IV) still do not have any other integrity controls.

Referential integrity: An integrity constraint that specifies that the value (or existence) of an attribute in one relation depends on the value (or existence) of the same attribute in another relation.

The SQL 1989 standard introduced a syntax for referential integrity control. **Referential integrity** involves two tables in a 1:*M* relationship. In the relational data model, a 1:*M* relationship causes the primary key of the table on the one-side to be a column in the table on the many-side of the relationship. Referential integrity means that a value in the matching column on the many-side must correspond to a value in the same column for some row in the table on the one-side. For example, consider the following expanded version of the definition of the BILLED table from Figure 8-1:

```
CREATE TABLE BILLED
  (PATIENT_NO INTEGER NOT NULL
    REFERENCES PATIENT,
   ITEM_CODE       SMALLINT NOT NULL
    REFERENCES ITEM,
   CHARGE       DECIMAL(7,2));
```

The REFERENCES clause for PATIENT_NO states that for each row of the BILLED table there must be exactly one row in the PATIENT table whose PATIENT_NO column (the primary key of that table) value is the same as the PATIENT_NO value in BILLED.

Referential integrity ensures there will never be a mismatch between related tables, even after updates and deletes. Full referential integrity is sometimes too restrictive. To deal with such restrictiveness, the latest SQL standard has added two additional clauses related to referential integrity: ON DELETE and ON UPDATE clauses. For the BILLED table, consider the following extension to the example above:

```
CREATE TABLE BILLED
  (PATIENT_NO INTEGER
    REFERENCES PATIENT,
    ON DELETE SET NULL,
  . . .
```

ON DELETE tells the DBMS what to do with rows, for example, in the BILLED table when a PATIENT row is deleted. ON DELETE SET NULL tells the DBMS to allow the deletion, but to set the PATIENT_NO in BILLED for corresponding rows to the null value. As an alternative, consider the following:

```
CREATE TABLE BILLED
  (PATIENT_NO INTEGER DEFAULT 9999
    REFERENCES PATIENT
    ON DELETE SET DEFAULT
    ON UPDATE CASCADE,
  . . .
```

ON DELETE SET DEFAULT tells the DBMS to allow the deletion, but to set the PATIENT_NO in BILLED for corresponding rows to the default for this column. ON UPDATE deals with, for example, what to do if a patient is assigned a new number. ON UPDATE CASCADE says that when a PATIENT_NO in the PATIENT table changes, all the corresponding PATIENT_NOs in the BILLED table should also change to the new value.

Another type of integrity control added in SQL-89 was global constraints, or assertions. For example, consider the following extension to the PHY table in Figure 8-1 and the following constraint on the MVCH database:

```
CREATE TABLE PHY
    (PHY__ID       CHAR(10) NOT NULL UNIQUE,
    PHY__PHONE     CHAR(8)
    SALARY         DECIMAL(9,2));
CREATE ASSERTION PHY__BUDGET
    CHECK (SELECT SUM(SALARY) FROM PHY <= 10000000);
```

The CHECK clause in the PHY__BUDGET assertion ensures that the salary budget for physicians is no greater than $10 million. This assertion could be changed each year as a new budget is approved.

Because of the importance of data integrity in general, and referential integrity in particular, features such as those illustrated above are likely to appear in most SQL systems in the near future. It is much better to include such controls as part of the data definitions than to rely on programmers to know and check these in each program they write. Without such referential integrity controls, a database can become full of orphan rows that can be either forgotten or mishandled.

Data Dictionary Facilities

Since RDBMSs typically store table, column, and view definitions, along with integrity rules, security constraints, and other data about data in tables, the RDBMS can itself be used to write queries and routines to produce data dictionary output. Further, a user who understands this definition structure can extend existing tables or build other tables to enhance the built-in features (for example, to include data on who is responsible for data integrity). A user is, however, often restricted from modifying the structure or contents of these definition tables directly, since the DBMS depends on them for its interpretation and parsing of queries.

Each SQL system keeps various internal tables for these definitions. In the dBASE SQL version, the following set of tables contains pertinent data definitions:

SYSDBS	Lists the name of each database, the user ID of the person who created the database, the date each database was created, and the full operating system path to the database.
SYSTABAUTH	Records the table and view privileges held by database users.
SYSCOLAU	Describes the privileges held by users to update columns in a table or updatable view.
SYSCOLS	Describes the columns in the tables and views.
SYSIDSX	Defines index characteristics.
SYSKEYS	Describes keys used in indexes.
SYSSYNS	Contains synonyms for table and view names.
SYSTABLS	Describes tables and views.
SYSTIMES	Used in multiuser environments to ensure the latest versions of internal tables are used.
SYSVDEPS	Describes the relationships between views and tables.
SYSVIEWS	Defines each view.

For example, SYSTABLS contains such information on tables as the table name, owner/creator user ID, and number of columns (among other items). SYSCOLS lists the names of all database columns, the associated table or view in which each column is defined (thus, a column name that is used in more than one table will appear in several rows of SYSCOLS), and data types.

Since these internal tables are also relational tables, a user can query them to discover, for example, which tables contain an ITEM__CODE column as follows:

```
SELECT TBNAME FROM SYSCOLS
    WHERE COLNAME = "ITEM__CODE";
```

The result would be

```
TBNAME
ITEM
BILLED
DET__BILL
```

given the definition of tables and views so far for our MVCH database. Rettig (1989) provides an excellent review of how to retrieve data definitions from the DB2 system catalog.

DATA RETRIEVAL AND MANIPULATION IN SQL

Some authors (for example, see Date, 1987a, Kroenke, 1983, and Ullman, 1980) distinguish among three different but related forms of relational calculus: tuple calculus, domain calculus, and transform languages. Ingres (Relational Technology, Inc., 1989) and the query language on which it is based, QUEL (Stonebraker et al., 1976), are representative of tuple calculus. A few rare implementations of domain calculus exist (see Date, 1987a, for a discussion). SQL is based on the transform language SEQUEL (Chamberlin et al., 1976).

General Structure of SQL Calculus

Commands in SQL (and other relational calculus systems) specify in a specific syntax which columns to manipulate, from what tables, and for what rows. For those already familiar with relational algebra-based products (like the dBASE and R:Base proprietary command languages), there are two fundamental differences between relational algebra and relational calculus:

1. calculus combines the SELECT and PROJECT commands and the binary operators (such as SUBTRACT) into one SELECT (or similar) statement that lists the column names to appear in the result (PROJECT), and uses a WHERE clause to specify the selection criteria; and

2. calculus also uses the WHERE clause to specify the intertable associations used for implicitly JOINing relations in the SELECT command.

Thus, whereas the JOIN operator of the relational algebra is a binary operator (and a table that is the combination of n relations must be generated in n-1 JOINs), one SELECT command can join numerous tables (implicitly). Several examples of SQL were given in Chapter 2.

Basic SQL Retrieval Command Structure

Most SQL data retrieval statements include the following three distinct clauses:

SELECT	Lists the columns (including expressions involving columns) from base tables or views to be projected into the table that will be the result of the command.
FROM	Identifies the tables or views from which columns will be chosen to appear in the result table, and includes the tables or views needed to join tables to process the query.
WHERE	Includes the conditions for row selection within a single table or view, and the conditions between tables or views for joining.

The first two are required, and the third is necessary when only certain table rows are to be retrieved. As an example, we can display the patient charges from the BILLED relation of Figure 8-1 for PATIENT_NO = 1234 as follows:

```
SELECT CHARGE
   FROM BILLED
      WHERE PATIENT_NO = 1234;
```

Two special keywords can be used along with the list of columns to display: DISTINCT and *. If the user does not wish to see duplicate rows in the result, then SELECT DISTINCT may be used. In the above example, if a patient had been charged the same amount for several items, the result of the query would have duplicate rows. SELECT DISTINCT CHARGE would display a result table without the duplicate rows. SELECT *, where * is shorthand for all columns, displays all columns from all the tables or views in the FROM clause, and SELECT table-name.* displays all columns from just the table listed before the *.

The default action for any SELECT command is to display the results on the screen. Some SQL implementations (including the dBASE version) also allow the result to be placed into a temporary table, so that this subset of the database does not have to be repeatedly derived. Care must be taken when using this feature, since the temporary table will not reflect any subsequent changes made to the data in the original tables (as a view does). For example,

```
SELECT CHARGE
   FROM BILLED
      WHERE PATIENT_NO = 1234
         SAVE TO TEMP TEMP_CHG (COST) KEEP;
```

stores the results of the query into a new database table, TEMP_CHG, and labels the stored column COST. The optional KEEP keyword tells SQL to actually make this a new permanent table in the database (if KEEP had not been included, the TEMP_CHG table would be automatically deleted at the end of the current SQL session). Some SQL implementations use an alternative syntax in which a table is created from the result of query. In this style, the equivalent of the above command would be:

```
CREATE TEMP_CHG (COST) AS
   (SELECT CHARGE
      FROM BILLED
         WHERE PATIENT_NO = 1234);
```

You may use AND, OR, and NOT logical operators to create complicated WHERE clauses, and you may use parentheses to properly group the logical operations. (We will see many examples of the use of logical operators later in this chapter.) It is important to note that the order of conditions in a compound WHERE clause is immaterial. While optimizing the query processing, the DBMS will determine if a particular sequence is better than any other.

You may also embed SELECT commands within search conditions in a WHERE clause. For example, suppose we wanted to display the BILLED row(s) that has the largest CHARGE value. Using a built-in function (to be discussed in the next section), we can write this query as follows:

```
SELECT * FROM BILLED
  WHERE CHARGE=(SELECT MAX(CHARGE) FROM BILLED);
```

The use of SELECT commands within SELECT commands is a feature of SQL that is used in various circumstances, which we will illustrate in several subsequent sections.

Built-in Functions   You may use functions such as COUNT, MIN, MAX, SUM, and AVG of specified columns in the column list of a SELECT command to specify that the resulting answer table is to contain aggregated data instead of row-level data. All of these functions appear in most SQL implementations. For example,

```
SELECT COUNT(*)
  FROM ATTENDS
    WHERE PATIENT_NO = 1234;
```

would display the number of procedures performed on patient number 1234; that is, it would count the number of rows for patient 1234. This, however, is not the same as the number of distinct procedures performed on this patient when several physicians are involved in the same procedure (and hence there are multiple rows). To obtain the number of distinct procedures, we would modify the query as follows:

```
SELECT COUNT(DISTINCT PROCEDURE)
  FROM ATTENDS
    WHERE PATIENT_NO = 1234;
```

In this case, we are not counting the number of rows; we are counting the number of distinct values of a certain column.

When a simple column appears in the column list of a SELECT, that column name is used as the heading in the display of the results. For built-in functions and expressions, the DBMS makes up a name for the column. Each SQL system uses different conventions for making up these computed column headings. Some SQL implementations provide the programmer with a way to use a more meaningful heading. For example, the following version of the above query may be permitted:

```
SELECT COUNT(DISTINCT PROCEDURE) AS "NO. OF PROCEDURES"
  FROM ATTENDS
    WHERE PATIENT_NO = 1234;
```

This would use the column heading "NO. OF PROCEDURES" above the result.

Limitations on the use of data-aggregate functions vary from system to system. In SQL/DS and the dBASE IV version of SQL, data aggregates and individual row-level data may not be mixed in the same SELECT clause unless the results are grouped by all the row-level data; that is, data aggregation is a function of groups of rows, and row and group data cannot appear together. We will review the GROUP BY clause in a later section of this chapter. Sayles (1989) provides a review of the built-in functions in many SQL systems.

Displaying Constants and Calculated Values   You may include in the column list after the SELECT verb not only column names but also constants and expressions. Consider the following SQL query for the Mountain View Community Hospital database:

```
SELECT CHARGE, CHARGE*1.06
   FROM BILLED;
```

This simple query displays a list of the current charges alongside what those charges would be with a 6% increase.

You may also include constants in the column list. The SQL command

```
SELECT "The total number of procedures for", PATIENT__NO, "is",
   COUNT(PROCEDURE)
      FROM ATTENDS
         WHERE PATIENT__NO = 1234;
```

displays the same result for the data aggregation example from the prior sections, but this time in a more narrative, rather than columnar, form.

Computed values can also be used in a WHERE clause. For example, the query

```
SELECT PATIENT__NO
   FROM PATIENT
      WHERE (DATE__DISCH - DATE__ADMIT) > 10;
```

would list those patients who had stayed in the hospital for more than 10 days. (Note that in some SQL systems special functions would have to be used to allow arithmetic on dates.) In the dBASE version of SQL, a variety of built-in functions may be used in expressions, (such as UPPER NAME) to display a patient's name in all caps.

Sorting and Grouping the Result   If the resulting rows are desired in a sorted sequence, you may add an ORDER BY clause to the query to achieve ascending or descending sequence with a major and several minor sort keys. You use a GROUP BY clause to perform functions on groups of rows with common values. The following illustrates the use of ORDER BY and GROUP BY clauses. We can produce a list of the total charges per patient for major medical items (item codes in the range 500–800) for those patients with large major medical expenses (total charges over $50,000) as follows:

```
SELECT PATIENT__NO, SUM(CHARGE)
   FROM BILLED
      WHERE ITEM__CODE BETWEEN 500 AND 800
      GROUP BY PATIENT__NO
      ORDER BY PATIENT__NO
      HAVING SUM(CHARGE) > 50000
```

Here the GROUP BY clause is used to specify subtotal control breaks. This query will display a subtotal of CHARGE for each patient. Since PATIENT_NO is the grouping variable, it may be used in the SELECT column list. In fact, *every* non-aggregate column in the column list *must* be part of the GROUP BY in SQL. The ORDER BY phrase simply sorts the output into patient-number sequence for easier scanning. Some relational languages require ORDER BY to accompany each GROUP BY phrase, but often it is redundant since GROUP BY also sorts the results. When required, the ORDER BY along with the GROUP BY sorts rows together with the same GROUP BY value to facilitate subtotal calculations.

This example also includes a HAVING clause, which is necessary because of the qualification on group-level data. HAVING selects which groups will appear, in this case groups with total charges over $50,000. HAVING is like WHERE, except that it involves group-level data.

An optional DESC clause on the ORDER BY will sort the results in reverse sequence. Several columns may be listed after ORDER BY to create major and minor sort sequences, and each may be in ASC or DESC sequence. Also, ORDER BY can refer to columns by name or position from left to right in the column list. For example,

```
SELECT PATIENT_NO, SUM(CHARGE)
 FROM BILLED
  WHERE ITEM_CODE BETWEEN 500 AND 800
   GROUP BY PATIENT_NO
   ORDER BY 2 DESC, PATIENT_NO
   HAVING SUM(CHARGE) > 50000;
```

would show the results in descending total charge sequence, and then in ascending sequence by PATIENT_NO as a secondary sort key.

NULL in Qualifications In addition to being able to use AND, OR, and NOT in qualifications, some SQL systems allow other options and keywords. For instance, since SQL/DS recognizes a NULL value, qualifications can include NULL and NOT NULL. For example, WHERE DATE_DISCH IS NOT NULL would limit a query to only discharged patients. Care should be taken when using NULL in compound qualifications. SQL follows what is called *three-value logic*: true, false, and unknown. Research has shown that some complex queries based on three-value logic can generate unexpected results. When using NULL in qualifications, you should check the users' manual for what are called *truth tables*, which indicate how NULL will be interpreted in Boolean qualifications.

The IN Operator You may replace the OR operator by IN to simplify query writing. In addition, you need IN in some more complex queries (shown later in this chapter), so programmers frequently use IN instead of OR for consistency. For example, the query

```
SELECT PATIENT_NO FROM ATTENDS
  WHERE PHY_ID IN ("BAKER,J.","FISCUS,A.");
```

would display the patient numbers of all patients treated by BAKER,J. or FISCUS,A. The logical operator NOT may precede IN to specify the complement of a list of values.

The BETWEEN Operator As IN simplifies queries involving many OR conditions, the BETWEEN operator simplifies query writing for range qualifications. When a qualification says BETWEEN x and y, this is equivalent to $>= x$ AND $<= y$. (Note: BETWEEN may mean $> x$ AND $< y$ in some SQL systems.) For example, suppose we wanted to find all the patients who had been charged between \$200 and \$400 for item 207. The SQL query for this would be

```
SELECT PATIENT_NO
   FROM BILLED
      WHERE ITEM_CODE = 207 AND
         CHARGE BETWEEN 200 AND 400;
```

The LIKE Operator Frequently, with search conditions that involve character data, exact matches are not needed or may be problematic. Spelling errors on data entry, inconsistent use of upper- and lowercase, and various punctuation marks can result in missing desired data. At other times you cannot be specific about what data are sought (for example, when we are not sure of the spelling of a name or when we want all values that include a particular substring). The LIKE operator is useful in these circumstances.

LIKE uses two special character symbols: % and __. The symbol % means ignore zero or more characters, and __ means ignore exactly one character where these symbols are used. For example, the clause WHERE NAME LIKE 'Mc%' would qualify all people whose names begin with 'Mc', and WHERE LOCATION LIKE '__2%' would ask for rooms on the second floor in any building (the first position of the location code is a building number).

MULTIPLE TABLE OPERATIONS IN SQL

As we saw in Chapter 2, inquiry and reporting requirements often involve data from several related tables. In a relational system, data from related tables are combined into one table (or view), and then displayed or used as input to a form or report definition. Thus, the majority of relational database programming involves combining into one table data from two, three, or more related tables. In a relational database, all relationships from one table to another or within one table are either 1:M or 1:1. These relationships are implemented simply by having a column that comes from the same domain of values in each related table. That is, we can link two tables by finding matches on the common columns. We usually think of such matching as finding for each row in the table on the many-side (or one of the one-sides in a 1:1 relationship) of a relationship the one row of the table on the one-side of the relationship that matches the common column value.

How the linking of related tables is programmed varies among different types of relational systems. In SQL, the WHERE clause of the SELECT command is also used for multiple table operations. In fact, SELECT can include references to two, three, or more tables in the same command. SQL has two ways to use SELECT for combining data from related tables, which we illustrate below. Relational algebra systems (like the dBASE proprietary language, covered in Chapter 9) can refer to only one or two tables per command.

The most frequently used relational operation, which brings together data from two (or more) related tables into one resultant table, is called a **join**. SQL specifies a join implicitly by referring in a WHERE clause to the matching of common

Join: A relational operation that causes two tables with a common domain to be combined into a single table.

columns over which tables are joined. You may join two tables when each one contains a column that has the same domain of values, a condition that is frequently referred to as *having common columns*. The result of a join operation is a single table with columns possibly from all the tables being joined and with each row containing data from rows in the different input tables with matching values for the common columns.

An important rule of thumb in forming join conditions is the following: There should be one WHERE condition for each pair of tables being joined. Thus, if four tables are to be combined, three conditions would be necessary. For example, a query for the MVCH database of Figure 8-1 might involve the four related tables BILLED, ITEM, PATIENT, and ROOM. The three conditions would involve matching: (1) ITEM__CODE in BILLED and ITEM, (2) PATIENT__NO in BILLED and PATIENT, and (3) PATIENT__NO IN PATIENT and ROOM (or BILLED and ROOM).

There are many possible types of joins in relational database queries (although each SQL implementation may support only some of these types). Three types of joins are described in this chapter: equi-join, natural join, and outer join (see Figure 8-2).

Figure 8-2

Examples of join commands

PATIENT

PATIENT_NO.	DATE_DISCH.
1234	05/20/83
0675	06/23/83
2345	02/28/83

BILLED

B_PATIENT_NO.	B_CHARGE
2345	23.00
2345	65.00
1234	80.50
1234	125.00

BILL_DATA

PATIENT_NO.	DATE_DISCH.	B_PATIENT_NO.	B_CHARGE
1234	05/20/83	1234	80.50
1234	05/20/83	1234	125.00
2345	02/28/83	2345	23.00
2345	02/28/83	2345	65.00

(a) Result of equi-join

BILL_DATA

PATIENT_NO.	DATE_DISCH.	B_CHARGE
1234	05/20/83	80.50
1234	05/20/83	125.00
2345	02/28/83	23.00
2345	02/28/83	65.00

(b) Result of natural join

BILL_DATA

PATIENT_NO.	DATE_DISCH.	B_CHARGE
1234	05/20/83	80.50
1234	05/20/83	125.00
2345	02/28/83	23.00
2345	02/28/83	65.00
0675	06/23/83	?

Note: ? indicates a NULL value.

(c) Result of outer join

Equi-join

With an **equi-join**, the joining condition is based on *equality* between values in the common columns. For example, in Figure 8-2a there is a row in the result table (called BILL—DATA) whenever there is a match between PATIENT—NO in the PATIENT table and PATIENT—NO in the BILLED table. Notice that with an equi-join the common columns both appear (redundantly) in the result table (so that both PATIENT—NOs appear in BILL—DATA).

It is also possible to define joins based on inequality conditions; for example, "greater than" joins, "less than" joins, "not equal" joins, and so on. We show several examples of inequality joins later in this chapter.

Equi-join: A join in which the joining condition is based on equality between values in the common columns. Common columns appear (redundantly) in the result table.

Natural Join

A **natural join** is the same as an equi-join, except that one of the duplicate columns is eliminated. For example, Figure 8-2b shows the BILL—DATA table for a natural join. This table is the same as the one in Figure 8-2a except that the second PATIENT—NO column has been eliminated.

The natural join is the most commonly used form of join operation. The SQL command for the join operation in Figure 8-2b is the following:

Natural join: The same as an equi-join, except that one of the duplicated columns is eliminated in the result table.

```
SELECT BILLED.PATIENT—NO, DATE—DISCH, CHARGE
  FROM PATIENT, BILLED
    WHERE PATIENT.PATIENT—NO = BILLED.PATIENT—NO;
```

The SELECT clause identifies the attributes to be displayed (PATIENT—NO must be prefixed with a table name, since this column appears in both tables), the FROM clause identifies the tables from which attributes are selected, and the WHERE clause specifies the joining condition for common columns. The two PATIENT—NOs in the WHERE clause must be prefixed by the associated table name; otherwise, it would be ambiguous which PATIENT—NO was being referenced.

Note that the sequence in which the table names appear in the FROM clause is immaterial. The query optimizer part of the DBMS will decide in which sequence to process each table. Whether indexes exist on common columns will influence the sequence in which tables are processed, as will which table is on the 1 and which is on the M side of 1:M relationships. If you find that a query takes significantly different amounts of time depending on the sequence in which you list tables in the FROM clause, the DBMS does not have a very good query optimizer.

Outer Join

Often in joining two tables, we find that a row in one table does not have a matching row in the other table. For example, in Figure 8-2 there is an entry for patient number 0675 in the PATIENT table, but no entry for this patient in the CHARGES table. (Perhaps no charges have yet been billed to this patient.) As a result, with an equi-join or natural join, there is no entry for this patient in BILL—DATA (see Figures 8-2a and 8-2b).

Knowing that some patient has no charge may be important management information. This information may be produced by using an **outer join**: rows that do not have matching values in common columns are also included in the result

Outer join: A join in which rows that do not have matching values in common columns are nevertheless included in the result table.

table. Null values appear in columns where there is no match between tables. Figure 8-2c shows an entry for patient number 0675 with a null value for CHARGE. Compare Figures 8-2a, 8-2b, and 8-2c carefully to make sure you understand each of these join operations.

Although still not found in many relational systems, the outer join (available in Oracle) is appearing in newer versions of systems and is likely, in some form, to become a standard feature. The advantage of the outer join is that information is not lost. In Figure 8-2c, patients with no charges can be handled in the same table as patients with charges. Unless otherwise stated in this section, all joins will be natural joins. In those systems that do not have an outer join, the UNION command can be used; the use of UNION for the BILL_DATA answer table is illustrated later in this chapter.

Table Name Abbreviations

When columns from several different tables are referenced in one command, the DBMS must be able to identify unambiguously which columns are found in which table. Such column identification is especially difficult when the system permits you to use the same column name in several tables (which you might do if the columns have the same domain of values). As we saw above, the way SQL handles duplicate column names is to prefix a column name with the associated table name: tablename.columnname.

You may create an abbreviation for a query as part of the FROM clause, as in the following example:

```
SELECT R.EXTENSION
  FROM ROOM R, ATTENDS AT
    WHERE AT.PROCEDURE = 'Tonsillectomy' AND
       AT.PATIENT_NO = R.PATIENT_NO;
```

(*Note:* in dBASE's SQL, the single letters A through J may not be used as abbreviations.) This query displays the telephone numbers of all patients who are in the hospital for a tonsillectomy. These abbreviations are needed only when column names are not unique; when a table is joined with itself (a self-join, to be illustrated below), and with so-called correlated subqueries (also illustrated below). The abbreviation applies only to the one command, so subsequent commands in an interactive session must restate any abbreviation needed.

Joining by Subqueries

The preceding SQL example illustrates one of the two basic approaches for joining two tables: the joining technique. Besides the joining technique, SQL provides the subquery technique, which involves placing one (inner) query (SELECT, FROM, WHERE) within the WHERE or HAVING clause of another (outer) query. The inner query provides values for the search condition of the outer query.

The joining technique for query construction, in contrast to the subquery approach, is useful when data from several relations are to be retrieved and displayed, and the relationships are not necessarily nested. We can use the joining technique to determine the items and associated descriptions charged to PATIENT NO 1234, as follows:

```
SELECT ITEM.ITEM__CODE, DESCRIPT
   FROM ITEM, BILLED
      WHERE ITEM.ITEM__CODE = CHARGE.ITEM__CODE AND
         PATIENT__NO = 1234;
```

The equivalent subquery-style query, which may be easier for some people to understand and compose, would be

```
SELECT ITEM__CODE, DESCRIPT
   FROM ITEM
      WHERE ITEM__CODE =
         (SELECT ITEM__CODE FROM BILLED
            WHERE PATIENT__NO = 1234);
```

The subquery approach may be used for this query because we only need to display data from the table in the outer query.

When an inner query returns a *set* of values and the matching is on equality to any of the values, then the keyword IN is used. Suppose we wanted to display the ITEM__CODE and DESCRIPT columns for all work performed on patient 1234 in Mountain View Community Hospital. In SQL's subquery approach, we would write

```
SELECT ITEM__CODE, DESCRIPT
   FROM ITEM
      WHERE ITEM__CODE IN
         (SELECT ITEM__CODE FROM BILLED
            WHERE PATIENT__NO = 1234);
```

The qualifiers NOT, ANY, and ALL may be used in front of IN or logical operators such as =, >, and < (see Figure 8-3 later in this section for examples). Since IN works with zero, one, or many values from the inner query, many programmers simply use IN instead of = for all queries, even if the equal sign would work.

Suppose that as part of a hospital audit we wanted to know what patients had been charged more than twice the average rate for X-ray work (ITEM__CODE = 307). We would specify this query in SQL as follows:

```
SELECT DISTINCT PATIENT__NO
   FROM BILLED
      WHERE ITEM__CODE = 307
         AND CHARGE >
         (SELECT 2 * AVG(CHARGE)
            FROM BILLED
               WHERE ITEM__CODE = 307);
```

This query also illustrates that a table (BILLED) can be compared with itself, even using an inequality (>) operator (an inequality join). In this illustration, the inner query acts as a function that calculates a constant to be compared to a column (CHARGE) value.

In summary, you can use the subquery approach when qualifications are nested (that is, one is within another) or when qualifications are easily understood in a nested way. Nesting uses pairwise joining of *one and only one* column in an inner query with *one* column in an outer query (the exception to this is when a subquery is used with the EXISTS keyword). You can display data only from the table(s) referenced in the outer query. Up to 16 levels of nested queries are typically supported. Queries are processed inside out, although a special type of subquery, a correlated subquery, is processed outside in.

Correlated Subqueries

Correlated subqueries: In SQL, a subquery in which processing the inner query depends on data from the outer query.

In the preceding subquery examples, it was necessary to examine the inner query before considering the outer query. That is, the result of the inner query was used to limit the processing of the outer query. In contrast, for other kinds of queries, called **correlated subqueries**, the processing of the inner query depends on data from the outer query. That is, the inner query is somewhat different for each row referenced in the outer query. In this case, the inner query must be computed *for each* outer row, whereas in the earlier examples, the inner query was computed *only once* for all rows processed in the outer query.

Suppose we wanted to know which patients had been charged more than twice the average rate for any type of work performed on them. We can answer this question with correlated subqueries in which we modify one of the preceding queries so that ITEM_CODE in the inner query refers to the ITEM_CODE in the outer query as each row is processed:

```
SELECT DISTINCT PATIENT_NO, ITEM_CODE
  FROM BILLED PA
    WHERE CHARGE >
      (SELECT 2*AVG(CHARGE)
        FROM BILLED PB
          WHERE PA.ITEM_CODE = PB.ITEM_CODE);
```

In this query, as each row of the PA table is processed, the inner query computes the average charge across all BILLED rows for the item mentioned in the PA row. If the charge in the current PA row is more than twice this average, then the PATIENT_NO and ITEM_CODE from the current PA row are included in the result table (if they have not already been included).

When to Use Correlated Subqueries Correlated subqueries may seem difficult to write at first, but once you understand that your query needs to process one table for each row of another table, the use of correlated subqueries becomes clear. Situations in which multiple events have to happen or not happen together usually call for correlated subqueries. In contrast, noncorrelated subqueries are used when rows from one table are going to be selected based on a value computed from the rows of another table. Sometimes, depending on how you conceive a query, you can answer the same question by either noncorrelated or correlated subqueries.

Qualified Subqueries

SQL includes several other operators to handle situations in which more complex conditions about the results of the subquery occur. These operators are [NOT] EXISTS, ALL, and ANY. In WHERE clauses, the logical operator EXISTS (NOT EXISTS) restricts the display of outer table rows to situations in which subqueries have (have not) *any* qualified rows; that is, where there is (is not) a null set as the result. For example, suppose we wanted to know the patient numbers of patients who had been charged for both treatments 307 and 807. We would write this query as follows in SQL:

```
SELECT DISTINCT PATIENT_NO
   FROM BILLED BA
      WHERE EXISTS
         (SELECT * FROM BILLED BB
              WHERE BA.PATIENT_NO = BB.PATIENT_NO AND
              BA.ITEM_CODE = 307 AND BB.ITEM_CODE = 807);
```

In this correlated subquery example, both the outer query and the subquery refer to the same relation, BILLED. We distinguish rows from each reference to the BILLED table by two abbreviations, BA and BB. The subquery will be true if the same patient (qualified by the first WHERE clause of the subquery) has two BILLED rows, one for item 307 and another for item 807 (qualified by the second WHERE condition of the subquery). That is, the first WHERE clause of the inner query ensures that the BILLED row of the inner query deals with the same patient as referenced by the current row of the outer query. The second WHERE condition of the inner query checks that these two BILLED rows are for the two desired treatments. Also note that in the case of the EXISTS operator, the inner query is evaluated simply as true or false, so we can use SELECT *, rather than SELECT of one column.

We can use the ALL operator (among other uses) as a substitute for the MAX or MIN built-in function and thus often create more understandable queries. Suppose we wanted to audit charging practices in Mountain View Community Hospital. One of the audit tests is to determine the numbers and names of all patients who had been charged more for item 125 than all patients were charged for item 126, two similar laboratory tests. An SQL query for this inquiry follows:

```
SELECT PATIENT_NO, NAME
   FROM PATIENT
      WHERE PATIENT_NO IN
         (SELECT PATIENT_NO
              FROM BILLED
                 WHERE ITEM_CODE = 125 AND
                    CHARGE >ALL
                 (SELECT CHARGE
                    FROM BILLED
                       WHERE ITEM_CODE = 126));
```

The ANY operator finds rows for which the column mentioned in the WHERE clause has a value less than or greater than any (some) value from another column. Suppose we wanted to know the numbers and names of all patients who had been charged more for item 125 than any patient had been charged for item 126. That is, in this audit test, we expect that all the item 125 charges should be less than all the item 126 charges. An SQL query for this inquiry follows:

```
SELECT PATIENT_NO, NAME
   FROM PATIENT
      WHERE PATIENT_NO IN
         (SELECT PATIENT_NO
              FROM BILLED
                 WHERE ITEM_CODE = 125 AND
                    CHARGE >ANY
                 (SELECT CHARGE
                    FROM BILLED
                       WHERE ITEM_CODE = 126));
```

Other Multiple Table Operations

Because relational query languages like SQL are set-oriented languages (that is, commands operate on and generate sets of rows), the equivalent of various set operations may also be available.

Appending Query Results Together   The UNION command combines the result of two queries into one table as long as the two tables being combined have compatible corresponding columns. That is, the two tables must have the same number of columns, and the corresponding columns must have the same data type. This property is called *union compatibility*. The results from more than two queries may be combined by inserting UNION between each query.

UNION automatically sorts the result table in sequence by all the columns in the column list, from left to right. If this is not the desired sequence, you may insert an ORDER BY clause, but only after the last SELECT. If you include an ORDER BY, you may specify only column numbers, not names (since the same column names may not be used in all SELECTs involved in the UNION).

UNION is often used to produce the results of an outer join when an outer join operator is not provided in an SQL implementation. For example, we could produce a list of charges for all patients, even those for whom there were no charges so far (so that we could work with patients with zero charges) by using UNION in the following query:

```
SELECT BILLED.PATIENT__NO, NAME, CHARGE
  FROM BILLED, PATIENT
    WHERE BILLED.PATIENT__NO = PATIENT.PATIENT__NO
UNION
SELECT PATIENT__NO, NAME, 0
  FROM PATIENT
    WHERE PATIENT__NO NOT IN
      (SELECT PATIENT__NO
         FROM BILLED);
```

The equivalent Oracle outer join command would be

```
SELECT PATIENT.PATIENT__NO, NAME, CHARGE
  FROM PATIENT, BILLED
    WHERE PATIENT.PATIENT__NO = BILLED.PATIENT-NO (+);
```

where the (+) indicates that the outer join is to be performed.

The MINUS and INTERSECT Operators   Depending on the implementation, both set difference (MINUS) and set intersection (INTERSECT) operators may be available. You may use MINUS and INTERSECT only on union-compatible tables. Both of these can be very helpful in simplifying query writing. Suppose we wanted to know which of the patients who have been treated by Dr. Wilcox have not been charged for anything yet. We can write this query using the MINUS operator:

```
SELECT DISTINCT PATIENT__NO
  FROM ATTENDS
    WHERE PHY__ID = "Wilcox"
MINUS
SELECT DISTINCT PATIENT__NO
  FROM BILLED;
```

The first query finds all the patients treated by Dr. Wilcox. The second query determines which patients have been billed so far. Any patient number in the result of the first query and not in the second (the first set minus the second set) satisfies the query. Note that the sequence in which we list these two queries is important, since A − B does not necessarily equal B − A in set mathematics.

This same query can be written without a MINUS operator by using the following subquery approach:

```
SELECT DISTINCT PATIENT_NO
  FROM ATTENDS
  WHERE PHY_ID= "Wilcox" AND
     PATIENT_NO NOT IN
        (SELECT DISTINCT PATIENT_NO
          FROM BILLED);
```

As an example of the use of INTERSECT, suppose we wanted to know which patients had been treated by both Dr. Wilcox and Dr. Snyder. We can write this query using the INTERSECT operator:

```
SELECT DISTINCT PATIENT_NO
  FROM ATTENDS
    WHERE PHY_ID = "Wilcox"
INTERSECT
SELECT DISTINCT PATIENT_NO
  FROM ATTENDS
    WHERE PHY_ID = "Snyder";
```

We could also use a subquery to produce the same result as an INTERSECT:

```
SELECT DISTINCT PATIENT_NO
  FROM ATTENDS
    WHERE PHY_ID = "Wilcox" AND
      PATIENT_NO IN
          (SELECT PATIENT_NO
            FROM ATTENDS
              WHERE PHY_ID = "Snyder");
```

Figure 8-3 shows some additional examples of SQL queries.

DATA MAINTENANCE IN SQL

We have waited until now to explain SQL data maintenance commands because these commands may include SELECT commands within a maintenance operation. The SQL data maintenance operators work on tables or updatable views. The operators are

INSERT   Places a new row in a table based on values supplied in the statement, copies one or more rows derived from other database data into a table, or extracts data from one table and inserts them into another.

UPDATE   Changes values in one or more specified rows of a table by replacing current values with constants or the results of calculations.

DELETE   Deletes one or more qualified rows of a table.

Figure 8-3

Examples of SQL commands

What patients (display in PATIENT_NO order) have been charged more than $300 for item 307?

```
SELECT          PATIENT_NO
FROM            BILLED
WHERE           ITEM_CODE = 307 AND
                    CHARGE > 300
ORDER BY        PATIENT_NO;
```

What physicians have not treated patient 1234?

```
SELECT          PHY_ID
FROM            PHY
WHERE           PHY_ID NOT IN
                (SELECT PHY_ID
                 FROM ATTENDS
                 WHERE PATIENT_NO = 1234);
```

Create a new table (called WORK) containing the physician IDs, phone numbers, what procedures they have performed, and on what patients (only for physicians who have performed procedures).

```
SELECT          AT.PHY_ID, PHY_PHONE, PATIENT_NO,
                PROCEDURE
FROM            PHY, ATTENDS AT
WHERE           PHY.PHY_ID = AT.PHY_ID
SAVE TO TEMP    WORK    KEEP;
```

How many procedures have been performed on patient 1234?

```
SELECT          COUNT(*)
FROM            ATTENDS
WHERE           PATIENT_NO = 1234;
```

How many (distinct) physicians have treated patient 1234?

```
SELECT          COUNT (DISTINCT PHY_ID)
FROM            ATTENDS
WHERE           PATIENT_NO = 1234;
```

What patients have total charges greater than $1000?

```
SELECT          PATIENT_NO
FROM            BILLED
GROUP BY        PATIENT_NO
HAVING          SUM(CHARGE) > 1000:
```

What is the total charge for items 307 and 415 to each patient who has been billed for both items? (Assume a patient who is billed for either of these items is billed only once for that item.)

```
SELECT DISTINCT   CA.PATIENT_NO, CA.CHARGE + CB.CHARGE
FROM              BILLED CA, BILLED CB
WHERE             CA.ITEM_CODE = 307 AND
                  CB.ITEM_CODE = 415 AND
                  CA.PATIENT_NO = CB.PATIENT_NO
```

Some SQL systems also have a command that permits rows to be transferred from an external file to a database table. Such an insert command is useful for batch loading of data, where the external file, containing new rows, was created by a separate data entry or text editor program.

Adding Data to a Table

In SQL, we could add one new row to the BILLED relation as follows:

```
INSERT INTO BILLED
  VALUES (1234,,220.00);
```

The sequence in which we list the values must correspond to the sequence in which the associated columns were defined for the table. A null value, if permitted, will be stored for any column not included (as for the second column in the example above). If values were to be supplied for the columns in a different sequence, we would follow the table name by the list of column names (in parentheses) for the columns (in sequence) to receive data.

In addition, one or more rows may be copied from one table to another. Suppose there were also an OUT__PAT relation in the database of Figure 8-1, for patients receiving treatment without occupying a hospital sleeping room. Further, assume that the structure of the OUT__PAT table is the same as the PATIENT table. When an outpatient is admitted for overnight, we could copy (without destroying) the demographic data as follows:

```
INSERT INTO PATIENT
  SELECT *
    FROM OUT__PAT
      WHERE PATIENT__NO = 1234;
```

Whole groups of rows can be copied when the WHERE clause involves secondary keys.

Batch Input   Some versions of SQL (for example, SQL/DS) have a special command for entering multiple rows as a batch: the INPUT command. For example, if we wanted to enter a batch of rows for the BILLED table, we would say

```
INPUT BILLED;
```

and then enter the values for each of the new rows. Again, the values must be entered in the sequence in which the columns were defined, with one input line for each new row. The keyword END is entered at the beginning of a line to tell SQL when all the data have been entered.

In addition, some SQL versions have a batch input command to load data from a nondatabase text file. For example,

```
COPY BILLED
  (format information)
    FROM "BILLED.TXT";
```

might tell SQL to append new rows to the BILLED table from records found in the BILLED.TXT ASCII operating system file. Usually such a command needs to include a description of the format of the data in the text file (for example, the width of each field, which field corresponds to which database column, and what delimiters are used between fields or at the end of each record).

Deleting Database Contents

Rows can be deleted individually or in groups. Suppose some BILLED rows had been entered for an ITEM (say ITEM_CODE 444) that was no longer a billable item. BILLED rows for this item could all be eliminated by the command

```
DELETE FROM BILLED
   WHERE ITEM_CODE = 444;
```

The simplest form of DELETE eliminates all rows of a table, as in

```
DELETE FROM PATIENT;
```

which would delete all patient rows.

Deletion must be done with care when rows from several relations are involved. For example, if we delete a PATIENT row before deleting associated BILLED rows, we will have a referential integrity violation. (*Note:* Including the ON DELETE clause with a field definition can mitigate such a problem.) Suppose we wish to delete all treatments performed by physicians in a given department (these physicians have the same phone extension, X3422). In this case, to preserve database integrity, we must delete the ATTENDS rows before we can delete the PHYs rows, as follows:

```
DELETE FROM ATTENDS
   WHERE PHY_ID IN
     (SELECT PHY_ID
       FROM PHY
           WHERE PHY_PHONE = "X3422");
DELETE FROM PHY
   WHERE PHY_PHONE = "X3422";
```

One restriction on this type of DELETE, which involves a subquery, is that the table from which rows are being deleted cannot be referenced inside the subquery.

Unlike the dBASE proprietary language illustrated in Chapter 2, SQL actually eliminates the affected database records with the DELETE command. You should therefore always execute a SELECT command first to display the records that would be deleted and visually verify that only the desired rows are qualified.

Changing Database Contents

To update data in SQL we must inform the DBMS what relation, columns, and rows are involved. Suppose an incorrect charge were entered for patient 1234 and item 307. The following SQL UPDATE statement would institute an appropriate correction:

```
UPDATE BILLED
   SET CHARGE = 322.50
     WHERE PATIENT_NO = 1234
       AND ITEM_CODE = 307;
```

The SET command can also change a value to NULL by SET *columname* = NULL. As with DELETE, the WHERE clause in an UPDATE command may contain a subquery, but the table being updated may not be referenced in the subquery.

Modifying Data Through a View

Views are primarily intended for ease of data retrieval, but it is possible under limited circumstances to modify (INSERT, DELETE, and UPDATE) base-table data by referring to a view. In SQL, view data modification in views is limited by the following restrictions:

1. Only views that are simple row-and-column subsets of a single base table are updatable (that is, the view cannot include such operations as join, GROUP BY, DISTINCT, or any data aggregation function).

2. A column in a view derived from mathematical expressions involving base data may not be updated.

3. A view defined from another view is not updatable.

4. A new row may not be inserted into a view table when the base table affected would have a missing value for a column defined as NOT NULL.

One feature of view definition that was not mentioned in the prior section on defining views is the WITH CHECK OPTION. If this option is included in the view definition, all INSERTs and UPDATEs against this view will be checked to ensure that the new or changed row does still fit the view definition. For example, consider the following simple view for a selected subset of items:

```
CREATE VIEW SOME__ITEMS
   AS SELECT *
      FROM ITEM
          WHERE ITEM__CODE BETWEEN 200 AND 300
             WITH CHECK OPTION;
```

This view can be used to insert new rows or change existing rows in the ITEM table. Attempts to insert through this view an item with a code outside this range, however, will be rejected. The check option is not inherited; thus, a view created from another view does not implicitly have the check option of the original view. Keller (1986) provides further discussion of interpreting and handling updates through a view.

TRANSACTION INTEGRITY FACILITIES

Relational DBMSs are no different from other types of database managers in that one of their primary responsibilities is to ensure that database maintenance is properly and completely handled. Data maintenance is defined in units of work called *transactions*, which involve one or more data manipulation commands. A transaction is the complete set of closely related update commands that must all be done or none of them should be done, for the database to be valid. For example, an accounting clerk in Mountain View Community Hospital might try to enter the data from a form completed by a nurse that indicates all the items used for and to be charged to a patient for a given day. Unless the whole form is accurate, policy states that the form must be returned to the originating nurse for correction and verification, and no charges should be made until the form is completely correct. Thus, either all BILLED rows from this form are to be entered into the database or none of them should be. Here, the business transaction is all the insertions of BILLED rows from the form; there is not a separate transaction for each item on the form.

What we need are commands to define the boundaries of a transaction, to commit the work of a transaction as a permanent change to the database, and to purposely and properly abort a transaction, if necessary. In addition, we need data recovery services to clean up after abnormal termination of database processing in the middle of a transaction. For example, maybe the whole form of items to be charged to a patient is accurate, but in the middle of entering the information on the form, the computer system might malfunction or lose power. In this case, we do not want some of the changes made and not others. It's all or nothing at all if we want a valid database.

In dBASE's SQL, the following commands are available to control such transaction integrity:

BEGIN TRANSACTION	Creates a log file and starts recording all changes (insertions, deletions, and updates) to the database in this file.
END TRANSACTION	Takes the contents of the log file and applies them to the database (thus making the changes permanent), and then empties the log file.
ROLLBACK WORK	Asks SQL to empty the log file.

These commands are entered in the same way as other SQL commands. The BEGIN and END TRANSACTION commands define the boundary of a transaction. Database changes do not become part of the database until the END TRANSACTION is executed. Until then, the changes are recorded only in a log or suspense file. It makes sense to include only data modification and retrieval commands between the BEGIN and END. Although retrieval commands are innocuous in a transaction, there is no harm in including them. On the other hand, commands like CREATE, GRANT, and REVOKE should not appear within a transaction.

Standard SQL takes a slightly different approach. For example, in SQL/DS the relevant transaction integrity commands are

AUTOCOMMIT {ON/OFF}	Specifies whether changes to a table are made permanent after each data modification command (ON) or only when work is explicitly made permanent (OFF) by the COMMIT WORK command.
COMMIT WORK	Specifies that all changes made to a database since the last COMMIT WORK command (these have been kept in a log file since the last COMMIT) are to be made permanent (useful only when AUTOCOMMIT is OFF); the log file is emptied and a new transaction begins.
ROLLBACK WORK	Informs SQL/DS to undo all changes made to the database (empty the log file) since the last COMMIT WORK command, and to begin a new transaction.

BACKOUT

Informs SQL/DS to nullify all changes made since the last SAVE (sub) command during the execution of an INPUT command (only relevant if AUTOCOMMIT is ON).

Successful program termination results implicitly in a COMMIT WORK command, and an aborted program induces a ROLLBACK WORK command.

In SQL/DS, the effects of any data maintenance commands do not occur immediately. If changes are *not* to be automatically made by the DBMS (AUTOCOMMIT OFF), then all changes are held in a log file until the user explicitly issues the command that defines the end of one transaction and the beginning of the next (COMMIT WORK). If, before executing this command, the user enters ROLLBACK WORK, then the log file is cleared, and the database retains the same contents that were present before the transaction began (and users have no idea that any changes were attempted).

If changes are to be automatically made (AUTOCOMMIT ON), then they still are not made until the next SQL command is given or an END command is issued; END indicates that the transaction is complete (in this case each transaction is composed of a single SQL command). Before the issue of END or the next command, a ROLLBACK WORK will undo the changes of the last modification command. Although the AUTOCOMMIT ON feature is convenient, it does force one to do work one command at a time, which may not correspond to the logical units of business transactions.

SET AUTOCOMMIT is an interactive command, so a given user session of SQL/DS can be dynamically controlled for appropriate integrity measures. Since each SQL INSERT, INPUT, UPDATE, and DELETE command typically works only on one table at a time and some data maintenance (such as deletion of all patient data for a given patient from the Mountain View Community Hospital database) requires updating of multiple tables for the work to be complete, these transaction integrity commands are very important in clearly defining whole units of database changes that must be completed in full for the database to retain integrity.

Further, some SQL systems have concurrency controls that handle the updating of a shared database by concurrent users, and also can journalize database changes, so that a database can be recovered after abnormal terminations in the middle of a transaction or to undo erroneous transactions. For example, in a banking application, the update of a bank account balance by two concurrent users should be cumulative. Such controls are transparent to the user in SQL; no user programming is needed to ensure proper control of concurrent access to data. SQL was designed from the beginning to be used in a multiuser environment. Other systems, like the original dBASE product, were designed as single-user systems. We will see in Chapter 9 that special commands are needed in programs written in the dBASE proprietary language to control concurrent access. To ensure the integrity of a particular database, you must be sensitive to transaction integrity and recovery issues and must make sure that application programmers are appropriately informed of when these commands are to be used.

SUMMARY

This chapter has covered the SQL language for relational database definition and manipulation. This standard has been criticized for many flaws, and in reaction to these, and to increase the power of the language, extensions are constantly under review by the ANSI X3H2 committee and other standards bodies responsible for the SQL standard.

Some of the flaws identified for SQL follow:

- Inefficient syntax, in which many queries can be written in several different ways (sometimes with vastly different processing speeds)
- Permitting duplicate rows in relations
- Inadequate support of subqueries (for example, not all of the relational operators can be used in subqueries)
- Inadequate support of true, false, and unknown logical operations and handling of unknown or missing values in data aggregation functions (like MAX and AVG)

The potential extensions to SQL (which now appear in some SQL implementations and will be added to others in the future) include

- Specification of a default value clause for column definitions; options would include NULL, a specified constant for that column, or a global default value constant
- Integrity clause that can be included with a column definition
- Primary key and foreign key clauses to specify referential integrity restrictions
- Allowing UNION, MINUS, and INTERSECT to be used in view definitions, in subqueries, and in INSERT commands
- Allowing the range points in a BETWEEN expression to be listed either smaller-to-larger value or larger-to-smaller value

Relational systems were criticized for many years because of their relative inefficiency compared with network systems. However, with recent performance improvements, with judicious use of key indexes, or with implementation on a database machine, a database designer can now construct relational databases that can be efficiently processed. The inclusion of SQL commands in a third-generation host language can provide the detailed data processing controls still necessary for customized programming. SQL commands along with other DBMS modules—report writers, graphics generators, screen and form painters, and a variety of other related tools—make many relational DBMSs, such as dBASE IV, SQL/DS, DB2, Oracle, and Ingres, very comprehensive system development environments. Increasingly, SQL-based relational systems are being used to initially develop and iteratively evolve all types of information systems.

We suggest that no one DBMS language or architecture, even SQL or relational, will be totally dominant. First, different applications require different data management capabilities. Second, different organizations have various data processing traditions and skills that will naturally make them tend to select different technologies. Third, the large installed base of database applications means that it can be very expensive to convert all organizational data and programs to one DBMS. And finally, there is no reason to doubt that a new Charles Bachman or Ted Codd is already at work on a new generation of DBMS. In fact, systems for the object-oriented data model (see Chapter 5) are now appearing, and many believe these will be superior to relational systems.

CHAPTER REVIEW

Key Terms

Correlated subqueries

Equi-join

Join

Natural join

Null value

Outer join

Referential integrity

Relational DBMS (RDBMS)

REVIEW QUESTIONS

1. Define each of the following terms:
   - a. view
   - b. relational calculus
   - c. integrity constraint
   - d. equi-join
   - e. natural join
   - f. outer join
   - g. subquery
   - h. correlated subquery
   - i. joining technique
   - j. INTERSECT
   - k. MINUS
   - l. null value
   - m. COMMIT
   - n. ROLLBACK
   - o. BEGIN TRANSACTION
   - p. END TRANSACTION

2. Explain the following statement regarding SQL: Any query that can be written using the subquery approach can also be written using the joining approach, but not vice-versa.

3. Explain the difference between the ability to query the data definition catalog in SQL and the capabilities of a data dictionary/directory.

4. Explain why JOIN is called a binary operator. How is JOIN accomplished, in general, in SQL?

5. Drawing on material covered in prior chapters, explain the factors to be considered in deciding whether to create a key index for a table in SQL.

6. Explain why it is sometimes necessary to prefix a column name with a table name in SQL statements.

7. Explain the purpose of a view in SQL.

8. Explain why it is necessary to limit the kinds of updates performed on data when referencing data through a view.

9. Explain how a view can be used for data security.

10. Suppose you are a user of the dBASE SQL version, and you are unfamiliar with the tables stored on your system. What on-line facilities exist to help you learn what data is kept on your system?

11. What is the difference between COUNT and COUNT DISTINCT in SQL? When will these two commands generate the same and different results?

12. When would you use an outer join instead of a natural join?

13. What is the purpose of the COMMIT command in SQL? How does COMMIT relate to the notion of a business transaction (such as entry of a customer order or issuing a customer invoice)?

PROBLEMS AND EXERCISES

1. Match the following terms to the appropriate definitions.

   ____ equi-join   a. a standard relational query and definition language

   ____ natural join   b. provides rapid access to rows

   ____ outer join   c. accomplishes JOIN within WHERE clause

   ____ relational algebra d. also called a virtual table

   ____ relational calculus e. All rows are kept in a result table.

___ SQL	f. Changes to a table are made permanent.
___ view	g. Redundant columns are kept.
___ index	h. uses SELECT, PROJECT, and JOIN commands
___ COMMIT	i. Changes to a table are undone.
___ ROLLBACK	j. Redundant columns are not kept.
___ database machine	k. a third generation programming language in which SQL commands are embedded
___ null value	l. hardware that performs DBMS functions
___ host language	m. missing or nonexisting value

Problems 2–7 are based on the Lakewood College database from Chapter 4. The 3NF relations for that application are repeated below.

STUDENT NO.	STUDENT NAME	MAJOR
38214	Bright	IS
69173	Smith	PM
. . .		

STUDENT (STUDENT NO., STUDENT NAME, MAJOR)

INSTRUCTOR NAME	INSTRUCTOR LOCATION
Codd	B104
Kemp	B213
Lewis	D317
. . .	

INSTRUCTOR (INSTRUCTOR NAME, INSTRUCTOR LOCATION)

COURSE NO.	COURSE TITLE	INSTRUCTOR NAME
IS 350	Database	CODD
IS 465	Sys anal	KEMP
PM 300	Prod mgt	LEWIS
QM 440	Op res	KEMP
. . .		

COURSE (COURSE NO., COURSE TITLE, INSTRUCTOR NAME)

STUDENT NO.	COURSE NO.	GRADE
38214	IS 350	A
38214	IS 465	C
69173	IS 465	A
69173	PM 300	B
69173	QM 440	C
. . .		

REGISTRATION (STUDENT NO., COURSE NO., GRADE)

2. Write a full database description using the SQL data definition language (shorten, abbreviate, or change any data names as needed for the SQL version you might use). Assume the following attribute data types:

STUDENT NO. (integer, primary key)
STUDENT NAME (25 characters)
MAJOR (5 characters)
INSTRUCTOR NAME (25 characters, primary key)
INSTRUCTOR LOCATION (5 characters)
COURSE NO. (6 characters, primary key)
COURSE TITLE (10 characters)
GRADE (1 character)

3. Define the following view using an SQL view definition.

STUDENT NO.	STUDENT NAME	MAJOR	COURSE NO.	GRADE
38214	Bright	IS	IS 350	A
38214	Bright	IS	IS 465	C
69173	Smith	PM	IS 465	A
69173	Smith	PM	PM 300	B
69173	Smith	PM	QM 440	C

4. Write an SQL command to create an index called FIND_GRADE for the concatenated primary key (STUDENT_NO. and COURSE_NO.) in the REGISTRATION relation.
5. Before any row can be entered in the REGISTRATION table, the COURSE to be entered must already exist in the COURSE table (referential integrity). Write an SQL assertion that will enforce this constraint.
6. Write SQL retrieval commands for each of the following queries:
   a. Display the instructor location for the instructor Lewis.
   b. Display the student number and student name for all information system (IS) majors.
   c. Display the total number of students who are IS majors.
7. Write an SQL retrieval command to produce the table shown in Problem 3 above. Note the similarity between the view definition (Problem 3) and the retrieval command (Problem 7). Under what conditions would each of these commands be used?
8. Write SQL commands to answer the following question from the Mountain View Community Hospital database of Figure 8-1: What physicians have performed a tonsillectomy?
9. Write SQL commands to answer the following question from the database of Figure 8-1: What patients (display NAME) have been charged for the item TELEVISION?
10. Write an SQL query to answer the following question about Mountain View Community Hospital: What patients (display PATIENT_NO) are being treated by Dr. Wilcox and not Dr. Franklin?
11. Write an SQL query to answer the following question about Mountain View Community Hospital: What patients (display PATIENT_NO) have not been treated by Dr. Jefferson?
12. Write SQL commands to find those physicians that have not yet treated any patients at Mountain View Community Hospital.
13. Assume that the ITEM relation of Figure 8-1 is altered to also include STD_CHG, the standard charge for an item. Write the SQL commands to display the patient numbers for patients who have been charged above standard.

Problems 14–20 are based on the Pine Valley Furniture database from Chapter 2.

14. Create in SQL the Pine Valley Furniture database for the conceptual data model in Figure 2-7. Use other figures in Chapter 2 to help you choose column data types, lengths, indexes, etc.
15. Write an SQL command to display the order number, customer number, order date, and promised shipping date for orders promised for shipping prior to November 20, 1993.
16. Write an SQL query to display the order number, customer number, product number, order date, and order quantity for all orders of only products M128 or E125, but only if the order quantity is greater than 15.
17. Write an SQL query to display customer number, name, and order number for all customers and their orders; include customers who do not have any orders.
18. Write an SQL query to produce a list of all the products and the number of times each product has been ordered.
19. Write an SQL query to list the order number and order quantity for all customer orders for which the order quantity is greater than the average order quantity of that product. *Hint*: This involves a correlated subquery.

20. Write an SQL command to create a new temporary database table that would hold the following data: product numbers and the associated total quantity order of each, across all customer orders. Then use this temporary table in another SQL command to list the products that have total quantity ordered greater than twice the average total quantity ordered across all products.

REFERENCES

Ashton-Tate. 1992. *dBASE IV Language Reference.* Scotts Valley, Calif.: Ashton-Tate (a Borland Company).

Chamberlin, D. D., M. M. Astrahan, K. P. Eswaran, P. P. Griffiths, R. A. Lorie, J. W. Mehl, P. Reisner, and B. W. Wade. 1976. "SEQUEL: A Unified Approach to Data Definition, Manipulation and Control." *IBM Journal of Research and Development* 20 (Nov.): 560–74.

Codd, E. F. 1970. "A Relational Model of Data for Large Shared Data Banks." *Communications of the ACM* 13 (June):377–87.

———. 1982. "Relational Database: A Practical Foundation for Productivity." *Communications of the ACM* 25 (Feb.):109–17.

———. 1985a. "Does Your DBMS Run by the Rules?" *Computerworld* (Oct. 21):49–64.

———. 1985b. "Is Your DBMS Really Relational?" *Computerworld* (Oct. 14), ID/1–ID/9.

Date, C. J. 1987a. *An Introduction to Database Systems.* Vol. 1. 4th ed. Reading, Mass.: Addison-Wesley.

———. 1987b. "Where SQL Falls Short." *Datamation* (May 1):83, 84, 86.

IBM Corp. 1991. *SQL Reference for VM and VSE.* Nov. Form SH09–8087. Endicott, N.Y.: IBM Corp.

ISO. 1987. *Database Language SQL.* International Organization for Standardization.

——— 1989. *Database Language SQL.* International Organization for Standardization.

——— 1991. *Database Language SQL.* International Organization for Standardization.

Keller, A. M. 1986. "The Role of Semantics in Translating View Updates." *IEEE Computer* (Jan.):63–73.

Kroenke, D. 1983. *Database Processing.* 2d ed. Chicago: Science Research Associates.

Melton, J. 1993. "Changing of the Guard." *Database Programming & Design.* (March):31–32.

Melton, J., and K. Kulkarni. 1992a. "Is the SQL Standard Too Large?" *Database Programming & Design* (July):21, 22, 24, 26.

——— 1992b. "Out With the Old." *Database Programming & Design* (August):26–27.

Oracle Corp. 1988. *Oracle Application Tools for MS-DOS User's Guide.* Menlo Park, Calif.: Oracle Corp.

Relational Technology, Inc. 1989. *INGRES/SQL Reference Manual.* (Release 6.3). Nov. Alameda, Calif.: Relational Technology (division of ASK Computer Systems).

Rettig, M. 1989. "Gourmet Guide to the DB2 Catalog." *Database Programming & Design* 2 (Feb.):26–32.

Sayles, J. S. 1989. "All in a Row." *Data Based Advisor* 7 (Dec.):36–42.

Stonebraker, M. R., E. Wong, P. Kreps, and G. Held. 1976. "The Design and Implementation of Ingres" *ACM-TODS* 1 (Sept.):189–222.

Technical Committee X3H2—Database. 1986. *Database Language SQL.* (Jan.). American National Standards Institute.

Technical Committee X3H2—Database. 1989. *Database Language SQL.* American National Standards Institute.

Ullman, J. D. 1980. *Principles of Database Systems.* Potomac, Md.: Computer Science Press.

9

Implementing a
dBASE IV Database

LEARNING OBJECTIVES

After studying this chapter, you should be able to:

- Write one- and two-table queries using the dBASE IV programming language.
- Contrast the SQL and dBASE languages as examples of relational calculus and relational algebra languages, respectively.
- Explain the efforts to use the dBASE language as the basis for an industry standard of Xbase database products.
- Use various dBASE commands to restrict retrieval of data to selected rows and columns, as desired, in queries.
- Explain the differences in using indexes versus sorting of data for retrieval and display of data.
- Use dBASE commands to maintain data in a dBASE database.
- Write a dBASE program, and use macros and functions in a program.

INTRODUCTION

In the prior chapter on SQL we saw examples of one prevalent, standard, structured database management language. Although SQL was developed in IBM Corporation research labs, it has evolved through the efforts of a standardization body representing a broad spectrum of the database and programming industry. SQL began as a mainframe database language, but its use has expanded to all computer platforms.

Besides SQL, two other main approaches to database processing have emerged to dominate the industry—the dBASE relational algebra-based language and the Query-by-Example (QBE) style. We devote this chapter to dBASE and the following chapter to QBE. We illustrate QBE using Paradox 4.0. We use the Pine Valley Furniture database from Chapter 2 for our illustrations in these chapters.

The evolution of dBASE, in contrast to what we learned about SQL, has been driven by a few vendors of PC database systems. Various lawsuits by Ashton-

Tate stalled initial efforts by several companies and the IEEE society to define a dBASE language standard (Hawkins, 1992). Now that rights to dBASE have been clarified, standardization efforts have been renewed through the American National Standards Institute (ANSI). Today, an active and viable industry exists in dBASE-related PC relational database products. Such so-called Xbase products (database systems, language compilers, add-ons to dBASE, and dBASE applications) are broadly accepted in the computer industry.

In this chapter, we examine the dBASE approach to database processing, concentrating on those features unique to the dBASE programming language. This chapter does not present a complete, in-depth description of dBASE—the goal is not to make you a skilled dBASE programmer. Instead, the purpose of this chapter is to prepare you to understand rapidly *any* Xbase package you might use by reviewing the broad range of salient features of the dBASE language. In addition, you will be able to compare the capabilities of various packages (using dBASE, SQL, QBE, and other approaches) and know what features to evaluate.

We will assume familiarity with the basic relational terminology and database design presented in Chapters 2, 3, and 6. You may also want to read the appendix "Codd's 12 Rules for a Truly Relational System" to review the basic principles on which PC relational systems are built. Further, since dBASE is primarily a PC product, you need to understand the role of database processing on personal computers. An understanding of the relationship between database processing on PCs or local area networks (LANs) and departmental minicomputers or corporate mainframes is necessary for proper management of corporate data. Without this understanding, a multiple-unit company can create many databases and cause exactly the same problems associated with file processing systems, as outlined in Chapter 1. If you are not already familiar with database processing on personal computers, you should read the appendix "An Overview of PC-DBMSs."

THE STRUCTURE AND COMPONENTS OF PC RELATIONAL SYSTEMS

With the growing popularity of microcomputers, many vendors have developed PC-RDBMSs. A PC-RDBMS such as dBASE IV is a multiple-component product that frequently includes the following:

- The *core DBMS*, which provides data definition, a relational query language, and data definition and retrieval functions (repository).

Run-time version: The portion of the DBMS needed to run an existing database application.

- An optional **run-time version** of the DBMS (basically the database control program—see Chapter 12) that allows only prewritten (and precompiled) programs to execute (that is, the user cannot enter ad hoc, interactive queries). This facility reduces the main memory requirements and allows software developers to bundle the DBMS with application software without requiring the purchaser to buy the complete DBMS.

- A *programming language* that provides IF-THEN-ELSE logic, forms input and output, and presentation of menus and prompts to interactive users. Programs can then be stored in command files to be used by nonprogrammers or to provide frequently used routines for inclusion in interactive sessions.

- A *menu-driven front end* that uses menus or forms to prompt the user in completing each clause of each DBMS data definition, retrieval, modification, or other command. This user-friendly aid often displays the actual structured query on the screen as menu selections are made. This allows the user to verify visually the correctness of the query as interpreted, to be able to use the DBMS quickly without extensive training, and to learn the structured language by actually doing some database processing.

- A *screen painter or forms designer* that supports building CRT screen forms similar to the manual forms found in the organization that make data entry and updating easy. The screen painter provides such features as drawing boxes, applying color and intensity, displaying cross-reference data (for example, automatically displaying the customer's name when given the customer number), making data entry pleasant, and reducing entry errors.

- A *report writer* that supports extensive reporting features beyond those provided by the query or programming languages. Typical features are subtotals and totals, custom report layouts, control breaks, data value formatting, statistical analysis, page numbering and dating, and column labeling.

- A *business graphics* module that allows quick summarization of database contents in pie charts, line graphs, bar charts, and other business graphical formats.

- An **application generator** that supports building complete application systems from multiple stored programs and tree-structured menus to guide the user to the desired program in the application system (for example, to programs for entry of a new customer, a customer order, or for printing a product sales summary report).

- *File import/export utilities* that allow data to be entered into or extracted from a database and files used by other popular PC packages (for example, electronic spreadsheet and desktop publishing systems).

- A *natural language or tabular language processor* that allows a user to express a query in Englishlike statements or select desired data by filling in a form or template on the screen.

Application generator: A programming language that allows a database application to be built from existing programs, screen and report definitions, and from custom-built menus.

Usually the standard version of the PC-RDBMS is designed for single-user database access. Special versions of the DBMS are required for local area network environments or when interacting with both mainframe and PC databases. We discuss the unique issue of multiuser systems in Chapter 13.

Relational PC-DBMS Styles

The main structural difference between relational systems is the style of their query languages. The three major general styles are (1) relational calculus (typical of most systems that originated on mainframes), (2) relational algebra (typical of the original style of many PC products), and (3) Query-by-Example. A relational algebra query specifies the ordered steps used in generating the result. A relational calculus query is purely descriptive, containing no method for achieving the desired relation. Chapter 8 covered the dominant relational calculus language, SQL. The Query-by-Example approach is illustrated in Chapter 10 using Paradox 4.0.

A **relational algebra** language like dBASE IV has unary and binary table operators, whereas a relational calculus language like SQL allows more than two tables to be referenced in one command. Thus, relational algebra decomposes complicated retrieval statements into many statements, each of which deals with operations on one or two tables. A single relational algebra statement can be simpler to construct than a relational calculus statement. However, the full effect of database processing cannot be seen in relational algebra unless you analyze potentially many statements.

Relational algebra: A data manipulation language that provides a set of operators for manipulating one or two files.

dBASE: A STANDARD FOR PC RELATIONAL SYSTEMS

dBASE has significant market penetration. According to Grauer and Barber (1992), there are over three million copies of dBASE installed on six continents. dBASE has existed longer than the IBM PC! Starting out under the name Vulcan, dBASE has evolved into dBASE IV version 1.5, and a Microsoft Windows version was about to be released by Ashton-Tate, division of Borland International, as this book went to press.

E. F. Codd published the seminal article on relational database theory and relational algebra in 1970 (Codd, 1970). dBASE is arguably the first successful commercial DBMS to follow from this ground-breaking work. Today, two software company giants—Borland International with dBASE IV and Microsoft with FoxPro—dominate the dBASE and related product market. Because of the influence of these two vendors, dBASE is ensured many more years of a prominent position in the database field.

Since dBASE is a product name trademarked by Ashton-Tate, the field generally refers to the wide range of systems that use derivatives of the dBASE programming language as **Xbase products**. Besides Borland and Microsoft, other major Xbase products are the following:

Xbase products: Database systems and utilities based on the dBASE programming language.

- **Clipper**, from Nantucket Corporation (recently bought by Computer Associates International). Clipper is a compiler for a dBASE language program; Clipper has no interactive "Control Center" as in dBASE IV.

- **dbFast for Windows**, also from Computer Associates International. dbFast is also a compiler for a dBASE language program, but it is designed for Microsoft Windows rather than MS-DOS.

- **dBMAN V for MS-DOS**, from Verasoft Corporation. dBMAN is a work-alike to dBASE III Plus that is also available for several forms of the UNIX operating system.

- **Emerald Bay Database Server**, from Emerald Bay Group. The EB database server is a LAN-based DBMS that uses a database engine that follows the dBASE language, not SQL, the language of most database servers. (Emerald Bay Group was founded by Wayne Ratliff, the author of the first dBASE.)

- **Genifer**, from Bytel Corporation. Genifer is a screen formatter and report and menu generator that can be used with dBASE and other Xbase products.

- **ERwin/DBF**, from Logic Works, Inc. ERwin/DBF is a forward- and reverse-engineering tool for dBASE; ERwin/DBF can generate dBASE table definitions from ER diagrams or build ER diagrams from dBASE file structures.

- **dBASE IV for UNIX**, from Borland International. dBASE for UNIX is a natural addition to the Borland family of products, and helps to establish dBASE more broadly in the database processing field.

To some degree, dBASE has become a pawn in the struggle for size and market penetration between major software vendors (Borland, Microsoft, and Computer Associates). On the other hand, if ownership of a leading Xbase product is part of the image of being a major software firm, the importance of dBASE has only been reinforced by recent corporate acquisitions.

An Xbase product is characterized primarily by its inclusion of a relational algebra programming language similar to that in dBASE III or dBASE IV. Although some systems also include a menu-driven interface like the dBASE Control Center or an SQL language capability, it is the relationship to the dBASE command language that ties these systems together. The primary purpose of this chapter is to provide you with a sound foundation in this language; we use dBASE IV exclusively for illustration. For a more thorough comparison of Xbase products and analysis of the Xbase industry, see Hawkins (1992), Perschke (1992), Pinneau (1992), Ricciardi (1992), and Schaffhauser (1992).

dBASE Terminology and Concepts

In this section we review some basic dBASE terminology and concepts used throughout the chapter. Since the intent of this chapter is to give you a conceptual overview of the Xbase style of DBMS, this section is purposely short. For the same reason, we do not provide formal definitions of specific dBASE terminology. You may want to refer to a separate dBASE text if you are going to use dBASE extensively in a database course.

dBASE IV contains two main components: the Control Center and the dot prompt. The Control Center, shown extensively in Chapter 2, is a menu-driven interface that prompts a user in interactive use of dBASE. The dot prompt is a command line interface in which dBASE language commands are entered and executed one line at a time. Looping and conditional branching commands are not effective in the dot prompt since execution is interactive for each line. However, prewritten programs that include such logic may be run from the dot prompt. In this chapter, we will focus on the dBASE command language as used with either the dot prompt or stored programs. Although SQL commands may also be entered as commands, we do not address this capability of dBASE here (see Chapter 8).

dBASE recognizes the concept of a database by grouping related data, queries, forms, reports, labels, and programs into a catalog, which is a collection of related files. A catalog for the Pine Valley Furniture Company database illustrated throughout this book appears in Figure 2-11. This particular catalog is called PVF and is stored on the A: floppy disk drive (.CAT is the DOS standard file extension used by dBASE to distinguish a catalog file). You may store many catalogs on one floppy or hard disk. The catalog used by dBASE at any time is called the *active catalog*.

Using a dBASE File   Before a file may be used in dBASE it must be put into *use* and assigned to a specific file work area. A work area is an area of memory where you can open a database file, together with its index files. The dBASE USE command performs this function. The basic structure of the USE command is

```
. USE filename [IN work area number]
```

where *filename* is the name of a data file in the active catalog. In the above notation, lowercase words stand for names or symbols that you would enter, and a clause in brackets [. . .] is optional. Besides the IN clause, other optional clauses for the USE command include

```
INDEX index file list
ORDER index name OF multiple index file
ALIAS alias name [EXCLUSIVE] [NOUPDATE] [NOLOG] [NOSAVE]
AGAIN
```

The INDEX clause specifies which database files containing indexes should be opened when the data file is placed in use. If an index file is not opened, it will not be updated if the file contents change. Later in the chapter, we explain that an index file may contain several (up to 47) tags or individual key indexes.

A tag is a name for an index. The ORDER clause is used to specify which tags to open. Up to 10 index files may be open at a time.

The ALIAS clause allows you to specify an alternative name for a file. Usually you use it to create an abbreviation for a file name, as when CUSTOMER is short-ened to CU to minimize keystrokes in subsequent commands. The optional choices after the ALIAS specification deal with file and record locking in a multiuser environment. We discuss these options later in this chapter under multiple-user considerations.

Once a file is placed in use, two other dBASE constructs—the record pointer and filter—influence which records from the file are processed. Each file has a record pointer that contains the relative record number (or position) of the current, or active, record in the file. Many dBASE commands act on the current record, and other commands simply change the value of the record pointer. Other com-mands work on whole files. A filter is a set of instructions that restrict the actions of subsequent commands to certain records or fields in a file. A filter is a kind of mask that limits database activity to the desired portion of a database.

DATABASE DEFINITION IN dBASE

Since the purpose of this chapter is to provide you with an understanding of the dBASE style of database language, we provide only a brief overview of data def-inition features. You should refer to the section ''Database Definition in dBASE IV'' in Chapter 2 for examples.

Given a set of database requirements (say in entity-relationship notation) trans-lated into relational notation (as outlined in Chapter 6), the designer of a dBASE database has only a few data definition choices:

- Name, data type, length, and format (for example, number of decimal places) for each field

- Columns or combinations of columns for which to create primary or second-ary key indexes (see Chapter 7 for a discussion of indexes)

Data Types

The six field types in dBASE—character, numeric, floating-point, logical, memo, and date—were briefly described in Chapter 2. All of these, except memo, are similar to corresponding data types found in any programming language, so we do not address them here. Since a memo field data type is typically included in modern DBMSs, we introduce this data type here.

A **memo field** is a long, variable-length character string. Usually, a memo field contains unstructured data (for example, a salesperson's comments about a cus-tomer, an open-ended response to a market research question, or custom text for different types of potential customers to be inserted into a form letter). A memo field has a predefined width in the database file in which it is specified, but a memo field is not actually stored as part of the database file. Rather, a pointer to a location in a separate memo file is stored. For example, if CUSTOMER.DBF is the DOS file that contains the CUSTOMER database file, then the CUSTOMER.DBT file would contain values for all memo fields for the

Memo field: A long, varia-ble-length character string; usually stored in a separate file from the other fields in the associated record.

CUSTOMER database file. Each memo field value may be up to 64K in length, but space is allocated only for what is needed to store the entered values. A file may have several memo fields.

Besides giving a field a data type, dBASE has no other data integrity control. There is no capability within the dBASE file definition, for example, to do the following:

- To state that a field may not contain a null (or empty) value
- To specify a default value
- To limit values to a specified range of values or to a value found in another database file
- To specify a field as computed from other fields within the same file

Such capabilities must be controlled through forms or programs. This is a noticeable limitation of dBASE since enforcement of such data integrity rules cannot be ensured unless these rules are stored as part of the file definition.

Additional Table Definition Features

PC-RDBMSs are frequently used to prototype an application to meet changing database needs. Thus, it is very convenient to be able to redefine a database or define new database files from existing ones. Obviously, care should be taken in using these features. It is advisable to back up files before making changes that affect the structure of the database.

In dBASE IV, we can completely redefine any aspect of a file; for example, a column name, data type, and length can all be changed. Fields may be added or deleted. The definition of a file is changed via the dBASE MODIFY STRUCTURE command. The MODIFY command has several restrictions: you may not rename a field and change its type or length at the same time, and you may not insert or delete fields as well as change field names in one step.

MODIFY STRUCTURE causes the normal data definition screen to appear. You move through the screen making the desired changes, and exit and save the changes when you are done. dBASE makes a backup copy of any data, memo, and index files before it rebuilds the files. It then automatically appends the data from the backup files to the new files without requiring any further commands.

You do not have to specify a table structure from scratch in dBASE IV; the structure definition can itself be stored as data in one table, and you can create a new data table from this definition table. For example, the dBASE commands

```
. USE PRODUCT
. COPY TO ITEMDEF STRUCTURE EXTENDED
```

create a table ITEMDEF that contains the five fields that define each data element in a table (see Figure 2-12 for the PRODUCT table): field name, field type, field width, number of decimal places, and an index flag. Each row in ITEMDEF is the definition of a field from the PRODUCT table. Data modification statements (to be covered later) can then be used to change the contents of the ITEMDEF table. That is, we can change field names or lengths, add new fields, delete fields, and so on, as appropriate for the new file being created. For example, this new file might specify field names that are local to a particular department. The ITEMDEF file could also be created and populated as is any other data file, rather than copied from an existing file structure. Then, the command

```
. CREATE ITEM FROM ITEMDEF
```

would define a new table, ITEM, for which field definitions would come from the contents of the ITEMDEF table. This command does not store data in ITEM but only defines the table structure. This CREATE (table) FROM (structure) command is especially useful as part of a prewritten program to perform all the necessary data definition building functions for a novice user. A similar command,

```
. COPY STRUCTURE TO filename [FIELDS field list]
```

combines the above steps into one command (obviously without the ability to first change the table definitions). The above COPY command says, ''Copy the structure of the current database file to the named file, optionally including in the definition of the new file only the fields from the current file that are listed in the field list.''

Index Definition in dBASE

Indexes were introduced in Chapter 7 as an efficient means for providing rapid random and sequential processing of data. You will recall from the discussion in Chapter 7 that an index is a separate file maintained outside the data file being indexed. The DBMS can quickly scan an index to find a pointer to one or several records that satisfy a key qualification, or the DBMS can access the index in the defined sequence to retrieve records in sorted order. In contrast, a sorted file provides for fast access to records only in the sequence that was used for sorting. Further, only one sort can be maintained, unless multiple copies of a data file are kept, each in different sorted orders. Thus, the ability to index a database file is an important feature that provides users with flexible ways to access data.

In fact, in dBASE, your only physical database design choice is the creation of primary and secondary key indexes. We introduced dBASE indexing in Chapter 2. On the data definition screen (see, for example, Figure 2-12 for the PRODUCT table), we can designate individual fields for the creation of an index. Figure 2-13 illustrated various options available for customizing an index. The equivalent dBASE command to create an index is INDEX; its syntax follows:

```
. INDEX ON key expression TO index filename [UNIQUE]
  or
. INDEX ON key expression
    TAG tag name [OF index filename]
    [FOR condition] [UNIQUE] [DESCENDING]
```

The first form of INDEX creates an index file with a .NDX extension, which is compatible with older versions of dBASE. The second form of INDEX, with the TAG clause, uses the latest dBASE capabilities. Because of the importance of indexes in relational database processing, we explain more details of dBASE indexing than of other data definition features.

Tag: In dBASE, a key index contained in a multiple-index file.

Multiple-index file: In dBASE, a file that contains up to 47 key indexes.

dBASE Indexes   Figure 9-1 depicts the dBASE indexing system for a hypothetical data file DATA. An index **tag** is one index in a **multiple-index file** (or .MDX file) of several indexes. Each multiple-index file can have up to 47 tags. Each data file has associated with it a so-called production .MDX file that has the same file name as the data file. All tags are stored in the production .MDX file unless

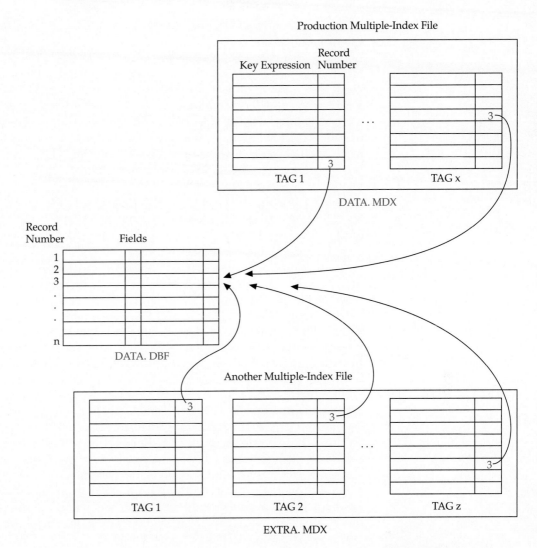

Figure 9-1

dBASE indexing system

another is specified in the OF clause of an INDEX command. The advantage of a multiple-index file is that it allows you to organize the same data table in up to 47 different ways all at once. Different multiple-index files can be used for different sets of tags.

One multiple-index file is open for each table at a time. You designate one of the tags in an open multiple-index file as the master index. The master index determines the sequence in which records will be displayed. You use the dBASE command SET ORDER TO TAG *tag name* to make a specific tag the current master index. All indexes associated with the opened multiple-index file are active, so dBASE can use any of them to speed database processing. However, when you want data records displayed, only the master index controls the display sequence.

Opening and Closing an Index   As mentioned above, you use the INDEX clause of the USE command to state which .MDX file to open. If you do not specify an .MDX file to open, dBASE assumes you want to open the production index file. You use the TAG clause to specify which tag to open as the master. CLOSE INDEX closes an open index file, but never closes the production index file.

As long as an index is open (all the tags in the current master index and any single index files mentioned when the file is put into use are open), it will be updated whenever the associated base table is changed. That is, each appending of a new record or change in an existing record causes index maintenance overhead. If you forget or decide not to open an index, you can execute a REINDEX command to update all single and multiple indexes without creating new indexes. Updating a file with all indexes open can significantly delay update times, so a user may elect not to open all single indexes during file updating. Updates to the index are then in a sense batch-processed via the REINDEX command. Reindexing is important; otherwise indexes and tables will not agree.

Tag Specification   Each tag is a specific key index. The key expression may simply be a field name. In addition, a key expression may contain a concatenation of alphanumeric fields, subtractions of numeric fields, functions of fields, and combinations of these and other options.

Index values are case-sensitive. This sensitivity to case and the requirement of exact matches in order to find records based on index values can cause sticky problems for text-data search strings (the key value we are seeking) and keys. Several options are available in dBASE to deal with this problem. First, the SET EXACT OFF command says that if each character in the search string matches the corresponding character in the index key entry, consider the row found even if the entire length of both strings does not match. This command solves the problem of trailing blanks. A second option is to index a character field by applying the UPPER or LOWER string function in the key expression to change all characters to the same case, if case is, in fact, immaterial. In this situation, the key expression is, for example, UPPER(*fieldname*), not just *fieldname*. Then each search string must be similarly converted to find the matching key values. This and other indexing problems, such as numeric data left-justified in text fields, or ignoring leading articles (*a, and, the*) are discussed in Nebel (1989).

Multiple-key (or concatenated key) indexes may be created by forming one key expression involving string operators to append the different fields to each other. A concatenated key has more than one field. For example, to form a concatenated key index CHGINDEX on ORDER_NO and PRODUCT_NO in the REQUEST table of the Pine Valley Furniture database, the dBASE INDEX command would be

```
. INDEX ON STR(ORDER_NO) + PRODUCT_NO
    TO CHGINDEX UNIQUE
```

The INDEX command causes the current contents of the table to be indexed. The STR( ) function converts the numeric ORDER_NO into a character string to concatenate with the character field PRODUCT_NO to form the index value. The UNIQUE keyword restricts index entries to one entry per key value (a primary key).

Other Index Options   Two additional clauses of the INDEX command not already explained are the FOR and DESCENDING options. You use FOR to index records that meet a specified condition. For example, assume you want to create an index of products that includes only those that have stocked out, that is, those with QOH equal to zero. You could create this index with the command

```
. INDEX ON PRODUCT_NO TAG REORDER
    FOR QOH = 0 UNIQUE
```

Using this index as the master, you could then issue FIND or SEEK commands to find specific, stocked-out products.

DESCENDING builds the index in descending sequence. This clause causes records to be displayed in reverse order, rather than in ascending order, which is the default.

Deleting an Index   If you create an index and then decide that it is no longer of any use, you can eliminate it by using the command

```
. DELETE TAG tag name [OF index filename]
```

Data Dictionary Facilities

The data dictionary (or repository) is an important part of database management systems. The repository of most relational systems is active and integrated, which means that it contains the actual database description used by the DBMS. Most database users primarily use only a small portion of a single database regularly, and various other databases less frequently. As a result, users are unfamiliar with most of the data available to them. Thus, when a somewhat different query arises or an unfamiliar report is seen, a user may not know which data to use or how to interpret the data reported. The data repository is the source that tells which data is stored where, how it is formatted, who created it, and a host of other "data about data."

As mentioned earlier, dBASE has a feature called a *catalog* that allows tables and associated screen forms, labels, reports, and other definitions in the repository to be logically grouped, usually because of their common use in applications. Thus, an organization may have an accounting catalog, an engineering catalog, and a marketing catalog. Catalogs help to isolate not only data manipulation but also definition access to only relevant portions of all the data maintained. This approach is very helpful when multiple databases are stored on the same medium. The SET CATALOG TO command informs dBASE which catalog to use. The active catalog may be changed during an interactive session or within a program.

Table 9-1 lists and defines the various data definition access and manipulation commands built into dBASE IV. The main command to show the definition of a

TABLE 9-1   Selected dBASE IV Data Dictionary Commands

dBASE Command or Function	Explanation
LIST STRUCTURE	Shows definition of specified table
LIST FILES	Lists all database files in the current directory
LIST STATUS	Shows information about the current dBASE IV session, including all open files, indexes, and filter formulas
FILE(*filespec*)	Tests for the existence of a specified filename
TAGNO(*tag name*)	Returns the index number for the specified index
KEY(*tag name*)	Returns the key expression for the specified index
CATALOG( )	Returns the name of the active catalog file

Figure 9-2

Example of LIST
STRUCTURE command

```
. USE REQUEST
. LIST STRUCTURE
Structure for database: A:\REQUEST.DBF
Number of data records:      28
Date of last update    : 05/29/92
Field  Field Name  Type        Width    Dec    Index
    1  ORDER_NO    Numeric        5               Y
    2  PRODUCT_NO  Character      4               Y
    3  ORDER_QTY   Numeric        3               N
** Total **                     13
.
```

table is LIST STRUCTURE. The use of this command for the REQUEST table in Pine Valley Furniture is shown in Figure 9-2. The output from LIST STRUCTURE echos the table definition information, plus information on the number of current records in the table, the date of last update, and the total record length.

Summary of Database Definition Commands

In this section, we reviewed the dBASE data definition capabilities. dBASE provides basic data definition facilities, but lacks some important features. In particular, dBASE is missing important data integrity controls as part of table and field definitions. dBASE also lacks a currency data type. dBASE does have a relational view capability, which can be very helpful in making a database easy to use. Reasonable security features exist (we discuss security controls in DBMSs in Chapter 12), and the data definitions and other database status information can be retrieved from the built-in data dictionary.

DATA RETRIEVAL AND MANIPULATION IN dBASE IV

The dBASE data manipulation language follows the relational algebra style, whereas SQL (covered in Chapter 8) follows the relational calculus style. There are several important differences between these two approaches: number of files used in a command, ability to retrieve single records, and use of indexes. First, all commands in an algebra language operate on either one or two files, but never more than two files. A calculus language may work on three, four, or even more files within one command. For example, one calculus data retrieval command in SQL could join together data from the PRODUCT, REQUEST, CUORDER, and CUSTOMER files in the Pine Valley Furniture database. In an algebra language, such an operation would have to be performed in three incremental steps that would join pairs of files.

Second, a calculus language is set-oriented whereas an algebra language is record-oriented. For example, as we saw in Chapter 8, the result of every SQL retrieval command is a complete set of records that satisfy some qualification. This result can be displayed or stored in a new database table. There is no ability to read the first record that satisfies the qualification, and then read the next, and so forth. Thus, it is difficult to view each qualified record and make specialized processing choices. In contrast, dBASE has easy-to-use commands that retrieve qualified records one at a time. A program can then perform any other operations before reading another record.

Finally, indexes are transparent in calculus languages and explicit in algebra languages. That is, we never had to consider in any query illustrated in Chapter 8 whether indexes existed or not on fields involved in the query; we simply wrote the query the same way in either case. In contrast, we use different commands in the dBASE language when fields are or are not indexes. Further, although several commands may be permitted in some cases, one command may be considerably more efficient than another, depending on the existence of indexes. Thus, the programmer has more decisions to make when using dBASE.

Filters

The results of any dBASE query can be limited by a restriction placed on files called a *filter*. A **filter** associated with a database table limits database processing to the records that satisfy the filter condition. Because filters affect all other retrieval and modification commands, we introduce this dBASE feature first. In the dBASE command language, the equivalent of the conditions in a view is the SET FILTER TO command. Specific conditions may be specified with the SET FILTER command, or the command may specify a file in which the conditions are stored. Each database file may have an active filter. The following commands display the records from the Customer file for those customers with more than a 5% discount.

Filter: In dBASE, a condition placed on a file that makes it appear as if the file contains only records that meet the given condition.

```
. USE CUSTOMER
. SET FILTER TO DISCOUNT > 5
. LIST
```

All subsequent queries to the Customer table would be restricted to this set of records, just as if these were the only kind of records in the Customer file. However, commands that involve specific record positions ignore any active filter. For example, the following commands display the second record in the Customer table, regardless of its discount value.

```
. GOTO 2
. DISPLAY
```

Single-Table Commands

The two most basic single-table dBASE data retrieval commands are DISPLAY and LIST. These commands show the contents of a table in tabular form on the specified output device, typically the PC screen. These are nearly identical commands with subtle differences. For example, the commands DISPLAY ALL and LIST produce the same results, except that DISPLAY ALL pauses after each new screen full of data is shown.

The simple command

```
. DISPLAY
```

shows the fields in the current record of the file in use. The full syntax for the DISPLAY and LIST commands is the same; using LIST, this syntax is

```
LIST [expression list] [OFF] [scope]
  [FOR condition] [WHILE condition] [TO PRINTER/TO FILE filename]
```

The optional expression list is a comma-separated set of field names or expressions from the file in use. When an expression list is present, only the listed fields and expressions are shown in the result. An expression is any typical arithmetic formula of fields, possibly including functions of fields using special functions available in the language. For example, the commands

```
. USE PRODUCT
. LIST PRODUCT_NO, UNIT_PRICE*QOH
```

produce the following result:

```
Record # PRODUCT_NO   UNIT_PRICE*QOH
       1 M128                 2000.00
       2 E350                 2535.00
       3 E125                 1564.00
       4 E177                  933.00
       5 T100                  491.90
       6 T160                  332.00
       7 O100                 1582.00
       8 O625                  995.00
       9 O800                    0.00
      10 B975                 2250.00
      11 B985                 2376.00
      12 B381                  450.00
      13 R210                  500.00
```

If you do not want to have column headers, then entering the following command before the above commands suppresses header display:

```
. SET HEADING OFF
```

When you include the optional OFF clause, the display of the record numbers is suppressed.

The scope clause limits the display to a range of specific physical records in the file. The options for scope are

- ALL, for all the records in the file (this is the default scope for the LIST command)
- NEXT *n*, for *n* records beginning with the current one (NEXT 1 is the default with the DISPLAY command)
- RECORD *n*, for a specific relative record in the file
- REST, for all the records from the current position to the end of the file

The FOR clause also limits the display to specified records, but in this case the limit is based on record contents, not physical position. The FOR condition is a typical Boolean expression of one or more simple conditions; the operators .AND., .OR., and .NOT. may be used. For example, the following commands

```
. USE PRODUCT
. LIST PRODUCT_NO,ROOM,FINISH,UNIT_PRICE
  FOR ROOM = "LIVING" .OR. FINISH = "BIRCH"
```

result in

```
Record #  PRODUCT__NO  ROOM    FINISH   UNIT__PRICE
       1  M128         STUDY   BIRCH        200.00
       5  T100         LIVING  BIRCH        245.95
       6  T160         LIVING  BIRCH        332.00
      10  B975         LIVING  MAPLE        225.00
      11  B985         LIVING  MAPLE        198.00
      12  B381         DINING  BIRCH        150.00
```

The scope of records considered in a LIST or DISPLAY command is also implicitly limited by any SET FILTER or SET DELETED command. We explained SET FILTER earlier. SET DELETED says how to handle records that have been marked for deletion, but not yet eliminated. SET DELETED OFF, the default, means that records marked for deletion are ignored in subsequent commands; SET DELETED ON means to include such records.

The WHILE clause is also used to limit the display to qualified records; however, using WHILE is more complicated than using the FOR clause. LIST WHILE *condition* requires that a SET ORDER command be used first to organize the records in a particular index sequence related to the WHILE condition, and then a FIND command (explained below) must be executed to position the record pointer on the first record that satisfies the WHILE condition. LIST WHILE then displays the records until the condition is not met. Thus, LIST FOR scans the whole file looking for records that satisfy the condition, whereas LIST WHILE follows one particular sorted order and stops immediately when the condition fails. Obviously, LIST WHILE may be more efficient than LIST FOR with a large file, but it is of more limited value because the WHILE condition must relate to one index expression.

The TO PRINTER/TO FILE *filename* clause is used to redirect the output from the default device, the PC screen, to either the printer or a specified file.

Locating Desired Records   As mentioned earlier, relational algebra languages are record-oriented; that is, such languages have commands to locate a record that satisfies a specific condition and other commands to find the next such record, and so on. dBASE has three such table-search commands, each used in slightly different circumstances: LOCATE, FIND, and SEEK. Table 9-2 summarizes the appropriate use of these three commands. Each command finds the desired record (that is, positions the record pointer in a file), but these commands do not show the contents of the found record.

TABLE 9-2   Table-Search Commands

Command	Condition	Single Index Search	To Find Next Record
LOCATE	Complex	N	CONTINUE
FIND	Simple	Y	SKIP
SEEK	Simple, but may include a memory variable	Y	SKIP

The syntax of the LOCATE command is

```
LOCATE [FOR condition] [scope] [WHILE condition]
```

LOCATE searches from the beginning of a file (unless the scope indicates otherwise) for the first record that satisfies the specified condition. The condition may be any Boolean expression; because of this, indexes are *not* used to speed the search. Once a LOCATE is executed, a CONTINUE command searches for the next record with the same condition. When the dBASE function FOUND( ) returns a value of .F. or the function EOF( ) returns a value of .T., you know there are no more records that satisfy the condition. The following interactive example shows the use of LOCATE and CONTINUE to find the high-priced products (over $500) that are in limited supply (less than 4 units on hand).

```
. LOCATE FOR UNIT_PRICE > 500 .AND. QOH < 4
Record = 2
. DISPLAY
Record# PRODUCT_NO DESCRIPT   ROOM     FINISH      UNIT_PRICE QOH
     2 E350        TABLE      DINING   OAK             845.00   3
. CONTINUE
Record = 8
. DISPLAY
Record# PRODUCT_NO DESCRIPT   ROOM     FINISH      UNIT_PRICE QOH
     8 O625        DESK       STUDY    MAHOGANY        995.00   1
. CONTINUE
Record = 9
. DISPLAY
Record# PRODUCT_NO DESCRIPT   ROOM     FINISH      UNIT_PRICE QOH
     9 O800        CREDENZA   STUDY    MAHOGANY        875.00   0
. CONTINUE
End of LOCATE scope
```

LOCATE is a very general search command, since the search condition can be any legitimate expression, but LOCATE may be slow, since it does not take advantage of any indexes. You should avoid using LOCATE for large databases found in business transaction-processing applications.

In contrast, FIND offers a rapid way to locate a record, but the condition must involve a single index. The syntax of FIND is

```
FIND key value
```

Memory variable: A nondatabase field defined within a program that is used to store intermediate results, keyboard input, and other data not associated with a database file.

FIND uses the current master index for the file in use (the SET ORDER command is used to specify the master index). FIND, like LOCATE, ignores records masked by a SET FILTER or SET DELETED OFF command. The key value must be either a literal or the name of a character memory variable preceded by the & symbol. A **memory variable** is a nondatabase field defined within a dBASE program or procedure that is used to store intermediate results and other data not associated with a database file. FIND searches for an exact match with the key value unless preceded by a SET EXACT OFF or SET NEAR ON commands. SET EXACT OFF allows for partial key searches. If there is not an exact match, SET NEAR positions the record pointer on the next indexed record after where the key value would be if it were in the index. The following example illustrates FIND and the effect of these SET commands.

```
. SET ORDER TO PRODUCT_NO
Master index: PRODUCT_NO
. SET EXACT ON
. SET NEAR OFF
. FIND E177
. DISPLAY
Record# PRODUCT_NO DESCRIPT       ROOM    FINISH  UNIT_PRICE QOH
      4 E177       CHAIR W/OARM  DINING  OAK        155.50   6
. FIND M128
Find not successful
. SET EXACT OFF
. FIND M128
. DISPLAY
Record# PRODUCT_NO DESCRIPT       ROOM    FINISH  UNIT_PRICE QOH
      1 M128       BOOKCASE      STUDY   BIRCH      200.00  10
. FIND T103
Find not successful
. DISPLAY

.
. SET NEAR ON
. FIND T103
Find not successful
. DISPLAY
Record# PRODUCT_NO DESCRIPT       ROOM    FINISH  UNIT_PRICE QOH
      6 T160       TABLE COFFEE  LIVING  BIRCH      332.00   1
```

Not illustrated above is the SKIP command. SKIP *n* works as CONTINUE does for LOCATE; that is, SKIP moves the record pointer ahead *n* records in the index sequence. SKIP can be used to pick every *n* records or, if *n* is calculated from some form of random-number generator, to randomly sample records from a file. By itself SKIP moves to the next record in sequence.

Whereas FIND is typically used in interactive mode, SEEK is typically used as part of a program. SEEK works just as FIND does, except that the key value may be any valid expression of the same data type as the index. The search performed by SEEK, as with LOCATE and FIND, is limited by any SET FILTER or SET DELETED command. Often, SEEK is used to search for a record with a key value that matches that entered by a user. For example, the program would present a formatted screen on which the user would enter a product number. dBASE would store this entry in a memory variable, and then SEEK would look through the PRODUCT_ NO index for a product record with the value found in the memory variable.

Built-in Functions

Several functions available in dBASE allow easy calculation of summary data for a file. The available functions are listed in Table 9-3. The results of AVERAGE and SUM may be displayed or stored in a memory variable (if one expression is averaged) or a memory array (if there are several expressions averaged). Also, these functions support expressions as arguments, not just simple fields, as with TOTAL. COUNT involves no fields for display. Since COUNT results in only one value, that result may be stored in a memory variable or displayed. Each of these commands is also affected by a SET FILTER command on the file. With TOTAL, the file must be either indexed or sorted (we discuss sorting next) on the key field, so that the subtotals by key value can be computed.

TABLE 9-3 dBASE Function Commands

Command	Explanation
AVERAGE [*expression list*] [*scope*] [FOR *condition*] [WHILE *condition*] [TO *memvar* / TO ARRAY *array name*]	Computes the arithmetic mean of numeric expressions
COUNT [TO *memvar*] [*scope*] [FOR *condition*] [WHILE *condition*]	Computes the number of records that satisfy a specified condition
SUM [*expression list*] [TO *memvar* / TO ARRAY *array name*] [*scope*] [FOR *condition*] [WHILE *condition*]	Computes the total value of specified numeric expressions
TOTAL ON *key field* TO *filename* [FIELDS *field list*] [*scope*] [FOR *condition*] [WHILE *condition*]	Computes the total value of numeric fields grouped by key field value in a file and creates a second database file to contain the results

In addition to these specific built-in functions, a more general data-aggregation function, the CALCULATE command, provides the ability to compute a wider range of summary data for a file. The syntax of CALCULATE is

```
CALCULATE [scope] option list
  [FOR condition] [WHILE condition]
  [TO memvar / TO ARRAY array name]
```

The option list is a set of comma-delimited functions of expressions involving file fields. Table 9-4 lists the supported functions. For example, the following command computes the average and maximum inventory values of products and the number of products for Pine Valley Furniture:

```
. CALCULATE AVG(UNIT_PRICE*QOH),MAX(UNIT_PRICE*QOH),CNT( )
    13 records
AVG(UNIT_PRICE*QOH) MAX(UNIT_PRICE*QOH)  CNT( )
            1231.45                2535      13
```

As before, a SET FILTER limits the scope of such calculations.

Sorting a File

As we have seen, you can control the sequence in which records are processed by a SET ORDER command if the file is indexed on a key that corresponds to the desired sequence. When a file is not indexed as desired, or when you have a one-time need for a specific data display order, you can use the SORT command. SORT creates a new table from the table in use, including only those records that meet record qualifications and SET FILTER and SET DELETED conditions. Thus, SORT causes data redundancy, and it creates a separate file that is physically in exactly

TABLE 9-4   Options in the CALCULATE Command

Option	Explanation
AVG (*expression*)	Average
CNT ( )	Number of records in file
MAX (*expression*)	The largest value
MIN (*expression*)	The smallest value
NPV (*rate,flows,initial*)	The net present value, where *rate* is a decimal value for the discount, *flows* is any valid expression of a database field that is the series of signed cash flow values, and *initial* is a numeric expression (usually negative) for the initial investment
STD (*expression*)	The standard deviation
SUM (*expression*)	The sum of all values
VAR (*expression*)	The population variance

the desired sequence. That is, SORT uses extra secondary memory and creates a potential for inconsistency if the original file changes, but SORT yields a file that is quickly processed in the specified sequence. The syntax of the SORT command is

```
SORT TO filename ON field1 [sort order]
  [,field2 [sort order] ...] [ASCENDING/DESCENDING]
  [scope] [FOR condition] [WHILE condition]
```

You may sort on one or more fields, and for each you may specify a particular sort order: ascending (/A) or descending (/D) order. You may also specify /C, which sorts without differentiating between upper- and lowercase. For example, /DC for a field specifies descending order ignoring the distinction between upper- and lowercase characters. ASCENDING or DESCENDING covers all fields for which a sort order is not explicitly given. You can use the file generated by SORT as you would any database file. This file is automatically defined by dBASE with no indexes. If you want to use FIND or SEEK to search this file, you must issue an INDEX command.

MULTIPLE-TABLE OPERATIONS IN dBASE IV

As mentioned earlier in the chapter, one of the main characteristics of a relational algebra language like the dBASE command language is that you must do multiple table operations in steps, each involving a pair of tables. In contrast, using a relational calculus language like SQL, you retrieve data from many tables in one (possibly complex) statement. Further, we saw for SQL that tables could be combined in several different ways: what we called *equi-join*, *natural join*, and *outer join*. In dBASE, there is only one such way to combine matching rows from two tables: the JOIN command. The dBASE JOIN command creates the natural join of two tables (see Chapter 8 for a definition of different types of joins). There is no command in dBASE to create an outer join.

The JOIN Command

JOIN creates a new database file by combining matching records from two database files open in separate work areas. Two files may be joined if they have one or more fields in common, that is, field values that come from the same domain. The field names do not have to be the same to do a join. The syntax of the JOIN command is

```
JOIN WITH file TO filename FOR condition
   [FIELDS field list]
```

JOIN takes the file in the current work area and tries to match each record with one or more records in the other file, on the basis of the given condition. The result is a new file that includes all the fields (or only the listed fields if the FIELDS clause is included) from the two tables. Thus, without the optional FIELDS clause, the result is a natural join. The FOR clause limits the JOIN to records that meet only certain qualifications. Although typically the FOR condition includes equality of values on the common fields that permit the tables to be joined, inequality comparisons may also be used.

Suppose you wanted to see data from both the CUORDER and CUSTOMER files. You need to join these two files on the common field, CUST__NO. In dBASE, you would use the following commands:

```
. SELECT 2
. USE CUSTOMER
. SELECT 1
. USE CUORDER
. JOIN WITH CUSTOMER TO CUSTORD FOR CUST__NO = B->CUST__NO
    14 records joined
. USE CUSTORD
. DISPLAY STRUCTURE
Structure for database: A:\CUSTORD.DBF
Number of data records: 14
Date of last update: 09/15/93
Field Field Name   Type        Width   Dec   Index
    1 ORDER__NO    Numeric         5            N
    2 CUST__NO     Numeric         4            N
    3 ORDER__DATE  Date            8            N
    4 PROM__DATE   Date            8            N
    5 NAME         Character      20            N
    6 ADDRESS      Character      20            N
    7 CTY__ST__ZIP Character      30            N
    8 DISCOUNT     Numeric         2            N
** Total **                       98
```

The two files are opened in separate work areas. The JOIN command specifies an equality match for the two CUST__NO fields. The symbol B-> qualifies the second CUST__NO field to come from the B, or number 2, work area. Since there are 14 CUORDER records, and each has a matching CUSTOMER record, the resultant table has 14 records. The DISPLAY STRUCTURE shows the definition of this table, which was automatically generated by dBASE. You can now use the CUSTORD file as you would any other database table. Although they are not shown here, you could include other qualifications as part of a compound condition in the FOR clause (for example, to restrict the resultant table to records with only specified discounts).

As an example of an inequality join, suppose you wanted to find the REQUEST records that ask for more units of a product than are currently on hand. The following dBASE JOIN builds a result table with relevant data for this inquiry.

```
. SELECT 2
. USE PRODUCT
. SELECT 1
. USE REQUEST
. JOIN WITH PRODUCT TO OVER
  FOR PRODUCT_NO = B->PRODUCT_NO .AND.
    ORDER_QTY > B->QOH
   13 records joined
. USE OVER
. DISPLAY STRUCTURE
Structure for database: A:\OVER.DBF
Number of data records: 13
Date of last update: 09/15/93
Field Field Name  Type      Width  Dec  Index
    1 ORDER_NO    Numeric      5         N
    2 PRODUCT_NO  Character    4         N
    3 ORDER_QTY   Numeric      3         N
    4 DESCRIPT    Character   12         N
    5 ROOM        Character   10         N
    6 FINISH      Character   10         N
    7 UNIT_PRICE  Numeric      7     2   N
    8 QOH         Numeric      3         N
** Total **                  55
```

This query has a compound joining condition: REQUEST and PRODUCT records are joined by equal PRODUCT_NOs and by ORDER_QTY greater than the quantity on hand, QOH. The following LIST command shows specific field values for the records in the OVER table created from this join.

```
. LIST PRODUCT_NO,ORDER_NO,ORDER_QTY,QOH
Record# PRODUCT_NO ORDER_NO ORDER_QTY QOH
      1 M128         61392        30  10
      2 T160         61392         3   1
      3 E350         61394         6   3
      4 B381         61395         6   3
      5 O625         61397         3   1
      6 O800         61397         2   0
      7 O100         61398        10   4
      8 M128         61399        20  10
      9 E177         61400         8   6
     10 E350         61401         4   3
     11 E125         61402        12   8
     12 E177         61403        20   6
     13 E125         61403        24   8
```

SET RELATION Command

JOIN explicitly links two files based on a joining condition, and creates a third database file with fields from the joined tables. In contrast, the SET RELATION command implicitly links one file, a base file, with one or more other files, each based on common field values. The result is that a record in the base file appears to have appended to it the field values from the records linked to it. That is, as the record pointer is moved in the base file, so are the record pointers moved to the associated records in linked files. SET RELATION requires that files be indexed on the common fields. The SET RELATION must be in a many-to-one direction, so that each link matches with only one record in the other file.

The general syntax of SET RELATION is

```
SET RELATION TO [expression INTO filename
    [, expression INTO filename ...]]
```

SET RELATION TO without any parameters removes the relation from the currently selected work area. Each file linked to the file in the current work area has an INTO clause.

For example, the REQUEST file is related in a many-to-one relationship to each of PRODUCT and CUORDER. The following example shows how you can use SET RELATION to synchronize the movement of pointers in these three files and how you can display data from each in one LIST command, as if all the data were in one file.

```
. SELECT 3
. USE PRODUCT ORDER PRODUCT__NO
Master index: PRODUCT__NO
. SELECT 2
. USE CUORDER ORDER ORDER__NO
Master index: ORDER__NO
. SELECT 1
. USE REQUEST
. SET RELATION TO PRODUCT__NO INTO PRODUCT, ORDER__NO INTO
CUORDER
. DISPLAY
Record# ORDER__NO PRODUCT__NO ORDER__QTY
      1    61384 M128                4
. SELECT 3
. DISPLAY
Record# PRODUCT__NO DESCRIPT ROOM  FINISH UNIT__PRICE QOH
      1 M128         BOOKCASE STUDY BIRCH      200.00  10
. SELECT 2
. DISPLAY
Record# ORDER__NO CUST__NO ORDER__DATE PROM__DATE
      1    61384 1273      11/04/93    11/21/93
```

The above example shows that as the current record is read first from Work Area 2 and then from Work Area 3, the record there corresponds to the REQUEST record (product M128 and order number 61384, respectively).

Further, data from all three files can be displayed in one DISPLAY command, since related rows are synchronized:

```
. DISPLAY PRODUCT_NO,C->DESCRIPT,ORDER_NO,
    B->CUST_NO,B->ORDER_DATE ALL
Record#  PRODUCT_NO  C->DESCRIPT  ORDER_NO  B->CUST_NO B->ORDER_DATE
      1  M128        BOOKCASE       61384      1273 11/04/93
      2  B381        CABINET        61384      1273 11/04/93
      3  R210        TABLE          61384      1273 11/04/93
      4  T100        END TABLE      61390      1273 11/06/93
      5  T160        TABLE COFFEE   61390      1273 11/06/93
      6  B975        TABLE          61391      1273 12/01/93
      7  B985        END TABLE      61391      1273 12/01/93
      8  M128        BOOKCASE       61391      1273 12/01/93
      9  M128        BOOKCASE       61392      1278 10/10/93
     10  O100        BOOKCASE       61392      1278 10/10/93
     11  T160        TABLE COFFEE   61392      1278 10/10/93
     12  E350        TABLE          61394      1278 01/03/94
     13  B975        TABLE          61395      2345 11/20/93
     14  B985        END TABLE      61395      2345 11/20/93
     15  B381        CABINET        61395      2345 11/20/93
     16  O100        BOOKCASE       61396      1069 11/22/93
     17  O625        DESK           61397      1069 11/10/93
     18  O800        CREDENZA       61397      1069 11/10/93
     19  M128        BOOKCASE       61398      1256 11/10/93
     20  O100        BOOKCASE       61398      1256 11/10/93
     21  M128        BOOKCASE       61399      1256 11/11/93
     22  E125        ARM CHAIR      61400      3211 12/01/93
Press any key to continue...
     23  E177        CHAIR W/OARM   61400      3211 12/01/93
     24  E350        TABLE          61400      3211 12/01/93
     25  E350        TABLE          61401      3434 11/02/93
     26  E125        ARM CHAIR      61402      3434 11/24/93
     27  E177        CHAIR W/OARM   61403      3434 12/15/93
     28  E125        ARM CHAIR      61403      3434 12/15/93
```

Other Multiple-Table Operations

Three other multiple-table operations (introduced in Chapter 8) are often helpful:

- Union, which appends two files with identical field types
- Difference, which finds the records that are in one file (or set of records) but not in another file (or set)
- Intersection, which finds the records that are common to two files or sets of records

dBASE has a version of union, but does not directly support either difference or intersection.

Union   You can union two files in dBASE with the APPEND FROM command. APPEND FROM copies records from a file to the end of the active database file. The FROM file may be a dBASE IV file, or it may be a dBASE III file, a comma-delimited ASCII, a space-delimited ASCII, several different types of spreadsheet, or a fixed-length-field ASCII file. The main limitation when appending two dBASE IV files is that only fields with identical names are included; that is, the result of APPEND FROM is the active file with potentially more rows, and these new rows will have blank values for fields that are not in the FROM file.

The complete syntax of the APPEND FROM command is

```
APPEND FROM filename
   [[TYPE] filespec] [REINDEX] [FOR condition]
```

The optional TYPE clause specifies the format of the FROM file. REINDEX causes the active file's indexes to be rebuilt after all new records are appended; otherwise the index is updated after each new record is inserted. A FOR clause may involve only fields that are in both files.

Difference   Finding the records that are in one set of records and not in another is a very common type of inquiry. Some examples of inquiries in Pine Valley Furniture that involve set difference follow:

- Which products have not been ordered?
- Which customers have not placed an order?
- Which customers have not paid any of their invoices?

In each of these cases, we want to take the set of product or customer numbers and eliminate those numbers that appear in another list; the list of numbers remaining is the desired result.

Because there is no direct approach in dBASE to perform set difference, there is no one way to calculate such a result. We illustrate one set of the steps necessary to perform the equivalent of difference in dBASE using a variation of the first example above. Specifically, we find the products that have not been ordered by customer 1273. The process involves six steps:

1. Copying the PRODUCT file to a temporary file, TEMP1, so the contents of the PRODUCT file are not destroyed by subsequent steps
2. Joining the REQUEST and CUORDER files into a temporary file, TEMP2
3. Copying the records from TEMP2 for customer 1273 into a temporary table, TEMP3
4. Defining a SET RELATION from TEMP1 to TEMP3 based on PRODUCT_NO
5. Deleting the records in TEMP1 that have a matching value in TEMP3 (that is, deleting those products that have been ordered by customer 1273)
6. Listing the records that remain in TEMP1

The dBASE commands and responses from an interactive dBASE session for these steps and our sample database follow:

Step 1.
```
. SELECT 1
. USE PRODUCT
. COPY TO TEMP1
   13 records copied
```

Step 2.
```
. SELECT 2
. USE CUORDER
. SELECT 1
. USE REQUEST
. JOIN WITH CUORDER TO TEMP2 FOR ORDER_NO = B->ORDER_NO
   28 records joined
```

Step 3.
```
. USE TEMP2
. COPY TO TEMP3 FOR CUST_NO = 1273
   8 records copied
```

Step 4.
```
. SELECT 2
. USE TEMP3
. INDEX ON PRODUCT_NO TAG PRODUCT_NO
 100% indexed      8 Records indexed
. SELECT 1
. USE TEMP1
. SET RELATION TO PRODUCT_NO INTO TEMP3
```

Step 5.
```
. DELETE FOR PRODUCT_NO = B->PRODUCT_NO
   7 records deleted
. PACK
   6 records copied
```

Step 6.
```
. LIST PRODUCT_NO
Record# PRODUCT_NO
      1 E350
      2 E125
      3 E177
      4 O100
      5 O625
      6 O800
```

In Step 1 the 13 PRODUCT records are copied into file TEMP1. In Step 2 each of the 28 REQUEST records is joined with its corresponding CUORDER record so that CUST_NO and PRODUCT_NO appear in the same file, TEMP2. In Step 3 only those records in TEMP2 that apply to the specified customer, 1273, are saved into file TEMP3. An index on PRODUCT_NO in file TEMP3 had to be created in Step 4 since the SET RELATION requires the INTO file to be indexed on the matching field. The PACK command in Step 5 eliminates the records marked for deletion by the DELETE command. Step 6 displays the result—the products that customer 1273 has not ordered.

The interested reader may want to refer to the section on "MINUS and INTERSECT Operators" in Chapter 8 and the section on "Sets" and the NO operator in Chapter 10 to see how set difference is handled in SQL and Paradox.

Intersection   Suppose we wanted to find which products had been ordered by both customers 1273 and 3434. This is an example of an inquiry that can be answered by set intersection. We first find the products ordered by customer 1273, then the products ordered by customer 3434, and then look for the common products. As with difference, there is no direct command for intersecting two sets of records in dBASE IV. However, we can use several dBASE commands to simulate set intersection by the following steps:

1. Join into file TEMP1 the CUORDER and REQUEST files, so that associated CUST_NO and PRODUCT_NO values are in the same record.

2. Copy into file TEMP2 the PRODUCT_NO field values for records from TEMP1 for customer 1273; do likewise into file TEMP3 for customer 3434; this step creates the two sets for intersection.

3. Join into file TEMP4 records from files TEMP2 and TEMP3 based on equality of PRODUCT_NOs; the contents of TEMP4 is the desired answer.

The commands and interactive session responses in dBASE follow:

Step 1.
```
. SELECT 2
. USE CUORDER
. SELECT 1
. USE REQUEST
. JOIN WITH CUORDER TO TEMP1 FOR ORDER_NO = B->ORDER_NO
   28 records joined
```

Step 2.
```
. USE TEMP1
. COPY TO TEMP2 FIELDS PRODUCT_NO FOR CUST_NO = 1273
   8 records copied
. COPY TO TEMP3 FIELDS PRODUCT_NO FOR CUST_NO = 3434
   4 records copied
```

Step 3.
```
. SELECT 2
. USE TEMP2
. SELECT 1
. USE TEMP3
. JOIN WITH TEMP2 TO TEMP4 FOR PRODUCT_NO = B->PRODUCT_NO
No records joined
. SELECT 2
. LIST
Record#  PRODUCT_NO
      1  M128
      2  B381
      3  R210
      4  T100
      5  T160
      6  B975
      7  B985
      8  M128
. SELECT 1
. LIST
Record#  PRODUCT_NO
      1  E350
      2  E125
      3  E177
      4  E125
```

As the two list commands verify, there are, in fact, no products in common for the two sets. Thus, the intersection is null, as indicated in the answer from dBASE to the join in Step 3.

View Queries

As illustrated in Chapter 2 (see Figures 2-31 and 2-32), a view is a virtual table (that is, it is not stored as a regular database table) composed of columns from one or more related base (or permanent) tables. Various views of the same data allow different users to see these data in ways convenient to each. A view is also a way to give the user the impression of manipulating data from just one table, which makes data manipulation easier. Views may be necessary since some database processing commands must work on only one base table or one view table, not on several tables in combination. (For example, a report might have to be based on only one table.) Views also help in database security, since we can restrict access to the database by permitting a user to use only views that contain the data he or she is authorized to see. Views are now common features of PC-RDBMSs, including dBASE.

dBASE IV uses a visual programming style called Query-by-Example for specifying a view, or what dBASE calls a **query view**. (Since Query-by-Example is the foundation for Paradox, we will cover this database query style in depth in Chapter 10.) The dBASE command to activate the query-view design screen is CREATE VIEW, and MODIFY VIEW is used to change a view definition. You call up a file skeleton or template of each base table from which columns are to be selected and then indicate which columns to include in the new view. dBASE allows the use of up to eight base tables to build a view (views may not be used to define other views). We do not repeat the basics of defining a view here. Review the material in Chapter 2 if necessary as a refresher.

A view is activated in the dBASE language by the SET VIEW TO *filename* command, where the named file contains the view definition. SET VIEW TO ? lists all the view files in the current catalog. After you issue the SET VIEW command, dBASE computes the results of other commands (like DISPLAY and LIST) using only the data in the view.

Recall that a view is a virtual file; that is, the view does not contain actual data, which are still stored in the base tables. dBASE builds the data from one or several base tables into a single virtual table whenever the view table is referenced. Thus, each SET VIEW TO command causes a query to be executed. Once executed, subsequent references in the same session to the view file use the created view table. To update the view contents, simply reexecute the SET VIEW TO command and refer to the same view.

Example View for Pine Valley Furniture   For managerial decision making and other activities, database contents are usually summarized by calculating simple statistics like counts, sums, and averages. We can also use views to perform such summaries. In Figure 9-3 we define a view showing the total quantity of dining room furniture ordered, grouped by product number. Thus, the quantity ordered from multiple REQUEST records is summed and displayed with the as-

Query view: In dBASE, a virtual table created from a Query-by-Example format; data may be retrieved from a query view as if it were a regular database file.

Figure 9-3

Total dining room orders view

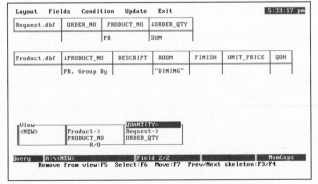

(a)   View definition

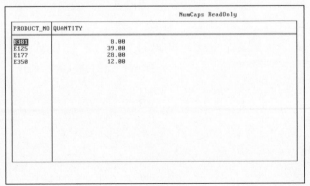

(b)   View table data

sociated product. We accomplished this by using the keyword SUM under the field to be summarized and the keyword Group By under the field on which the aggregation is made. The view definition in Figure 9-3a renames the sum of the ORDER_QTY fields as QUANTITY. This is a convenient feature, since those who use a view may have special terms for certain data that differ from standard field names and are more meaningful than names made up by the DBMS. However, renamed fields may not be edited via a view (the "R/O" below renamed fields means "read only"). The results appear in Figure 9-3b.

One final note about views is that frequently there are restrictions on updating the database via views. In dBASE IV, for example, only views that have simple data (that is, no aggregation) from one base table can be used to update the database. Otherwise, the updating might be ambiguous.

DATA MAINTENANCE IN dBASE IV

The typical operations of adding, deleting, and changing records are all possible in the dBASE IV programming language. In fact, there are several commands for adding and changing, suited for different circumstances.

Adding Data to a Table

The APPEND command allows you to add records to the end of the file in the current work area. APPEND is a screen-oriented data entry command for which a data entry form, like the ones in Figures 2-23 or 2-24, is displayed on the screen. That is, only one record from the file in the current work area is shown on the screen at a time.

A default form (see Figure 2-18 for the PRODUCT file in Pine Valley Furniture) is used unless a SET FORMAT command has been executed to pick a specific format for display. APPEND enforces all dBASE data validation rules (for example, data types) and any other validation rules associated with the form used for data entry. Note that APPEND does not check for duplicate or incomplete records. Since indexes are updated for appended records, duplicate key values will cause a record to be rejected if a key is defined as unique. Thus, data are not usually entered directly into a record via the APPEND command; that is, APPEND is used for limited, interactive data entry. Often, a program is written to capture the new data via a form, then the data is checked in the program for completeness and accuracy as well as consistency with other data. Once all the new data are validated, then the new data are stored (by the READ command) into a new record.

Deleting Database Contents

In the section on the difference operation, we saw the commands used to delete rows from a dBASE database: DELETE and PACK. The general structure of the DELETE command is

```
DELETE [scope] [FOR condition] [WHILE condition]
```

That is, DELETE eliminates records that satisfy given qualifications. The simple command DELETE eliminates the current record; otherwise, the default scope when a FOR or WHILE clause is present is ALL.

As noted earlier, DELETE does not actually erase records from the file; rather, it marks them for deletion. PACK erases all records that have been marked for deletion. Until PACK is executed, the marked records can still be used. In fact, marked records are shown when you enter DISPLAY and LIST commands; these records are flagged with an asterisk to indicate they are marked for deletion. Further, you can use the RECALL command (which has the same syntax as DELETE) to restore marked records. In addition, you may invoke a SET DELETED command to determine whether marked records are included or ignored by other dBASE commands.

Changing Database Contents

There are four commands in dBASE IV for changing database contents: EDIT (or CHANGE), BROWSE, REPLACE, and UPDATE.

Full-Screen Data Maintenance   EDIT and BROWSE are both full-screen editors that support changing and deleting existing records, and adding new records. The difference is that BROWSE shows records from a database file in a tabular format and EDIT uses a default or a custom form to show one record from a file or view at a time on the screen. You use BROWSE to quickly and visually scan a file, making changes in various records and fields. In contrast, EDIT is typically used within a dBASE program to present a user with a structured format through which to edit or add a record.

Both EDIT and BROWSE have many options, more than are appropriate to explain here. These options cover such functions as preventing the addition of new records; deactivating the standard dBASE edit menu bar; making all or selected fields "read only," so that only new records may be added or only certain fields may be changed; preventing the deletion of records; selecting only certain fields for display; controlling field display width; using windows to place a table image or form at a specific location on the screen; and limiting the records included in the EDIT or BROWSE to those with certain field values.

The operation of both BROWSE and EDIT is affected by any SET FILTER and SET ORDER commands on the file. Further, the use of BROWSE and EDIT may be limited by security levels and access restrictions. You may not change any calculated field, but such fields automatically change when the base data from which they are derived change.

It is very easy to switch between EDIT and BROWSE mode when you are in an interactive session. You simply press <F2> to move between these modes. Figure 9-4 shows the difference between BROWSE and EDIT modes. The screen in Figure 9-4a was generated from the following dBASE commands:

```
. USE PRODUCT
. BROWSE FIELDS PRODUCT_NO,DESCRIPT,UNIT_PRICE,QOH,
     VALUE=UNIT_PRICE*QOH
```

Here we have used the optional FIELDS clause to include only certain fields. VALUE is a calculated field defined for just this BROWSE command. Figure 9-4b shows what would appear on the screen if <F2> were pressed when displaying the screen in Figure 9-4a. This is a default EDIT screen, but only the fields from the BROWSE are shown. The EDIT command itself does not have a clause to

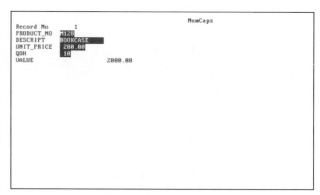

				NumCaps
PRODUCT_NO	DESCRIPT	UNIT_PRICE	QOH	VALUE
T120	BOOKCASE	200.00	10	2000.00
E350	TABLE	845.00	3	2535.00
E125	ARM CHAIR	195.50	8	1564.00
E177	CHAIR W/OARM	155.50	6	933.00
T100	END TABLE	245.95	2	491.90
T160	TABLE COFFEE	332.00	1	332.00
O100	BOOKCASE	395.50	4	1582.00
D625	DESK	995.00	1	995.00
O800	CREDENZA	875.00	0	0.00
B975	TABLE	225.00	10	2250.00
B985	END TABLE	198.00	12	2376.00
B301	CABINET	150.00	3	450.00
R210	TABLE	500.00	1	500.00

(a) BROWSE command   (b) EDIT command

Figure 9-4

Full-screen file editing

generate calculated fields, since EDIT presumes a default or existing custom form. However, when EDIT is entered from BROWSE, a default form is created that includes calculated fields.

Automated Data Maintenance   The REPLACE command is used to make specified changes to all records that satisfy certain conditions. That is, REPLACE is a type of batch updating. All records that satisfy the specified condition will be changed without user intervention or interaction.

The syntax of REPLACE is

```
REPLACE field WITH expression [ADDITIVE]
[, field WITH expression [ADDITIVE] ...]
[scope] [REINDEX] [FOR condition] [WHILE condition]
```

REPLACE overwrites the specified fields with the value of the given expression. One or several fields may be updated in one REPLACE command. The expression can be a constant or any legal dBASE arithmetic or character-string formula. ADDITIVE affects only memo fields and is not explained here. REINDEX causes dBASE to rebuild any index on an updated field after all replacements are made; otherwise, any affected index is rebuilt after each record is changed. A scope should be included if a FOR or WHILE clause is not; if there is no scope, FOR, or WHILE clause, only the current record is affected by the REPLACE.

To illustrate the use of REPLACE, suppose the cost of oak wood increased, causing Pine Valley Furniture to increase the unit price of all oak products by 10%. A REPLACE command to make this global change would be

```
REPLACE UNIT_PRICE WITH UNIT_PRICE*1.1 FOR FINISH="OAK"
```

The UPDATE command is used to replace fields in the current database file with data from another database file. The second file might have been created by batch input from a dBASE program that captures database changes in business transactions. That is, it is common for an organization not to actually update a database in real-time as transactions occur. Rather, updates are collected into a suspense file, and later applied after thorough validation. The second file may simply be another database file with related data, rather than a file with batched transactions.

The syntax of UPDATE is

```
UPDATE ON key field FROM work area
  REPLACE field WITH expression [, field WITH expression ...]
      [RANDOM] [REINDEX]
```

The file being updated must be the active file. *Work area* is the label of the work area where the second file is located. Each record in the second file must contain the primary key field of the file being updated. Each FROM file record is matched with a record in the updated file. The REPLACE command is then applied, involving expressions on fields from the two matching records. An expression can be simply a field name in the second file, or it may involve arithmetic on any fields from the matching records. Both files must be sorted in ascending order by the key field or indexed on this field; however, if RANDOM is used, then only the file to be updated needs to be indexed on the key field. REINDEX works as previously described with other commands.

Maintaining Transaction Integrity

A database transaction in dBASE IV is a series of data maintenance commands treated as a single unit of work. A single unit of work means that *all* the commands in the transaction must be completed successfully for the effects of the transaction to be valid. For example, all the product order lines of a customer order must be entered completely before the customer order is accepted.

The dBASE commands to manage transaction integrity—BEGIN TRANSACTION and END TRANSACTION—were discussed in Chapter 2 in the section on "Order Transaction." Therefore, we do not discuss these commands here. You may want to review this section in Chapter 2.

WRITING dBASE PROGRAMS

In this chapter we have already seen many of the data manipulation commands used in dBASE programs. In addition, there are process-control and input/output commands needed to build whole programs. It is not possible to cover in this chapter all the details of the dBASE programming language. Rather, we provide an overview of other dBASE programming language features not already addressed in this chapter.

In this section we review three forms of programming with dBASE IV:

1. Keyboard macros for coding a sequence of commands to a single keystroke
2. User-defined functions that calculate the value of a single variable from the input of several parameters
3. The use of the dBASE IV programming language for building a stored procedure

Macros

You may have already used keyboard macros in an electronic spreadsheet or word processor package. A **macro** is a sequence of keystrokes and commands that are assigned to a particular key or key combination. You activate a macro by pressing the assigned keystroke or selecting a macro from a menu of macros. You can also

Macro: A sequence of keystrokes assigned to a single keyboard key.

execute a PLAY MACRO command in a dBASE program. When a macro is activated, dBASE immediately reacts to the sequence of cursor movements, function keys, menu choices, and commands stored in that macro. Very simply, a macro is a way to execute a sequence of commands needed to perform a commonly used operation with a single keystroke. You can use macros to create a custom keyboard for an application. For example, you can map keyboard function keys to particular application functions, which will make your application easier to use. You may write an original macro for a particular database or use a prewritten macro found in a purchased or user-developed macro library. One library may contain up to 35 different macros. Macros may be nested; that is, one macro can use another macro inside it—but a macro may not refer to itself.

Creating a Macro   Typically you create a macro by recording it through the Macros submenu of the Tools menu in the dBASE Control Center (although a macro can be created outside the Control Center). You then enter the keystrokes sequentially. As keystrokes are entered, dBASE actually performs the steps so you can see if the macro code does what is expected. If user input is required, you press SHIFT-F10 to specify where a user-input break is required, and then continue coding the macro. When the macro is completely recorded, you press SHIFT-F10 again and select the End Recording option.

An Example Macro   The macro we selected for this example displays the number of orders received for a specific customer number entered by the user at an input break. This macro uses the CUORDER file from the Pine Valley Furniture database. This query is built by use of a query view, which counts the number of orders for a specified customer. Thus, the heart of the desired macro will be to build this view and display its results.

We have built this macro to be invoked only from the Control Center, but the cursor may be anywhere in the Control Center when the user starts the macro. Thus, the first step in the macro is to position the cursor to build the query. The complete macro is listed in Figure 9-5. In this figure, a word enclosed in { } stands for the keyboard key with that label (for example, {Esc} means the escape key). The macro has been recorded and assigned to the C key. Every command and key in this macro is exactly what we would use from the Control Center to build the view for this query, except for the {InpBreak}, which shows where we would input the desired customer number.

Figure 9-5

Order count macro

This macro is explained line by line as follows:

Line 1: This line first causes dBASE to exit the Control Center and enter the dBASE dot prompt command system ({Esc}Y). Then, since we only need to use the CUORDER file, all other files are closed (CLOSE ALL{Enter}).

Line 2: The USE command opens the file we need for this query (USE CUORDER{Enter}).

Line 3: This line returns control to the Control Center from which the view will be built (ASSIST{Enter}).

Line 4: Upon entering the Control Center, the cursor will be over the Data column. Thus, this line moves the cursor right to the Query column and selects the top option, *create*, there ({rightarrow} {Enter}).

Line 5: Query builds a default view that contains all the columns of the base table, so the first step here drops the default view ({F5}). Then the cursor is moved to the Order Number column in the file template, and the function COUNT is entered ({Tab}COUNT). Next the cursor is moved to the Customer Number column, where a user-input break is specified for the user to enter the desired customer number for selection ({Tab} {InpBreak}). After the user enters the customer number, control is returned to the macro. Next the cursor is moved back (left) one column to the Order Number field. The Fields menu is selected from the Query work surface and the "Add column to view" option is selected ({Shift-Tab} {Alt-f} {Enter}).

Line 6: Now the query can be executed to display the count ({F2}). A pause is inserted for the user to study the results ({InpBreak}). We are done with the query, so we exit the query work surface ({Alt-e} {Enter}).

Line 7: We are then asked if we want to save the query. Since this is an ad hoc request, the default "No" is chosen ({Enter}).

Since this macro was assigned to the C key, the macro can be executed from the Control Center by typing Alt-F10 followed by C.

Macros are quite helpful for reusing common sets of operations; however, a macro is a fixed sequence of commands and keyboard strokes; for more sophisticated requirements, other programming constructs are needed. The next section introduces those available in dBASE IV.

User-Defined Functions

We have already seen examples of various built-in functions in dBASE for manipulating character strings, maximum or minimum value, and mathematical calculations. Like many programming languages, dBASE also supports the specification of custom functions by the programmer. A function, similar to a macro, allows a standard procedure that calculates a specific value to be written once and reused wherever needed in a program.

A **user-defined function (UDF)** is a set of dBASE commands that returns a single value to the command line where it is used. A UDF may accept a parameter list for input to the function. The general structure of a UDF is

User-defined function (UDF): In dBASE, a set of commands that return a single value to the command line where the UDF is referenced.

```
FUNCTION function-name
PARAMETERS parameter-list
commands
RETURN(variable)
```

The PARAMETERS command assigns local names to the parameters being passed to the function. The variable after the RETURN command is a memory variable (that is, not part of any database table) calculated within the function. It is the value of this variable that is passed back to the command line where the function was used. A UDF does not change the value of any of the parameters passed to it. A value passed to a local parameter may actually be an expression; the commands in a function are usually arithmetic expressions. A UDF is stored in a dBASE procedure or program file for use within that procedure or program. Most database access commands are prohibited in a function—for example, APPEND, SORT, JOIN, BROWSE, and TOTAL (among many others).

The following is an example of a simple UDF that might be useful in writing programs for the Pine Valley Furniture database. This function calculates the extended discounted price for a line item on a customer order (that is, a row of the REQUEST table). The function definition is

```
FUNCTION Ex_Price
PARAMETERS E_Disc, E_Price, E_Qty
Result = (E_Price * E_Qty) * (1.0 - E_Disc)
RETURN(Result)
```

This function is used in the following dBASE program fragment, which needs the extended price value. In this fragment, we assume that data for a REQUEST table row have just been retrieved, and the product number, order number, and order quantity fields have been stored in memory variables R_prod, R_order, and R_qty, respectively. The following code retrieves the remaining needed data from other database files and then uses this function to display the extended price:

```
SELECT A
USE CUORDER INDEX ORDER_NO
FIND R_order
R_cust = CUST_NO
SELECT B
USE CUSTOMER INDEX CUST_NO
FIND R_cust
SELECT C
USE PRODUCT INDEX PRODUCT_NO
FIND R_prod
? Ex_Price(B->DISCOUNT,UNIT_PRICE,R_qty)
```

The first USE command opens the ORDER table and the order number index. The FIND command retrieves the order row for the order referenced in the REQUEST row. Then the second USE command opens the CUSTOMER table and the index for the customer number. The following FIND retrieves the customer record associated with the order row just found. The following USE and FIND similarly retrieve the correct PRODUCT record. From these commands, all three parameter values (discount from the customer table, unit price from the product table, and order quantity from the REQUEST table) have been found. The last line displays the result returned from the function (? is a shorthand notation in dBASE that says, "Display the result on the screen").

Procedures

The dBASE programming language includes the various query language commands we have already seen plus many other commands for process control (looping, branching, and conditional logic), data input from the screen, output to various devices, and setting the environment for the program. In this section we discuss the basic capabilities and commands of dBASE programs. The interested reader is referred to Krumm (1990) and Senn (1990) for excellent, more detailed tutorials.

Table 9-5 lists some additional dBASE IV programming language commands not already covered in this chapter. The commands are grouped into five categories:

1. Data manipulation for retrieval and maintenance
2. Input and output
3. Process logic for controlling the sequence of command execution
4. SET commands for specifying a program's environment (that is, defaults and options for the general execution of other commands)
5. Commands not included in the previous four groups

A program is stored in a program file (with a .PRG extension). You can create and change a file using a text editor or the dBASE MODIFY COMMAND statement. A program is run by executing the command

```
DO program-name
```

either interactively from the keyboard or by including this command in another routine (that is, one program may call another program). DO will automatically compile a program if only the source file exists. You can also instruct dBASE to start a program automatically when dBASE itself is activated.

A very common structure for a program is to have a main section that first opens files and conducts other initializing tasks, then executes calls to major task routines, and finally closes files and prints concluding messages. Since this structure may be nested several levels deep, programming is frequently based on subroutines. dBASE IV subroutines are called *procedures*.

A **procedure** is a named set of commands and can thus be either a whole program or a subroutine. A procedure is run by issuing the DO *procedure-name* command anywhere in a program or at the dBASE dot prompt. A procedure can be stored within a program, in a separate procedure file, or in a separate file of several procedures. Each procedure begins with the word PROCEDURE and ends with RETURN (but there is no parameter passed in the RETURN, as we saw above with a UDF). The SET PROCEDURE *procedurefile* command is used within a program to make a specific file of procedures active.

Procedure: In dBASE, a named set of commands used as a program or subroutine within a program or in a library of procedures.

Parameters may be passed to a procedure (both subroutines and programs), in which case the PARAMETERS command must be the first command in a procedure. As opposed to a function, a procedure may change the value of parameters passed to it.

To help you tie together all the screens, reports, and programs needed to build an information system, dBASE provides the Application Generator. An application generator is a tool for conveniently building applications from other objects— prewritten procedures, databases, forms, and reports. The generator helps you build menus, banners, and program linkages to form an application. An application generator is often used to build the skeleton of the main program of an application; then, you would modify the generated code to create custom features that cannot be automatically generated.

TABLE 9-5 Selected dBASE Programming Language Commands

Data Manipulation	
GO TO *n*	Position row pointer on a particular relative row in a table.
STORE	Place the value of an expression into a memory variable.
Input and Output	
@ . . . SAY	Display value at specified row and column on screen.
@ . . . GET	Display value at specified row and column on screen and prepare to read input. (A picture clause and valid range of values clause may be included.)
READ	Store into memory all data entered on the screen from @ . . . GET commands since the last READ or CLEAR command was executed.
Process Logic	
DO	Execute (call) another dBASE procedure or program.
DO CASE . . . END CASE	Select one action from a set of alternatives based on a condition that is true for one or none of the alternatives.
DO WHILE . . . END DO	Repeat a set of commands while a condition is true.
IF . . . THEN . . . ELSE	Conditionally process two sets of commands.
ON ERROR	Execute a specific command when a dBASE error occurs.
SCAN . . . ENDSCAN	For each row in the active table that meets the specified condition, execute the commands specified.
Setting Environment	
CARRY	Determines if values from the last row are carried forward to next row on APPEND, BROWSE, EDIT, INSERT, and CHANGE commands.
CLOCK	Turns on or off display of system clock in upper right corner of the screen.
DEVICE	Specifies output device for @ . . . SAY command.
MESSAGE	Displays a given user-defined message on the bottom line of the screen.
REPROCESS	Sets the number of times dBASE will retry a command when a record is locked (applies only to network applications).
STEP	Stops or does not stop program execution after each command.

(continues)

TABLE 9-5   Selected dBASE Programming Language Commands *(Continued)*

Other	
DEFINE PAD	Defines a line of a menu bar, including the prompt in the menu and any help message.
DEFINE POPUP	Defines a popup menu window.
ON SELECTION PAD	Defines what action to take when a specific menu option (pad) is selected on a menu bar.
ON SELECTION POPUP	Defines what action to take when a specific menu option on a popup menu is selected.
PRIVATE	Create memory variables local to current procedure.
RELEASE	Delete specified memory variables, and free that space in memory.

SUMMARY

This chapter has overviewed the salient features of the dBASE IV programming language and DBMS. dBASE, arguably the most popular PC relational DBMS, has tremendous power for creating and manipulating databases. A dBASE database consists of multiple files contained in the same catalog. Forms, reports, labels, query views, and other objects may also be included in a catalog.

dBASE follows the relational algebra style of language, in which commands work on one or two database files at a time. The heart of the dBASE language, as with any algebra language, is the JOIN command, which links two files on a common field. With JOIN, and the related SET RELATION command, you can gain access to data from related database files. dBASE supports the concept of a relational view, which is a way to construct a virtual file of data from multiple actual database files. A view can make subsequent programming easier and help in data security.

You can use the dBASE language to create sophisticated database applications. With the aid of custom forms and reports, menus, user-defined functions, and a host of programming language commands, you can build applications customized to the needs of an organization or user. dBASE databases can be used by one user on a stand-alone PC or shared among multiple users on a local area network.

As mentioned in the introduction, dBASE follows one of the three primary styles of relational database programming: relational algebra. The other two primary styles—SQL and Query-by-Example—are covered in Chapters 8 and 10, respectively. After reading these three chapters, you should have a basic but comprehensive understanding of implementing relational databases. For those with a further interest in such technologies, Chapter 11 reviews some advanced features from these three environments and introduces new database technology under the Microsoft Windows™ operating environment.

CHAPTER REVIEW

Key Terms

Application generator
Filter
Macro
Memo field
Memory variable

Multiple-index file
Procedure
Query view
Relational algebra

Run-time version
Tag
User-defined function (UDF)
Xbase products

REVIEW QUESTIONS

1. Define each of the following terms:
   a. relational algebra
   b. user-defined function (UDF)
   c. JOIN
   d. intersect
   e. UNION

   f. query view
   g. PACK
   h. Xbase
   i. dBASE catalog
   j. dBASE tag

   k. filter
   l. memo field
   m. memory variable
   n. macro
   o. dBASE procedure

2. What are the advantages of a run-time version of a PC-RDBMS?
3. Contrast the purpose and use of three dBASE commands: LOCATE, FIND, and SEEK.
4. Contrast the use of the EDIT and BROWSE dBASE commands.
5. Compare the capabilities and use of the SET RELATION TO and JOIN commands in dBASE.
6. Explain why updating data via a relational view can be done in only limited circumstances in dBASE IV.
7. Contrast the use of FOR and WHILE clauses in dBASE commands like LIST.
8. Explain the use of the scope clause in dBASE commands.
9. What purpose does the dBASE application generator serve?

PROBLEMS AND EXERCISES

1. Match the following terms to the appropriate definitions.

   ____ parameter   a. an individual index

   ____ dot prompt   b. data passed between procedures

   ____ tag   c. command line used in dBASE IV

   ____ SET RELATION   d. dBASE command that makes data from two or more files appear to be in one file

   ____ catalog   e. grouping of forms, reports, and other objects

   ____ intersection   f. a set-oriented relational language style that permits more than two files to be used in one command

   ____ relational algebra   g. a record-oriented relational language style that permits at most two files to be used in one command

   ____ relational calculus   h. a dBASE command to link two files based on common field values

   ____ union   i. those records that are common to two sets of records

Problems 2–11 are based on the Lakewood Community College database from Chapter 6 (the 3NF relations for that application are repeated here):

STUDENT NO.	STUDENT NAME	MAJOR
38214	Bright	IS
69173	Smith	PM
. . .		

STUDENT (STUDENT NO.,
STUDENT NAME, MAJOR)

INSTRUCTOR NAME	INSTRUCTOR LOCATION
Codd	B 104
Kemp	B 213
Lewis	D 317
. . .	

INSTRUCTOR (INSTRUCTOR NAME,
INSTRUCTOR LOCATION)

COURSE NO.	COURSE TITLE	INSTRUCTOR NAME
IS 350	Database	Codd
IS 465	Sys Anal	Kemp
PM 300	Prod Mgt	Lewis
QM 440	Op Res	Kemp
. . .		

COURSE (COURSE NO., COURSE
TITLE, INSTRUCTOR NAME)

STUDENT NO.	COURSE NO.	GRADE
38214	IS 350	A
38214	IS 465	C
69173	IS 465	A
69173	PM 300	B
69173	QM 440	C
. . .		

REGISTRATION (STUDENT NO.,
COURSE NO., GRADE)

2. Write dBASE commands to define this database (shorten, abbreviate, or change data names as required by the limitations of dBASE). Assume the following data types:

STUDENT NO. (integer, primary key)

STUDENT NAME (25 characters)

MAJOR (5 characters)

INSTRUCTOR NAME (25 characters, primary key)

INSTRUCTOR LOCATION (5 characters)

COURSE NO. (6 characters, primary key)

COURSE TITLE (10 characters)

GRADE (1 character)

3. Refer to your answer to Problem 2, and now select primary keys for each table. Justify your selection of primary keys. Also, suggest other indexes that you would create to make the processing of this database efficient (assume that the queries listed in Problem 4 are the only ones for this database).

4. Write dBASE IV commands for each of the following queries:
   a. Display the instructor location for the instructor Lewis.
   b. Display the student number and student name for all information systems (IS) majors.
   c. Display the total number of students who are IS majors.

5. Write dBASE IV commands to produce a table with columns STUDENT NO., STUDENT NAME, MAJOR, COURSE NO., and GRADE. (*Hint:* Data are contained in multiple base tables.)

6. What dBASE IV command would be used to accomplish the following?
   a. Add a new row to the end of the REGISTRATION table.
   b. Delete all rows for student number 56789 in the REGISTRATION table.
   c. Change the grade for student 38214 in IS 465 from C to B.

7. Write the dBASE command(s) necessary to display those students who have taken IS 465 but who have not taken IS 350.

8. Write the dBASE IV command(s) to display the names and locations of all instructors for courses taken by student number 69173.

9. Write the dBASE IV commands to display the STUDENT NO. and STUDENT NAME of those students who have taken a course from both instructor CODD and instructor KEMP.

Problems 10–14 are based on the Pine Valley Furniture database described in this chapter and in Chapter 2, with table definitions appearing in Figures 2-12 and 2-14 through 2-16. You are to use dBASE commands, not the dBASE Control Center, to answer these questions. Some questions can be answered with one command, and some require a small program of several dBASE commands.

10. Display the order number, customer number, product number, order date, and order quantity for orders of more than 15 units of products M128 or E125.
11. Display each product number and the total quantity ordered for each product.
12. Display order numbers, product numbers, and order quantity for all orders involving order quantities of 10 units.
13. Display the order number, customer number, order date, and promised shipping date for orders promised for shipping prior to November 20, 1993.
14. Display the order number and order quantity for all customer orders for which the order quantity is greater than the average order quantity.

REFERENCES

Codd, E. F. 1970. "A Relational Model of Data for Large Shared Data Banks." *Communications of the ACM* 13 (June):377–87.

Grauer, R., and M. Barber. 1992. *Database Management Using dBASE IV and SQL*. Watsonville, Calif.: Mitchell McGraw-Hill.

Hawkins, J. L. 1992. "ANSI Standard Xbase?" *Data Based Advisor* 10 (Sept.):10, 12, 14.

Krumm, R. 1990. *The Student Edition of dBASE IV, Programmer's Version*. Reading, Mass.: Addison-Wesley.

Nebel, S. E. 1989. "Five Index Tricks for dBASE." *DBMS* 2 (Dec.):54–62.

Perschke, S. 1992. "Xbase Enters the Modern Age." *DBMS* 5 (May):48–50, 52, 54.

Pinneau, S. 1992. "dBASE IV for UNIX." *DBMS* 5 (Feb.):30, 33, 35.

Ricciardi, S. 1992. "Xbase Development Systems." *PC Magazine* (May 26):301–4 ff.

Schaffhauser, D. 1992. "Mainframe Meets Micro . . . Computer Associates Buys Nantucket!" *Data Based Advisor* 10 (July):44, 46, 47.

Senn, J. A. 1990. *The Student Edition of dBASE IV*. Reading, Mass.: Addison-Wesley.

Query-by-Example: Implementing a Paradox 4.0 Database

LEARNING OBJECTIVES

After studying this chapter, you should be able to:

- Explain the capabilities of Query-by-Example (QBE) and its relationship to Paradox 4.0.
- Explain the advantages and disadvantages of QBE compared to SQL and the dBASE proprietary language.
- Write single- and multiple-table queries in Paradox.
- Define different types of join commands, and be able to use Paradox to write queries for each of these types of joins.
- Create indexes and understand other ways to tune the performance of a Paradox database.
- Write Paradox commands to add, delete, and change database contents.
- Describe a database transaction and understand how to control for transaction integrity in Paradox.
- Explain the general capabilities of relational database management systems and explain the different approaches of Paradox 4.0 and dBASE IV.

INTRODUCTION

In the preceding two chapters on relational implementations we have seen examples of systems that use structured command languages (SQL and the proprietary dBASE language). A different style of programming language, called *direct manipulation* (Shneiderman, 1983), gives users more of a visual programming environment. Relational DBMSs have been designed for a variety of users, not all of whom want to use a structured query language, no matter how much more productive and easy such a language may be compared to conventional procedural programming languages. The prime example of a direct-manipulation database language is Query-by-Example, or QBE.

In this chapter we examine the QBE approach to database processing. We use Paradox 4.0 as the particular system to illustrate the features of the QBE language.

Paradox has one of the most extensive and powerful QBE interfaces, so it is a fine example from which to learn the QBE style. We also introduce in this chapter a few of the unique features of Paradox, even when these features are not inherent in QBE. We do so because Paradox, like dBASE IV, is a very popular DBMS, and a database student should understand the features of Paradox in comparison to other leading systems.

This chapter does not present a complete, in-depth description of Paradox—the goal is not to make you a skilled Paradox programmer. Instead, our purpose is to prepare you to understand rapidly *any* QBE-based language. Thus, we do not introduce many terms specific to Paradox. You will, however, be able to compare the capabilities of various packages (using dBASE, SQL, and QBE) and know what features to evaluate from the material presented in Chapters 8 through 10.

We will assume familiarity with the basic relational terminology and database design presented in Chapters 2, 3, and 6. You may also want to read the appendix "Codd's 12 Rules for a Truly Relational System" to review the basic principles on which PC relational systems are built.

THE HISTORY AND IMPORTANCE OF QBE

Although QBE (like SQL) was originally developed for mainframe database processing, it has become prevalent in personal computer database systems as well. Query-by-Example was originally developed by Zloof (1977) and was first available for use with SQL/DS and DB2 database systems on IBM mainframes. The success of the first personal computer relational DBMS (PC-RDBMS) that was completely based on QBE, Paradox, has encouraged other products to adopt a QBE interface as one option. As we have seen in Chapter 2, dBASE IV uses a QBE-style interface in its Control Center. Many other systems also include a variation on QBE.

Coverage of QBE is essential for the understanding of modern database systems. This is true because QBE is considered a highly productive language in which to program. Not only is it visually quite different, but several research studies (for example, Greenblatt and Waxman, 1978; Thomas and Gould, 1975) have shown that even with relatively little training, student subjects found it easier to use than SQL or a relational algebra language (the style on which the dBASE language is based). A more recent study by Byrer (1991) further shows that the success of QBE is due not only to its being a direct-manipulation language. Byrer has demonstrated that QBE outperforms one other direct-manipulation database system, Superbase 4, in many ways. Thus, QBE has some unique capabilities that will probably help it to become even more of a standard direct-manipulation database interface than it already is.

QBE and End-User Computing

QBE is especially useful for end-user database programming. The visual programming environment gives the nonprogramming user a single view of data no matter what database task is performed. As we will see (and as was shown in Chapter 2), queries are developed interactively on a CRT screen in a format that resembles the desired output. That is, both queries and results are shown on the same work surface. This is very helpful for more complex operations, like joining together data from several tables to form an answer table.

Complete database applications can be written in QBE, but it is more common to use QBE for interactive querying or updating of a database. That is, QBE is particularly useful for ad hoc database processing. Rather than developing a complete application in QBE, it is more common to use QBE to prototype an application. QBE queries can be saved to a program file (called a *script* in Paradox), and these saved queries can then be enhanced by the addition of PAL, the Paradox programming language, commands.

The role of PC-RDBMSs like Paradox and dBASE is discussed in the appendix "An Overview of PC-RDBMSs." You may want to review this appendix as background to the current chapter.

QBE: THE BASICS

There is no official standard for QBE as has been defined for SQL (see Chapter 8 for a discussion of the SQL standardization efforts). For this reason, there is no minimal set of capabilities that a query interface must meet to be considered a QBE implementation. However, because QBE has evolved from research on database query languages and because it is a visual language, all vendors have adopted the same basic approach to QBE. Although there may be differences in certain operators, learning one QBE querying system (like Paradox) will allow you to quickly learn another QBE system.

You have already seen an example of a QBE query interface. The QBE interface in dBASE IV was shown in Figures 2-31a and 2-32, which you should review. Both data retrieval and data modification can be done via entering keywords, constants, and example data into the cells of a table layout. Because (as with most relational systems) data definitions are stored in internal tables, even data definition is done through a similar table layout interface.

The QBE interface that we describe for Paradox in this chapter looks basically like those found in dBASE IV and R:BASE (from Microrim, Inc.) on PCs, and in SQL/DS and DB2 on IBM mainframes. One difference with QBE and SQL/DS is that in this case QBE was intended to work *with* SQL, not as a stand-alone, complete language. That is, you would use the command language of SQL/DS to define a database, and then you would use the associated QBE interface (QBE is actually a separate program product from SQL/DS and DB2) for ad hoc queries and minor data modification. Paradox, in contrast, was developed as a total database system solution following the QBE style. In addition, Paradox includes the PAL programming language for writing complex series of related queries, looping statements, and other commands.

Paradox and QBE Terminology

Figure 10-1 shows a typical Paradox screen. This example illustrates the Pine Valley Furniture Cuorder data table as it would be displayed in Paradox. In Paradox terminology, each data column (like CUST NO) on this screen is called a *field*, and each row is called a *record*. This example Cuorder table has 14 records. A table also is one kind of Paradox object. Other types of objects are forms, reports, indexes, settings, and validity checks. All of the objects related to the same table are called an *object family*. All objects in the same family have the same DOS file name, but each type of object has a different file extension. Paradox does not have a concept like the catalog of dBASE IV. Thus, there is no true notion of a database

Figure 10-1

Typical Paradox screen

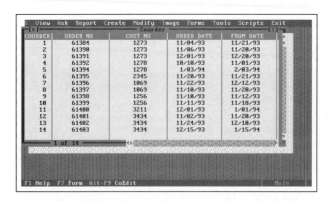

in Paradox. That is, there is no explicit grouping of tables and related objects into a named database. For this reason, different databases in Paradox are usually stored in different subdirectories or on different disks. The current DOS path where Paradox finds and stores objects is called the *working directory*.

Paradox refers to the data layout displayed on the screen as an *image*. You can enlarge, shrink, move, and erase an image. An image may be too wide or too long to fit completely on the screen at once. You can use cursor-movement keys or a mouse to move different parts of the image onto the screen. The data table in Figure 10-1 is one type of image. Another type of image is a query form, which is a layout of a particular table in which a query is specified. It is the query form that gives QBE its direct-manipulation flavor. For example, the top part of Figure 10-2 shows a simple query form for the Pine Valley Furniture Cuorder table. The query form has been filled in to display all the columns (each one with a $\sqrt{}$) for customer orders placed after December 1, 1993. The bottom part of Figure 10-2 shows the query result, or Answer table.

The PC screen serves as a window into the Paradox workspace. The workspace holds all the objects (data tables, query forms, reports, etc.) you have defined. It is possible to have, for example, many different query forms and data tables active in the workspace at one time. Cursor-movement keys or a mouse are used to move among the different images, as we demonstrate later in the chapter.

The result of any query is a special data table labeled the *Answer table*. An example Answer table is shown in Figure 10-2. A new Answer table is created each time a query form is processed; however, an Answer table can be made permanent by renaming it. In this way, an Answer table may then be used in subsequent queries. This is an important Paradox capability, which often makes the writing of complex queries simpler by building the ultimate result in steps.

Figure 10-2

Simple Paradox query

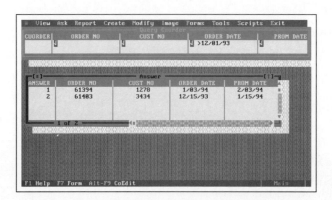

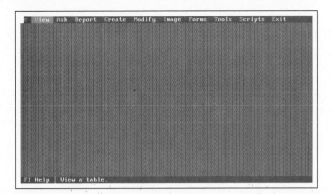

Figure 10-3

Paradox main menu

Overview of a Paradox Screen

Figure 10-3 shows the Paradox opening screen, with the ten-option main menu across the top. This screen is the equivalent of the dBASE Control Center. A brief explanation of the highlighted menu option (View in this example) appears on the bottom line.

You display this (or a similar) menu by pressing the <F10>, or menu, key. The menu key actually displays a context-sensitive menu that will differ from the one in Figure 10-3, depending on what Paradox operation is active. The ten options on the main menu are briefly explained in Table 10-1.

When you want Paradox to perform a specific function you press Do-It!, or the <F2> key, to execute a certain command. For example, the Answer table of Figure 10-2 is produced by pressing <F2> on the query form. Table definitions, data table updates, and form or report definitions are also saved or executed with Do-It! That is, Paradox does not perform many operations until you press <F2>.

TABLE 10-1 Paradox Main Menu Options

Menu Option	Description
View	Display a table on the screen.
Ask	Create a query to display selected columns from specified rows of one or more tables.
Report	Design, redesign, or print a customized report.
Create	Define a new data table.
Modify	Modify data table contents or structure.
Image	Rearrange the display of data on the screen or design a graph.
Forms	Design or redesign a customized screen form.
Tools	Run a variety of advanced options for data conversion and formatting, and for controlling Paradox operation.
Script	Record or play back stored programs.
Exit	Leave Paradox.

Such a keystroke is essential for a visual programming language like QBE. For example, in building the query in Figure 10-2, you can enter the values and symbols in the query form in any sequence you wish. It is not until all qualifications, keywords, and other elements have been entered into cells that you want the query to be executed, at which time you would press Do-It!

DATABASE DEFINITION IN PARADOX

In this section, we briefly overview the Paradox features for database definition, using the Pine Valley Furniture database from Chapter 2 for illustration. We show only the highlights here, since the purpose of this chapter is to review Query-by-Example, not Paradox.

Paradox 4.0 supports six types of data: alphanumeric, numeric, currency, date, memo, and short number (for small integer data). Unless otherwise controlled through Paradox ValChecks (data integrity controls to be reviewed later), any field may contain a null, or what Paradox calls a BLANK, value. The existence of a BLANK value can be checked in queries, as we will show later.

Paradox does not support virtual or calculated fields. Thus, a data table field may not be defined, for example, as the product of two other fields. Such calculations can be shown in data table displays, but the calculation may not be automatically stored as part of the record.

Data Definition Screen

Data definitions are driven by the creation of a table. You define a table via the Create option on the Paradox main menu (see Figure 10-3). Once defined, a table definition can be changed (restructured), and the structure of a table can be recalled. In addition, (part of) the definition of a table may be borrowed from an existing table structure. You can specify a primary key index as part of a table definition, and facilities exist in Paradox for creating secondary key indexes. Finally, data integrity and security restrictions may also be placed on a table.

If the new table resembles an existing table, you may use the Borrow option on the menu to populate the structure table with the field definitions from the existing table. You may then add, edit, or delete fields to meet the requirements of the new table. Fields from multiple tables may be borrowed. Borrowing an existing table definition must be done with care so as to not cause unwanted nonnormalized tables. Borrowing is helpful if you want to do the following:

- Reuse the precise names and data types for cross-reference and foreign keys.
- Create several tables by segmenting a relation. (For example, we might want to create different customer tables corresponding to different sales regions.)

As with dBASE IV in Chapter 2, the Pine Valley Furniture Paradox database contains four tables: Product, Customer, Cuorder, and Request. The corresponding dBASE IV table definitions were shown in Figures 2-12, 2-14, 2-15, and 2-16, respectively. Figure 10-4 shows the Paradox structure for the Cuorder table. We do not discuss the table definitions, since they parallel those in Chapter 2 (except for minor data type differences between dBASE IV and Paradox). The Cuorder table definition is displayed from the Restructure submenu under the Modify option on the main Paradox menu. This is where table definitions may be dis-

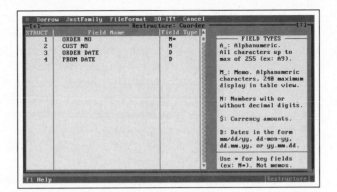

Figure 10-4

Paradox Cuorder table definition

played and modified (for example, fields renamed, deleted, added, and rearranged).

Index Definition in Paradox

You can create primary and secondary key indexes (see Chapter 7 for a discussion of indexes) as ways to design a database for efficient processing. After making these choices, you can sit back and relax, since you have no control over the location of records in a table, the structure of key indexes, the proximate location of related records from different tables for fast accessing of these records, or the maintenance of statistics that could help in optimizing query processing. Thus, you have very limited control of the internal schema definition, or physical database structure.

Primary Key Indexes　　You specify the primary key of a table by placing an asterisk at the end of the data type for the field or fields that compose the primary key when creating or restructuring a table. See, for example, the ORDER NO field in the Cuorder table definition of Figure 10-4. Paradox does not insist that each table have a primary key. Since such permissiveness violates pure relational database theory, we recommend that you assign a primary key to each table. When you specify a primary key, Paradox will do the following:

- Prohibit more than one record from having the same (composite) value in the key field(s).

- Show the rows of the table in ascending sequence by the primary key value (unless a different sorting order is specified in a query).

- Create a primary key index on the field(s), which can improve query response time.

A primary key may be simple (one field) or compound (multiple fields). In either case, Paradox requires that the primary key must be the first field(s) in the list of fields in the table definition.

Secondary Key Indexes　　A secondary key is a field for which multiple records may have the same value. For example, ROOM in the Product table could be a secondary key. In addition, a secondary key exists when such a field is used as part of the record-selection criterion of a query. Thus, whereas a primary key is an inherent characteristic of a table, secondary keys cannot be identified until queries are known.

Consider a query to display the complete contents of Product records for products that apply only to the Living room. Figure 10-5 shows this query and the result from our sample Pine Valley Furniture database. Since this query involves a qualification on a secondary key field, Paradox would, without the aid of an index, have to search through all Product records to find those that satisfy this query. If there are many Product records and such queries involving the ROOM field are frequently entered, then Paradox could improve overall database processing by creating an index on the ROOM field.

Paradox has two methods for creating secondary key indexes. The first involves the Paradox Application Language, PAL (equivalent to the dBASE programming language), which we will not illustrate. The second is an automatic method in which Paradox analyzes a query and builds indexes that would speed up query processing. For example, with the query of Figure 10-5 on the screen, you would press the <F10>, or menu key, and then select the Tools option. Then you would select the QuerySpeed option from the Tools menu. Figure 10-6 shows the result of these steps. For this example query, Paradox has determined that a secondary key index on the ROOM field would *not* improve database processing time. This may be true, since there are only a few records in our sample Product table, and scanning the whole table does not take much time. Paradox might also have decided that the cost of extra disk storage space for the index and of maintaining this index as ROOM values are added, changed, or deleted would be more than the potential time savings. For a more complex query, Paradox would consider all possible secondary key fields for potential indexing, and would selectively recommend those that might speed processing.

When an index is no longer helpful, it may be deleted. You do this through the Delete option on the Tools menu.

Figure 10-5

Paradox query involving a secondary key

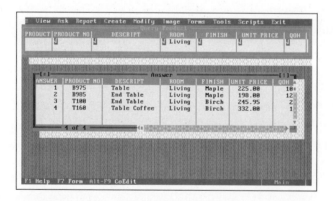

Figure 10-6

Result of QuerySpeed

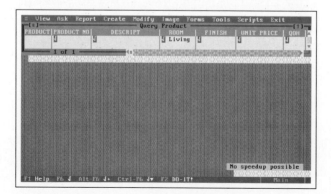

Data Integrity Controls

Paradox has rather extensive capabilities for controlling the integrity of data. Although these features are not part of QBE, the data integrity controls within Paradox illustrate advanced PC-RDBMS capabilities. Therefore, we review these capabilities in this section. The Paradox data integrity control features include

- Specifying minimum and/or maximum values for a field
- Assigning a default value for a field
- Defining a particular format, or picture, for a field
- Requiring a field to have a value (a NOT NULL type option)
- Establishing referential integrity restrictions (that is, requiring that a field value in one table match the value of a primary key field in some record in another table)
- Specifying whether to move the cursor to the next field or record when data for this field is complete

These options are called **validity checks**, or ValChecks, in Paradox. Validity checks are specified by first selecting the Modify option from the Paradox main menu, then choosing the DataEntry selection and entering the name of the table (or picking from a list of table names) on which you wish to place an integrity control. This selection displays an image of the table on the workspace. Then you press the <F10> key to call up the DataEntry menu, choose the ValCheck option, and then the Define option. You then move the cursor to the field on which you want to define a validity check and press <Enter>. Figure 10-7 shows the menu of validity checks for the QOH field of the Product table. Any of these options, except the TableLookup, would make sense for QOH. Two of the validity checks require further explanation for a clearer understanding: Picture and TableLookup.

Validity check: In Paradox, a data integrity control placed on a field.

Picture Format   A picture controls the data entry format for a field. It is also used to limit values to a certain set of options, and to automatically fill in characters in set positions within a value. A picture forces you to enter data exactly and completely. Obviously, you cannot specify a picture that violates the data type of the field involved; for example, you cannot require a numeric field to contain an alphabetic character.

A picture is composed of a sequence of special symbols that outline what is possible, position by position, for an entered value. For example, consider the PRODUCT NO field in the Product table. From the data analysis presented in Chapter 2, the integrity of this field could be accurately controlled with a '&###'

Figure 10-7

Choices for types of validity checks

TABLE 10-2 Example Paradox Validity Check Pictures

Example Picture	Explanation
###;,###	A six-digit number with a comma separating thousands from hundreds
X-####	A typical telephone extension, in which 'X- ' is automatically filled in when the user enters X, x, or a space at the beginning of the field
{20,40,60,75,100}W	A light bulb wattage field for bulbs of only the specified wattages
&*?	An alphabetic field with the first letter in uppercase and any number of following characters (up to the length specified in the field's data type)

picture. This picture says that the first character is any letter converted to uppercase, and the next three characters may only be digits.

A listing of all possible picture codes is beyond the scope of this chapter. Table 10-2 illustrates some possible pictures and example situations in which each would be useful. You can use such codes to carefully control data entry and maintenance. Paradox will reject any data entry for a field that violates a picture (or any other validity check) and display an appropriate error message indicating the type of validity check that was violated. The user must enter a value for each field of a record that meets all validity checks before the record may be saved.

TableLookup TableLookup is the most powerful of the Paradox data integrity control features. You can use this feature to do the following:

- Require that the values of a particular field exist in the primary key field of another table. This capability is called *referential integrity control*.

- Refer to another table where the acceptable values for a field can be found and then displayed. The user may browse this list of values and pick the desired value to be entered. This capability resembles a help system for data entry.

- Automatically copy values from a record in one table into the corresponding fields in the table being validated. This capability is helpful when tables are nonnormalized and the values for some of the fields being entered already exist. For example, a customer order table could be defined to contain certain customer data that also appear in the customer table, and the associated customer data for a new order could be automatically copied into the new order record from the customer table.

When you choose TableLookup from the menu in Figure 10-7, you are asked for the name of the data table into which lookup will occur. Usually, lookup involves a foreign key in one table and a lookup into the table that has that key as its primary key. For example, the Cuorder table might have a lookup on its CUST NO field into the Customer table. Remember that the field into which the lookup occurs must be to the first field of the target table. A lookup might also be used to match a field's value to a list of possible values found in a data table used as a code table. For instance, we might build a table that contains all the possible values for FINISH, and then use a lookup to validate entry of this field in the Product table. (Can you use a picture validity check for this same purpose?)

There are two primary options with TableLookup: JustCurrentField and AllCorrespondingFields. Consider, as mentioned above, a TableLookup validity check on the CUST NO field on the Cuorder table. JustCurrentField checks CUST NO against the values in the first field of all rows in the lookup table (Customer), or optionally copies a selected value from this field in the lookup table into the validated field. The HelpAndFill choice under JustCurrentField gives the user entering data the option to press the <F1>, or Help, key when entering a value for CUST NO. Pressing <F1> causes Paradox to display the list of possible CUST NO values, from which the user may search for (by moving the cursor through the list or by jumping to the value with the Zoom key, <Ctrl + Z>) and select (by pressing <F2>) the desired input value.

The second TableLookup option is AllCorrespondingFields. This form of validity check on the CUST NO field of the Cuorder table would not just validate the field against the Customer table's first-column values. In addition, values for all fields from the Customer table that have the *same* field names as those in the Cuorder table are automatically copied into the Cuorder table from the matching row in the Customer table. AllCorrespondingFields is useful when tables are nonnormalized. Since the Pine Valley Furniture database is normalized, there is no opportunity to use this option for this database. If we had implemented the Cuorder table shown in Figure 10-1 to also include an ADDRESS field, however, then we could specify an AllCorrespondingFields validity check on the CUST NO field to automatically include the ADDRESS value from the Customer table once a valid CUST NO is entered or selected from a help list.

Data Dictionary Facilities

Since you may not have created the database you are accessing, how can you find out what tables, fields, forms, and reports are available to you? The Info selection on the Tools menu of Paradox provides access to some of the internal definitions for data tables and related objects. This selection provides six options for accessing information about a database:

- Structure: Displays the fields and data types for a specified table.
- Inventory: Lists the table, script, or all files stored on the working directory.
- Family: Enumerates the forms, reports, and other objects associated with a table.
- Who: Lists the names of Paradox users currently signed on (relevant only in a network environment).
- Lock: Also for a network environment, this lists who has placed what type of lock on which tables.
- TableIndex: Lists secondary keys for a table.

Who and Lock deal with multiuser considerations to be discussed in Chapter 13. Examples for the Structure and Family options appear in Figure 10-8.

The structure and number of records of the Cuorder table appear in Figure 10-8a. This screen actually shows the contents of a temporary table, called the Struct table. This explains the meaning of the message at the bottom of the screen, "1 of 4", which means that the cursor is on the first record of the Struct table; this record corresponds to the ORDER NO field definition. You can change the con-

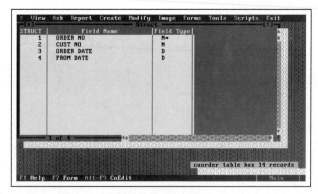

(a) Table structure

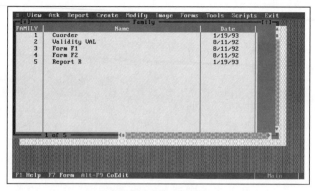

(b) Table family list

Figure 10-8

Paradox data dictionary
facilities

tents of the Struct table by pressing <F9> to go into edit mode at this point. After
exiting this screen, the Struct table (which exists until the session ends or another
Struct table is created) will appear on a list of data tables, and you can manipulate
it as you would any data table. Since it is possible in Paradox to rename this
temporary table, the structure of a table can be permanently saved.

Figure 10-8b lists the objects in the Cuorder table family, which includes the
Cuorder table itself, plus a validity check file, two forms definitions, and a report
definition. As before, this screen shows the contents of a special, temporary table
called Family, which you can edit and rename.

Summary of Data Definition Commands

The preceding remarks describe the salient data definition features of Paradox.
None of these capabilities are linked to the QBE style of relational database que-
rying, so they could be available with any relational system. What is unique about
QBE is the query interface, which is explained beginning in the next section.

SIMPLE DATA RETRIEVAL
IN QBE AND PARADOX

With any relational system, the result of a data retrieval is shown and stored in a
table. QBE is no different. What makes QBE unique is that the visual image of a
table is also used for writing queries. The visual image gives the user the sense of
directly manipulating the data. For most novice users, this visual approach will
be more natural, will require less training, and will make programming more
efficient.

Single-Table Displays

The simplest form of data retrieval is an unqualified display of the complete contents of one data table. This operation is available in Paradox through the View
option on the main menu. Figure 10-1 showed the result of viewing the Cuorder
table from our Pine Valley Furniture example database. In view mode, a table may
only be displayed, not edited. To edit the table, the user may press <F9>. Cursor-

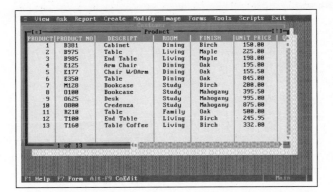

Figure 10-9

Viewing multiple tables on the workspace

movement keys or a mouse and scroll bars may be used to scroll right and left and scroll or page up and down throughout the view image. For a table with many rows, it may be tedious to use cursor keys to scan to a desired row. You can use the Zoom key, <Ctrl+Z>, to find a desired record.

It is possible to place multiple data table views onto the workspace. This is done by repeatedly calling View from the main menu without clearing the workspace (<F8> clears the current image from the workspace). For instance, Figure 10-9 shows the screen after first viewing the Customer table and then viewing the Product table. The cursor is located in the table most recently added to the workspace, the Product table in this case, which overlays the Customer table data. It is possible to move each table image, like a window in Microsoft Windows, but we allowed the table images to overlap here. You use UpImage (<F3>) and DownImage (<F4>) to move between images, or you can click the mouse on the arrow in the upper-right corner of a data table. Any number of images may be placed on the workspace.

Single-Table Queries

Although viewing table contents or zooming in on a particular record can be useful, we usually ask more complex questions of a database. QBE provides a simple, visual method for specifying qualified queries. Data for display may be limited to certain columns and records with desired values. This is done by filling in keywords, symbols, and values into a query form on the PC screen.

The discount rate query of Figure 2-8 is an example of a query that involves selected columns and rows. Figure 10-10 shows this query and its result in QBE, using the Paradox Ask function. You generate this screen by selecting Ask from

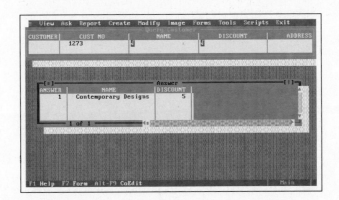

Figure 10-10

Discount rate query in QBE

the main menu and then picking the Customer table for querying. This places a blank Customer query form on the top of the screen. You enter the record qualifier of 1273 for CUST NO in this field and place a check mark (using <F6>) under the two fields to be displayed. The Customer table is too wide to show all columns on the screen, and the DISCOUNT field, one of the fields to be displayed, is the last field in the table. Therefore, we rotated the fields to get all the displayed fields on the screen (to show all the relevant parts of the query form in one figure). We rotated fields by placing the cursor first on ADDRESS and then on CITY ST ZIP and, in each case, pressing <Ctrl + R>, the Rotate key. Rotate moves a field to the right-most end of the image. Rotate can also be used on an Answer table to show fields in a sequence other than the one in which they are defined in the table structure. Once the query form is completed, you press <F2>, the Do-It! key, to process the query. The equivalent dBASE Control Center Discount Rate query was shown in Figure 2-29.

All Check Marks Are Not Created Equal   You may press <F6> under specific columns, or if you want to show all the fields, you may press <F6> with the cursor under the table name. The <F6> check mark ($\sqrt{}$) is a toggle, so if you want to remove a check mark, simply press <F6> under a field with a $\sqrt{}$. <F6> also indicates that the results are to be sorted in ascending order by that field value, and that rows with duplicate values in all checked fields are to be eliminated from the Answer table. <Alt + F6>, or the $\sqrt{}+$ key, works like <F6>, except that duplicates are included and the results are not sorted. (Data will be displayed in primary key sequence if no other sorting rules are specified.) <Ctrl + F6>, or $\sqrt{}\blacktriangledown$, specifies descending sequence and the elimination of duplicates.

Figure 10-11 shows the effects of these different check marks. In Figure 10-11a we use <F6> for both PRODUCT NO and ORDER QTY fields in the Request table, which results in an Answer table with 27 records (not all are shown). Duplicate rows are eliminated, and the answer is shown in ascending order first by PRODUCT NO and second by ORDER QTY. Figure 10-11b shows the effect of using the descending-order check marks, <Ctrl + F6>, for both fields. Again, 27 rows are in the Answer table. Finally, Figure 10-11c shows the use of <Alt + F6>. In this case all 28 Request table rows (two rows have the same values for PRODUCT NO and ORDER QTY fields) are included in the Answer table (not all can be shown on the screen). In Figure 10-11c the results are sorted in ascending order by ORDER NO and PRODUCT NO, since there is a primary key index on this combination of fields, even though ORDER NO is not in the Answer table.

Because this chapter concentrates on the QBE style database query language, we will skip many Paradox features. For example, the sorted forms of check marks assume that major to minor sort keys go from left to right on queries. If this is not the case, you can change the sequence in which fields are used for sorting. You can also rename an Answer table to make it a permanent part of a database, and you can save and later replay a query. If you need to use these features of Paradox, please refer to a Paradox manual or some other book on the Paradox language.

Selecting Qualified Records

What if you are only interested in certain records? We have seen in Figure 10-10 the basic approach to entering qualifications for which records to display from a table. This is done by placing conditions under the associated column. The condition can be an equality one, as in Figure 10-10, or it could involve a range or inequality condition. For example, instead of entering 1273 under the CUST NO

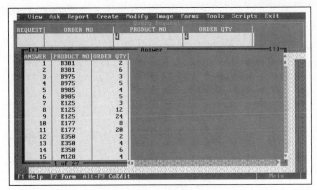

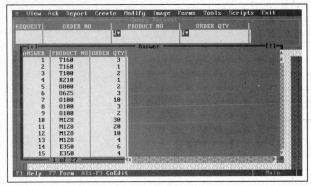

(a) Regular check mark

(b) Descending-order check mark

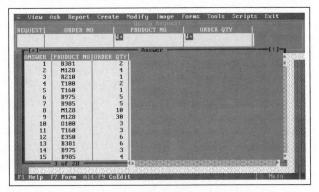

Figure 10-11

Different forms of check marks

(c) Include duplicates check mark

column in Figure 10-10, you could place >1273 or NOT 1273 under this field. You can also use the relational operators <, <=, and >=. You can use the keyword BLANK to select those records that have a null value for a field. Also, you can use the keyword TODAY to qualify a field value to today's date.

Arithmetic in Qualifications   Arithmetic can also be done within qualifications. For example, <TODAY+10 would qualify a date field value to a date no later than 10 days from now. Consider the query in Figure 10-12, which finds those Cuorder records for which shipment is promised within 10 days of when

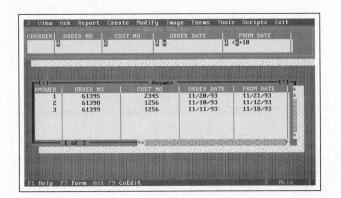

Figure 10-12

Example query with calculation in qualification

the order was entered. This query also introduces the Example entry (the high-lighted *x* under ORDER DATE and PROM DATE). Here, *x* refers to the value of ORDER DATE in a given row. So, the qualification under PROM DATE changes for each record, to be relative to whatever the ORDER DATE is for that record, not an absolute date. We will use Example entries extensively later for multiple-table queries, but they can also be very useful for qualifications within a single-table query.

Inexact Qualifications   There are also wildcard characters for finding records in which a value follows a certain pattern. The two wildcard characters in Paradox are @ to match any single number or character and .. to match any series of num-bers or characters. Suppose you want to find the customer record for Common-wealth Builder, but you don't know the exact spelling of this customer's name. In this case you might enter C..B.. as the qualification under the NAME field to find the desired customer.

An interesting Paradox qualification operator is LIKE. The LIKE operator finds records that are similar to, but not necessarily identical to, the value entered as the qualification. LIKE is useful for finding records when you are not sure of the spelling, or when data may have been entered in inconsistent ways. For example, data entry personnel may have been inconsistent in capitalizing words, or perhaps they have sometimes entered data with a punctuation mark and sometimes not (for example, *d'Angelo* versus *d Angelo*). An equality match is case-sensitive and looks for an exact comparison, but the LIKE operator ignores case and looks for similar but not necessarily identical values. Suppose you wanted to find any cus-tomer whose name is LIKE A B C Office Supply. Even though the stored data have ABC without embedded spaces, Paradox will find the correct record when you enter this LIKE phrase under the NAME field of the Customer table query form. Although LIKE is a very helpful operator, it is not as intelligent as we might like. For example, the following two qualifications will find ABC Office Supply in the database:

```
LIKE ABD Office Supply
LIKE Able Office Supply
```

However, Paradox will not find the desired record with the following two qual-ifications:

```
LIKE ABC Office
LIKE XYZ Office Supply
```

Records with Unique Qualifications   Another special qualification operator is ONLY. The query in Figure 10-13 finds those product descriptions that are associated only with Birch finishes. According to the query results, the products that are made only in Birch are a Cabinet and a Table Coffee. There are also Bookcase and End Table products made in Birch, but these are made in other finishes as well. We will see other examples of the ONLY operator later.

Queries with Compound Conditions   As you might expect from other da-tabase systems we have seen in this text, it is possible to write compound Boolean conditions with AND, OR, and NOT operators. One form of compound condition is an AND or an OR on the same field. Figure 10-14 contains a query for those products with unit price between $300 and $500. The two range conditions on UNIT PRICE separated by a comma indicate the AND condition. Figure 10-15

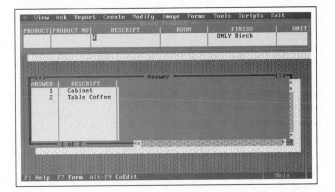

Figure 10-13

Example query with
ONLY operator

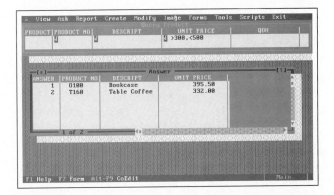

Figure 10-14

Example query with
AND condition on one
field

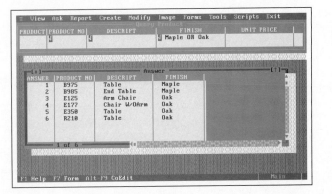

Figure 10-15

Example query with OR
condition on one field

shows the query you would write to find those products that are made of either Maple or Oak.

Conditions under different fields on the same row of a query form have an implied AND between them, and conditions on different rows of a query form have an implied OR between them. For example, consider the query of Figure 10-16. This query finds the Maple products that cost less than $400 or those products that are not made of Maple and cost more than $600.

Built-in Functions and Calculations   The typical built-in functions of AVERAGE, COUNT, MAX, MIN, and SUM are available in Paradox, and such summary values may be calculated on either all records or all unique records.

Figure 10-16

Example query with compound conditions on multiple lines

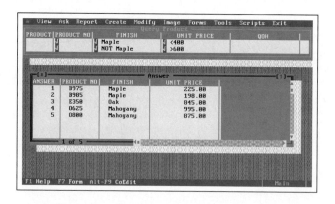

Also, you can mathematically combine or concatenate character field values to form a calculated result. Figure 10-17 illustrates use of one of these built-in functions, MAX. The query in Figure 10-17a shows the date of the most recent order for each customer. The check mark on CUST NO serves two purposes. First, the check mark says to include this field in the Answer table; second, it divides the records into groups on which the summary statistics are to be calculated. In this case, the MAX is calculated for each group, where a group is those records with the same CUST NO. Figure 10-17b shows how to use the MAX function to find the date of the most recent order. (There could, of course, be several customer orders for this same date, but we can't see if this is true from this figure.) Paradox will automatically label the desired value "Max of ORDER DATE," but we have used the AS operator to establish a specific field name of Most Recent Order for the Answer table.

You also can use built-in functions to select which *groups* to display. For example, you could replace CALC MAX under ORDER DATE in Figure 10-17a with MAX < 11/20/93, in this case, only those customers with orders no more recent than November 20, 1993, would appear in the Answer table. Such use of MAX is similar to the HAVING operator in SQL (see Chapter 8).

Calculating computed fields from database contents also uses the CALC function. For example, suppose you wanted to see the current product prices, as well as what the prices would be if they were increased by 7% for Maple finish products and 9% for all other products, and the difference between the current and possible new prices. A query to produce this result appears in Figure 10-18. Because the

Figure 10-17

Examples of queries with built-in functions

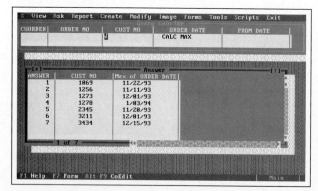
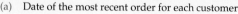

(a) Date of the most recent order for each customer

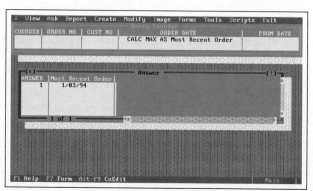

(b) Date of most recent order

expressions under the UNIT PRICE field are so long, the PRODUCT NO field does not show on the query form, but this field has been checked for display. Two lines are used in the query form to represent the two separate (OR) conditional calculations. Example elements are used in the calculations, and we defined a meaningful column heading for each computation.

There are subtle ways in which Paradox calculates certain functions that can give unexpected results. For example, the COUNT function can give some surprising results because it will ignore duplicate values unless told otherwise. Suppose you wanted to find out how many products there were for each pair of ROOM and FINISH values. The query in Figure 10-19 would seem to be a way to produce this result. The Answer table says there is only one product for each pair of values. This seems odd, since there are 13 products in the Product table and the total of the counts is not 13. Now, if you were to add the keyword ALL after COUNT, you would get the correct answer. AVERAGE and SUM functions automatically include duplicate values, so the ALL operator is not necessary with these. If, however, you want the AVERAGE or SUM of only the unique values, you must use the UNIQUE keyword to modify the calculation, as we used ALL here with COUNT.

Summary of Single-Table Queries

In this section we have shown the variety of Paradox querying capabilities for answering questions from one table of data. Many of these capabilities are used in building more complex queries as well. Actually, we have left out many

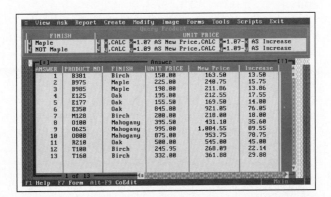

Figure 10-18

Example query with calculations

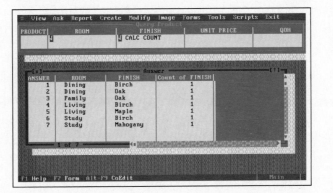

Figure 10-19

Subtlety of COUNT function

subtleties and options, since our goal is not to train you in Paradox. From the exposure here, you can explore and learn other options and master those presented in this section. Next we review the Paradox and QBE multiple-table querying capabilities that add significant power and ease to database processing.

MULTIPLE-TABLE OPERATIONS IN QBE AND PARADOX

As we saw in Chapter 2, inquiry and reporting requirements often involve data from several related tables. In a relational system, data from related tables are combined into one table, and then displayed or used as input to a form or report definition. Thus, the majority of relational database programming involves combining into one table data from two, three, or more related tables. In a relational database, all relationships from one table to another or within one table are either 1:*M* or 1:1. These relationships are implemented simply by including a column that comes from the same domain of values in each related table. That is, two tables can be linked by finding matches in the common columns. We usually think of this process as finding for each row in the table on the many-side (or one of the one-sides in a 1:1 relationship) of a relationship the one row of the table on the one-side of the relationship that matches the common column value.

In QBE we link tables by placing an example value under common columns in different query forms. We have used example values earlier in the chapter to link two related fields in one table (see the queries in Figures 10-12 and 10-18).

Join

In relational database terminology, a join is the operation of linking multiple related tables together in queries. There are several types of joins: equi-join, natural join, and outer join, to name the most common. These have been defined in Chapter 8 and illustrated in Figure 8-2; we will not define them again here. In this section, we examine several examples of these types of joins, as well as the self-join, in which a table is joined with itself.

Many examples of multiple-table queries in the Pine Valley Furniture Company database were described in Chapter 2. For example, consider the daily order log of Figure 2-9. This query displays the customer name, order number, and promised shipping date for all orders placed on a specified date. The data for this query come from two tables: Customer and Cuorder. Thus, these two tables must be linked by an example value on their common field, CUST NO. The dBASE IV version of this query written in the Control Center's QBE-type interface was shown in Figure 2-31. The Paradox version of this query appears in Figure 10-20.

The customer order history query of Figure 2-10 is another example of a multiple-table query. As you can see from the E-R diagram in Figure 2-10, this query involves four tables: Customer, Cuorder, Request, and Product. Remember, however, that each Cuorder record contains the CUST NO as a cross-reference from Cuorder to Customer. Thus, since we need only the CUST NO field for this query, we do not include the Customer file in the query. Similarly, we do not need the Product file, since the PRODUCT NO field is found in the Request table. An example value in the ORDER NO field is used to join the two remaining tables together. Figure 10-21 shows the Paradox QBE query to produce the order history data for customer 1273 during November of 1993.

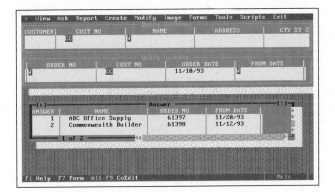

Figure 10-20

Paradox query for daily order log

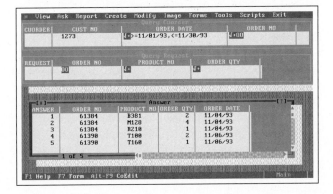

Figure 10-21

Paradox version of order history query

Frequently, complex multiple-table queries are difficult to write without breaking the query into more manageable parts. Paradox provides the capability to rename an Answer table (from the Tools option on the main menu). This makes a temporary Answer table a permanent database table, so that we can use the renamed table in subsequent queries. Since Paradox does not support a relational view (see Chapters 8 and 9 for discussions of views), such real intermediate tables are the only way to simplify query writing in Paradox.

Outer Join   The outer join operator for relational databases works like the natural join, except that rows in the tables being joined that do not have a match in other tables are also included in the result. For example, suppose you wanted to create a list of all the products in Pine Valley Furniture with their corresponding total units sold. A new or unpopular product may not have any entries in the Request table. Thus, you must do an outer join of the Product and Request tables, as is shown in Figure 10-22. (All products have sales, so no product has a sold value of 0 in the Answer table.) The inclusion operator (!) is placed directly after the example element in the table from which we want to include rows that have no match in the other table. You can place the ! on both tables you join if it is possible that rows in each might not have a match in the other table.

Self-Join   It is not uncommon to find a query that requires a table to be joined with itself. This type of query is called a **self-join** (or a *recursive join*). For example, suppose you want to know what orders have been placed that include any of the same products that were ordered on order 61395. Such a query might arise because

Self-join (recursive join): A join of a table with itself.

Figure 10-22

Example of outer join in Paradox

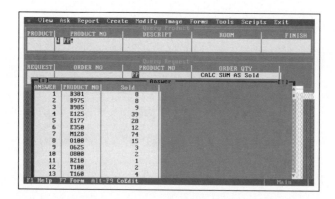

of, say, a packaging problem with this order, and you need to find if any other orders have had the same problem. A Paradox QBE query to answer this question appears in Figure 10-23. A self-join is done in one query template using two rows that have some value in common. In this case, we are looking for any record in the Request table that has a match to PRODUCT NO in any Request record for ORDER NO 61395. We use the qualifier "NOT 61395" in the second row, so that this order does not appear in the answer table.

Figure 10-24 shows a more extensive example of a combination of a self-join and a natural join. This figure answers the question, "What customers have pur-

Figure 10-23

Example of a self-join in Paradox

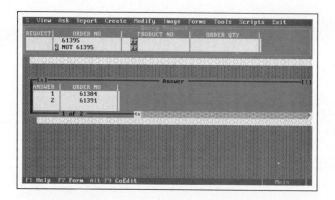

Figure 10-24

Example of a combination of a self-join and a natural join in Paradox

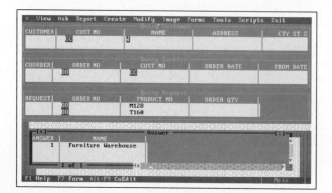

chased both products M128 and T160 on the same order?'' In the sample data used in this Pine Valley Furniture database, the customer Contemporary Designs also ordered both of these products, but they were purchased on different orders. In this query, the Customer and Cuorder tables are matched by a natural join, and the Cuorder and Request tables are also matched by a natural join. The self-join occurs within the Request table, where two records with specific PRODUCT NO values must have the same ORDER NO value.

Sets

As we have noted, it is often difficult even in QBE to answer a question in a single query. One way to deal with such difficult queries is to break a query into multiple steps, saving intermediate tables, as we have discussed. Paradox provides one other handy mechanism for helping to answer complex queries: a set. A **set** is a defined group of records about which you intend to ask further questions. It creates a shorthand for referring to the group of records, no matter how complex the definition of the set is. (A set provides some of the same convenience as a relational view.) A set is similar to the results of a subquery in SQL. Since a set is a group of records, you can compute the values for SUM, COUNT, and so on for the set. A set is used as a basis for comparison in query forms that are all resident on the workspace; that is, a set definition exists only in a workspace.

Set: In Paradox, a defined group of records.

 Suppose you want to know which Request record contained the largest value for ORDER QTY. You could, of course, view this table and scan for the row with the largest value for the ORDER QTY field. An actual Request table could be very long, however, and you can automate the process of finding the largest value by using a set. A query to answer this question appears in Figure 10-25. In this query the set of ORDER QTY values is given the set name x. The word SET must appear under the table name; only example elements, link values, and constant values may appear in the same line as the word SET; that is, no check marks or calculations may appear in this line. The second line of the query form says to display the row(s) from the Request table whose value for ORDER QTY is the maximum of all the values in the x set. The second line of the query form defines a group of records that Paradox compares to the set. Here, each group for comparison is composed of one row from the Request table (all the rows with the same values for ORDER NO and PRODUCT NO). Often, each group contains multiple rows from a table.

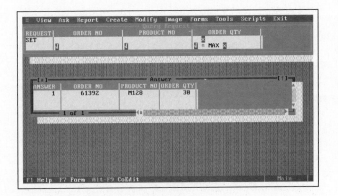

Figure 10-25

Paradox query with SET operator

Figure 10-26

Use of a set to find set difference

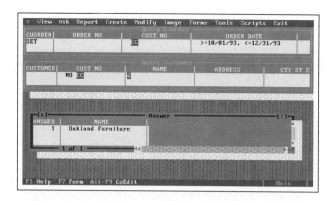

There are many uses for Paradox sets. Suppose you want to find those customers who did not buy anything from Pine Valley Furniture in the last quarter of 1993. That is, you want to know what customer numbers from records in the Customer table are not listed in the records of the Cuorder table for the fourth quarter of 1993. Figure 10-26 shows how you would answer this question using a Paradox set. As for most uses of a set, there are two major components to this query. The first component defines the set. In this case, the set CC is the group of CUST NO values for Cuorder records for the fourth quarter. The second component states by check marks what records to select in comparison to values in the set. The query on the Customer table defines groups of customers, in which each group (which is of size one in this case) of customers has the same customer NAME. The query says to show those NAME values (groups) whose associated CUST NO values do not appear in the CC set.

NO is one of four special operators that can be used to compare a group of values to the values in a set. These four operators are NO, ONLY, EVERY, and EXACTLY; they are defined in Table 10-3. We saw in Figure 10-13 a simple example of ONLY. In this case, since the set contained only one value and only one table was involved, a set definition was not necessary. This query said to display those product description groups that contain only Birch finished products. For this query, each group for comparison potentially contains more than one record.

Figure 10-27 illustrates queries involving sets and the ONLY operator for the Pine Valley Furniture database. The set includes Living and Dining room furni-

TABLE 10-3   Set Operators

Operator	Explanation of Group in Comparison to Set
NO	No value in the group equals a value in the set.
ONLY	The values in the group are only values from the set and no other values, but not necessarily all values from the set.
EVERY	The values in the group cover every value in the set (plus possibly additional values).
EXACTLY	The values in the group cover every and only those values in the set.

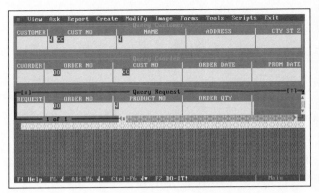

(a) Generation of table for records to be compared to the set

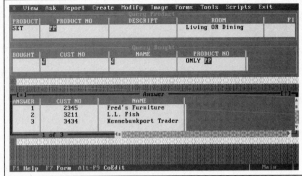

(b) Query and result for records only in the set

Figure 10-27

Example of SET with ONLY operator

ture, which are products with PRODUCT NOs B381, B975, B985, E125, E177, E350, T100, and T160 (8 of the 13 products in the sample database). Figure 10-27a shows a query that defines a table, Bought, of product numbers and the associated customer numbers and names for each Request record. This table was created to simplify subsequent queries. Figure 10-27b shows the query and result for those customers who have bought only products in this set. Each group being compared to the set consists of those Bought records that are for the same customer. In this case, therefore, a group of potentially more than one value is being compared to a set of 8 values. This clearly illustrates the mathematical set-manipulation nature of using a Paradox set:

- ONLY tests whether a comparison group is a subset of the defined set.
- NO is equivalent to subtracting the set from the group.
- EVERY tests whether a comparison group is a superset of the defined set.
- EXACTLY discovers if a comparison group and the defined set are equal.

The GroupBy Operator   In the preceding examples we displayed the groups of records that met the comparison to a defined set. Sometimes a query may call for such a comparison, but it is other data associated with the group that are to be displayed. Suppose you want to know the names of the customers in Pine Valley Furniture who have placed only small orders. Such customers are a potential problem due to the fixed cost of handling an order. In this case, the defined set is the order numbers for Request table rows with ORDER QTY smaller than 5 units. Each comparison group is the order numbers for a given customer (from the Cuorder table). If all of the order numbers in a group are in the defined set, then the customer has placed only small orders. What we want to display, however, are the customer names for those groups that satisfy the comparison (from the Customer table). This query requires the GroupBy Paradox operator, the <Shift+F6> key. The query and result appear in Figure 10-28. We see that three customers have placed only small orders. In Figure 10-28, the highlighted G represents the GroupBy selection. GroupBy was used since it is not the CUST NO that we want to display, but rather the NAME. The comparison of a group to a set works as we saw above. Instead of displaying the group field values that satisfy the comparison (no members of the group are in the defined set of ORDER NOs), the group is used as a cross-reference into the Customer table to find the associated NAME field.

Figure 10-28

Example of GroupBy
operator

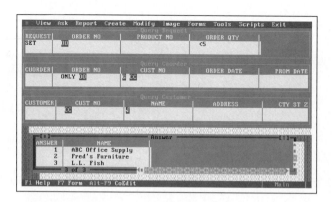

Other Multiple-Table Operations

Besides joining tables, many relational systems also provide means for three other relational operations: union, difference, and intersection (see Chapters 8 and 9 for a discussion of these operators). Union takes two lists of records and combines them into one list. This is often handy when you need to write several queries to find subsets of the records you want; you can then merge these subsets together into one final list. Difference finds values that are in one list but not in another (like the customer numbers from a customer table that do not appear in a customer order table). Intersection finds values that are common to two lists (like a list of customer numbers for those who have bought Birch furniture and another list of those who have bought Maple furniture). We have seen in the preceding discussion of sets that you can use ONLY to find the records in the intersection of two lists of values, and you can use NO to find the records that are in one list and not another (equivalent to difference).

Union is accomplished in Paradox by combining two tables (a source and a target) into one (the new target). These two tables might be saved Answer tables from two queries, or they might be a database table and an imported table from an external source (like a mailing list of customers), or any combination of these and other sources for tables. You perform this operation from the Tools selection on the main menu; you choose the Tools menu option More, and then choose the option Add. The two tables must have corresponding fields in the same order. Also, the two tables being combined must have compatible, but not necessarily identical, field types (some data conversion is supported). If the target table is keyed, you must specify what to do when a record being added has a key value that already exists in the target table. You may choose either to reject the duplicate record in the source table or to update the existing record in the target with the new values found in the corresponding source record.

The More menu under Tools also has a Subtract option, which is another way that Paradox supports the difference operation. Subtract deletes from the target table those matching records in the source table. If the target table is keyed, a match is simply on the key field; if the target table is not keyed, then all field values must match for deletion to occur.

Summary of Multiple-Table Operations

This section has reviewed a wide selection of ways to manipulate two, three, or more tables to answer questions that involve data from multiple tables. Obviously, the aim was not to teach the keystrokes of using Paradox. Rather, we have shown the kinds of operations that are possible in a QBE system; you should, if required, be able to negotiate with relative ease your way through the Paradox menu system to find the desired choices and operations.

DATA MAINTENANCE IN QBE AND PARADOX

You can use Query-by-Example for more than data retrieval; you can also modify data through queries by editing data in tables or forms. Also, as already discussed, you can add new data to a table by merging records from another table into it.

Data Maintenance Operations in Queries

Inserting new records, deleting selected existing records, and changing the values in selected existing records can all be done from update queries. Insertion involves copying values from one or more (source) tables into another (target) table. Deletion and change operate on one table to modify its contents. With each of these operations, Paradox also creates some temporary tables that you can use to undo maintenance operations when errors have occurred or you decide that the operation should not have been done.

Inserting New Records   Recall that when you use the Add operations in the More menu, source and target tables require compatible fields in the same sequence. Since this situation is not always the case, an INSERT query is a more general way to copy data from one or more tables into a target table. Also with an INSERT query, you can place a qualification on the source tables to copy only the desired records and fields into the target table. Finally, you can rearrange and combine fields in the source tables to populate the target table in a very customized fashion.

Suppose Pine Valley Furniture purchases an external mailing list of potential customers that it wants to combine with the records in its Customer table. This mailing list has been imported (Paradox can import from several formats) into a Paradox table called Newcusts, some sample contents of which appear in Figure 10-29a. Since the format of Newcusts customer data does not match the Customer table definition, we could not simply add these new records to the Customer table. Some of the potential customers were assigned a CUST NO, but not all, so those with a BLANK value for CUST NO are not to be inserted into Customer.

Figure 10-29

Example of INSERT query

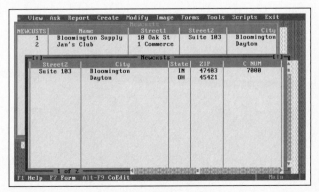

(a)   Records to insert

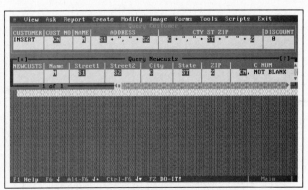

(b)   INSERT query

Figure 10-29b shows the INSERT query for this situation. The result of an INSERT query is a temporary table, called Inserted, which Paradox automatically creates. The Inserted table (not shown in Figure 10-29) contains the rows from the source table (Newcusts) that were inserted into the target table (Customer) in the target table format. To convert the Newcusts format into the Customer fields, string concatenations were specified for the ADDRESS and CTY ST ZIP Customer fields. Example values were used to specify which field from the source table was to be inserted under what field of the target table. The DISCOUNT for any potential customer is zero. Also, under the C NUM field in the Newcusts table is the restriction that only rows with nonblank values for the customer number are to be added. The contents of the one row that was inserted confirm that the insertion happened as desired.

The Inserted table exists until another INSERT query is run or until the end of the session. This table can be used, for example, to undo previous insertions if an error is discovered.

Deleting Records   A DELETE query removes selected rows from a table. A DELETE query looks like a display query, except that rows that would be displayed are deleted instead. For example, to delete all Birch products from the Product table, we would write a query to display the Birch products, but would also include the word DELETE under the Product table name in the query form. If no qualifications are entered under fields in the query form, then all records would be deleted from the specified table.

Changing Records   A CHANGETO query changes values in the selected rows of a table based upon value-substitution statements. A CHANGETO query, like a global search and replace in a word processor, changes all occurrences of a field, but in this case only in rows that satisfy any qualification included in the query. Suppose that Pine Valley Furniture wanted to reward all their customers who had purchased 40 or more units of products by setting their discount to the maximum value, 15%. Figure 10-30a shows the calculation of the total quantity ordered by each customer from data in the Request and Cuorder tables; this result was stored in a table called Custtot. Then Figure 10-30b shows the CHANGETO query necessary to update the discount field to 15%. This query finds in the Custtot table the CUST NOs for customers with 40 or more units purchased and then changes the Customer table DISCOUNT field for just these customers. The Changed table contains copies of the changed Customer records prior to the update. As before, the Changed table can be used to undo erroneous updates.

Figure 10-30

Example of CHANGETO
query

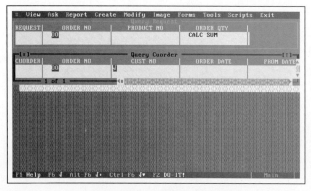

(a)   Calculation of intermediate result

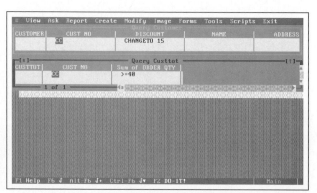

(b)   CHANGETO query

Data Maintenance Menu Commands

The data maintenance operations of INSERT, DELETE, and CHANGETO were, of course, designed for those kinds of data table modifications that you can control by database contents and queries. Other data maintenance requires user interaction to enter new or type over existing values. This latter type of data maintenance is also done visually via table images or forms on which a user enters values or presses special keys to perform desired functions.

The interactive data maintenance functions are found under the Modify option on the Paradox main menu. Three choices exist: DataEntry, Edit, and CoEdit. A fourth choice, MultiEntry, works with multitable forms, an especially helpful feature of Paradox that we review in Chapter 11. Since these interactive data maintenance features of Paradox are not QBE-related, we do not to discuss them here.

TRANSACTION INTEGRITY FACILITIES OF PARADOX

Paradox has very limited facilities for controlling transaction integrity. There are no commands for defining logical transaction boundaries as there are in SQL and dBASE IV (see the BEGIN and END TRANSACTION commands for dBASE described in Chapter 2). Paradox does have a command that aborts a transaction and returns the database to values before the current transaction began: the UNDO command. UNDO is accessible from the DataEntry and Edit menus, and can be invoked by pressing <Ctrl+U>.

A transaction has an implicit boundary in Paradox. A transaction begins when you move the cursor to a particular record or create a new record. A transaction ends when you move to another record or delete a record. In Edit mode, if you move away from an edited record and then come back to it, Paradox updates the existing transaction. Thus, a transaction can contain several changes to a record; also, one record may be involved in several transactions during one session. Each time you press UNDO, you undo one more transaction, in reverse chronological order. In CoEdit mode (that is, when you are editing a file when someone else is also editing records in the same file), UNDO restores the most recently changed record to its contents prior to the most recent editing. Once you press Do-It!, however, changes cannot be undone. Prior transactions cannot be undone.

OTHER PARADOX CAPABILITIES

Paradox has many other capabilities that have made it one of the most popular PC-RDBMSs on the market today. These additional features include custom screen (or form) and report generation. Because most PC-RDBMSs contain such modules, we devote part of Chapter 11 to form- and report-generation features, including the capabilities within Paradox. In addition, Paradox includes a proprietary programming language, PAL, the Paradox personal programmer (an application generator), and can generate simple business graphics. PAL, although different from the dBASE command language introduced in Chapter 9, has many similarities to its dBASE counterpart since each is a structured database processing language. Because we have already overviewed the dBASE language and the focus of this chapter is on QBE as illustrated by Paradox, we do not address PAL or these other capabilities of Paradox here.

SUMMARY

Query-by-Example is a powerful and visual database interface employed in several database management systems. QBE promotes easy and accurate database querying. When implemented as part of a complete DBMS, like Paradox 4.0, QBE provides flexible and extensive database processing capabilities.

In this chapter we covered the QBE style of writing queries. In QBE, a query is written by filling in values, keywords, and special symbols within the cells of a table image displayed on a CRT. Data retrieval and maintenance queries are all written using this one programming style. Helpful constructs, like sets and groups, aid a programmer in writing complex queries and programs.

We overviewed in this chapter the data definition features of Paradox 4.0, one DBMS based on QBE. Paradox supports both primary and secondary keys as well as data integrity constraints. A TableLookup feature can be used to enforce referential integrity links between tables.

We also showed how to use QBE within Paradox to write single- and multiple-table queries. Such queries can involve simple and compound qualification on one or several fields.

Paradox is an evolving product. As we were writing this chapter Borland International released its first version of Paradox for Windows. Paradox for Windows extends the notion of table objects as described in this chapter to a more complete object-oriented system of more general data and programming objects, properties, and methods. It uses a graphical user interface (GUI) to the database, and you may include graphics in forms and reports. We introduce Paradox for Windows in Chapter 11.

Database management systems are dynamic, evolving, and powerful software tools. A standard interface, like QBE, helps users to make the inevitable transition from one generation to the next of a given product. QBE, in particular, because it gives a user the impression of directly manipulating tables of data, is especially easy to use. We expect QBE to continue to be a style of database querying included not only in future releases of Paradox but also in many other products.

CHAPTER REVIEW

Key Terms

Self-join	Set	Validity check

REVIEW QUESTIONS

1. Define each of the following terms:
   a. LIKE operator
   b. direct manipulation
   c. Paradox object
   d. object family
   e. query form
   f. Answer table
   g. primary key
   h. secondary key
   i. validity check
   j. TableLookup
   k. Zoom
   l. join
   m. self-join
   n. outer join
   o. Paradox set
   p. INSERT query
   q. CHANGETO
2. Explain the difference between the JustCurrentField and AllCorrespondingFields options with a TableLookup validity check in Paradox.
3. Explain the process required to save the results of a Paradox query into a new database table.
4. Draw a diagram to illustrate the differences in comparing a group of records to a set using each of the four set operators: NO, ONLY, EVERY, and EXACTLY.

5. Outline the claimed benefits of a direct-manipulation language, like QBE, compared with other types of database query languages.
6. Explain how secondary key indexes can be created for use within Paradox.
7. Explain the purpose of a picture as a means for data validity checking.
8. What construct is used in Paradox to join two or more tables together?
9. Describe the differences in the results of using each of the three types of check mark keys in Paradox.
10. How many query forms must be placed on the workspace to specify a self-join?
11. What does Paradox do to help a user undo the effects of INSERT, DELETE, and CHANGETO queries?

PROBLEMS AND EXERCISES

1. Match the following terms to the appropriate definitions.

___ Query-by-Example   a. used with data type to indicate primary key

___ asterisk (*)   b. a set operator that matches every value and only those values in a set

___ secondary key   c. ensuring that a foreign key in one table matches the value of a primary key in another table

___ referential integrity   d. a direct-manipulation database language

___ EXACTLY   e. a set operator that identifies groups of records that match every value in a set

___ EVERY   f. a field for which multiple records may have the same value

Problems 2–8 are based on the Lakewood College database from Chapter 6. The 3NF relations for that application are repeated below.

STUDENT NO.	STUDENT NAME	MAJOR
38214	Bright	IS
69173	Smith	PM
. . .		

STUDENT (STUDENT NO., STUDENT NAME, MAJOR)

INSTRUCTOR NAME	INSTRUCTOR LOCATION
Codd	B 104
Kemp	B 213
Lewis	D 317
. . .	

INSTRUCTOR (INSTRUCTOR NAME, INSTRUCTOR LOCATION)

COURSE NO.	COURSE TITLE	INSTRUCTOR NAME
IS 350	Database	Codd
IS 465	Sys Anal	Kemp
PM 300	Prod Mgt	Lewis
QM 440	Op Res	Kemp
. . .		

COURSE (COURSE NO., COURSE TITLE, INSTRUCTOR NAME)

STUDENT NO.	COURSE NO.	GRADE
38214	IS 350	A
38214	IS 465	C
69173	IS 465	A
69173	PM 300	B
69173	QM 440	C
. . .		

REGISTRATION (STUDENT NO., COURSE NO., GRADE)

2. Develop a full database definition using Paradox for this database (shorten, abbreviate, or change data names as required by the limitations of Paradox). Assume the following attribute data types:

STUDENT NO. (integer, primary key)

STUDENT NAME (25 characters)

MAJOR (5 characters)

INSTRUCTOR NAME (25 characters, primary key)

INSTRUCTOR LOCATION (5 characters)

COURSE NO. (6 characters, primary key)

COURSE TITLE (10 characters)

GRADE (1 character)

3. Develop Paradox commands for the following:
    a. Validity check on the values of the GRADE field
    b. Validity check on the format of the COURSE NO. field
    c. Required value validity checks on all appropriate fields
4. Before any row can be entered in the REGISTRATION table, the COURSE to be entered must already exist in the COURSE table (referential integrity). Develop Paradox commands to enforce this constraint.
5. Write Paradox queries for each of the following:
    a. Display the instructor location for the instructor Lewis.
    b. Display the student number and student name for all information systems (IS) majors.
    c. Display the total number of students who are IS majors.
6. Write Paradox commands to perform the following operations:
    a. Delete all rows for student number 56789 in the REGISTRATION table.
    b. Change the grade for student number 38214 in IS 465 from C to B.
7. Write Paradox commands to find the minimum grade of all IS majors in IS 465.
8. Write Paradox commands to find the maximum grade given by each instructor.
9. Since Paradox does not support the relational view concept, what Paradox capabilities can be used to achieve some of the same objectives as for views?

Problems 10–16 are based on the Pine Valley Furniture database defined in this chapter.

10. Display the order number, customer number, product number, order date, and order quantity for orders of more than 15 units of products M128 or E125.
11. Display the customer number, name, and order numbers of all customer orders, and include in this list any customer who has no orders in the database.
12. Write a query that shows each product and the total quantity ordered for each product (be sure to include products that have never been ordered).
13. Write a query that lists all the product descriptions and associated rooms; include duplicates.
14. Find the average number of units on each line item (request) of a customer order.
15. Display a list of all the products and the number of times each product has been ordered.
16. Produce an Answer table using one or more queries that shows the order number, product number, and order quantity for all customer orders for which the order quantity is greater than the average order quantity of that product.

REFERENCES

Byrer, J. 1991. "The Relative Effectiveness of a Direct Manipulation Interface Versus Command-Based Interface in a Database Query Task Environment." Unpublished Ph.D. diss., Indiana University.

Greenblatt, D., and J. Waxman. 1978. "A Study of Three Database Query Languages." In *Database: Improving Usability and Responsiveness,* ed. B. Shneiderman. New York: Academic Press.

Shneiderman, B. 1983. "Direct Manipulation: A Step Beyond Programming Languages." *IEEE Computer* 16:57–69.

Thomas, J. C., and J. D. Gould. 1975. "A Psychological Study of Query by Example." *Proceedings of National Computer Conference.* New York: AFIPS Press.

Zloof, M. M. 1977. "Query-by-Example: A Data Base Language." *IBM Systems Journal* 16, no. 4:324–43.

Advanced Features and Graphical Interfaces for PC Database Systems

LEARNING OBJECTIVES

After studying this chapter, you should be able to:

- Explain the general capabilities of screen-design software, and be able to explain the features for character-based forms and screen design in dBASE IV and Paradox 4.0.
- Explain the general capabilities of report generators, and be able to explain the features for customized report design in dBASE IV and Paradox 4.0.
- Describe the salient characteristics of PC database systems as this technology evolves into graphical user interfaces, such as for the Microsoft Windows operating system environment.
- Identify object-oriented programming concepts embodied in PC-DBMSs that adopt a graphical user interface and graphical programming style.

INTRODUCTION

This chapter shows a variety of features of PC-DBMSs that were not covered in Chapters 8–10. Two major areas of features are covered:

1. application-development capabilities (screen and report generators) used to build systems with highly customized user interfaces
2. characteristics of new PC-DBMSs that use graphical rather than character-based user interfaces (illustrated by Paradox for Windows)

Chapters 8–10 concentrated on the salient capabilities of the data retrieval and maintenance commands present in the three dominant styles of relational database systems: SQL, Xbase, and QBE query languages. We illustrated primarily the data manipulation commands for single and multiple table operations in each language. What you learned in these chapters is very helpful for writing ad hoc, or interactive, data manipulation commands, and for writing programs for processing a database. With only these query languages, however, you cannot utilize highly stylized screens and reports. Most information systems require easy-to-use input screens and specialized reports with a variety of summary data and data

393

formatting. Consequently, our coverage of PC-DBMSs would be incomplete without addressing the user interface. The user interface with most information systems is through customized data entry and display screens (or forms) and printed reports. We illustrated some simple forms and reports in Chapter 2, so you probably have a general feel for such features.

A major trend in information systems is the transition from character-based user interfaces to graphical, or so-called GUI, user interfaces. This trend affects both user interfaces as well as programming principles. In the database arena the trend is resulting in new database systems, many of which are developed on object-oriented concepts. For brevity, we show in this chapter only one, typical example of this technology that was released as this book was being written: Paradox for Windows. Here, we will see some similarities with Paradox 4.0, but we will emphasize those elements that characterize how a character-based product changes as it evolves into a graphical interface. Other GUI interface products exist (like Microsoft's Access), but since the basic concepts are similar, we show only Paradox for Windows. We expect fierce competition for market share in GUI-based PC-DBMSs as vendors rapidly introduce many additional products.

DATA ENTRY AND DISPLAY FORMS

Typically, modern information systems—whether they be transaction processing, management information systems, decision support systems, or executive information systems—collect and display data via customized screen displays. For data entry, often these displays resemble manual forms traditionally used for data capture. On-screen forms, in comparison to line-by-line data entry, are easier to use and follow, make people less prone to errors, and are more flexible. Features such as multiple-screen forms, boxes and color, automatic fill-in of default values, and on-screen menus make all this possible.

In this section we review the form-design capabilities of dBASE IV and Paradox 4.0 (Borland International, 1992a, 1992b). These capabilities are typical of what is available in a variety of character-based database systems. Later in the chapter we will see how a graphical database system differs. We begin with dBASE IV and then address Paradox more extensively, since Paradox has more advanced features.

dBASE Forms for Input and Output

We introduced the creation of dBASE forms in Chapter 2. You can invoke the form designer either by the dBASE CREATE (or MODIFY) SCREEN command at the dot prompt or from the Control Center, as shown in Chapter 2. The dBASE screen-designer module creates a screen-format file containing commands that place text on the screen and capture keyboard input. Such a file can be created command-by-command, but using the forms designer is much easier. After this generation, you can edit the file to add features that you could not include from the screen designer or to make the code more efficient. You use the dBASE SET FORMAT command in a program or at the dot prompt to specify which stored screen design to apply to each database file. Once you enter the SET command, all subsequent entry and display of data with the associated file will utilize the specified form.

A major limitation of the dBASE form designer is that a form is associated with only *one* file or query view. Thus, if you want a form that combines data from several database files (for example, customer and order), you must first join the related files into an intermediate file or create a query view with the combined data. Obviously, you cannot change the original database tables by entering or modifying data through a form on an intermediate file, but such data maintenance is possible with a query view. We will see later in this chapter that Paradox, in contrast, supports multiple-table forms. An intermediate table is redundant data, so it must be reconstructed each time the report is used if the original data is dynamic.

Another limitation of dBASE forms is that only one record from a file may appear on one instance of a form. For example, you cannot show all requested line items on one customer order on one form in dBASE. You can overcome this limitation by using a query view that does a self-join to merge data from several records into one record. Again, we will see later that the Paradox screen designer does not have this restriction.

The above two limitations of the dBASE form designer mean that you cannot build the customer order screen of Figure 2-6a directly from CUSTOMER, CUORDER, PRODUCT, and REQUEST tables. dBASE has a screen management construct called *windows*, discussed later, that can help you work around these limitations. With the windows capability (not to be confused with the Microsoft Windows operating environment), you would define two forms, one for customer and order data and one for a single line item and associated product data, and then place both forms on the screen at once in two windows. These windows, however, are not linked, so data in the line item window would not automatically change as a new order appeared in the customer order window.

Figure 11-1 shows a custom-designed form to display a PRODUCT record from the Pine Valley Furniture Company database (this is the same as Figure 2-23). You could use this display to enter a new record and to display or modify an existing PRODUCT record. The screen cursor is currently over the UNIT PRICE field, and a special prompt for this field appears on the bottom line of the screen. dBASE processes this screen as a whole object. That is, you may move from field to field on the screen, entering or changing values in any desired sequence, by either pressing the <Tab> key or moving the cursor with a mouse. Data in the record displayed is not stored or modified in the database, however, until you press <PageUp> or <PageDown> to move to a different record, or you press <Ctrl + End> to save the current record. Changes to a record on the screen are cancelled by pressing <Esc>. That is, dBASE separates the functions of entering data into the form from storing data in the database. You can press other special keys to delete the currently displayed record (<Del>) and to show an empty form to enter a new record (<Ins>). A form can be used from the Control Center, and the EDIT and BROWSE commands in dBASE programs also work with a form.

Figure 11-1

Sample dBASE product form

Figure 11-2

Sample dBASE product
form design

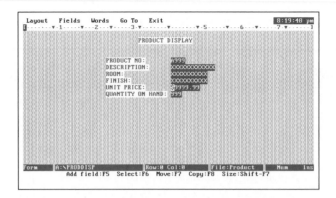

Forms are most easily defined via the form-design screen activated from the Control Center or the CREATE or MODIFY SCREEN commands. Figure 11-2 shows the form-design screen for the product form in Figure 11-1 (this is the same as Figure 2-19). The form itself is laid out in the hashed area of the screen. Each field on the form is placed at a particular row and column. What is shown for each field is a coded picture that specifies the permissible data. For example, the PRODUCT NO field value must begin with an alphabetic character followed by three digits. You enter the picture for a field from a menu under the Field menu, one of the menu options listed at the top of the form-design screen.

You add a new field to a form by placing the cursor on the first position on the screen where the field is to be located, and then pressing <F5> (or selecting the Add Field option from the Field menu). As shown on the prompt line at the bottom of the form-design screen in Figure 11-2, you may also move, copy, and resize fields (that is, increase or decrease the space allocated on the form for a field). You may also place text for instructions or field labels on the form. You may use the Word menu to have dBASE left-, center-, or right-align text between the form's margins. Refer to the section on "Product and Customer Transactions" in Chapter 2 for illustrations of many of the screen-design features available.

Since our purpose in this chapter is to make you aware of user interface design features in PC database systems, not teach you the details of using a particular form designer, we do not review each of the form-design menu choices in dBASE. In general, from the screen-design menus, you can create many special effects and enforce many controls on forms-based data entry and display, including the following:

- Defining calculated fields for display (dBASE computes a calculated field only when a record is retrieved into a form, so a calculated field does not dynamically change on the screen as the base fields in the calculation are modified or entered.)

- Defining a multiple-screen form (that is, one that is longer than one screen; a dBASE form may be up to 80 columns wide)

- Using foreground and background colors to highlight data

- Defining templates and pictures to force certain data entry and display formats (for example, displaying CR or DB next to positive or negative numbers, enclosing negative numbers in parentheses, and centering data within a field template)

- Converting all letters to uppercase

- Defining a multiple-choice field, which allows the user to pick from a preset list of possible field values
- Specifying that a blank field receives either a default value or the value found in the same field in the previous record
- Setting data integrity controls for the smallest or largest values for a field

It is interesting that many of the above data entry and maintenance controls are specified with each screen, rather than as part of the field or record definition. dBASE has chosen, however, to not enforce global restrictions on a database in return for flexibility of data entry, maintenance, and display. This flexibility can lead to improper data. If in designing a form you forget to apply, for example, a certain field format or default value, erroneous data may be entered. On the other hand, if different default values, different smallest or largest values, or other controls vary by circumstance, dBASE allows you to specify these varying controls.

The dBASE form designer is actually a special kind of code generator. A **code generator** is a module of a DBMS that helps you to design an object—screen, report, or menu—and which then automatically produces the program instructions required to create the object. That is, the dBASE form designer creates a file that contains all of the form definition commands, all of which are commands in the dBASE proprietary language. You could have entered these commands yourself, but it is much easier to let a form designer do it for you from a visual image of the form you want. You can, however, modify this source code file or copy it into a program you write if you want to enhance the form or develop more complex screen-handling logic with the generated form as a starting point.

Figure 11-3 contains the code generated for the product display form of Figure 11-2. The first, or initialization, section of the code defines variables local to this routine and sets certain status variables to a desired state. Code is also generated to remember the values of these status variables before the form is used, so they can be restored after a user is done with the form. The second section of the generated code writes all the text to the screen and specifies where on the screen and with what format and data integrity controls different fields are displayed or entered. For example, the Unit_price field is captured on row 8 beginning in column 42. A picture format of "9999.99" is applied to Unit_price, a minimum value of 0 is specified in the RANGE statement, and a message is defined for placement on the bottom screen line. The final, or exit, section of the code restores the status variables and releases the RAM used for the local variables.

As stated earlier, a SET FORMAT command activates use of a specified form with subsequent full screen editing commands (READ, EDIT, APPEND, INSERT, CHANGE, and BROWSE). For example, the following commands in a program would cause the screen in Figure 11-1 to display product M128 data for editing:

```
.USE PRODUCT
.SET FORMAT TO PRODDISP
.EDIT FOR PRODUCT_NO="M128"
```

Screen Windows   A form is designed independently of where it might be placed on a screen. The default is that a form is a full-screen display, so placement of text and data in a particular line and column is relative to the full-screen boundaries. However, in different instances you might want the same form (or any data display) to appear in different locations on the screen. The dBASE construct to handle this is a window.

A window is a rectangular area of the screen that is defined in a DEFINE WINDOW command by the absolute location of its upper left-hand and lower

Code generator: A module of a DBMS that produces the program instructions that define a form, report, or menu. A code generator usually builds these instructions from a visual image of the object drawn by the designer of the object.

Figure 11-3

dBASE code for product form

```
*-------------------------------------------------------------------------
* Name.......: PRODDISP.FMT
* Date.......: 5-27-92
* Version....: dBASE IV, Format 1.5
* Notes......: Format files use "" as delimiters!
*-------------------------------------------------------------------------

*-- Format file initialization code
------------------------------------------

*-- Some of these PRIVATE variables are created based on CodeGen and may not
*-- be used by your particular .fmt file
PRIVATE ll_talk, ll_cursor, lc_display, lc_status, ll_carry, lc_proc

IF SET ("TALK") = "ON"
 SET TALK OFF
 ll_talk = .T.
ELSE
 ll_talk = .F.
ENDIF
ll_cursor = SET("CURSOR") = "ON"
SET CURSOR ON

lc_status = SET("STATUS")
*-- SET STATUS was OFF when you went into the Forms Designer.
IF lc_status = "ON"
   SET STATUS OFF
ENDIF

*-- @ SAY GETS Processing.
-------------------------------------------------------

*-- Format Page: 1
@ 1,32 SAY "PRODUCT DISPLAY"
@ 4,23 SAY "PRODUCT NO:"
@ 4,41 GET Product_no PICTURE "A999"
@ 5,23 SAY "DESCRIPTION:"
@ 5,41 GET Descript PICTURE "XXXXXXXXXXXX"
@ 6,23 SAY "ROOM:"
@ 6,41 GET Room PICTURE "XXXXXXXXXX"
@ 7,23 SAY "FINISH:"
@ 7,41 GET Finish PICTURE "XXXXXXXXXX"
@ 8,23 SAY "UNIT PRICE:"
@ 8,41 SAY "$"
@ 8,42 GET Unit_price PICTURE "9999.99" ;
   RANGE REQUIRED 0 ;
   MESSAGE "Price per unit of product"
@ 9,23 SAY "QUANTITY ON HAND:"
@ 9,41 GET Qoh PICTURE "999" ;
   RANGE 0 ;
   DEFAULT 0
*-- Format file exit code
-------------------------------------------------------

*-- SET STATUS was OFF when you went into the Forms Designer.
IF lc_status = "ON"   && Entered form with status on
   SET STATUS ON      && Turn STATUS "ON" on the way out
ENDIF
IF .NOT. ll_cursor
   SET CURSOR OFF
ENDIF

RELEASE lc_fields,lc_status
*-- EOP: PRODDISP.FMT
```

right-hand corners. You can define a window to include special border symbols and specify foreground, background, and enhanced character colors for the window. When you activate a window by an ACTIVATE WINDOW command, all subsequent displays to the screen, whether from a form or any dBASE output, are directed to that window. Thus, depending on which window is activated, the same form may appear at different locations on the screen. Further, by defining several windows for concurrent display, you can place different forms on the screen at the same time. Data in the various windows are not, however, automatically synchronized. For example, suppose a screen contains two windows, one with customer data and one with customer order data. When the window with customer order data switches to a different order, the window with customer data will not automatically switch. You can make the windows change by writing a dBASE program to rewrite the data in both windows.

Paradox Forms for Data Input and Output

Paradox has most of the same form-design capabilities found in dBASE. In addition, Paradox supports the design of forms for displaying

- Multiple records from the same table in a tabular format (a multirecord form)
- Multiple pages (up to fifteen pages per form)
- A record in one table along with related records from one or more associated tables (This is a multitable form in which scrolling potentially affects all the records from all related tables.)
- A form embedded within another form, even when the two tables associated with the two forms are not related (an option in constructing a multiple-table form, in which case scrolling is not synchronized, or linked, across rows from the two forms)

In each case, a form is no wider than the screen, but may be longer than one screen. Also, one field may wrap between lines, which is not possible in table-view mode. You can add colors and various types of borders to a form to make it more appealing and readable.

The basic form definition capabilities in Paradox are similar to what we saw in Chapter 2 and in the preceding section for dBASE IV. For example, each table has a standard default form. Figure 11-4a shows a custom form for the CUORDER table in Pine Valley Furniture that you could use for viewing or editing data in the CUORDER table. This form design is shown by choosing the Forms option on the Paradox main menu, then selecting Change from the Forms menu, and finally

Figure 11-4

Paradox form

(a)   Custom form-design screen

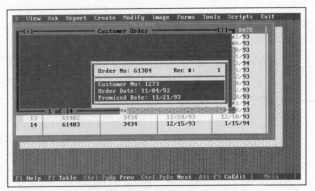

(b)   Viewing a record with a custom form

choosing Form 1 from the various forms defined for this table. The cursor is on line 6, column 33, on page 1 of 1 of the form, which is the beginning of the position where the ORDER NO field was placed. The status indicator on the bottom line of the screen says this is a regular field from the table and gives the field name.

We placed field titles on this form next to where fields are located, and we added a double line border and colors to make certain fields stand out more. For example, the dark part of the form is a blue color on the screen. Other special effects, like intense, reverse, and blinking characters, may be set. The record number, which is automatically generated by Paradox, may be included on the form.

To use a specific form while in view or edit mode, you press the menu key, <F10>. You select the Image option, and then the PickForm choice. You indicate which form (associated with the table now on the workspace) you wish to use, and then the image on the workspace switches to the form. The use of the custom CUORDER form for viewing a record is shown in Figure 11-4b. Here, since we were in table-view mode, Paradox overlaps the form onto the work surface, on top of the table view of the CUORDER table.

Besides placing fields from the table associated with the form wherever we want on the screen layout, we can

- Indicate that a field is a regular field; that is, it can be changed by data entry and editing.

- Indicate that a field is for display only. You may enter or edit data in the field, or even move the cursor to the field on the screen.

- Place calculated fields. These, of course, may not be modified by data entry or editing, and they are not actually stored with the table; various functions, like absolute value, trigonometric operations, square root, and rounding, can be part of a calculated field's expression.

- Place literals, like the titles for the different fields on the form.

- Erase a field from a form or modify a field's display format.

- Define an area on a form, and then move or erase the area's contents.

Since the basic Paradox features for form design are similar to those available in dBASE, we will not repeat a discussion of these capabilities for Paradox. Instead, we address in the next section two unique capabilities of Paradox: multiple-table and multiple-record forms.

Multiforms in Paradox

Many business transactions require entry of data into several data tables. Paradox supports such transactions through *multitable forms*. You may use a multitable form to display or edit data. In Edit mode, a transaction is bounded by a multitable form, so transaction integrity control better matches business activities when a transaction is handled via a multitable form rather than several single-table forms.

A multitable form actually contains several forms, one for each table. One form is called the *master*, and the others are called *detail* or *embedded* forms. A master form often is associated with the table that is on the one side of the one-many relationships between the tables associated with all the forms on a multitable form, but this is not always the case. Four possibilities for linked forms exist: one-one, one-many, many-one, and many-many. Just as with joining in queries, linked forms are based on common field values in the tables associated with the master and detail forms. The detail forms are designed first, so that they can be embedded into the master when it is defined. A detail form may not have any embedded forms.

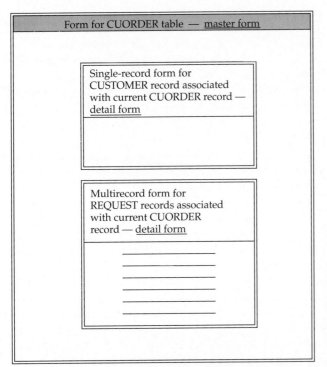

Form for CUORDER table — <u>master form</u>

Single-record form for
CUSTOMER record associated
with current CUORDER record —
<u>detail form</u>

Multirecord form for
REQUEST records associated
with current CUORDER
record — <u>detail form</u>

Structure of embedding forms

(b) Form-design screen

(c) Embedded multirecord form-design screen

(d) Use of multitable form for viewing data

Figure 11-5

Paradox multitable form

Figure 11-5a shows the relationships between master and detail forms for data associated with a customer order in Pine Valley Furniture. The focus of data for the screen is a single customer order, so a form on the CUORDER table is the master form. Since there is one customer related to each customer order, we linked a single-record embedded form for the CUSTOMER table to this master form. Linking is done by matching CUST NO values in the two tables. Since there are potentially several line items related to each customer order, we linked a multirecord embedded form on the REQUEST table to this master form. In this case linking is done by matching ORDER NO values in the CUORDER and REQUEST tables. Because an embedded form cannot itself contain an embedded form, we cannot include PRODUCT table data (like a description) in this screen. If we had joined REQUEST and PRODUCT data into a temporary table, then we could tie the embedded multirecord form to this temporary table to show product data.

Note that tables involved in a multitable form do not have to be linked or related. For example, it would be possible to design a form that had one area for

Customer table records and another for Product table records, even though these two tables do not have a direct linkage in the Pine Valley Furniture database. In the case of unlinked tables on a multitable form, each master and embedded form works independently, so as you scan through the records in one form while the records in the other form do not change in synchronization.

Either the master or detail forms may be display-only. A display-only form is useful for reference purposes when you need to protect the contents from unwanted changes. For example, you could design a form that contains a row from the PRODUCT table and associated rows from the REQUEST table in the Pine Valley Furniture database. The purpose of the form would be to maintain PRODUCT data (like unit price), but the REQUEST data is shown for only information purposes. In this case, we can make the embedded form with the REQUEST data display-only.

A multitable form is, however, most useful when you want to place on one screen the related records from two or more tables (up to seven tables can be on one multitable form in Paradox 4.0). For example, consider the multitable form depicted in Figure 11-5b, which corresponds to the general relationships of forms in Figure 11-5a. The master form in this example is associated with the CUORDER table. There are two embedded forms on this master form. The top shaded area refers to a form for the CUSTOMER table, and contains the data about the customer on an order. In this case, this linkage is from an instance on the many side of a relationship to the one record on the one side (from CUORDER to CUSTOMER). In contrast, the bottom shaded area refers to a form (Form 2) for the REQUEST table. Here, the reference is from the one to the many side of a relationship. Form 2 for the REQUEST table is a multirecord form that displays multiple rows from the REQUEST table. For this CUORDER master form, this embedded REQUEST table form will show the multiple REQUEST records associated with (linked to) a given CUORDER record. The cursor for the screen shown in Figure 11-5b is on row 14, column 29, which is within the bottom embedded form. The status information on the bottom line of the screen indicates the embedded reference just described. Each embedded form must be designed before it can be placed on a master form.

The definition of the *multirecord form* embedded within this CUORDER form is shown in Figure 11-5c. A multirecord form contains the same fields from a specified number of rows from the same table, in this case eight records of the REQUEST table. In designing this form, we assumed that no more than eight line items would appear on any one customer order. In no case can a multirecord form exceed one screen in length.

Figure 11-5d shows the use of this CUORDER form for viewing a CUORDER record and the associated customer and request data. In view mode, <PageUp> and <PageDown> move forward and backward between master table records; the associated customer and request data change along with the master data. This is because the master and detailed forms were specified as linked, or synchronized, when the master form was created.

In Edit mode, you may enter or change values for any of the CUORDER table data on this form. For example, you could enter a new ORDER NO to correct a previous data entry mistake. This is an especially interesting editing example. In a multitable form, any change to a value in a linked field in a *master* table cascades to the associated field in the linked *detail* table (you **may not**, however, display and hence change the value of the linked field in a *detail* form). In this instance, changing the ORDER NO in the CUORDER table on this multitable form would automatically change the ORDER NO foreign key in each of the REQUEST records associated with it.

Paradox protects other forms of referential integrity as well. For example, you may not delete a master record on the one-side of a one-to-many relationship if there are any associated detail records. However, you may change (modify, add, or delete) records on the many-side of a relationship in the associated form. Such cascading changes and referential integrity control occur only through multitable forms, not when you edit data with forms for just one table.

While in edit mode, you can tell Paradox to insert a new CUORDER record by pressing <Insert>. When you fill in or change the CUST NO, Paradox will link the CUORDER record to the associated CUSTOMER table record. You move between the master and embedded forms by the ImageUp (<F3>) and ImageDown (<F4>) keys. So, after you enter or correct the CUST NO field, if you press <F3> the associated CUSTOMER form will be automatically filled in. You use <F3> and <F4> to move to the embedded REQUEST form to enter or change the associated line items on the order. Pressing <Delete> will erase the current record; for example, pressing <Delete> on any line in the embedded REQUEST form deletes that record from REQUEST. You cannot delete a master record if there are any detail records that depend on it. For example, you cannot delete a CUORDER record until you first delete all associated REQUEST records; however, you may delete a CUORDER record without first deleting the associated CUSTOMER record. In fact, deleting a CUORDER record would not delete the associated CUSTOMER record even if this were the only CUORDER record for that CUSTOMER. The link between the CUORDER record and the REQUEST records, the ORDER NO field, is automatically created from the form definitions. You press Do-It! to save the new record.

Although multirecord and multitable forms are very powerful and helpful data entry and viewing options, sometimes you cannot design a form to do exactly what you want. For example, an embedded table form may not itself be a multitable form; that is, multitable forms may not be nested. Many times, as in this situation, the limitations of Paradox forms can be overcome by creating intermediate tables, that is, by joining related tables, and then basing a form on the intermediate table. Alternatively, third normal form can be violated to overcome this limitation of Paradox. Smith (1991) discusses several tricks to circumvent limitations of Paradox multitable forms.

GENERATING CUSTOM REPORTS

The output from an information system is often a report produced on a printer or displayed on a PC or terminal screen. A report differs from a form in that a form is based on one row from one table, whereas a report typically lists many rows with summary statistics at specified control breaks. The design of report programs can, as with forms, take considerable programming. Fortunately, many DBMSs provide a report generator that, in a style similar to forms, allows you to lay out a report on the screen; the generator then produces the detailed code needed to process the report. We overview the report-generator features of PC-DBMSs by discussing both dBASE IV and Paradox 4.0.

dBASE IV Report Generator

The creation of custom dBASE reports was introduced in Chapter 2. The dBASE CREATE (or MODIFY) REPORT command invokes the same report-design screen as shown in Figure 2-34. The dBASE report-designer module creates a report format file containing commands that summarize data and print detailed, or record-level, data, group-level data, and overall summary data from the records of a file. The dBASE REPORT FORM command is used in a program or at the dot prompt to specify which stored report design to use and which records in a file to include in the report. A custom report may be directed to the screen, a printer, or a file.

As with forms, the code produced by the dBASE report generator contains dBASE proprietary language commands. Thus, you could write this from scratch, but the visual layout and automatic generation of the commands is much easier. You can edit a report code file to add commands or to include the report-printing code within a larger program.

A limitation of the dBASE report designer is that a report is associated with only one file or view. Thus, if you want a report that combines data from several database files, you must first join the related files into an intermediate file or create an equivalent query view. We will see in the next section that Paradox, in contrast, supports multiple-table reports. An intermediate table is redundant data, so it must be reconstructed each time the report is used if the original data is dynamic.

The illustrations in the section on "Report Writer Features for Database Processing" in Chapter 2 sufficiently show the capabilities of the dBASE report generator. You may want to review this section now. We repeat below in Figure 11-6 the customer order history report layout found in Figure 2-35. dBASE includes report layout features typical of report generators, including the following:

- Creating page headers and footers. For example, in Figure 11-6, the report title, page number, and date have been placed into the Header Band.

- Printing an introductory section on the first page of a report. (No such section is included in Figure 11-6.)

- Creating summarized fields of grand totals, averages, and so forth to appear at the end of a report. For example, we could place a grand total of the QTY ORDERED column into the Footer band in Figure 11-6.

- Calculating and printing summarized data for groups of records, possibly using nested groups. For example, in Figure 11-6 we have indicated in the Group 1 band that the total quantity ordered for each customer is to be displayed after printing all the detailed records for each customer.

- Adding lines, boxes, and other special symbols to make the report more readable. In Figure 11-6, for example, we have added special column headings, bars to separate columns, and a double underscore above the group total figures.

- Making page breaks occur at specified logical points—for example, after each subgroup of data.

- Creating calculated fields from file data and placing these within the report

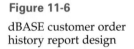

Figure 11-6

dBASE customer order history report design

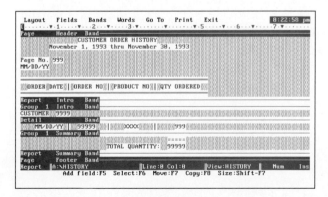

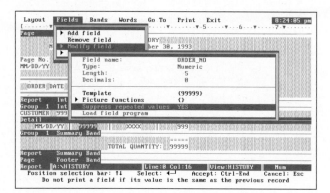

Figure 11-7

"Suppress repeated values" menu window

along with raw, detailed data. For example, if unit price were included in each detail row of the report defined in Figure 11-6, we could also place a calculated field of price times quantity on each detail line.

- Suppressing repeating values (that is, the same value occurring in sequential rows for the same field). This is shown in Figure 11-7 by choosing YES for the "Suppress repeated values" option on the Modify Field submenu within the Fields menu for the ORDER__NO field.

- Defining display formats for fields, so that separator characters or certain picture formats are used. In Figure 11-6, we used a specific format for the ORDER__DATE field.

- Selecting special print fonts and styles—for example, boldface, underline, italic, and subscripts.

dBASE supports two types of printed reports: column and form layout. A typical column report, like the report defined in Figures 11-6 and 11-7, contains one print line for each row from the associated database file or view, and data appear in perfectly aligned columns on the page. The report may include elements for a report introduction, header, footer, and summary, as illustrated with the different report bands. In contrast, a form layout allows you to place fields from a record in multiple print lines, and there may be no sense of columns of data on the page. A form layout is useful when printing data on preprinted forms, such as W-2 statements, invoice forms, or bank checks. Multiple records, however, are printed one after another with a form layout report.

Paradox Report Generator

Although the Paradox report generator has many of the same general capabilities as the dBASE report generator, there are a few additional, interesting features:

- Reports based on data from up to five tables

- Placing calculated fields computed from data in the report plus fields from other related tables (lookup tables)

- Wrapping long field values onto several lines

- Range output, which is actually a printing feature that allows you to select a specific set of pages to print if all you need to do is replace erroneous pages from a previously printed report

There is no exact equivalent to a multitable form with Paradox reports, but it is possible to show fields from other related, or lookup, tables. To use lookup tables, the report must be based on the table on the many-side of each relationship, called the *master* table, and lookup tables may not be nested. For example, a report for Pine Valley Furniture based on the REQUEST table could have fields from the CUORDER table (for instance, ORDER DATE) and from the PRODUCT table (for instance, DESCRIPT). There is a direct link from REQUEST to each of these tables, but the report could not refer to the CUSTOMER table, because it is only related to REQUEST by way of the CUORDER table. You could create a temporary table by joining the CUORDER and CUSTOMER tables and then implicitly, through lookup to the temporary table, data from CUORDER and CUSTOMER could appear on a custom report for the REQUEST table.

Reports are designed and changed via the Report option on the Paradox main menu. As with most report generators, you can do the following in Paradox:

- Create your own column headings and change the display format for fields.
- Place titles and other descriptive data at various locations on a report.
- Specify date and page numbers to appear in page headers or footers.
- Locate calculated fields on report lines. A calculated field is the result of horizontal, or record-level, arithmetic—for example, multiplying unit price by order quantity to get an extended price per printed line.
- Organize report detail lines into nested groups of records and print summary statistics on each group and on all records.
- Create free-form reports that are actually mailing labels, printed forms, form letters, or other styles that print one record per printed page or document.
- Force page breaks as desired.
- Define page width, length, and margins to handle different printers or pre-printed forms.
- Embed printer codes to obtain large, condensed, highlighted, and other special printing features.

Figure 11-8 contains a default tabular report layout for the REQUEST table. Because of the way the Paradox report designer shows the report layout, the last two digits of the page number are truncated on the right edge of the screen image. The layout is divided into bands, as is done in dBASE, as follows:

- *Report band*: This is the outer-most (implied) band in the report layout. Any text or fields in this band will print once for the whole report.
- *Page band*: Items in this band are printed on each page. Figure 11-8 includes page header information (some blank lines, date, title, and page number) that will print at the top of every page, and some blank lines for the bottom of every page.

Figure 11-8

Default Paradox REQUEST table report design

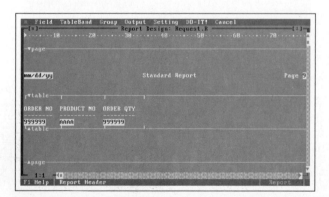

- *Table band*: This is the inner-most band (in any report layout), which shows the detailed data. Typically, as in the layout in Figure 11-8, the fields from the master table are placed in this band. Paradox has automatically placed these fields in the sequence specified in the table definition, with default formats based on field types.

The layout defines a precise way that data will be printed. For example, the blank lines are significant: they show spacing above and below the detail lines and at the top and bottom of every page. Various options exist to control, for example, how often certain column headings appear.

In Figure 11-6 we showed a dBASE custom tabular report layout for the customer order history report. Figures 11-9a and 11-9b show the equivalent Paradox custom report definition. These two figures show overlapping portions of the total report definition work surface. This layout introduces one additional type of band, the group band:

- *Group band*: A group band specifies how to arrange the detail table records. In this case, we defined three group bands on the CUST NO, ORDER DATE, and ORDER NO fields, respectively. That is, all the REQUEST records associated with the same CUST NO value are first sorted together and grouped in ascending sequence. Within each of these groups, records will print sorted first by ORDER DATE and second by ORDER NO.

There are several key elements to this report layout. First, the REQUEST table has been linked to the CUORDER table by the common field, ORDER NO. This allows the report to look up values from the associated CUORDER record for each REQUEST detail table record. In essence, this permits the report to be designed as if each REQUEST record also contained the field values from its associated CUORDER record. This, for example, allows us to have CUST NO as the first group field, even though CUST NO is not in the REQUEST table. The notation Cuorder−>CUST NO shows that this field comes from a linked table. ORDER NO has to be a primary key (that is, indexed and only one record per value) for Paradox to permit linking these tables.

Second, we defined a group header and footer for the CUST NO group. In the header we placed the label "CUSTOMER" and the CUST NO field for the group. This is one way to have a record value print only once per group. In the group footer we defined a total for the ORDER QTY field. Such summary values are the result of columnar arithmetic, so we can place the sum, average, count, max, and min values of a column in the group band (usually in the footer). The screen cursor in Figure 11-9b is on the summary field in this footer. (See the second status line

Figure 11-9

Custom Paradox customer order history report design

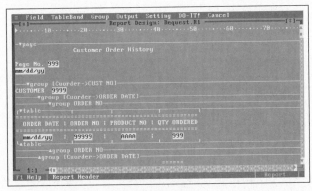

(a)   First section

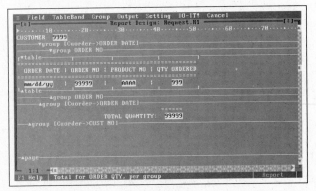

(b)   Last section

CUSTOMER ORDER HISTORY

Page No. 1
12/17/93

ORDER DATE	ORDER NO.	PRODUCT NO.	QTY. ORDERED
CUSTOMER 1069			
11/10/93	61397	O625	3
		O800	2
11/22/93	61396	O100	2
		TOTAL QUANTITY:	7
CUSTOMER 1256			
11/10/93	61398	M128	10
		O100	10
11/11/93	61399	M128	20
		TOTAL QUANTITY:	40
CUSTOMER 1273			
11/04/93	61384	B381	2
		M128	4
		R210	1
11/06/93	61390	T100	2
		T160	1
12/01/93	61391	B975	5
		B985	5
		M128	10
		TOTAL QUANTITY:	30
CUSTOMER 1278			
1/03/93	61394	E350	6
10/10/93	61392	M128	30
		O100	3
		T160	3
		TOTAL QUANTITY:	42
CUSTOMER 2345			
11/20/93	61395	B381	6
		B975	3
		B985	4
		TOTAL QUANTITY:	13
CUSTOMER 3211			
12/01/93	61400	E125	3
		E177	8
		E350	2
		TOTAL QUANTITY:	13
CUSTOMER 3434			
11/02/93	61401	E350	4
11/24/93	61402	E125	12
12/15/93	61403	E125	24
12/15/93	61403	E177	20
			60

(c) Sample report

of the screen, which says that the cursor is in this footer and that the field under the cursor is the "Total for ORDER QTY, per group.") This summary field was placed on the report via the Field option on the Report menu (the Report menu is activated by pressing <F10> when on the report layout workspace). The Field option allows the selection of regular (that is, actual table fields), summary (like this total quantity), calculated (for example, the product of two table fields), today's date or time, page number, and the record number for a detail line.

Third, as mentioned above, three groups were defined (up to 16 are allowed). The ORDER DATE and ORDER NO groups may seem superfluous (that is, there are no summary statistics for them), but they are necessary for one of the formatting features we want on this report. We do not want repeating values for ORDER DATE and ORDER NO to appear within the same customer group. Suppression of repeating values is controlled at the group, not the detail record, level within the Paradox report generator, so these two groups had to be defined to specify the suppression of repeating values on these fields.

Each group band can be defined in Paradox on any of three options:

- A field in the detail or any linked table; that is, as with CUST NO, a new group is formed each time the field changes value, and all records with the same value are sorted together for printing.

- Records with a range of values in a particular field. For example, we might want to group detail records by month or year for a date field.

- A specific number of records. For example, you can use this option when you are printing on a preprinted form that has a fixed number of lines of space.

It is not possible to define a group based upon changes in values for a calculated field. You can define group heading or summary data with any of these types of groups. Also, you can choose a sort direction for records within the group.

Fourth, since this report is based on the REQUEST table, we explicitly placed the CUORDER fields on this layout. That is, we started with the default layout in Figure 11-8 and linked the REQUEST table to the CUORDER table via the proper menu selections. Then, using the Field menu, we placed the desired CUORDER fields where we wanted them on the report layout. We also changed the default column widths and placement of fields within the report columns to create the desired format with column separators.

An example printed report for this layout definition appears in Figure 11-9c. Since the full REQUEST table was the master for this report layout, there is no date range. Rather, all sample REQUEST records are printed. We could have created an intermediate table with an insert data modification query to populate a table with just those REQUEST records that were within a desired date range. Then this report definition would have been defined relative to this intermediate table. In fact, we could have created a Paradox script that first emptied this intermediate table of any contents from a previous printing of the report and then populated the table with the desired data.

DATABASE SYSTEMS
FOR MICROSOFT WINDOWS

Two major computing trends are changing the nature of database management systems: graphical user interfaces and object-oriented programming. These two trends come together under Microsoft's Windows operating system and other similar environments (like OS/2, Motif, Apple System 7, and UNIX X-Windows).

Database systems for Microsoft Windows were just being released as we wrote this book, so an extensive explanation of this new type of database management system is not possible. A brief overview, however, is necessary since this new database technology presents significant conceptual differences from prior DBMSs, especially in the user interface and systems development environment.

We provide this overview by reviewing the salient features of one early market entry, Paradox for Windows, from Borland International (Borland International, 1992c). This is a suitable product to illustrate, since you have already seen examples using the DOS version of this product in Chapter 10 and earlier in this chapter. Also, the principles on which Paradox for Windows are based are illustrative of many Windows database systems.

Paradox for Windows combines elements of relational databases with object-oriented programming. That is, data are stored in simple tables with foreign and cross-reference keys linking these tables. Further, each field, record, table, form, report, and so on is considered an individual object, whose properties can be changed independently of other objects with which it is associated. Objects may be nested within each other, and methods may be assigned to an object. We will illustrate the object-oriented principles later in this section. You may want to refer to Chapter 5 on object-oriented data modeling, where we introduced concepts of object, method, encapsulation, and inheritance. We assume in this section that you have a basic familiarity with these object-oriented concepts. We also assume that you have some familiarity with Microsoft Windows.

The Windows Environment for Database Processing

As a Windows application, Paradox for Windows draws on standard Windows user interfaces. Consider Figure 11-10, which displays the contents of the CUSTOMER table from the Pine Valley Furniture database. We generated this view of the CUSTOMER table by selecting the typical Windows File menu option, and then selecting the Open and Table options from subsequent drop-down menus. We chose the CUSTOMER database table from a typical Windows scroll list window, and then Paradox displayed the CUSTOMER table contents in the window in the center of the screen shown in Figure 11-10. As with any window, you can resize and move this CUSTOMER table window on the screen.

Figure 11-10

CUSTOMER table display in Paradox for Windows

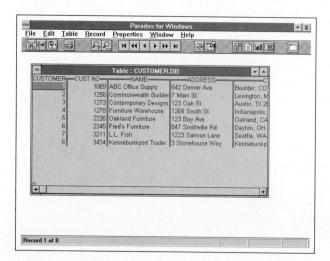

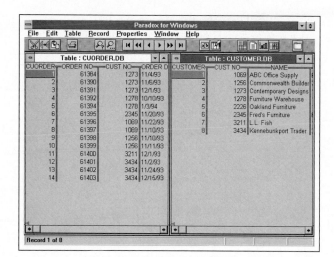

Figure 11-11

Two table windows

Multiple tables can be placed on the screen, each in its own window. Figure 11-11 shows the CUSTOMER and CUORDER tables as two tiled windows on the screen. The Windows menu is used to select the style of display: tiled (as shown), cascaded (overlapping in a stair-step fashion), or as icons (reduced to just a symbol). You can move between windows by placing the cursor in the desired window and clicking the left mouse button.

Figures 11-10 and 11-11 also illustrate the Paradox for Windows SpeedBar, the third row of icons at the top of the screen. When the cursor (not visible on the screen) is located over one of these icons, the location of the cursor is verified by a message in the lower left-hand corner of the screen. As in all Windows applications, you may highlight any part of the screen by dragging the mouse over a rectangular section. When you click the left mouse button on the Copy icon in the SpeedBar, the highlighted portion is copied to the Windows Clipboard. You could then switch to another Windows application (possibly a spreadsheet or word processing program) and paste this data onto the screen there. The Paradox SpeedBar changes depending on context; that is, there are different SpeedBars when you design a form and when you write a query. You may activate many SpeedBar functions, as in a DOS environment, by typing a certain function key or special key combination.

Linking with Other Applications

One Microsoft Windows feature implemented in Paradox for Windows is **OLE**, or **Object Linking and Embedding**. This Windows capability allows you to place an object from another Windows application (like a graphics package or word processor) onto a Paradox screen. Paradox acts as an OLE client (that is, Paradox can use objects from an OLE server application), but Paradox cannot, yet, be an OLE server application to other Windows software. This direct referencing of data in other applications relates to a Paradox for Windows concept called a *container object*. A **container object** is an object that completely surrounds all objects within it and controls the behavior of objects within it. For example, when you move, delete, or change the properties of a container object, all contained objects are similarly changed. An OLE object is a foreign object. That is, when you double-click on an OLE, the application associated with the OLE object is opened so you

Object Linking and Embedding (OLE): A Microsoft Windows capability in which an object from one application can be referenced from within another application.

Container object: In Paradox for Windows, an object that completely surrounds another object.

can manipulate this object (you cannot manipulate it in Paradox for Windows since this is not a Paradox object). This OLE feature greatly expands the possible contents of a database, form, or report. Container objects are used throughout Paradox for Windows, and they are not limited to only OLE.

Forms

Paradox for Windows forms are very similar to those we saw earlier in this chapter for the DOS version of Paradox. However, the object orientation of Paradox for Windows makes it much easier to design and customize a form. Each field, title, and feature of a form is an object, whose properties (for example, location, color, font, size, and associated methods) can be easily changed. Further, container objects on a form allow you to design a form with nested objects, which also makes it much easier to customize a screen display.

Figure 11-12 contains the default form for the CUSTOMER table from the Pine Valley Furniture database. This figure is generated from the form design desktop, so containers are indicated by the lines on the screen. As with Paradox for DOS, Paradox for Windows supports forms with embedded forms (in which case, the embedded form is simply treated as an object, like a field or text label). We will discuss here only a simple form, since we want to emphasize the object-oriented form-design features.

The third row of symbols on the form design desktop is the relevant SpeedBar. The icons in this SpeedBar cover cutting, copying, and pasting areas on the form; adding text and changing fonts; drawing boxes and adding graphics (like a company logo) on the form, including OLE objects; creating buttons (like an OK button with an associated method) for giving a user options; and creating multirecord forms. The rulers show exact placement of the form elements. In Figure 11-12, we see that there is a container object for each row of the table, which contains a text label object and a field object.

The form is modified by dragging objects to new locations and adding other objects. Further, we can easily change the properties of any object. We can inspect and then modify properties by first selecting the object and then calling the *Object Inspector* on that object. The Object Inspector displays the properties of the selected

Figure 11-12

Default Paradox for Windows CUSTOMER table form

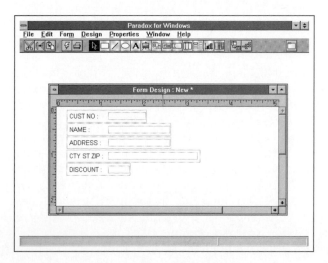

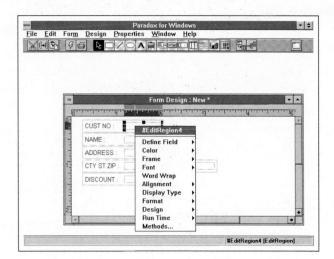

Figure 11-13

Object Inspector for
CUST NO field

object. In Figure 11-13 we have selected the customer number (CUST NO) field on the form. We did this by clicking the left mouse button twice with the cursor over this field. The first click selected the container that holds this field, and the second click chose the field itself. Then, we clicked the right mouse button to activate the Object Inspector. The menu lists the properties relevant to this type of object:

- *Define Field*: The name of the field to be displayed in this object
- *Color*: The background color of the object, which you can choose from a color palette when you select this menu option
- *Frame*: The style of frame, or pattern that surrounds an object (for example, single or double lines, and line thickness)
- *Font*: This is the type style for characters that appear in the object (for example, typeface, size, bold or italics, and color)
- *Word Wrap*: A yes/no choice on whether text in the object is word-wrapped at the right margin; if yes, the object can be horizontally resized
- *Alignment*: A specification of whether text in the object is to be right-justified, left-justified, centered, or both right- and left-justified
- *Display Type*: A specification of the general format of the display of field contents, including labeled, unlabeled, radio button, and check box
- *Format*: An indication of the format used to display field contents (for example, the style for a date field type)
- *Design*: Indicates if the object display grows or shrinks to fit the size of the data
- *Run Time*: This sets various parameters active when the form is used, like whether the field is read only and how to interpret the Tab key
- *Methods*: This is relevant to certain types of fields in which you want to associate certain methods (or programs written in the proprietary ObjectPAL language) with certain field values or button selections

The property menu displayed depends on the type of object you select, so Figure 11-13 is relevant for a database field object. Object Inspector allows you to quickly customize objects without programming, thus accelerating systems development.

Queries

You can create queries that involve from 1 to 24 tables in Paradox for Windows. The style of querying is Query-by-Example (QBE), as it is for Paradox for DOS. Because we have already covered QBE extensively in Chapter 10, we will show in this section only one example of a multiple-table query within the Windows query interface.

Figure 11-14 shows the Paradox for Windows version of the order history query illustrated in Figure 10-21 for Paradox for DOS. Figure 11-14a shows the initial query design desktop. We generated this screen by selecting the File menu, and then specifying that a new Query was desired. Paradox then displayed a list of database files from which we chose the CUORDER table. Each field has a default width in the query image, which is why the field names are truncated. You can change the space allocated for a field on the query image by placing the cursor over the vertical bar to the right of a field and, while holding down the left mouse button, dragging the field separator to expand or contract the field width. The small squares in each field are buttons. Holding down the left mouse button with

Figure 11-14

Order history query

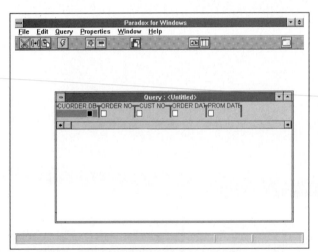

(a)　CUORDER table query image

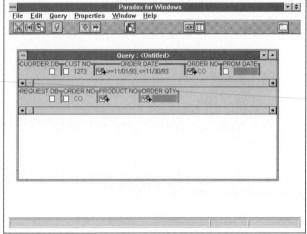

(b)　Query

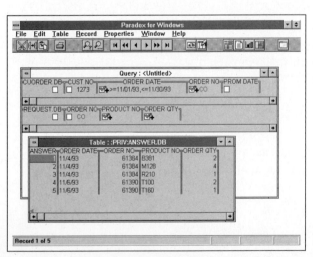

(c)　ANSWER table

the cursor on one of these buttons displays a menu of the different kinds of check marks we saw in Chapter 10. You then drag the highlight bar to the desired type of check mark, and release the mouse button to make your selection.

The cursor in Figure 11-14a is placed over the Add Table icon in the SpeedBar. Figure 11-14b shows the result of adding the REQUEST table to the desktop and filling in all the query image entries. In Figure 11-14b, we moved the CUST NO by dragging it left one column from where it was in Figure 11-14a. We entered the proper check marks, field qualifications, and example values for joining the two tables. Figure 11-14c shows the ANSWER table, which appears as a separate window. Not shown in this figure is how we changed the format of the ORDER NO column in the ANSWER table. The ORDER NO field has numeric format, with a default style that includes two decimal places. We changed this to an integer by clicking the right mouse button over any value in this column, and then choosing an integer data format. This again illustrates the powerful Object Inspector feature of Paradox for Windows.

Now is an appropriate time to reiterate that Paradox for Windows operates as a typical Windows application. For example, you will notice that each window in Figure 11-14 has buttons and a slide to scroll left and right and contains window maximize and minimize icons. A consistent interface across Windows applications greatly reduces the time required to learn any new Windows program.

Data Modeling

The last feature of Paradox for Windows we illustrate reinforces the benefits of using a graphical user interface in developing a database application. A **Paradox data model** is a graphical representation of the relationships between the tables you use in a document (form or report). The data model tells the document designer what fields can be placed on the document and the linkages between these fields. A data model is an easy way to tell Paradox for Windows what it needs to know to build a multitable form or report. The data modeling capability of Paradox is a form of visual programming in which Paradox uses an E-R type diagram to generate code for a form or report definition.

Consistent with the relational data model underlying Paradox, tables can be linked in a data model only by common fields in the tables. You can specify only binary 1:1, 1:*M*, or *M*:1 relationships. A 1:1 (or *M*:1) relationship in Paradox data modeling is called a *single-valued relationship*, in which one record can relate to

Paradox data model: A graphical representation of the relationships between tables used in a form or report. This data model is used to visually lay out data required during form or report design.

```
              PVF CUSTOMER ORDER

     ORDER NO.:  61384      CUSTOMER NO.:  1273

     NAME:                  Contemporary Designs
     ADDRESS:               123 Oak St.
     CITY STATE ZIP:        Austin, TX 28384

     ORDER DATE: 11/04/93   PROMISED DATE: 11/21/93

     PRODUCT     DESCRIPTION     QUANTITY       UNIT
       NO.                        ORDERED      PRICE

       M128       Bookcase          4         200.00
       B381       Cabinet           2         150.00
       R210       Table             1         500.00
```

(a) Order entry screen

Figure 11-15
Sample customer order

(continues)

(continued)

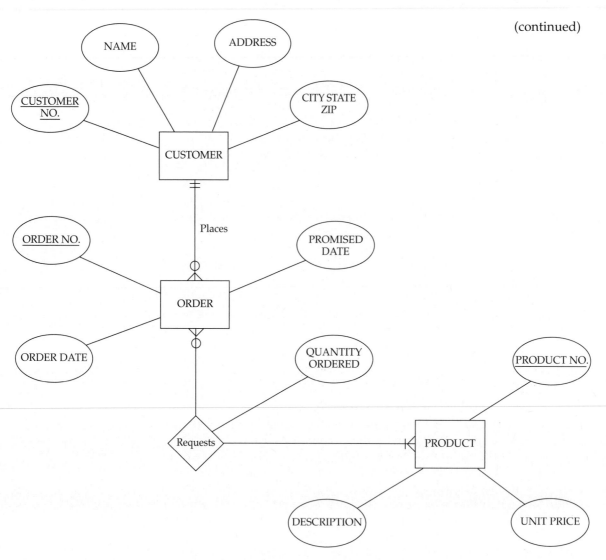

(b) E-R diagram for order entry screen

zero or one record in the other table. A 1:*M* relationship is called a *multivalued relationship*, in which one record can relate to zero, one, or many records in the other table.

We can use the data modeling capability of Paradox for Windows to help in the design of a form to enter new customer orders at Pine Valley Furniture. We repeat in Figure 11-15 the contents of Figure 2-6, which illustrates a possible layout and E-R diagram for a customer order entry screen. As shown in Figure 11-15b, this form includes data from CUSTOMER, ORDER, REQUEST, and PRODUCT entities.

Figure 11-16 shows where we start in defining such a data model for building a customer order entry form. This figure was generated by first selecting the File menu, and choosing to build a New object, and finally a Form object. The CUORDER table was then selected from the scroll list on the left of the screen, and Paradox placed an icon for this table in the design area on the right of the screen. We chose the CUORDER table first since this is the master table for the

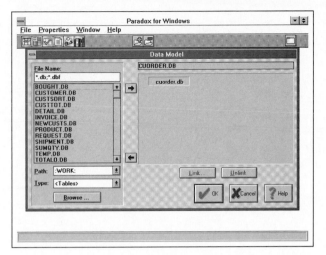

Figure 11-16

Starting to build a data model

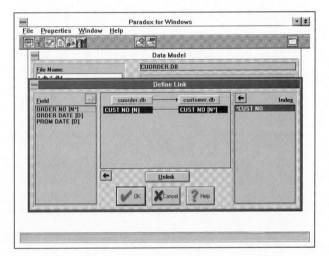

Figure 11-17

Data model to connect CUORDER and CUSTOMER tables

form; that is, as in Paradox for DOS, the master table is the starting point of the form. We next selected the CUSTOMER table from the scroll list. We then connected the CUORDER and CUSTOMER tables. We eventually created the screen that appears in Figure 11-17. Paradox determined that this was a single-valued link. Initially, Paradox tried to link the two tables by the primary keys of each table. We then chose the CUST NO field from the CUORDER table in the field list on the left of the screen, since this is the proper linking field.

We added the other two tables (REQUEST and PRODUCT) needed for the customer order screen to the data model and linked them as done above. The final data model is shown in Figure 11-18. This clearly shows the *M*:1 relationships from CUORDER to CUSTOMER and from REQUEST to PRODUCT and the 1:*M* relationship from CUORDER to REQUEST. When we click the mouse over the OK button, Paradox automatically produces the initial form layout of Figure 11-19.

We then used the object-oriented features of the form designer to drag the containers around the layout, to change field labels, to add a screen title, and to modify the width of columns and number of rows in the multirecord grid on the screen. The final form design we created is shown from the form-design desktop in Figure 11-20. Figure 11-21 shows this form with some sample data. In Figure

Figure 11-18

Final data model for customer order form

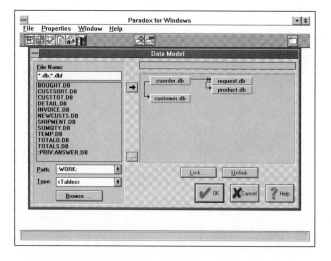

Figure 11-19

Initial customer order form design

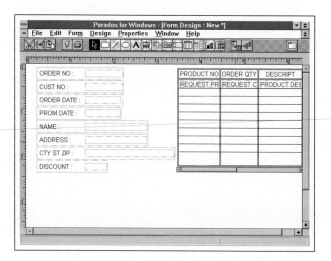

Figure 11-20

Final customer order form design

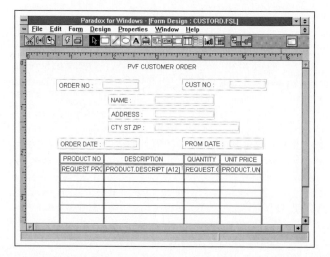

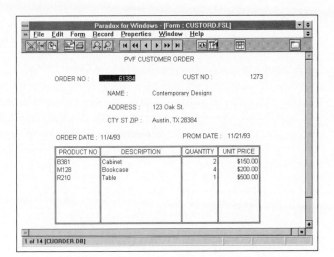

Figure 11-21

Sample customer order screen

11-21, the ORDER NO field is currently highlighted. We can press <PageUp> and <PageDown> to move between CUORDER records. As we do so, all the data changes accordingly. If we were to change the CUST NO field value, different NAME, ADDRESS, and CITY ST ZIP field values would appear, those for the new CUST NO value. Values may not be entered in these associated fields. Likewise, once a PRODUCT NO is entered in a row of the embedded table, the associated DESCRIPTION and UNIT PRICE field values are displayed. Only the QUANTITY value can be entered along with the PRODUCT NO.

SUMMARY

A DBMS is a central technology in the development of modern information systems. A DBMS by itself, however, is not sufficient for you to design easy-to-understand user interfaces. Many system developers also use screen- (or form-) designer modules and report-generator modules to more quickly define custom user interfaces. In this chapter we have reviewed the essential features of screen- and report-design modules of dBASE and Paradox to illustrate the power of these components of a database development environment. Such custom screen- and report-design tools are available with most DBMSs, whether on a PC, minicomputer, or mainframe computer.

We have also illustrated in this chapter how the modern database development environment is changing as graphical user interfaces (GUIs) and object-oriented programming emerge in DBMSs. In systems development, GUI interfaces and object-oriented programming principles are creating a more visual paradigm for interaction with database systems. An example of this is the data modeling feature of Paradox for Windows. With data modeling, the designer of a form or report draws a chart similar to an entity-relationship diagram on the screen. Paradox then automatically generates a document with the data from this chart in a format consistent with the relationships between entities. Such a visual scheme for designing forms and reports suggests opportunities for a more visual environment for other database functions, like querying.

We have now finished our review of relational database systems. We have seen in Chapters 8–11 that relational technology is not static. It is evolving with the whole computer industry. SQL, Xbase, and QBE remain popular, yet changing, standards for relational systems. DBMS vendors are adding to and adapting these standards with better graphical capabilities, programming concepts, and tools that support more rapid systems development.

Not all database systems installed in organizations today, however, are relational. Many information systems were developed in the 1960s–1980s with DBMSs that followed the hierarchical and network data models. These "legacy" technologies are an important part of current information processing environments. We turn our attention in the next section of the text to this important installed base of database systems.

CHAPTER REVIEW

Key Terms

Code generator
Container object

Object Linking and
Embedding (OLE)

Paradox data model

REVIEW QUESTIONS

1. Define each of the following terms:
   a. multirecord form
   b. multitable form
   c. master table
   d. detail table
   e. dBASE window
   f. Object Inspector
   g. single-valued relationship
   h. multivalued relationship
   i. graphical user interface
2. Explain how you might overcome the limitation of a form or report designer that restricts a single form or report to only one database file.
3. Discuss the advantages and disadvantages of storing data entry integrity controls with a form rather than with the field and record definitions, as is done in dBASE IV.
4. Explain the differences between a dBASE IV window and the concept of a window in the Microsoft Windows operating environment.
5. Discuss the advantages of a multitable form over several single-table forms for the entry of a business transaction.
6. Explain the purpose of a display-only form in Paradox for DOS.
7. For a report generator (like the standard dBASE IV report generator) that requires that a report design include fields from only *one* database table or view, discuss the relative advantages and disadvantages of creating an intermediate table versus a query view from the multiple tables required for a report.
8. List the different types of bands that may appear on a Paradox report design and briefly explain the purpose of each.
9. Discuss the benefits of the Object Linking and Embedding (OLE) feature of Microsoft Windows for database processing.

PROBLEMS AND EXERCISES

1. Match the following terms to the appropriate definitions.

   ____ form

   ____ code generator

   a. a screen display that requires more than one full screen of data

   b. a feature of Paradox for Windows that shows and permits editing the properties of a database object

____ container object

c. a stylized display of data from one database record and possibly other related records

____ Object Inspector

d. a module of a DBMS that produces the program instructions that define a form, report, or menu

____ field suppress

e. in Paradox for Windows, an object that completely surrounds another object

____ multiple-page form

f. the ability to stop printing repeating values of the same field in a report definition

2. Design and create a Paradox report to show product order history. This report should be similar to the one in Figures 11-6 and 11-7, except that the detailed data should be grouped by product number instead of customer number. In this report, show group totals *and* a grand total of quantity ordered. Include product description as well as product number in the group header.

3. Develop the screen definition of Figure 11-2 in dBASE. Augment this form to include another row of data that is a calculated field of the UNIT PRICE times the QUANTITY ON HAND.

4. In Chapter 9 on dBASE we introduced the SET RELATION command. Investigate how this command might be used to build a dBASE form that contains related rows from both CUSTOMER and CUORDER tables. That is, rather than creating a temporary table that joins these two tables, can SET RELATION be used to simplify creating a form involving two related tables?

5. Design a Paradox 4.0 multiform that shows customer order data about a particular product. For each product, show the product number and description, and for each order associated with the product, show the order number, quantity ordered, and promised delivery date. *Hint:* First decide which table is associated with the master form and which tables are associated with any embedded forms. Also, remember that an embedded form may not have an embedded form within it.

6. Redesign the customer order history report of Figure 11-6 (dBASE) or Figure 11-9 (Paradox) to show orders in reverse chronological order and to calculate a grand total of quantity ordered across all customers.

7. Use Paradox for Windows with the Pine Valley Furniture database to show the names of customers who have bought both products E350 and T160.

8. On the Answer table to the query for Problem 7 above, use the Object Inspector to change the name column so that values are centered, not left-justified, in the column.

9. In the customer order form of Figure 11-20, use the Object Inspector to change the background color of the column headings of the table of product data.

10. Use Paradox for Windows to develop the same form described in Problem 5.

REFERENCES

Borland International. 1992a. *Using dBASE IV*. Scotts Valley, Calif.: Ashton-Tate, a Borland International, Inc. Company.

Borland International. 1992b. *Paradox, Version 4.0, User's Guide*. Scotts Valley, Calif.: Borland International, Inc.

Borland International. 1992c. *Paradox for Windows, Version 1.0, User's Guide*. Scotts Valley, Calif.: Borland International, Inc.

Smith, B. J. 1991. "Multi-Table Form Tricks." *Data Based Advisor* 9 (Nov.):39–44.

Data Administration and Distributed Databases

Apple Computer, Inc.

DISTRIBUTED DATABASES FOR DISTRIBUTED CONTROL

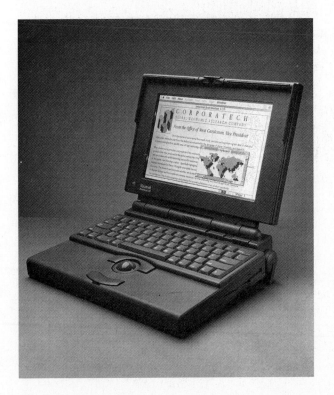

Part IV consists of two chapters. In Chapter 12 we describe data administration, which is the custodian of an organization's data and is responsible for developing procedures to protect and control data resources. In Chapter 13 we describe the important client/server architecture and distributed databases. The topics in these chapters are especially relevant for a large, global firm such as Apple Computer Corporation. In the past few years, Apple Computer has grown from a $2 billion company to a company with over $6 billion in annual sales. Its manufacturing operations, information systems, users, and databases are spread across the globe.

Apple Computer (headquartered in Cupertino, California) provides an excellent example of a distributed database environment. To illustrate some of the issues described in Part IV, consider the Apple Computer assembly plants located in Cork, Ireland, and Singapore, Malaysia. Control of the assembly process is achieved through a three-layer, computer-based architecture.

The first layer consists of compact Macintosh computers that are used as workstations on the shop floor. These workstations enable the capture of data that reflects up-to-the-minute assembly and workflow activities. The workstations enable such tasks as optically scanning UPC labels on component parts in order to identify them by part number. Other tasks include collecting and passing information about the status of quality-control testing during the production process.

Data are passed to and from the second layer, which consists of Macintosh II computers serving as communication servers. These servers continually poll the first-layer workstations in a round-robin fashion. Standardized information requests are passed as SQL commands to the server. This enables the maintenance of a database that stores the status of jobs in process as well as job-routing information.

The servers also pass data to and from the third layer of this architecture. This upper layer is a Digital Equipment Corporation VAX host computer. While the number varies, there are an average of eight workstations to each Macintosh II server and 18 servers. The number of servers is scheduled to triple in the future.

The INGRES database management system is used to maintain the job and routing database files. These database files are stored on both the VAX host and the Macintosh II communication servers; thus it is necessary to maintain the consistency of the data across these platforms. As the factory receives update information affecting the manufacture of products to fill customer orders, the host computer database is updated in real time. As a result, shop floor control is also in real time. This provides optimal flexibility in terms of meeting customer demands.

By redundantly storing the databases at two levels in this architecture, manufacturing can continue to be supported whenever the host computer is unavailable. In such a situation, the redundant databases on the Macintosh II servers provide necessary job-control and routing information for assembly operations in a manufacture-for-stock production environment. This system enables Apple to maximize use of the production assembly facilities.

12

Data Administration

LEARNING OBJECTIVES

After studying this chapter, you should be able to:

- Define the key terms *data administration*, *database administration*, *data steward*, *repository*, *locking*, *versioning*, *deadlock*, *transaction*, and *encryption*.
- List several major functions of data administration and of database administration.
- Describe where data administration should report in an organization and the reasons for this reporting relationship.
- Describe the role of an information repository and how it is used by data administration.
- Describe the function of a database management system (DBMS) and the major components of a DBMS.
- Compare the optimistic and pessimistic systems of concurrency control.
- Describe the problem of database security, and list five techniques that are used to enhance security.
- Describe the problem of database recovery, and list four basic facilities that are included with a DBMS to recover databases.

INTRODUCTION

Organizations are increasingly recognizing that data and information are resources that are too valuable to be managed casually. According to a study conducted by the Center for the Study of Data Processing of Washington University (Herbert and Hartog, 1986), data utilization (that is, "assuring that data are made available to the right person in a timely manner") is the second most important issue in MIS management (the first is aligning MIS with business goals). Further, this issue moved from ninth place (1984) to fourth place (1985) and then to its second-place position.

There are many causes of poor data utilization:

1. Multiple definitions of the same data entity and inconsistent representations of the same data elements in separate databases, which makes linking data across different databases hazardous
2. Missing key data elements, which makes existing data useless
3. Low levels of data quality due to inappropriate sources of data or timing of data transfers from one system to another
4. Not knowing what data exist, where to find them, and what they really mean

One organizational response to the data utilization issue is to create a new function called *data administration*. The person who heads this function is called the *manager of data administration* or, more popularly, the *data administrator*. Actual experience with computer databases has established a fundamental principle: The data administration function is *essential* to the success of managing the data resource. Establishing this function is an indication of top management's commitment to data resource management. When the data administration function is not established, or when it is weakly established, the chances of success of the database approach are significantly diminished.

DATA ADMINISTRATION FUNCTIONS

Databases are shared resources that belong to the entire enterprise, not the property of a single function or individual within the organization. Data administration is the custodian of the organization's data, in much the same sense that the controller is custodian of the financial resources. Like the controller, data administration must develop procedures to protect and control the resource. Also, data administration must resolve disputes that may arise when data are centralized and shared among users, and must play a significant role in deciding where data will be stored and managed.

Data administration is responsible for a wide range of functions, including database planning, analysis, design, implementation, maintenance, and protection. Also, data administration is responsible for improving database performance and for providing education, training, and consulting support to users. The data administrator must interact with top management, users, and computer applications specialists.

Selecting the data administrator and organizing the function are extremely important. The data administrator must be a highly skilled manager and must be capable of resolving differences that normally arise when significant change is introduced into an organization. The data administrator should be a respected, senior-level middle manager selected from within the organization, rather than a technical computer expert or a new individual hired for the position.

Several concepts, methods, and tools are available to help data administration manage the data resources to achieve high utilization (as defined above). A database and a database management system (DBMS) are fundamental components of a data administrator's portfolio. A repository or data dictionary/directory is needed so that all database users know exactly what the word *data* means, what data are available where, who controls access to the data, how data are stored, when they are maintained, and where they are used. The use of a repository is covered in considerable detail later in this chapter.

Data Administration, Database Administration, and Data Stewards

The manager of the data administration function requires a high level of both managerial and technical skills. On the one hand, this person must be capable of enlisting cooperation from users, who may at first resist the idea of giving up their private data to a shared database. Also, these users must be convinced of the benefits of adhering to a set of standard definitions and procedures for accessing the database. On the other hand, the data administrator must be capable of managing a technical staff and dealing with technical issues such as query optimization and concurrency control.

To resolve the managerial versus technical complexity of data administration, numerous organizations today are creating both data administration and database administration functions. **Data administration** is a high-level function that is responsible for the overall management of data resources in an organization, including maintaining corporate-wide data definitions and standards. **Database administration** is a technical function that is responsible for physical database design and for dealing with technical issues such as security enforcement, database performance, and backup and recovery. We provide a more detailed discussion of the functions of data administration and database administration and their organizational placement in the next section.

Recently the concept of a data steward has emerged in the data resource management field. A **data steward** manages a specific logical data resource or entity (for example, customer, product, or facility) for all business functions and data processing systems that originate or use data about the assigned entity. A data steward is the focal point for coordinating all data definitions, quality-control and improvement programs, access authorization, and planning for the data entity for which he or she is responsible. Data stewards may be coordinated by the data administrator or may collectively satisfy the responsibilities of data administration.

Usually a data steward is a user-manager from a business department that originates data about a data entity or has primary interest in that entity. The intent of data stewardship is to distribute (not decentralize) data administration to those most knowledgeable of and dependent on high-quality data for key data entities.

An enterprise information model would be used to identify the key data entities to be assigned to data stewards. A data steward manages an enterprise data entity not just for the good of his or her own area of the organization but also to promote organizational data sharing and access. When the organization distinguishes local data from organizational data, a particular unit may appoint data stewards for entities local to that unit.

Data administration: A high-level function that is responsible for the overall management of data resources in an organization, including maintaining corporate-wide definitions and standards.

Database administration: A technical function that is responsible for physical database design and for dealing with technical issues such as security enforcement, database performance, and backup and recovery.

Data steward: Manages a specific logical data resource or entity for all business functions and data processing systems that originate or use data about the assigned entity.

Functions of Data and Database Administration

In this section we delineate the functions of data administration and database administration in greater detail. We use the concept of a database system life cycle to provide a framework for this discussion. As shown in Figure 12-1, there are six stages in the life cycle of a typical database system:

1. Database planning
2. Database analysis

Figure 12-1

Stages in a database system life cycle

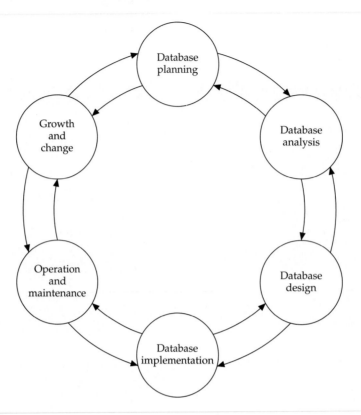

3. Database design

4. Database implementation

5. Operation and maintenance

6. Growth and change

Although these functions are performed more or less in the order given above, there is considerable interaction among the various stages, as Figure 12-1 shows. Also, the manner in which these functions are performed varies from one organization to the next and is influenced by the use of specific methodologies and CASE tools. (We discuss CASE tools later in this chapter.)

Following is a brief discussion of the major stages in the database system life cycle.

Planning   The purpose of database planning is to develop a strategic plan for database development that supports the overall organizational business plan. Although the responsibility for developing this plan rests with top management, data administration provides major inputs to the planning process. Database planning was described in Chapter 3. The major output from database planning is an enterprise data model.

Analysis   The process of analysis is concerned with identifying data entities currently used by the organization, precisely defining these entities and their relationships, and documenting the results in a form that is convenient to the design effort that is to follow. In addition to identifying current data, requirements analysis attempts to identify new data elements (or changes to existing data elements) that will be required in the future. We described the processes and tools of analysis in Chapters 4 and 5. The result of analysis is a conceptual data model.

Design   The purpose of database design is to develop a logical database architecture that will meet the information needs of the organization, now and in the future. There are two stages in database design: logical design (described in Chapter 6) and physical design (described in Chapter 7). Although the data administrator has primary responsibility for database design, he or she must work closely with users and system specialists in performing these design activities. The output of logical design is normalized relations. The result of physical design is a database definition for a particular DBMS.

Implementation   Once the database design is completed, the implementation process begins. The first step in implementation is the creation (or initial load) of the database. The database is simply an empty superstructure until it has been "populated" with actual data values. Database administration manages the loading process and resolves any inconsistencies that arise during this process.

Operation and Maintenance   Database operation and maintenance is the ongoing process of updating the database to keep it current. Examples of updating include adding a new employee record, changing a student address, and deleting an invoice. Maintenance includes activities such as adding a new field, changing the size of an existing field, and so on.

Users are responsible for updating and maintaining the database; data administration is responsible for developing procedures that ensure that the database is kept current and that it is protected during update operations. Specifically, data administration must perform the following functions:

1. Assign responsibility for data collection, editing, and verification
2. Establish appropriate update schedules
3. Establish an active and aggressive quality-assurance program, including procedures for protecting, restoring, and auditing the database

Growth and Change   The database is a model of the organization. As a result, it is not static but reflects the dynamic changes in the organization and its environment. Data administrators must plan for change, such as adding new record types, accommodating growth, and so on. They must also monitor the performance of the database (both efficiency as well as user satisfaction) and take whatever corrective actions are required to maintain a high level of system performance and success.

Figure 12-2 presents a breakdown of the major functions within each of the life-cycle phases. This figure also shows which of the functions are normally performed by data administration and which are typically performed by database administration. Notice that data administration is normally responsible for the following functions: database planning, conceptual design, and logical database design. Database administration is typically responsible for physical database design and much of database implementation, operation, and maintenance. Several functions, such as specifying database access policies, conducting user training, and managing growth and change, may be the responsibility of both groups.

The actual allocation of responsibilities between data administration and database administration varies from one organization to the next. No doubt the definition of each of these functions will continue to evolve as organizations gain experience with information resource management.

Figure 12-2

Functions of data administration

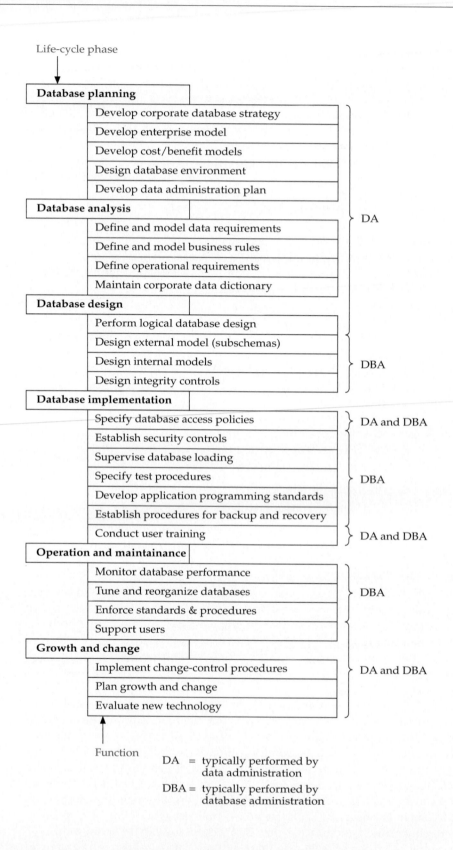

Life-cycle phase

Database planning
| Develop corporate database strategy |
| Develop enterprise model |
| Develop cost/benefit models |
| Design database environment |
| Develop data administration plan |

Database analysis
| Define and model data requirements |
| Define and model business rules |
| Define operational requirements |
| Maintain corporate data dictionary |

} DA

Database design
| Perform logical database design |
| Design external model (subschemas) |
| Design internal models |
| Design integrity controls |

} DBA

Database implementation
| Specify database access policies | } DA and DBA
| Establish security controls |
| Supervise database loading |
| Specify test procedures |
| Develop application programming standards |
| Establish procedures for backup and recovery |

} DBA

| Conduct user training | } DA and DBA

Operation and maintainance
| Monitor database performance |
| Tune and reorganize databases |
| Enforce standards & procedures |
| Support users |

} DBA

Growth and change
| Implement change-control procedures | } DA and DBA
| Plan growth and change |
| Evaluate new technology |

Function

DA = typically performed by data administration

DBA = typically performed by database administration

Organizing the Data Administration Function

This section addresses three key management issues that arise in organizing the data administration function. The way in which top management resolves these issues is a good indication of their acceptance of information resource management. The three issues are (1) initiating the data administration function, (2) selecting the data administrator, and (3) integrating the data administration function into the organization (including decentralized and other types of structures).

Initiating the Data Administration Function   Data administration and its primary tool, the repository (or data dictionary), are often viewed as extraneous and unessential to data management, yet nothing could be further from the truth. Data administration produces valuable results, but those anxious to have access to data often see it as a bottleneck or extra step in that process. Data administration is developed over several years and usually evolves from a system-planning or project management function.

Wherever data administration obtains its start, several steps are essential to ensure its success from the beginning:

1. Obtain management support for and commitment to the rationale for the function and its role in database development. This may require conducting a survey of other organizations to identify practical justification for data administration. Also essential here is determining the relationship of data administration and any data system planning group(s).

2. Determine the requirements for a repository, and acquire financial support to buy or develop a repository appropriate for the database environment.

3. Train the data administration staff in database planning, database trends, data security and recovery, and other areas in which the staff will be involved.

4. Develop standards of operation (for example, data-naming conventions) and measures of performance (for example, meeting project deadlines) for data administration staff so they recognize that their job has professional practices and that their good performance can be identified and rewarded.

Many organizations acquire a DBMS before a data administration function is (formally) established, yet logic would indicate that this puts the cart before the horse (or the resource before the manager). In such an organization, the DBMS is used to implement a series of unrelated applications that do not share data. Thus, expectations for database management may not be high, and user experience may not be conducive to change. The practical consequence of a situation like this is that the data administration function does not usually start with a clean slate. Database design practices, data ownership, multiple databases, multiple or no data dictionaries, and an essentially active but unorganized data management function are very likely to be already in place when the data administration function is started. The first chore then is to convince those with vested interests that methods must be changed. Thus, above all, data administration is an agent of change that must be sensitive to organizational history and politics, as well as existing technology, systems, and attitudes.

Because of the inertia of past practices, data administration often begins with a new, major application of system planning, and then slowly integrates other data and systems under its management. A phased introduction is almost always the wisest way to start the data administration function.

Selecting the Data Administrator A review of the functions of the data administrator (see Figure 12-2) indicates that this person must possess an unusual collection of managerial, analytical, and technical skills. In reviewing the full range of responsibilities, however, it is apparent that the job is more managerial than technical. The data administrator must perform the following typical managerial functions:

1. *Planning:* Developing a comprehensive plan for the organization's data resource

2. *Organizing:* Organizing and staffing the data administration function

3. *Supervising:* Supervising the data administration staff

4. *Communicating:* Communicating with managers, users, and computer specialists

5. *Controlling:* Developing procedural controls for maintaining and protecting the data resources

Thus, the organization should define the data administrator position as a management position. The ideal candidate is a person with at least middle-management experience (line or staff), a broad knowledge and "sense" of the enterprise (including its politics), and stature as a manager. Such a person requires some familiarity with computer-based information systems but does not have to be a computer or database expert.

Other candidates for the data administrator position might include business analysts, user-oriented systems analysts, or a data administrator with relevant experience in another, similar organization. However, a manager with experience in the enterprise is usually preferred.

Highly technical computer specialists such as system programmers are not usually good candidates for data administrator. Selecting such persons normally results from an overly narrow, technical definition of the data administration function. Most of these individuals do not have the managerial experience, aptitude, or desire to be a data administrator; however, they might be assigned to the data administration staff.

Integrating the Data Administration Function In most organizations today, the data administration function is located somewhere within the information systems organization. Where that function is placed within the IS organization varies from one enterprise to another, depending on the role and tasks assigned to data administration. In some organizations, data administration is viewed as a narrow technical function and is assigned to support services or even to computer operations (this indicates that, regardless of its title, the role is really that of database administration). In other organizations, data administration is viewed as a high-level managerial function that reports directly to the chief information officer.

If an organization wishes to manage information as a resource, it must place data administration at a high level within the IS organization. Figure 12-3 shows one such organization structure, in which data administration reports directly to the chief information officer (CIO). In this example of an organization, the functions shown within data administration are data analysis, database design, and database administration.

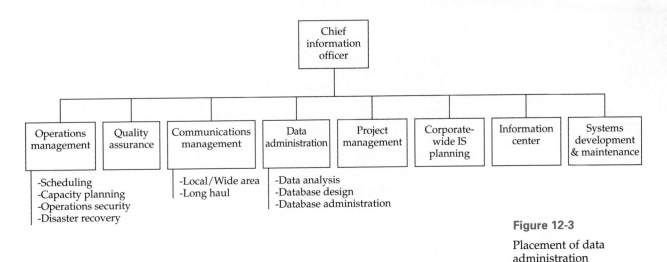

Figure 12-3

Placement of data administration

DATA ADMINISTRATION TOOLS

Data administration uses a variety of computer software tools to support its various activities. In this section we describe three related software products that are used by data administrators: repositories, CASE tools, and database management systems. The relationship among these components of the database environment was introduced in Chapter 1 (see Figure 1-13).

Repositories

Data administrators are responsible for managing one of the most important databases in the enterprise—the information repository, or metadata that describes an organization's data and data processing resources. Information repositories are replacing data dictionaries in many organizations. While data dictionaries are simple data-element documentation tools, information repositories are used by data administrators and other information specialists to manage the total information processing environment.

Repository Environment   The role of an information repository is shown in Figure 12-4. This diagram shows the components of a repository and the environment in which a repository is used. In the application development environment, people (either information specialists or end users) use CASE tools, high-level languages, and other tools to develop new applications. In the production environment, people use applications to build databases, keep the data current, and extract data from databases.

An **information repository** combines information about an organization's business information and its application portfolio (Bruce, Fuller, and Moriarty, 1989). Business information is the data stored in the corporate databases, while the application portfolio consists of the application programs that are used to manage business information. The information repository describes business information and applications in terms of components called *objects* (as described in Chapter 5).

An **information repository dictionary system (IRDS)** is a computer software tool that is used to manage and control access to the information repository. It provides facilities for recording, storing, and processing descriptions of an organ-

Information repository: Stores metadata that describes an organization's data and data processing resources. Manages the total information processing environment. Combines information about an organization's business information and its application portfolio.

Information repository dictionary system (IRDS): A computer software tool that is used to manage and control access to the information repository.

Figure 12-4

Role of an information
repository

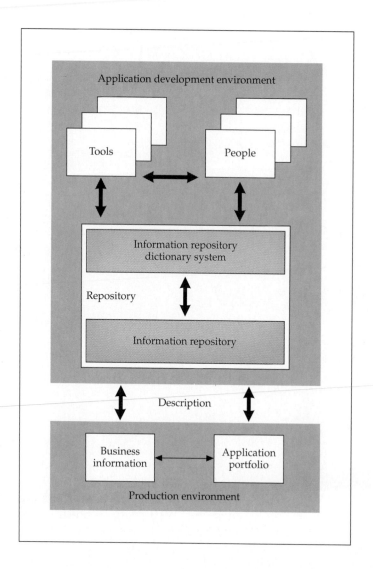

ization's significant data and data processing resources (Lefkovitz, 1985). The term
repository is used by some vendors to refer to the combination of the information
repository and the IRDS.

Using a Repository The repository is an essential tool for data administration
and is used by both data administration and database administration throughout
the entire database system life cycle. An information repository serves as a source
of information for each of the following:

1. Users who must understand data definitions, business rules, and relationships among data objects

2. Automated CASE tools that are used to specify and develop information
   systems

3. Applications that access and manipulate data (or business information) in
   the corporate databases

An organization may use a repository in one of three modes, depending on the nature of the repository and the objectives of the organization.

1. *Passive mode.* The repository is primarily a documentation tool used by people, not by automated tools or applications.

2. *Active-in-development.* The repository is used by people as a documentation tool and by automated development tools (such as CASE tools) during application development. That is, automated tools make use of the repository to generate data structures, documentation, databases, models, and other components of the application environment. As an illustration, when a database analyst develops an entity-relationship diagram using a CASE tool, the E-R diagram is stored in the repository. However, the repository is not used to actively support application programs in the production environment.

3. *Active-in-production.* In this mode, the repository is more than a documentation and development tool. It is the mechanism through which application programs obtain metadata in the production environment. All data integrity, data validation, and security-access rules are enforced through the information repository, and changes to these rules are made in the repository.

Many organizations use a repository initially in the passive mode, then progress to the active-in-development mode, and finally go on to the active-in-production mode. The active-in-production mode is preferred, since all components of the information systems environment have a single, centralized source of organizational metadata.

CASE Tools

If you review the functions of data administration (Figure 12-2), you will notice that data administrators (and database administrators) are responsible for numerous tasks that involve data modeling and design. Fortunately, CASE tools are now available to automate or at least assist in the performance of many of these tasks.

Computer-aided software engineering (CASE) is technology for automating software and database development and maintenance tasks (McClure, 1989). CASE tools are designed to support (or automate) the various stages of the system development life cycle, as shown in Figure 12-5.

Figure 12-6 presents a sample problem to be addressed using the diagramming facilities of CASE tools. This problem involves a simple video store that rents videos to customers on a cash basis. The analyst is to develop a data flow diagram and entity-relationship diagram based on this description.

Two such diagrams are shown in Figure 12-7. Figure 12-7a shows a level 0 (or high-level) data flow diagram. In this diagram, sources and destinations of data (such as CUSTOMER) are represented by squares. Processes such as "RENT TAPE TO CUSTOMER" are represented by rounded rectangles, and data flows are represented by arrows. Finally, a database (such as RENTAL DATABASE) is represented by an open-ended rectangle. Compare this diagram to the narrative description (Figure 12-6) to see how this diagram flows for the video store.

An entity-relationship diagram for the video store is shown in Figure 12-7b. This diagram shows four entities: CUSTOMER, TITLES, TAPES, and RENTAL (the primary key for each entity is also shown). Each instance of TAPES represents a copy of the TITLES entity.

Figure 12-5

System development life cycle (Source: Lyon, 1993. Reprinted with permission of Technical Enterprises, Inc. From *Data Management Review* vol. 3, no. 6, p. 18. Copyright 1993.)

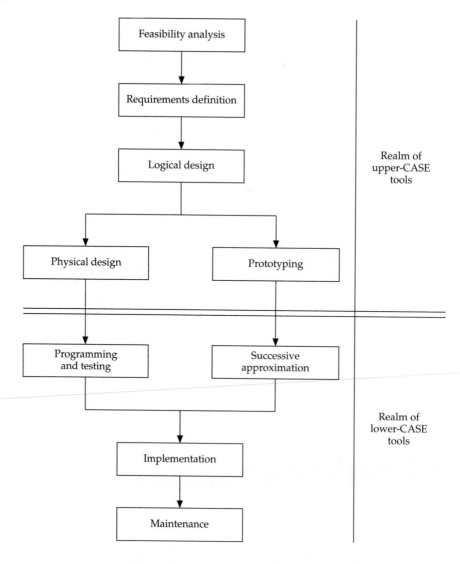

Among the numerous benefits that data administrators and software developers gain from using CASE tools are the following:

1. Improved productivity in development
2. Improved quality through automated checking
3. Automatic preparation and updating of documentation
4. Encouragement of prototyping and incremental development
5. Automatic preparation of program code from requirements definitions
6. Reduced maintenance efforts

Unfortunately, not all CASE tools are sufficiently integrated at present to support all of the tasks shown in Figure 12-8 or to provide all of the above benefits. For example, some are predominantly upper-CASE (early life-cycle step) tools, and others are predominantly lower-CASE (later life-cycle step) tools. Integrated tools continue to emerge, however, and will undoubtedly be used as standard development environments during the remainder of this decade.

Our sample problem concerns a local video rental store (we named it Captain Video, although it has nothing to do with the real store). The following is a brief description of the business. No decision has yet been made on which parts of the business will require computer support, or what type of technology will be used.

EVENTS LIST

1. Customer rents tape(s) and makes rental payment.
2. Customer returns tape and may pay late charge of $1 per day.
3. Time to notify overdue borrowers.
4. Time to report rentals.
5. Captain Video submits new tape.
6. Captain Video submits rate change on some movie titles.
7. Customer changes address.
8. Customer requests particular movie title.

OTHER DETAILS

The standard time period for a rental is two days after the borrowed tape is rented. If the customer fails to return the tape in time, then it is time to send a tape overdue notice to the customer address with the title and copy number and past due return date. A tape is a cassette of video tape with a prerecorded movie that can be rented. Each tape has a movie title and a copy number. All copies of a movie have the same rental rate. Not all movies have the same rental rate. A rental is the lending of a tape to a person (previous or new customer) in exchange for cash. A rental has a check-out date, a return date, and a rental charge. If a tape is late, there is a standard $1 per day late charge upon return (no drop box). A customer can rent more than one tape at a time. A tape can be rented, on the shelf waiting to be rented or overdue. This video store has no membership plan and they don't take American Express. All transactions are in cash on-the-spot; no deposits are accepted.

Figure 12-6

Sample problem for CASE tool diagramming

Database Management Systems

A **database management system (DBMS)** is a software application system that is used to create, maintain, and provide controlled access to user databases. Database management systems range in complexity from a PC-DBMS (such as Ashton-Tate's dBASE IV) costing a few hundred dollars to a mainframe DBMS product (such as IBM's DB2) costing several hundred thousand dollars. The major components of a full-function DBMS are shown in Figure 12-9, and a brief description of each of these components follows.

DBMS Engine   The engine is the central component of a DBMS. This module provides access to the repository and the database and coordinates all of the other functional elements of the DBMS. The DBMS engine receives logical requests for data (and metadata) from human users and from applications, determines the secondary storage location of those data, and issues physical input/output requests to the computer operating system. The engine provides services such as

Database management system (DBMS): A software application system that is used to create, maintain, and provide controlled access to user databases.

DBMS engine: The central component of a DBMS. Provides access to the repository and the database and coordinates all of the other functional elements of the DBMS.

Figure 12-7

CASE tool diagrams

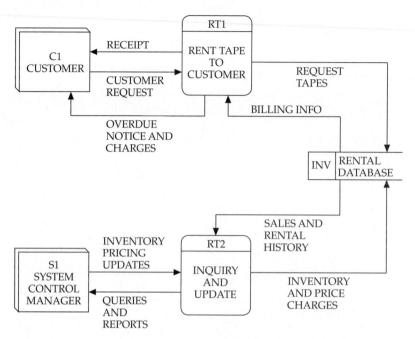

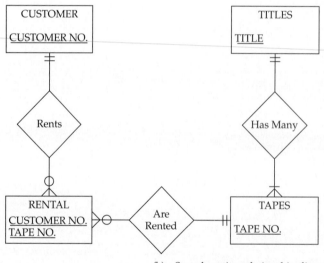

(a) Sample level 0 data flow diagram

(b) Sample entity-relationship diagram

memory and buffer management, maintenance of indexes and lists, and secondary storage or disk management.

Interface subsystem: Provides facilities for users and applications to access the various components of the DBMS.

Interface Subsystem The **interface subsystem** provides facilities for users and applications to access the various components of the DBMS. Most DBMS products provide a range of languages and other interfaces, since the system will be used both by programmers (or other technical persons) and by users with little or no programming experience. Some of the typical interfaces to a DBMS are the following:

1. A data definition language (or data sublanguage), which is used to define database structures such as records, tables, files, and views

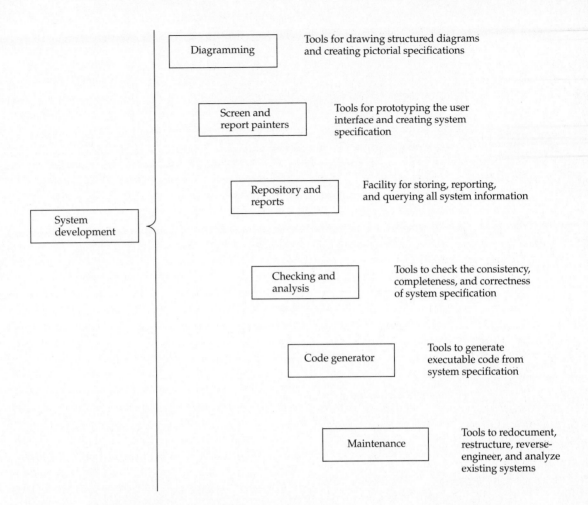

Figure 12-8

Tasks performed by CASE tools

2. An interactive query language (such as SQL), which is used to display data extracted from the database and to perform simple updates

3. A graphic interface (such as Query-by-Example) in which the system displays a skeleton table (or tables), and users pose requests by suitable entries in the table

4. A forms interface in which a screen-oriented form is presented to the user, who responds by filling in blanks in the form

5. A DBMS programming language (such as the dBASE IV command language, which is a procedural language that allows programmers to develop sophisticated applications)

6. An interface to standard third-generation programming languages such as BASIC and COBOL

7. A natural language interface that allows users to present requests in free-form English statements

We present examples of many of these interfaces in following chapters.

Information Repository Dictionary Subsystem   The information repository dictionary subsystem is used to manage and control access to the repository (the IRDS was described in a previous section; see Figure 12-4). In Figure 12-9 we choose to show the IRDS as a component that is integrated within the DBMS.

Database management system

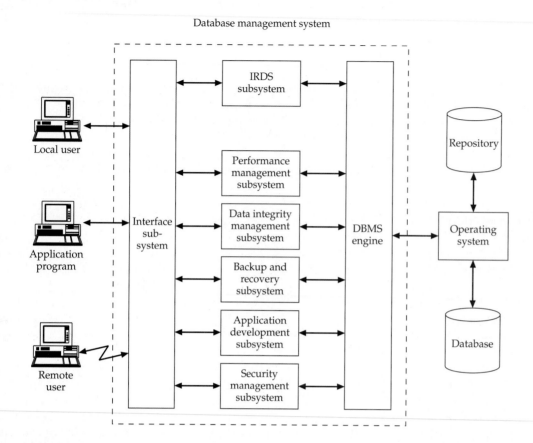

Figure 12-9

Components of a DBMS

Notice that the IRDS uses the facilities of the database engine to manage the repository.

Performance management subsystem: Subsystem that provides facilities to optimize (or at least improve) DBMS performance.

Performance Management Subsystem   The **performance management subsystem** provides facilities to optimize (or at least improve) DBMS performance. Two of its important functions follow:

1. *Query optimization:* Structuring SQL queries (or other forms of user queries) to minimize response times
2. *DBMS reorganization:* Maintaining statistics on database usage and taking (or recommending) actions such as database reorganization, creating indexes, and so on to improve DBMS performance

Data integrity management subsystem: Subsystem that provides facilities for managing the integrity of data in the database and the integrity of metadata in the repository.

Data Integrity Management Subsystem   The **data integrity management subsystem** provides facilities for managing the integrity of data in the database and the integrity of metadata in the repository. There are three important functions:

1. *Intrarecord integrity:* Enforcing constraints on data item values and types within each record in the database
2. *Referential integrity:* Enforcing the validity of references between records in the database (discussed in Chapter 7)
3. *Concurrency control:* Assuring the validity of database updates when multiple users access the database (discussed in a later section).

Backup and Recovery Subsystem   The **backup and recovery subsystem** provides facilities for logging transactions and database changes, periodically making backup copies of the database, and recovering the database in the event of some type of failure. (We discuss backup and recovery in greater detail in a later section.)

Application Development Subsystem   The **application development subsystem** provides facilities that allow end users and/or programmers to develop complete database applications. It includes CASE tools (described in a previous section) as well as facilities such as screen generators and report generators. (We describe many of these features in Chapter 11.)

Security Management Subsystem   The **security management subsystem** provides facilities to protect and control access to the database and repository. (We discuss security management in a later section.)

CONCURRENCY CONTROL

Databases are shared resources. We must expect and plan for the likelihood that several users will attempt to access and manipulate data at the same time. With concurrent processing involving updates, a database without **concurrency control** will be compromised due to interference between users. There are two basic approaches to concurrency control: a pessimistic approach (involving locking) and an optimistic approach (involving versioning). We summarize both of these approaches in the following sections.

The Problem of Lost Updates

The most common problem that is encountered when multiple users attempt to update a database without adequate concurrency control is that of lost updates. Figure 12-10 shows a common situation. John and Marsha have a joint checking

> **Backup and recovery subsystem:** Subsystem that provides facilities for logging transactions and database changes, periodically making backup copies of the database, and recovering the database in the event of some type of failure.
>
> **Application development subsystem:** Subsystem that provides facilities that allow end users and/or programmers to develop complete database applications.
>
> **Security management subsystem:** Subsystem that provides facilities to protect and control access to the database and repository.
>
> **Concurrency control:** Concerned with preventing loss of data integrity due to interference between users in a multiuser environment.

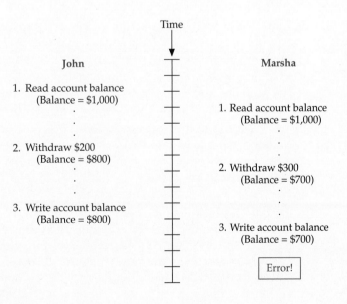

Figure 12-10

Lost update (no concurrency control)

account, and they both want to withdraw some cash at the same time, each using an ATM terminal in a different location. Figure 12-10 shows the sequence of events that might occur, in the absence of a concurrency control mechanism. John's transaction reads the account balance (which is $1,000), and he proceeds to withdraw $200. Before the transaction writes the new account balance ($800), Mary's transaction reads the account balance (which is still $1,000). She then withdraws $300, leaving a balance of $700. Her transaction then writes this account balance, which replaces the one written by John's transaction. The effect of John's update has been lost due to interference between the transactions, and the bank is unhappy.

Locking Mechanisms

> **Locking:** Any data that is retrieved by a user for updating must be locked, or denied to other users, until the update is completed (or aborted).

Locking mechanisms are the most common type of concurrency control mechanism. With **locking**, any data that is retrieved by a user for updating must be locked, or denied to other users, until the update is completed (or aborted). Locking data is much like checking a book out of the library—it is unavailable to others until it is returned by the borrower.

Figure 12-11 shows the use of record locks to maintain data integrity. John initiates a withdrawal transaction from an ATM. Since John's transaction will update this record, the application program locks this record *before* reading it into main memory. John proceeds to withdraw $200, and the new balance ($800) is computed. Marsha has initiated a withdrawal transaction shortly after John, but her transaction cannot access the account record until John's transaction has returned the updated record to the database and unlocked the record. The locking mechanism thus enforces a sequential updating process that prevents erroneous updates.

> **Locking level (granularity):** The extent of the database resource that is included with each lock.

Locking Level   An important consideration in implementing concurrency control is choosing the locking level. The **locking level** (also called **granularity**) is the extent of the database resource that is included with each lock. Most commercial products implement locks at one of the following levels:

1. *Database.* The entire database is locked and becomes unavailable to other users. This level has limited application, such as during a backup of the entire database (Rodgers, 1989).

2. *Table.* The entire table containing a requested record is locked. This level is appropriate mainly for bulk updates that will update the entire table, such as giving all employees a 5% raise.

3. *Block or page.* The physical storage block (or page) containing a requested record is locked. This level is generally not desirable, since a page may contain records of more than one type.

4. *Record level.* Only the requested record (or row) is locked. This is the most commonly implemented locking level; all other records are available to other users. It does impose some overhead at run time when several records are involved in an update.

5. *Field level.* Only the particular field (or column) in a requested record is locked. This level may be appropriate when most updates affect only one or two fields in a record. For example, in inventory control applications the quantity-on-hand field changes frequently, but other fields (such as description and bin location) are rarely updated. Field-level locks require considerable overhead and are seldom used.

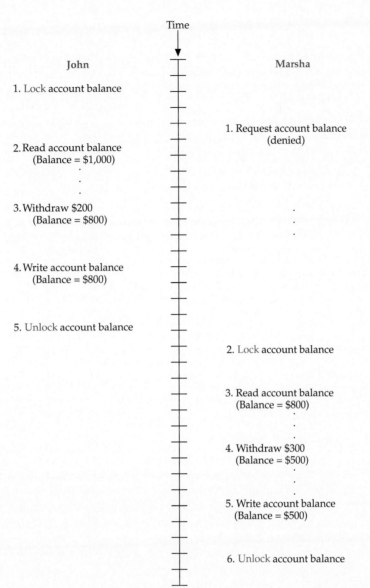

Figure 12-11

Updates with locking

Time

John   Marsha

1. Lock account balance

                                                        1. Request account balance
                                                           (denied)

2. Read account balance
   (Balance = $1,000)
          .
          .

3. Withdraw $200
   (Balance = $800)   .
                                                                 .

4. Write account balance
   (Balance = $800)

5. Unlock account balance

                                                        2. Lock account balance

                                                        3. Read account balance
                                                           (Balance = $800)
                                                                  .
                                                                  .

                                                        4. Withdraw $300
                                                           (Balance = $500)
                                                                  .
                                                                  .

                                                        5. Write account balance
                                                           (Balance = $500)

                                                        6. Unlock account balance

Types of Locks   So far, we have discussed only locks that prevent all access to locked items. In reality, the database administrator today can generally choose between two types of locks: shared and exclusive.

1. **Shared locks.** Shared locks (also called *S locks*, or *read locks*) allow other transactions to read (but *not* update) a record (or other resource). A transaction should place a shared lock on a record (or data resource) when it will only read (but not update) that record. Placing a shared lock on a record prevents another user from placing an exclusive lock on that record.

2. **Exclusive locks.** Exclusive locks (also called *X locks*, or *write locks*) prevent another transaction from reading (and therefore updating) a record until it is unlocked. A transaction should place an exclusive lock on a record when it is about to update that record (Descollonges, 1993). Placing an exclusive lock on a record prevents another user from placing *any* type of lock on that record.

Shared lock (S lock or read lock): Allows other transactions to read (but not update) a record (or other resource).

Exclusive lock (X lock or write lock): Prevents another transaction from reading (and therefore updating) a record until it is unlocked.

Figure 12-12

The problem of deadlock

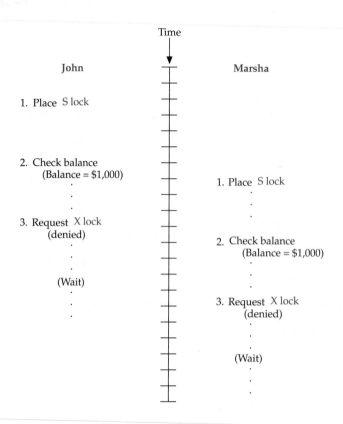

Figure 12-12 shows the use of shared and exclusive locks for the checking account example. When John initiates his transaction, the program places an S lock on his account record (since he is reading the record to check the account balance). When John requests a withdrawal, the program attempts to place an exclusive lock (X lock) on the record (since this is an update operation). However, as you can see in the figure, Marsha has already initiated a transaction that has placed an S lock on the same record. As a result, his request is denied; remember that if a record has an S lock, another user cannot obtain an X lock.

Deadlock   Locking (say at the record level) solves the problem of erroneous updates but may lead to another problem, called **deadlock**: an impasse that results when two (or more) transactions have locked a common resource, and each must wait for the other to unlock that resource. Figure 12-12 shows a simple example of deadlock. John's transaction is waiting for Marsha's transaction to remove the S lock from the account record, and vice versa. Neither person can withdraw money from the account, even though the balance is more than adequate.

Figure 12-13 shows a slightly more complex example of deadlock. In this example, User A has locked record X and User B has locked record Y. User A then requests record Y (intending to update) and User B requests record X (also intending to update). Both requests are denied, since the requested records are already locked. Unless the DBMS intervenes, both users will wait indefinitely.

Managing Deadlock   There are two basic ways to resolve deadlocks: deadlock prevention and deadlock resolution. When **deadlock prevention** is employed, user programs must lock all records they will require at the beginning of a transaction (rather than one at a time). In Figure 12-13, User A would have to

Deadlock: An impasse that results when two (or more) transactions have locked a common resource, and each must wait for the other to unlock that resource.

Deadlock prevention: User programs must lock all records they will require at the beginning of a transaction (rather than one at a time).

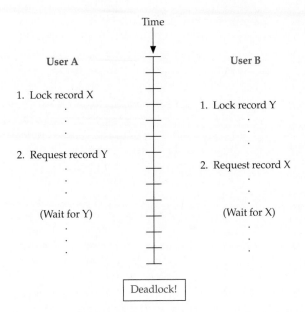

Figure 12-13

Another example of
deadlock

lock both records X and Y before processing the transaction. If either record is already locked, the program must wait until it is released.

Locking records in advance prevents deadlock. Unfortunately, it is often difficult to predict in advance what records will be required to process a transaction. A typical program has many processing parts and may call other programs. As a result, deadlock prevention is not often practical.

The second (and more common) approach is to allow deadlocks to occur, but to build mechanisms into the DBMS for detecting and breaking the deadlocks. Essentially, these **deadlock resolution** mechanisms work as follows. The DBMS maintains a matrix of resource usage, which, at a given instant, indicates what subjects (users) are using what objects (resources). By scanning this matrix, the computer can detect deadlocks as they occur. The DBMS then resolves the deadlocks by "backing out" one of the deadlocked transactions. Any changes made by that transaction up to the time of deadlock are removed, and the transaction is restarted when the required resources become available. We will describe the procedure for backing out shortly.

> **Deadlock resolution:** Allows deadlocks to occur but builds mechanisms into the DBMS for detecting and breaking the deadlocks.

Versioning

Locking (as described above) is often referred to as a *pessimistic* concurrency control mechanism, because each time a record is required, the DBMS takes the highly cautious approach of locking the record so that other programs cannot use it. In reality, in most cases other users will not request the same documents, or they may only want to read them, which is not a problem (Celko, 1992).

A newer approach to concurrency control, called **versioning**, takes the *optimistic* approach that most of the time other users do not want the same record, or if they do, they only want to read (but not update) the record. With versioning, there is no form of locking. Each transaction is restricted to a view of the database as of the time that transaction started, and when a transaction modifies a record, the DBMS creates a new record version instead of overwriting the old record.

> **Versioning:** There is no form of locking. Each transaction is restricted to a view of the database as of the time that transaction started, and when a transaction modifies a record, the DBMS creates a new record version instead of overwriting the old record.

The best way to understand versioning is to imagine a central records room, corresponding to the database (Celko, 1992). The records room has a service window. Users (corresponding to transactions) arrive at the window and request documents (corresponding to database records). However, the original documents never leave the records room. Instead, the clerk (corresponding to the DBMS) makes copies of the requested documents and timestamps them. Users then take their private copies (or versions) of the documents to their own workplace and read them and/or make changes. When finished, they return their marked-up copies to the clerk. The clerk merges the changes from marked-up copies into the central database. When there is no conflict (for example, when only one user has made changes to a set of database records), that user's changes are merged directly into the public (or central) database.

Suppose instead that there is a conflict; for example, two users have made conflicting changes to their private copy of the database. In this case, the changes made by one of the users are committed to the database. (Remember that the transactions are timestamped, so that the earlier transaction can be given priority.) The other user must be told that there was a conflict, and his work cannot be committed (or incorporated into the central database). He must check out another copy of the data records and repeat the previous work. Under the optimistic assumption, this type of rework will be the exception rather than the rule.

Figure 12-14 shows a simple example of the use of versioning for the checking account example. John reads the record containing the account balance, successfully withdraws $200, and the new balance ($800) is posted to the account with a COMMIT statement. Meanwhile, Marsha has also read the account record and requested a withdrawal, which is posted to her local version of the account record. However, when the transaction attempts to COMMIT it discovers the update conflict, and her transaction is aborted (perhaps with a message such as, "Cannot complete transaction at this time"). She can then restart the transaction, working from the correct starting balance of $800.

The main advantage of versioning over locking is performance improvement. Read-only transactions can run concurrently with updating transactions, without loss of database consistency.

Figure 12-14

The use of versioning

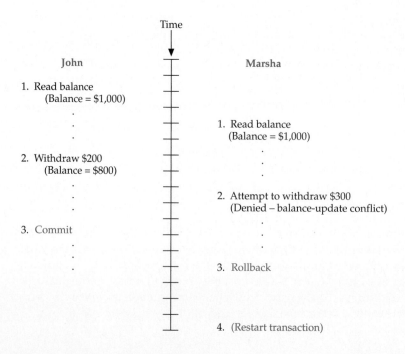

DATABASE SECURITY

Corporations and government agencies are putting more and more sensitive data on computers. As the number and sophistication of user access paths to the database increase, data become vulnerable to unwanted access or corruption. A recent survey of computer security professionals estimates the annual losses from computer abuse at over $500,000,000 nationally. Among the survey respondents, the average installation experienced losses of over $100,000 and 365 person-hours per year (Bloombecker, 1989).

Database security is defined as protection of the database against accidental or intentional loss, destruction, or misuse. As we noted earlier in the chapter, data administration is responsible for developing overall policies and procedures to protect databases. Data administration uses several facilities provided by data management software in carrying out these functions. The most important security features of data management software follow:

Database security: Protection of the database against accidental or intentional loss, destruction, or misuse.

1. Views or subschemas, which restrict user views of the database
2. Authorization rules, which identify users and restrict the actions they may take against the database
3. User-defined procedures, which define additional constraints or limitations in using the database
4. Encryption procedures, which encode data in an unrecognizable form
5. Authentication schemes, which positively identify a person attempting to gain access to a database

Views

A view (defined in Chapter 2) is a subset of the database that is presented to one or more users. To illustrate, the PART and VENDOR relations shown in Figure 7-16 are base tables that are part of a larger database. Suppose that a particular user requires a view that associates PART__NAME with VENDOR__NAME. We can provide this list by defining the following view in SQL:

```
CREATE VIEW PART__VENDOR
  AS SELECT PART__NAME, VENDOR__NAME,
    FROM PART, VENDOR
    WHERE PART.VENDOR__NO = VENDOR.VENDOR__NO;
```

If the user enters this query:

```
SELECT *
  FROM PART__VENDOR
  ORDER BY PART__NAME
```

the following result will appear:

```
PART__NAME     VENDOR__NAME
gizmo          Artcraft
thumzer        Choicetops
whatsit        Artcraft
widget         Deskmate
```

Although views promote security by restricting user access to data, they are not adequate security measures, because unauthorized persons may gain knowledge of or access to a particular view. Also, several persons may share a particular view; all may have authority to read the data, but only a restricted few may be authorized to update the data. Finally, with high-level query languages, an unauthorized person may gain access to data through simple experimentation. As a result, more sophisticated security measures are normally required.

Authorization Rules

Authorization rules: Controls incorporated in the data management systems that restrict access to data and also restrict the actions that people may take when they access data.

Authorization rules are controls incorporated in the data management system that restrict access to data and also restrict the actions that people may take when they access data. For example, a person who can supply a particular password may be authorized to read any record in a database but cannot necessarily modify any of those records.

Fernandez, Summers, and Wood (1981) have developed a conceptual model of database security. Their model expresses authorization rules in the form of a table (or matrix) that includes subjects, objects, actions, and constraints. Each row of the table indicates that a particular subject is authorized to take a certain action on an object in the database, perhaps subject to some constraint. Figure 12-15 shows an example of such an authorization matrix. This table contains several entries pertaining to records in an accounting database. For example, the first row in the table indicates that anyone in the Sales Department is authorized to insert a new customer record in the database, provided that the customer's credit limit does not exceed $5,000. The last row indicates that the program AR4 is authorized to modify order records without restriction. Data administration is responsible for determining authorization rules.

Implementing Authorization Rules   Most contemporary database management systems do not implement an authorization matrix such as the one shown in Figure 12-15; they normally use simplified versions. There are two principal types: authorization tables for subjects and authorization tables for objects. Figure 12-16 shows an example of each type. In Figure 12-16a, for example, we see that salespersons (who are probably identified by passwords) are allowed to modify customer records but not delete these records. In Figure 12-16b, we see that order records can be modified by persons in Order Entry or Accounting but not by salespersons. A given DBMS product may provide either one or both of these types of facilities.

Figure 12-15

Authorization matrix

Subject	Object	Action	Constraint
Sales Dept.	Customer record	Insert	Credit limit LE $5,000
Order trans.	Customer record	Read	None
Terminal 12	Customer record	Modify	Balance due only
Acctg Dept.	Order record	Delete	None
Luke Skywalker	Order record	Insert	Order amt LT $2,000
Program AR4	Order record	Modify	None

Figure 12-16

Implementing
authorization rules

	Customer records	Order records
Read	Y	Y
Insert	Y	N
Modify	Y	N
Delete	N	N

(a) Subjects (salespersons)

	Salespersons (password BATMAN)	Order entry (password JOKER)	Accounting (password TRACY)
Read	Y	Y	Y
Insert	N	Y	N
Modify	N	Y	Y
Delete	N	N	Y

(b) Objects (order records)

Authorization tables such as those shown in Figure 12-16 are attributes of an organization's data and their environment; they are therefore properly viewed as metadata. Thus, the tables should be stored and maintained in the repository. Since authorization tables contain highly sensitive data, they themselves should be protected by stringent security rules. Normally, only selected persons in data administration have authority to access and modify these tables.

User-Defined Procedures

Some DBMS products provide user exits (or interfaces) that allow system designers or users to create their own **user-defined procedures** for security, in addition to the authorization rules we have just described. For example, a user procedure might be designed to provide positive user identification. In attempting to log on to the computer, the user might be required to supply a procedure name in addition to a simple password. If a valid password and procedure name are supplied, the system then calls the procedure, which asks the user a series of questions whose answers should be known only to that password holder (such as mother's maiden name).

User-defined procedures:
User exits (or interfaces) that allow system designers to define their own security procedures in addition to the authorization rules.

Encryption

For highly sensitive data (such as company financial data), data encryption can be used. **Encryption** is the coding (or scrambling) of data so that they cannot be read by humans. Some DBMS products include encryption routines that automatically encode sensitive data when they are stored or transmitted over communications channels. For example, encryption is commonly used in electronic funds transfer (EFT) systems. Other DBMS products provide exits that allow users to code their own encryption routines.

Encryption: The coding (or scrambling) of data so that they cannot be read by humans.

Any system that provides encryption facilities must also provide complementary routines for decoding the data. These decoding routines must be protected by adequate security, or else the advantages of encryption are lost, and they also require significant computing resources.

Authentication Schemes

A long-standing problem in computer circles is how to positively identify persons who are trying to gain access to a computer or its resources. Passwords cannot, of themselves, ensure the security of a computer and its databases, because they give no indication of who is trying to gain access.

To circumvent this problem, the industry is developing devices and techniques to positively identify any prospective user. The most promising of these appear to be **biometric devices**, which measure or detect personal characteristics such as fingerprints, voice prints, retina prints, or signature dynamics. To implement this approach, several companies have developed a **smart card**—a thin plastic card the size of a credit card, with an embedded microprocessor. An individual's unique biometric data (such as fingerprints) are stored permanently on the card. To access a computer, the user inserts the card into a reader device (a biometric device) that reads the person's fingerprint (or other characteristic). The actual biometric data are then compared with the stored data, and the two must match for the user to gain computer access. A lost or stolen card would be useless to another person, since the biometric data would not match.

Biometric device: Measures or detects personal characteristics such as fingerprints, voice prints, retina prints, or signature dynamics.

Smart card: A thin plastic card the size of a credit card with an embedded microprocessor.

DATABASE RECOVERY

Database recovery is data administration's response to Murphy's law. Inevitably, databases are damaged or lost because of some system problem that may be caused by human error, hardware failure, incorrect or invalid data, program errors, computer viruses, or natural catastrophes. Since the organization depends so heavily on its database, the database management system must provide mechanisms for restoring a database quickly and accurately after loss or damage.

Database recovery: Mechanisms for restoring a database quickly and accurately after loss or damage.

Basic Recovery Facilities

A database management system should provide four basic facilities for backup and recovery of a database:

1. *Backup facilities*, which provide periodic backup copies of the entire database
2. *Journalizing facilities*, which maintain an audit trail of transactions and database changes
3. A *checkpoint facility*, by which the DBMS periodically suspends all processing and synchronizes its files and journals
4. A *recovery manager*, which allows the DBMS to restore the database to a correct condition and restart processing transactions

Backup facilities: An automatic dump facility that produces a backup copy (or *save*) of the entire database.

Backup Facilities   The DBMS should provide **backup facilities** that produce a backup copy (or *save*) of the entire database. Typically, a backup copy is produced at least once per day. The copy should be stored in a secured location where it is protected from loss or damage. The backup copy is used to restore the database in the event of catastrophic loss or damage.

Journalizing facilities: An audit trail of transactions and database changes.

Transaction log: Contains a record of the essential data for each transaction that is processed against the database.

Journalizing Facilities   A DBMS must provide **journalizing facilities** to produce an audit trail of transactions and database changes. As Figure 12-17 shows, there are two basic journals, or logs. First, there is the **transaction log**, which contains a record of the essential data for each transaction that is processed against the database. Data that are typically recorded for each transaction include the

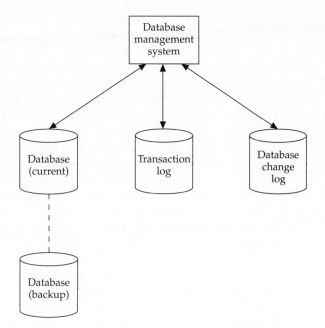

Figure 12-17

Database audit trail

transaction code or identification, time of the transaction, terminal number or user ID, input data values, records accessed, and records modified.

The second kind of log is the **database change log**, which contains before- and after-images of records that have been modified by transactions. A **before-image** is simply a copy of a record before it has been modified, and an **after-image** is a copy of the same record after it has been modified.

Checkpoint Facility   A **checkpoint facility** in a DBMS periodically refuses to accept any new transactions. All transactions in progress are completed, and the journal files are brought up to date. At this point, the system is in a *quiet state*, and the database and transaction logs are synchronized. The DBMS writes a special record (called a *checkpoint record*) to the log file. The checkpoint record contains information necessary to restart the system.

A DBMS may perform checkpoints automatically (which is preferred) or in response to commands in user application programs. Checkpoints should be taken frequently (say, several times an hour). When failures do occur, it is often possible to resume processing from the most recent checkpoint. Thus, only a few minutes of processing work must be repeated, compared with several hours for a complete restart of the day's processing.

Recovery Manager   The **recovery manager** is a module of the DBMS that restores the database to a correct condition when a failure occurs, and resumes processing user requests. The type of restart used depends on the nature of the failure. The recovery manager uses the logs shown in Figure 12-17 (as well as the backup copy, if necessary) to restore the database.

Database change log: Contains before- and after-images of records that have been modified by transactions.

Before-image: A copy of a record (or memory page) before it has been modified.

After-image: A copy of a record (or memory page) after it has been modified.

Checkpoint facility: A facility by which the DBMS periodically refuses to accept any new transactions. The system is in a *quiet state*, and the database and transaction logs are synchronized.

Recovery manager: A module of the DBMS that restores the database to a correct condition when a failure occurs, and resumes processing user requests.

Recovery and Restart Procedures

The type of recovery procedure that is used in a given situation depends on the nature of the failure, the sophistication of the DBMS recovery facilities, and operational policies and procedures. Following is a discussion of the techniques that are most frequently used.

Restore/Rerun: Involves reprocessing the day's transactions (up to the point of failure) against the backup copy of the database.

Restore/Rerun   The **restore/rerun** technique involves reprocessing the day's transactions (up to the point of failure) against the backup copy of the database. The most recent copy of the database (say, from the previous day) is mounted, and all transactions that have occurred since that copy (which are stored on the transaction log) are rerun.

The advantage of restore/rerun is its simplicity. The DBMS does not need to create a database change journal, and no special restart procedures are required. However, there are two major disadvantages. First, the time to reprocess transactions may be prohibitive. Depending on the frequency of making backup copies, several hours of reprocessing may be required. Processing new transactions will have to be deferred until recovery is completed, and if the system is heavily loaded, it may be impossible to catch up. The second disadvantage is that the sequencing of transactions will often be different from when they were originally processed, which may lead to quite different results. For example, in the original run, a customer deposit may be posted before a withdrawal. In the rerun, the withdrawal transaction may be attempted first and may lead to sending an insufficient funds notice to the customer. For these reasons, restore/rerun is not a sufficient recovery procedure and is generally used only as a last resort in database processing.

Transaction Integrity   A database is updated by processing transactions that result in changes to one or more database records. If an error occurs during the processing of a transaction, the database may be compromised, and some form of database recovery is required. Thus, to understand database recovery, we must first understand the concept of transaction integrity.

A *business transaction* (defined in Chapter 2) is a sequence of steps that constitute some well-defined business activity. Examples of business transactions are "Admit Patient" (in a hospital) and "Enter Customer Order" (in a manufacturing company). Normally, a business transaction requires several actions against the database. For example, consider the transaction "Enter Customer Order." When a new customer order is entered, the following steps may be performed by an application program:

1. Input order data (keyed by user).
2. Read CUSTOMER record (or insert record if a new customer).
3. Accept or reject the order (if Balance Due plus Order Amount does not exceed Credit Limit, accept the order; otherwise, reject it).
4. If the order is accepted: Increase Balance Due by Order Amount. Store the updated CUSTOMER record. Insert the accepted ORDER record in the database.

In processing a transaction, we want the changes to the database to be made only if the transaction is processed successfully, in its entirety. In this case, we say that the changes are *committed*. If the transaction fails at any point, we say that it has *aborted*, and we do not want any of the changes to be made. For example, suppose that the program accepts a new customer order, increases Balance Due, and stores the updated CUSTOMER record. However, suppose that the new ORDER record is not inserted successfully (perhaps there is a duplicate Order No. key, or perhaps there is insufficient file space). In this case, we want the transaction to abort.

To maintain transaction integrity, the DBMS must provide facilities for the user or application programmer to define **transaction boundaries**—that is, the logical beginning and end of transactions. The DBMS should then commit changes for successful transactions and reject changes for aborted transactions. Transaction boundaries were illustrated in Chapter 2 in the section an "Order Transaction" and in Chapter 8 in the section on "Transaction Integrity Facilities."

Backward Recovery   With **backward recovery** (also called **rollback**), the DBMS backs out of or undoes unwanted changes to the database. As Figure 12-18a shows, before-images of the records that have been changed are applied to the database. As a result, the database is returned to an earlier state; the unwanted changes are eliminated.

Backward recovery is used to reverse the changes made by transactions that have aborted, or terminated abnormally. To illustrate the need for backward recovery (or UNDO), suppose that a banking transaction will transfer $100 in funds from the account for customer A to the account for customer B. These steps are performed:

1. The program reads the record for customer A and subtracts $100 from the account balance.

2. The program then reads the record for customer B and adds $100 to the account balance.

Now the program writes the updated record for customer A to the database. However, in attempting to write the record for customer B, the program encounters an error condition (such as a disk fault) and cannot write the record. Now the database is inconsistent—record A has been updated but record B has not—and the transaction must be aborted. An UNDO command will cause the recovery manager to apply the before-image for record A to restore the account balance to its original value (the recovery manager may then restart the transaction and make another attempt).

Transaction boundaries: The logical beginning and end of transactions.

Backward recovery (rollback): Used to back out of or undo unwanted changes to the database. Before-images of the records that have been changed are applied to the database, and the database is returned to an earlier state. Used to reverse the changes made by transactions that have been aborted or terminated abnormally.

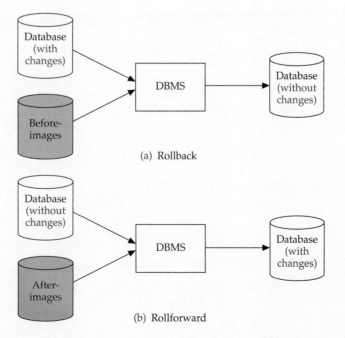

(a) Rollback

(b) Rollforward

Figure 12-18

Basic recovery techniques

Forward recovery (rollfor-ward): Starts with an earlier copy of the database. After-images (the results of good transactions) are applied to the database, and the data-base is quickly moved for-ward to a later state.

Forward Recovery   With **forward recovery** (also called **rollforward**), the DBMS starts with an earlier copy of the database. By applying after-images (the results of good transactions), the database is quickly moved forward to a later state (see Figure 12-18b). Forward recovery is much faster and more accurate than restore/rerun, for the following reasons:

1. The time-consuming logic of reprocessing each transaction does not have to be repeated.
2. Only the most recent after-images need to be applied. A database record may have a series of after-images (as a result of a sequence of updates), but only the most recent, "good" after-image is required for rollforward.

The problem of different sequencing of transactions is avoided, since the results of applying the transactions (rather than the transactions themselves) are used.

Types of Database Failure

A wide variety of failures can occur in processing a database, ranging from the input of an incorrect data value to complete loss or destruction of the database. Four of the most common types of errors are aborted transactions, incorrect data, system failure, and database loss or destruction. Each of these types of errors is described in the following sections, and the most common recovery procedure is indicated (see Figure 12-19).

Aborted transaction: A transaction that is in pro-gress terminates abnor-mally.

Aborted Transactions   As we noted earlier, a transaction frequently requires a sequence of processing steps to be performed. An **aborted transaction** terminates abnormally. Some reasons for this type of failure are human error, input of invalid data, hardware failure, and deadlock. A common type of hardware failure is the loss of transmission in a communications link when a transaction is in progress.

When a transaction aborts, we want to "back out" the transaction and remove any changes that have been made (but not committed) to the database. The re-covery manager accomplishes this by backward recovery (applying before-images for the transaction in question). This function should be accomplished automati-cally by the DBMS, which then notifies the user to correct and resubmit the transaction.

Incorrect Data   A more complex situation arises when the database has been updated with incorrect, but valid, data. For example, an incorrect grade may be recorded for a student, or an incorrect amount input for a customer payment.

Incorrect data are difficult to detect and often lead to complications. To begin with, some time may elapse before an error is detected and the database record

Figure 12-19

Responses to database failure

Type of failure	Recovery technique
Aborted transaction	Rollback
Incorrect data	(1) Backward recovery (or)(2) Compensating transactions (or)(3) Restart from checkpoint
System failure (database intact)	(1) Rollback (or)(2) Restart from checkpoint
Database destruction	Rollforward

(or records) corrected. By this time, numerous other users may have used the erroneous data, and a chain reaction of errors may have occurred as various applications made use of the incorrect data. In addition, transaction outputs (such as documents and messages) based on the incorrect data may be transmitted to persons. An incorrect grade report, for example, may be sent to a student, or an incorrect statement sent to a customer.

When incorrect data have been introduced, the database may be recovered in one of the following ways:

1. If the error is discovered soon enough, backward recovery may be used. (However, care must be taken to ensure that all subsequent errors have been reversed.)

2. If only a few errors have occurred, a series of compensating transactions may be introduced through human intervention to correct the errors.

3. If the first two measures are not feasible, it may be necessary to restart from the most recent checkpoint before the error occurred.

Any erroneous messages or documents that have been produced by the erroneous transaction will have to be corrected by appropriate human intervention (letters of explanation, telephone calls, etc.).

System Failure   In a system failure, some component of the system fails, but the database is not damaged. Some causes of system failure are power loss, operator error, loss of communications transmission, and system software failure.

When the system crashes, some transactions may be in progress. The first step in recovery is to back out those transactions using before-images (backward recovery). However, it may not be possible to restart from this point after a system crash, since status information in main memory is likely to be lost or damaged. The safest approach is to restart from the most recent checkpoint before the system failure. The database is rolled forward by applying after-images for all transactions that were processed after that checkpoint.

Database Destruction   In the case of **database destruction**, the database itself is lost, or destroyed, or cannot be read. A typical cause of database destruction is a disk drive failure (or *head crash*).

Database destruction: The database itself is lost, or destroyed, or cannot be read.

A backup copy of the database is required for recovery in this situation. Forward recovery is used to restore the database to its state immediately before the loss occurred. Any transactions that may have been in progress when the database was lost are restarted.

HANDLING MISSING OR ERRONEOUS DATA

It is not uncommon in database management to encounter situations where data are missing, lost, or incomplete. When data are not normalized or when they are duplicated for high operational performance, different data values for the same data item may disagree, causing ambiguity or uncertainty as to the real data value (which may have to be handled as missing the real value).

As we will see in later chapters, many DBMSs now support a NULL VALUE that can be used to represent missing data, but although missing data can be represented, reporting involving missing values may be cumbersome. For example, if the gender of some employees is missing and the age of some other employees is missing, any comparison or relationship between age and gender is questionable, since it would not be based on the same employees. According to Babad and Hoffer (1984), there are six possible methods for dealing with missing data:

1. *Initialization of data fields.* Initialization ensures that all data elements are set to some value and that computations can always be performed; however, the lack of data is masked, and computations may be biased.

2. *Automatic defaults.* Common default values are zero, the smallest or largest possible value for numerical fields, or a blank space for non-numeric fields. NULL VALUE also fits into this category. Although similar to initialization methods, defaults can be applied at any time data are found to be missing.

3. *Deducing values.* The DBMS can compensate for missing data by inferring values. The most common derived value would be to use the mean of some set of values—either all values from all record instances, some appropriate or categorized subset, or simply the range of possible values. More sophisticated methods could estimate the missing value from audit trails or from characteristics of similar records. It might even be possible to represent the missing value by a confidence interval or range (set in the case of discrete data) of likely values.

4. *Track missing data.* No matter how values may be stored in the place of missing data, it is equally important to tag or identify data as missing. Use of NULL VALUE or some special code does this, but no value is actually stored. It may even be desirable to know for how long the value has been unknown or what attempts have been made to find the correct value. A tag stored with the missing value can indicate that the value stored was entered by some user, estimated in some way, reconstructed from an audit trail, or reviewed for reasonableness on the same day, among many possible annotations.

5. *Determine impact of missing data.* How we handle missing data may depend on how the missing data will affect those who use it. If data are listed in a report merely for descriptive purposes, then simply showing a null value may be sufficient. If the value would be crucial in putting a core summary statistic over an important threshold (for example, cause a reorder of an expensive inventory item), then the missing value should cause a message to either find the missing value or interpret the results with caution. Vassiliov (1981) discusses this situation in detail.

6. *Prevent missing data.* Even if complete prevention of missing data is not possible, the incidence of missing data can be greatly reduced by certain procedures. In batch processing, pre-edit programs can scan for missing data and validate all data elements. (A major source of missing data is an invalid field value that has been eliminated by an edit check at data load time.) Reports of missing and invalid data elements can lead to an immediate search for actual values before the data have to be entered into the database. Grouping transactions into logical sets and forcing the whole set to be valid before any single transaction takes effect is another procedure that can be used to prevent missing data. (For example, make sure that a patient discharge, which affects patient, bed, and charges data, can be processed as a whole.) To avoid erroneous handling by application programs, programmers can write special utilities to scan for missing data, especially unrelated records.

No data model explicitly recognizes the possibility of missing data, yet it is an everyday fact of life for a living database. If the problem is not dealt with during database design, a database can evolve into a low integrity state and cause interrupted or erroneous data processing. A database designer must therefore design the database and database utilities to deal with the inevitable situation of missing or ambiguous data.

SUMMARY

In this chapter we define the functions of data administration, the major tools that are used by data administrators, and several key data management issues.

Data administration is a high-level management function that is responsible for developing an enterprise data model and for maintaining corporate-wide data standards. Database administration is a technical function that is responsible for physical database design and for dealing with technical issues such as security, performance, and backup and recovery. Recently, the concept of a data steward has emerged—a person who manages a specific logical data resource for all business functions.

There is a database system life cycle that includes the following stages: planning, analysis, design, implementation, operation and maintenance, and growth and change. Data administration is normally responsible for database planning, analysis, and logical database design. Database administration is typically responsible for physical database design and much of database implementation, operation, and maintenance. Some functions, such as specifying database access policies, conducting user training, and managing growth and change, may be the responsibility of both groups.

To be successful, data administration must have support and commitment from top management. The head of data administration (or the data administrator) must have a high level of management skills, as well as technical skills. Data administration should normally report directly to the chief information officer (or head of information systems) within the organization. In a decentralized organization, data administration may be decentralized along with other information system functions, but it is often desirable to have a corporate data administration group to coordinate the efforts of decentralized data administrators.

Data administration uses a variety of computer software tools to support its activities. Information repositories are knowledge bases that describe an organization's data and applications. Repositories may be passive or active, depending on their role in managing the IS environment. An information repository should be carefully selected to ensure a good fit with an organization's needs.

CASE (or computer-aided software engineering) tools are used to automate software and database development and maintenance tasks. Upper-CASE tools support the earlier stages of the system development life cycle, including requirements definition, analysis, and design. Lower-CASE tools are those that automate functions later in the life cycle, such as code generation, testing, and maintenance. Both types of tools are used extensively by data administrators.

A database management system (or DBMS) is a software application system that is used to create, maintain, and provide controlled access to user databases. The central component of a DBMS is the engine, which provides access to both the repository and the database. A typical DBMS also provides an interface subsystem, and facilities for data integrity, backup and recovery, security management, and applications development.

Concurrency control is concerned with preventing loss of data integrity due to interference among users in a multiuser environment. The DBMS should provide facilities for concurrency control. There are two classes of concurrency control mechanisms: pessimistic and optimistic. The pessimistic approach uses record locking. There are two types of locks: shared (which allows other users to read but not update a record) and exclusive (which prevents other users from reading a record). Optimistic concurrency uses a technique called *versioning*, in which each user has a private copy, or version, of all records to be modified, and any update conflicts are managed by the DBMS.

Database security is concerned with protecting a database against accidental or intentional loss, destruction, or misuse. DBMS software provides security control through facilities such as user views, authorization rules, encryption, and authentication schemes. However, adequate security also requires physical security of the data center and its environment.

Database recovery procedures are required to restore a database quickly after loss or damage. A DBMS may provide four types of facilities for backup and recovery: backup copies of the database, journalizing facilities, a checkpoint facility, and a recovery manager. Depending on the situation, three types of recovery may be used: restore/rerun (after complete failure), backward recovery (after a data error or failed transaction), and forward recovery (after a system failure).

A common problem in database management results when data are missing, lost, or incomplete. Although missing data (or null values) can be represented in many systems, using these data can lead to erroneous or ambiguous results. There are several possible ways to handle missing data, and data administrators must establish policies for dealing with these and other issues described earlier.

CHAPTER REVIEW

Key Terms

Aborted transaction

After-image

Application development
  subsystem

Authorization rules

Backup and recovery
  subsystem

Backup facilities

Backward recovery
  (rollback)

Before-image

Biometric device

Checkpoint facility

Concurrency control

Data administration

Data integrity
  management
  subsystem

Data steward

Database administration

Database change log

Database destruction

Database management
  system (DBMS)

Database recovery

Database security

DBMS engine

Deadlock

Deadlock prevention

Deadlock resolution

Encryption

Exclusive lock (X lock,
  or write lock)

Forward recovery
  (rollforward)

Information repository

Information repository
  dictionary system
  (IRDS)

Interface subsystem

Journalizing facilities

Locking

Locking level (granularity)

Performance management
  subsystem

Recovery manager

Restore/rerun

Security management
  subsystem

Shared lock (S lock, or
  read lock)

Smart card

Transaction boundaries

Transaction log

User-defined procedure

Versioning

REVIEW QUESTIONS

1. Give a concise definition for each of the following terms:
   a. database management system
   b. information repository
   c. data administration
   d. database administration
   e. information repository dictionary system
   f. computer-assisted software engineering
   g. concurrency control
   h. deadlock
   i. authorization rules
2. Contrast the following terms:
   a. data administration; database administration
   b. information repository; information repository dictionary system
   c. deadlock prevention; deadlock resolution
   d. backward recovery; forward recovery
   e. active-in-development; active-in-production
   f. upper-CASE tools; lower-CASE tools
   g. optimistic concurrency control; pessimistic concurrency control
   h. shared locks; exclusive locks
3. What is the function of a data steward?
4. Briefly describe six stages in the life cycle of a typical database system.
5. Briefly describe four steps that are required to ensure the success of data administration.
6. Briefly describe three modes for using an information repository.
7. List and briefly describe six tasks that are typically performed by CASE tools.
8. List six benefits that are often achieved through the use of CASE tools.
9. What is the advantage of optimistic concurrency control, compared to pessimistic?
10. What is the difference between shared locks and exclusive locks?
11. What is the difference between deadlock prevention and deadlock resolution?
12. Briefly describe five security features commonly used in data management software.
13. What are authentication schemes? How are biometric devices used for this purpose?
14. Briefly describe four DBMS facilities that are required for database backup and recovery.
15. What is transaction integrity? Why is it important?
16. List and briefly describe four common types of database failure.
17. List and briefly describe six techniques for dealing with missing data.

PROBLEMS AND EXERCISES

1. Match the following terms to the appropriate definitions.

   ___ optimistic concurrency control   a. has upper and lower versions

   ___ data administration   b. prevents interference between
                                                   transactions

   ___ database management system   c. coding data for security

   ___ information repository   d. typically uses locking

   ___ database administration   e. high-level management function

   ___ CASE tools   f. uses waiting for resources

   ___ concurrency control   g. a logical unit of work

   ___ deadlock   h. restores a database

___ encryption	i. primarily a technical function
___ transaction	j. typically uses versioning
___ recovery manager	k. software application system
___ pessimistic concurrency control	l. stores metadata

2. Fill in the two authorization tables for Mountain View Community Hospital below, based on the following assumptions (enter Y for yes or N for no):
   (1) Nurses, physicians, and administrators may read patient records but may not perform any other operations on these records.
   (2) Persons in admissions may read and/or update (insert, modify, delete) patient records.
   (3) Nurses may read patient charges but may not insert, modify, or delete these records. Nurses may not access physician or employee records.

a.

	Patient records	Patient charges	Physician records	Employee records
Read				
Insert				
Modify				
Delete				

Authorizations for Nurses

b.

	Nurses	Physicians	Admissions	Administrator
Read				
Insert				
Modify				
Delete				

Authorizations for Patient Records

3. For each of the situations listed below, decide which of the following recovery techniques is most appropriate:
   (1) Backward recovery
   (2) Forward recovery (from latest checkpoint)
   (3) Forward recovery (using backup copy)
   (4) Compensating transactions
   a. A phone disconnection occurs while a user is entering a transaction.
   b. A disk module is dropped and is damaged so that it cannot be used.
   c. A lightning storm causes a power failure.
   d. An incorrect amount is entered and posted for a student tuition payment. The error is not discovered for several weeks.
4. For the concurrent update situation shown in Figure 12-10, what balance would be shown if the transaction for Marsha was processed and the results stored before the transaction for John?
5. HallMart Department Stores runs a multiuser DBMS on a local area network file server. Unfortunately, at the present time the DBMS does not enforce concurrency control. One HallMart customer had a balance of $250.00 when the following three transactions were processed at about the same time:
   (1) Payment of $250.00
   (2) Purchase on credit of $100.00
   (3) Merchandise return (credit) of $50.00

Each of the three transactions read the customer record when the balance was $250.00 (that is, before the other transactions were completed). The updated customer record was returned to the database in the order shown above.

  a. What was the *actual* balance for the customer after the last transaction was completed?

  b. What balance *should* have resulted from processing these three transactions?

6. Fill in the following authorization tables for Pine Valley Furniture Company (Y or N) based on the following assumptions:

  (1) Salespersons may read, insert, or modify (but not delete) customer records. They may not access employee records.

  (2) Employees of the personnel department may read and/or update employee records.

  (3) Quality inspectors may read employee records (although sensitive fields such as Salary are hidden). They may not update these records.

  (4) Salespersons may read product records but may not update these records.

  (5) Persons other than quality inspectors and the personnel department may not access employee records.

a.

	Customer records	Employee records	Product records
Read			
Insert			
Modify			
Delete			

Authorizations for Salespersons

b.

	Accountants	Quality inspectors	Personnel Department	President
Read				
Insert				
Modify				
Delete				

Authorizations for Employee Records

7. For each of the situations described below, indicate which of the following security measures is most appropriate:

  (1) Authorization rules

  (2) Encryption

  (3) Authentication schemes

  a. A national brokerage firm uses an electronic funds transfer system (EFTS) to transmit sensitive financial data between locations.

  b. A manufacturing firm uses a simple password system to protect its database but finds it needs a more comprehensive system to grant different privileges (such as read versus create or update) to different users.

  c. A university has experienced considerable difficulty with unauthorized users who access files and databases by appropriating passwords from legitimate users.

8. Customcraft, Inc., is a mail-order firm specializing in the manufacture of stationery and other paper products. Annual sales of Customcraft are $25 million and are growing at a rate of 15% per year. After several years' experience with conventional data processing systems, Customcraft has decided to organize a data administration function. At present, they have four major candidates for the data administrator position:

  a. John Bach, a senior systems analyst with three years' experience at Customcraft, who has attended recent seminars in structured systems design and database design

    b. Margaret Smith, who has been production control manager for the past two years after a year's experience as programmer/analyst at Customcraft

    c. William Rogers, a systems programmer with extensive experience with DB2 and Oracle, the two database management systems under consideration at Customcraft

    d. Ellen Reddy, who is currently database administrator with a medium-size electronics firm in the same city as Customcraft

      Based on this limited information, rank the four candidates for the data administrator position, and state your reasons.

9. Referring to Problem 8, rank the four candidates for the position of database administrator at Customcraft. State your reasons.

10. Visit an organization that has implemented a database approach. Evaluate each of the following:

    a. The organizational placement of the data administration function

    b. The functions performed by data administration and database administration

    c. The background of the person chosen as head of data administration

    d. The status and usage of an information repository (passive, active-in-design, active-in-production)

    e. The procedures that are used for security, concurrency control, and backup and recovery

11. Find a recent article describing an incident of computer crime. Was there evidence of inadequate security in this incident? What security measures described in this chapter might have been instrumental in preventing this incident?

REFERENCES

Babad, Y. M., and J. A. Hoffer. 1984. "Even No Data Has a Value." *Communications of the ACM* 27 (Aug.):748–56.

Bloombecker, J. J. 1989. "Short-Circuiting Computer Crime." *Datamation* 55 (Oct. 1):71–72.

Brown, R. 1988. "Data Integrity and SQL." *Database Programming & Design* 1 (Mar.):36–45.

Bruce, T., J. Fuller, and T. Moriarty. 1989. "So You Want a Repository." *Database Programming & Design* 2 (May):60–69.

Celko, J. 1992. "An Introduction to Concurrency Control." *DBMS* 5 (Sept.):70–83.

Descollonges, M. 1993. "Concurrency for Complex Processing." *Database Programming & Design* 6 (Jan.):66–71.

Fernandez, E. B., R. C. Summers, and C. Wood. 1981. *Database Security and Integrity*. Reading, Mass.: Addison-Wesley.

Herbert, M., and C. Hartog. 1986. "MIS Rates the Issues." *Datamation* (Nov. 15):79–86.

Jaqua, D. J. 1988. "SQL Database Security." *Database Programming & Design* 1 (July):25–35.

Lefkovitz, H. C. 1985. *Proposed American National Standards Information Resource Dictionary System*. Wellesley, Mass.: QED Information Sciences.

Lyon, L. 1989. "CASE and the Database." *Database Programming & Design* 2 (May):28–33.

McClure, C. 1989. *CASE Is Software Automation*. Englewood Cliffs, N.J.: Prentice-Hall.

Rodgers, U. 1989. "Multiuser DBMS under UNIX." *Database Programming & Design* 2 (Oct.): 30–37.

Vassiliov, Y. 1981. "Functional Dependencies and Incomplete Information." *Proceedings of the 6th International Conference on Very Large Data Bases*. Montreal, Canada:260–269.

Weldon, J. 1981. *Data Base Administration*. New York: Plenum Press.

Winkler-Parentz, H. B. 1989. "Can You Trust Your DBMS?" *Database Programming & Design* 2 (July):50–59.

Client/Server and Distributed Databases

LEARNING OBJECTIVES

After studying this chapter, you should be able to:

- Define the key terms *client/server architecture, local area network,* and *distributed database.*
- List several major advantages of the client/server architecture, compared to other computing approaches.
- Distinguish between a file server and a database server, and contrast how each is used in a local area network.
- Describe four major strategies for distributing data.
- Describe two advantages and two disadvantages of data replication in a distributed database.
- Describe three major functions of a distributed DBMS.
- Describe four types of transparency that are design goals in a contemporary DBMS.
- Briefly describe the two-phase commit protocol and its role in a distributed DBMS.

INTRODUCTION

The advances in personal computer technology and the rapid evolution of graphical user interfaces, networking, and communications are changing the way today's computing systems are being used to meet ever more demanding business needs. In many organizations, previously stand-alone personal computers are being linked together to form networks that support work-group computing (this process is sometimes called *upsizing*). At the same time, other organizations (or even the same organizations) are *downsizing* mainframe applications to take advantage of the greater cost-effectiveness of networks of personal computers and workstations. As technology continues to evolve, users are increasingly capable of interconnecting various platforms efficiently and transparently to distribute data and applications across heterogeneous platforms and networks.

463

In this chapter we describe several related trends and new technologies in database management, each of which deals with these new computing paradigms. These technologies are LAN-based DBMSs, client-server DBMSs, and distributed databases. We do not deal directly with shared database issues in a centralized host computer environment, since these issues were discussed in detail in Chapter 12.

A variety of new opportunities and competitive pressures are driving the trend toward these database technologies. Corporate restructuring, such as mergers, acquisitions, and consolidations, makes it necessary to connect or (in some cases) replace existing stand-alone applications. Similarly, corporate downsizing has given individual managers a broader span of control, thus requiring access to a wider range of data. Applications are being downsized from expensive mainframes to networked microcomputers and workstations that are much more user-friendly and cost-effective. However, data traffic congestion on traditional LANs with a simple database server can cause serious performance problems. Thus, IS professionals increasingly recognize the need to separate the user interface front end from the database engine back end to allow more flexible system development environments. New standards for open systems are emerging that support distributed computing and distributed databases. Finally, as distributed database management software matures, the trend to distributed databases seems likely to accelerate.

LOCAL AREA NETWORKS

Personal computers and workstations can be used as stand-alone systems to support local applications. However, organizations have discovered that if data are valuable to one employee, they are probably also valuable to other employees in the same work-group or in other work-groups. By interconnecting their computers, workers can exchange information electronically and can also share devices (such as laser printers) that are too expensive to be used by a single user only.

A *local area network (LAN)*, which was introduced in Chapter 1, supports a network of personal computers, each with its own storage, that are also able to share common devices (such as a hard disk) and software (such as a DBMS) attached to the LAN. Each PC and workstation on a LAN is typically within 100 feet of the others, with a total network cable length of under 1 mile. At least one PC is designated as a file server, where the shared database is stored. The LAN modules of a DBMS add concurrent access controls, possibly extra security features, and query- or transaction-queuing management to support concurrent access from multiple users of a shared database.

File Servers

File server: A device that manages file operations, and is shared by each of the client PCs that are attached to the LAN.

In a basic LAN environment (see Figure 13-1), all data manipulation occurs at the workstations where data are requested. One or more file servers are attached to the LAN. A **file server** is a device that manages file operations and is shared by each of the client PCs that are attached to the LAN. Each of these file servers act as additional hard disks for each of the client PCs. For example, your PC might recognize a logical F: drive, which is actually a disk volume stored on a file server on the LAN. Programs on your PC refer to files on this drive by the typical path specification, involving this drive and any directories, as well as the filename.

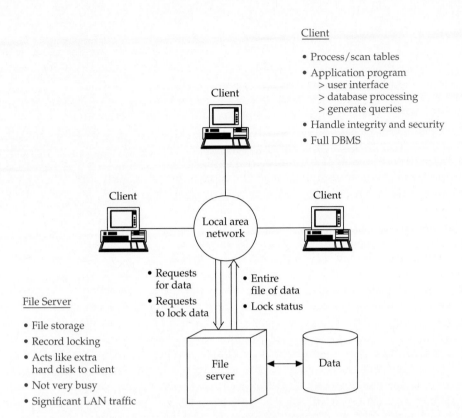

Figure 13-1

File server model

Client

- Process/scan tables
- Application program
  > user interface
  > database processing
  > generate queries
- Handle integrity and security
- Full DBMS

Client

Client   Client

Local area network

- Requests for data
- Requests to lock data

- Entire file of data
- Lock status

File Server

- File storage
- Record locking
- Acts like extra hard disk to client
- Not very busy
- Significant LAN traffic

File server

Data

In a LAN environment, each client PC is authorized to use the DBMS when a database application program runs on that PC. Thus, there is one database but many concurrently running copies of the DBMS, one on each of the active PCs. The primary characteristic of a client-based LAN database is that all data manipulation is performed at the client PCs, not at the file server. The file server acts simply as a shared data storage device. Software at the file server queues access requests, but it is up to the application program at each client PC, working with the copy of the DBMS on that PC, to handle all data management functions. For example, data security checks and file and record locking are initiated at the client PCs in this environment.

Limitations of File Servers

There are three limitations when using using file servers on local area networks. First, considerable data movement is generated across the network. For example, when an application program running on a client PC in Pine Valley Furniture wants to access the Birch products, the whole Product table is transferred to the client PC and then scanned at the client to find the few desired records. Thus, the server does very little work, the client is busy with extensive data manipulation, and the network is transferring large blocks of data. Consequently, a client-based LAN places considerable burden on the client PC to do functions that have to be performed on all clients, and creates a high network traffic load.

Second, each client workstation must devote memory to a full version of the DBMS. This means that there is less room for an application program on the client

PC, or a PC with larger RAM is needed. Further, because the client workstation does most of the work, each client must be rather powerful to provide a suitable response time. In contrast, the file server does not need much RAM and need not be a very powerful PC, since it does little work.

Third, and possibly most important, the DBMS copy in each workstation must manage the shared database integrity. In addition, each application program must recognize, for example, locks and take care to initiate the proper locks. Thus, application programmers must be rather sophisticated to understand various subtle conditions that can arise in a multiple-user database environment. Programming is more complex, since you have to program each application with the proper concurrency, recovery, and security controls.

Client/server architecture:
A form of LAN in which a central database server or engine performs all database commands sent to it from client workstations, and application programs on each client concentrate on user interface functions.

Database server: The (back-end) portion of the client/server database system which provides database processing and shared access functions.

CLIENT/SERVER ARCHITECTURE

A recent improvement in LAN-based PC-RDBMSs is the **client/server architecture,** in which application processing is divided (not necessarily evenly) between client and server. The client workstation is responsible for managing the user interface, including presenting data, and the database server is responsible for database storage and access. Figure 13-2 shows the client/server architecture.

In the client/server architecture, all database recovery, security, and concurrent access management is centralized at the server, whereas this is the responsibility of each user workstation in a simple LAN. These central DBMS functions are performed by the **database server** in a client/server environment. Some people refer to the central DBMS functions as the *back-end functions*, whereas the application programs on the client PCs are *front-end programs*. Further, in the client/server architecture the server executes all data qualification statements, so that

Figure 13-2

Client/server
architecture

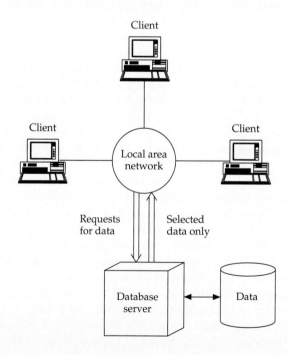

only data that match the requested criteria are passed across the network to client stations.

Functions of the Client and Server

According to Sinha (1992) and O'Lone and Williamson (1991), a client is a process that interacts with the user and has the following characteristics:

- The client presents the user interface; that is, the client application program controls the PC screen, interprets data sent to it by the server, and presents the results of database queries.

- The client forms queries or commands in a specified language (often SQL) to gather the data needed by the application, and then sends these queries to the server; often, the preparation of queries is transparent to the user, since the user interface does not resemble this query language.

- The client functions are performed on a separate computer from the database server functions; hence, neither the client nor the database server are complete application environments themselves.

The server is also a process and has the following characteristics:

- The server responds to queries from clients, checks the syntax of these commands, verifies the access rights of the user, executes these commands, and responds with desired data or error messages.

- The server hides the server system from the client and from the end user, so that the user is completely unaware of the server's hardware and software.

Thus, a client/server architecture is an example of a loosely coupled system, which separates functions on specialized processors. The server and different clients may even run different operating systems.

A client/server database is different from a centralized database system on a mainframe. The primary difference is that each client is an intelligent part of the database processing system. The application program is running on the client, not on the host or server. The application program handles all interactions with the user and local devices (printer, keyboard, screen, etc.). Thus, there is a division of duties between the server (database server) and the client. The database server handles all database access and control functions, and the client handles all user interaction and data manipulation functions. The client PC sends database commands to the database server for processing.

The client can be running any application system that can generate the proper commands (often SQL) to the server. For example, the application program might be written in Quattro Pro (an electronic spreadsheet package), a report writer, a sophisticated screen painter, or any fourth-generation language that has an **application program interface**, or API, for the database engine. An API calls library routines that transparently route SQL commands from the front-end client application to the database server. An API might work with existing front-end software, like a third-generation language or custom report generator, and it might include its own facilities for building applications. When APIs exist for several program development tools, then you have considerable independence to develop client applications in the most convenient front-end programming environment, yet still draw data from a common server database.

APIs have evolved so that it is possible to have clients with heterogeneous operating systems (for example, DOS, OS/2, UNIX, and System 7 from Apple)

Application program interface (API): Software that allows a specific front-end program development platform to communicate with a particular back-end database server, even when the front end and back end were not built to be compatible.

running applications against a common database. Some APIs can also interface not only to DOS and UNIX PC-based servers, but also to mainframe hosts running IBM's DB2 or SQL/DS.

Client/Server Advantages

A client/server architecture provides several significant benefits (Berson, 1992):

1. It allows companies to leverage the benefits of microcomputer technology. Today's workstations deliver impressive computing power at a fraction of the costs of mainframes.
2. It allows most processing to be performed close to the source of data being processed, thereby improving response times and reducing network traffic.
3. It facilitates the use of graphical user interfaces (GUIs) and visual presentation techniques commonly available for workstations.
4. It allows for and encourages the acceptance of open systems.

Issues in Client/Server Database Design

Among important issues to consider in the design of client/server database systems (Sinha, 1992; O'Lone and Williamson, 1991) are the following:

1. The server must be able to grow in power and capacity as more clients are added, or it may become a bottleneck.
2. Often a gateway (or translation software) from the server to one or more mainframes may be necessary to transfer data between databases. Frequently, a client/server system is part of an overall database strategy in an organization, in which a mainframe serves as a central warehouse or clearinghouse between data capture applications and distributed data presentation applications.
3. Capabilities must be provided at the server for database recovery, backup, security, and uninterrupted power.
4. Client/server computing is more complex because proper database processing requires close communication between clients and servers across a network; further, specialized and expensive tools (database server, APIs, and operating systems) are necessary.
5. There is currently a lack of standards on the exact distribution of database processing between the client and the server, data transfer protocols, access schemes for databases distributed across several servers on a LAN, and global data dictionary facilities for locating distributed data.
6. Sophisticated front-end software, now often using a graphical user interface (GUI), requires high-end and expensive client workstations.

Survey of Servers for Client/Server Databases

Some leading software database servers for a client/server environment are

- DB2/2 from IBM Corporation
- Oracle Server from Oracle Corporation

- SQLBase Server from Gupta Technologies
- Microsoft's SQL Server
- SQL Server from Sybase, Inc.
- Borland's Interbase Client/Server DBMS

Some client/server environments use mainframe host database systems, such as IBM's DB2, as the database server. In fact, some industry watchers speculate that many mainframe computers will become strictly database hubs or servers, providing a kind of central warehouse function. That is, either client PCs will access the mainframe database to retrieve data, or the mainframe will act as a clearinghouse into which raw data are stored and checked for integrity before they are distributed to decentralized or distributed databases.

Further, a special-purpose computer, called a **database computer**, can provide the server functions (Teradata, a division of NCR Corporation, is one leading supplier of database computers). Typically, a database computer uses a parallel computing architecture to simultaneously process different parts of a database. A query is broken down into parts (for example, different sets of rows from the same table) that a query processor can scan in parallel. Thus, because of mainframe servers and database computers, not all database software servers are PC-DBMSs.

Database computer: A specially designed computer that contains a customized operating system and the run-time components of a DBMS.

Many other vendors of relational DBMSs are attempting to migrate their products into the client/server environment. However, products that were not designed from the beginning under a client/server architecture may have problems adapting to this new environment (see Radding, 1992, for a discussion of such issues). This is because new issues and new spins on old issues arise in this new environment; examples include query optimization, distributed databases, data administration of distributed data, CASE tool code generators, cross-operating-system integration, and more. In general, there is a lack of tools for database design and performance-monitoring in a client/server environment.

Survey of Front-end Application Development and API Tools

Since each database server uses a slightly different version of SQL, different front-end tools, or at least different versions of front-end tools, are required with different database servers and different client operating systems. Some popular front-end tools include the following:

- SQL Link from Borland, which allows Paradox programs to access SQL Server (from both Microsoft and Sybase), Oracle Server, IBM's DB2/2, and several other database servers
- DataEase SQL, which allows programs written in the DataEase language to access SQL Server, Database Manager, and Oracle Server databases
- Q+E add-in to the Excel electronic spreadsheet system, which allows access to SQL Server, Database Manager, and Oracle Server databases from within Excel
- @SQL add-in to Lotus 1-2-3 versions 2.01 and 2.2, which supports access to SQL Server databases
- SQLWindows version 3.1 from Gupta Technologies, which provides screen painters, a report writer, and context-sensitive help features to SQL Base, SQL Server, Oracle, IBM's Data Manager, DB2, Btrieve, Teradata, and other servers
- PowerBuilder from Powersoft Corporation, which provides a variety of

object-oriented programming tools to build client applications that access Sybase and Microsoft SQL Server, SQL Base, Oracle, DB2, and other database servers

- Object/1 version 3.0 from mdbs, Inc., which is an object-oriented programming environment for an OS/2 client and SQL Server, Oracle, OS/2 Data Manager, and mdbs's MDBS IV server product

McGoveran (1992) outlines some important considerations in selecting front-end and API tools:

- The range of SQL commands that the tool can generate. For example, can subqueries be generated?
- The granularity of data updating. For example, can the front-end application control the definition of a database transaction to include one or several database records?
- Can the tool handle many-to-many relationships?
- What does the tool assume about how concurrency control is handled at the server?
- Can the tool access data from multiple databases on multiple servers?

Comprehensive and thorough surveys of front-end and back-end tools for client/server databases quickly become out of date because of the rapid rate of technology development in this field. Given this caveat, the interested reader is referred to Garcia (1991), Kelly (1992), Mann (1992), and Watterson (1992) for larger lists and descriptions of features for client/server tools.

DISTRIBUTED DATABASES

Distributed database: A single logical database that is spread physically across computers in multiple locations that are connected by a data communications link.

When an organization is geographically dispersed, it may choose to store its databases on a central computer or to distribute them to local computers (or a combination of both). A **distributed database** is a single logical database that is spread physically across computers in multiple locations that are connected by a data communications network. We emphasize that a distributed database is truly a database, not a loose collection of files. The network must allow the users to share the data; thus a user (or program) at location A must be able to access (and perhaps update) data at location B. The sites of a distributed system may be spread over a large area (such as the United States or the world), or over a small area (such as a building or campus). The computers may range from micros to large-scale computers or even supercomputers.

Decentralized database: A database that is stored on computers at multiple locations; however, the computers are not interconnected by a network, so that users at the various sites cannot share data.

It is important to distinguish between distributed and decentralized databases. A **decentralized database** is also stored on computers at multiple locations; however, the computers are not interconnected by a network, so that users at the various sites cannot share data. Thus a decentralized database is best regarded as a collection of independent databases, rather than having the geographical distribution of a single database.

Objectives and Trade-offs

A major objective of distributed databases is to provide ease of access to data for users at many different locations. To meet this objective, the distributed database system must provide what is called **location transparency**, which means that a user (or user program) requesting data need not know the location of the data. Any request to retrieve or update data at a nonlocal site is automatically forwarded by the system to that site. Ideally, the user is unaware of the distribution of data, and all data in the network appear as a single logical database.

Compared to centralized databases, there are numerous advantages to distributed databases. The most important of these are the following:

- *Increased reliability and availability.* When a centralized system fails, the database is unavailable to all users. A distributed system will continue to function at some reduced level, however, even when a component fails. The reliability and availability will depend (among other things) on how the data are distributed (discussed in the following sections).

- *Local control.* Distributing the data encourages local groups to exercise greater control over "their" data, which promotes improved data integrity and administration. At the same time, users can access nonlocal data when necessary. Hardware can be chosen for the local site to match the local, not global, data processing work.

- *Modular growth.* Suppose that an organization expands to a new location or adds a new work group. It is often easier and more economical to add a local computer and its associated data to the distributed network than to expand a large central computer. Also, there is less chance of disruption to existing users than is the case when a central computer system is modified or expanded.

- *Lower communication costs.* With a distributed system, data can be located closer to their point of use. This can reduce communication costs, compared to a central system.

- *Faster response.* Depending on how data are distributed, most requests for data by users at a particular site can be satisfied by data stored at that site. This speeds up query processing since communication and central computer delays are minimized. It may also be possible to split complex queries into subqueries that can be processed in parallel at several sites, providing even faster response.

A distributed database system also faces certain costs and disadvantages:

- *Software cost and complexity.* More complex software (especially the DBMS) is required for a distributed database environment. We discuss this software later in the chapter.

- *Processing overhead.* The various sites must exchange messages and perform additional calculations to ensure proper coordination among the sites.

- *Data integrity.* A by-product of the increased complexity and need for coordination is the additional exposure to improper updating and other problems of data integrity.

- *Slow response.* If the data are not distributed properly according to their usage, or if queries are not formulated correctly, response to requests for data can be extremely slow. These issues are discussed later in the chapter.

Location transparency: A design goal for a distributed database, which says that a user (or user program) requesting data need not know the location of the data.

Options for a Distributed Network

We have defined a distributed database as one that is spread across computers in multiple locations that are connected by a data communications network (or networks). As Figure 13-3 shows, there are a variety of ways to configure such a network.

- In a *fully connected network*, each site (or computer) is physically linked to every other site. This approach provides the greatest reliability and flexibility, but it is also the most costly to install.
- A *partially connected network* has links between only some of the sites. Links are generally installed between sites where the traffic density is greatest.
- A *tree-structured network* is a hierarchical arrangement of nodes. It is often used in organizations that have a hierarchical organization structure that corresponds to the network.
- A *star network* connects numerous satellite computers with a central computer (computer C in Figure 13-3). This approach is common in companies with branch locations that must communicate with a central corporate computer.
- A *ring network* interconnects sites in a closed loop. This approach is often used to link personal computers in a local area network.

In practice, these options are often combined. For example, Figure 13-4 shows a common distributed processing approach in a manufacturing company that combines the tree-structured and ring approaches. The network contains three types of computers: a corporate mainframe, departmental computers (for engineering and manufacturing), and microcomputers or workstations. The corporate database (including personnel, marketing, and financial data) is maintained on the corporate computer. The engineering and manufacturing departmental computers each manage databases relative to their respective areas. The engineering computer is networked to several workstations (powerful microcomputers) for computer-aided design and computer-aided manufacturing (CAD/CAM).

In manufacturing, numerous personal computers are linked in a local area network (ring). These PCs perform a variety of functions, such as controlling machines and robots, controlling materials-handling equipment, and reading manufacturing data. The local area network (LAN) has a dedicated database server that manages a local database (which might contain work assignments, move-

Figure 13-3

Alternative network configurations

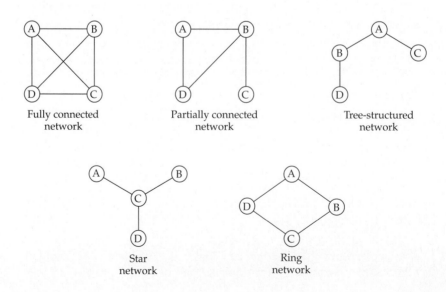

Fully connected network

Partially connected network

Tree-structured network

Star network

Ring network

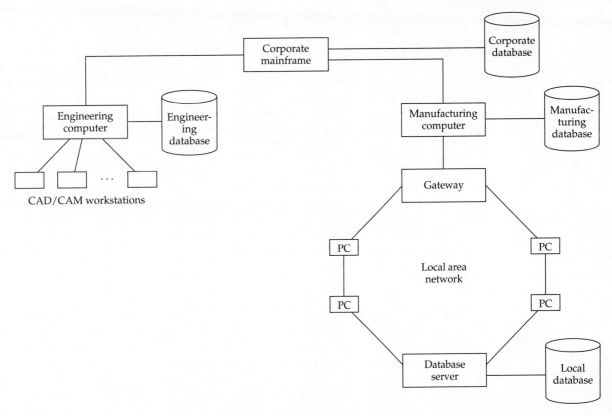

Figure 13-4

Distributed processing system for a manufacturing company

ments of materials, and so on). Notice that this database is centralized with respect to the local area network but in the overall scheme is just one component of the distributed database.

The LAN communicates with the manufacturing computer by means of a *gateway*—a microcomputer with special software to coordinate such communications.

Options for Distributing a Database

How should a database be distributed among the sites (or nodes) of a network? We discussed this important issue of physical database design in Chapter 7, which introduced an analytical procedure for evaluating alternative distribution strategies. In that chapter we noted that there are four basic strategies for distributing databases:

1. Data replication
2. Horizontal partitioning
3. Vertical partitioning
4. Combinations of the above

We will explain and illustrate each of these approaches using relational databases. The same concepts apply (with some variations) for other data models, such as hierarchical and network.

Suppose that a bank has numerous branches located throughout a state. One of the base relations in the bank's database is the Customer relation. Figure 13-5

Figure 13-5

Customer relation for a
bank

ACCT NO.	CUSTOMER NAME	BRANCH NAME	BALANCE
200	Jones	Lakeview	1000
324	Smith	Valley	250
153	Gray	Valley	38
426	Dorman	Lakeview	796
500	Green	Valley	168
683	McIntyre	Lakeview	1500
252	Elmore	Lakeview	330

shows the format for an abbreviated version of this relation. For simplicity, the
sample data in the relation apply to only two of the branches (Lakeview and
Valley). The primary key in this relation is account number (ACCT NO.).
BRANCH NAME is the name of the branch where customers have opened their
accounts (and therefore where they presumably perform most of their transactions).

Data Replication   One option for data distribution is to store a separate copy
of the database at each of two or more sites. The Customer relation in Figure 13-5
could be stored at Lakeview or Valley, for example. If a copy is stored at every
site, we have the case of *full replication.*

There are two advantages to data replication:

1. *Reliability:* If one of the sites containing the relation (or database) fails, a
copy can always be found at another site.

2. *Fast response:* Each site that has a full copy can process queries locally, so
queries can be processed rapidly.

There are also two primary disadvantages:

1. *Storage requirements:* Each site that has a full copy must have the same storage capacity that would be required if the data were stored centrally.

2. *Complexity and cost of updating:* Whenever a relation is updated, it must be
updated at each site that holds a copy. This requires careful coordination,
as we will see later.

For these reasons, data replication is favored where most transactions are read-
only and where the data are relatively static, as in catalogs, telephone directories,
train schedules, and so on. CD-ROM storage technology has promise as an economical medium for replicated databases.

Horizontal partitioning:
Distributing the rows of a
table into several separate
tables.

Horizontal Partitioning   With **horizontal partitioning,** some of the rows of a
table (or relation) are put into a base relation at one site, and other rows are put
into a base relation at another site. More generally, the rows of a relation are
distributed to many sites.

Figure 13-6 shows the result of taking horizontal partitions of the Customer
relation. Each row is now located at its home branch. If customers actually conduct
most of their transactions at the home branch, the transactions are processed locally and response times are minimized. When a customer initiates a transaction
at another branch, the transaction must be transmitted to the home branch for
processing and the response transmitted back to the initiating branch (this is the
normal pattern for persons using automated teller machines, or ATMs). If a customer's usage pattern changes (perhaps because of a move), the system may be
able to detect this change and dynamically move the record to the location where

ACCT NO.	CUSTOMER NAME	BRANCH NAME	BALANCE
200	Jones	Lakeview	1000
426	Dorman	Lakeview	796
683	McIntyre	Lakeview	1500
252	Elmore	Lakeview	330
(a) Lakeview Branch			

ACCT NO.	CUSTOMER NAME	BRANCH NAME	BALANCE
324	Smith	Valley	250
153	Gray	Valley	38
500	Green	Valley	168
(b) Valley Branch			

Figure 13-6
Horizontal partitions

most transactions are being initiated. In summary, horizontal partitions for a distributed database have three major advantages:

1. *Efficiency:* Data are stored close to where they are used and separate from other data used by other users or applications.

2. *Local optimization:* Data can be stored to optimize performance for local access.

3. *Security:* Data not relevant to usage at a particular site are not made available.

Thus, horizontal partitions are usually used when an organizational function is distributed, but each site is concerned with only a subset of the entity instances (frequently based on geography).

Horizontal partitions also have two primary disadvantages:

1. *Inconsistent access speed:* When data from several partitions are required, the access time can be significantly different from local-only data access.

2. *Backup vulnerability:* Since data are not replicated, when data at one site become inaccessible or damaged, usage cannot switch to another site where a copy exists; data may be lost if proper backup is not performed at each site.

Vertical Partitioning With the **vertical partitioning** approach, some of the columns of a relation are projected into a base relation at one of the sites, and other columns are projected into a base relation at another site (more generally, columns may be projected to several sites). The relations at each of the sites must share a common domain, so that the original table can be reconstructed.

To illustrate vertical partitioning, we use an application for the manufacturing company shown in Figure 13-4. Figure 13-7 shows Part relation with PART NO. as the primary key. Some of these data are used primarily by manufacturing, while

Vertical partitioning: Distributing the columns of a table into several separate tables.

PART NO.	NAME	COST	DRAWING NO.	QTY ON HAND
P2	Widget	100	123-7	20
P7	Gizmo	550	621-0	100
P3	Thing	48	174-3	0
P1	Whatsit	220	416-2	16
P8	Thumzer	16	321-0	50
P9	Bobbit	75	400-1	0
P6	Nailit	125	129-4	200

Figure 13-7
Part relation

Figure 13-8

Vertical partitions

PART NO.	DRAWING NO.
P2	123-7
P7	621-0
P3	174-3
P1	416-2
P8	321-0
P9	400-1
P6	129-4

(a) Engineering

PART NO.	NAME	COST	QTY ON HAND
P2	Widget	100	20
P7	Gizmo	550	100
P3	Thing	48	0
P1	Whatsit	220	16
P8	Thumzer	16	50
P9	Bobbit	75	0
P6	Nailit	125	200

(b) Manufacturing

others are used mostly by engineering. The data are distributed to the respective departmental computers using vertical partitioning, as shown in Figure 13-8. Each of the partitions shown in Figure 13-8 is obtained by taking projections (that is, selected columns) of the original relation. The original relation in turn can be obtained by taking natural joins of the resulting partitions.

In summary, the advantages and disadvantages of vertical partitions are identical to those for horizontal partitions. However, horizontal partitions support an organizational design in which functions are replicated, often on a regional basis, while vertical partitions are typically applied across organizational functions with reasonably separate data requirements.

Figure 13-9

Data distribution strategies (Source: Copyright © *Database Programming & Design*, April 1989, Vol. 2, No. 4. Reprinted by permission of Miller Freeman Publications.)

Combinations of Operations   To complicate matters further, there are almost unlimited combinations of the preceding strategies. Some data may be stored centrally, while other data are replicated at the various sites. Also, for a given relation, both horizontal and vertical partitions may be desirable for data distribution. Figure 13-9 is an example of a combination strategy:

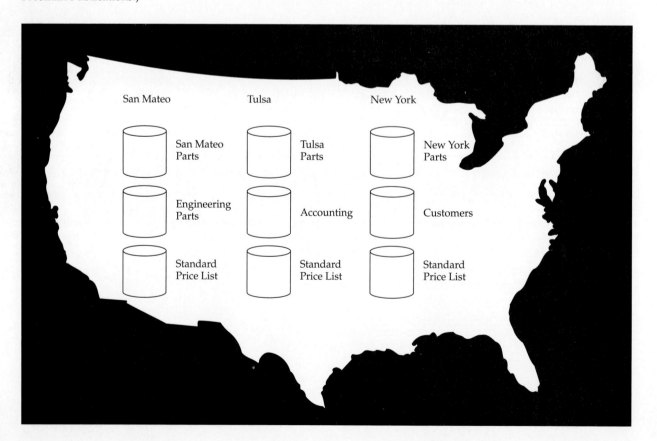

1. Engineering Parts, Accounting, and Customer data are each centralized at different locations.

2. Standard parts data are partitioned (horizontally) among the three locations.

3. The Standard Price List is replicated at all three locations.

The overriding principle in distributed database design is that data should be stored at the sites where they will be accessed most frequently (although other considerations, such as security, data integrity, and cost, are also likely to be important). The data administrator plays a critical and central role in organizing a distributed database in order to make it distributed, not decentralized.

DISTRIBUTED DBMS

To have a distributed database, there must be a database management system that coordinates the access to data at the various nodes. We will call such a system a *distributed DBMS*. Although each site may have a DBMS managing the local database at that site, a distributed DBMS is also required to perform the following functions:

1. Determine the location from which to retrieve requested data.

2. If necessary, translate the request at one node using a local DBMS into the proper request to another node using a different DBMS and data model.

3. Provide data management functions such as security, concurrency and deadlock control, query optimization, and failure recovery.

Conceptually, there could be different DBMSs running at each local site, with one master DBMS controlling the interaction across database parts. Such an environment is called a *heterogeneous distributed database* (Goldring, 1990). Although ideal, complete heterogeneity is not practical today; limited capabilities exist with some products when each DBMS follows the same data architecture (for example, relational).

Figure 13-10 shows one popular architecture for a computer system with a distributed DBMS capability. Each site has a local DBMS that manages the database stored at that site. Also, each site has a copy of the distributed DBMS and the associated distributed data dictionary/directory (DD/D). The distributed DD/D contains the location of all data in the network, as well as data definitions. Requests for data by users or application programs are first processed by the distributed DBMS, which determines whether the transaction is local or global. A **local transaction** is one in which the required data are stored entirely at the local site. A **global transaction** requires reference to data at one or more nonlocal sites to satisfy the request. For local transactions, the distributed DBMS passes the request to the local DBMS; for global transactions, the distributed DBMS routes the request to other sites as necessary. The distributed DBMSs at the participating sites exchange messages as needed to coordinate the processing of the transaction until it is completed (or aborted, if necessary). This process may be quite complex, as we will see.

The DBMS (and its data model) at one site may be different from that at another site; for example, site A may have a relational DBMS, while site B has a network DBMS. In this case, the distributed DBMS must translate the request so that it can be processed by the local DBMS. The capability for handling mixed DBMSs and

Local transaction: In a distributed database, a transaction that requires reference only to data that are stored at the site where the transaction originates.

Global transaction: In a distributed database, a transaction that requires reference to data at one or more nonlocal sites to satisfy the request.

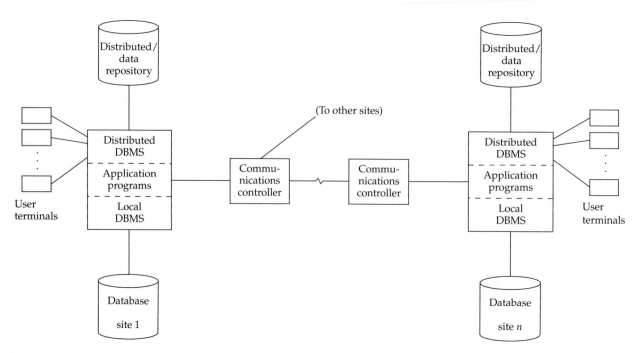

Figure 13-10

Distributed DBMS
architecture

data models is a state-of-the-art development that is beginning to appear in some commercial DBMS products.

In our discussion of an architecture for a distributed system (Figure 13-10), we assumed that copies of the distributed DBMS and DD/D exist at each site (thus the DD/D is itself an example of data replication). An alternative is to locate the distributed DBMS and DD/D at a central site, and other strategies are also possible. However, the centralized solution is vulnerable to failure and therefore is less desirable.

A distributed DBMS should isolate users as much as possible from the complexities of distributed database management. Stated differently, the distributed DBMS should make transparent the location of data in the network as well as other features of a distributed database. Traiger et al. (1982) define four objectives of a distributed DBMS that, when met, ease the construction of programs and the retrieval of data in a distributed system. These objectives, which are described below, are the following: location transparency, replication transparency, failure transparency, and concurrency transparency. We also describe query optimization, which is an important function of a distributed DBMS.

Location Transparency

Although data are geographically distributed and may move from place to place, with *location transparency* users (including programmers) can act as if all the data were located at a single node. To illustrate location transparency, consider the distributed database in Figure 13-9. This company maintains warehouses and associated purchasing functions in San Mateo, California, Tulsa, Oklahoma, and New York City. Their engineering offices are in San Mateo and their sales offices are in New York City. Suppose that a marketing manager in San Mateo, California, wanted a list of all company customers whose total purchases exceed $100,000.

From a terminal in San Mateo, with location transparency the manager could enter the following request:

```
SELECT *
  FROM CUSTOMER
  WHERE TOTAL__SALES > 100,000;
```

Notice that this SQL request does not require the user to know where the data are physically stored. The distributed DBMS at the local site (San Mateo) will consult the distributed DD/D and determine that this request must be routed to New York. When the selected data are transmitted and displayed in San Mateo, it appears to the user at that site that the data were retrieved locally (unless there is a lengthy communications delay!).

Now consider a more complex request that requires retrieval of data from more than one site. For example, consider the Parts logical file in Figure 13-9, which is geographically partitioned into physically distributed database files stored on computers near their respective warehouse location: San Mateo parts, Tulsa parts, and New York parts. Suppose that an inventory manager in Tulsa wishes to construct a list of orange-colored parts (regardless of location). This manager could use the following query to assemble this information from the three sites:

```
SELECT DISTINCT PART__NO, PART__NAME
  FROM PART
  WHERE COLOR = 'Orange'
  ORDER BY PART__NO;
```

In forming this query, the user need not be aware that the parts data exist at various sites (assuming location transparency) and that therefore this is a global transaction. Without location transparency, the user would have to reference the parts data at each site separately and then assemble the data to produce the desired results.

The above examples concern read-only transactions. Can a local user also update data at a remote site (or sites)? With today's distributed DBMS products, a user can certainly update data stored at one remote site (such as the Customer data in this example). Thus a user in Tulsa could update bill-of-material data stored in San Mateo. A more complex problem arises in updating data stored at multiple sites (such as the Vendor file). We discuss this problem in the next section.

To achieve location transparency, the distributed DBMS must have access to an accurate and current data dictionary/directory that indicates the location (or locations) of all data in the network. When the directories are distributed (as in the architecture shown in Figure 13-9), they must be synchronized so that each copy of the directory reflects the same information concerning the location of data. Although much progress has been made, true location transparency is not yet available in most systems today.

Replication Transparency

Although the same data item may be replicated at several nodes in a network, with **replication transparency** (sometimes called *fragmentation transparency*) the programmer (or other user) may treat the item as if it were a single item at a single node.

To illustrate replication transparency, see the Standard Price List file (Figure 13-9). An identical copy of this file is maintained at all three nodes (full replica-

Replication transparency: A design goal for a distributed database, which says that although a given data item may be replicated at several nodes in a network, a programmer or user may treat that data item as if it were a single item at a single node. Also called *fragmentation transparency*.

tion). First, consider the problem of reading part (or all) of this file at any node. The distributed DBMS will consult the data directory and determine that this is a local transaction (that is, it can be completed using data at the local site only). Thus the user need not be aware that the same data are stored at other sites.

Now suppose that the data are replicated at some (but not all) sites (partial replication). If a read request originates at a site that does not contain the requested data, that request will have to be routed to another site. In this case the distributed DBMS should select the remote site that will provide the fastest response. The choice of site will probably depend on current conditions in the network (such as availability of communications lines). Thus the distributed DBMS (acting in concert with other network facilities) should dynamically select an optimum route. Again, with replication transparency the requesting user need not be aware that this is a global (rather than local) transaction.

A more complex problem arises when one or more users attempt to update replicated data. For example, suppose that a manager in New York wants to change the price of one of the parts. This change must be accomplished accurately and concurrently at all three sites, or the data will not be consistent. With replication transparency, the New York manager can enter the data as if this were a local transaction and be unaware that the same update is accomplished at all three sites. However, to guarantee that data integrity is maintained, the system must also provide concurrency transparency and failure transparency, which we discuss next.

Failure Transparency

Each site (or node) in a distributed system is subject to the same types of failure as in a centralized system (erroneous data, disk head crash, and so on). However, there is the additional risk of failure of a communications link (or loss of messages). For a system to be robust, it must be able to *detect* a failure, *reconfigure* the system so that computation may continue, and *recover* when a processor or link is repaired (Korth and Silberschatz, 1986).

Error detection and system reconfiguration are probably the functions of the communications controller or processor, rather than the DBMS. However, the distributed DBMS is responsible for database recovery when a failure has occurred. The distributed DBMS at each site has a component called the **transaction manager** that performs the following functions:

1. Maintains a log of transactions and before-and-after database images
2. Maintains an appropriate concurrency control scheme to ensure data integrity during parallel execution of transactions at that site

For global transactions, the transaction managers at each participating site cooperate to ensure that all update operations are synchronized. Without such cooperation, data integrity can be lost when a failure occurs. To illustrate how this might happen, suppose (as we did earlier) that a manager in New York wants to change the price of a part in the Standard Price List file (Figure 13-9). This transaction is global: every copy of the record for that part (three sites) must be updated. Suppose that the price list records in New York and Tulsa are successfully updated; however, due to transmission failure, the price list record in San Mateo is not updated. Now the data records for this part are in disagreement, and an employee may access an inaccurate price for that part.

With **failure transparency,** either all the actions of a transaction are committed or none of them are committed. Once a transaction occurs, its effects survive hard-

Transaction manager: In a distributed database, a software module that maintains a log of all transactions and maintains an appropriate concurrency control scheme.

Failure transparency: A design goal for a distributed database, which guarantees that either all the actions of each transaction are committed or else none of them are committed.

ware and software failures (Traiger et al., 1982). In the vendor example, when the transaction failed at one site, the effect of that transaction was not committed at the other sites. Thus the old vendor rating remains in effect at all sites until the transaction can be successfully completed.

Commit Protocol

To ensure data integrity for update operations, the cooperating transaction managers execute a **commit protocol**, which is a well-defined procedure (involving an exchange of messages) to ensure that a global transaction is either successfully completed at each site or else aborted. The most widely used protocol is called a **two-phase commit.** First, the site originating the global transaction sends a request to each of the sites that will process some portion of the transaction. Each site processes the subtransaction (if possible), but does not immediately commit (or store) the result to the local database. Instead, the result is stored in a temporary file. Each site notifies the originating site when it has completed its subtransaction. When all sites have responded, the originating site now initiates the two-phase commit protocol:

1. A message is broadcast to every participating site, asking whether that site is willing to commit its portion of the transaction at that site. Each site returns an "OK" or "not OK" message.

2. The originating site collects the messages from all sites. If all are "OK," it broadcasts a message to all sites to commit the transaction. If one or more responses are "not OK," it broadcasts a message to all sites to abort the transaction.

This description of a two-phase commit protocol is highly simplified. For a more detailed discussion of this and other protocols, see Date (1983) and Korth and Silberschatz (1986).

Concurrency Transparency

We described the problem of concurrency control for a single (centralized) database earlier in this chapter. Recall that when multiple users access (and update) a database, data integrity may be lost unless locking mechanisms are used to protect the data from the effects of concurrent updates. The problem of concurrency control is more complex in a distributed database, since the multiple users are spread out among multiple sites and the data are often replicated at several sites, as well.

The objective of concurrency management is easy to define but often difficult to implement in practice. Although the distributed system runs many transactions concurrently, **concurrency transparency** allows each transaction to appear as if it were the only activity in the system. Thus when several transactions are processed concurrently, the results must be the same as if each transaction were processed in serial order. Some interesting examples of how these four objectives can be realized in a distributed database are contained in Edelstein (1990).

The transaction managers (introduced above) at each site must cooperate to provide concurrency control in a distributed database. Two basic approaches may be used: locking (introduced Chapter 12) and timestamping. A few special aspects

Commit protocol: An algorithm to ensure that a transaction is successfully completed, or else it is aborted.

Two-phase commit protocol: An algorithm for coordinating updates in a distributed database.

Concurrency transparency: A design goal for a distributed database, with the property that although a distributed system runs many transactions, it appears that it is the only activity in the system. Thus, when several transactions are processed concurrently, the results must be the same as if each transaction was processed in serial order.

of locking in a distributed database are discussed in Date (1983). The next section reviews the timestamping approach.

Timestamping With this approach, every transaction is given a globally unique timestamp, which generally consists of the clock time when the transaction occurred and the site ID. **Timestamping** ensures that even if two events occur simultaneously at different sites, each will have a unique timestamp.

The purpose of timestamping is to ensure that transactions are processed in serial order, thereby avoiding the use of locks (and the possibility of deadlocks). Every record in the database carries the timestamp of the transaction that last updated it. If a new transaction attempts to update that record and its timestamp is *earlier* than that carried in the record, the transaction is assigned a new timestamp and restarted. Thus, a transaction cannot process a record until its timestamp is *later* than that carried in the record, and therefore it cannot interfere with another transaction.

To illustrate timestamping, suppose that a database record carries the timestamp 168, which indicates that a transaction with timestamp 168 was the most recent transaction to successfully update that record. A new transaction with timestamp 170 attempts to update the same record. This update is permitted, since the transaction's timestamp is later than the record's current timestamp. When the update is committed, the record timestamp will be reset to 170. Now, suppose instead that a record with timestamp 165 attempts to update the record. This update will not be allowed, since the timestamp is earlier than that carried in the record. Instead, the transaction timestamp will be reset to that of the record (168), and the transaction will be restarted.

The major advantage of timestamping is that locking and deadlock detection (and the associated overhead) are avoided. The major disadvantage is that the approach is conservative, in that transactions are sometimes restarted even when there is no conflict with other transactions.

Timestamping: In distributed databases, a concurrency control mechanism that assigns a globally unique timestamp to each transaction. Timestamping is an alternative to the use of locks in distributed databases.

Query Optimization

With distributed databases, the response to a query may require that data be assembled from several different sites (although with location transparency, the user is unaware of this need). The way in which the user formulates the query may have a drastic impact on the response time. Date (1983) provides an excellent yet simple example of this problem. Consider the following situation adapted from Date. A simplified procurement (relational) database has the following three relations:

```
SUPPLIER (SUPPLIER NO., CITY)        10,000 records, stored in
                                     Detroit
PART (PART NO., COLOR)               100,000 records, stored in
                                     Chicago
SHIPMENT (SUPPLIER NO., PART NO.)    1,000,000 records, stored in
                                     Detroit
```

and a query is made (in SQL) to list the supplier numbers for Cleveland suppliers of red parts:

```
SELECT      SUPPLIER.SUPPLIER_NO
FROM        SUPPLIER, SHIPMENT, PART
WHERE  SUPPLIER.CITY = 'Cleveland'
   AND       SUPPLIER.SUPPLIER_NO = SHIPMENT.SUPPLIER_NO
   AND       SHIPMENT.PART_NO = PART.PART_NO
   AND       PART.COLOR = 'Red';
```

Each record in each relation is 100 characters long, there are 10 red parts, a history of 100,000 shipments from Cleveland, and a negligible query computation time compared with communication time. Also, there is a communication system with a data transmission rate of 10,000 characters per second and a 1-second access delay to send a message from one node to another.

Date identifies six plausible query-processing strategies for this situation and develops the associated communication times; these strategies and times are summarized in Table 13-1. Depending on the choice of strategy, the time required to satisfy the query ranges from 1 second to 2.3 days! Although the last strategy is best, the fourth strategy is also acceptable.

In general, this example indicates that it is often advisable to break a query in a distributed database environment into components that are isolated at different sites, then determine which site has the potential to yield the fewest number of qualified records, and then move this result to another site where additional work is performed. Obviously, more than two sites require even more complex analyses and more complicated heuristics to guide query processing.

TABLE 13-1   Query-Processing Strategies in a Distributed Database
Environment (Adapted from Date, 1983)

Method	Time
Move PART relation to Detroit, and process whole query at Detroit computer.	16.7 minutes
Move SUPPLIER and SHIPMENT relations to Chicago, and process whole query at Chicago computer.	28 hours
JOIN SUPPLIER and SHIPMENT at the Detroit computer, PROJECT these down to only tuples for Cleveland suppliers, and then for each of these, check at the Chicago computer to determine if associated PART is red.	2.3 days
PROJECT PART at the Chicago computer down to just the red items, and for each, check at the Detroit computer to see if there is some SHIPMENT involving that PART and a Cleveland SUPPLIER.	20 seconds
JOIN SUPPLIER and SHIPMENT at the Detroit computer, PROJECT just SUPPLIER_NO and PART_NO for only Cleveland SUPPLIERs, and move this qualified projection to Chicago for matching with red PARTs.	16.7 minutes
Select just red PARTs at the Chicago computer and move the result to Detroit for matching with Cleveland SUPPLIERs.	1 second

Evolution of Distributed DBMS

Distributed database management is a relatively new and emerging technology. Current releases of distributed DBMS products do not provide all of the features described in the previous sections. For example, some products provide location transparency for read-only transactions but do not yet support global updates. To illustrate the evolution of distributed DBMS products, we briefly describe three stages in this evolution: remote unit of work, distributed unit of work, and distributed request.

In the following discussion the term *unit of work* refers to the sequence of instructions required to process a transaction. That is, it consists of the instructions that begin with a "begin transaction" operation and end with either a "commit" or a "rollback" operation (Date, 1983).

Remote Unit of Work   The first stage allows multiple SQL statements to be originated at one location and executed as a single unit of work on a *single* remote DBMS. Both the originating and receiving computers must be running DB2. The originating computer does not consult the data directory to locate the site containing the selected tables in the remote unit of work. Instead, the originating application must know where the data reside and connect to the remote DBMS prior to each remote unit of work. Thus the remote unit of work concept does not support location transparency.

A remote unit of work allows updates at the single remote computer. All updates within a unit of work are tentative until a commit operation makes them permanent or a rollback undoes them. Thus transaction integrity is maintained for a single remote site; however, an application cannot assure transaction integrity when more than one remote location is involved (Conte, 1989). Referring to the database in Figure 13-9, an application in San Mateo could update the Part file in Tulsa and transaction integrity would be maintained. However, that application could not simultaneously update the Part file in two or more locations and still be assured of maintaining transaction integrity. Thus the remote unit of work also does not provide failure transparency.

Distributed Unit of Work   A distributed unit of work allows various statements within a unit of work to refer to *multiple* remote DBMS locations. This approach supports some location transparency, since the data directory is consulted to locate the DBMS containing the selected table in each statement. However, all tables in a *single* SQL statement must be at the same location. Thus, a distributed unit of work would not allow the following query, designed to assemble parts information from all three sites in Figure 13-9:

```
SELECT DISTINCT  PART__NO, PART__NAME
FROM             PART
WHERE            COLOR = 'ORANGE'
ORDER BY         PART__NO;
```

Similarly, a distributed unit of work would not allow a single SQL statement that attempts to update data at more than one location. For example, the following SQL statement is intended to update the part file at three locations:

```
UPDATE      PART
SET         UNIT__PRICE = 127.49
WHERE  PART__NO = 12345
```

This update (if executed) would set the unit price of part number 12345 at $127.49 at Tulsa, San Mateo, and New York (Figure 13-9). The statement would not be acceptable as a distributed unit of work, however, since the single SQL statement refers to data at more than one location. The distributed unit of work does support protected updates involving multiple sites, provided that each SQL statement refers to a table (or tables) at one site only. For example, suppose in Figure 13-9 we want to increase the balance of part number 12345 in Tulsa and at the same time decrease the balance of the same part in New York (perhaps to reflect an inventory adjustment). The following SQL statements could be used:

```
UPDATE      PART
SET         BALANCE = BALANCE - 50
WHERE   PART_NO = 12345 AND LOCATION = 'TULSA'
UPDATE      PART
SET         BALANCE = BALANCE + 50
WHERE   PART_NO = 12345 AND LOCATION = 'NEW YORK';
```

Under the distributed unit of work concept, either this update will be committed at both locations, or else it will be rolled back and (perhaps) attempted again. We conclude from these examples that the distributed unit of work supports some (but not all) of the transparency features described earlier in this section.

Distributed Request   The distributed request allows a single SQL statement to refer to tables in more than one remote DBMS, overcoming a major limitation of the distributed unit of work. The distributed request supports true location transparency, since a single SQL statement can refer to tables at multiple sites. However, the distributed request may or may not support replication transparency or failure transparency. It will probably be some time before a true distributed DBMS, one that supports all of the transparency features we described earlier, appears on the market.

SUMMARY

This chapter covered various issues and technologies involved in the sharing of data by multiple people across space and time. We described the client/server architecture, which is being used both to network personal computers and workstations (upsizing) and to replace older mainframe applications (downsizing). We described some of the components of the client/server architecture, including local area networks, database servers, application programming interfaces, and application development tools.

The two types of local area network shared databases—file server and client/server—were compared, and we saw that the newer client/server technologies have significant advantages over the older file servers. These advantages include less network traffic, greater flexibility to develop applications in convenient environments, and a more sensible distribution of duties to form a cooperative computing situation.

We saw that a distributed database is a single logical database that is spread across computers in multiple locations connected by a data communications network. The network must allow the users to share the data as transparently as possible. There are numerous advantages to distributed databases. The most important of these are the following: increased reliability and availability of data, local control by users over their data, modular (or incremental) growth, reduced communication costs, and faster response to requests for data. There are also several costs and disadvantages of distributed databases: software is more costly and complex, processing overhead often increases, maintaining data integrity is often more difficult, and if data are not distributed properly, response to requests for data may be very slow. Both the advantages and disadvantages should be considered by an organization that is considering distributed database management.

There are several options for distributing data in a network: data replication, horizontal partitioning, vertical partitioning, and combinations of these approaches. With data replication, a separate copy of the database (or part of the database) is stored at each of two or more sites. Data replication can result in improved reliability and faster response; however, additional storage capacity is required, and it may be difficult to keep the data updated at each of the sites. With horizontal partitioning, some of the rows of a relation are placed at one site, and other rows are placed in a relation at another site (or several sites). On the other hand, vertical partitioning distributes the columns of a relation among different sites. The objectives of data partitioning include improved performance and security.

To have a distributed database, there must be a distributed DBMS that coordinates the access to data at the various nodes. Requests for data by users or application programs are first processed by the distributed DBMS, which determines whether the transaction is local (can be processed at the local site) or global (requires access to data at nonlocal sites). For global transactions, the distributed DBMS consults the data directory and routes the request to nonlocal sites as necessary.

A distributed DBMS should isolate users from the complexities of distributed database management. By location transparency, we mean that although data is geographically distributed, it appears to users as if all of the data were located at a single node. By replication transparency, we mean that although a data item may be stored at several different nodes, the user may treat the item as if it were a single item at a single node. With failure transparency, either all the actions of a transaction are completed at each site, or else none of them are committed. With concurrency transparency, although the distributed system runs many transactions concurrently, each transaction appears to be the only activity in the system. Few (if any) distributed DBMS products today provide all of these forms of transparency; however, these products are improving, and most of these features will probably evolve in future releases.

CHAPTER REVIEW

Key Terms

Application program interface (API)	Decentralized database	Replication transparency
Client/server architecture	Distributed database	Timestamping
Commit protocol	Failure transparency	Transaction manager
Concurrency transparency	File server	Two-phase commit protocol
Database computer	Global transaction	Vertical partitioning
Database engine	Horizontal partitioning	
	Local transaction	

REVIEW QUESTIONS

1. Define each of the following terms:
   a. centralized database
   b. decentralized database
   c. distributed database
   d. application programming interface
   e. replication transparency
   f. database computer
   g. failure transparency
   h. concurrency transparency
   i. location transparency
   j. database server
   k. front-end program
   l. heterogeneous distributed database
2. Explain the relative advantages of centralized, decentralized, and distributed databases.
3. What are the advantages and disadvantages of replicated databases?
4. What are the advantages and disadvantages of partitioned databases?
5. Explain how deadlock can occur in a distributed database.
6. Contrast the following terms:
   a. partitioned data; replicated data
   b. location transparency; replication transparency
   c. failure transparency; concurrency transparency
   d. locking; timestamping
   e. remote unit of work; distributed unit of work
   f. file server; database server
7. What is the purpose of the two-phase commit protocol? Briefly describe each of the two phases.
8. What are the major advantages and issues of the client/server architecture?
9. Briefly describe four types of transparency in a distributed database environment.
10. What do we mean by cooperative processing? Why is this approach becoming popular?
11. What are the typical functions of a database server?

PROBLEMS AND EXERCISES

1. Match each of the following terms with the most appropriate definition:

   ___ star network
   ___ two-phase commit
   ___ horizontal partition
   ___ replication transparency
   ___ location transparency
   ___ remote unit of work
   ___ distributed request
   ___ distributed database

   a. supports a single remote DBMS
   b. satellite computers connected to a central computer
   c. used to preserve data integrity
   d. Rows of a table are distributed to nodes.
   e. User is unaware that data are distributed to several nodes.
   f. one logical database allocated to several physical nodes
   g. supports true location transparency
   h. User is unaware that data are duplicated in network.

2. The following statements refer to the distributed database shown in Figure 13-9. Name the type of transparency (location, replication, failure, concurrency) that is indicated by each statement.

    a. End users in New York and Tulsa are updating the Engineering Parts database in San Mateo at the same time. Neither user is aware that the other is accessing the data, and the system protects the data from lost updates due to interference.

    b. An end user in Tulsa deletes an item from the Standard Price List at that site. Unknown to the user, the distributed DBMS also deletes that item from the Standard Price List in San Mateo and New York.

    c. A user in San Mateo initiates a transaction to delete a part from San Mateo parts and simultaneously to add that part to New York parts. The transaction is completed in San Mateo but due to transmission failure is not completed in New York. The distributed DBMS automatically reverses the transaction at San Mateo and notifies the user to retry the transaction.

    d. An end user in New York requests the balance on hand for part number 33445. The user does not know where the record for this part is located. The distributed DBMS consults the directory and routes the request to San Mateo.

3. The following questions refer to the distributed database shown in Figure 13-9.

    a. Write a SQL statement that will update the Standard Price List by increasing the UNIT_PRICE of PART_NO 56789 by 10%.

    b. Indicate whether the statement you wrote in part (a) is acceptable under each of the following protocols:

     (i) Remote unit of work

     (ii) Distributed unit of work

    (iii) Distributed request

4. The following questions refer to the distributed network shown in Figure 13-9.

    a. Write one SQL statement that will increase the BALANCE in PART_NO 56789 in San Mateo Parts by 10%, and another SQL statement that will decrease the BALANCE in PART_NO 12345 in New York Parts by 10%.

    b. Indicate whether the statement you wrote in part (a) is acceptable under each of the following protocols:

     (i) Remote unit of work

     (ii) Distributed unit of work

    (iii) Distributed request

5. Visit an organization that has installed distributed database management. Explore the following questions:

    a. Is this truly a distributed database? If so, how are the data distributed: replication, horizontal partitioning, vertical partitioning?

    b. What commercial distributed DBMS software products are used? What are the advantages, disadvantages, and problems with this system?

    c. To what extent does this system provide each of the following: location transparency, replication transparency, concurrency transparency, failure transparency, query optimization?

    d. Does this system most closely resemble remote unit of work, distributed unit of work, or distributed request?

    e. What are the organization's plans for future evolution of this system?

6. Speculate on why you think a truly heterogeneous distributed database environment is not possible today. What are the difficulties in delivering on this environment?

7. Explain the major factors at work in creating the drastically different results for the six query processing strategies outlined in Table 13-1.

REFERENCES

Conte, P. 1989. "In Search of Consistency." *Database Programming & Design* 2 (Aug.):42–45.

Date, C. J. 1983. *An Introduction to Database Systems.* Vol. 2. Reading, Mass.: Addison-Wesley.

Edelstein, H. 1990. "Distributed Databases." *DBMS* 3 (Sept.):36–48.

Garcia, A. 1991. "Client/Server Directory: Back Ends and Front Ends." *Data Based Advisor* 4 (Oct.):64–77.

Goldring, R. 1990. "The Long Road to Heterogeneous Distributed DBMS." *Database Programming & Design* 3 (July):33–35.

Kelly, S. 1992. "Database Servers." *DBMS Buyer's Guide* (Summer):35–40.

Korth, H. F., and A. Silberschatz. 1986. *Database System Concepts.* New York: McGraw-Hill.

Mann, M. 1992. "Windows Databases Give Users More Flexibility." *PC Week* (August 10): 87–92.

McGoveran, D. 1992. "Looking Beneath the Surface." *Data Based Advisor* 10 (March):58–61.

O'Lone, E. J., and A. Williamson. 1991. "Client/Server Computing." In *DATAPRO Managing Data Networks*, portfolio #2025.

Radding, A. 1992. "DBAs Find Tools Gap in C/S." *Software Magazine* (Client/Server Special Section) 12 (Nov.):33–38.

Schur, S. G. 1989. "Building an Active Distributed Database." *Database Programming & Design* 2 (April):46–51.

Sinha, A. 1992. "Client-Server Computing." *Communications of the ACM* 35 (July):77–98.

Smith, B. J. 1992. "More Scripts You Can Count On." *Data Based Advisor* 10 (March):42–46.

Sprague, R. H., and B. C. McNurlin. 1986. *Information Systems in Practice.* Englewood Cliffs, N.J.: Prentice Hall.

Traiger, I., J. Gray, C. Galtieri, and B. Lindsay. 1982. "Transactions and Consistency in Distributed Database Systems." *ACM Transactions on Database Systems* 7 (Sept.): 323–342.

Watterson, K. 1992. "Status: OS/2 Front Ends." *Data Based Advisor* 10 (Aug.):49–59.

PART V

Legacy Database Systems

McDonnell Douglas Corporation

MANUFACTURING SUPPORT WITH IMS

Classical database management system technologies have been used in industry for over two decades. One of the most widely adopted is IBM's Information Management System (IMS). IMS is a hierarchical DBMS that supports high-volume processing applications where speed in data retrieval and data processing performance is critical. As an example, consider the use of IMS within the McDonnell Aircraft Company (MCAIR) component of the McDonnell Douglas Corporation. MCAIR manufactures major fighter aircraft products in the defense contracting industry including the Air Force F-15, Navy F-18, and Marine Corps AV-8B.

The aircraft manufacturing process is supported by an on-line Bill of Materials and Automated Planning Application running under IBM's IMS. This manufacturing application system was first developed in the mid-1970s and has since undergone significant enhancement. The foundation of the system is three Hierarchical Indexed Direct Access Method (HIDAM; see Chapter 14) databases that are logically related to one another. These databases are organized with numerous secondary indexes for alternative data retrieval.

One type of data stored in these databases is the bill-of-materials description of all materials used to manufacture and assemble major end-item components of the various aircraft under production. The databases also store engineering data about materials used to build aircraft parts, such as raw material size, tensile strength, raw material type, and data describing the geometric properties of aircraft parts. Special manufacturing application programs can access the databases in order to store and retrieve routing plans that describe the actual production sequence to be followed during the assembly process. This enables the firm to schedule and balance resource requirements during the assembly process.

As you might imagine, these HIDAM databases are quite large. Data for over 1.5 million aircraft parts are stored in the databases. This requires about 8,000 cylinders of storage capacity on IBM 3380 direct access storage devices. This equates approximately to *4 billion bytes* (gigabytes) of storage capacity!

Two types of Information System organizations support this and other IMS manufacturing and business applications at MCAIR. One organizational unit is responsible for maintaining data integrity. This group includes 10–12 database professionals. Additionally, each computer-based system like the Bill of Materials and Automated Planning Application is supported by a team of application programmers and analysts. This particular system is maintained by about 20 programmers and analysts.

This system provides information support to a very large base of concurrent users. Peak demand can result in 800 or more concurrent users in an on-line environment! IMS is able to provide the high level of data retrieval performance necessary to enable this heavy usage workload. The system is available on-line 24 hours a day, 6½ days a week, and provides MCAIR management with up-to-the-minute information about the status of the aircraft manufacturing process.

Hierarchical Database Systems

LEARNING OBJECTIVES

After studying this chapter, you should be able to:

- Describe and illustrate IMS physical databases and the IMS database description language.
- Describe and illustrate IMS logical databases and the method of defining logical database records.
- Provide an overview of IMS data structures.
- Describe and illustrate the main features of DL/I, the IMS data manipulation language.

INTRODUCTION

The earliest database management systems were based on the hierarchical data model. As database requirements have become better understood, these systems have had to evolve to handle a broader range of data structures. However, many organizations today continue to use hierarchical database management systems because of the investment they have in these products and in the related application programs.

The leading hierarchical DBMS still in use today is IBM's Information Management System (IMS) (IBM Corp., 1989). IMS was developed during the mid-1960s in response to the data processing needs of the aerospace industry. This development was undertaken as a joint project of IBM and North American Aviation. Since its introduction in the late 1960s, IMS has evolved through several versions. The current version is IMS/ESA (Information Management System/Extended System Architecture). IMS is widely used among installations with IBM mainframe computers.

The IMS development team chose the hierarchical structure because they agreed with the philosopher who observed that all views of life are hierarchical in nature. They began by developing a physical hierarchical view, which unfortunately does not always mirror life. Finally, through logical relationships and other improvements, IMS was able to model life by becoming a logical hierarchical system.

IMS PHYSICAL DATABASES

Physical database record (PDBR): In IMS, a hierarchical arrangement of segments.

Segment: In IMS, a named set of related fields.

Root: In IMS, the top segment in a physical database record.

Child: In IMS, a subordinate segment below the root.

The physical database record is a basic building block in IMS. A **physical database record (PDBR)** consists of a hierarchical arrangement of segments. A **segment**, in turn, consists of a set of related fields. The top segment (or entry point) in a PDBR is called the **root** segment. A PDBR, then, consists of a root segment plus a hierarchical arrangement of subordinate segments called **child** segments.

Figure 14-1 shows a typical IMS physical database record. This PDBR contains information about departments, about equipment that is assigned to each department, and about employees assigned to each department. DEPARTMT is the name of the root segment type for this PDBR, and EQPMENT and EMPLOYEE are child segment types. The EMPLOYEE segment, in turn, has two child segments, DEPENDNT and SKILL. These segments contain information about each employee's dependents and skills, respectively.

PDBR Occurrences

The physical database record shown in Figure 14-1 is a PDBR *type*. An occurrence of this PDBR type is shown in Figure 14-2. This occurrence represents data for one department (ACCTG) and contains two EQPMENT segments and two EMPLOYEE segments. The first employee (Evans) has three dependents and two skills. The second employee (Thomas) has one skill and no dependents.

Each occurrence of a root segment represents one PDBR occurrence. Thus, all the segments constitute one such PDBR occurrence (the ENGRG root segment shown would constitute a second occurrence of this record type).

Figure 14-1

IMS physical database record

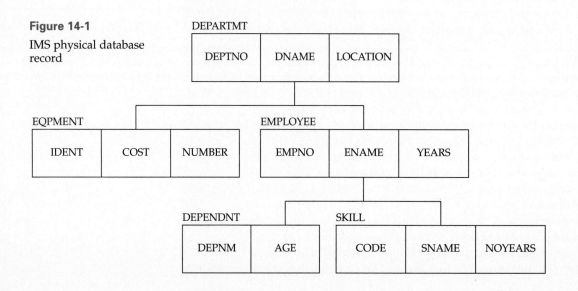

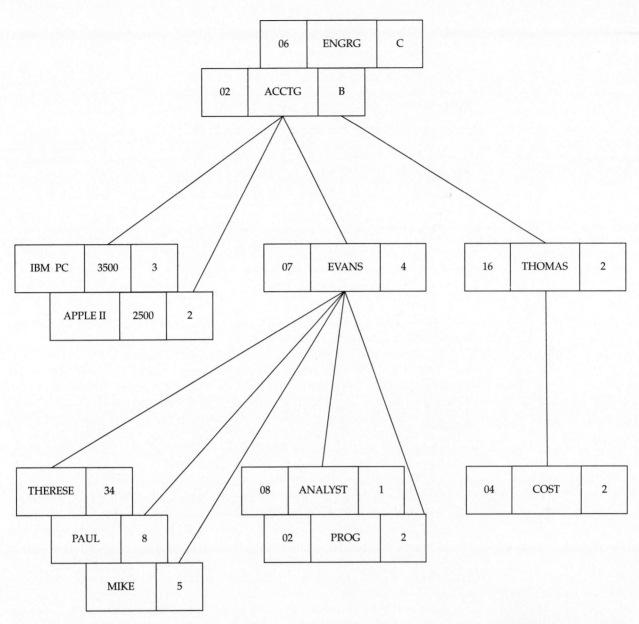

Figure 14-2

An occurrence of the PDBR

Database Description

Each IMS physical database record type is defined by a **database description (DBD)**. The DBD appears as a set of macro statements that define the segments and fields within a PDBR. These macro statements are coded by a programmer or database analyst and then assembled into object form and stored in a library by the IMS control program.

Figure 14-3 shows a skeleton DBD for the department database. The statements have been numbered for reference in the following discussion; normally, these statement numbers are omitted.

Statement 1 assigns the name DEPTDB to the database shown in Figure 14-1. Statement 2 then defines the root segment. This segment type is assigned the name

Database description (DBD): In IMS, the definition of a physical database record type.

Figure 14-3

Database description (DEPTDB)

```
 1    DBD     NAME=DEPTDB
 2    SEGM    NAME=DEPARTMT, BYTES=27, PARENT=0
 3    FIELD   NAME=(DEPTNO, SEQ), BYTES=3, START=1
 4    FIELD   NAME=DNAME, BYTES=20, START=4
 5    FIELD   NAME=LOCATION, BYTES=4, START=24
 6    SEGM    NAME=EQPMENT, PARENT=DEPARTMT, BYTES=29
 7    FIELD   NAME=(IDENT, SEQ), BYTES=15, START=1
 8    FIELD   NAME=COST, BYTES=10, START=16
 9    FIELD   NAME=NUMBER, BYTES=4, START=26
10    SEGM    NAME=EMPLOYEE, PARENT=DEPARTMT, BYTES=42
11    FIELD   NAME=(EMPNO, SEQ), BYTES=10, START=1
12    FIELD   NAME=ENAME, BYTES=30, START=11
13    FIELD   NAME=YEARS, BYTES=2, START=41
14    SEGM    NAME=DEPENDNT, PARENT=EMPLOYEE, BYTES=32
15    FIELD   NAME=(DEPNM,SEQ), BYTES=30, START=1
16    FIELD   NAME=AGE, BYTES=2, START=31
17    SEGM    NAME=SKILL, PARENT=EMPLOYEE, BYTES=28
18    FIELD   NAME=(CODE, SEQ), BYTES=6, START=1
19    FIELD   NAME=SNAME, BYTES=20, START=7
20    FIELD   NAME=NOYEARS, BYTES=2, START=27
```

DEPARTMT and is defined as 27 bytes in length. All names in IMS are limited to a maximum length of eight characters.

Statements 3 to 5 define the three field types that are included in DEPARTMT. Each FIELD-definition statement defines the name, length, and starting position within the segment. Statement 3 contains the clause NAME=(DEPTNO, SEQ). This clause defines DEPTNO to be the sequence field for the DEPARTMT root segment type. As a result, physical database record occurrences within the DEPTDB database are sequenced in ascending department-number sequence.

Statement 6 defines the EQPMENT segment type. The clause PARENT= DEPARTMT in this statement defines EQPMENT as a child segment of DEPARTMT. The segment is 29 bytes in length.

Statement 7 defines the IDENT field type within the EQPMENT segment type. The clause NAME=(IDENT, SEQ) means that for each occurrence of a parent DEPARTMT segment type, occurrences of the child EQPMENT segment type are stored in ascending sequence according to the IDENT field. Thus, for example, in Figure 14-2, the segment for APPLE II occurs before the segment for IBM PC. All occurrences of child segments of a particular parent occurrence are referred to as **twins**.

Twins: In IMS, all occurrences of child segments of the same parent occurrence.

Statements 8 to 20 define the remaining segment types and field types in the department database. Multiple physical databases will often be needed to represent a given conceptual database model effectively and efficiently.

IMS LOGICAL DATABASES

Logical database (LDB): In IMS, all occurrences of a logical database record (LDBR) type.

External views of individual users in IMS are reflected in logical database records (LDBRs). A **logical database (LDB)** consists of all occurrences of a logical database record (LDBR) type. Each LDBR type is a subset of a corresponding PDBR type (or more than one PDBR type). An LDBR may differ from the corresponding PDBR in the following ways:

1. Any segment type (except the root segment) of a PDBR may be omitted from an LDBR. If any segment type in the PDBR is omitted, then all of its dependents are also omitted.

2. Any field types that occur in a PDBR may be omitted in the corresponding LDBR.

Example LDBRs

Two examples of logical database records derived from the department physical database are shown in Figure 14-4. Figure 14-4a is an "equipment" LDBR that contains the DEPARTMT and EQPMENT segment types. Figure 14-4b is a "personnel" LDBR that contains the DEPARTMT, EMPLOYEE, and SKILL segment types. Each of these LDBR types represents the view of a different user. Notice that each LDBR type contains DEPARTMT as its root segment, as required.

Although not shown in Figure 14-4, any of the fields in a PDBR segment may be omitted in the corresponding LDBR segment. For example, the YEARS field in the EMPLOYEE segment could be omitted in the LDBR shown in Figure 14-4b.

Program Communication Block

Each LDBR type is defined by a series of statements called a **program communication block (PCB)**. The PCB for the personnel LDBR is shown in Figure 14-5.

Statement 1 defines the program communication block. The clause TYPE = DB is required for each PCB that defines a database (as opposed to an on-line transaction). The clause DBNAME = DEPTDB specifies that the DBD for the underlying database is DEPTDB (as defined in Figure 14-3).

The clause KEYLEN = 19 defines the maximum length of the concatenated key for the hierarchical path in this LDBR. In the LDBR shown in Figure 14-4b, the hierarchical path consists of the DEPARTMT, EMPLOYEE, and SKILL segment types. The fields on which these segments are sequenced, and the field lengths, are the following: DEPTNO, 3 bytes; EMPNO, 10 bytes; and CODE, 6 bytes. Thus, KEYLEN = 3 + 10 + 6, or 19 bytes. The KEYLEN clause is used by IMS to reserve space for concatenated keys in retrieving segments.

Program communication block (PCB): In IMS, a series of statements that define a logical database record (LDBR).

Figure 14-4

Examples of logical database records

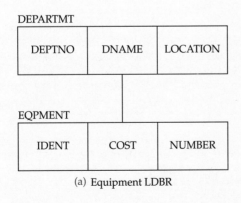

(a) Equipment LDBR

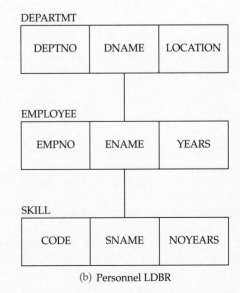

(b) Personnel LDBR

Figure 14-5

Program communication block for personnel LDBR

```
1    PCB      TYPE=DB, DBDNAME=DEPTDB, KEYLEN=19
2    SENSEG   NAME=DEPARTMT, PROCOPT=G
3    SENSEG   NAME=EMPLOYEE, PROCOPT=G
4    SENSEG   NAME=SKILL, PROCOPT=G
```

Statements 2 to 4 define the segments from the PDBR that are to be included in this LDBR. The term SENSEG means "sensitive segment." Segments from the PDBR that are included in an LDBR are said to be *sensitive* (the term can also be applied to fields that are to be included). In this PCB, the sensitive segments are, of course, DEPARTMT, EMPLOYEE, and SKILL.

The term PROCOPT in Figure 14-5 stands for "processing options." The PRO-COPT clause specifies the operations that a user of this LDBR can perform against each segment. In Figure 14-5, the clause PROCOPT=G specifies that a user can only "get" (G), or retrieve, each segment occurrence. Other options that can be specified are I ("insert"), R ("replace"), and D ("delete"). Also, any combination of these options may be specified.

Caution must be used in specifying and using the delete (D) option in IMS. When an occurrence of a sensitive segment is deleted, all children of that segment are also deleted, whether they are sensitive or not. For example, the LDBR in Figure 14-4b is sensitive to the EMPLOYEE and SKILL segment types, but not to the DEPENDNT segment type. Suppose that a user deletes an EMPLOYEE segment occurrence. All DEPENDNT segment occurrences for that employee are also deleted, even though the user may not be aware of their existence.

The sensitive segment feature of IMS offers two significant advantages:

1. *Data independence:* A new type of segment can be added to the database without affecting existing users. The LDBR for the existing user is not sensitive to this new segment type.

2. *Data security:* A user cannot access particular segment types if the user view (LDBR) is not sensitive to those segment types.

Program Specification Block

Program specification block (PSB): In IMS, the set of all program communication blocks (PCBs) for a given user.

Each user may have one or more program communication blocks. The set of all PCBs for a given user is called a **program specification block (PSB)**. The PSB for each user is assembled and stored in a system library by the IMS control program. The control program extracts the PSB from the library when a user program is executed.

IMS INTERNAL MODELS

IMS offers the user a wide variety of physical data organizations and access methods. Choosing the best internal model for each application requires a detailed knowledge of both IMS and the pattern of data usage defined during physical design. In this section, we provide only a brief overview of the IMS data structures.

Overview of IMS Internal Model

Figure 14-6 shows an overview of the IMS data structures and access methods that constitute the internal model. As shown in this illustration, IMS supports four types of databases:

- Hierarchical sequential access method (HSAM)
- Hierarchical indexed sequential access method (HISAM)
- Hierarchical direct access method (HDAM)
- Hierarchical indexed direct access method (HIDAM)

The IMS control program contains routines to process each of these four data structures. Also, each of these routines "calls" (or uses) one of several standard access methods. The access methods used by IMS (and shown in Figure 14-6) are the following:

- Sequential access method (SAM)
- Indexed sequential access method (ISAM)
- Virtual storage access method (VSAM)
- Overflow sequential access method (OSAM)

The function of each of these access methods is to retrieve a physical record (possibly containing several stored records) and to present a stored record to the IMS control program.

HSAM

The simplest IMS data structure is the hierarchical sequential access method (HSAM). With this organization, the segments that make up a physical database record are stored in physical sequence within one or more stored records. The

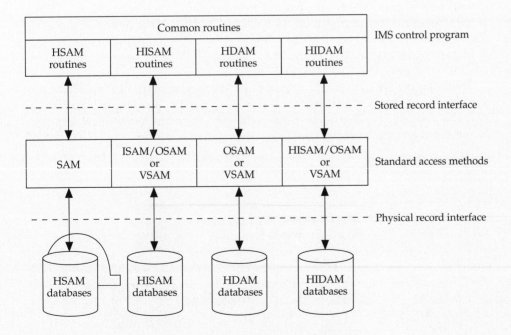

Figure 14-6

Overview of IMS internal models

Hierarchical sequence: In IMS, a top-down, left-to-right ordering of segments within a physical database record (PDBR).

root segment is stored first, followed by its dependent segments. The segments are stored in **hierarchical sequence**, which is a top-to-bottom, left-to-right ordering within the PDBR. Thus, the hierarchical sequence is represented by physical adjacency in HSAM.

Figure 14-7 shows an HSAM organization for the department database (DEPTDB). The segment occurrences in this figure are taken from the PDBR occurrence shown in Figure 14-2. The segment occurrences are stored in two fixed-length stored records. First, the root segment (DEPARTMT 02) is stored, followed by the two EQPMENT segments in sequential order. The remaining segments are stored in hierarchical sequence as they appear within the PDBR. When the first stored record is filled, the remaining segments continue in the next stored record. Since fixed-length stored records are used, some unused space often results.

Although simple, HSAM has the same disadvantages as any physical sequential organization of records. Locating a particular segment requires an extensive sequential scan (each stored segment has a code that identifies the segment type for retrieval). Also, insertions and deletions are difficult to manage. As a result, HSAM has very limited use in most IMS installations. Normally, this method is used for historical or archival files.

HISAM

The hierarchical indexed sequential access method (HISAM) provides an indexed sequential organization for segments. As a result, the segments of a physical database record can be retrieved either sequentially or by direct access. HISAM uses either ISAM or VSAM as its underlying access method (ISAM and VSAM are described in Chapter 7). ISAM is used with a special IMS access method called OSAM (overflow sequential access method).

A HISAM organization for the department database is shown in Figure 14-8. In this example, two data sets (or physical storage files) are used, an ISAM data set and an OSAM data set. Each of these data sets is divided into fixed-length stored records. When an IMS database is first loaded, each root segment that is stored causes a new ISAM stored record to be created. This root segment is stored at the front of the record (in Figure 14-8, DEPARTMT 02 is the first root segment). The remainder of that record is then filled with additional dependent segments in hierarchical sequence (in Figure 14-8, the first EQPMENT segment for department 02 is placed in the ISAM record).

If all dependent segments for a particular root segment fit into one ISAM record, then no OSAM record is required. However, if the dependent segments overflow this record (as in Figure 14-8), then they are stored in hierarchical sequence in an OSAM record. A pointer containing the relative address of the OSAM record

Figure 14-7

HSAM organization for DEPTDB

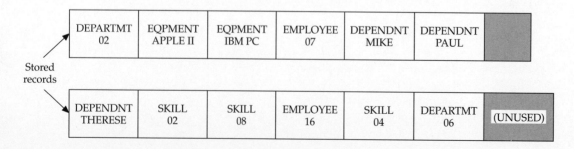

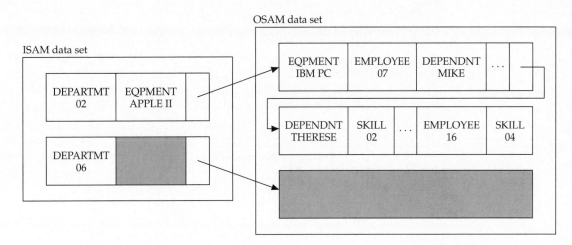

Figure 14-8

HISAM organization for DEPTDB

is placed in the last segment. If the first OSAM record is filled, a second record is created, and so on. As shown in the figure, one ISAM record and two OSAM records were required for all the segments for department 02.

The segments in a physical database record may be processed sequentially by following the pointers, such as those shown in Figure 14-8. Also, each root segment can be located by direct access using the ISAM index. Thus, HISAM provides the advantages of both sequential and direct access.

When VSAM is used, the ISAM data set is replaced by a VSAM key-sequenced data set. Also, the OSAM data set is replaced by a VSAM entry-sequenced data set. Thus, the segments are stored within VSAM control intervals and managed by the VSAM indexes.

HISAM is not often used in most IMS installations. It should be used only when no logical relationships exist and adds and deletes are minimal (that is, the database is not volatile).

HDAM and HIDAM

HDAM and HIDAM are both direct access methods. Both permit direct access to the root segment of a PDBR occurrence and therefore are frequently used. The dependent segments of that occurrence can then be accessed directly by following pointer chains. The main difference between HDAM and HIDAM is in the technique for addressing root segments, as we will now explain.

Pointer Structures   HDAM and HIDAM both use pointers to represent the hierarchical sequence of segments within a PDBR occurrence. As Figure 14-9 shows, the hierarchical sequence may be represented either by hierarchical pointers or by child/twin pointers.

The use of hierarchical pointers is shown in Figure 14-9a. These pointers are simply "threaded" through the segments in hierarchical sequence. The last segment in the PDBR occurrence (in this case, 04 COST 2) does not contain a pointer to the next root segment. Hierarchical pointers are most efficient when the segments within a PDBR are normally processed in hierarchical sequence.

The use of child/twin pointers is shown in Figure 14-9b. Each parent segment contains a pointer to its first child segment occurrence. Each child segment oc-

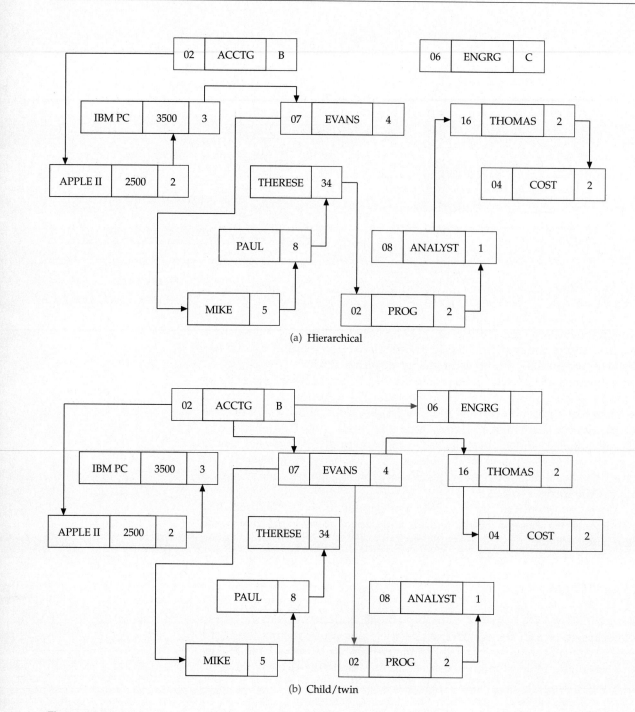

(a) Hierarchical

(b) Child/twin

Figure 14-9

HDAM and HIDAM
pointer structures

currence then contains a pointer to the next twin segment (if one exists). Also, each parent may optionally contain a pointer to the last (as well as first) child occurrence. Child/twin pointers are most efficient when only certain parent/child occurrences within a PDBR are normally processed each time (rather than the entire sequence).

Although not shown in Figure 14-9, both hierarchical and child/twin pointers may be bidirectional. That is, between any two segments, backward as well as forward pointers may be used.

HDAM   Hierarchical direct access method (HDAM) provides direct access to root segments by means of a hashing algorithm. Segments are stored in fixed-length stored records. The hashing algorithm generates a relative record address that provides the location of a root segment occurrence. The dependent segments may then be accessed by following the segment pointers (hierarchical or child/twin).

When an HDAM database is initially loaded, the root segments may be loaded in any order (key sequence is not necessary). However, all dependent segments for each root segment must be loaded in hierarchical sequence after the root segment. Dependent segments are stored as closely as possible to the root segment.

When two root segments collide (hash to the same relative address), the second root segment is placed in the next available stored record that contains sufficient space. A pointer to the second root segment is then placed in the first root segment (several colliding root segments may be linked by such a pointer chain).

HIDAM   Hierarchical indexed direct access method (HIDAM) also provides direct access to root segments. However, instead of using a hashing algorithm, HIDAM uses a dense index to locate root segment occurrences. Root segments are linked to dependent segments by pointers, as with HDAM.

The main advantage of HDAM (compared with HIDAM) is the speed of access where direct access is required. HDAM should be used where random access is required almost exclusively. Sequential processing with HDAM is difficult or inefficient.

On the other hand, the main advantage of HIDAM is that both random and sequential access are handled effectively. Thus, HIDAM is probably the most frequently used of all access methods in IMS.

Specifying the Internal Model

In IMS, the mapping of a physical database into storage is defined by adding additional statements to the database description (such as the one in Figure 14-3). For example, if HISAM is to be used, the following statement would be added to DBD:

```
ACCESS=HISAM
```

Additional entries are required to define the access method (such as VSAM versus ISAM) and the type of pointers to be used (hierarchical versus child/twin). Full specification of the internal model is often quite complex and is beyond the scope of this text.

IMS DATA MANIPULATION

The IMS data manipulation language is called Data Language I (DL/I). DL/I consists of a set of commands that are used with a host language (COBOL, PL/I, or assembler language). The application program invokes (or uses) these commands by means of subroutine calls.

Table 14-1 presents an overview of the DL/I commands. We describe and illustrate each of these commands below. The syntax is simplified in the following examples for ease of presentation. The examples are based on the department database (Figure 14-2).

TABLE 14-1 Summary of DL/I Operations

Operations	Explanation
GET UNIQUE (GU)	Direct retrieval of a segment
GET NEXT (GN)	Sequential retrieval of a segment
GET NEXT WITHIN PARENT (GNP)	Sequential retrieval under current parent
GET HOLD (GHU, GHN, GHNP)	As above, but allow subsequent DLET/REPL
REPLACE (REPL)	Replace existing segment
DELETE (DLET)	Delete existing segment
INSERT (ISRT)	Add new segment

GET UNIQUE (GU)

The GET UNIQUE (GU) command is used to retrieve a specific segment occurrence. The segment may be a root segment or a dependent segment. The segment desired is specified in parentheses by a qualifying condition, called a *segment search argument* (SSA). For example, suppose that we want to retrieve the segment for department 06 (a root segment). The following command would be used:

```
GU DEPARTMT (DEPTNO=06)
```

In this example, the SSA is DEPTNO = 06. The GU command will retrieve the *first* segment that satisfies the SSA (presumably there is only one occurrence for each department).

Now suppose that we want to retrieve the segment for EVANS (EMPNO = 07) in ACCTG (DEPTNO = 02). The following commands would be used:

```
GU DEPARTMT (DEPTNO=02)
   EMPLOYEE (EMPNO=07)
```

In this example, a hierarchical path is specified. The GU command will retrieve only the segment at the *bottom* of this path. Thus, the employee segment for EVANS (but not the parent department segment) will be retrieved.

The SSA may be omitted from a DL/I command. For example, consider the following commands:

```
GU DEPARTMT
   EQPMENT (IDENT=APPLE II)
```

With this command, DL/I will retrieve the *first* occurrence of an EQPMENT segment that satisfies the indicated SSA. It will scan DEPARTMT segments sequentially until this first dependent segment is located.

GET NEXT (GN)

GET NEXT (GN) is used for sequential retrieval of occurrences of a particular segment type. For example, suppose that we use the following commands:

```
GU DEPARTMT (DEPTNO=02)
   EQPMENT
GN EQPMENT
```

The GU command will cause the first EQPMENT segment (APPLE II) for DEPARTMT 02 to be retrieved. The GN command will then cause the next EQPMENT segment (IBM PC) to be retrieved.

The GN command cannot be executed until a current position has been established in the database. In the preceding example, the GU command establishes the starting position by retrieving the first EQPMENT segment.

Now suppose that we add another GN command to the above example:

```
GU DEPARTMT (DEPTNO=02)
   EQPMENT
GN EQPMENT
GN EQPMENT
```

These commands will attempt to retrieve a third EQPMENT segment. However, referring to Figure 14-2, we see that there are only two such segments under DEPARTMT 02. Will this result in an error condition? The answer is that it will not. Instead, DL/I will retrieve the next EQPMENT segment in the database under a new root segment. In fact, we can retrieve *all* EQPMENT segments in the database with the following commands:

```
     GU DEPARTMT
        EQPMENT
MORE GN EQPMENT
        GO TO MORE
```

GET NEXT WITHIN PARENT (GNP)

Like GET NEXT, GET NEXT WITHIN PARENT (GNP) causes sequential retrieval of segment occurrences. However, unlike GN, only occurrences under the current parent segment are retrieved. For example, if we wish to retrieve all DEPENDNT segments for EVANS in ACCTG, we can use the following commands:

```
     GU DEPARTMT (DEPTNO=02)
        EMPLOYEE (EMPNO=07)
        DEPENDNT
NEXT GNP DEPENDNT
        GO TO NEXT
```

In this example, the GU command retrieves the first DEPENDNT segment for this employee. The GNP then sequentially retrieves the remaining segments for the same employee (EVANS has three dependents). When the last segment is retrieved, DL/I will return a status message indicating that there are no more subordinate DEPENDNT segments for this employee.

The GNP command can be used to retrieve *all* subordinate segment occurrences under a current parent. For example, suppose that we wish to retrieve all segment occurrences for DEPARTMT 02:

```
     GU DEPARTMT (DEPTNO=02)
NEXT GNP
        GO TO NEXT
```

Since no segment type is specified for GNP, the loop will cause all subordinate segments to be retrieved in hierarchical sequence. DEPARTMT 02 has ten subordinate segments (see Figure 14-2).

GET HOLD

There are three GET HOLD commands: GET HOLD UNIQUE (GHU), GET HOLD NEXT (GHN), and GET HOLD NEXT WITHIN PARENT (GHNP). These commands function in exactly the same manner as GU, GN, and GNP, respectively. However, the GET HOLD versions must be used to retrieve segments that are going to be replaced (REPL) or deleted (DLET).

Replacement (REPL)

The replace (REPL) command is used to replace a segment occurrence with an updated version of the same segment. First, the segment must be retrieved by using one of the GET HOLD commands. The segment is then modified, and the REPL command writes the updated segment.

Look again at Figure 14-2. Suppose that we wish to change the age of the DEPENDNT PAUL from 8 to 9. The following commands could be used:

```
GHU DEPARTMT (DEPTNO=02)
    EMPLOYEE (EMPNO=07)
    DEPENDNT (DEPNM=PAUL)
    MOVE '9' TO AGE
    REPL
```

Deletion (DLET)

A segment to be deleted must first be retrieved by using one of the GET HOLD commands. For example, suppose that we wish to delete the skill PROG for EVANS in ACCTG. The following commands would be used:

```
GHU DEPARTMT (DEPTNO=02)
    EMPLOYEE (EMPNO=07)
    SKILL (CODE=02)
DLET
```

A DLET command deletes not only a particular segment, but all of its subordinate children (there are some exceptions to this rule, but they are beyond the scope of this text). For example, the following command will delete the root segment for DEPARTMT 02 plus all ten of its subordinate segments:

```
GHU DEPARTMT (DEPTNO=02)
DLET
```

As a result, you must be cautious in using this command. In general, the processing options (PROCOPT) specification in the PCB should limit the delete operation to only a few qualified users.

Insertion (ISRT)

ISRT allows the user to insert a new segment into the database. To insert a new subordinate segment, the parent segment must already exist in the database. For example, suppose that we wish to insert a new DEPENDNT occurrence for EVANS in ACCTG. The following commands could be used:

```
MOVE 'CHRIS' TO DEPNM
MOVE '0' TO AGE
ISRT DEPARTMT (DEPTNO=02)
     EMPLOYEE (EMPNO=07)
     DEPENDNT
```

First, the new segment to be inserted is built in the application program output area (indicated by the first two statements above). Next, the ISRT statement defines the hierarchical path to the segment to be inserted. The new segment occurrence is inserted in sequence among the existing child occurrences for the specified parent.

ADVANCED IMS FEATURES

So far, we have described the basic features of IMS. All these features are based on a purely hierarchical data model. In this section, we describe two additional features that extend IMS beyond this hierarchical model: logical databases and secondary indexing.

Logical Databases

Earlier in this chapter, we defined a logical database record (LDBR) as a subset of an IMS physical database record (PDBR). More generally, an LDBR may be defined as a subset of one or more PDBRs. In this section, we describe how an LDBR can be defined as a subset of two PDBRs.

Suppose that the department database (DEPTDB) illustrated in Figure 14-1 already exists. Now suppose that the organization wants to create a project database (PROJDB). The structure of this proposed database is shown in Figure 14-10a. The root segment type is PROJECT, and the dependent segment is EMPLOYEE.

One possible approach is to create a new PDBR type with the structure shown in Figure 14-10a. However, the new EMPLOYEE segment occurrences will contain the same data that already exist in the EMPLOYEE segments within the department database. A better approach (which avoids this redundancy) is to link the new PROJECT segment with the existing EMPLOYEE segment by means of a logical pointer segment (see Figure 14-10b). There are two PDBR types in this figure: DEPTDB and PROJDB. The logical pointer segment (called EMPLPROJ) links the two databases. EMPLPROJ is the *physical* child of PROJECT and the *logical* child of EMPLOYEE.

As shown in Figure 14-10c, the new PROJECT database may now be represented as a logical database. The LDBR type in this figure is a subset of the two PDBR types shown in Figure 14-10b. The logical database shown in Figure 14-10c does not actually exist. However, a user application program may process the data as if it existed in this form.

Figure 14-10

Logical databases

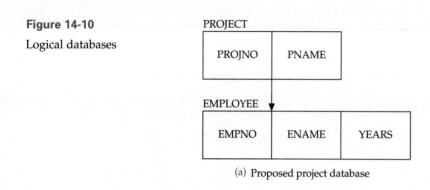

(a) Proposed project database

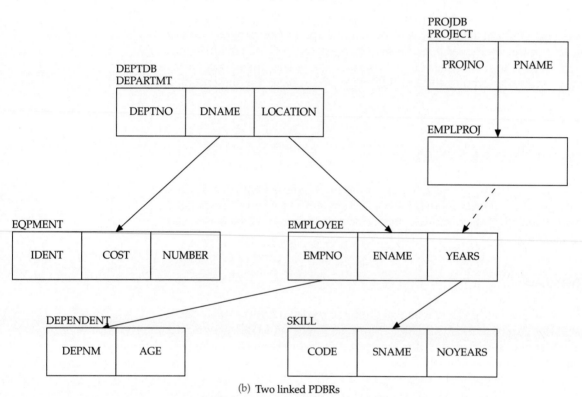

(b) Two linked PDBRs

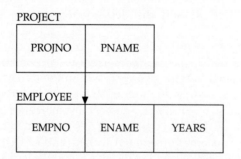

(c) One LDBR based on the first two PDBRs (PROJEMP)

Database Description   Building a logical database is a three-step process. The first step is defining a physical database description of the project database. In Figure 14-11a, statements 1 to 4 are similar to those in Figure 14-3, and the project segment is defined with two fields. Statement 5 is the description of the EMPLPROJ pointer segment. This statement identifies PROJECT as the physical parent, and EMPLOYEE (in DEPTDB) as the logical parent. The P in this entry denotes that the pointer in EMPLPROJ is a logical pointer. If there are data related to the combination of a project and an employee (called *intersection data*), these data can be stored in the EMPLPROJ segment.

The second step is to amend the Department physical database description (Figure 14-3) by adding an LCHILD (logical child) statement, as shown in Figure 14-11b. Statement 11 in this figure indicates that EMPLOYEE has a logical child called EMPLPROJ in the PROJDB database. This statement is then followed by the FIELD statements for EMPLOYEE.

The third step in building our logical database is to define the logical database itself. As see in Figure 14-11c, this process is rather straightforward. In statements 1 and 2, the database is named and is defined as logical. In statement 3, the PROJECT segment is defined, and the source of the data to be used is shown to be the PROJDB. In statement 4, the EMPLOYEE is defined, and the source of its data is the EMPLOYEE segment in the DEPTDB database and the EMPLPROJ segment in the PROJDB database.

There are two important restrictions in defining logical databases:

1. The root of a logical database must also be the root of a physical database. In Figure 14-10, PROJECT is the root of the PROJEMP (logical database) and PROJDB (physical database).

2. A logical child segment must have one physical parent and one logical parent. In Figure 14-10, EMPLPROJ is the physical child of PROJECT and the logical child of EMPLOYEE.

In this section, we have presented a simplified description of IMS logical databases. In reality, additional entries would be required. For a complete discussion of this topic, see IBM Corp. (1989).

```
1   DBD     NAME=PROJDB
2   SEGM    NAME=PROJECT, BYTES=27, PARENT=0
3   FIELD   NAME=(PROJNO, SEQ), BYTES=7, START=1
4   FIELD   NAME=PNAME, BYTES=20, START=8
5   SEGM    NAME=EMPLPROJ, PARENT=((PROJECT), (EMPLOYEE, P, DEPTDB))
```

(a) Physical DBD

```
10  SEGM    NAME=EMPLOYEE, PARENT=DEPARTMT, BYTES=42
11  LCHILD  NAME=(EMPLPROJ, PROJDB)
```

(b) Change to EMPLOYEE segment of DEPTDB database

```
1   DBD      NAME=PROJEMP, ACCESS=LOGICAL
2   DATASET  LOGICAL
3   SEGM     NAME=PROJECT, SOURCE=(PROJECT, DATA, PROJDB)
4   SEGM     NAME=EMPLOYEE, PARENT=PROJECT,
             SOURCE=((EMPLPROJ, DATA, PROJDB), (EMPLOYEE, DATA, DEPTDB))
```

(c) Logical DBD for PROJEMP logical database

Figure 14-11

Building the logical database

Processing a Logical Database   A logical database is accessed in exactly the same way as a physical database. The programmer does not have to know whether the database is physical or logical.

Loading a logical database is another matter. Again, it is a three-step process, assuming the logical database has been correctly defined. First, the data must be loaded onto the first physical database (DEPTDB in our example). Second, the data must be loaded onto the other physical database (PROJDB). Finally, an IMS utility is run that causes the two databases to be logically connected.

Once the logical database has been loaded, a user can process it exactly as if it were a physical database. That is, DL/I commands can be used to retrieve and manipulate the logical database. For example, suppose that we wish to retrieve all EMPLOYEE segments for employees who are assigned to PROJECT ABCD. The following DL/I commands would be used:

```
        GU PROJECT (PROJECTNO=ABCD)
            EMPLOYEE
NEXT GNP EMPLOYEE
            GO TO NEXT
```

Notice that in filling this request, the program will retrieve segments from two physical databases.

Secondary Indexing

One of the important features of IMS is the ability to access databases using multiple keys. As an example, we normally access the DEPTDB by department number. If we now need to access the DEPTDB by location, we could use a logical database, but a better approach would be to use a secondary index. Like HIDAM databases, secondary indexes are implemented by means of a physical index database. To implement a secondary index, we must change the DBD of the database to be indexed (DEPTDB in our example).

We would need to add the following two statements to the DBD (Figure 14-3) immediately after the LOCATION field statement:

```
LCHILD NAME=(LOCINDX, LOCDB), POINTER=INDX
 XDFLD NAME=XLOCN, SRCH=LOCATION
```

The first (or LCHILD) statement specifies that this database (DEPTDB) is indexed by a segment called LOCINDX (location index). That index is defined in a database called LOCDB. The POINTER=INDX entry specifies that LOCINDX is indeed an index (not a data record). The second (or XDFLD) statement identifies the field that is indexed; in this example, it is LOCATION, as specified by the SRCH=LOCATION entry. The NAME=XLOCN entry specifies that the variable name XLOCN will be used in referring to the indexed field.

Defining a Secondary Index   The secondary index database is described as shown in Figure 14-12. Statement 1 is a regular DBD statement and assigns the name LOCDB to this database. Statement 2 assigns the name LOCINDEX to the segment in an index, and statement 3 defines the field (LOCATION) on which the secondary index is defined. This is the only field in the LOCINDEX segment.

```
1   DBD     NAME=LOCDB, ACCESS=INDEX
2   SEGM    NAME=LOCINDEX, BYTES=4
3   FIELD   NAME=LOCATION, BYTES=4, START=1
4   LCHILD  NAME=(DEPARTMT, DEPTDB), INDEX=XLOCN
```

Figure 14-12

DBD for secondary index

Statement 4 is the LCHILD that connects the index database to the LOCATION field in the DEPTDB. A secondary index database such as this one is loaded using IMS utilities.

Using a Secondary Index   When an IMS database is loaded, any secondary indexes that have been defined by the user are automatically constructed by IMS. Also, IMS automatically maintains the secondary indexes as the database is modified.

To use a secondary index, the user specifies DL/I commands that invoke the variable names for the indexed field. To return to our original example, suppose that we wish to retrieve the segment for the department whose location is B100. The following statement will be used:

```
GU DEPARTMT (XLOCN=B100)
```

This statement causes IMS to retrieve the B100 index segment within LOCDB. That segment contains a pointer to the B100 data segment within DEPARTMT, which is the target segment.

In this example, we assume that values of the indexed field are unique (e.g., there is only one B100 segment). However, an IMS secondary index may also be defined for fields that do not have unique values. For example, there may be more than one department at a given location. Therefore, a secondary index for LOCATION must accommodate nonunique values. Minor modifications are required in the secondary index definition for this case [for details, see IBM Corp. (1989)].

Case Example: Mountain View Community Hospital

In this section, we illustrate the use of IMS to implement a database for Mountain View Community Hospital. An entity-relationship diagram of a database for this hospital is shown in Figure 4-30. Figure 14-13 shows an IMS implementation of this database.

Database Definition

Three distinct physical databases are shown in Figure 14-13. These databases are linked together by logical pointers for reasons already described. A DBD for the PHYSICIAN database is shown in Figure 14-14 (we will ask you to develop DBDs for the remaining databases in the chapter problems).

Two segment types are defined in the PHYSICIAN database: PHYSICN (for physician) and TREATMT (for treatment). Notice that in statement 8, a logical child is defined for the TREATMT segment. This logical child is the treatment

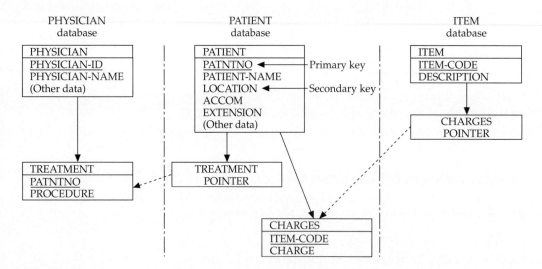

Figure 14-13

IMS database structures
(Mountain View Community Hospital)

Figure 14-14

DBD for PHYSICIAN
database (Mountain
View Community
Hospital)

```
1   DBD      NAME=PHYSDB
2   SEGM     NAME=PHYSICN, BYTES=17, PARENT=0
3   FIELD    NAME=(PHYSID, SEQ), BYTES=10, START=1
4   FIELD    NAME=PHYPHONE, BYTES=7, START=11
5   SEGM     NAME=TREATMT, PARENT=PHYSICN, BYTES=19
6   FIELD    NAME=(PATNTNO, SEQ), BYTES=4, START=1
7   FIELD    NAME=PROCEDUR, BYTES=15, START=5
8   LCHILD   NAME=(TREATPTR, PATNTDB)
```

pointer (TREATPTR) in the PATIENT database (PATNTDB). This pointer links the PATIENT and PHYSICIAN databases.

Database Manipulation

To illustrate database manipulation, we use DL/I statements to retrieve data from the hospital databases. All the statements are based on the database structures shown in Figure 14-13.

Simple Retrieval   To retrieve patient data for patient number 1234, we use the following command:

```
GU PATIENT (PATNTNO=1234)
```

Indexed Retrieval   To retrieve patient data for the patient in location 4321, we use the following command:

```
GU PATIENT (XLOCN=4321)
```

This command assumes that there is a secondary index for the LOCATION field. Also, we assume that XLOCN is the variable name for the indexed field LOCATION.

Retrieval of Child Segments   To calculate total charges for patient number 1234, we use the following commands:

```
        MOVE 0 TO TOTAL
          GU PATIENT (PATNTNO=1234)
             CHARGES
             ADD CHARGE TO TOTAL
   MORE GNP CHARGES
             ADD CHARGE TO TOTAL
             GO TO MORE
```

The GET UNIQUE (GU) statement retrieves the first CHARGES segment for this patient (if one exists). The amount of the CHARGE is added to the running total (TOTAL). The GNP statement is then executed repeatedly to retrieve additional charges, and TOTAL is updated until there are no more charges for that patient.

Retrieval Using Logical Records   To retrieve all TREATMT segments for patient number 1234, we use the following commands:

```
          GU PATIENT (PATNTNO=1234)
             TREATMT
   MORE GNP TREATMT
             GO TO MORE
```

In this retrieval, the PATIENT and TREATMT segments exist in separate databases. However, use of the treatment pointer (TREATPTR) allows the user to manipulate the TREATMT segment as a child of PATIENT.

SUMMARY

In this chapter, we have presented an introduction to IMS, a database management system based on the hierarchical data model. In IMS, data are viewed as hierarchical arrangements of segments. A data manipulation language called Data Language I (DL/I) allows the user to retrieve data by traversing the tree structure.

Although the design of IMS dates from the late 1960s, a stream of enhancements has been added to provide new features. Thus, through the use of logical databases, the user can model limited networks. Also, secondary indexing permits access on fields other than primary keys. However, because these features are quite complex, IMS tends to be used only in relatively sophisticated data processing shops where considerable technical expertise is available.

Many other hierarchical DBMS products (not described in this chapter) are also available. Although it represents older technology, the hierarchical model remains a viable alternative for some DBMS implementations. However, it should be evaluated against the more recent network and relational systems.

CHAPTER REVIEW

Key Terms

Child	Program communication	Physical database record
Database description (DBD)	block (PCB)	(PDBR)
Hierarchical sequence	Program specification block	Root
Logical database (LDB)	(PSB)	Segment
		Twins

REVIEW QUESTIONS

1. Give a concise definition for each of the following terms:
   a. segment
   b. root segment
   c. logical database record
   d. physical database record
   e. database description
   f. program communication block
2. Contrast the following terms:
   a. physical database record; logical database record
   b. program communication block; program specification block
   c. root segment; child segment
   d. hierarchical pointers; child/twin pointers
3. Define each of the following acronyms:
   a. IMS
   b. PDBR
   c. LDBR
   d. PCB
   e. PSB
   f. GNP
   g. LCHILD
   h. SENSEG
4. Describe each of the following access methods briefly, and indicate the conditions favoring its use:
   a. HSAM
   b. HISAM
   c. HDAM
   d. HIDAM
5. Describe two ways in which an LDBR may differ from a PDBR.
6. Describe two advantages of the sensitive-segment feature in IMS.
7. Why must caution be used in deleting a root segment with the DL/I DLET command?
8. Describe two restrictions in defining logical databases.

PROBLEMS AND EXERCISES

Problems 1 to 4 are based on the following hierarchical database structure for Pine Valley Furniture Company:

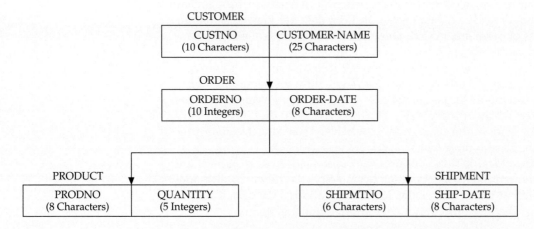

1. Write an IMS database description (DBD) for the database shown.
2. Based on the DBD in Problem 1, write a program communication block (PCB) for a logical database record that contains the CUSTOMER, ORDER, and PRODUCT segments (but omits the SHIPMENT segment).
3. Write DL/I statements for each of the following retrievals:
   a. CUSTOMER segment for customer number ABCD
   b. ORDER segment for order number 1234, customer number ABCD
   c. All ORDER segments for customer number ABCD
   d. All PRODUCT segments for customer number ABCD, order number 1234

4. Write DL/I statements for the following updates:
   a. Change the QUANTITY for product number 10 in order number 1234 for customer number ABCD from 3 to 2.
   b. Delete shipment number WXYZ for order number 6789 from customer number ABCD.
   c. Add shipment number CDEF to order number 6789 from customer number ABCD (shipment date is 6/18/9X).
5. Write an IMS database description for the ITEM database in Figure 14-13. Assume the following data item characteristics:

ITEM CODE	10 Characters
DESCRIPN	25 Characters

6. Write an IMS database description for the PATIENT database (Figure 14-13). Include the logical pointers. Assume the following data item characteristics:

PATNTNO	10 Characters
PATNAME	25 Characters
LOCATION	5 Characters
ACCOM	6 Characters
EXTENSN	4 Integers
ITEMCODE	10 Characters
CHARGE	Decimal XXXX.XX

7. In Figure 14-13, LOCATION is identified as a secondary key in the PATIENT segment. Write an IMS secondary index DBD for this field.
8. One logical database record derived from the hospital database (Figure 14-13) appears as follows:

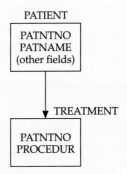

Write an IMS DBD for this logicial record.

9. Write DL/I statements for the following retrievals in the hospital database (Figure 14-13):
   a. CHARGE segment for item number 1234, patient number ABCD
   b. All CHARGE segments for patient number ABCD
   c. All TREATMENT segments for patient number ABCD performed by physician number P10
10. Referring to Figure 14-2, what segment(s) will be retrieved for each of the following statements?
    a. GU DEPARTMT (DEPTNO=02)
        EQPMENT (IDENT=APPLE II)
    b. GU DEPARTMT (DEPTNO=02)
        EMPLOYEE (EMPNO=07)
        SKILL (CODE=02)

c.   GU DEPARTMT (DEPTNO=02)
         EMPLOYEE (EMPNO=07)
         DEPENDNT (DEPNM=THERESE)
NEXT GNP DEPENDNT
         GO TO NEXT

REFERENCES

Date, C. J. 1981. *An Introduction to Database Systems*. 3d ed. Reading, Mass.: Addison-Wesley.

IBM Corp. 1989. *IMS/ESA Version 3 General Information Manual*. IBM form no. GC26-4275-0.

Network and CODASYL Implementations

LEARNING OBJECTIVES

After studying this chapter, you should be able to:

- Explain the interaction between a host language application program, a DBTG DBMS, operating systems, and a database during database processing.
- Explain the data independence that is created by having separate schema and subschema DDLs, DML, and DMCL.
- Describe the role of each of the following in tuning the performance of a DBTG database: area, VIA location mode, prior and owner pointers, singular (or system) sets, and sort keys.
- Use sets to depict various types of relationships.
- Use various set membership clauses to implement semantic controls on the existence and processing of data.
- Explain record-at-a-time navigation through a network database.

INTRODUCTION

The purpose of this chapter is to review the implementation of the network data model in industry standards and in commercial database management systems. You may want to review "The Network Data Model" section in Chapter 7 before proceeding.

The implementation of the network data model is an interesting example of the influence of industry standards and of individual vendors. The Conference on Data Systems Languages (CODASYL) through its Data Base Task Group (DBTG) is a standards organization that has developed and issued descriptions of languages for defining and processing data. The initial report describing a network database implementation was issued in 1971 (CODASYL, 1971). Subsequent reports and updates describing most network DBMSs were issued in 1978 and 1981 (see references at end of this chapter).

Although represented on the original DBTG, IBM Corporation did not sign or endorse these standards and to this day has not implemented a network DBMS.

But many other hardware vendors and numerous software firms have chosen to develop systems following the CODASYL guidelines (even for IBM computers). At the same time, IBM has installed IMS, its hierarchical DBMS, in many of its customers' data centers. Again, these events indicate that variety is the hallmark of database.

The CODASYL Committee is a voluntary group of individuals who represent hardware and software vendors, universities, and major developers and users of data processing systems. Their original charge had been to discuss changes to the COBOL programming language and to write position papers in this area. Member organizations were in no way bound to implement these positions in their program products. It had become clear that COBOL needed radical extension to support multiple-file (database) data processing, and the DBTG was formed.

In 1963, General Electric (later Honeywell Information Systems) began to market Integrated Data System (IDS), the forerunner of network DBMSs. The generally accepted leader of the development of IDS was Charles Bachman. Although Bachman was not on the DBTG itself, several individuals from Honeywell were represented, along with Richard Schubert of B.F. Goodrich Chemical Company, a primary user of IDS. Through these individuals, and because IDS was the most fully developed DBMS by this time, the structure of IDS (and the ideas of Charles Bachman) greatly influenced the deliberations of the DBTG. Even today, many organizations draw ''Bachman diagrams'' to represent network databases.

Although pleased with the capabilities of IDS, B.F. Goodrich worked on expanding these functions to meet more of the DBTG guidelines. Interest grew in the computing community in bringing a DBTG network DBMS to the marketplace. John Cullinane approached B.F. Goodrich and purchased the rights to further develop and market their initial DBTG implementation along with the existing CULPRIT report-writer product. He named his new product Integrated Database

TABLE 15-1 Summary of Some Network DBMSs

Package	Vendor	Equipment	Comments
CODASYL DBMSs			
IDMS	Cullinet Software (Division of Computer Associates)	IBM 360/370, 30xx, 43xx, variety of operating systems, DEC VAX under VMS operating system, several minis, and a few other mainframes	Various related packages, including Integrated Data Dictionary, CULPRIT report-writer, OnLine English natural language, distributed database facility, and Application Development System (ADS/O)
PR1ME DBMS	PR1ME Computer	Various PR1ME mini and supermini computers under PR1MOS operating system	
DMS-170	CDC	Variety of hardware under NOS operating system	
DBMS 11	DEC	DEC VAX under VMS operating system	
IDS II	Honeywell Information Systems	Variety of HIS computers	Extension of first network DBMS; works with many host languages
DMS-1100	Univac (UNISYS)	Exec 8 and more recent operating systems for Univac 1100 computer family	Popular nonprocedural language MAPPER

Management System (IDMS), which is still, today, the leading DBTG DBMS on IBM (and other) computers.

Many network DBMSs exist today. Most of these are DBTG implementations, but several significant exceptions have appeared. Table 15-1 lists several of these network DBMSs and pertinent information about them. Since DBTG network DBMSs dominate, most of this chapter reviews the definition and processing of data using these DBMSs. Also addressed are recent extensions to network DBMSs that provide non-network views of a database managed by a network DBMS. This topic is an important development that creates a great deal of confusion in distinguishing between DBMSs.

There are actually three official versions of the DBTG guidelines (1971, 1978, and 1981 reports); we have chosen to emphasize the 1978 report because most DBTG DBMSs today come closest to following these guidelines. Some exceptions will be noted when appropriate. Because of its prominence among IBM computer installations, we will draw heavily on IDMS as an example of a DBTG implementation. For greater depth on the DBTG model, Olle (1980) provides an excellent coverage of these guidelines through several minor modifications published in 1973.

INTRODUCTION TO CODASYL DBTG GUIDELINES

To begin to understand the DBTG guidelines and implementations of this data model, we must start by analyzing the concept of a DBMS that underlies the work of the DBTG. Figure 15-1 shows the conceptual database management system envisioned by the DBTG. This diagram indicates that a DBMS is conceived as software that works in conjunction with an operating system to service multiple, concurrently executing user programs.

DBMS Operation

To comprehend the nature of a DBTG DBMS, it is important to understand the operational sequence of events that occurs when such a DBMS is used. This sequence is depicted with numbered arrows in Figure 15-1 and can be summarized as follows:

1. A user program "calls" the DBMS with a request for service (retrieval, maintenance, and so on), which has been written using special data manipulation language (DML) statements. These statements are included in a host language (e.g., COBOL) user program.

2. The DBMS analyzes the request for service by matching the parameters of the request with a stored version of a definition of the database (called a *schema*) and a definition of the part of the database applicable to this program (called a *subschema*). These two data definitions have been predefined via data description languages (DDLs) and are maintained and stored separately from user programs in a library of data definitions.

3. As long as the request for service contains no inadmissible components (e.g., improper security passwords or references to data outside the invoked subschema), the DBMS composes a series of I/O commands for the access methods of the operating system.

CONCEPTUAL DATABASE
MANAGEMENT SYSTEM

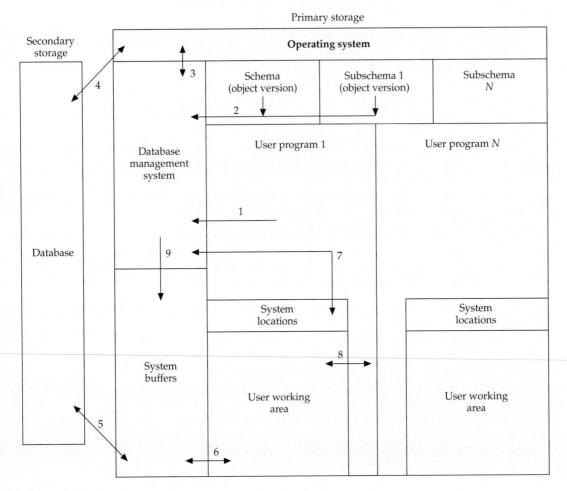

Figure 15-1

CODASYL conceptual
database management
system (*Source:*
CODASYL, 1971)

4. The operating system interacts with secondary storage devices to initiate database access.

5. The operating system performs the appropriate retrieval or modification of database contents, using data buffers managed by the DBMS. These buffers contain blocks of data transferred between main and secondary memory in which data are formatted as defined by the schema.

6. In the case of data retrieval, data are then moved from the system buffers to a user work area or data section of the calling user's program (steps 5 and 6 are reversed for maintenance). This transfer also often includes the reformatting of data and the elimination of data in blocks not included in the subschema.

7. The DBMS then sets status-variable values in the user program with messages and error codes to indicate the nature of any problems, if any, that arose during database interaction.

8. The user program is then free to further manipulate the data it has received from the database or to compose new records for database maintenance.

9. While each user program is executing, the DBMS manages the system buffers so that, for example, if a request for data is made that asks for data already in a system buffer, the DBMS can bypass steps 3 to 5 and provide the data immediately to the calling program.

Although the outline of this interaction could be interpreted in several ways, the resulting guidelines specified an implementation in which user calls occur at the record level; that is, the user program includes DML statements to retrieve or write *each* record required for processing, one at a time from each database file.

A CODASYL Database

There are two perspectives on a CODASYL database: a comprehensive and a local perspective. The comprehensive perspective is called a **schema**, which is a definition of the complete database. It describes what is in the database and the linkages between data. It describes the record types and fields from a data model, as well as some physical constructs of how data are to be organized on disk. A local perspective is called a **subschema**, which covers a restricted view of a database. A subschema is a subset, possibly with some redefinition, of its associated schema. A given database will have one schema, but may have several associated subschemas, each for a different program or groups of programs. Each program invokes one subschema, which then becomes that program's view into the database.

Schema: In the CODASYL data model, the description of a database.

Subschema: In the CODASYL data model, the description of that subset of a database used by a program that accesses the database. A subschema may be a subset of its associated schema, and may redefine some records and fields within the schema.

DBTG Languages

The DBTG guidelines also specified or implied various new languages. Figure 15-2 illustrates the relationships between these languages and the roles of each in defining and using a network database. First is a schema **data description language** (schema DDL), used to define the global database. As previously mentioned, this is a combination of implementation-independent and -dependent statements. Since the schema DDL does not, however, cover all internal/physical declarations, a **device media control language (DMCL)** was proposed to specify assignment of data to particular devices, data block contents and format, database update audit trail options, and so on.

Also proposed were standards for a subschema data description language (subschema DDL) for specifying database structure to program compilers. Several user programs are allowed to share the same subschema. Originally, only a COBOL subschema DDL was proposed, but today a FORTRAN subschema DDL also exists. Each language requires its own subschema DDL since the idea was to define the external database in a syntax that can be easily translated into the data definitions of a programming language.

Finally, standards for a **data manipulation language (DML)**, also host-language-specific, were proposed. Initially, only a COBOL version was outlined, but today a FORTRAN version also exists. The DBTG assumed a host-language environment in which there would be extensions to an already existing language (as opposed to defining a new self-contained language for database manipulation). These extensions would be handled either by vendors creating new language compilers to translate the expanded vocabulary or by preprocessors (as illustrated in Figure 15-2) that would translate only the new language statements within a program into standard language sentences (usually CALL statements with parameters derived from the raw DML statement). The output from the DML preprocessor would then be given to a standard language compiler.

Data description language (DDL): The language component of a DBMS that is used to describe the logical (and sometimes physical) structure of a database. Different DDLs may exist to describe either the whole database or particular views of part of a database.

Device media control language (DMCL): A language used with a CODASYL DBMS to specify the physical design of a database.

Data manipulation language (DML): A language component of a DBMS that is used by a programmer to access and modify the contents of a database.

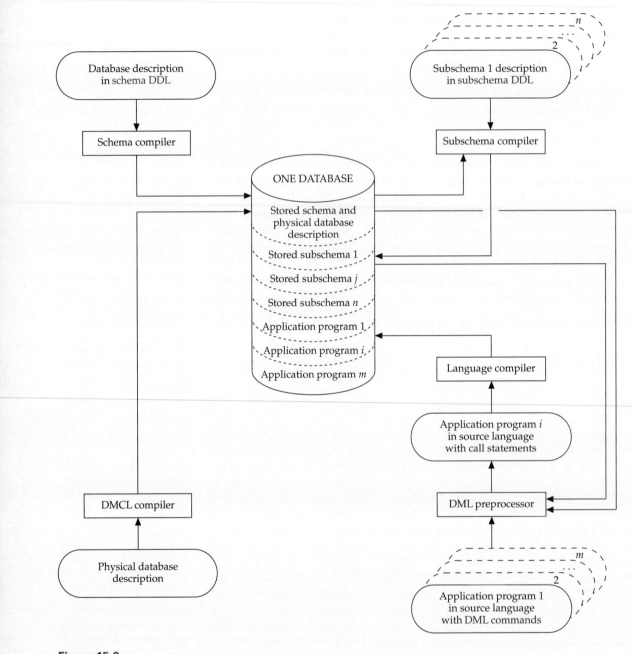

Figure 15-2

DBTG languages and
compilation cycles

The DBTG proposals also called for extensive capabilities to define security
controls in the schema DDL. Many initial implementations of the DBTG model
chose not to include these capabilities since it was felt that, given computing
power in the early 1970s, database processing performance would be seriously
deterred by such overhead. Today, inclusion of security controls is a standard
feature of DBTG implementations. Also standard today are nonprocedural (non-
record-at-a-time) query languages for DBTG implementations that permit retrieval (but often *not* update) to be accomplished in fewer statements and less
programming time than in conventional procedural languages like COBOL or
FORTRAN.

This, then, is an overview of the DBTG DBMS environment. The following sections address the DBTG model and its languages in greater detail.

DBTG SCHEMA DDL: THE CONCEPTUAL/INTERNAL DATABASE

The DBTG schema DDL uses some familiar terminology but has certainly done its part to create new terms. On occasion, this terminology has been disturbing enough to cause CODASYL to change terms to clarify usage of the data model. The schema DDL has many clauses and various options in most of the clause parameters. It is beyond our purpose here to cover all features of the schema DDL, so we will show only the most salient and frequently used features and parameters. The general structure of a DBTG schema definition for a simplified version of a database for Pine Valley Furniture is shown in Figure 15-3a. The structure

```
SCHEMA NAME IS _____
   [ON ERROR...]
   [PRIVACY LOCK...]
{AREA NAME IS _____
   [ON ERROR...]
   [PRIVACY LOCK...]}*
{RECORD NAME IS _____
   LOCATION MODE...
   [KEY IS...]**
   {WITHIN...}*
   [ON ERROR...]
   [PRIVACY LOCK...]
   [level-no data-base-data-name
    |((|PICTURE...| or |TYPE...|)
        |OCCURS...|) or
        (|SOURCE...|)|
        |RESULT...|
        |CHECK...|
        | FOR (ENCODING OR DECODING)...|
        [ON ERROR...]
        [PRIVACY...]|}
[SET NAME IS _____
      OWNER IS...
      [SET IS DYNAMIC or PRIOR|
      ORDER IS...
      [ON ERROR...]
      [PRIVACY LOCK...]
      {MEMBER IS _____
       INSERTION IS _____
       RETENTION IS _____
      [KEY IS...]
      |SEARCH KEY IS...|
      |CHECK IS...|
      |SET SELECTION...|
      [ON ERROR...]
      [PRIVACY LOCK...]}}]
END SCHEMA
```

   *Deleted in 1981 CODASYL revision, but still a part of most DBMSs.
  **Added in 1981 version, but not yet present in most DBMSs.
   [...]-0, 1 or many occurrences of clause
   {...}-1 or many occurrences of clause
   |...|-0 or 1 occurrence of clause

(a) Schema DDL   (continues)

Figure 15-3

General structure of DBTG schema definition

Figure 15-3

(continued)

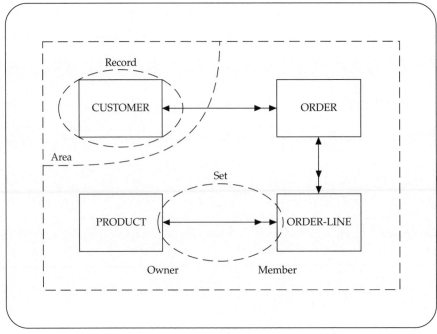

Schema

(b) Schema diagram

illustrated here generally obeys the 1978 DBTG guidelines; exceptions are indicated with footnotes. Figure 15-3b illustrates via a network diagram the parts of a network data model that correspond to the various sections of the schema DDL.

The structure shown in Figure 15-3a can be broken into three general segments. The first segment defines contiguous physical storage regions, called *areas*, into which all data values will be stored. Because this deals with the physical or metaphysical database, the 1981 guidelines have dropped this segment (and related clauses) to make the schema more independent of implementation.

The second segment describes all the record types or files and the data item contents that compose the database. The third segment defines the database representation, called *sets*, of all pairwise record type relationships designed in the conceptual database. The data model is a simple network, and link and intersection record types (called *junction records* by IDMS) may exist, as well as sets between them (ORDER-LINE is an example of an intersection record in Figure 15-3b). Thus, the complete network of relationships is represented by several pairwise sets; in each set some (one) record type is owner (at the tail of the network arrow) and one or more record types are members (at the head of the relationship arrow). Usually, a set defines a 1:*M* relationship, although 1:1 is permitted.

Two types of clauses that can appear at various points in a schema will not be addressed in detail here; these are the ON ERROR and PRIVACY clauses. ON ERROR can be used to indicate that certain user-defined procedures are to be invoked in case of specified errors in data or commands. PRIVACY LOCKs specify passwords or procedures that are used to verify that certain database manipulations are authorized for users of the database.

Before we explain the schema DDL, it is worth mentioning that you may have the most trouble understanding three components of DDL: LOCATION MODE,

SET SELECTION, and set membership clauses. Carefully study examples and discussions that involve these most frequently misunderstood parts of a DBTG database definition.

Areas or Realms

Consider the simplified Pine Valley Furniture database of Figure 15-3b. If this database were large enough to require many disk cylinders or disk packs, processing could become very expensive. If a significant amount of data processing were related to customer geographical regions (e.g., sales reports produced by region or new orders batched by region), then it might be advantageous to cluster CUSTOMER and ORDER records (at least) from a common geographical region close together in the physical database for more rapid access between these records. Similarly, suppose that marketing applications concentrate record usage on CUSTOMER and ORDER records, and that production applications primarily use PRODUCT and ORDER-LINE record types. In this case, it is advantageous to cluster CUSTOMER and ORDER records close together, but separate from a cluster of PRODUCT and ORDER-LINE records, in order to provide rapid access between records that are used together in data processing.

An **area** (or **realm** in recent CODASYL terminology) is a named, contiguous portion of secondary memory. Operationally, this is equivalent to a range of adjacent pages of some physical disk file. The purpose of the area designation is to control the physical proximity of records, as illustrated in the Pine Valley Furniture cases of geographical regions and segregated data processing. The database of a schema will reside in one or more areas. Each area is named in the schema, and the definition of each record specifies which area or areas will hold records of that type (the WITHIN clause).

Area: In a CODASYL database, a named, contiguous area of secondary storage. Also called *realm*.

A skeleton of a schema for this Pine Valley Furniture situation would be

```
AREA NAME IS SOUTH
...
RECORD NAME IS CUSTOMER
...
   WITHIN SOUTH, EAST, WEST AREA-ID IS CUST-REGION
...
   1 CUST-REGION; TYPE IS CHARACTER 10
...
RECORD NAME IS ORDER
...
   LOCATION MODE IS VIA ORDERS-FOR-CUSTOMER SET
   WITHIN AREA OF OWNER
...
SET NAME IS ORDERS-FOR-CUSTOMER
   OWNER IS CUSTOMER
...
   MEMBER IS ORDER
...
```

In this example, it is assumed that three areas were desirable: SOUTH, EAST, and WEST (area definitions for EAST and WEST are similar to the one for SOUTH). CUSTOMER records are automatically placed in the proper area by the DBMS when a new record is stored. The customer's region (and area) name, loaded into the CUST-REGION field of a CUSTOMER record instance by a data entry program, is used to specify proper placement. ORDER records are placed in the same region as their associated CUSTOMER record (that is, their owner is the ORDERS-FOR-CUSTOMER set). Thus, if data processing requirements frequently require ORDER records associated with a given CUSTOMER record, then these records can be accessed more rapidly than if placement is not controlled. For this reason, a set is said to define an access path to "walk" through a database from owner record to members (or vice versa). This placement of ORDER records near their related CUSTOMER record is controlled by the WITHIN clause of the ORDER record (makes all ORDERs closer to all CUSTOMERs than to other records) and the LOCATION MODE clause of the ORDER record (places a specific ORDER close to its particular CUSTOMER record instance).

Records

> **Record type:** A named entity, instances of which describe individual occurrences of the entity. See also *record*.

The second major data construct in the DBTG model is that of a record type. A **record type** is a named entity, instances of which describe individual occurrences of the entity. We define a record type by specifying how the physical location of a record instance is determined (LOCATION MODE clause) and by a list of data element (or data-base-data-name) definitions.

> **LOCATION MODE:** In a CODASYL database, the method used to determine the disk address of records of a particular record type when those records are stored or accessed.

LOCATION MODE of a Record   LOCATION MODE is a physical construct that has been removed in recent guidelines but is still present in most commercial implementations. **LOCATION MODE** specifies the method that will be employed to determine the precise disk address of an instance of a record when it is stored. Two methods are popular: CALC and VIA. Table 15-2 briefly summarizes the use of each of these methods.

Data processing frequently requires referring to records by logical key value. For example, a data entry operator may input a product number from a sales form and expect to see associated data for completing the entry of a customer order. The CALC LOCATION MODE would be appropriate to support this need.

The CALC LOCATION MODE is illustrated in the following partial record definitions:

```
RECORD NAME IS PRODUCT
LOCATION MODE CALC USING PRODUCTNO DUPLICATES NOT ALLOWED
...
  1 PRODUCTNO; PICTURE 9999.
...
RECORD NAME IS ORDER-LINE
LOCATION MODE CALC USING PRODUCTNO, ORDERNO
  DUPLICATES NOT ALLOWED
...
  1 PRODUCTNO; PICTURE 9999.
  1 ORDERNO; PICTURE 9999.
```

CALC was designed to specify that record instances will be stored and found by hashing on key values. For the preceding PRODUCT record, PRODUCTNO is a primary key (since DUPLICATES NOT ALLOWED); for the ORDER-LINE record given here, the concatenated key is PRODUCTNO plus ORDERNO, which is also unique. If duplicates are allowed, then the DBMS will permit two or more records to have the same hash key value. Otherwise, when not allowed, the DBMS will enforce, during storing and modification, the primary key property by returning error codes for data manipulation commands that would cause a violation

TABLE 15-2   **DBTG Record Placement Control Using LOCATION MODE**

LOCATION MODE	Explanation	Examples

CALC	Indicates that a record instance will be placed and may be accessed in secondary memory based on a value for a primary or secondary key. Usually, this is implemented by key-value hashing, but index methods are possible. That is, the database can be entered directly at a given record if a CALC key value is known.	`RECORD NAME IS PRODUCT`
		`  LOCATION MODE IS CALC`
		`  USING PRODUCTNO`
		`  DUPLICATES NOT ALLOWED`
		—defines a single, primary key
		
		`RECORD NAME IS CUSTOMER`
		`  LOCATION MODE IS CALC`
		`  USING CUST-ZIP`
		`  DUPLICATES ARE FIRST`
		—defines a single, secondary key

VIA	Indicates that a record instance will be placed in secondary memory close to its parent record instance for *one* specified set. This helps to improve performance when used with a frequently referenced set. VIA and CALC may not both be used on same record; use of VIA prevents access to record on a key value.	`RECORD NAME IS ORDER-LINE`
		`  LOCATION MODE IS VIA`
		`  ITEMS-ON-ORDER SET`
		`. . .`
		`SET NAME IS`
		`  ITEMS-ON-ORDER`
		`OWNER IS ORDER`
		`. . .`
		`MEMBER IS ORDER-LINE`
		—specifies that an ORDER-LINE instance should be stored close to its ORDER owner instance

of the duplicates clause. The CALC key must be defined as fields within the record being CALCed, even if part of the key can be found in a related record (in this case, PRODUCTNO of ORDER-LINE is also in the related PRODUCT record).

Some DBTG systems permit only one LOCATION MODE clause; others permit several LOCATION MODE or the more recent KEY IS clauses. Some DBTG systems even permit a database designer to use other than hashing methods for implementing CALC mode (e.g., indexes). In general, the CALC mode must be interpreted as any keyed access method (entry point into a database) using primary or secondary keys, as allowed by the DBMS. The use of CALC does not preclude accessing a record by its association with other records; it simply says that records will be *physically placed* (and can be found) based on key values.

On other occasions, users of an information system do not know primary key values for desired records, but instead know the key for some associated record. For example, we might know a product number but not know the numbers of customers who have open orders for this product.

The second LOCATION MODE alternative, designed to provide efficient record access by association, is VIA. VIA means that a record will be placed as close to its associated owner record instance as the DBMS can find *for the specified set*. The use of VIA in the DBTG model prevents a user from accessing a record directly by a key value. LOCATION VIA should be used for a given record when much data processing of this record involves first accessing an associated owner record before instances of this type are required (that is, access via relationships between records, since records to be retrieved are known only by their association with other records).

Consider again the ORDER-LINE record type. Although each of these record instances could be identified by a concatenated key of ORDERNO plus PROD-UCTNO, careful review of data processing might indicate that ORDER-LINE records are retrieved or stored only after first retrieving associated PRODUCT or ORDER records. After additional review, we determine that ORDER-LINE records are more often processed along with ORDER records than with PRODUCT records. We could then use the following LOCATION MODE clause in the definition of the ORDER-LINE record:

```
RECORD NAME IS ORDER-LINE
LOCATION MODE IS VIA ITEMS-ON-ORDER SET
...
SET NAME IS ITEMS-ON-ORDER
OWNER IS ORDER
...
MEMBER IS ORDER-LINE
...
```

Figure 15-4 illustrates the effect these schema commands might have on the database of Figure 15-3b (Pine Valley Furniture).

A record can be located VIA only one set in the DBTG model, so ORDER-LINEs cannot also be specified to be placed close to PRODUCT. It should be emphasized here the VIA does not establish which owner record instance is, in fact, the owner of a given member instance, but only that a member instance will be *placed* close to its owner instance. The SET SELECTION clause in the SET definition controls the method of determining ownership; we will discuss this clause later. As illustrated in Figure 15-4, a record type located VIA one set may participate as owner or member in other sets and may be accessed through these other sets; the most efficient access for the record will be through the set on which it is VIA. If a set member record instance located VIA its owner changes ownership (by a RECONNECT or similar command), its location will not change to be close to its new owner. Thus, after the ownership change, the member will not necessarily exhibit rapid access from its owner VIA the designated set.

In the most recent CODASYL guidelines, LOCATION MODE has been eliminated in favor of a more general and logical clause called KEY IS. Under the latest guideline, not yet implemented in all commercial systems, each record type may have one or more single or concatenated primary or secondary keys with either ascending or descending logical orderings maintained. Assuming a primary key of CUSTOMERNO in the CUSTOMER record of Figure 15-3b, we could include (in place of the LOCATION MODE clause)

```
KEY CUSTOMERNO IS ASCENDING CUSTOMERNO
DUPLICATES ARE NOT ALLOWED
```

and for the secondary key of PRODUCTNO in the ORDER-LINE record, we could include

```
KEY PRODUCTNO IS ASCENDING PRODUCTNO
DUPLICATES ARE FIRST
```

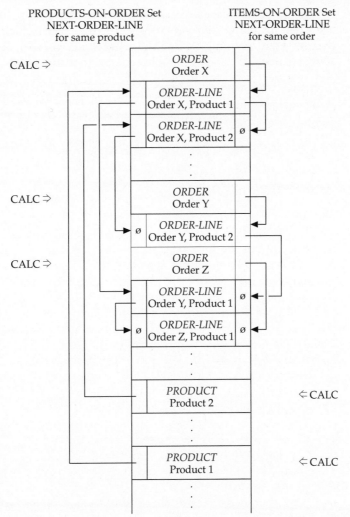

PRODUCTS-ON-ORDER Set
NEXT-ORDER-LINE
for same product

ITEMS-ON-ORDER Set
NEXT-ORDER-LINE
for same order

Figure 15-4

VIA placement control
for ITEMS-ORDERED set

DUPLICATES ARE NOT ALLOWED specifies a primary key. The use of FIRST or LAST indicates how to sequence records for storage and retrieval with duplicate secondary key values. FIRST means that a new record with a duplicate value will be stored as the first record (first on a chain) among any with the same value for PRODUCTNO; use of LAST would tell the DBMS to store the new record last (in this key sequence) after all existing records (on a chain) with this same PRODUCTNO value. A KEY IS clause will cause some type of key access method, like hashing or indexing, to be employed, depending on the implementation.

Although not part of the most current CODASYL guidelines, LOCATION MODE has been presented here because most DBTG systems use some form of this clause, even if the KEY IS clause is also supported.

Data Elements in a Record Definition   A record type may have no data elements, which is the case of a link record. Link records are possible because the DBTG data model can be classified as a simple network model. In most cases, a record type will have one or more data elements, or data-base-data-names, as part of its definition. A record type must contain data elements for each component of each key and for each data element used for sorting members of a set.

The schema not only defines what data elements are to be in each record, but also their format of representation in the database (which may be different from that for corresponding fields in user working storage). Thus, each data element must have exactly one of the following as part of its definition:

- PICTURE clause
- TYPE clause
- SOURCE clause
- OCCURS clause (not allowed in some systems)
- OCCURS and PICTURE clauses
- OCCURS and TYPE clauses

and any of the other clauses shown in Figure 15-3a, with a few limitations.

The PICTURE format is similar to that used in COBOL. Both character and numeric formats are supported. A PICTURE is used to define a display format for data elements. Consequently, data are stored using the computer's typical coding scheme (e.g., EBCDIC or ASCII). TYPE is used to cause more efficient storage formats to be used. TYPE can specify base (BINARY or DECIMAL), scale (FIXED or FLOAT), and mode (REAL or COMPLEX); length specifications for arithmetic data, or BIT or CHARACTER strings; or DATA-BASE-KEY. For example, the PRODUCT file for Pine Valley Furniture could be defined as a DBTG record type as follows:

```
RECORD IS PRODUCT
LOCATION MODE CALC USING PRODUCTNO
...
  1 PRODUCTNO ; PIC 9999.
  1 DESCRIPTION ; PIC X(20).
  1 FINISH ; PIC X(8).
  1 ROOM ; PIC X(2).
  1 PRICE ; TYPE DECIMAL 6,2.
```

Here most data elements are to be used for display purposes. PRICE will be stored in the computer system's DECIMAL format, with four integer digits and two decimal places (some DBTG systems have a DOLLAR TYPE in which TYPE DOLLAR 4 would be identical to this specification).

An OCCURS clause may be used with PICTURE or TYPE to indicate a repeating group of elementary data items. In addition, an OCCURS clause may appear by itself to specify a repeating data aggregate. For example, we could expand the definition of PRODUCT above to include a set of PRICEs, depending on quantity purchased. Part of the record definition might then look like this:

```
RECORD IS PRODUCT
...
1 PRICE-SCHEDULE ; OCCURS 3 TIMES.
  2 QTY-UPPER ; PICTURE 99999.
  2 QTY-PRICE ; DECIMAL 6,2.
```

In this example, a three-tiered price schedule capability has been designed for each product. If different products have a different number of quantity-price breaks, then

```
RECORD IS PRODUCT
...
1 NO-BREAKS ; TYPE IS DECIMAL 2.
1 PRICE-SCHEDULE ; OCCURS NO-BREAKS TIMES.
  2 QTY-UPPER ; PICTURE 99999.
  2 QTY-PRICE ; DECIMAL 6,2.
```

would allow for 0 to 99 different quantity-price breaks for each PRODUCT.

Other Data-Element Clauses   Any data element can be further defined in a schema by CHECK and coding clauses. A CHECK clause specifies validation criteria to be checked each time the associated data element changes value or a new value is added. Implementations vary, but most permit specification of a list of legitimate values or ranges of values or the execution of a more general user procedure.

Coding clauses inform the DBMS what to do to ENCODE or DECODE a data-element value. Again, implementations vary, but the effect of such clauses is to define code tables so that long, standard character strings that are input can be converted to more compact codes to save storage space (and vice versa for reporting). For example, coding could be used for the DESCRIPTION of the PRODUCT record. Such coding could equate TABLE with a stored value of TA, WALL UNIT with a stored value of WU, and so on, to reduce space and eliminate wasted characters (if variable-length records are not supported). Entry of WALL UNIT for DESCRIPTION would result in only WU being stored; display of a TA stored value would result in TABLE actually being reported.

Relationship Definitions: Sets

A **set** is the definition of a directed relationship from an owner record type to one or more member record types. A set usually defines a 1:*M* relationship, say, an ORDERS-FOR-CUSTOMER set from CUSTOMER as owner to ORDER as member. A set may also define a 1:1 relationship, but this is unusual. A set may not define an *M:N* relationship, since the DBTG model prescribes a simple network data model. One can generally assume that a set is implemented as a ring data structure with the owner at the head of the chain and with the last member pointing to the owner. Other structures (bidirectional chains, pointer arrays, owner pointers, and so forth) can be defined in clauses not being considered here.

Figure 15-5a illustrates a segment of the database for Pine Valley Furniture. Figure 15-5b shows a skeleton of the schema DDL necessary to define this part of the database. The figure includes a complete definition for the PRODCUT-VENDOR-LINK record. Assuming that this is only a link record, no data elements are defined, although some "data about data" (e.g., pointers to maintain sets) may be allocated from the compilation of the schema DDL.

The inclusion of a set, say, from PRODUCT or ORDER-LINE, in the schema of Figure 15-5b informs the schema DDL compiler to establish some type of data structure to permit rapid access from an instance of a PRODUCT record to instances of associated set ORDER-LINE members (and possibly vice versa). Whenever records are inserted, deleted, or modified in either of these files, the DBMS will perform much of the maintenance of the overhead data to continue correct record association. This schema in Figure 15-5b illustrates that a record type may be an owner of several sets and also a member of several sets; some DBTG systems even permit the same record type to be both owner and member of the same set!

Set: In a network data model, a one-to-many association between two record types, where the first record type is called the *owner* and the second is called the *member*.

Figure 15-5

Skeleton of the schema
for part of Pine Valley
Furniture database

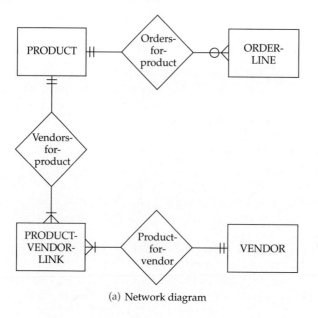

(a) Network diagram

```
SCHEMA NAME IS PINE
...
RECORD NAME IS PRODUCT
   LOCATION MODE IS CALC USING PRODUCTNO
...
1 PRODUCTNO ; PIC 9999.
...
RECORD NAME IS ORDER-LINE
   LOCATION MODE IS VIA ORDERS-FOR-PRODUCT SET
...
RECORD NAME IS VENDOR
   LOCATION MODE IS CALC USING VENDORNO
...
1 VENDORNO ; PIC 9999.
...
RECORD NAME IS PRODUCT-VENDOR-LINK
   LOCATION MODE IS VIA VENDORS-FOR-PRODUCT SET
SET IS ORDERS-FOR-PRODUCT
   OWNER IS PRODUCT
   ...
   MEMBER IS ORDER-LINE
   ...
SET IS VENDORS-FOR-PRODUCT
   OWNER IS PRODUCT
   ...
   MEMBER IS PRODUCT-VENDOR-LINK
   ...
SET IS PRODUCTS-FOR-VENDOR
   OWNER IS VENDOR
   ...
   MEMBER IS PRODUCT-VENDOR-LINK
   ...
```

(b) Schema definition

However, a set is not the only means of relating records in the DBTG model.
Consider the same PRODUCT to ORDER-LINE relationship just discussed. If both
record types contain PRODUCTNO and if this data element is used in a KEY IS
clause in each record definition, then associated records may also be rapidly retrieved by accessing records by this logical key. Nevertheless, a set is the usual
means employed in a DBTG database to represent a relationship, since this is the

only way the DBMS will know about the relationship! If sets are not used to represent relationships, then the implementation is not any richer in structure and capabilities than multiple random access files.

Member Insertion Sequence   When a member instance is inserted into a set, the DBMS must know what basis to use to determine where in the chain of existing members to place the new record. The typical choices available are

FIRST:	at the beginning of the chain
LAST:	at the end of the chain (FIRST and LAST support chronological order of members by date/time of entry)
SORTED:	based on the value of some field in the member record
NEXT:	immediately after the most recently accessed member of the set
PRIOR:	immediately before the most recently accessed member of the set

We will discuss later in this chapter the difficult decision of choosing whether to sort members of a set. Very simply, the trade-off is between saving sorting time when data are reported versus storage space for the key field (this may be part of the record anyhow) and extra member-insertion time to scan for the right place in the member chain. Long chains can, of course, be costly to scan, and frequent maintenance and infrequent reporting in sequence may negate the benefit of a sorted set.

Loop Relationship   Several types of 1:*M* relationships need special illustration if we are to explain their representation in schema DDL. The first is a loop relationship. Figure 15-6 shows such a relationship and indicates a skeleton of the schema parts required to represent this relationship between customers within the same parent organization under several different implementations in the DBTG model. This loop relationship would help to ascertain the total purchasing behavior of a client for which several purchasing agents or divisions are individual buyers.

Figure 15-6a illustrates the basic loop relationship and the most direct way, if permitted, to represent this type of relationship. This representation requires that the DBMS support use of the same record type as both owner and member of the same set. In this case, both the parent organization as well as the individual buying groups are represented as CUSTOMERs (which, of course, they probably are).

The approach of Figure 15-6b is to define an additional ORGANIZATION record type, instances of which own a set of CUSTOMER member instances for that parent organization. Data manipulation statements can be used to move from one member to another in a given set instance or from a member instance to the associated owner instance. The approach of Figure 15-6c is, if permitted by the particular DBMS, to define a secondary key on the PARENT-ORG data element of the CUSTOMER record type; data manipulation statements can then be used to access all CUSTOMER records with a common value for this secondary key. In all of these cases, it is still possible to define a primary key of CUSTOMERNO for the CUSTOMER record.

Singular Sets   Singular or system relationships (called *one-of-a-kind* in IDMS) are easy to represent in a DBTG schema. The purpose of a singular relationship is to arrange all the instances of some record type into sorted sequence under a common owner: the "system."

Figure 15-6

Alternative representations of a loop relationship in the CODASYL model

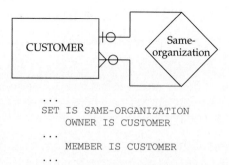

```
...
SET IS SAME-ORGANIZATION
    OWNER IS CUSTOMER
...
        MEMBER IS CUSTOMER
...
```

(a) Loop relationship with the same owner and member

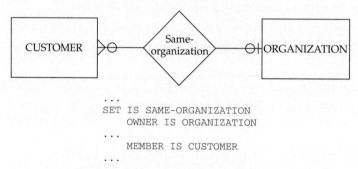

```
...
SET IS SAME-ORGANIZATION
    OWNER IS ORGANIZATION
...
    MEMBER IS CUSTOMER
...
```

(b) Loop relationship using two record types

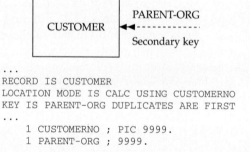

```
...
RECORD IS CUSTOMER
LOCATION MODE IS CALC USING CUSTOMERNO
KEY IS PARENT-ORG DUPLICATES ARE FIRST
...
    1 CUSTOMERNO ; PIC 9999.
    1 PARENT-ORG ; 9999.
...
```

(c) Loop relationship using secondary key

Suppose we wanted to arrange all CUSTOMER records into ascending order by CUST-ZIPCODE to avoid the cost of sorting all CUSTOMER records for each mailing. Figure 15-7 illustrates the skeleton of the definition of a singular set that accomplishes this desired sequencing. CUSTOMER records can all be retrieved as members under one common parent (the singular system) in the zip code order because of the use of the ORDER IS SORTED clause and the KEY IS clause of the member specification for the set. Thus, now we would have two access points into CUSTOMER: (1) The primary key of CUSTOMERNO is CALCed to provide direct addressing, and (2) the CUST-ZIPCODE set is used to access CUSTOMERs in zip code order.

Singular sets can also be used to logically group together records with a common characteristic (e.g., all customers who have exceeded their credit limit); that is, not all record instances from the set-member record type *must* be included in the set.

```
...
RECORD IS CUSTOMER
    LOCATION MODE IS CALC USING CUSTOMERNO
...
1 CUSTOMERNO ; PIC 9999.
1 CUST-ZIPCODE ; PIC 99999.
...
SET IS CUST-SORT
    OWNER IS SYSTEM
    ORDER IS SORTED BY DEFINED KEYS
    ...
    MEMBER IS CUSTOMER
    ...
    KEY IS ASCENDING CUST-ZIPCODE
        DUPLICATES ARE LAST
...
```

Figure 15-7

Example of a schema DDL for a singular set

It is very important to understand the distinct difference between singular sets and sets with an actual owner record. Singular sets create *one* set instance; other sets create one set instance *for each owner*. Thus, whereas sorted member records in a singular set provide a logical ordering for *all* the records of the member record type, sorted members in regular sets create logical orderings of a *subset* of member records, those with a common parent/owner.

Sets with Multiple Member Types   Any set definition contains reference to only one owner record type but may include several member record-type clauses. This capability permits the representation of class relationships or any relationship in which a single owner-record instance can be associated with many member instances, each of different types. Some DBTG systems permit all members to be sorted by such options as record name (all members of the same type sorted together under a common parent), database key (that is, physical address sequence, which is convenient for efficiently traversing a member chain), or key values in each member record type.

Figure 15-8 illustrates a typical situation where CUSTOMER records are related to both OPEN- and CLOSED-ORDERs. The CUSTOMER-ORDERS set definition places into a common set instance all OPEN- and CLOSED-ORDERs, in ORDERNO sequence, for each CUSTOMER owner. The sorting option is used here simply to facilitate reporting of order data. A hazard of such a set with multiple members is that long member chains can be created; if individual sets are not established from owner to each member type (e.g., CUSTOMER to only OPEN-ORDER), processing for only one of the member-type records can be degraded by having to access unwanted set members.

Multiple Relationships Between Records   Any number of sets may be defined between the same pair of record types. For example, if Pine Valley Furniture writes both blanket and special orders (*blanket* means an order for a series of deliveries over some extended time period, and *special* means a one-time, stand-alone order), then we might want to define two sets between CUSTOMER and ORDER: Blanket-for-Customer and Special-for-Customer. In this way, users interested in only one type of customer order could use the specialized set to find only orders of the desired type without wasted accesses to unwanted types. Multiple sets between the same pair of record types can also be used to handle different sorting sequences (e.g., orders by sale date, or orders by due date).

Figure 15-8

DBTG schema for a set with two member record types

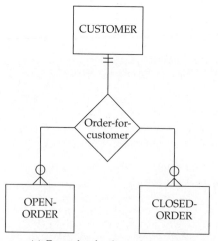

(a) Example of a class relationship

```
RECORD IS CUSTOMER
...
RECORD IS OPEN-ORDER
...
1 O-ORDERNO ; PIC 9999.
...
RECORD IS CLOSED-ORDER
...
1 C-ORDERNO ; PIC 9999.
...
SET IS ORDERS-FOR-CUSTOMER
OWNER IS CUSTOMER
ORDER IS SORTED BY DEFINED KEYS
    DUPLICATES NOT ALLOWED
...
MEMBER IS OPEN-ORDER
...
    KEY IS ASCENDING O-ORDERNO
        DUPLICATES ARE NOT ALLOWED
...
MEMBER IS CLOSED-ORDER
...
    KEY IS ASCENDING O-ORDERNO
        DUPLICATES ARE NOT ALLOWED
...
```

(b) Schema DDL for class relationship

Many-to-Many Relationships Because the CODASYL network standard is a simple network architecture, many-to-many relationships have to be implemented using link records. Figure 15-9 illustrates, by way of an instance diagram, the result of representing an *M:N* relationship between PRODUCT and VENDOR. In this case, an intersection record containing the vendor's PRICE for that product is used to link a PRODUCT to a VENDOR when that vendor supplies that product. We assume here that meaningful data, PRICE, need to be retained on each PRODUCT-VENDOR relationship instance. If no such meaningful data exist, then the structure remains the same as in Figure 15-9, except there would be only pointers in the PRODUCT-VENDOR-LINK record. Since meaningful data exist most of the time when there is an *M:N* relationship, the creation of the extra link record is almost always needed. In fact, it is recommended so that even if meaningful data are not recognized until after the database is implemented, the structure of the database will stay the same (thus minimizing reprogramming). Note that each

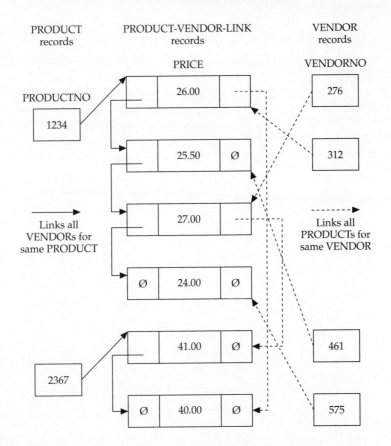

PRODUCT records   PRODUCT-VENDOR-LINK records   VENDOR records

Figure 15-9

Example of records and sets implementations for a many-to-many relationship

VENDOR and PRODUCT record is stored only once, but a PRODUCT-VENDOR-LINK record instance appears each time a vendor can supply some product. As will be seen later, the three record types and two sets of this figure can be used to find both the vendors of a given product and the products of a given vendor. That is, sets may be processed from either owner to member or member to owner.

Set Qualifications A set may optionally be defined to be DYNAMIC or PRIOR. DYNAMIC means that this set has no specific member record type, but an instance of any record other than of the owner type may become associated in this set to a given owner instance. Use of DYNAMIC is rare. PRIOR, on the other hand, can be an important feature. Specification of SET IS PRIOR causes the DBMS to implement for the associated set a method that allows the set to be processed as efficiently in the backward (prior) direction as in the forward (next) direction. The effect is to create a bidirectional chain capability, although the guidelines do not specify that a bidirectional chain is *the* way PRIOR must be implemented.

Set-Member Definition The set membership clauses are an important part of a schema. Not only do they provide a necessary companion to the OWNER IS clause, but they are instrumental in set integrity control and, hence, relationships in a database. In addition, it is important to study this section of a schema carefully because three of its clauses—INSERTION, RETENTION, and SET SELECTION— typically are difficult to understand for people getting their first exposure to database management. Further, you should be aware that INSERTION is called CONNECTION and RETENTION is called DISCONNECTION by some DBTG systems.

Any set may have one or more MEMBER IS and associated clauses, one each for each record type related to the set owner in the relationship represented by the set. In explaining these clauses, we will use sets with only *one* member record type.

For the purpose of explaining set membership clauses, consider the database shown in Figure 15-10a and a possible schema definition for this database shown in Figure 15-10b. The situation depicted here is an inventory accounting database for unique, serial-numbered, limited-life products stored at various warehouses. For this situation, we will assume that the organization permits transshipment of

Figure 15-10

Illustration of set membership clauses

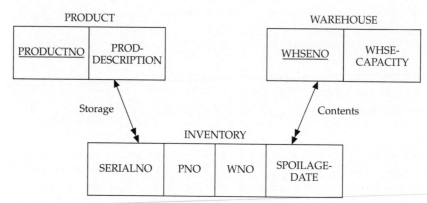

(a) Sample inventory database

```
SCHEMA IS INVENTORY
AREA NAME IS STOCK
RECORD NAME IS PRODUCT
   LOCATION MODE IS CALC USING PRODUCTNO
   1 PRODUCTNO ; PIC 9999.
   1 PROD-DESCRIPTION ; PIC X(20).
RECORD NAME IS WAREHOUSE
   LOCATION MODE IS CALC USING WHSENO
   1 WHSENO ; PIC 99.
   1 WHSE-CAPACITY ; PIC 999999.
RECORD NAME IS INVENTORY
   LOCATION MODE IS VIA STORAGE SET
   1 SERIALNO ; PIC 99999.
   1 PNO ; PIC 9999.
   1 WNO ; PIC 99.
   1 SPOILAGE-DATE ; PIC 999999.
SET NAME IS STORAGE
   OWNER IS PRODUCT
   ORDER IS FIRST
   MEMBER IS INVENTORY
      INSERTION IS AUTOMATIC
      RETENTION IS FIXED
      CHECK IS PRODUCTNO IN PRODUCT=PNO
      SET SELECTION IS BY VALUE OF PRODUCTNO
SET NAME IS CONTENTS
   OWNER IS WAREHOUSE
   ORDER IS SORTED BY DEFINED KEYS
   MEMBER IS INVENTORY
      INSERTION IS AUTOMATIC
      RETENTION IS MANDATORY
      KEY IS ASCENDING PNO DUPLICATES ARE FIRST
      CHECK IS WHSENO IN WAREHOUSE=WNO
      SET SELECTION IS STRUCTURAL WHSENO=WNO
END SCHEMA
```

(b) Schema DDL for inventory database

products between warehouses. This example would be typical of certain chemical or pharmaceutical products. This situation is another example of an *M:N* relationship and illustrates how such a relationship would be defined in the DDL.

The STORAGE set relates a generic product to particular serial-numbered instances of that product stored in warehouses. An analysis of reporting requirements involving records of this set indicates that no special set ordering of INVENTORY members for the associated PRODUCT owner is necessary, so ORDER IS FIRST is chosen to speed member-record creation (since a new record would be inserted in a chained set at the beginning of the chain, which we have seen is the easiest point to insert in a single-directional chain).

Controlling Member Insertion   Since an INVENTORY record may not logically exist unless it is for an already existing PRODUCT, INSERTION IS AUTOMATIC is used. This means that the DBMS will automatically link a new INVENTORY record to its associated PRODUCT owner when we store a new INVENTORY record in the database.

The other choice for INSERTION IS is MANUAL, which means that we would have to explicitly and separately program when to connect a new INVENTORY record in a data entry program. AUTOMATIC saves a minimal amount of program coding. MANUAL would be appropriate if a member record might not have an owner record in a set when initially stored in a database. For example, a set from department to employee might have INSERTION IS MANUAL, since many employees when hired are not immediately assigned to a department.

The CONTENTS set also uses INSERTION IS AUTOMATIC, since it is assumed that a particular serial-numbered part must reside in some warehouse. The INSERTION IS clause is an effective mechanism for enforcing certain semantic data requirements (that is, existence dependencies upon original entry of a record). The appropriate value of AUTOMATIC or MANUAL for any given set can be established only after a careful analysis of the meaning of data and relationships involved in a set.

Controlling Member Retention   Similar to the INSERTION IS clause is the RETENTION IS clause. In the STORAGE set, RETENTION IS FIXED is used. This means that once a serial number is associated to a generic PRODUCT record, it must be *permanently* associated with the same PRODUCT. The only way to change the association to another PRODUCT would be to delete the INVENTORY record and reenter it under a new owner PRODUCT.

On the other hand, since individual parts may be transshipped from one warehouse to another, RETENTION IS MANDATORY is used in the CONTENTS set. MANDATORY says that the member record, in order to exist, must always have some WAREHOUSE owner (the part has to be somewhere!), but that the particular owner may change. In terms of the data manipulation language to be introduced later, MANDATORY allows us to RECONNECT INVENTORY records as required to indicate current location of a part.

A third option for RETENTION IS, not illustrated here, is OPTIONAL. This choice means that we may actually DISCONNECT a member record from any owner and leave the member unowned for as long as is appropriate. For example, a part is not really in any warehouse during transshipment. To permit an INVENTORY record to have no WAREHOUSE owner during this period, we would use RETENTION IS OPTIONAL. OPTIONAL also permits the deletion of an owner record without having to delete members. For example, if a warehouse is closed, the associated part records will still exist until the parts are moved to a new location.

RECONNECTing records can have a subtle effect on database performance. If, for example, INVENTORY records are located VIA the CONTENTS set instead of the STORAGE set, an INVENTORY record that changed its association to other than its original WAREHOUSE would *not* be physically moved to now be near its current WAREHOUSE owner record in the physical database.

The RETENTION IS clause also provides a method to include semantic controls, after original loading of data, of proper database record associations and data manipulation. Table 15-3 summarizes the impact of various combinations of INSERTION and RETENTION options. Be aware, however, that the terms FIXED, MANDATORY, and OPTIONAL have not had the same meanings in all versions of the DBTG guidelines. Until 1978, FIXED did not exist, and MANDATORY meant FIXED. If you are using a DBTG DBMS, read the reference manuals carefully to determine what is implemented by that vendor.

Cross-Reference Key Control   The CHECK IS clauses provide yet another level of semantic control of record associations. Each of these clauses in the example of Figure 15-10 requires that key values in both member and owner of a set instance must be identical. These clauses provide an extra protection that the correct semantic connection will occur when records are originally inserted into the database or CONNECTed to an owner. To fully appreciate the usefulness of the CHECK IS clause, you must understand the function of the SET SELECTION clause.

TABLE 15-3   **Summary of DBTG Semantic Controls in Set Membership Clauses**

	Automatic	Manual
FIXED	Member record *must* have an owner when it is stored and will continue to have *same* owner until member is deleted. DBMS will automatically CONNECT member to owner, based on SET SELECTION clause, when member is stored.	Member record is permitted to *not* have an owner when it is stored, but once CONNECTed to an owner, it *must* keep same owner until member is deleted. DBMS will *not* CONNECT member to owner until told to do so by user program.
MANDATORY	Member record *must* have an owner when it is stored, but member can be RECONNECTed to other owners as required. DBMS will automatically CONNECT member to owner, based on SET SELECTION clause, when member is stored.	Member record is permitted to *not* have an owner when it is stored, and once CONNECTed may be RECONNECTed to other owners as required. DBMS will *not* CONNECT member to owner until told to do so by user program.
OPTIONAL	Member record *must* have an owner when it is stored, but member can be RECONNECTed to other owners or DISCONNECTed from any owner as required. DBMS will automatically CONNECT member to owner, based on SET SELECTION clause, when member is stored.	Member record is permitted to *not* have an owner when it is stored; once CONNECTed, if ever, it may be RECONNECTed or DISCONNECTed as required. DBMS will *not* CONNECT member to owner until told to do so by user program.

Determining a Member's Owner Instance   Whereas the INSERTION and RETENTION clauses control *when* and *whether* a record type must have an owner, the SET SELECTION clause determines *which instance* of the owner record type of a set should become the "proud parent."

For the STORAGE set in Figure 15-10, SET SELECTION IS BY VALUE OF PRODUCTNO means that when a new INVENTORY record is stored in the database (if INSERTION IS AUTOMATIC) or CONNECTed to a PRODUCT owner, the DBMS will use the current value in PRODUCTNO from user working storage as a key to find the appropriate owner. Thus, PRODUCT must have a keyed access (e.g., LOCATION MODE IS CALC or a KEY IS clause, whichever the DBMS uses) on the data element referenced (in this case, PRODUCTNO). This type of SET SELECTION clause forces the DBMS to find the owner record automatically and forces the DBMS user to make sure that the correct PRODUCTNO is in memory. As long as PNO is correctly recorded, the CHECK IS clause on this set is a validity check that set selection was done properly. This form of the SET SELECTION clause is more often used when the member record type does *not* contain the key of the owner record.

The SET SELECTION clause of the CONTENTS set is the one that is more appropriate when a member record contains the key of the associated owner record instance. SET SELECTION IS STRUCTURAL means that the DBMS is to find the associated owner record for a new member when it is stored (if INSERTION IS AUTOMATIC) or CONNECTed by using the value of a data element in the member (e.g., WNO) as the key value of the owner (e.g., WAREHOUSENO). In this case, the CHECK IS clause is of no operational value, since the SET SELECTION clause guarantees that the check will not be violated.

Proper use of INSERTION, RETENTION, CHECK, and SET SELECTION clauses requires practice. Although use of these clauses forces a database designer to deal with many details, these clauses provide valuable tools for semantic controls of database maintenance and processing. A database programmer also needs to be aware of these clauses in order to interpret error messages that indicate breaches of these integrity constraints.

Many DBTG DBMSs also permit a SET SELECTION THRU CURRENT OF SET option. This version is difficult to understand until one understands the DBTG data manipulation language and a construct used there called *currency indicators*. Basically, this form differs from the others in that the DBMS does not have to find the owner record, but uses the last owner record instance retrieved. This is, in fact, often the most efficient choice for SET SELECTION, especially in interactive programs. For example, if when entering a new INVENTORY record the program first finds the record for the WAREHOUSE indicated for the part, why make the DBMS find it again in order to store the INVENTORY record? The proper WAREHOUSE owner is "current"ly in working storage and does not need to be refound.

A SET SELECTION clause is not found in certain DBTG systems. In these (in particular, IDMS), the owner for a new member record being inserted into the database is essentially the most recently retrieved record of each set, which must be an instance of the proper owner record type for each set.

Sorting Members   Finally, we need to explain the ORDER IS SORTED clause for the CONTENTS set. An analysis of reporting requirements from this database indicated that warehouse contents frequently were desired in PRODUCTNO (PNO) sequence for easy reading. The ORDER IS SORTED and KEY IS clauses cause the database to automatically maintain member INVENTORY records in this sequence (usually via a sorted list), thus avoiding sorting of records or report lines for each report.

Other Set-Member Clauses Not illustrated in Figure 15-10 but appearing in Figure 15-3 is the SEARCH KEY IS clause of the member section of a set definition. The set itself establishes a method (usually a chain) to access all member instances, possibly in a sorted sequence, under a common owner record instance. The SEARCH KEY IS clause defines direct access from an owner instance to a member with a specific key value. That is, SEARCH KEY IS establishes functionally a key index in each owner record that points to each member record. For example, in the database of Figure 15-10a, we might want to create a way to identify/access for each WAREHOUSE the INVENTORY that will spoil each day. To do so, we would include in the member clause of the CONTENTS set the clause

```
SEARCH KEY IS SPOILAGE-DATE DUPLICATES ALLOWED.
```

The design of efficient network databases depends on careful study of database usage maps, as shown in Figure 7-4. These figures help a database designer to

- Identify frequent entry points into the database (need for CALC keys)
- Identify high-activity access paths (possible use of VIA LOCATION MODE)
- Identify entry into database to a subset of records or a group of records of same type in sorted sequence (possible use of system or singular set)
- Search through members of a set in a sorted sequence (possible use of ORDER IS SORTED to sort member records)

As a summary of this section on DBTG schema definition, Figure 15-11 contains schema DDL for the Mountain View Community Hospital database of Figure 7-21. Numbered lines are explained in the notes to the figure.

Figure 15-11

Schema for Mountain View Community Hospital

```
* * * * * * * * * * * * * * * * * * * * * * * * * * * * * * * * * * * * * * * * * * * * * * *
    SCHEMA DESCRIPTION.
* * * * * * * * * * * * * * * * * * * * * * * * * * * * * * * * * * * * * * * * * * * * * * *
    SCHEMA NAME IS MVCH.
(1) FILE DESCRIPTION.
    FILE NAME IS MVCHFILE         ASSIGN TO MVCHDS
                                  DEVICE TYPE IS 3380.
    FILE NAME IS JOURNAL          ASSIGN TO SYSJRNL.
* * * * * * * * * * * * * * * * * * * * * * * * * * * * * * * * * * * * * * * * * * * * * * *
    AREA DESCRIPTION.
* * * * * * * * * * * * * * * * * * * * * * * * * * * * * * * * * * * * * * * * * * * * * * *
(2) AREA NAME IS MVCH-CHG         RANGE IS 770351 THRU 770420
                                  WITHIN FILE MVCHFILE
                                     FROM 1 THRU 70.
    AREA NAME IS MVCH-PHY         RANGE IS 770421 THRU 770586
                                  WITHIN FILE MVCHFILE
                                     FROM 71 THRU 160.

* * * * * * * * * * * * * * * * * * * * * * * * * * * * * * * * * * * * * * * * * * * * * * *
    RECORD DESCRIPTION.
* * * * * * * * * * * * * * * * * * * * * * * * * * * * * * * * * * * * * * * * * * * * * * *
    RECORD NAME IS ROOM.
(3) RECORD ID IS 100.
    LOCATION MODE IS CALC         USING LOCATION
                                  DUPLICATES NOT ALLOWED.
    WITHIN MVCH-PHY AREA.
      02 LOCATION                 PIC 9999.
      (other data items)
* * * * * * * * * * * * * * * * * * * * * *
```

(Continues)

Figure 15-11

(continued)

```
* * * * * * * * * * * * * * * * * * * *
      RECORD NAME IS PATIENT.
      RECORD ID IS 101.
      LOCATION MODE IS CALC          USING PATIENT-NO
                                     DUPLICATES NOT ALLOWED.
      WITHIN MVCH-CHG AREA.
         02 PATIENT-NO               PIC 9999.
         (other data items)
* * * * * * * * * * * * * * * * * * * *
      RECORD NAME IS PHYSICIAN.
      RECORD ID IS 102.
      LOCATION MODE IS CALC          USING PHYSICIAN-ID
                                     DUPLICATES NOT ALLOWED.
      WITHIN MVCH-PHY AREA.
         02 PHYSICIAN-ID             PIC X(10).
         02 PHYSICIAN-PHONE          PIC 9(7).
* * * * * * * * * * * * * * * * * * * *
      RECORD NAME IS ITEM.
      RECORD ID IS 103.
      LOCATION MODE IS CALC          USING ITEM-CODE
                                     DUPLICATES NOT ALLOWED.
      WITHIN MVCH-CHG AREA.
         02 ITEM-CODE                PIC 999.
         02 DESCRIPTION              PIC X(15).
* * * * * * * * * * * * * * * * * * * *
      RECORD NAME IS TREATMENT.
      RECORD ID IS 104.
 (4)  LOCATION MODE IS VIA           TREATED SET.
      WITHIN MVCH-PHY AREA.
         02 PHYSICIAN-ID             PIC X(10).
         02 PATIENT-NO               PIC 9999.
         02 PROCEDURE                PIC X(15).
* * * * * * * * * * * * * * * * * * * *
      RECORD NAME IS CHARGES.
      RECORD ID IS 105.
 (5)  LOCATION MODE IS VIA           INCURRED SET.
      WITHIN MVCH-CHG AREA.
         02 PATIENT-NO               PIC 9999.
         02 ITEM-CODE                PIC 999.
         02 CHARGE                   PIC 9999V99 COMP-3.
* * * * * * * * * * * * * * * * * * * * * * * * * * * * * * * * * * * * * * * * *
      SET DESCRIPTION.
* * * * * * * * * * * * * * * * * * * * * * * * * * * * * * * * * * * * * * * * *
      SET IS ASSIGNED.
      ORDER IS FIRST.
 (6)  MODE IS CHAIN.
 (7)  OWNER IS ROOM                  NEXT DBKEY POSITION IS 1.
 (8)  MEMBER IS PATIENT              NEXT DBKEY POSITION IS 4
                                     LINKED TO OWNER
                                        OWNER DBKEY POSITION IS 5
 (9)                                 OPTIONAL AUTOMATIC.

* * * * * * * * * * * * * * * * * * * *
      SET IS RECEIVED.
(10)  ORDER IS LAST.
(11)  MODE IS CHAIN                  LINKED TO PRIOR.
      OWNER IS PATIENT               NEXT DBKEY POSITION IS 1
                                     PRIOR DBKEY POSITION IS 2.
      MEMBER IS TREATMENT            NEXT DBKEY POSITION IS 1
                                     PRIOR DBKEY POSITION IS 2
                                     LINKED TO OWNER
                                        OWNER DBKEY POSITION IS 5
(12)                                 FIXED MANUAL.
```

(Continues)

Figure 15-11

(continued)

```
* * * * * * * * * * * * * * * * * * *
      SET IS TREATED.              LINKED TO PRIOR.
(13)  ORDER IS SORTED.             NEXT DBKEY POSITION IS 1
      MODE IS CHAIN                PRIOR DBKEY POSITION IS 2.
      OWNER IS PHYSICIAN           NEXT DBKEY POSITION IS 3
                                   PRIOR DBKEY POSITION IS 4
      MEMBER IS TREATMENT          LINKED TO OWNER
                                      OWNER DBKEY POSITION IS 6
                                   FIXED AUTOMATIC
                                   ASCENDING KEY IS PATIENT-NO
                                      DUPLICATES ARE FIRST.


* * * * * * * * * * * * * * * * * * *
      SET IS INCURRED.
      ORDER IS SORTED.
      MODE IS CHAIN.
      OWNER IS PATIENT             NEXT DBKEY POSITION IS 3.
      MEMBER IS CHARGES            NEXT DBKEY POSITION IS 1
                                   FIXED MANUAL
                                   ASCENDING KEY IS ITEM-CODE
                                      DUPLICATES ARE LAST.


* * * * * * * * * * * * * * * * * * *
      SET IS PROVIDED.
      ORDER IS LAST.
      MODE IS CHAIN.
      OWNER IS ITEM                NEXT DBKEY POSITION IS 1.
      MEMBER IS CHARGES            NEXT DBKEY POSITION IS 2
                                   LINKED TO OWNER
                                      OWNER DBKEY POSITION IS 3
                                   FIXED AUTOMATIC.
```

Notes

(1) Logical file names used in schema are matched with physical data set names and devices.
(2) Areas are assigned to page ranges in logical files. In this schema, we have chosen to have two areas: MVCH-CHG, which contains those record types related to the patient bill, and MVCH-PHY, which contains all other record types.
(3) RECORD ID simply assigns a number to identify each record type uniquely in the data dictionary.
(4) VIA is chosen here to group TREATMENT records close to PHYSICIAN records, since it is assumed that these related records are frequently used together in programs.
(5) Similar assumption as in (4), but this time for PATIENT and CHARGES records.
(6) This is a mandatory clause that simply says to create a chain from owner through members.
(7) The NEXT DBKEY POSITION clause specifies which relative pointer in the record associated with this clause (in this case, ROOM) is to be used for the next in chain pointer for this set.
(8) Again, the NEXT DBKEY POSITION clause specifies the pointer position (in this case in PATIENT); the LINKED TO OWNER indicates that each member record is to have a pointer (the pointer in the position specified) to its owner record to support rapid access to owner.
(9) OPTIONAL AUTOMATIC is used to allow PATIENTs to exist without being assigned a hospital location, but originally a PATIENT record can only be entered if the patient is admitted and placed in some location. The reader should recall that IDMS does not have a SET SELECTION clause, as noted in the text.
(10) ORDER IS LAST is used to keep TREATMENT records in approximately ascending order by treatment date.
(11) LINKED TO PRIOR establishes backward chaining as well as forward chaining. The PRIOR clauses in the OWNER and MEMBER definitions indicate where in these records to find the PRIOR pointers.
(12) FIXED MANUAL is used here and in the INCURRED set to handle emergency treatment situations in which treatment is performed (and charges incurred) before the patient is admitted.
(13) ORDER IS SORTED is used to keep TREATMENT records grouped together by PATIENT (see ASCENDING KEY clause in member definition); DUPLICATES ARE FIRST is used in the member clause to keep TREATMENT records in reverse chronological order under each PATIENT.

DBTG SUBSCHEMA DDL: EXTERNAL DATABASES

Each user of a database usually wants to use only a portion of a global, conceptual database. This portion may strictly be a subset but may also redefine, into more local terminology and different structures, selected components (records, data elements, sets) of the database. Further, as a means to secure the database against accidental damage by naive users or to ensure legislated, organizational, or personal privacy, a particular user may be limited in what components of the database he or she may use and what data manipulations may be performed on the visible data.

The CODASYL Data Base Task Group provided for these capabilities by specifying subschemas. As defined earlier in this chapter, a subschema is a defined subset of an associated database that gives a program invoking the subschema a customized view of the database. The view of the database as seen from a subschema may differ from the database definition in that selected data elements, records, sets, and areas may be omitted; data elements, records, sets, and areas may be renamed using terms more understandable to a class of users; and data element formats (PICTURE, TYPE, length) may be changed to suit specialized data processing needs. Subschema capabilities in some DBTG systems even permit the subschema to define logical records that are combinations of data elements from several related schema records; this capability is similar to the "view" concept in relational databases and can be considered the result of an implicit combination of record joins.

Subschemas provide a mechanism for data independence, since they yield a consistent view of the database to a group of programs; if the schema changes but the local view is unaffected, then programs (which use a subschema, not the schema) are also unaffected.

Over the years, subschema DDLs have been developed for COBOL, FORTRAN, PL/I, and assembler languages. A subschema is defined separately from any application program that uses it; a subschema is stored in a subschema library, managed by the DBMS, and can be invoked or included in an application program when that program is compiled, link edited, or loaded, depending on the DBMS.

Figure 15-12 illustrates the IDMS subschema DDL via the Patient Bill user view for the Mountain View Community Hospital schema definition in Figure 15-11. Each subschema is named and is matched to a particular schema.

Areas, records, data elements, and sets to be included in the subschema are defined, along with restrictions on the use of data manipulation commands on these structural components. Also, depending on the features of the DBMS, this

```
ADD SUBSCHEMA OF PATIENT-BILL
    OF SCHEMA MVCH.

ADD AREA ...

ADD RECORD PATIENT
    ELEMENT PATIENT-NO.

ADD RECORD ITEM
    ELEMENTS ARE ALL.

ADD RECORD CHARGES
    ELEMENTS ARE ALL.

ADD SET INCURRED.

ADD SET PROVIDED.
```

Figure 15-12

IDMS subschema for Patient Bill (Mountain View Community Hospital)

Figure 15-13

Example of IDMS logical
record definition in a
subschema

```
ADD LOGICAL RECORD IS DETAILED-BILL
    ELEMENTS ARE PATIENT, CHARGES, ITEM
ADD LOGICAL PATH OBTAIN DETAILED-BILL
    SELECT FOR FIELDNAME EQ PATIENT-NO
        FIND PATIENT WHERE CALCKEY IS
            PATIENT-NO OF REQUEST
        OBTAIN EACH CHARGES WITHIN INCURRED
        OBTAIN OWNER WITHIN PROVIDED
```

division may include privacy specifications and explanations of derivation of logical records as combinations of base records from the subschema. Some DBTG
systems permit data names to be redefined into localized terms.

IDMS is one such DBTG DBMS that has a facility to define logical records and
the process of deriving them (called a logical path). Figure 15-13 illustrates how
the logical record concept could be used to define a DETAILED-BILL logical record for an identified patient.

In this case, the DBMS would automatically and transparently construct a
DETAILED-BILL record for each CHARGES instance of each PATIENT record
instance (that is, DETAILED-BILL represents the complete printed line item on
the patient bill). We derive a DETAILED-BILL logical record by first using the
current value of PATIENT-NO to FIND (that is, locate but not load any PATIENT
data in working storage) a uniquely identified PATIENT; the application programmer must make sure that the proper PATIENT-NO is in working storage before
requesting a DETAILED-BILL record. Then the DBMS would OBTAIN (that is,
transfer data element values into working storage) a CHARGES record for this
PATIENT and conclude by OBTAINing the ITEM owner of this CHARGES in the
PROVIDED set.

The operational benefit of a logical record, as will be seen later, is to reduce
the application programmer's burden by creating virtual data that do not have to
be constructed step by step in the application program. The result is less program
coding (hence, faster development), less chance of erroneous data processing
(since common, complicated data accesses can be coded into the subschema by a
senior database programmer), and often a more understandable data model presented to the programmer (since excessive details have been masked from the
programmer).

COBOL DML: RETRIEVING AND
MAINTAINING DATA

We choose to illustrate here the data processing capabilities in the COBOL programming language for accessing and manipulating a DBTG database. As mentioned before, this is not the only procedural language possible, but it is the one
you are most likely to encounter in business data processing. As you will see in
the next section, nonprocedural language access is also possible with many DBTG
systems.

Procedural, step-by-step (record-by-record) processing of a database requires
frequent reference to some relative position in the database from which to move.
That is, we must know some current position in order to find the next record on
a chain or to identify a position for record insertion or deletion. This logic is an
integral part of processing a DBTG database.

Currency Indicators

The term used in the DBTG data manipulation language (DML) for relative position is *currency indicator*. In fact, the DBMS is constantly keeping track of numerous currency indicators. A **currency indicator** is a variable that holds the physical address (database key) of the record instance most recently accessed or manipulated in a specified category of records. These categories result in the following currency indicators important in various DML statements:

1. Current of run-unit: the most recent instance of any database record referenced (that is, retrieved or maintained by some DML command, such as FIND, OBTAIN, CONNECT, or STORE)

2. Current of record type: for each record type in the subschema, the most recent record instance referenced

3. Current of set: for each set in the subschema, the most recent set record instance (owner or member) referenced

4. Current of area: for each area in the subschema, the most recent record occurrence referenced

Currency indicators are updated each time a record instance is accessed. Currency indicator updating may be suppressed, under application program control, to maintain a desired reference point. An application programmer must be well aware of the effect that each DML command has on currency indicator status.

Figure 15-14 shows an action diagram (AD) for a situation we will use to illustrate the maintenance of currency indicators. An **action diagram** shows the sequence of steps needed to produce specific output from a database. The double-line bar shows a repetition loop. The lines with arrows show record accesses. The situation illustrated here depicts part of the data processing necessary to produce

Currency indicator: In a CODASYL DBMS, a variable that holds the physical address (database key) of the record instance most recently accessed or manipulated. Each program invokes several currency indicators, each for different categories of records: each record type, each set, each area, and the database as a whole.

Action diagram: A map or diagram that shows a sequence of actions or steps needed to retrieve certain data or produce certain results from a database.

FOR ALL SALESPERSONS

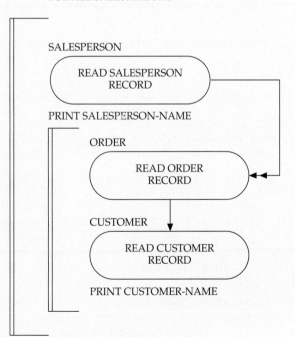

Figure 15-14

Action diagram for all customers by salesperson

a summary of the customers handled by each salesperson at Pine Valley Furniture. Figure 15-15 contains a network instance diagram and an accompanying table that illustrates the detailed maintenance of currency indicators. There is no need to sort the data in any way, so the process begins by accessing the first salesperson on file. To understand Figure 15-15, it is important to remember that user working storage contains only one instance of each record type at a time. Each time we OBTAIN (read) another ORDER record, for example, the prior ORDER record in main memory is overwritten.

In Figure 15-15b, a currency indicator is highlighted each time it is updated. A circle indicates that the currency indicator actually changes value; a box signifies that it was updated but no value change occurred. Logical values for currency indicators are used for clarity; currency indicators, in practice, are physical or relative disk addresses. Numbers on the arrows in the diagram (Figure 15-15a) correspond to the movement through the database caused by execution of the DML statements in the table.

Several events shown in Figure 15-15 require explanation. The first step in the table can occur without any currency indicator values established, since it accesses an absolute, not relative, record (the first SALESPERSON record found in the SALES-AREA). All the OBTAIN NEXT ORDER commands require that there be an established value for CURRENT OF SOLD-SET. Since there is no NEXT ORDER after orders X.2 and X.1, the DBMS would return an error message to the calling program and leave currency indicators unchanged after execution of these commands. The OBTAIN CURRENT SALESPERSON is necessary in step 7 to establish the proper value for CURRENT OF RUN-UNIT so that step 8 will work as desired (if CURRENT OF RUN-UNIT remained X.2, step 8 would actually access Salesperson T again).

Figure 15-15

Example of currency indicator maintenance in a DBTG DBMS

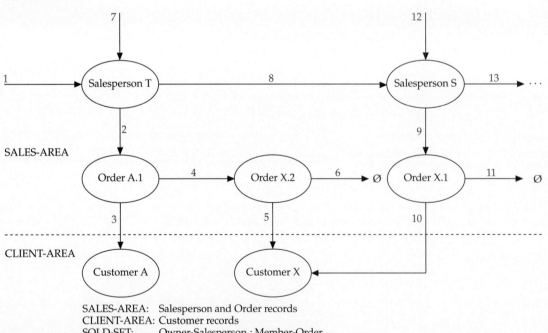

SALES-AREA: Salesperson and Order records
CLIENT-AREA: Customer records
SOLD-SET: Owner-Salesperson ; Member-Order
BOUGHT-SET: Owner-Customer ; Member-Order

(a) Sample database   (continues)

Figure 15-15

(continued)

DML command	CURRENT OF RUN-UNIT	Records			Sets		Areas	
		CURRENT OF SALESPERSON	CURRENT OF ORDER	CURRENT OF CUSTOMER	CURRENT OF SOLD-SET	CURRENT OF BOUGHT-SET	CURRENT OF SALES-AREA	CURRENT OF CLIENT-AREA
1 OBTAIN FIRST SALESPERSON WITHIN SALES-AREA	(T)	(T)			(T)		(T)	
2 OBTAIN NEXT ORDER WITHIN SOLD-SET	(A.1)	T	(A.1)		(A.1)	(A.1)	(A.1)	
3 OBTAIN OWNER WITHIN BOUGHT-SET	(A)	T	A.1	(A)	A.1	(A)	A.1	(A)
4 OBTAIN NEXT ORDER WITHIN SOLD-SET	(X.2)	T	(X.2)	A	(X.2)	(X.2)	(X.2)	A
5 OBTAIN OWNER WITHIN BOUGHT-SET	(X)	T	X.2	(X)	X.2	(X)	X.2	(X)
6 OBTAIN NEXT ORDER WITHIN SOLD-SET	[X]	T	[X.2]	X	[X.2]	[X]	[X.2]	X
7 OBTAIN CURRENT SALESPERSON	(T)	[T]	X.2	X	(T)	X	(T)	X
8 OBTAIN NEXT SALESPERSON WITHIN SALES-AREA	(S)	(S)	X.2	X	(S)	X	(S)	X
9 OBTAIN NEXT ORDER WITHIN SOLD-SET	(X.1)	S	(X.1)	X	(X.1)	(X.1)	(X.1)	X
10 OBTAIN OWNER WITHIN BOUGHT-SET	(X)	S	X.1	[X]	X.1	(X)	X.1	[X]
11 OBTAIN NEXT ORDER WITHIN SOLD-SET	X	S	[X.1]	X	[X.1]	X	[X.1]	X
12 OBTAIN CURRENT SALESPERSON	(S)	[S]	X.1	X	(S)	X	(S)	X
13 OBTAIN NEXT SALESPERSON WITHIN SALES-AREA	–	–	–	–	–	–	–	–

(b) Currency indicators

Overview of DML Commands   In addition to currency indicators, special data elements defined automatically in the user working area by the subschema compiler can be used for application program control. These data elements include the following:

- DB-STATUS: a code that is set after each DML command and that contains a value indicating the type of error, if any, that occurred; although implementation-dependent, this code is usually composed of an indicator for the type of command on which the error occurred (e.g., FIND) and several other characters symbolizing the specific error encountered (e.g., no next record found in set).

- DB-RECORD-NAME, DB-SET-NAME, DB-AREA-NAME, and DB-DATA-NAME: codes in which the DBMS places the subschema names for the record, set, area, and data element (where applicable) for the error that has just occurred (e.g., step 6 in Figure 15-15 would result in DB-RECORD-NAME equaling ORDER, DB-SET-NAME equaling SOLD-SET, DB-AREA-NAME equaling SALES-AREA); DB-DATA-NAME is applicable only on operations involving data elements (usually for violations of CHECK clauses on data values).

The DBTG COBOL DML commands can be divided into three categories: retrieval statements, modification statements, and control statements. Table 15-4 lists the various DML commands included in each of these categories.

TABLE 15-4   Typical COBOL DML Commands

Retrieval

FIND	Locates record in database
GET	Transfers record to working storage
OBTAIN	Combines FIND and GET
	With each command, we can retrieve
	• unique record
	• duplicate record
	• next or prior record in set or area
	• owner of a member record

Modification

STORE	Puts a new record into database and links it to all sets in which it is an automatic member
MODIFY	Changes data values in an existing record
CONNECT	Links an existing member record into a set occurrence
DISCONNECT	Removes (unlinks) an existing member record from its current set occurrence
RECONNECT	A combination of DISCONNECT and CONNECT to unlink a record from its current set and link it to a new set occurrence of the type
ERASE	Deletes record from database, DISCONNECTs it from all set occurrences in which it participates, and deletes other records for which this is an owner in set

Control

COMMIT	Makes permanent all database updates made since last COMMIT command executed
ROLLBACK	Aborts all updates since last COMMIT and restores database to status at time of last COMMIT
KEEP	Places concurrent access controls on database records

Data Retrieval

In record-at-a-time processing, records can be retrieved on the basis of

- Unique key or address value (entry into database)
- Next with same or duplicate key value (secondary key)
- First, last, next, or prior in set or area, possibly in a specified order (related-records navigation)
- Owner of a member record in a set (usually used to change from processing along one set to processing along another)
- Search key within a sorted set or indexed records

Further, since retrieval is the basis for navigating/moving through a database, we might want to (1) locate only the position of a record in order to verify its existence or as a reference point for subsequent movement (FIND); (2) once located (that is, current of run-unit), put the record's data into working storage for processing (GET); or (3) combine the first two steps into one for both data manipulation and subsequent movement (OBTAIN). In addition, we may want to retain exclusive access to data while retrieving in order to prohibit other programs from updating data. (The need to do this depends on the concurrency control of the DBMS; see Chapter 12.)

To understand some of these data retrieval capabilities, consider again the subschema in Figure 15-12 for the Mountain View Community Hospital Patient Bill user view; Figure 15-16a shows a variety of processing using this subschema. Recall that the DBTG COBOL DML contains statements that extend the standard COBOL examples; all the following examples represent parts of a COBOL program necessary to perform the data retrieval function specified (the IDMS COBOL DML is used as an example DML; IDMS uses the variable ERROR-STATUS instead of DB-STATUS).

Suppose we simply wanted to retrieve data for a specified patient (PATIENT-NO 1234). To do so, we need to store the desired key value (1234) in the PATIENT-NO field of the PATIENT record in working storage and then issue the proper

Figure 15-16

Mountain View Community Hospital subschema

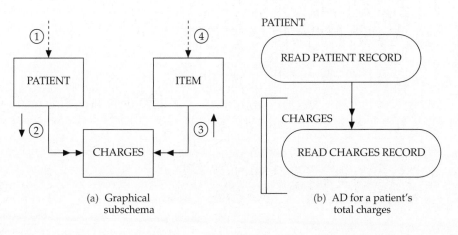

(a) Graphical subschema

(b) AD for a patient's total charges

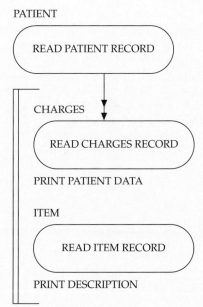

(c) AD for description of all items for which a patient is charged

DML OBTAIN command in order to enter the database along the path labeled (1) in Figure 15-16a. This would be accomplished by

```
MOVE '1234' TO PATIENT-NO IN PATIENT.
OBTAIN CALC PATIENT.
IF ERROR-STATUS=0 THEN NEXT SENTENCE
    ELSE...error routine...
```

The preceding OBTAIN command would make the PATIENT record for PATIENT-NO 1234 current of run-unit, current of PATIENT record type, and current of INCURRED set. If we then wished to calculate this patient's total charges, we would continue accessing along path (2) in Figure 15-16a with the following code (see Figure 15-16b for an AD of the procedure):

```
MOVE 0 TO TOT-CHARGE.
    OBTAIN FIRST CHARGES WITHIN INCURRED.
    PERFORM ADD-CHARGES UNTIL ERROR-STATUS NOT = 0.
    IF NOT end-of-set
      PERFORM error-routine.
ADD-CHARGES.
    ADD CHARGE IN CHARGES TO TOT-CHARGE.
    OBTAIN NEXT CHARGES WITHIN INCURRED.
```

In this example, CHARGES record instances related to the current of INCURRED set are (logically) sequentially retrieved and processed as required. At the first iteration, the set PATIENT owner (PATIENT-NO 1234) is current of set. The looping terminates when ERROR-STATUS indicates that there are no more CHARGES records within this set instance; any other error code in ERROR-STATUS indicates an unexpected error in the database, which may require user intervention or even termination of the program. It is highly advisable to fully use the error-monitoring capabilities of the DBMS after every DML statement (some implementations have ON ERROR clauses as part of each DML command).

As a final example of retrieval statements, consider a reporting requirement to display the description of all the items charged to a specified patient (again, PATIENT-NO 1234). In this case, all three subschema records have to be accessed, but no data from the CHARGES record for this patient are desired. Figure 15-16c illustrates an AD for this retrieval, which is frequently referred to as a "V" retrieval since a path resembling a V is formed by accessing records in steps (1), (2), and then (3) in Figure 15-16a. The following DML statements could be used to retrieve the necessary data:

```
        MOVE '1234' TO PATIENT-NO IN PATIENT.
        OBTAIN CALC PATIENT.
        IF ERROR-STATUS = 0 THEN NEXT SENTENCE
            ELSE ... error routine ...
        Display or print desired PATIENT data.
LOOP.
        FIND NEXT CHARGES WITHIN INCURRED.
        IF ERROR-STATUS = error code for no next record in set
            THEN terminate this procedure.
        IF ERROR-STATUS = some other error code
            THEN ... error routine ...
        OBTAIN OWNER WITHIN PROVIDED.
        IF ERROR-STATUS = any error code
            THEN ... error routine ...
        Display or print DESCRIPTION in ITEM.
        GO TO LOOP.
```

In this example, note that current of INCURRED set was not affected by accessing a CHARGES owner in the PROVIDED set. CHARGES records act in the same way as link records in this example; since link records have no meaningful contents, only FIND needs to be used to retrieve them.

Data Maintenance and Control

Data maintenance within the DBTG model, although limited to only six commands (see Table 15-4), requires careful development because of the various semantic controls that may be specified in a DBTG schema (refer to Table 15-3 for a summary of these controls). Further, to ensure the integrity of a database against concurrent record update and abnormal program termination in the middle of a set of update statements, data maintenance routines require careful design.

When a database (or database area) is opened by a program, most DBTG DMLs require a specification of the mode of processing to be performed by the program (retrieval or update). If the mode is retrieval, then the DBMS will prohibit use of any data modification command in the program. If the mode is update, then two options are often permitted. The first, PROTECTED, means that concurrent update is prevented but that concurrent retrieval is allowed. The second, EXCLUSIVE, prevents any concurrent use of the database (or area).

In addition, many DBTG DMLs permit record-level controls, called *locks*, to maintain a finer level of concurrent update management. In IDMS, for example, a program can place a SHARED lock on a record to prevent other run-units from updating a record temporarily while permitting retrieval. An EXCLUSIVE lock prohibits any other activity on a record until the lock is released. Exclusive locks are implicitly placed on a record that is altered by a STORE, MODIFY, or ERASE DML command.

Further control can be imposed to protect the integrity of a database from abnormal termination of a program during a series of related maintenance statements. Consider the situation of entering a new customer order into the Pine Valley Furniture database. Roughly, the procedure to enter this information into the database is as follows:

1. Accept order header data and enter a new ORDER record.
2. Accept PRODUCTNO, QUANTITY-ORDERED, and so on, for a LINE-ITEM and store the line item.
3. If there are more LINE-ITEMs, then repeat step 2.

Suppose that after accepting and storing the ORDER data and several LINE-ITEM records, a batch update program encounters an error that invalidates the whole customer order. The error necessitates aborting the whole logical transaction and deleting all the previously entered data for this order. Using the ORDERNO in working storage and the set between ORDER and LINE-ITEM, the program could ERASE these records one by one. A simpler approach, however, is to have the DBMS automatically perform these deletions. The beginning of the logical transaction is indicated by some special DML control statement (a START TRANSACTION, COMMIT, or some other command). Another special DML command (typically ROLLBACK or ABORT) is executed to restore the database to the previous commit point.

Storing a New Record We will illustrate the data modification statements using the Mountain View Community Hospital subschema of Figures 15-12 and 15-16a and some variations. Consider the situation of storing the charge for an additional item charged to a patient. Since (from the schema in Figure 15-11)

CHARGES is an AUTOMATIC member of the PROVIDED set and a MANUAL member of the INCURRED set, we will have to use a CONNECT command to insert the CHARGE into the proper INCURRED set instance. Further, since the SET SELECTION of the INCURRED set is implicitly THRU CURRENT OF SET, we will have to first make the proper PATIENT record current. A CHARGES record instance is automatically linked to the correct ITEM owner in the PROVIDED set by common key values. The logical access path for this storage is step (1), then step (2) in Figure 15-16a. The DML for this update for PATIENT-NO 1234 would be as follows:

```
/* Verify patient record exists and make it current */
MOVE '1234' TO PATIENT-NO IN PATIENT.
FIND CALC PATIENT.
IF ERROR-STATUS = 0 THEN NEXT SENTENCE
    ELSE ... error routine ...
/* Build new CHARGES record in working storage */
MOVE 150 TO CHARGE IN CHARGES.
MOVE '1234' TO PATIENT-NO IN CHARGES.
MOVE 307 TO ITEM-CODE IN CHARGES.
STORE CHARGES.
IF ERROR-STATUS = 0 THEN NEXT SENTENCE
    ELSE ... error routine ...
/* Connect manual set member */
CONNECT CHARGES TO INCURRED.
IF ERROR-STATUS = 0 THEN NEXT SENTENCE
    ELSE ... error routine ...
...
```

Deleting an Existing Record The schema for this database (see Figure 15-11) indicates that CHARGES is a FIXED member of both sets (INCURRED and PROVIDED). We may simply delete a CHARGES for PATIENT-NO 1234 and ITEM-CODE 307 in the case of misbilling by first FINDing the desired PATIENT (based on its CALC key), then searching for CHARGES for ITEM-CODE 307 among the members of the INCURRED set instance for PATIENTNO 1234, and then ERASEing the proper CHARGES record. This is the same logical access path as in Figure 15-16b, but in this case searching can stop once the desired CHARGES record for deletion is found. Thus, we would

```
/* Find desired PATIENT record */
MOVE '1234' TO PATIENT-NO IN PATIENT.
FIND CALC PATIENT.
IF ERROR-STATUS = 0 THEN NEXT SENTENCE
    ELSE ... error routine ...
/* Search for desired CHARGES record within INCURRED set */
LOOP.
    OBTAIN NEXT CHARGES WITHIN INCURRED.
    IF ERROR-STATUS = error code for no next record in set
        THEN indicate error and terminate.
    IF ERROR-STATUS = some other error code
        THEN ... error routine ...
    IF ITEM-CODE IN CHARGES NOT = 307
        THEN GO TO LOOP.
    ERASE CHARGES.
    IF ERROR-STATUS = 0 THEN NEXT SENTENCE
        ELSE ... error routine ...
    ...
```

Changing a Member Record's Owner   RETENTION IS FIXED prevents us from moving a CHARGES to a different owner record, which is a natural semantic for this database. If, however, we had indicated RETENTION IS MANDATORY for CHARGES in the PROVIDED set, we could then RECONNECT (but not DISCONNECT) CHARGES records in this set. Suppose we want to change the CHARGES stored earlier to the 413 ITEM-CODE. To do so, we must first find the record for PATIENT-NO 1234 [access (1) in Figure 15-16a], then verify that the new ITEM record owner exists [access (4) in Figure 15-16a], then search through the CHARGES records under the desired patient looking for the CHARGES record to be reconnected [access (2) in Figure 15-16a]. Thus, assuming that we had used MANDATORY, not FIXED, for the PROVIDED set, we would

```
            /* Find the desired PATIENT record */
            MOVE '1234' TO PATIENT-NO IN PATIENT.
            FIND CALC PATIENT.
            IF ERROR-STATUS = 0 THEN NEXT SENTENCE
                ELSE ... error routine ...
            /* Find the ITEM to which CHARGES is to be connected */
            MOVE 413 TO ITEM-CODE IN ITEM.
            FIND CALC ITEM.
            IF ERROR-STATUS = 0 THEN NEXT SENTENCE
                ELSE ... error routine ...
            /* Search in INCURRED set for CHARGES to be reconnected */
LOOP.
        OBTAIN KEEP EXCLUSIVE NEXT CHARGES WITHIN
                INCURRED.
        IF ERROR-STATUS = error code for no next record in set
                THEN indicate error and terminate.
        IF ERROR-STATUS = some other error code
                THEN ... error routine ...
        IF ITEM-CODE IN CHARGES = 307 THEN NEXT SENTENCE
                ELSE GO TO LOOP.
        /* Change CHARGES record and reconnect to new owner */
        MOVE 413 TO ITEM-CODE IN CHARGES.
        RECONNECT CHARGES TO PROVIDED.
        IF ERROR-STATUS = 0 THEN NEXT SENTENCE
                ELSE ... error routine ...
        COMMIT
```

The KEEP EXCLUSIVE clause on the OBTAIN command prevents any other run-unit from retrieving or modifying this CHARGES record while this run-unit is updating it. The COMMIT command releases this concurrency lock and makes the updates permanent (that is, the updates may not be aborted and undone after this point). KEEP EXCLUSIVE and COMMIT are vocabulary particular to IDMS but are representative of the data maintenance controls available in DBTG COBOL DMLs.

To illustrate DISCONNECT, suppose that miscellaneous charges (ITEM-CODE 999) do not have an ITEM record and that to support storage of such charges, we had made CHARGES an OPTIONAL member of the PROVIDED set. The logical access path for this situation is the same as in the previous example, except that the operation will be to DISCONNECT the record rather than to RECONNECT it. We could then change the charge for ITEM-CODE 413 to ITEM-CODE 999 for PATIENT-NO 1234 by

```
/* Find the desired PATIENT record */
MOVE '1234' TO PATIENT-NO IN PATIENT.
FIND CALC PATIENT.
IF ERROR-STATUS = 0 THEN NEXT SENTENCE
    ELSE ... error routine ...
/* Find the ITEM from which CHARGES is to be disconnected */
MOVE 413 TO ITEM-CODE IN ITEM.
FIND CALC ITEM.
IF ERROR-STATUS = 0 THEN NEXT SENTENCE
    ELSE ... error routine ...
/* Search in INCURRED set for CHARGES to be disconnected */
LOOP.
    OBTAIN KEEP EXCLUSIVE NEXT CHARGES WITHIN
        INCURRED.
    IF ERROR-STATUS = error code for no next record in set
        THEN indicate error and terminate.
    IF ERROR-STATUS = some other error code
        THEN ... error routine ...
    IF ITEM-CODE IN CHARGES = 307 THEN NEXT SENTENCE
        ELSE GO TO LOOP.
    /* Disconnect CHARGES record and change contents */
    DISCONNECT CHARGES FROM PROVIDED.
    IF ERROR-STATUS = 0 THEN NEXT SENTENCE
        ELSE ... error routine ...
        MOVE 999 TO ITEM-CODE IN CHARGES.
    MODIFY CHARGES.
    IF ERROR-STATUS = 0 THEN NEXT SENTENCE
        ELSE ... error routine ...
    COMMIT.
```

Note that in this and the prior example, we had to OBTAIN, not just FIND, CHARGES in order to MODIFY its contents. It is also worth emphasizing again that it is wise not to execute the COMMIT until after all aspects of the logical transaction are complete. If we were to COMMIT after each DML modification command (e.g., after the DISCONNECT above), and then for some reason the user program aborted before the MODIFY command, the database would be left in a low integrity state, with only part of the total update done.

Special Maintenance Considerations In addition to deleting a record instance, the ERASE command can have a much broader effect on database contents. Assuming the original schema and subschema from Figures 15-11 and 15-12, respectively, consider deletion of an ITEM record occurrence. Since CHARGES are FIXED members of the PROVIDED set (the same would be true of MANDATORY), they cannot exist without an ITEM owner. If we ERASE an ITEM record in this case, the CHARGES records associated with this ITEM would also automatically be erased by the DBMS.

If CHARGES were an OPTIONAL member of the PROVIDED set, then we could choose what to do with CHARGES members (and members of any other set owned by ITEM) when deleting an ITEM owner. If we were to use

```
ERASE ITEM PERMANENT MEMBER.
```

then any MANDATORY or FIXED member for a set owned by ITEM would also be ERASEd, but OPTIONAL members (such as CHARGES under the preceding assumption) would only be automatically DISCONNECTed. If we

```
ERASE ITEM SELECTIVE MEMBER.
```

then all MANDATORY or FIXED members would be ERASEd, but OPTIONAL members would also be ERASEd *if* they do not currently have a member in any other set (e.g., INCURRED) occurrence. In the case of CHARGES records, since each must be a member of some INCURRED set, none would be ERASEd. This would apply only to members that are OPTIONAL members of other sets. All members can be ERASEd regardless of other set membership by using ERASE ITEM ALL.

Logical Record Processing in IDMS

In Figure 15-13, we introduced the IDMS logical record construct that can be defined in a subschema. The purpose of a logical record is to define a simple view of the database that consolidates several database records into one virtual record. Logical records can be used to simplify OBTAIN, STORE, MODIFY, and ERASE processing by permitting *one* such DML statement to implicitly retrieve and appropriately process a group of related records.

Figure 15-13 contains a definition for a DETAILED-BILL logical record. We can use this logical record to produce a listing of all charges for a given PATIENT (say, PATIENT-NO 1234) by

```
PRINT-LIST.
   OBTAIN NEXT DETAILED-BILL WHERE PATIENT-NO = '1234'
      ON LR-NOT-FOUND GO TO AFTER-LIST.
   Display or print data from CHARGES and ITEM records
      (but not PATIENT, since logical record definition uses FIND for
      PATIENT record)
   . . .
   GO TO PRINT-LIST.
AFTER-LIST.
   . . .
```

The ON error clause also represents a logical/symbolic way to check database error codes instead of using detailed IF statements involving ERROR-STATUS and other variables.

NETWORK DATABASE DESIGN ISSUES AND ADVANCED TOPICS

The network data model presents a database designer with many options to customize a database for efficient processing. Many of the design decisions have been ignored or covered very briefly in the previous sections. This section elaborates on the topics of prior sections, introducing more subtle points and advanced options, and also focuses on particular network implementation design decisions.

Because network systems frequently are used for high-volume, transaction-processing applications, efficient database design is important. Further, most of the topics addressed here deal with basic structural choices for a database, which do not exhibit data independence. Thus, redesign to incorporate or change these design elements would typically require application program maintenance; for this reason, it is important to design the database in the best way possible the first time.

Record Placement Control

Two internal network model constructs control the physical absolute and relative placement of records: areas and LOCATION MODE. Areas are physically contiguous disk tracks that are opened and closed together. In designing a database, we would be more likely to create an area and to place selected records in that area if

- We wanted a single level of security control (that is, by area) on all the designated records.
- Database navigation time would be noticeably improved by restricting placement of the related records to relatively nearby disk tracks (that is, to minimize disk head movement).

LOCATION MODE is determined by how records will be accessed. CALC is used when some application program will *know* (from user entry or other database records) the key of a record (or records in the case of a secondary key) to be accessed. That is, the application needs direct entry into the database on that record type. Such entry points would be apparent from a composite usage map like that in Figure 7-4. Choice of CALC requires the key to be a field (or fields, for a concatenated key) in the record being CALCed (so storage space is necessary to support CALC). The ability to CALC a record is unaffected by changes in set membership for that record. The existence of a primary key for a record type that is itself meaningful business data (e.g., ORDERNO for an order, LADINGNO for a shipment) usually means that the record should be CALCed, whereas records with artificial primary keys or concatenated keys are less likely for CALC. One easy way to decide whether a record should be CALCed is to determine if it is a member of any set—if it is not a member of any set, it should be CALCed.

A database designer will usually begin by CALCing the obvious entry points; other record types are then considered for VIA. Since many of the record types not CALCed may be members of several sets, the issue is really: VIA *which* set? A composite usage map (see, for example, Figure 7-4) is very useful. The set chosen for VIA would be the one associated with the path into the record that has the largest frequency of access. One caution with VIA: Since record placement is related to the owner of a member record when the member is first stored, MANDATORY and OPTIONAL sets (in which ownership may change) are not attractive as VIA sets.

Record Data Elements

Three particular database design issues arise when determining the data elements of a record. First is the issue of whether to include the key of the associated owner record (and any of the other nonkey owner data) in the member record of a set. For example, consider the ORDER-LINE record in Figure 15-3b. Since pointers will be maintained by the DBMS for the two sets in which ORDER-LINE participates, PRODUCTNO and ORDERNO are not necessary in order to access the owner PRODUCT or ORDER for a particular ORDER-LINE. However, if we want to sort ORDER-LINE records in the ORDER to ORDER-LINE set by PRODUCTNO, then we must include PRODUCTNO in ORDER-LINE.

Owner nonkey data can be stored in a member to make accessing the owner in order to retrieve the data unnecessary, but this causes redundancy from unnormalizing the data. Thus, such storage would typically only be done when real-time processing requirements necessitate squeezing every extra record access out of a program.

The second design issue for data elements deals with the creation of repeating groups or definition of a separate record type. Use of a repeating group is not really feasible when repeating data are or could be related to multiple base records. That is, repeating data are very similar to the members of a set, and if the repeating data are members of only one set, then they can be embedded within the owner as a repeating group. For example, consider Figure 15-17, which depicts EMPLOYEE and DEPENDENT data, as well as other personnel data entities. Since the collection of DEPENDENT data for a particular EMPLOYEE is related only to the EMPLOYEE, this could easily be designated as repeating group data in the EMPLOYEE record type. On the other hand, ASSIGNMENT data are not a characteristic of just EMPLOYEE, but also JOB. Although we could make ASSIGNMENT a repeating group within EMPLOYEE (thus, denormalizing the database), we would then have to either duplicate it as a repeating group within JOB or create a *M:N* relationship between JOB and EMPLOYEE, which is not allowed in many network systems.

The third data element design issue is whether to store derived or calculated data for an entity in the associated record (and recalculate them as the parameters change) or to recalculate them in an application program as they are needed each time. For example, some users of a database may want to manipulate the price and quantity ordered of products; other users, in accounting, perhaps, may only want to see the derived product amount due. But can we be sure that all accounting user programs will calculate amount due correctly?

The DBTG guidelines introduced the concept of virtual data, or data that appear to exist in a record but that do not physically reside in an instance of that record. Two clauses, the SOURCE and the RESULT clauses, deal with the distinction between ACTUAL and VIRTUAL data elements. These clauses and options together allow the database to appear to contain data that, at least in the form or location perceived, do not actually exist.

If the SOURCE clause is associated with a given data element definition, it signifies that a value for that data element is to be the same as a specified data element from its owner in a designated set. For example, ORDERNO in an instance of an ORDER-LINE record from Figure 15-3b (Pine Valley Furniture Company) must have the same value as the ORDERNO in its associated ORDER record. SOURCE provides a form of integrity control of the database. Use of SOURCE prohibits use of PICTURE or TYPE on the same data element, since these are implied from the "source" data element. An appropriate SOURCE clause for this example would be

```
RECORD IS ORDER-LINE
...
1 ORDNO; ACTUAL SOURCE IS ORDERNO OF OWNER
        ITEMS-ON-ORDER SET.
```

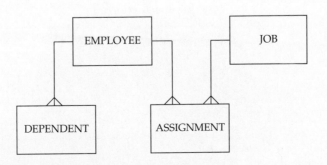

Figure 15-17

Repeating group data in a network

In this case, ACTUAL specifies that ORDNO is to be redundantly stored again in the ORDER-LINE record. Use of VIRTUAL instead of ACTUAL would tell the DBMS to allow use of ORDNO as if it were a data element of the ORDER-LINE record, but retrieve it from the associated ORDER record instead (and save the redundant space).

The RESULT clause also utilizes the ACTUAL and VIRTUAL designations. The RESULT clause says that the data element to which it applies is to be calculated or derived from a procedure involving other data elements from the same record; from all members for this record, in which the owner is some set (e.g., to calculate a total across all members, the equivalent of a class attribute in the semantic data model); or from some more general calculation. If ACTUAL RESULT is specified, then the derived value is constantly maintained by the DBMS and stored in the record. If VIRTUAL RESULT is specified, then the derived value is calculated by the DBMS each time a record instance is retrieved and appears to be included in the physical record, but it actually only exists in the user's working storage area (or subschema).

Sets

Since it is a set that provides navigation through a network database, the choice as to which sets to include directly affects database processing performance. A database designer will certainly choose to build a set for each relationship between record types in the conceptual data model of the database. The issue is whether to build extra, redundant sets. Such redundant sets serve two purposes:

1. **To maintain different member sorting sequences for the same relationship** (e.g., one set between CUSTOMER and ORDER for ORDERs in promised delivery date sequence and another set in salesperson sequence). Recall that each time we choose to sort the members of a set, the sorting variable must be included in the member records (e.g., salesperson ID might have to be included in the ORDER record only if we were to sort ORDERs on this in some set). A database designer, to be able to decide on this type of sorted set, needs to understand not only access paths in the composite usage map but also desirable member-access sequence. A sorted set saves scanning members until the desired one or group is found in a random sequence and saves a post-database access sort to rearrange the data.

2. **To "shortcut" access along several component links.** For example, consider the network database of Figure 15-18a. To determine the products ordered

Figure 15-18

Redundant set for processing efficiency

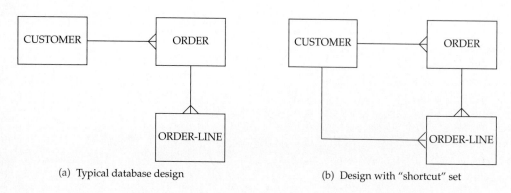

(a) Typical database design   (b) Design with "shortcut" set

by a given customer, we must enter the database on customer and navigate to ORDER, then to ORDER-LINE. In Figure 15-18b the redundant, transitive link from CUSTOMER to ORDER-LINE can be used to navigate directly to ORDER-LINE from CUSTOMER. Such shortcuts can only be made along a set of (nested) 1:1 or 1:M relationships. A shortcut 1:M link from CUSTOMER to PRODUCT, which is along a M:N transitive relationship, is infeasible since the same PRODUCT record can have only one owner for the set, yet it must be able to have several in the actual relationship.

The additional set-design issues of choice of singular sets, and insertion and retention controls have been covered adequately in prior sections.

DEVICE MEDIA CONTROL LANGUAGE

Although the schema DDL specifies some internal database characteristics, the schema still has a great deal of data independence from the internal database. The device media control language (DMCL) is used to complete the database definition.

Because the DMCL is used to prescribe physical database characteristics, its use should be limited to the database administrator. PR1ME Computer, in fact, has made this implicit by calling their version of the DMCL for their DBTG DBMS the Database Administrator Control Program (DBACP) and by requiring that a user have special computer system privileges in order to perform most of the DBACP functions.

In IDMS, the DMCL is used to:

- Specify the number of secondary memory pages to keep in a main memory buffer area (this would specify the size of the system buffers block in Figure 15-1)

- Specify the characteristics of each area, such as the number of characters per page in the area, amount of space for expansion of variable-length records, and alias names for the area

- Define the physical characteristics of journal files used to store record and transaction images useful in database recovery

Similar functions are performed by most DMCLs or equivalent utilities. In general, these functions allocate physical space for the database, specify which options to use (if any) for representing sets, name all the various physical operating system files and/or data sets used to construct the database, and indicate whether and how to create audit trails and data modification journals.

NONPROCEDURAL ACCESS: QUERY AND NATURAL LANGUAGES

Most vendors of DBTG systems provide nonprocedural query languages for ad hoc, interactive retrieval of data and/or report writer programs for nonprocedural production of customized reports. For example, PR1ME provides DBMS/Query (or DISCOVER) with its DBTG DBMS. Cullinet provides OnLine Query (OLQ) as a query langauge, IDMS/CULPRIT as a report writer, and OnLine English (OLE) as a natural language processor. (OnLine English is marketed by Cullinet, but is one version of Intellect, a product of Artificial Intelligence Corp.) Further, Cullinet now has a new version of IDMS, IDMS/R, which includes a relational-like query language. Their claim is that this marriage of network data storage with relational access provides both high performance and ease of access.

Query Languages

Query languages permit an interactive programmer, often a non–data processing professional, to write record retrievals using expressions that specify which records are desired without having to go through the process of record-by-record retrieval. Often such query languages resemble relational calculus; thus, it is possible to give an end user a relational-like view of a network database.

As an example of a query language for a network database, we will present a few sample queries using Cullinet's OnLine Query (OLQ). For this illustration, consider the inventory database of Figure 15-10. We could retrieve the first sequential PRODUCT record in the database by

```
(1) GET FIRST SEQUENTIAL PRODUCT RECORD
```

and OLQ would immediately display the contents of this record on the terminal. We could then retrieve the first INVENTORY for this PRODUCT by

```
(2) GET FIRST INVENTORY BELONGING TO THIS PRODUCT
```

and could continue to retrieve other INVENTORY records one by one using

```
(3) REPEAT WITH LAST
```

Otherwise, if we wanted to see all the INVENTORY records for this PRODUCT, we could issue the following command immediately after (1):

```
(4) GET ALL INVENTORY BELONGING TO THIS PRODUCT
```

Such query languages are helpful in that they can rapidly produce the result of a simple end-user question, check on the contents of a database after a series of COBOL data maintenance program executions, or provide a user with a prototype of the type of report that could be produced in a fancier format by a batch report writer or COBOL report program. These languages do, however, have a precise grammar and syntax that must be learned by anyone who wishes to write a query. Release 10.0 of OLQ from Cullinet has a menu-driven front end for end users.

Natural Languages

Natural language system: A language subsystem based on artificial intelligence that allows the user to carry on a dialogue with the computer in an unstructured version of English or another language.

A **natural language system** eliminates the need to learn a specific grammar, vocabulary, and syntax. OnLine English (OLE) from Cullinet is an English-language query system that enables users to obtain computer-stored information by means of simple request. OLE accepts and interprets a freely worded request, retrieves the appropriate data, and performs all processing necessary to display the results in a meaningful format. The capacity to accept everyday English phrases is a powerful feature of OnLine English that distinguishes it from traditional query systems.

Consider again the inventory database of Figure 15-10. After a user signs on and is greeted by OLE, Figure 15-19 illustrates some possible dialogue between OLE and the user. In this figure, OLE prompts and responses are shown in capital letters and user questions in lowercase. Prior to processing each English question, OLE displays a structured query version of its interpretation of the original question. The user can abort the processing at this point in order to restate the query if OLE has misinterpreted the question. If the user uses key words such as *average*, *minimum*, or *bar graph*, OLE will generate the appropriate result.

Given that such nonprocedural languages exist for access to a network database, why should we ever program in COBOL? First, most of these facilities are limited to data retrieval and reporting; data update is usually not supported. Second, the computer time required to dynamically translate query or English statements into the record-level commands adds significant overhead to computer processing. A prewritten procedural language routine would execute the same type of retrieval much faster (but, of course, would take significantly more time to code). The trade-off, basically, is between machine efficiency and programmer efficiency. When rapidly developed, ad hoc, frequently modified, or one-time reports are desired, nonprocedural languages are suitable; if high-volume transaction processing or repeated rapid-response queries characterize the computing work load, then procedural languages will be more appropriate for processing the network database.

```
PLEASE ENTER YOUR FIRST REQUEST
What are the fields in the inventory file?
FIELDS IN THE INVENTORY FILE
SNO   PNO   WNO
NEXT REQUEST
What is the SNO and PNO of all inventory in 04 warehouse?
PRINT THE SNO AND PNO OF ALL INVENTORY WITH WNO=04
THE NUMBER OF RECORDS TO RETRIEVE IS 3
     SNO       PNO
    12345     1234
    72843     5436
    92371     3476
NEXT REQUEST
Where is part 1234 stored?
PRINT THE WNO OF ALL INVENTORY WITH PNO = 1234
THE NUMBER OF RECORDS TO RETRIEVE IS 2
     WNO
     04
     12
NEXT REQUEST
How many warehouses are there?
COUNT THE WAREHOUSE
ANSWER: 16
NEXT REQUEST
   ...
```

Figure 15-19

Example of IDMS OnLine English dialogue

SUMMARY

This chapter has reviewed the major network data model implementation, the CODASYL DBTG model (and IDMS, a leading commercial product). Although the discussion has been dominated by an examination of record-level access to data, we have also shown example query languages for access data in network databases. Such query and natural languages can provide a relational-like front-end view of a network database.

The network data model has been much maligned since the introduction of the relational model. Criticisms have primarily focused on issues of ease-of-use and processing complex queries, which generally favor the relational model. However, in practice, the network data model DBMSs have continued to be popular data management technologies, usually because of the better performance possible by the explicit record-level processing. Today, because of relational-like query language front ends, we can "have our performance and ease of use, too."

CHAPTER REVIEW

Key Terms

Action diagram	Data manipulation language	Natural language system
Area	(DML)	Record type
Currency indicator	Device media control language	Schema
Data description language	(DMCL)	Set
(DDL)	LOCATION MODE	Subschema

REVIEW QUESTIONS

1. Define each of the following terms:
   - a. CODASYL DBTG
   - b. IDS
   - c. DDL
   - d. DML
   - e. DMCL
   - f. schema
   - g. subschema
   - h. area
   - i. host language
   - j. LOCATION MODE
   - k. manual insertion
   - l. automatic insertion
   - m. fixed retention
   - n. mandatory retention
   - o. optional retention
   - p. CALC location mode
   - q. virtual data
   - r. currency indicator
   - s. search key
   - t. IDMS logical record
   - u. natural language

2. Contrast the functions of the three DBTG retrieval commands FIND, GET, and OBTAIN.
3. Discuss the advantages of using a network DBMS with a relational-like query language.
4. Describe the use of the system buffers shown in Figure 15-1. When are data moved in and out of these buffers? What effect would paging in a virtual-memory operating system have on buffer contents?
5. Describe the role of a computer operating system in database access under the DBTG guidelines.
6. Explain why there are different subschema DDLs, one for each host programming language.
7. Explain why a record may not have a CALC key and also be located VIA some set.
8. Explain the factors to consider for selecting among FIRST, LAST, and SORTED for the ORDER IS clause of a set definition.

9. Explain the benefit of the IDMS logical record construct.
10. Explain the purpose of the IDMS COMMIT command, and discuss where in a program this command can be usefully placed.
11. Under what circumstances (database schema characteristics) is the DML command RE-CONNECT permitted?
12. Discuss the various uses of a singular set.

PROBLEMS AND EXERCISES

1. Match each term with the appropriate definition:

___ DBTG

a. language used to state data retrieval and modification operations

___ schema

b. diagram indicating navigation path or steps through a database

___ subschema

c. task force that developed the CODASYL network standard

___ status variable

d. most recent record accessed

___ DDL

e. a natural language processor

___ DML

f. contains error codes and other data about command execution

___ VIA location mode

g. command that makes recent database changes a part of the actual database

___ virtual data element

h. data that are not actually stored in the database but appear as if they are

___ singular set

i. a database description for a DBMS

___ RECONNECT

j. command that changes a set member's owner

___ current of set

k. view of a database used by an application program

___ logical access map

l. placement of a member instance close to its owner instance

___ COMMIT

m. language used to define a database

___ Intellect

n. used to sort all records of some type into sequence

2. Consider the entities of AGENT, POLICY, CLIENT, BENEFICIARY, and INSURANCE COMPANY in an independent insurance agency. Design a DBTG network diagram (similar to Figure 15-5a) for this situation.
3. For the database designed in Problem 2, suggest several data processing requirements for which use of more than one area would be beneficial in the schema.
4. Specify the LOCATION MODE clause for each record type in Problem 2, and justify your choice of mode and duplicates specification.
5. For each of the sets in your answer to Problem 2, specify and justify INSERTION and RETENTION clauses. Write complete set definitions for this problem.
6. Consider the entities of PROJECT, GENERAL TASK, and EMPLOYEE in a project management or job shop organization. Design a DBTG network diagram (similar to Figure 15-5a) for this situation.
7. For the situation in Problem 6, assume there is a need to report the employees working on a project in order by their job classification. Write the schema DDL necessary to support this requirement through the database structure.

8. Consider the situation of an automobile dealership and entities OWNER, VEHICLE, SALE, and SALESPERSON. Assume all the usual relationships between these entities plus the association of a sale to vehicles traded in on that sale. Design a DBTG network diagram (similar to Figure 15-5a) for this situation, and write the schema DDL, using data items of your choice.

9. In the situation in Problem 8, assume that the dealership's general manager frequently sends promotional mailings to owners of vehicles on file. To minimize mailing costs, she wishes this to be printed in customer zip code order. Add to your schema and network diagram for Problem 8 the constructs necessary to support this data processing.

10. Review the alternatives of representing a loop relationship presented in Figure 15-6. Evaluate each of these and suggest situations in which each would be a desirable approach.

11. For the database schema of Problem 8, draw a logical access map, and then write the COBOL and DML commands necessary to change ownership of a vehicle. Assume any data elements you believe are essential; include skeletons of database error checks.

12. For the database of Problem 2, write the COBOL and DML commands required to enter a new policy into the database. Assume any data elements you believe are essential; include skeletons of database error checks.

13. Consider again the database of Problem 2. Draw a logical access map and action diagram, and then write the COBOL and DML commands required (skeleton of the code is all that is necessary) to produce a report of the policy numbers and anniversary dates for each policy of each client. The policy numbers and dates are to be grouped by client; the clients are not be printed in any particular logical order.

14. In the preceding database design problems, you were not given much information about the data processing requirements of the situation, but instead were asked to design the database in more general terms. Specifically, what clauses of a DBTG schema are affected by knowledge of particular data processing requirements? How is each affected?

15. Consider again the data processing required in Problem 13. Design some sample data for this problem, and develop an illustration of currency indicator maintenance, as in Figure 15-15, for your sample data and the program fragment you wrote for Problem 13.

REFERENCES

ANSI X3H2. 1981. *Proposed American National Standard for a Data Definition Language for Network Structured Databases*. American National Standards Institute.

CODASYL. 1971. *Data Base Task Group April 71 Report*. New York: Association for Computing Machinery.

CODASYL COBOL Committee. 1978. *COBOL Journal of Development*. Available from Federal Department of Supply and Services, Hull, Quebec, Canada.

CODASYL Data Description Language Committee. 1978. *DDL Journal of Development*. Available from Federal Department of Supply and Services, Hull, Quebec, Canada.

Computer Associates International. 1988. *IDMS-DB/DC DML Reference*. Garden City, N.Y.: Computer Associates International.

Computer Associates International. 1988. *IDMS/RDDL References*. Garden City, N.Y.: Computer Associates International.

Computer Associates International. 1988. *IDMS/R Concepts and Facilities*. Garden City, N.Y.: Computer Associates International.

Olle, T. W. 1980. *The CODASYL Approach to Data Base Management*. Chichester, England: Wiley.

Tsichritzis, D., and F. Lochovsky. 1982. *Data Models*. Englewood Cliffs, N.J.: Prentice-Hall.

Appendix A

CODD'S RULES FOR A TRULY RELATIONAL SYSTEM

So-called RDBMSs appear in many forms and with fervent marketing. How can a system that truly follows the principles of relational databases (with the associated functional capabilities) be easily distinguished from a system that does not? The founder of relational database theory, E. F. (Ted) Codd, has outlined 12 rules to test whether a product that is claimed to be "fully rational" really is. These rules are summarized at the end of this appendix.

Clearly a purist, Codd admits that "no existing DBMS product that I know of can honestly claim to be fully relational at this time" when compared with these rules (Codd, October 14, 1985). The situation has not changed since then. Even the ANSI SQL standard comes under criticism by Codd as not complying, although he says it can be readily modified to comply.

The 12 rules and Codd's arguments are all based on a single foundation principle, which he calls Rule Zero:

> Rule Zero. For any system that is advertised as, or claimed to be, a relational database management system, that system must be able to manage databases entirely through its relational capabilities.

This is a tall order and one that, in practice, DBMSs following other data models have never had to meet in their own context in order to be considered network, hierarchical, or whatever. This and other rules are designed with users in mind; that is, they are designed to create an easy-to-use and consistent structure and user interface. Codd's orientation is that "any DBMS that advises users to revert to some nonrelational capabilities to achieve acceptable performance—for any reason other than compatibility with programs written in the past on nonrelational database systems—should be interpreted as an apology by the vendor" (Codd, October 14, 1985, ID/4).

Rather than leaving these rules and the comparison of products against them as an academic debate, Codd argues that there are practical consequences for insisting on rule compliance (Codd, October 21, 1985). Some of these are:

- Rules 1 and 4 allow a database administrator always to know exactly what kinds of data are recorded. Hence, they minimize the time needed to determine the data available while also reducing the data redundancy that would result if this information were unknowable.

- Rule 3 helps users of all types to avoid making foolish and costly mistakes (for example, miscalculating summary data when null values are coded in some uninterpretable way).
- Rule 5 supports interactive program testing, which can mean improved programmer productivity.
- Rules 8–11 contribute to lower program development and maintenance costs due to the inevitable system changes that occur in decision support and information retrieval application systems.

People who firmly believe that RDBMSs are superior to other types of DBMSs argue that abusing the term *relational* reduces its meaning to the lowest common features of systems to which it is applied. Others—many of whom are proponents of commercial products that existed before the general popularity of relational systems—claim that user satisfaction with a tool and the ability of that tool to solve user problems should override definitions and categorization of products. Even with standards, vendors are motivated to enhance and otherwise distinguish their product from that of others. As long as this occurs, definitional debates are inevitable.

The following are Codd's 12 rules for a truly relational system.

RULE 1: Information Representation.

> All information in a relational database is represented explicitly at the logical level and in exactly one way—by values in tables.

Interpretation: Even metadata (that is, table names, column names, etc.) are all stored in tables; coupled with Rule 4, data definitions are accessible via the relational manipulation sublanguage. Thus, database administrators and developers of application and system software have access to up-to-date data definitions. "All information" can be widely interpreted. A reasonable definition of "all information" is any data or metadata defined or entered into the database. This would include, for example, integrity rules and user names (since such names appear in security rules), but would reasonably exclude procedure/program documentation on references to database data. The reference to "logical level" means that physical constructs such as pointers and indexes are not represented and need not be explicitly referenced in query writing, even if they exist.

RULE 2: Guaranteed Access.

> Each and every datum (atomic value) in a relational database is guaranteed to be logically accessible by resorting to a combination of table name, primary key value, and column name.

Interpretation: This specifies a minimal accessibility in terms of content—the names of data and the one and only one primary key value. Thus, no data are to be accessible only by artificial paths, such as linked lists or physical sequential scanning. This rule is based on the fact that the relational data model deals only with data at a functional or logical level, devoid of physical constructs, and is a consequence of Rule 1.

RULE 3: Systematic Treatment of Null Values.

> Null values (distinct from the empty character string or a string of blank characters and distinct from zero or any other number) are supported for representing missing information and inapplicable information in a systematic way, independent of data type.

Interpretation: Given this rule, "nulls not allowed" can be specified to provide data integrity on primary keys or any other column for which nonexisting values are inappropriate. The systematic, uniform representation means that only one technique needs to be employed to deal with null values. Further, the treatment of null values must be persistent and be applied at any value change in order to maintain integrity.

RULE 4: Dynamic On-Line Catalog Based on Relational Model.

> The database description is represented at the logical level in the same way as ordinary data, so that authorized users can apply the same relational language to its interrogation as they apply to the regular data.

Interpretation: Thus, only one data model is used for both data and metadata, and only one manipulation sublanguage needs to be learned. In addition, it would be possible to then extend the catalog of definitions to become more like a data dictionary by including any data about data appropriate for an application. Data definitions are stored in only one place, given this rule. A subtle consequence of this rule and Rule 1 is that the distinction between data and metadata is no longer clear since both can serve as the basis for information to and inquiry by a user.

RULE 5: Comprehensive Data Sublanguage.

> A relational system may support several languages and various modes of terminal use. However, there must be at least one language whose statements can express all of the following items: (1) data definitions, (2) view definitions, (3) data manipulation (interactive and by program), (4) integrity constraints, (5) authorization, and (6) transaction boundaries (begin, commit, and rollback).

Interpretation: The key word in this rule is *comprehensive.* The six specific items indicate that Codd does expect that most of the functions of a DBMS outlined in Chapter 12 are provided within the syntax of one language. The objective of this rule is to create a comprehensive environment that does not have to be left in order to accomplish another task. For example, if in the process of manipulating data the user decides to retain a result or record some new data, he or she does not have to exit one environment and enter another in order to define the new data, and then reenter the original to populate the new tables. Although the benefits of this rule are clear in concept, the motivation for this rule may not seem obvious from an analysis of relational theory. However, it is a consequence, in part, of Rule 4 since data definitions must be accessible from the manipulation sublanguage.

RULE 6: View Updating.

> All views that are theoretically updatable are also updatable by the system.

Interpretation: A view is "theoretically updatable" if there is an update (insert, delete, or modify) procedure that, when applied at any point in time to the base tables of a view, will have the same effect as the requested modification of the view. That is, the update of the base tables necessary to effect the change in the view must be unambiguously derivable by the system. For example, increasing an extended price column value in a view (where extended price is the multiple of price from a product base table and quantity from an order base table) does not have an unambiguous meaning in terms of base table data, so the relational DBMS would not have to be able to perform this update. But, updating a product description in a view that combines product and order base data could be interpreted unambiguously as an update of product description in the product base table, and must be supported according to this rule.

RULE 7: High-Level Insert, Update, and Delete.

> The capability of handling a base relation or a derived relation (that is, view) as a single operand applies not only to the retrieval of data but also to the insertion, update, and deletion of data.

Interpretation: This basically means that all operators are set operators, not record or tuple operators. Thus, a set of table rows can be deleted in one statement or a set of rows can all be modified in a common way in one command.

RULE 8: Physical Data Independence.

> Application programs and terminal activities remain logically unimpaired whenever any changes are made in either storage representations or access methods.

Interpretation: Again, "any changes" implies a very pure view of physical data independence. One typical example of the physical data independence advocated here would be that a query or program would be written the same no matter whether an index exists or not on a column qualified in the query; programs in a network system would probably change depending on the existence of an index, hashing function, or the like. This rule also implies that constructing an optimum retrieval sequence to compose the result of a query is the responsibility of the DBMS, not the user.

RULE 9: Logical Data Independence.

> Application programs and terminal activities remain logically unimpaired when information-preserving changes of any kind that theoretically permit unimpairment are made to the base tables.

Interpretation: This and Rule 8 permit a database designer to make changes, to evolve, or to correct database definitions at any point without having to completely redefine or reload the database (and take it out of service to do so). As long as information is not lost from the restructuring, no application programs or inquiry activities should have to change. To comply with this rule, it must be possible to preserve prior definitions through views, and these views must be able to be updated (Rule 6) as long as the database restructuring does not lose information. For example, the splitting of a table into two caused by recognition of new data requirements and the need to eliminate a transitive dependency (that is, a new entity is identified where only one domain of the entity was needed before the change) should not cause existing application procedures to change, because the split table can be virtually reconstructed in a view.

RULE 10: Integrity Independence.

> Integrity constraints specific to a particular relational database must be definable in the relational data sublanguage and storable in the catalog, not in the application programs.

Interpretation: This rule covers the ability to define as part of the database definitions controls on the values that columns may assume. Such rules may restrict values to be within a certain range, to be one of a set of permitted values, to be not null (if this column is part of a primary key, then this is called *entity integrity*), and to be a value from some other column of the database (that is, a non-null foreign key value must match some current value from a row of the table with that as primary key, so-called referential integrity). Even user-defined constraints (such as no more than five line items per order) should be possible. These integrity rules must be able to change over time; when changed, violations must be identified, and existing programs or inquiries must still be able to work.

RULE 11: Distribution Independence.

> The data manipulation sublanguage of a relational DBMS must enable application programs and inquiries to remain logically the same whether and whenever data are physically centralized or distributed.

Interpretation: In a distributed database, data are physically dispersed across several remote computer sites, and data processing requests at any one of those sites may require data stored at several of the sites. Each program treats the database as if it were all local, so distribution and redistribution do not change the logic of programs. It is important to note that this rule does not say that to be fully relational the DBMS must support a distributed database, but it does say that the data manipulation language would remain the same if and when this capability were introduced and when data are redistributed.

RULE 12: Nonsubversion.

> If a relational system has a low-level (single-record-at-a-time) language, that low level cannot be used to subvert or bypass the integrity rules and constraints expressed in the higher-level relational language (multiple-records-at-a-time).

Interpretation: This basically means that all data manipulation language supported by the relational DBMS must rely only on the stored database definition (including integrity rules and security constraints) for control of processing. This and Rule 5 imply that it should not be possible, nor is it necessary to access a relational database using any language that bypasses the data definitions catalog.

Appendix B

AN OVERVIEW OF PC-RDBMSs

Several trends suggest that PC-RDBMSs are becoming a prominent, if not the preferred, platform for building sophisticated application systems. These trends include

- The increasing power of personal computers
- The migration of mainframe DBMSs to PCs
- The increasing capabilities of PC-RDBMSs
- The cooperation of mainframe or LAN host and PC data management tools into a client-server computing environment (See Chapter 13 for more details on this trend.)

Typically, a PC-RDBMS includes or has available as add-on elements screen formatters, report writers, query languages, interfaces to procedural programming languages like C or Pascal, and special procedural or command languages for database processing. PC-RDBMSs are used not only to build personal computer applications, but also to prototype applications to be migrated to mainframes. They are used to build sophisticated applications involving database processing on workstations and local area network servers.

Unique Characteristics of PC-RDBMSs

PC-RDBMSs are unique primarily because of the operating environment for database processing. With mainframe systems, database processing occurs in a highly developed, multiprogramming, multiuser environment. Concurrent access to the database must be controlled, and security protection is essential because of the shared data. In the PC arena, in contrast, there are varying environments, which are discussed in the following sections.

Single-User Stand-Alone Approach   The single-user stand-alone approach remains a very common PC-DBMS environment. Here, a single user at a time uses a PC dedicated to that user's processing. The database is private in the sense that the user can take the diskettes away after use to prohibit other users from accessing the data. Further, the database on the PC is separate from any other database, including those on the mainframe from which some of the PC database may have been extracted. Thus, data may be duplicated, and synchronization of updating is a problem with which designers and users must deal.

Multiuser Stand-Alone Approach   In the multiuser stand-alone approach, a hard-disk-based database is shared among several concurrent users, who may all be using the same microprocessor with a multiprogramming-type operating system. More typically, they share a hard-disk file or database server from several PCs in a local area network (LAN). The LAN may also provide a gateway for access to other databases. Concurrency control and security may be limited or handled at a very coarse level (for example, file-level rather than record- or element-level lockout for update control). Here, as in the prior situation, the PC database is maintained separately from any mainframe database. This is, in fact, a major advantage, since unstructured, end-user access to the separate LAN database does not harm the performance of mainframe databases. Mainframe databases become high-volume warehouses that supply multiple-user databases (what some firms call *retail outlets*).

Mainframe Link Approach   The mainframe link is a specialized class of PC-RDBMSs, in which the same or very similar DBMS products are provided at both the PC and mainframe computers. A communications link (hardware and software) is provided as part of the PC package. From the PC, a user can access a mainframe database as she would from a terminal. This access is done in so-called terminal emulation mode, in which the PC is made to act as a special terminal, such as an IBM 327x. The user can also have selected data from the mainframe transferred to the PC (often using the same type of retrieval command as in any data access statement but with an extra clause to specify that the destination of the result is a file, database, or table on the PC). And finally, the user can manipulate data at the PC using the same language and range of commands as on the mainframe. Thus, users familiar with the mainframe product require minimal training time to learn the PC version. The benefit is that the PC can relieve a mainframe doing production database processing from also having to perform ad hoc inquiry processing. Performing both production and ad hoc processing can be expensive to support and can degrade the performance of the production database. Besides ORACLE, products such as PC/FOCUS (by Information Builders, Inc.) and PC/Nomad (by Must Software International) are examples of the mainframe link approach.

Multifunction Package Approach   Multifunction packages have integrated DBMS functions along with other management support tools. For example, several spreadsheet packages (for example, Lotus 1-2-3, Quattro Pro, Framework, and Microsoft Works) combine some simple RDBMS functions with spreadsheet and graphics capabilities. This class of PC-RDBMS should continue to expand as more general decision support system generators are created for personal computers.

Client-Server Approach   This is the newest PC-RDBMS environment, and is undergoing rapid change and growth in acceptance. In essence, the client-server approach blends the best of the mainframe (or host) and PC worlds. With a client-server database, database processing functions are distributed between client PCs on user desktops and a centralized PC database server. The database and core elements of the DBMS reside on the server. Clients run the application programs written in the database processing language. Language commands that cause database access are sent from the client to the server; the server returns to the client the requested data. Each client works in parallel with other clients in manipulating, formatting, and displaying data. Data integrity, security, and update control are managed centrally and transparently to each client at the server. Client workstations relieve the server from processing all user programs, yet the control of a central database exists. For many organizations, a client-server environment has become the preferred approach.

Other Differences In addition to these environmental differences, a PC-RDBMS differs from its mainframe counterparts in the size of the database that it can manage. As word sizes and operating system capabilities on PCs expand, larger databases are becoming possible via PC-RDBMSs. A PC-RDBMS is also limited by the processing speed of a personal computer, especially the time required to access hard-disk or diskette storage. Actually, newer microprocessors (for example, the Intel 80386 or later processors) have processing speeds and main memory capacities equal to or greater than some minicomputers. Thus, the real limitation is the disk input/output rates.

The Role of PC-RDBMS in Data Management

A PC-DBMS has several distinct features that make it attractive as part of a general data management strategy:

1. A PC-DBMS provides *mainframelike DBMS functions* for organizations or organizational units that do not require the power of a mini- or mainframe computer.

2. A PC-DBMS allows computer users in organizations that have an existing mainframe DBMS to develop *end-user database applications that are truly independent from production, high-transaction-volume databases*. Thus, the costly, unstructured end-user access does not degrade production database processing and does not interfere with the performance of these production databases.

3. Newer PC-DBMS technologies essentially permit an organization to create *a type of distributed database* (decentralized with planned transfer of data between databases). This achieves greater host performance and also reduces communication traffic in the computer network (see Chapter 13 for a discussion of distributed databases).

4. For those already using personal computers for management support, a PC-DBMS provides an additional *powerful tool to manage and present relevant data and information*.

5. A PC-DBMS and a database are *portable*, since for many of these products the DBMS and databases can be easily transported by moving diskettes. This not only benefits mobile managers but also means that the same DBMS and database can be used on mixed, yet compatible, machines (for example, several PCs running the MS-DOS operating system). This portability also affects education—students learning a DBMS can do so at home or in a classroom or laboratory. Further, they can learn without disrupting other students (when their errors crash the DBMS or destroy a file of input transactions, it only affects their own workspace).

The principles of database management hold whether we deal with mainframe or PC databases. The major issues are shareability, integrity, consistency, security, and accessibility. PC and mainframe databases should all be managed as part of an organizational plan for the data resource. PC databases create a special burden on data administration and can be quite redundant and inconsistent, so integrity of data may be difficult to manage. Further, the security of such distributed and independently managed data can be a challenge to ensure.

PC-RDBMSs and End-User Computing

End-user computing: An approach to data processing in which users who are not computer experts satisfy their own computing needs through the use of high-level software and languages such as electronic spreadsheets and relational database management systems.

End-user computing involves the development and use of computer-based applications by managers, executives, and occupational professionals, with little or no involvement by trained information system professionals. The proliferation of personal computers and the ease of use of spreadsheet, file management, word processing, business graphics, and desktop publishing software have opened new opportunities for the explosive, and potentially uncontrolled, deployment of systems in organizations.

Personal computer database applications can range from very simple data systems to databases with as complex a structure as any mainframe system. Today, personal computer DBMSs should *not* be treated as toy systems. They are sophisticated software packages that can either effectively solve significant data management problems or can be abused. Users of a PC-DBMS should be thoroughly trained in

- The use of the package
- Principles of good database design and documentation
- The need for proper backup and recovery practices
- The application of appropriate data security measures

In addition, the experience with end-user computing to date suggests that organization-wide support systems and policies are needed to manage the use of PC-DBMSs. Most organizations will standardize on one or just a few PC-DBMSs to more effectively provide training and consulting support. This control also means that the organization can write agreements with DBMS vendors that can result in significant savings from large-quantity purchases.

Equally important is the need to manage data as a corporate resource, which requires that databases on personal computers be defined and designed to be consistent with corporate methods. For example, data-element naming conventions should still be applied. The need for a database on a PC should be reviewed by a data administrator or end-user consulting specialist to help the user determine if a PC-DBMS is the appropriate technology. If a PC-DBMS is appropriate, these advisors can help determine the best source of data for the PC database (for example, a mainframe database, local data entry, or possibly an external public data source). The end-user consultant can also help the user establish a local area network or PC-mainframe connection if the database is to be used by multiple employees.

Experience with PC databases and DBMSs should be shared throughout an organization. An information center or computer club is an excellent forum. A newsletter or users' group can also promote better utilization of the DBMS and inform those using the PC-DBMS about issues of organization-wide data management.

Glossary of Terms

Aborted transaction A transaction that is in progress terminates abnormally. See also *Backward recovery, Transaction boundaries.*

Action diagram A map or diagram that shows a sequence of actions or steps needed to retrieve certain data or produce certain results from a database.

After-image A copy of a record (or memory page) after it has been modified. See also *Before-image.*

Alias An alternative name given an attribute. See also *Synonym.*

Anomalies Errors or inconsistencies that may result when a user attempts to update a table that contains redundant data. There are three types of anomalies: insertion, deletion, and modification anomalies. See also *Normalization.*

Application development subsystem Subsystem that provides facilities that allow end users and/or programmers to develop complete database applications.

Application generator A programming language that allows a database application to be built from existing programs, screen and report definitions, and from custom-built menus. See also *Code generator.*

Application program interface (API) Software that allows a specific front-end program development platform to communicate with a particular back-end database engine, even when the front end and back end were not built to be compatible. See also *Client/server architecture, DBMS engine.*

Area In a CODASYL database, a named, continuous area of secondary storage. Also called *realm.*

Attribute A named property or characteristic of an entity that is of interest to the organization.

Authorization rules Controls incorporated in the data management systems that restrict access to data and also restrict the actions that people may take when they access data. See also *Security management subsystem.*

Backup and recovery subsystem Subsystem that provides facilities for logging transactions and database changes, periodically making backup copies of the database and recovering the database in the event of some type of failure. See also *Checkpoint facility, Database change log, Restore/rerun, Transaction log.*

Backup facilities An automatic dump facility that produces a backup copy (or *save*) of the entire database. See also *Checkpoint facility.*

Backward recovery (rollback) Used to back out or undo unwanted changes to the database. Before-images of the records that have been changed are applied to the database and the database is returned to an earlier state. Used to reverse the changes made by transactions that have been aborted or terminated abnormally. See also *Aborted transaction, Forward recovery.*

Balanced tree (B-tree) A tree in which all leaves are the same distance from the root.

Base table A table in the relational data model that most likely corresponds to one physical file in secondary storage. See also *Relation, View.*

Before-image A copy of a record (or memory page) before it has been modified. See also *After-image.*

Binary relationship A relationship between instances of two entity classes. This is the most common type of relationship encountered in data modeling.

Biometric device Measures or detects personal characteristics such as fingerprints, voice prints, retina prints, or signature dynamics.

Boyce-Codd normal form (BCNF) A relation in which every determinant is a candidate key. See also *Normalization.*

Branching factor (degree of a tree) The maximum number of children allowed per parent in a tree.

Business area A cohesive grouping of functions and entities that forms the basis for information systems development.

Business function A related group of business processes that support some aspect of the mission of an enterprise.

Business rules Specifications that preserve the integrity of the logical data model. See also *Deletion rule, Insertion rule, Referential integrity constraint, Triggering operation, Validity check.*

Business transaction All the data about one business event, which might cause several database transactions to add, delete, or change database records. See also *Transaction boundaries.*

CALC A record-access strategy in the CODASYL data model in which records are stored and accessed by supplying a primary key value. See also *Hashed file organization, LOCATION MODE.*

Candidate key An attribute (or combination of attributes) that uniquely identifies each instance of an entity type. See also *Composite key, Primary key.*

Cardinality The number of instances of entity B that can (or must) be associated with each instance of entity A.

Categorization The concept that an entity comes in various subtypes. See also *Generalization, ISA relationship.*

Centralized data distribution All data are located at a single site.

Checkpoint facility A facility by which the DBMS periodically refuses to accept any new transactions. The system is in a quiet state and the database and transaction logs are synchronized. See also *Backup facilities, Restore/ rerun.*

Child In IMS, a subordinate segment below the root.

Class-subclass See *Generalization.*

Client A software application that requests services (such as communications management) from one or more servers. See also *Client/server architecture.*

Client/server architecture A form of LAN in which a central database server or engine performs all database commands sent to it from client workstations, and application programs on each client concentrate on user interface functions. See also *Application program interface, Client, Local area network.*

Clustering attribute Any nonkey attribute in a record (or row) that is used to cluster (or group together) the rows that have a common value for this attribute.

Clustering index An index defined on the clustering attribute of a file.

Code generator A module of a DBMS that produces the program instructions that define a form, report, or menu. A code generator usually builds these instructions from a visual image of the object drawn by the designer of the object. See also *Application generator.*

Commit protocol An algorithm to ensure that a transaction is successfully completed, or else aborted. See also *Two-phase commit protocol.*

Complex network data model A type of network data model that supports M:N (as well as 1:N) relationships.

Composite entity See *Gerund.*

Composite key A primary key that contains more than one attribute.

Composite usage map A concise reference to the estimated volume and usage of data in the database.

Computer-aided software engineering (CASE) tools Software tools that provide automated support for some portion of the system development process. See also *Integrated CASE toolset.*

Concatenated key See *Composite key.*

Conceptual data model A detailed model that captures the overall structure of organizational data, while being independent of any database management system or other implementation consideration. A conceptual data model includes the relevant entities, relationships, and attributes, as well as the business rules and constraints that define how the data are used.

Concurrency control Concerned with preventing loss of data integrity due to interference between users in a multiuser environment.

Concurrency transparency A design goal for a distributed database, with the property that although a distributed system runs many transactions, it appears that each one is the only activity in the system. Thus, when several transactions are processed concurrently, the results must be the same as if each transaction was processed in serial order. See also *Failure transparency, Location transparency, Replication transparency.*

Connection A mapping from one object class to another.

Connectivity See *Cardinality.*

Container object In Paradox for Windows, an object that completely surrounds another object. See also *Encapsulation.*

Correlated subqueries In SQL, a subquery in which processing the inner query depends on data from the outer query.

Critical success factor (CSF) An internal or external business-related result that is measurable and has a major influence on whether an organization meets its goals.

Currency indicator In a CODASYL DBMS, a variable that holds the physical address (database key) of the record instance most recently accessed or manipulated. Each program invokes several currency indicators, each for different categories of records: each record type, each set, each area, and the database as a whole.

Data Facts concerning things such as people, objects, or events.

Data administration A high-level function that is responsible for the overall management of data resources in an organization, including maintaining corporate-wide definitions and standards. See also *Database administration, Data steward.*

Data description language (DDL) The language component of a DBMS that is used to describe the logical (and sometimes physical) structure of a database. Different DDLs may exist to describe either the whole database or particular views of part of a database.

Data flow diagram (DFD) A graphic model of the flow, use, and transformation of data through a set of processes.

Data independence The separation of data descriptions from the applications that use the data.

Data integrity management subsystem Subsystem that provides facilities for managing the integrity of data in the database and the integrity of metadata in the repository.

Data item See *Attribute*.

Data manipulation language (DML) A language component of a DBMS that is used by a programmer to access and modify the contents of a database.

Data steward Manages a specific logical data resource or entity for all business functions and data processing systems that originate or use data about the assigned entity. See also *Data administration, Database administration*.

Database A shared collection of logically related data, designed to meet the information needs of multiple users in an organization.

Database administration A technical function that is responsible for physical database design and for dealing with technical issues such as security enforcement, database performance, and backup and recovery. See also *Data administration, Data steward*.

Database application system The data definitions, stored data, transactions, inquiries, screens, reports, and other programs needed to capture, maintain, and present data from a database.

Database change log Contains before- and after-images of records that have been modified by transactions. See also *Journalizing facilities*.

Database computer A specially designed computer that contains a customized operating system and the run-time components of a DBMS.

Database description (DBD) In IMS, the definition of a physical database record type.

Database destruction The database itself is lost or destroyed, or cannot be read.

Database management system (DBMS) A software application system that is used to create, maintain, and provide controlled access to user databases.

Database recovery Mechanisms for restoring a database quickly and accurately after loss or damage. See also *Aborted transaction, Backward recovery, Forward recovery*.

Database security Protection of the database against accidental or intentional loss, destruction, or misuse.

Database server The (back-end) portion of the client/server database system running on the server and providing database processing and shared access functions. See also *Client/server architecture, DBMS engine, File server*.

DBMS engine The central component of a DBMS. Provides access to the repository and the database and coordinates all of the other functional elements of the DBMS. See also *Database engine*.

Deadlock An impasse that results when two (or more) transactions have locked a common resource, and each must wait for the other to unlock that resource.

Deadlock prevention User programs must lock all records they will require at the beginning of a transaction (rather that one at a time).

Deadlock resolution Allows deadlocks to occur but builds mechanisms into the DBMS for detecting and breaking the deadlocks.

Decentralized database A database that is stored on computers at multiple locations; however, the computers are not interconnected by a network, so that users at the various sites cannot share data. See also *Distributed database*.

Degree The number of entity types that participate in a relationship.

Deletion rule A row should not be deleted from the referenced table if there is a matching row (or rows) in the referencing table. See also *Business rules*.

Depth The number of levels between the root node and a leaf node in a tree.

Determinant The attribute on the left-hand side of the arrow in a functional dependency; A is a determinant in the following functional dependency: A→B. See also *Candidate key, Primary key*.

Device media control language (DMCL) A language used with a CODASYL DBMS to specify the physical design of a database.

Distributed database A single logical database that is spread physically across computers in multiple locations that are connected by a data communications link. See also *Decentralized database, Partitioned data distribution, Replicated data distribution*.

Domain The set of all data types and ranges of values that an attribute may assume.

Domain-key normal form (DK/NF) A relation is in domain-key normal form if and only if every constraint on the relation is a logical consequence of key constraints and domain constraints. See also *Normalization*.

Encapsulation The property that the attributes and methods of an object are hidden from the outside world and do not have to be known to access its data values or invoke its methods. See also *Container object*.

End-user computing An approach to data processing in which users who are not computer experts satisfy their own computing needs through the use of high-level software and languages such as electronic spreadsheets and relational database management systems.

Encryption The coding (or scrambling) of data so that they cannot be read by humans.

Enterprise data model A high-level conceptual data model for an organization. An enterprise data model shows the entities and the relationships among the entities.

Enterprise modeling The first step in database development, in which the scope and general contents of a database are specified.

Entity A thing (e.g., person, place, event, or concept) about which an organization chooses to record data. See also *Weak entity*.

Entity instance (instance) A single occurrence of an entity type.

Entity-relationship data model (E-R model) A detailed, logical representation of the entities, associations, and data elements for an organization or business area. See also *Conceptual data model*.

Entity-relationship diagram (E-R diagram) A graphical representation of an E-R model.

Entity type A collection of entities that share common properties or characteristics.

Equi-join A join in which the joining condition is based on equality between values in the common columns. Common columns appear (redundantly) in the result table.

Exclusive lock (X lock or write lock) Prevents another transaction from reading (and therefore updating) a record until it is unlocked. See also *Locking, Locking level, Shared lock.*

Exclusive relationship The subtypes of a supertype are mutually exclusive, and each instance of the supertype is categorized as exactly one subtype. See also *Categorization.*

Exclusive subclasses Each instance of an object must be an instance of exactly one of the subclasses.

Exhaustive subclasses There are no other subclasses.

Exhaustive subtypes All subtypes are defined for a supertype. See also *Categorization.*

Existence dependency An instance of one entity cannot exist without the existence of an instance of some other (related) entity. See also *Weak entity.*

Failure transparency A design goal for a distributed database, which guarantees that either all the actions of each transaction are committed or else none of them are committed. See also *Concurrency transparency, Location transparency, Replication transparency.*

Fifth normal form (5NF) A relation is in fifth normal form if it is in fourth normal form and does not have a join dependency. See also *Normalization.*

File organization A technique for physically arranging the records of a file on secondary storage devices.

File server A device that manages file operations, and is shared by each of the client PCs that are attached to the LAN. See also *Local area network, Server.*

Filter In dBASE, a condition placed on a file that makes it appear as if the file contains only records that meet the given condition.

First normal form (1NF) A relation that contains no repeating groups. See also *Normalization.*

Foreign key An attribute that appears as a nonkey attribute in one relation and as a primary key attribute (or part of a primary key) in another relation. See also *Null value, Referential integrity.*

Forward recovery (rollforward) Starts with an earlier copy of the database. After-images (the results of good transactions) are applied to the database, and the database is quickly moved forward to a later state. See also *Backward recovery.*

Fourth normal form (4NF) A relation is in fourth normal form if it is in BCNF and contains no multivalued dependencies. See also *Normalization.*

Fragment See *Partitioned data distribution.*

Fragmentation transparency See *Replication transparency.*

Functional decomposition The process of breaking the functions of an organization down into progressively lower levels of detail.

Functional dependency A particular relationship between two attributes. For any relation R, attribute B is functionally dependent on attribute A if, for every valid instance of A, that value of A uniquely determines the value of B. The functional dependence of B on A is represented as A→B. See also *Determinant, Normalization.*

Generalization The concept that some things (entities) are subtypes of other, more general things. See also *Categorization, ISA relationship.*

Generalization hierarchy A hierarchical grouping of objects that share common attributes and methods.

Gerund A many-to-many relationship that the data modeler chooses to model as an entity type with several associated one-to-many relationships with other entity types.

Global transaction In a distributed database, a transaction that requires reference to data at one or more nonlocal sites to satisfy the request. See also *Local transaction, Transaction boundaries.*

Hashed file organization The address for each record is determined using a hashing algorithm. See also *CALC.*

Hashing algorithm A routine that converts a primary key value into a relative record number (or relative file address). See also *CALC.*

Hierarchical database model A data model in which records are arranged in a top-down structure that resembles a tree. See also *Logical database model.*

Hierarchical sequence In IMS, a top-down, left-to-right ordering of segments within a physical database record (PDBR).

Homonym A single name that is used for two different data items (for example, the term *invoice* used to refer to both a customer invoice and a supplier invoice).

Horizontal partitioning Distributing the rows of a table into several separate tables. See also *Partitioned data distribution, Vertical partitioning.*

Hybrid data distribution The database is partitioned into critical and noncritical fragments. Noncritical fragments are stored at only one site, while critical fragments are stored at multiple sites. See also *Distributed database.*

Identifier See *Primary key.*

Identifying relationship A relationship in which the primary key of the parent entity is used as part of the primary key of the dependent entity.

Identity An external identifier for each object that is not accessible to and cannot be modified by any other object or application.

Index A table or other data structure that is used to determine the location of rows in a table (or tables) that satisfy some condition. See also *Primary key.*

Indexed file organization The records are either stored sequentially or nonsequentially, and an index is created that allows the user to locate individual records.

Indexed nonsequential The records in an indexed organization are stored nonsequentially, and a full index (frequently called an *inverted index*) is required.

Indexed sequential The records are stored sequentially by primary key value, and a simple index (called a *block index*) is used.

Information Data that have been processed and presented in a form suitable for human interpretation, often with the purpose of revealing trends or patterns.

Information engineering A formal, top-down methodology that uses a data orientation to create and maintain information systems.

Information repository Stores metadata that describes

an organization's data and data processing resources. Manages the total information processing environment. Combines information about an organization's business information and its application portfolio. See also *Repository*.

Information repository dictionary system (IRDS) A computer software tool that is used to manage and control access to the information repository.

Information resource management (IRM) The concept that information is a major corporate resource and must be managed using the same basic principles used to manage other assets.

Information process A process that converts data into information.

Information systems architecture A conceptual blueprint or plan that expresses the desired future structure for the information systems in an organization.

Inheritance The property that, when entity types or object classes are arranged in a hierarchy, each entity type or object class assumes the attributes and methods of its ancestors (that is, those higher up in the hierarchy).

Insertion rule A row should not be inserted in the referencing table unless there already exists a matching entry in the referenced table. See also *Business rules*.

Instance See *Entity instance*.

Integrated CASE (I-CASE) toolset A set of CASE tools that can support all phases of the system development process.

Interface subsystem Provides facilities for users and applications to access the various components of the DBMS.

Inverted index See *Indexed nonsequential*.

ISA relationship The relationship between each subtype and its supertype. See also *Generalization*.

Join A relational operation that causes two tables with a common domain to be combined into a single table. See also *Equi-join, Natural join, Outer join, Self-join*.

Join dependency A relation that has a join dependency cannot be divided into two (or more) relations such that the resulting tables can be recombined to form the original table.

Journalizing facilities An audit trail of transactions and database changes. See also *Database change log, Transaction log*.

Key See *Primary key*. See also *Candidate key*.

Leaf node A node in a tree that has no child nodes.

Local area network (LAN) A system that permits computing devices to communicate with one another over distances that range from a few feet to several miles. See also *Client/server architecture*.

Local transaction In a distributed database, a transaction that requires reference only to data that are stored at the site where the transaction originates. See also *Global transaction, Transaction boundaries*.

LOCATION MODE In a CODASYL database, the method used to determine the disk address of records of a particular record type when those records are stored or accessed. See also *CALC, VIA*.

Location transparency A design goal for a distributed database, which says that a user (or user program) requesting data need not know the location of the data. See also *Concurrency transparency, Failure transparency, Replication transparency*.

Locking Any data that is retrieved by a user for updating must be locked or denied to other users, until the update is completed (or aborted). See also *Exclusive lock, Shared lock*.

Locking level (granularity) The extent of the database resource that is included with each lock.

Logical database (LDB) In IMS, all occurrences of a logical database record (LDBR) type.

Logical database design The process of mapping logical data models to structures that are specific to a target DBMS.

Logical database model A design that conforms to the data model for a class of database management systems. See also *Hierarchical database model, Network database model, Relational database model, Object-oriented database model*.

Macro A sequence of keystrokes assigned to a single keyboard key.

Memo field A long, variable-length character string; usually stored in a separate file from the other fields in the associated record.

Memory variable A nondatabase field defined within a program that is used to store intermediate results, keyboard input, and other data not associated with a database file.

Message connection A communications path between sending and receiving object classes.

Message map A diagram that shows the flow of messages superimposed on the message connections.

Method (or service) A processing routine that is encapsulated in an object and operates on the data described within that object.

Methodology A process (or related series of steps) to accomplish a design goal, together with a set of design objects that are manipulated to support the process.

Multiple-index file In dBASE, a file that contains up to 47 key indexes.

Multivalued attribute An attribute that can have more than one value for each entity instance.

Multivalued dependency A type of dependency that exists when there are at least three attributes (for example, A, B, and C) in a relation, and for each value of A there is a well-defined set of values for B and a well-defined set of values for C, but the set of values of B is independent of set C. See also *Functional dependency*.

Natural join The same as an equi-join except that one of the duplicated columns is eliminated in the result table.

Natural language system A language subsystem based on artificial intelligence that allows the user to carry on a dialogue with the computer in an unstructured version of English or another language.

Network database model A data model in which each record type may be associated with an arbitrary number of different record types. See also *Complex network data model, Simple network data model*.

Nonexclusive subtype Subtypes may overlap, and an instance of the supertype may simultaneously belong to more than one subtype.

Nonexhaustive subtype   Some (but not all) of the subtypes have been defined for a supertype.

Normal form   A state of a relation that can be determined by applying simple rules regarding dependencies to that relation. See also *Boyce-Codd normal form, Domain-key normal form, Fifth normal form, First normal form, Fourth normal form, Second normal form, Third normal form.*

Normalization   The process of converting complex data structures into simple, stable data structures. See also *Functional dependency, Well-structured relation.*

Null value   A special column value, distinct from 0, blank, or any other value, that indicates that the value for the column is missing or otherwise unknown. See also *Foreign key, Primary key.*

Object   A structure that encapsulates (or packages) attributes and methods that operate on those attributes. See also *Encapsulation, Inheritance.*

Object class   A logical grouping of objects that have the same (or similar) attributes and behavior (or methods).

Object instance   One occurrence (or materialization) of an object class.

Object Linking and Embedding (OLE)   A Microsoft Windows capability in which an object from one application can be referenced from within another application.

Object-oriented database model   A database model in which data attributes and methods that operate on those attributes are encapsulated in structures called *objects.*

Outer join   A join in which rows that do not have matching values in common columns are nevertheless included in the result table.

Paradox data model   A graphical representation of the relationships between tables used in a form or report. This data model is used to visually lay out data required during form or report design.

Partial functional dependency   A dependency in which one or more nonkey attributes are functionally dependent on part (but not all) of the primary key. See also *Second normal form (2NF).*

Partitioned data distribution   The database is divided into disjoint (nonoverlapping) partitions. Each partition (also called a *fragment*) is assigned to a particular site. See also *Distributed database.*

Performance management subsystem   Subsystem that provides facilities to optimize (or at least improve) DBMS performance.

Physical database design   The process of mapping the database structures from logical design to physical storage structures such as files and tables. Indexes are also specified, as well as access methods and other physical factors.

Physical database record (PDBR)   In IMS, a hierarchical arrangement of segments.

Physical process   A process that converts tangible inputs into tangible outputs.

Pointer   A field containing data that can be used to locate a related record.

Primary key   A candidate key that has been selected as the identifier for an entity type. Primary key values may not be null. Also called an *identifier.* See also *Candidate key, Foreign key, Index.*

Procedure   In dBASE, a named set of commands used as a program or subroutine within a program or in a library of procedures.

Process   A well-defined set of logical tasks performed repeatedly in support of one or more business functions. A process converts inputs into outputs, and has definite boundaries (beginning and ending points).

Program communication block (PCB)   In IMS, a series of statements that define a logical database record (LDBR).

Program specification block (PSB)   In IMS, the set of all program communication blocks (PCBs) for a given user.

Query view   In dBASE, a virtual table created from a Query-by-Example format; data may be retrieved from a query view as if it were a regular database file. See also *View.*

Read lock   See *Shared lock.*

Realm   See *Area.*

Record   See *Record type.*

Record type   A named entity, instances of which describe individual occurrences of the entity.

Recovery manager   A module of the DBMS that restores the database to a correct condition when a failure occurs, and resumes processing user requests. See also *Backward recovery, Forward recovery.*

Recursive foreign key   A foreign key in a relation that references the primary key values of that same relation.

Recursive structure   A repeating group.

Recursive relationship   See *Unary relationship.*

Referential integrity   An integrity constraint that specifies that the value (or existence) of an attribute in one relation depends on the value (or existence) of the same attribute in another relation. See also *Referential integrity constraint.*

Referential integrity constraint   A business rule that addresses the validity of references by one object in a database to some other object (or objects) in the database. See also *Business rules.*

Relation   A named, two-dimensional table of data. Each relation consists of a set of named columns and an arbitrary number of unnamed rows. See also *Base table.*

Relational algebra   A data manipulation language that provides a set of operators for manipulating one or two files.

Relational database model   A data model that represents data in the form of tables or relations.

Relational DBMS (RDBMS)   A database management system that manages data as a collection of tables in which all data relationships are represented by common values in related tables.

Relationship   An association between the instances of one or more entity types that is of interest to the organization. See also *Gerund.*

Repeating group   A set of two or more multivalued attributes that are logically related.

Replicated data distribution   A full copy of the database is assigned to more than one site in the network. See also *Distributed database.*

Replication transparency   A design goal for a distributed database, which says that although a given data item may be replicated at several nodes in a network, a programmer or user may treat that data item as if it were a single item at a single node. Also called *fragmentation transparency*. See also *Concurrency transparency, Failure transparency, Location transparency*.

Repository A knowledge base of information about the facts that an enterprise must be able to access and the processes it must perform to be successful. See also *Information repository dictionary system*.

Restore/rerun Involves reprocessing the day's transactions (up to the point of failure) against the backup copy of the database. See also *Checkpoint facility*.

Rollback See *Backward recovery*.

Rollforward See *Forward recovery*.

Root In IMS, the top segment in a physical database record.

Root node The node at the top of a tree.

Run-time version The portion of the DBMS needed to run an existing database application.

S lock See *Shared lock*.

Schema A description of the overall logical structure of a database, expressed in a special data definition language. See also *Logical database model*.

Schema In the CODASYL data model, the description of a database. See also *Subschema*.

Second normal form (2NF) A relation is in second normal form if it is in first normal form and every nonkey attribute is fully functionally dependent on the primary key. Thus no nonkey attribute is functionally dependent on part (but not all) of the primary key. See also *Partial functional dependency*.

Security management subsystem Subsystem that provides facilities to protect and control access to the database and repository. See also *Authorization rules*.

Segment In IMS, a named set of related fields.

Self-join (recursive join) A join of a table with itself.

Sequential file organization The records in the file are stored in sequence according to a primary key value.

Server A software application that provides services (such as database management) to requesting clients. See also *File server*.

Set In a network data model, a one-to-many association between two record types, where the first record type is called the *owner* and the second is called the *member*.

Set In Paradox, a defined group of records.

Shared lock (S lock or read lock) Allows other transactions to read (but not update) a record (or other resource). See also *Exclusive lock, Locking*.

Simple network data model A type of network data model that supports 1:N (but not M:N) relationships. See also *Complex network data model*.

Smart card A thin plastic card the size of a credit card with an embedded microprocessor.

Strategic information systems planning An orderly means of assessing the information needs of an organization and defining the systems and databases that will best satisfy those needs.

Structured query language (SQL) A standard fourth-generation query language for relational database systems.

Subschema A logical description of a user's view (or program's view) of data, expressed in a special data definition language.

Subschema In the CODASYL data model, the description of that subset of a database used by a program that accesses the database. A subschema may be a subset of its associated schema, and may redefine some records and fields within the schema. See also *Schema*.

Subtree A node and all the descendants of that node.

Subtype A subset of a supertype that shares common attributes or relationships distinct from other subsets. See also *Categorization*.

Supertype A generic entity type that is subdivided into subtypes. See also *Generalization*.

Synonym Two different names that are used to describe the same data item (for example, *car* and *automobile*). See also *Alias*.

Tag In dBASE, a key index contained in a multiple-index file.

Ternary relationship A simultaneous relationship among instances of three entity types. See also *Gerund*.

Third normal form (3NF) A relation is in third normal form if it is in second normal form and no transitive dependencies exist. See also *Transitive dependency*.

Time stamp A time value (such as date and time) that is associated with any data value. See also *Timestamping, Versioning*.

Timestamping In distributed databases, a concurrency control mechanism that assigns a globally unique timestamp to each transaction. Timestamping is an alternative to the use of locks in distributed databases. See also *Time stamp, Versioning*.

Transaction boundaries The logical beginning and end of transactions.

Transaction log Contains a record of the essential data for each transaction that is processed against the database. See also *Journalizing facilities*.

Transaction manager In a distributed database, a software module that maintains a log of all transactions and maintains an appropriate concurrency control scheme.

Transaction map A diagram that shows the sequence of logical database accesses.

Transitive dependency A functional dependency between two (or more) nonkey attributes in a relation. See also *Third normal form (3NF)*.

Tree A data structure that consists of a set of nodes that branch out from a node at the top of the tree (thus the tree is upside down).

Triggering operation (trigger) An assertion or rule that governs the validity of data manipulation operations such as insert, update, and delete. See also *Business rules*.

Twins In IMS, all occurrences of child segments of the same parent occurrence.

Two-phase commit protocol An algorithm for coordinating updates in a distributed database.

Unary relationship (recursive relationship) A relationship between the instances of one entity type.

User-defined function (UDF)   In dBASE, a set of commands that return a single value to the command line where the UDF is referenced.

User-defined procedures   User exits (or interfaces) that allow system designers to define their own security procedures in addition to the authorization rules.

Validity check   In Paradox, a data integrity control placed on a field. See also *Business rules.*

Versioning   There is no form of locking. Each transaction is restricted to a view of the database as of the time that transaction started, and when a transaction modifies a record, the DBMS creates a new record version instead of overwriting the old record. See also *Time stamp, Timestamping.*

Vertical partitioning   Distributing the columns of a table into several separate tables. See also *Horizontal partitioning, Partitioned data distribution.*

VIA   A record-access strategy in the CODASYL data model in which records are stored and accessed through a set relationship. See also *LOCATION MODE.*

View   A virtual table in the relational data model in which data from real (base) tables are combined so that programmers can work with just one (virtual) table instead of the several or more complete base tables.

Weak entity   An entity type that has an existence dependency.

Well-structured relation   A relation that contains a minimum amount of redundancy and allows users to insert, modify, and delete the rows in a table without errors or inconsistencies. See also *Normalization.*

Work-group computing   The use of computing resources for decision support and other applications by a team.

Write lock   See *Exclusive lock.*

X lock   See *Exclusive lock.*

Xbase products   Database systems and utilities based on the dBASE programming language.

Glossary of Acronyms

ANSI American National Standards Institute

API Application Program Interface

ASCII American Standards Code for Information Interchange

BCNF Boyce-Codd Normal Form

CAD/CAM Computer-Aided Design/Computer-Aided Manufacturing

CASE Computer-Aided Software Engineering

CD-ROM Compact Disk–Read-Only Memory

COBOL COmmon Business Oriented Language

CODASYL Committee On DAta SYstem Languages

CRT Cathode Ray Tube

CSF Critical Success Factor

DA Data Administrator (or Data Administration)

DBA Database Administrator (or Database Administration)

DBC Database Computer

DBD Database Description

DBMS Database Management System

DBTG Data Base Task Group

DB2 Data Base2 (an IBM Relational DBMS)

DDL Data Definition Language

DMCL Device Media Control Language

IDS Integrated Data System (an early network DBMS)

DFD Data Flow Diagram

DK/NF Domain-Key Normal Form

DL/I Data Language I (part of IMS)

DML Data Manipulation Language

DOS Disk Operating System

E-R Entity-Relationship

ERD Entity-Relationship Diagram

FORTRAN FORmula TRANslator

GUI Graphical User Interface

HDAM Hierarchical Direct Access Method

HIDAM Hierarchical Indexed Direct Access Method

HISAM Hierarchical Indexed Sequential Access Method

HSAM Hierarchical Sequential Access Method

IBM International Business Machines

I-CASE Integrated Computer-Aided Software Engineering

ID Identifier

IDMS/R Integrated Database Management System/Relational (a relational DBMS from Computer Associates)

IMS Information Management System (an IBM hierarchical DBMS; current version is IMS/ESA, or Information Management System/Extended System Architecture)

IRDS Information Repository Dictionary System

IRM Information Resource Management

IS Information System

ISA Information Systems Architecture

ISAM Indexed Sequential Access Method

ISO International Standards Organization

LAN Local Area Network

LDB Logical Database

LDBR Logical Database Record

MB Million Bytes

MIS Management Information System

M:1 Many-to-One

M:N Many-to-Many

ODBMS Object Database Management System

OLE Object Linking and Embedding

O-O Object-Oriented

OODM Object-Oriented Data Model

OSAM Overflow Sequential Access Method

OS/2   Operating System/2
PAL   Paradox Application Language
PC   Personal Computer
PCB   Program Communication Block
PC-DBMS   Personal Computer–Database Management System
PC-RDBMS   Personal Computer–Relational Database Management System
PDBR   Physical Database Record
P.K.   Primary Key
QBE   Query-by-Example
RDBMS   Relational Database Management System

SAM   Sequential Access Method
SQL   Structured Query Language
SQL/DS   Structured Query Language/Data System (an IBM relational DBMS)
UDF   User-Defined Function
VSAM   Virtual Storage Access Method
1:M   One-to-Many
1NF   First Normal Form
2NF   Second Normal Form
3NF   Third Normal Form
4NF   Fourth Normal Form
5NF   Fifth Normal Form

Index

(*Italicized* page number indicates that term is defined on that page.)